9ᵗ Wov.

13
2⟌65   +18
33   +12
        +15   392-404
        +7   430-445

286-283

D0518764

Josephine

An Introduction *to* MUSIC

An Introduction *to* MUSIC

BY DAVID D. BOYDEN

PROFESSOR OF MUSIC
UNIVERSITY OF CALIFORNIA, BERKELEY

With a Preface by Sir Thomas Arm ro

and a Foreword by Percy A. Scholes

FABER AND FABER LIMITED

London

13641

First published in England 1959
by Faber and Faber Limited
Second edition 1971
Printed in Great Britain by
John Dickens & Co Ltd, Northampton
All rights reserved

ISBN 0 571 04745 9 (Hard Bound Edition)
ISBN 0 571 09149 0 (Faber Paper Covered Edition)

Preface by Sir Thomas Armstrong

I AM VERY glad that this book has been made available to British students, because it seems to be one of the best summaries of the subject that have appeared in any language that I am familiar with, and also because it comes at a very opportune time. The public to whom this kind of book is addressed has passed beyond the stage of the more elementary kinds of musical appreciation which were necessary a generation ago, and is now prepared for the more detailed discussion which Dr. Boyden offers.

His book provides a complete scheme, and is adapted not only to the needs of the ordinary lover of music, but also to the requirements of the senior forms of schools where music is taken seriously. Especially valuable are the illustrations, both musical and pictorial, which are drawn from a wide area, and illustrate the subject in an intelligent way. Most helpful too, will be the suggestions that Dr. Boyden offers for advanced study of particular topics, the book lists, which are carefully compiled and are up to date, and the suggestions for planned listening.

In connection with any discussion of this subject a word of warning is necessary, and the introduction that the author provides is an indication that he is aware of some dangers. Knowledge about music is a very different thing from knowledge of music, and the basic difficulty of what is called musical appreciation is that of keeping the direct musical experience at the very heart of the endeavour. It is all very well to know the history of a thing, and it may be true, as Sir Percy Buck used to say, that until you know the history of a thing you cannot understand it; but it is also true that no kind of information can take the place of direct musical experience. How is a pupil to re-enact when his attention is elaborately drawn, well before the performance, to the modulation which the composer intended as a surprise? There is a well known passage in one of Peacock's novels, where the proud owner is taking his friends round an ornamental garden. As they pass through a carefully planned hedge an entrancing view breaks upon them. 'This is what I call "the Surprise",' says the proud owner. 'And what do you call it,' his friend asks, 'the second time you go round the garden?' But in a well-composed piece of music, owing to the carefully laid plans of a good composer, the surprise remains: a surprise not only the second time, but on countless occasions to the end of one's musical life. This, of course, is because the composer has so well prepared his stroke that it continues to be a surprise to the ear, and also to the mind which is building up through the ear its complete understanding of the work concerned.

The ear is an all-important thing. Dr. Boyden states that the training of the ear is one of the aims of his book, and he is right to realize that the whole purpose of his splendid endeavour rests upon the reader's ability to develop his own ear, without which the mind cannot have reliable data. Unless he can hear keenly, clearly, and with extreme sensitiveness to shades and qualities of tone, the music that the composers have written will not mean even to the most devoted listener what it should mean; and all Dr. Boyden's information will be beside the point. The training of the ear, I need hardly insist, is not a matter of a few minutes practice each day, but a lifelong process, and indeed, one might almost say, a way of living. The musician is a man who works, thinks, and lives in the medium of sound; his musical character depends upon its effectiveness, precision, and dependability of his hearing. When this factor is reliable, and only then, his knowledge, experience, and insight can develop to the farthest point of their capability.

I can recommend this book to students, teachers, and all those of the general public who are seriously interested in music. Although directed to an American public, it is written clearly, in language that will be understood by all English speaking people; it is free from pretentiousness and self-conscious avoidance of technical terms. There are a few differences in terminology that might puzzle an English reader: we speak of 'bar' instead of 'measure'; we call an 'eighth' note and a 'quarter' note a 'quaver' and a 'crochet'; where we should speak of the fourth 'note' of the scale, an American would speak of the fourth 'tone'; and what we call a 'melodic' minor, an American musician would call a 'pure' minor or the 'Aeolian mode'. Apart from these small differences of terminology, there is nothing in Dr. Boyden's text which should be other than clear to British readers, and I feel sure that his work will receive a warm welcome.

THOMAS ARMSTRONG

Foreword by Percy A. Scholes

I AM HONOURED by the suggestion that I should provide a Foreword for a book that I have gone through in proof and greatly admire—admire beyond any of the other books on its subject so far as I am acquainted with them. Professor Boyden, of course, understands both his subject and his prospective readers—which two forms of understanding are the obvious conditions to be met if such a book is to succeed in its purpose.

The book now before us has, of course, had a good many predecessors. So far as I know, however, these do not date back very far; indeed I can trace their stream merely up to the beginning of the nineteenth century—which is rather strange!

It seems to me that the very first suggestion of a public need of such books came from the famous historian of music, Dr. Charles Burney, who prefaced the first of his four big-volumed *History of Music* with an "Essay on Musical Criticism" in which these words occur:

> There have been many treatises published on the art of musical composition and performance but none to instruct ignorant lovers of music how to listen or to judge for themselves.

That very sensible complaint appeared in 1789, and had, apparently, no result. But we find Burney himself about twenty years later being taught "how to listen and judge for himself." He had never appreciated Bach. In those days few musicians did, very little Bach being published. Burney had brought back from his German tour a manuscript copy of part of the "48" but it was very defective, and it was not until Samuel Wesley (who had become a Bach enthusiast—one of the very pioneers of the Bach cult), in 1807, took his revered octogenarian friend in hand and gave him a definite series of "Bach Appreciation Lessons," as we should nowadays call them, that the fine old fellow began to realize what riches he had been overlooking in Bach.

The first person to give a public lecture on Musical Appreciation, and the first person to publish a treatise on it, seems to have been the Swiss Hans Georg Nägeli, whose lectures were given in various German cities in 1824, the treatise following a couple of years later (*Vorlesungen über Musik mit besonderer Berücksichtigung der Dilettanten*—"Lectures on Music with Particular Regard to Amateurs"). Then six years later (1830) there followed a work by that active Belgian musicologist, Fétis—*La Musique mise à la portée de tout le monde* ("Music Brought Within Everybody's Reach"). This enjoyed an immediate and overwhelming success. I have traced no fewer than nineteen editions. I am not at all sure that I have succeeded in compiling a complete list but it includes editions in English, Italian, Spanish, German, Portuguese, and Russian. The four translations into English include one in the United States— the first work of its sort there to appear.[1]

So far as I recall the first printed work of the nature of a treatise on Musical Appreciation was that by Ridley Prentice, a Professor of the Royal Academy of Music, who in the 1880's embarked on a campaign of popularization of music in various London suburbs by means of "Monthly Popular Concerts" and "Twopenny Concerts" and produced an excellent series of books (six grades of them) called *The Musician* and designed to be a "Guide and Companion to the Pianoforte Student . . . helping him to understand music better, and consequently to enjoy it more." Soon across the Atlantic the same idea was taken up by W. S. Matthews, Editor of *The Musician,* who in 1888 published his *How to Understand Music.* He was a brilliant pianist and believed that there should be much hearing of classical music played by the teacher to his pupils. I do not know when the American term (for it is American in origin) "Music Appreciation" came into use, but at a meeting of the *Musical Association* (Britain's great musicological body) in 1895, a touring party of distinguished American musicians was welcomed and one of them (my own old friend, Professor Waldo Pratt) read a paper, in the report of which the following occurred:

> The lecturer then gave some particulars concerning the effort being made in America to develop musical appreciation by including it in the educational curriculum.

From that period onwards efforts to provide the intelligent portion of the population with what the author of the present book calls "An Introduction to Music"[2] became increasingly common. So about 1897 we find

[1] The young Mendelssohn sneered at Fétis's idea, making the quite illogical remark, *"What is the good of talking so much about music? It is better to compose well."* And yet Mendelssohn, as a youth, had spent hours with Goethe for the purpose of playing and explaining to him at his request some of the masterpieces of music!

[2] A better term, by the way, than "Appreciation of Music," which, being ambiguous, is subject to misunderstanding as capable of meaning "evaluation."

the successive publication on the two sides of the Atlantic of Oliviera Prescott's quickly popular *About Music and What it is Made Of* and Krehbiel's *How to Listen to Music*. Then H. G. Wells in a series of articles called *Mankind in the Making*, in discussing school education, is seen pleading for a "type of music teaching which will enable the listener to distinguish the threads and the values of a musical composition, to have a quickened ear rather than a disciplined hand."

Ten years later a six-volume work jointly by the American authors Thomas Whitney Surette and Daniel Gregory Mason, *The Appreciation of Music*, enjoyed considerable success, as did a series of lectures in various English towns by Surette, under the aegis of the University Extension Board of Oxford University. Kobbé's book at about the same period, *How to Appreciate Music*, was another useful American effort.

The advent of the phonograph now became an important influence, the Victor Talking Machine Company establishing a definite Educational Department directed by our veteran, Dr. Frances Clark (happily, still amongst us), who, after five years, was able to report a list of no fewer than three thousand cities in various parts of the United States whose school activities included music appreciation. Peter Dykema (Columbia University), Will Earhart (Pittsburgh), and Mary Regal (Springfield, Mass.) are names that stand out prominently at this period.

A Miss A. Langdale (of whom I know nothing beyond the name) served as a useful link between American and British pioneers and inspired the vigorous Stewart Macpherson of the Royal Academy of Music, who, in the objects of the Music Teachers' Association which he founded, prominently included the impressing on Heads of Schools the duty of "stimulating and maintaining amongst teachers a recognition of the important and often overlooked fact that music is a literature and should be taught and studied from that point of view." Macpherson's own books and others by his followers enjoyed (and in their own country still enjoy) great popularity.

There, then, is a brief synopsis of the early history of the big educational movement to which Professor Boyden's contribution is now before us. May it enjoy the popularity it deserves and thus tend to widen the circle of music lovers amongst the author's own compatriots—and, I hope, amongst my own countrymen also. I am sure Professor Boyden has shown himself to be a practical man, and I hope and believe that he will attain the success which his practical effort in a good cause manifestly deserves.

PERCY A. SCHOLES

Oxford

Contents

CONCERNING THE SECOND EDITION   xxi

INTRODUCTION   x.iii

PART I. THE FUNDAMENTALS

1. *The Enjoyment and Understanding of Music*   3

2. *The Elements of Music. Rhythm, the First Element.*   9
   THE LISTENING PROCESS AND THE FUNDAMENTALS   9
   THE ELEMENTS OF MUSIC   10
   RHYTHM, THE FIRST ELEMENT   12
   MATERIAL FOR FURTHER STUDY   19

3. *Melody, the Second Element*   21
   PRELIMINARIES   21
   THE ORGANIZATION OF MELODIES   26
   MELODY AND SIMPLE FORMS   33
   MATERIAL FOR FURTHER STUDY   35

4. *Harmony, the Third Element*   42
   PRELIMINARIES   42
   THE RELATION OF RHYTHM TO POLYPHONY AND HARMONY   44
   CONSONANCE AND DISSONANCE   46
   HARMONY   48
   THE MELODIC DISSONANCES OF COUNTERPOINT   51
   MATERIAL FOR FURTHER STUDY   52

5. *The Larger Forms*   55
   FORM IN GENERAL   55
   THE LARGER FORMS   57
   MINUET. SCHERZO.   57
   THE RONDO   58
   THE THEME AND VARIATIONS   59
   OSTINATO. CHACONNE. PASSACAGLIA.   60
   THE FUGUE AND THE SONATA FORM AS COMPLEX EXPRESSIONS OF
       COUNTERPOINT AND HARMONY   61
   THE FUGUE   61
   ANALYSIS OF FUGUE III FROM BACH'S "THE ART OF THE FUGUE"   64

    THE SONATA FORM   67
    HOW TO "TELL" SONATA FORM   71
    MODIFICATIONS OF SONATA FORM   72
    THE COMPOSITE INSTRUMENTAL FORMS   73
    ANALYSIS OF HAYDN'S "DRUM ROLL" SYMPHONY   74

6. *Tone Color the Fourth Element*   84
    TONE COLOR   84
    THE HUMAN VOICE   85
    INSTRUMENTS IN GENERAL   87
    INDIVIDUAL CHOIRS AND INSTRUMENTS   90
    INSTRUMENTATION AND ORCHESTRATION   106

7. *Aspects of Performance*   108
    WHAT THE CONDUCTOR DOES   108
    THE IMPORTANCE OF PERFORMANCE AND INTERPRETATION   110

8. *Music and Description*   115
    PRELIMINARIES   115
    THE TEXT AND VOCAL FORMS   118
    PROGRAM MUSIC—MUSIC THAT TELLS A STORY   122

9. *Beauty and Related Questions*   126

PART II. THE DEVELOPMENT AND REPERTORY OF MUSIC

10. *The Development of Music to 1600*   133
    THE ORIGINS OF MUSIC   133
    FOLK MUSIC   134
    GREGORIAN CHANT   137
    THE MIDDLE AGES   140
    THE FOURTEENTH CENTURY: ARS NOVA. MACHAUT. LANDINI.   145
    THE EARLY FIFTEENTH CENTURY: DUNSTABLE. BINCHOIS. DUFAY.   147
    THE LATE FIFTEENTH CENTURY: JOSQUIN DES PREZ   149
    THE SIXTEENTH CENTURY: THE LATE RENAISSANCE   152
    SACRED MUSIC: PALESTRINA. LASSO. BYRD.   152
    SECULAR MUSIC: MARENZIO. MORLEY. WEELKES. WILBYE. DOWLAND.   155
    INSTRUMENTAL MUSIC   157

11. *The Seventeenth Century: Opera and Related Forms. Sacred
    Music.*   161
    THE BAROQUE (1600–1750)   161
    OPERA AND RELATED FORMS: MONTEVERDI. LULLY. PURCELL.   167
    SACRED MUSIC: GABRIELI. MONTEVERDI. CARISSIMI. SCHÜTZ.   175

12. *The Instrumental Music of the Seventeenth Century*   179
    RICERCAR. CANZONA. FANTASIA.   181
    PRELUDE AND TOCCATA. FRESCOBALDI.   181
    THE DANCE SUITE   183

THE SONATA: THE CHURCH SONATA, THE CHAMBER SONATA. CORELLI.   184

THE VARIATION. THE OSTINATO. CHACONNE AND PASSACAGLIA.   186

13. *The Early Eighteenth Century: Opera and Secular Cantata. Sacred Music.*   189

PRELIMINARIES   189

OPERA AND SECULAR CANTATA: ALESSANDRO SCARLATTI. HANDEL. RAMEAU. PERGOLESI. "THE BEGGAR'S OPERA."   193

SACRED MUSIC: HANDEL. BACH.   200

14. *The Instrumental Music of the Early Eighteenth Century*   212

THE CONCERTO GROSSO: CORELLI. TORELLI. VIVALDI. BACH. HANDEL.   212

THE SOLO CONCERTO: VIVALDI. BACH.   215

THE SONATA: BACH. DOMENICO SCARLATTI.   217

THE EVOLUTION OF OLDER FORMS: BACH. HANDEL. COUPERIN.   220

BACH AND HANDEL COMPARED   225

15. *Instrumental Music of the Classic Period*   229

THE CLASSIC PERIOD (1750–C.1820)   229

STYLES IN ART AND MUSIC: THE ROCOCO. THE MATURE CLASSIC STYLE.   231

THE SONATA   238

THE SYMPHONY: HAYDN'S "DRUM ROLL." MOZART'S "JUPITER." BEETHOVEN'S "EROICA."   240

THE SOLO SONATA: C. P. E. BACH. HAYDN. MOZART. BEETHOVEN.   245

CHAMBER MUSIC   246

THE CHAMBER MUSIC OF HAYDN, MOZART, AND BEETHOVEN   250

THE SOLO CONCERTO   256

MATERIAL FOR FURTHER STUDY   258

TWO MOZART CONCERTOS   260

16. *Opera and Sacred Music of the Classic Period*   264

THE OPERA SERIA. THE GLUCK "REFORM."   265

THE COMIC OPERA: PERGOLESI. MOZART.   268

SACRED MUSIC: HAYDN. MOZART.   274

HAYDN AND MOZART COMPARED   276

17. *The Early Nineteenth Century*   282

ROMANTICISM   282

FORMS AND STYLES OF ROMANTIC MUSIC   284

LUDWIG VAN BEETHOVEN   286

THE SONG. THE SHORT PIANO PIECE. SCHUBERT. SCHUMANN. CHOPIN.   293

18. *The Sonata, Symphony, and Concerto After Beethoven*   298

THE SONATA AND SYMPHONY IN GENERAL   298

INDIVIDUAL WORKS: SCHUBERT. BRAHMS. TCHAIKOVSKY. BRUCKNER AND MAHLER.   300

THE CONCERTO IN THE NINETEENTH CENTURY   312

19. *Orchestral Program Music*   316

THE CONCERT OVERTURE   316

THE PROGRAM SYMPHONY: BERLIOZ   318
THE SYMPHONIC POEM: LISZT. RICHARD STRAUSS.   324

20. *Sacred Music and Opera in the Nineteenth Century*   329
SACRED MUSIC: BEETHOVEN. LISZT. MENDELSSOHN. BERLIOZ. VERDI.
    BRAHMS. FAURÉ. THE RUSSIANS.   329
OPERA: MEYERBEER. AUBER. GOUNOD. BIZET. OFFENBACH. GILBERT
    AND SULLIVAN. ROSSINI. BELLINI. DONIZETTI. BEETHOVEN. WEBER.   332

21. *The Operas of Wagner and Richard Strauss*   341

22. *Verdi*   351
    "FALSTAFF"   355

23. *Nationalism in Music*   359
NATIONALISM IN RUSSIA: GLINKA. "THE FIVE." RUBINSTEIN. TCHAI-
    KOVSKY.   360
NATIONALISM IN BOHEMIA: SMETANA. DVOŘÁK.   365
NATIONALISM IN SCANDINAVIA: GRIEG   366

24. *After Wagner and Between Two Wars*   368
REGER. WOLF.   368
VERISMO: PUCCINI   370
ENGLAND: ELGAR   371
FRENCH INSTRUMENTAL MUSIC: FRANCK. FAURÉ AND THE FRENCH
    SONG.   372

25. *Impressionism: Debussy. Ravel. Reactions: Satie.*   377
DEBUSSY   377
RAVEL   386
REACTIONS: SATIE   389

26. *The Music of the Twentieth Century: An Introduction.*   392
THE COMPOSER AND THE PUBLIC   392
THE REVOLT AGAINST ROMANTICISM. NEW DIRECTIONS: ATONALITY.
    PRIMITIVISM. FOLK-MUSIC IDIOMS.   397
AFTER 1918: TWELVE-TONE MUSIC. NEOCLASSICISM. POST-WEBERN
    COMPOSERS. ELECTRONIC AND CHANCE MUSIC.   400

27. *The New Vienna School of Schoenberg, Webern, and Berg.*
    Expressionism and Free Atonality. The Twelve-Tone and
    Serial Techniques.   404
SCHOENBERG   408
WEBERN   419
BERG   426

28. *Stravinsky. His Russian Background and Early Works. Neo-*
    classicism in France. Neoclassic and Serial Works.   430
STRAVINSKY AND NEOCLASSICISM   434
STRAVINSKY'S NEOCLASSIC WORKS   435
STRAVINSKY'S STYLE   440

CONTENTS

29. *Bartók and the Folk-Music Idiom. Hindemith and Neoclassicism.*   445

    BARTÓK   445

    HINDEMITH   455

30. *Music Under the Soviets: The Impact of the State on Music. The Ballet. Prokofiev. Shostakovich. Khachaturian.*   460

    PROKOFIEV   463

    SHOSTAKOVICH   469

    KHACHATURIAN   479

31. *Other Leading Composers and Other Countries*   480

    FRANCE: "THE SIX"—HONEGGER, MILHAUD, POULENC   480

    ITALY: MALIPIERO. DALLAPICCOLA.   483

    SPAIN: FALLA   484

    FINLAND: SIBELIUS   485

    ENGLAND: DELIUS. VAUGHAN WILLIAMS. BLISS. WALTON. BRITTEN.   487

32. *Music in the New World: The United States. Latin America.*   490

    THE UNITED STATES   490

    BLOCH AND IVES: A STUDY IN CONTRAST   492

    THE AVANT-GARDE. COWELL.   496

    THE NATIONALISTS: HARRIS. HANSON. GERSHWIN. MOORE.   497

    INDIVIDUALISM AND EUROPEAN CURRENTS: SESSIONS. THOMPSON. COPLAND. PISTON. THOMSON.   499

    THE "YOUNGER" GENERATION: SCHUMAN. BARBER. MENOTTI.   503

    COMPOSERS IN LATIN AMERICA: VILLA-LOBOS. CHÁVEZ.   505

33. *The Avant-garde*   507

    NEW SOUNDS, INSTRUMENTS, AND INSTRUMENTAL USAGE. NEW DIRECTIONS.   508

    THE SPREAD OF SERIAL MUSIC. THE POST-WEBERN COMPOSERS. TOTAL ORGANIZATION. LEIBOWITZ. BOULEZ. MESSIAEN. BABBITT.   511

    NONSERIAL CHROMATICISTS: CARTER. KIRCHNER.   514

    MICROTONE MUSIC: BARTH. HÁBA. CARRILLO. PARTCH.   517

    FORERUNNERS OF ELECTRONIC SOUND. VARÈSE. "NOISE" AS RAW MATERIAL.   519

    ELECTRONIC MUSIC. TAPE-RECORDER MUSIC. MUSIQUE CONCRÈTE.   520

    STOCKHAUSEN.   522

    ALEATORY ("CHANCE") MUSIC. JOHN CAGE AND OTHERS.   524

APPENDIX I. *Notation: How Music Is Written Down*   531

    1. NOTATION OF PITCH   531

     MATERIAL FOR FURTHER STUDY   534

    2. NOTATION OF TIME   535

APPENDIX II. *The Order of the Mass. The Complete Text of the Ordinary.*   542

APPENDIX III. *Glossary*   546

INDEX   *follows p.* 554

Illustrations

FOLLOWING PAGE 146

1   *The London Symphony Orchestra making the film* Instruments of the Orchestra.

2A *The Griller Quartet.*

2B *The double-bass section, BBC Symphony Orchestra.*

3A *Oboes and English horn, BBC Symphony Orchestra.*

3B *Bassoons and double bassoon, BBC Symphony Orchestra.*

4A *The clarinets and the bass clarinet, BBC Symphony Orchestra.*

4B *The harp, London Symphony Orchestra.*

5A *The flutes, San Francisco Symphony Orchestra.*

5B *The percussion section, BBC Symphony Orchestra.*

6A *French horn section, BBC Symphony Orchestra.*

6B *Brasses, San Francisco Symphony Orchestra.*

7A *"Sumer is icumen in" (facsimile).*

7B *"Sumer is icumen in" in modern notation (original version, according to Manfred Bukofzer).*

8A *Bach's* Chaconne *for unaccompanied violin (facsimile of the autograph).*

8B *Bach's* Chaconne *in an edited version (Joachim and Moser).*

9A *The minnesinger Herr Reinmar playing the vielle (about 1300).*

9B *Performing the chanson "Jouyssance vous donneray" of Sermisy (about 1531).*

10 *Two churches famous for music:* A. *Notre-Dame in Paris;* B. *Saint Mark's in Venice.*

11A *Singing and dancing Machaut's* virelai, *"Dame, a vous sans retollir" (late fourteenth century).*

11B *Baude Cordier's chanson "Belle bonne" (about 1400).*

12A *Dowland's song "Shall I sue" (1600).*

12B *Detail from Jan Brueghel's painting "Hearing" (about 1620), showing a large number of contemporary instruments.*

13A *Jan van Hemessen's "Clavichord Player" (about 1534).*

13B   *A harpsichord made by Jean Couchet in Flanders (about 1650).*

14A   *The clavichord mechanism.*

14B   *The harpsichord mechanism.*

15   *Instruments of the seventeenth and early eighteenth centuries in playing position:* A. *The viol from Simpson's "The Division-Violist" (1659);* B. *The recorder from Hotteterre's "Principes de la Flute traversière . . ." (1708);* C. *The lute as played by Charles Mouton (flourished in the seventeenth century).*

16A   *French painting depicting the dance* La Volta *at the wedding of the Duke de Joyeuse and Princess Margarethe of Lorraine (1581).*

16B   *"The Concert," an engraving by Picart after a painting by Domenichino (early seventeenth century).*

FOLLOWING PAGE 306

17   *Baroque opera sets from Cesti's* Il Pomo d'Oro *(1667). Designs by Burnacino:* A. *"The Garden of Joy" (Act I, Scene 15);* B. *"The Mouth of Hell" (Act II, Scene 6).*

18A   *French court ballet (1625) during the youth of Louis XIV and Lully. Detail taken from a water color of Daniel Rabel (1578?–1637).*

18B   *Dancing the minuet accompanied by the strings. French engraving (1682).*

19A   *The opera house in Vienna where Cesti's* Il Pomo d'Oro *was first performed.*

19B   *Louis XIV and his family. Painting by Largillière (about 1710).*

20   *Composers' autographs: Purcell, Handel, Bach, Arne, Berlioz, Liszt.*

21A   *Architecture of the late baroque: interior of the "Wies" Church in Bavaria, built by Zimmermann (1757).*

21B   *The Rococo Theater, Schwetzingen, Baden (built in 1715).*

22A   *Claudio Monteverdi (1644).*

22B   *Henry Purcell. Painting by Closterman.*

22C   *Antonio Vivaldi from an engraving by I. Caldwall (1725).*

22D   *Johann Sebastian Bach. Painting by Hausmann (1748).*

23   *Two views of Handel:* A. *A painting by Denner;* B. *A caricature by a disgruntled contemporary (1754).*

24A   *The Young Mozart (1767).*

24B   *Beethoven (1815). Portrait by Christoph Heckel.*

24C   *Niccolò Paganini. Lithograph by Begas (before 1831).*

25A   *The "Wolf Glen" Scene from Weber's opera* Der Freischütz. *Drawn by Moritz von Schwind.*

25B   *Wagner's plan for the Festival Theater in Bayreuth (1876).*

26A *French* contredanse (*1805*).

26B *Monet: "Impression: Sunrise" (1872).*

27A *The waltz, Vienna. A mid-nineteenth-century engraving.*

27B *A scene from a performance of Wagner's* Tannhäuser *at Bayreuth (1954).*

28A *Richard and Cosima Wagner (1872).*

28B *Giuseppe Verdi. Portrait by Boldini (1886).*

28C *Franz Liszt playing to his friends in Vienna, by Kriehuber (1846). Kriehuber, Berlioz, Czerny, Liszt, and the violinist Ernst.*

29A *Claude Debussy as a Young Man (1884). Painting by Marcel Baschet.*

29B *Detail of Georges Seurat's painting "The Parade" (1889).*

30A *Jean Cocteau at the piano with "The Six": Milhaud, Auric, Honegger, Tailleferre, Poulenc, and Durey.*

30B *Scene from Martha Graham's ballet* Appalachian Spring (*1944*). *Music by Aaron Copland.*

31A *Portrait of Igor Stravinsky by Edward Weston (before 1936).*

31B *"The Three Musicians" by Pablo Picasso (1921).*

32A *Arnold Schoenberg (1947).*

32B *Berlin Philharmonic Hall (1963). New type of construction.*

FOLLOWING PAGE 402

33A Parade *designed by Picasso, music by Satie (1917).*

33B *Kandinsky, "Improvisation 30" (expressionist painting; 1913).*

34A *Anton Webern.*

34B *Stravinsky,* Orpheus, *autograph (1947).*

35A *Béla Bartók playing a folk instrument.*

35B *Paul Hindemith with his viola.*

36A *Serge Prokofiev.*

36B *Benjamin Britten.*

37A *Charles Ives and his wife.*

37B *Roger Sessions.*

38A *Bartolozzi. New sounds and chords on woodwinds (1967).*

38B *Pierre Boulez.*

39A *Karlheinz Stockhausen at work.*

39B *A score of electronic music: Stockhausen's "Electronic Study II."*

40A *Jackson Pollock: "Number 1" (1948).*

40B *John Cage.*

Concerning the Second Edition

THE FIRST EDITION of this book appeared more than a dozen years ago, and since then a number of changes have taken place in the world of music. Many new and often problematical works have been composed, and sometimes our perspective has changed toward pieces already in the repertory. Consequently, it is not happenstance that the first edition of *An Introduction to Music* has been completely rewritten from the time of Debussy on, taking account of new attitudes and relating in some detail the progress and development of music since 1945.

In general, the coverage with respect to individual composers is more detailed than in the earlier part of the book, and this change in emphasis seemed justified on the grounds that the information on the giants of the present is somewhat less accessible to the general reader than that of the great composers of the past. By the same token, the focus on composers has shifted the emphasis away from discussion of music by types, such as the sonata, symphony, concerto, and opera.

While the sections on the twentieth century have been rewritten and amplified, the substance of the earlier part of the book has been left much as it was, the changes consisting largely of bringing the Listening and Reading Suggestions up to date and correcting those errors of detail that appear inevitable in any large-scale effort. On the other hand, in keeping with the amplified coverage, the Glossary has been enlarged to ensure that all terms used in this book will be defined and understood in context.

One word about the dating of pieces of music, particularly in the sections on the twentieth century. As far as possible, or unless otherwise stated, the date given for any piece is that of the completion of the work, as opposed to the date of first performance or first appearance in print. Sometimes these dates are close together; but where they are not, especially when a work may wait years for a first performance, it clearly affords a fairer picture of a composer's development when the actual

xxiv   CONCERNING THE SECOND EDITION

date of a work's completion is given rather than that of the first performance or first printing.

As in the first edition, I have been the grateful recipient of much advice
and counsel. To single out two persons, among many others, who have
helped me: I wish to thank Professor Eve Meyer for detailed suggestions
concerning fundamental problems of organization; and Professor Gerald
Abraham has put me in his debt by reading and criticizing the sections
on the twentieth century.

Last but not least: I have been much gratified by the reception accorded
the first edition, and I hope that the second will continue to fill a need and
enjoy the response given the first.

DAVID D. BOYDEN

Berkeley, California
April 27, 1969

Introduction

W HEN IT COMES TO MUSIC, everyone agrees about one thing: you can't learn anything about music unless you listen to it. This could be called the "what" of our subject. And here general agreement ends. On the "how" and the "why" there are innumerable opinions. How to introduce anyone to music and why one method is better than another are subjects of long debate.

The "how" and the "why" of music have a broader application, however, and the two main parts of this book are devoted to "how" and "why" as well as "what." Part I is concerned with the fundamentals of music: "how" music is made. Part II, "The Development and Repertory of Music," discusses the "what" of music as a whole and "why" this or that happens. Naturally, all these things are related. The what and the how, in particular, illuminate each other, and listening to music becomes increasingly vivid as we do so on music's own terms. The fundamental how in Part I is essentially a short cut to understanding and listening to music as a whole. On the other hand, to study the fundamentals apart from music itself is to explore a vacuum, and any explanation of the fundamental processes of music is worthless unless it gives us a better insight into the music itself. The aim of this book is simply to train the ear and direct the mind toward the end of understanding and enjoying the literature of music. The fundamentals in Part I—rhythm, melody, harmony, tone color, and so on—are illustrated by pieces of music drawn as far as possible from Part II. In the latter, the same pieces (and a number of others) are discussed in a different way, namely, as they developed over the ages in their cultural and musical context.

After much thought I have arranged Part II chronologically, although it is not usual to do so in a book of this kind. It seems to me that the whole development of music is easier to follow in this way, and the important why of our subject—after all, one of its most fascinating aspects—becomes much clearer. Viewed in this manner, the complex development and reactions of music from one age to another become more vivid, and the relationship of music's forms and styles of expression is easier to explain and clarify. What happened to the sonata, the concerto, or the symphony—to select several examples—and why it happened, can hardly be explained satisfactorily in any other way, particularly in view of the fact that a sonata or concerto of Bach is quite different from a sonata or concerto of Beethoven, Tchaikovsky, or Bartók. At the same time I have tried to make the individual sections complete in themselves, as far as it is possible to do so, and they may be read in a different order from the one in which I have presented them. The cross references will help considerably to establish a relationship between the sections, whether they are read in chronological order or not. The coverage of the literature of music is perhaps more comprehensive than is usual in an introductory text, but this has seemed desirable in order to present a clear picture of the development of music from earliest to most recent times; and it has seemed practical in view of the comprehensive selection of music now available on phonograph records.

This book assumes no previous knowledge on the part of the reader. However, Part I is planned as an indispensable adjunct to Part II, and certain sections of the latter depend on a knowledge of the earlier part. A considerable amount of Part II does not rely on Part I and can be understood without it; but in the discussions of music in its own terms, especially in the analyses of pieces of music, the reader should be familiar with the corresponding sections of Part I to derive the most benefit from the discussion.

In both parts I have made numerous suggestions for listening and for reading. On the whole I think it is preferable to pursue the listening suggestions first, for reasons already mentioned and because any book on music must depend on this kind of musical co-operation from the reader. All the music suggested for listening is recorded, as well as most of the music mentioned in the body of the text. The readings give sources of additional information on a subject, sometimes along musical and sometimes along biographical lines. For those who wish to pursue still further certain phases of the fundamentals presented in Part I, I have added sections called "Material for Further Study."

Every book is written with a particular point of view and with someone in mind. My point of view is implicit in what I have just said, and while writing this book I have tried to keep constantly in mind my own experience in the college classroom and the introductory college course in music for which this book is primarily intended. I hope, too, that this book will find a wider and more general usefulness than the immediate goal to which it aims: that it will not be without value for the music student and especially for the general reader who wishes to expand his musical horizon in terms of the what, how, and why of music.

TO THE TEACHER

Every teacher who has helped me has had something of the missionary spirit; he has wanted to share his feelings, discoveries, and enthusiasms for his subject with others. For this reason, if for no other, I hope to be pardoned for mentioning some of the trials and errors of my own experience as they are reflected in this book.

To me the most crucial problem in any class is the transformation of the students from passive note-takers to active participants. I have found that this transformation takes place in the degree that the student is in contact with music. At first, the more active and physical this contact is, the better. It has surprised me, for instance, to discover how enthusiasm can be generated by insisting that students clap rhythms, conduct, or move to music. Each student his own Toscanini is an excellent motto. If a class is not too large, its members can learn rapidly how to beat simple two and three time. Insisting on a vigorous and accurate beat accomplishes wonders.

In my view, good illustrations lie at the heart and center of effective instruction. Besides the music itself, visual aids, diagrams, and analogies of one sort or another have helped me greatly, and I have incorporated a number of suggestions of this kind in the book. For example, illustrating the role of tonality by different *levels* in a visual drawing has proved fruitful; and, as far as I know, the application of the idea of levels to an older idea of "verbal" sonata form is my own invention (see p. 72). I have found also that illustration and participation by members of the class are stimulating to other members. In a class of general students there are often surprisingly wide and varied talents, musical and otherwise, which I try to discover at the beginning. Thus I have had dancers who were able to reconstruct, among other dances, the *pavane* and *galliard* according to the *Orchésographie* of Thoinot Arbeau (1589); and dancing for a class to the music of a sixteenth-century *pavane* has awakened interest in a way that nothing else could. Some classes, depending on their size and the aptitude of the students, can accomplish a great deal by singing. Each class is different, and each teacher has a different problem in terms of the size of his class and the variety of background and zeal of his students.

I have firm convictions about the necessity of introducing the student to the fundamental concepts of music, but I have no special brief as to how this should be done. The *idea* essential to many basic concepts of music can, I believe, be grasped and explained in general terms; and I have tried to make such a complicated but essential notion as modulation clear by simple analogies (see p. 51). I have no feelings, one way or the other, about how far the teacher should go in asking the student to learn note and time values, although I have given a large number of musical illustrations and included a section in the Appendix on the notation of pitch and time. Paradoxically, I believe that a score helps the majority of students, and I have urged its use in class and in the course of this book. My whole feeling about this is that a student absorbs the fundamentals gratefully and willingly to the degree that he sees that they are helping him to enjoy and listen to music better. If learning to read music can serve this end, it will, I think, prove highly advantageous.

A word about the coverage and arrangement of Part II and the suggestions for listening and reading. I have already mentioned my feelings about the chronological arrangement, and, as I have said, the coverage of the repertory is very full. This has been done because the general student has become aware of more and more music as the radio and especially the phonograph have widened the usual repertory. Furthermore, I believe that broadening the musical horizon is a sound aim. In this respect Part II looks considerably beyond what I expect to cover in two semesters of college work, but I have never believed in a course that is purely definitive and self-enclosed in its aims. The arrangement of the fundamentals in Part I is calculated in terms of listening in depth, so to speak. Obviously, the same piece can be heard to advantage again and again in different contexts, and for this reason I have suggested a relatively small number of pieces to illustrate quite different things. Assignments that are cumulative or comparative in terms of a fairly small number of pieces have been valuable for me. At the same time, I have added sections—"Material for Further Study"—of comparatively difficult material to be used as needed for advanced students or perhaps in a second, or later, semester. In an average class devoting two semesters to an introduction to music, I try to use the basic fundamentals coupled with such of the repertory as I can cover in the first semester; and, in the second, a review of the fundamentals (sometimes including the materials for further study) and more of the repertory. I hope that the book will prove flexible in this regard. I have found that the greatest problem in a class of this kind is the establishment of a balance between the fundamentals and the repertory. This, of course, is where the teacher comes in; and I am well aware that no text, not even the best, can rival the effectiveness of a teacher of genuine gifts and enthusiasm for his subject. The present text is planned as a framework within which the teacher can operate—to free him from making explanations that can be read and studied outside of class. If I have succeeded in this aim, that in itself will more than recompense the labor of writing the book.

Some time ago I read a sentence in *The Manchester Guardian Weekly* (December 24, 1953, p. 14) which has haunted me ever since. In an article entitled "The Teaching of English in America," David Daiches says, ". . . as a result of a rather scholastic training in critical methodology, he [the American student of English] often finds himself equipped with a technique (and a vocabulary) of analysis which bears no relation at all to the reasons why he in fact enjoys works of literature." If we were to substitute "listening," or "looking," for "analysis," Daiches's remark would summarize an age-old problem in teaching the arts at least, and in music, point to our central responsibility of showing the student how to listen in the fundamental terms of music without bogging down in technicalities. This raises a fundamental question as to what kind of listening is directly related to the enjoyment of music. I have never been able to answer this question even in so limited a sphere as that of my own enjoyment of and addiction to music, and I can only surmise from what students have told me that a judicious introduction to the fundamentals of music in relation to the literature of music has been valuable to them. Perhaps in the long run the situation comes down to something that can be illustrated by a personal anecdote. Years ago I wrote a letter to the critic Samuel Chotzinoff, taking him to task for his radio commentary on a series of Beethoven broadcasts by Toscanini. In his reply Chotzinoff wrote, "The only legitimate use for a critic is to create excitement around music and its creators." That is not all of a teacher's responsibility but it is a most important part.

In writing this book, I have been the grateful recipient of much generous help and advice from colleagues, assistants, and friends. At the University of California my assistants, Alan Rich, Martin Chusid, and Mrs. Sydney Charles, have helped me in numerous ways. My former students, Richard Irwin and Harry Edwall, have given me the benefit of their classroom experience. My colleagues, Professors Edgar Sparks, Alexander Ringer, Albert Elkus, Edward Lawton, Joseph Kerman, Seymour Shifrin, and Isabel Hungerland have aided me with their advice and criticism. Helen Farnsworth, Althea Doyle, and Joan Sinnott, secretaries to the Music Department of the University of California, have done me many favors. I am indebted to one of my former graduate students, Dr. E. J. Simon, for information on the transformation of the baroque to the Classic concerto. Professors William Austin of Cornell University, Arnold Elston of the University of Oregon, and Louise Rood of Smith College have advised me on special problems.

I also owe a debt of gratitude for their interest and advice to my personal friends, among them, Dr. and Mrs. Lovell Langstroth, Mr. and Mrs. Jon Cornin, Dr. and Mrs. Martin Kamen, Mr. Roger Levenson, Mr. Alfred Frankenstein, music and art critic of the San Francisco *Chronicle,* and Mr. Francis Scheetz.

To Percy Scholes, one of the pioneers in teaching music to a general audience, I wish to extend thanks for advice on the last stages of this book —as well as for the help I received from his book on the history of music appreciation. I am grateful to Eric Rahn for sending me pictures of the San Francisco Symphony Orchestra. Jeremy Noble of London rendered me invaluable aid by collecting examples and illustrations. Mlle. Martine Martenet of Rivaz, Switzerland, managed to type the final manuscript in time to meet a deadline. I am greatly obliged to Paul Hooreman of Lausanne, Switzerland, for the use of certain plates from his two valuable books, *Musiciens à travers les temps* (Paris, 1952) and *Danseurs à travers les temps* (Paris, 1953). The members of the staff of Alfred A. Knopf, Inc., particularly Tom Bledsoe, my editor, have throughout exhibited an amazing patience and understanding.

To my classes, I owe a debt that I can never repay, for it has always seemed to me that a teacher learns more from his students than they from him. And finally, to my long-suffering family, I owe both a debt and apologies. Without the help and encouragement of my wife, I do not believe that I could have surmounted the hurdles and discouragements that the writing of a book of this kind entails.

DAVID D. BOYDEN

Berkeley, California
March 1, 1956

Part One:

THE FUNDAMENTALS

1. *The Enjoyment and Understanding of Music*

> *The Artist . . . speaks to our capacity for delight and wonder, to the sense of mystery surrounding our lives; to our sense of pity, and beauty, and pain; to the latent feeling of fellowship with all creation—to the subtle but invincible conviction of solidarity that knits together the loneliness of innumerable hearts, to the solidarity of dreams, in joy, in sorrow, in aspirations, in illusions, in hope, in fear which binds men to each other, which binds together all humanity—the dead to the living and the living to the unborn.*
>
> JOSEPH CONRAD in *The Conditions of Art*

OF ALL THE ARTS, music is one of the most difficult to discuss. It is a complicated matter to define something that cannot be seen or touched but only heard and felt. Besides, how can one describe the most important thing in music, its power to appeal directly to the deepest and most varied emotions? The fact is that no one can communicate his own emotional experience *directly* to another person. Still, there are ways of listening that will permit anyone to hear music better, to glimpse the unsuspected vistas of the great literature of music, and to enjoy more fully the immense variety of emotions hidden in its depths.

Why do people love and enjoy music? This is a frustrating question because many of the pleasures of music are intuitive, and it is impossible to explain them in rational terms. There is an inexplicable mystery in being drawn to a succession of sounds that have been given beauty, coherence, and expression by a great mind and spirit. As Conrad says in the remarkable passage quoted above, "The Artist . . . speaks to our capacity for delight and wonder," and somewhere in the emotional experience of each individual who is moved by music the composer touches a common ground of sympathy and experience. The sheer brilliance of some performances thrills an audience, and in others the volume of sound or the immensity of the conception of a work leaves the individual "crushed by a tremendous emotion," as Berlioz wrote in his *Mémoires*. The shades of tone color of individual voices or instruments in the orchestra may be a source of delight. Some listeners confess to hearing music entirely in this way; and some to translating sound into a spectrum of color. An individual or audience is often stirred instinctively by the rhythmic animation and drive of music, by sudden contrasts of loud and soft, by the excitement of a *crescendo,* or even by the suspense of a dramatic silence.

For many persons there is great pleasure in direct contact with music. Clapping, walking, moving, marching, or dancing to music puts the individual in special physical touch with it. Playing an instrument or singing may lead one still deeper into its inner recesses. Taking part in a performance is often the source of unique rewards and pleasures that can best be appreciated by those who have experienced them. The physical excitement and even exaltation that may come to a chorus singer taking part in an inspired performance of a masterpiece are emotions quite different in character from those of the audience. Group activities of this sort reveal music as the most social of the arts; and, paradoxically, the individual preserves, as well as loses, his identity in a common effort to achieve emotional expression.

Physical and intuitive pleasure is the first and most natural reaction to music—and perhaps the most powerful. But there are obviously many other delights and satisfactions in music, and few music lovers remain satisfied for long merely with their basic physical response to music. They see about them others enjoying the fascinating inner world of a piece of music: its patterns of melody and rhythm, the continual movement of its forms, and the intricate meshing of voices and instruments. They hear a fugue, but its subtlety escapes them; and the complex relations of a symphony, apparently so enjoyable to others, leave them cold.

Musical pleasure is not a simple thing to analyze. At first it is a subtle mixture of physical response and our conscious efforts to penetrate the basic stuff of music itself. Gradually everything that we know and feel about music is fused in an organic compound of interrelated pleasures. Who can say how a knowledge of a composer's life contributes to an enjoyment of his music, or how an ability to play or sing—or any other special skill in music—adds to what one instinctively feels? Then, too, music never exists in a vacuum. Every piece of music has some relation to the culture of which it is a part—an exciting discovery to many people. The medieval cathedrals express their time, but so does a medieval motet —if we have the wit and musical understanding to discover it. The Romanticism of the nineteenth century is reflected just as surely in Verdi as in Victor Hugo, in Wagner as in Nietzsche. In our own time the clean, objective functionalism of architecture has corresponding analogies in the music of Stravinsky and others. Our pleasures in music are not simple or static. Over the years they become an inseparable blend of intuitive response, of our appreciation of music in its own terms, and of all the peripheries of our knowledge and experience.

Strangely enough, one of the chief pleasures of music has nothing to do with actual listening to music, and perhaps for this reason it is seldom mentioned. This pleasure comes from talking about music and communicating our feelings and reactions to others. Many individuals "appreciate" music instinctively, but they want to know and be able to say why they do. Consciously or unconsciously, they are striving to experience the pleasure of expressing their feelings about music. To be able to do so in the vocabulary of music, which no longer seems to them a rather esoteric jargon, increases their pleasure and excites their intellect.

The pleasure of talking about music is a source of infinite satisfaction to those who know anything about music and a corresponding misery to those who do not. As a matter of fact, it is often the misery factor as much as love of music that drives the nonmusician to try to explore its mysteries. A similar point has been amusingly made, in a characteristically perverse way, by Stephen Potter: [1]

> The general aim in music is to make other people feel outside it— or outsiders, compared to yourself. Don't look too solemn when music is played; on the contrary, be rather jolly about your musical appreciation. Say, "yes, it's a grand tune isn't it?" and bawl it out in a *cracked, unmusical* voice. Say, "Ludwig suggests that this theme represents the galloping hooves of the Four Horsemen of the Apocalypse. But to me it's just a grand tune."

The emotional experience of music is not always an unmixed pleasure, for although it can bring us joy, it can also give us pain. Consciously or not, the listener identifies himself with the emotions aroused by the music of the composer. A dance tune may carry one along pleasantly with its rhythm and recall some associated pleasure in the past; but the tremendous drive and emotional intensity of a Beethoven symphony may appeal to emotions "too deep for tears." Words, too, are often an aid in the expression of a poignant idea by giving specific form to an emotional situation that in turn is intensified by the matchless powers of music. Thus in Verdi's *Otello* the heart-rending death scene of Desdemona and Otello is conveyed to the audience by words and by the stage action, but the agony of the situation is intensified a hundredfold by the extraordinary power of Verdi's music. Here the audience shares the emotional experience of Verdi and Shakespeare, but this experience cannot be called pleasure in the ordinary sense. In this case music shows its power to move the deepest emotions and to cleanse the spirit by a catharsis that may be an exhausting emotional experience for the individual.

What anyone hears and enjoys in music is closely related to his training and experience, and to his vantage point. As Fritz Kreisler says, "It is cultural background, intellectual training, specialization, and execution that make the difference in the appreciation of music." The trained lis-

[1] In his book *Lifemanship* (New York: Henry Holt & Co., Inc., 1950) p. 72.

tener hears music, and experiences it, according to his emotional capacity, in a manner different from the untrained listener. The performer receives a different impression than the audience; and even individual performers playing the same piece hear the music quite differently, as would, for example, a violinist, the conductor, and the percussion player in the same orchestra. Both J. S. Bach and Mozart preferred to play the viola in the string ensemble because it took them into the middle of the harmony; and there is the celebrated story of the bassoonist in Bizet's *Carmen* who went to a performance of this opera on his day off, only to discover to his amazed excitement that, while he was playing "um-pah, um-pah" in the "Toreador Song," the violins and singers were playing a wonderful tune.

Enjoying and understanding music are inseparable from being familiar with music; and this process in turn is bound up with the manner and extent of listening to music. The first necessity for a musician, says William Schuman, is to become a virtuoso listener; and, one might add, to become acquainted with all kinds of music. It is human nature to accept and like the familiar and reject what is strange or unexplained.

Even with relatively familiar music a listener must be prepared to take an alert and informed attitude toward listening in order to absorb a composition to greatest advantage. This is no single road to understanding music, but certain attitudes are essential. In short, music should be listened to attentively, it should be listened to as a whole, and it should be listened to on its own terms.

In an age of "background" music the first lesson is to listen attentively, because "music to read by," or "mood listening," is not music that is really heard or music that gives much pleasure *as music*. Listening to a piece of music *as a whole* is obviously foreign to the experience of certain concertgoers who are accustomed to skim off the melody and dismiss the rest. Everyone loves a beautiful melody, but the lack of it is not necessarily disastrous to a piece of music, any more than the lack of a pretty face is necessarily fatal to a woman's charm. Nevertheless, many a piece is dismissed with the remark "this piece has no melody." This comment usually means that the piece has no easily remembered tune, which may be quite true. But it is also true that this criticism may be no more significant with respect to the piece in question than it would be to criticize an apple because it is not an orange.

This apple-orange criticism is not valid in certain cases, because there are different types of melodic material that assume quite different functions in the whole scheme of a piece of music. Some melodies are self-contained and beautiful in *themselves* as melodies and are easily perceived as such. But other "melodies" are designed not for what they are in themselves but for *what they will become* in relation to the other parts of the ensemble and to the composition as a whole. A fugue, for example, may depend on using a single melody in such a way that one melodic idea or motive (not necessarily a *tune*) furnishes the musical material for *all* the parts of the ensemble and for the entire piece. As such, the prime essential of this melody (or "subject," as it is properly called in the case of a fugue) is not to be "pretty," but to contain germs of musical ideas that can be extended to some length. The fugue is one classic case of the importance of listening to the whole of a piece of music, of hearing the relation of all the parts, and of not condemning a work for lacking a type of melody that is foreign to its nature.

Similarly, to avoid further embarrassment of the "apple-orange" variety, one ought to listen to music on its own terms. A piece that tells a story may be heard in one way; a piece without a story, in another. A sonata has to be heard as a sonata, not as the story of David and Goliath. On the other hand, in a piece about "David and Goliath"—and there is such—one may reasonably expect to find some reference to the slinging of the stone, as naïve as this may seem.

There are many reasons why music is "way over my head," as many casual concert-goers complain. A fundamental one is that understanding music on its own terms involves a kind of listening that recognizes the basic conventions of music and also the various forms and styles of expression evolved by composers in the past. This listening process is a means of unlocking the vast treasure house of music, best approached in a spirit of open-minded sympathy, particularly in the case of music of early times, music of other cultures (for example, the music of the Orient), and music of our own times—"this modern stuff." Audiences have frequently rejected a masterpiece merely because it was new and strange. The history of music and art is filled with unjust criticisms born of unfamiliarity and lack of sympathy. Beethoven's Third Symphony, the *Eroica,* one of the greatest of all works of art, was a trying experience for some listeners at its first hearing; and, in our own time, Stravinsky's *Le Sacre du Printemps* (*Rite of Spring*) created a riot at its first performance in Paris in 1913.

These instances show that the enjoyment of some music depends on a sympathetic hearing and the effort to understand it. This is especially so, ironically enough, with regard to music of our own time and music of early times. Some critics have dismissed "old" music as "crude" and imperfect, partly on the theory that art evolves in a continuous line toward the perfection of the present. The truth is that individual masterpieces must be perceived and enjoyed wherever they exist, although they may be emotional expressions of an age quite different from our own. Leonardo da Vinci was not a "primitive" artist because he lived and painted in the fifteenth century. Nor would anyone claim that the technique of painting has continually improved so that painting today is the best of all times. Absurd as such an idea may seem in painting, discussions of music still suffer from comparable arguments. In reality, composers of the fifteenth century such as Josquin des Prez (c. 1450–1521), an almost exact contemporary of Leonardo, produced great masterpieces in a mode of expression quite different from that of our own time, just as Leonardo's work is distinguished in the manner of technique and subject matter from the art of today. The best expressions of the human mind and spirit of any age are worth the effort to overcome the momentary strangeness that may be caused by the mode of expression in which they are cast.

Listening to music on its own terms has many emotional and intellectual rewards whose variety and intensity vary according to the effort, capacity, and temperament of the individual. There are also many by-products of the listening process. Not the least of these is the growing awareness of the limitless emotional horizon of the musical experience.

2. The Elements of Music. Rhythm, the First Element.

THE LISTENING PROCESS AND THE FUNDAMENTALS

> *Excerpt from a student's criticism of a course on music appreciation given by the author:*
>
> *"In discussing your course the other day, I tried to attack it for the 'technical' part, but on thinking it over, it is obvious that because I now have an inkling of what some of the techniques of music are all about, I am more able to begin understanding it.*
>
> *"P.S. The laudatory remarks are not intended to influence my grade."*

FOR THE BOGEY WORD "technical," the student could just as well have written *"fundamental."* What are the fundamentals of music? Although their extent could be debated, the hard core of the fundamentals is the basic stuff of music, the elements from which it is composed—*rhythm, melody, harmony,* and *tone color*—and the *forms* created by the interaction of these elements. An awareness of the fundamentals is merely knowing and hearing what is going on in the music, the application of the intelligence to hearing. This awareness sharpens the sense of discrimination by changing a passive attitude to an active and informed one. We cannot appreciate to the full what we do not understand, whether it is the music itself or the composer's problem of musical creation.

There is a myth, as persistent as it is erroneous and confusing, that studying music in terms of its fundamentals destroys a love of music. If this were true, those who have the deepest and most intimate knowledge of music—for example, the composer who wrote the music—ought to like it the least. The fact is that fundamental knowledge is arid and dangerous only when it becomes separated from what it is meant to serve, and particularly if it becomes the master where it should be the servant. The same danger is implicit in much of the learning process, especially in the study of the other arts and literature. How many persons have been driven from a love of English or foreign literature by the grammarians, or from a love of great music by the wrong emphasis at the wrong time on fundamentals for their own sake, divorced from the great literature of music?

Just how basic knowledge will contribute to an enjoyment of music is a highly individual and unpredictable matter. For instance, will learning the meaning of the notes on the printed page increase musical enjoyment? No experienced person would be rash enough to make such a claim dogmatically and categorically. But learning to read music, or at least to recognize the notes, can increase enjoyment if this knowledge permits the listener to follow a score, to discuss music more specifically with someone else, or to enjoy the musical experience of singing or playing. In short, learning to read music is merely a means toward an end, namely, the pleasure and understanding that come from hearing music as a whole and from being able to discuss it in a more articulate and informed way.[1]

In most cases the untrained listener must start his directed listening by apprehending the fundamentals of music *iargely as concepts.* It is a matter of time, experience, and training before these fundamentals become an organic part of a person's subconscious hearing. Nevertheless, anyone who has comprehended the *idea* of harmony or counterpoint cannot but hear music in a different and better manner than before, and such ideas will doubtless help the listener to *understand* much better. It will also help him to appreciate the magnitude of the composer's task and the scope of music in general. It may or may not increase his enjoyment of music, because enjoyment is so dependent on individual taste. In this area the individual must be trusted to enjoy what he truly hears.

Real technique, in the sense that the professional composer or performer uses the word, is attained only by the man who will give his lifetime to the study of music. The untrained listener cannot hope to attain a proficiency in composition or in performance without years of work. But the listener can hope for a heightened awareness of music through a comprehension of its basic concepts. As a matter of fact, the average listener often possesses a good ear; he lacks only the knowledge to direct his listening and to realize how the fundamental elements of music are at work in what he hears.

THE ELEMENTS OF MUSIC

In any art there are certain basic materials with which the artist works. In music these elements are rhythm, melody, harmony, and tone color. Dynamics and expression are also elementary to music, but they cannot be as decisively indicated as the elements mentioned. Not all the elements are necessarily present in any one piece. For example, folk song and various types of chant lack the element of harmony.

It is something of a problem to discuss the elements of music individ-

[1] Information about the notation of pitch and duration, and other symbols of written and printed music is in the Appendix, to be used as needed.

ually, because each is almost inseparably related to the others. Rhythm is
the only element that has a life of its own. The drum can by itself define
a rhythmic pattern; in fact, the rhythmic factor in the work and play of
our daily lives is so common that it needs no further comment. Still, if
rhythm has a life of its own apart from music, it is in such cases no longer
an element of music. Melody and rhythm, in the musical sense, are inseparably bound to each other, and (apart from the most primitive music)
melody can hardly be discussed at all apart from rhythm. The succession
of tones in a melody is given life, flow, and unique character through the
rhythm employed. Melody, in the broad sense of a rhythmic succession of
tones, is the most important element in music. This is why the lack of a
well-defined melody is so strongly felt. Melody is the most pervasive element in the development of music. It is the constant in a field of variables.

Another element, the dimension of depth, is added to music when several melodies sound together, as in *counterpoint (polyphony)*, or when a
melody is accompanied by chords, as in *harmony*. Historically speaking,
this element is unquestionably a later phenomenon than melody and
rhythm; it is also particularly connected with the development of music in
the Occident. Harmony distinguishes Occidental from Oriental music,
which has developed largely along melodic and rhythmic lines. The elements of depth may be called by the inclusive name of *harmony,* although
harmony and counterpoint will be distinguished in a more precise sense
in later discussions.

Tone color, a term derived by analogy from painting, refers to the particular shades (or *timbre*) of individual voices, instruments, and their
many combinations. Every sound has its particular quality or acoustical
property (see Chapter 6). The voice has a property different from the oboe
or the trombone, and even individual voices have many subtle shades of
timbre within their general limits of tone color. The timbre of a particular
voice or instrument is the element that often appeals most directly to
the ear.

Form, the organization of a piece of music, is sometimes considered an
element of music. Actually it is a result of combining elements rather than
a primary element, in the same way that a building is the result of shaping
stones, wood, or other materials into an organized structure.

Dynamics and expression are also important, often decisive, properties
of music, but they are less amenable to precise indication and control by
the composer than the things already mentioned. The final determination
of the degree of dynamics and expression rests with the performer, who
interprets more or less conscientiously and according to his training, ability, and temperament such indications as the composer has noted in the
score. Since the nineteenth century, composers have tried to regulate these
and similar aspects of music more exactly by refinements of notation (cf.
the metronome markings on p. 15), but the most careful indications with

respect to dynamics and expression must be, by their very nature, somewhat relative. How loud is "loud" and how expressive is *espressivo,* how sweet is *dolce* and how marked is *marcato?* Everything in musical performance is more or less relative. But a composer can indicate his intentions far more accurately with respect to duration, pitch, and even tone color than he can with regard to dynamics and expression.

RHYTHM, THE FIRST ELEMENT

> *On what is all musical movement based? On the relationship of impulse, activity, and repose.*
>
> RALPH KIRKPATRICK

There is nothing in music harder to define than rhythm.[2] In the most general sense, rhythm is concerned with regulating and ordering the time relationship of tones either by accents or by patterns of long and short notes. Because rhythm is concerned with the duration and accentual patterns of tones, it is responsible for the flow of music.

As most commonly understood, rhythm is identified with meter, that is, a regularly recurring accent or stress on the first beat of every bar, so that one feels the strong pulse ("strong" beat)

ONE two, ONE two

in a measure of duple time, or

ONE two three, ONE two three

in a measure of triple time, and so on. The unstressed beats are called "weak" beats. The visible sign of this kind of rhythm is the bar line (see p. 537), which immediately precedes the first regularly accented note of a measure. Regular recurrence of stress is a necessity for group dancing, for marching, and to some extent for any group activity performed to music. It might be called the *ensemble* accent, and it has permeated so much music that the phrase "the tyranny of the bar line" was coined to describe its sway.

Suggestions for Study

Since clapping or conducting to music is the best way to demonstrate meter—dancing being less practical under most circumstances—try clapping or conducting the following or similar pieces as they are played on the phonograph or on the piano. (For the conductor's beat, see p. 539.) Which of the following pieces begins on the "upbeat" and which on the "downbeat"? (For these terms, see p. 539.)

Strauss, *Blue Danube Waltz* (in three).

A Sousa march.

Haydn, Minuet from the "Drum Roll" Symphony (in three).

[2] For the notation of time, see the Appendix.

Bach, Gavotte from the Orchestral Suite in C major (in *alla breve:* two half-note beats to the measure).

Less common rhythms can be beaten with the conductor's gestures already given. For example, the second movement of Tchaikovsky's Sixth Symphony is in $\frac{5}{4}$ time, which the composer has phrased as

ONE two, ONE two three (2 plus 3);

and sometimes as

ONE two three, ONE two (3 plus 2);

and sometimes as

ONE two three four five.

METER AND RHYTHM

An absolutely fixed and regular accent becomes extremely monotonous and has somewhat the same effect as the singsong of perfectly regular accent in poetry. The word *rhythm* is sometimes used in a special sense to describe accents other than the regular stress on the first beat of the measure. As explained below, accents of this sort may come from the phrasing of the melody, from accents that are added to "normally" weak beats, and from syncopations of various sorts. Much contemporary music has revolted against regularity of meter and either dispenses with the time signature or uses varying meters throughout.

The first of the kinds of accents just described is an accent used at the beginning of a melodic phrase (sometimes a slur ⌒ indicates the number of notes in the phrase). Just as in a sentence or a spoken phrase, the beginning of a musical phrase tends to start with a slight stress and to end with a tapering off or dropping of the voice. These strengths and weaknesses in the accentuation do not necessarily coincide with the strong and weak beats of the meter, and it is the subtle conflict between the accent of the meter and the accent of the phrase that makes a good deal of variety and interest in music. The Haydn "Drum Roll" Symphony furnishes a good example of this conflict at the opening of the *allegro* of the first movement. The note pattern is $\frac{6}{8}$ (beat in 2):

Ex. 1

etc.

According to the meter, there should be a stress on the first note of the measure and a subordinate accent on the fourth of the six eighths. This is contradicted by the accents of the short phrases. The metric accent is supplied by the other parts of the harmony or is simply felt, and it is the contradiction of the ensemble accent and the accent of the single melody that gives such a lilt to the phrase. The end of a melodic phrase, irrespective of its position in the measure, is normally *unaccented*.

The same regularity of meter and irregularities of other accents exist in poetry. Of the following two examples, the first, as every schoolboy knows, uses a perfectly regular iambic tetrameter:

> The Stág at éve had drúnk his fíll
>
> Where dánced the móon on Mónan's ríll,
>
> > Sir Walter Scott in "The Lady of the Lake"

This is very nice, it "dances," and it satisfies us, provided that the regular meter does not persist too long. The other example, also basically iambic —this time iambic pentameter—has regular *and* irregular accent, and consequently is entirely different in its impression. It is the first quatrain of Shakespeare's Sonnet No. 107, and it begins with two of the most haunting lines ever written by Shakespeare or any one else:

> Nót mine own féars, nór the prophétic sóul
>
> Of the wíde world dréaming on thíngs to cóme,
>
> Can yét the léase of mý true lóve contról,
>
> Suppósed as fórfeit tó a cónfined dóom.

Lines three and four of this sonnet are quite regular. But not lines one and two; and no punishment could fit the crime of forcing these first two lines into the iambic pentameter in which a sonnet is supposed to be composed.

TEMPO

The speed at which a piece of music is played is called the *tempo*. Normally one feels the tempo in relation to how fast one plays the kind of note indicated in the denominator of the time signature. For example, a rapidly played quarter note in $\frac{3}{4}$ time would generally mean that the piece sounds fast. However, the situation is sometimes different in very fast or very slow tempos. In rapid $\frac{6}{8}$ time the very speed of the movement makes one hear two groups of three eighth notes each, not six individual eighth notes; the tempo is felt in relation to how fast the two basic groups are heard, rather than the six individual notes. Most *gigues* (or jigs), such as *The Irish Washerwoman,* are in $\frac{6}{8}$ (or $\frac{12}{8}$) and are heard basically in two (or four), not in six (or twelve). Time signatures that can be broken down into groups in this way are called *compound*. Incidentally, $\frac{12}{8}$ time divides into four groups of three each, *not* three groups of four each.

If compound signatures are used in slow time, every beat is heard, and the note value indicated by the denominator of the time signature is the counting unit. In slow $\frac{12}{8}$ time, for instance, twelve eighth notes are heard. In very slow time the speed of the counting unit indicated is sometimes so slow that the ear can scarcely comprehend it; the ear hears and the performer counts the subdivision of the beat. In very slow $\frac{4}{4}$, for example M. M. $\quarternote = 40$, it is usual to count eight beats at M. M. $\eighthnote = 80$. (The meaning of "M. M." is explained below.)

Tempo is indicated either by general terms (usually in Italian) or by absolute statements such as metronome markings. A slow tempo is indicated by such terms as *adagio, largo,* or *lento;* a moderate tempo, by *andante,* or *moderato;* moderately fast, by *allegretto;* fast, by *allegro* or *vivace;* and very fast, by *allegro assai, presto,* or *prestissimo*. These terms are just a sampling. Others are contained in the Glossary.

These terms indicate tempo only within general and relative limits, and sometimes hint at the mood; *allegro* means "cheerfully," and *vivace* means "vivaciously." However, tempo can be indicated with mathematical exactness. The statement M. M. $\quarternote = 120$ means that the quarter notes are played 120 to the minute or two per second. An indication of this kind is called a *metronome marking*—a metronome being an apparatus which marks exactly the time indicated, usually by waving a kind of inverted pendulum whose movements to and fro can be regulated by a sliding weight. The visual movement of the pendulum is usually accompanied by corresponding ticktocks. The abbreviation M. M. (or simply M.) means "Mälzel Metronome," and refers to Mälzel, who invented the metronome in 1816.

The decisive factor in tempo is how fast the basic unit of beat is played, not how it is notated. Suppose a piece of music has the time signature $\frac{3}{4}$, M. M. $\quarternote = 80$. This indicates that the quarter note is the unit of beat and that there are eighty beats to the minute. However, the same music could be written in $\frac{3}{8}$ time, M. M. $\eighthnote = 80$, and it would sound to the ear precisely as fast as the first example since the beat in both cases is eighty to the minute.

When the individual note becomes too fast to count comfortably, as frequently happens in compound time, the metronome marking and the general tempo marking apply, as a rule, to the speed of the large beat. In $\frac{12}{8}$ time, if the eighth were marked to be played at M. M. $\eighthnote = 240$, the individual eighth note would be much too fast to count comfortably, and the measure would be counted by the player and beaten by the conductor to the dotted quarter (see p. 537) at M. M. ♩. = 80.

To summarize: tempo is felt in relation to the speed of the counting unit of beat and to the rapidity of the subordinate notes connected with each of these beats.

The tempo can be modified by various indications. To increase the speed, the term *accelerando* is used; to decrease, *ritardando* or *rallentando.* *Tempo rubato* ("stolen time") means not to maintain a strictly regular time (for a more exact definition of *rubato* see the Glossary); *a tempo,* to return to the original time; *fermata* (or "hold") indicated ⌢ means to hold at will beyond the indicated time value of the note (for others terms, see the Glossary). The term *agogics* is sometimes used to indicate collectively all the subtleties involved in modification of tempo from strict time. An agogic accent results from the length of a note rather than from other factors.

"CROSS" ACCENTS AND SYNCOPATION

Sometimes an accent occurs on a beat that is normally unaccented in the measure. This "cross" accent may be indicated by an accent mark, or it may simply be felt for one of various reasons (cf. Material for Further Study, below). For instance, a *sarabande* (a certain type of dance) often has an accent on beat two. A well-known example is Bach's *Chaconne* for solo violin, the opening of which has features of the *sarabande* rhythm:

Ex. 2

No accent mark is given by Bach, but we feel an accent on beat two since the piece begins on beat two and since the note value heard on the second beat is longer than the notes that precede and follow. Another example of the same kind of thing is furnished by the second theme of the first movement of Schubert's "Unfinished" Symphony:

Ex. 3

The term *syncopation* refers to an accent that comes "off" the beat— that is, an accent that comes on a subdivision of the beat. If the music goes

ONE   two   three   (Ex. 4a),

then the pattern that follows in Example 4b (cf. the third and fourth notes)

Ex. 4

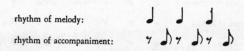

introduces an accent that is "off" the beat. It breaks the stride of the beat. Syncopation is a special property of "jazz," but it is common in almost all music. The music of Haydn, Beethoven, and Brahms—to mention three prominent composers—is full of syncopation in varying degrees of complexity. To take a simple instance, many accompanying figures are syncopated, being just "off" the beat:

Ex. 5

rhythm of melody:

rhythm of accompaniment:

Suggestion for Study

Clap the basic meter while singing a melody that has various "cross" accents or syncopations. For a simple example of syncopation in *alla breve,* see the opening of *Bourrée* I and *Bourrée* II of Bach's Orchestral Suite in C major.

THE ORGANIZING POWER OF RHYTHM

In some pieces melody or harmony may be the chief organizing force. In others, however, the rhythm is doubtless the primary factor, the chief element of coherence. In certain primitive music, investigators have found that a song sung by different singers may vary somewhat with respect to words or melody, but not with respect to rhythm. In this case the conclusion is that rhythm is more decisive than the melody or the words.[3]

This important aspect of rhythm is not by any means limited to primitive music. The entire opening movement of Bach's Third "Brandenburg" Concerto is dominated by the motive:

Ex. 6

Beethoven begins the *allegretto* of his Seventh String Quartet (Op. 59, No. 1, in F major) with the motive, reiterated on a single note:

[3] For a case of this kind among the American Indians, see Curt Sachs, *Rhythm and Tempo* (New York: W. W. Norton & Company, Inc.; 1953) p. 36.

Ex. 7

While the motive is not as basic to the Beethoven movement as it is to the Bach "Brandenburg" Concerto, its importance in binding the whole movement together cannot be denied.

On a much smaller scale, the force of rhythmic patterns may be observed in well-known tunes. In "America," there are two *basic* rhythmic patterns of two measures each:

Ex. 8

		PATTERN:
My country, 'tis of thee		A
Sweet land of liberty,		A
Of thee I sing:		B
Land where my fathers died,		A
Land of the pilgrim's pride,		A
From ev'ry mountain side		A' (varied)
Let freedom ring.		B' (varied)

The regularity of the grouping of the above patterns into two measures each is also a factor. The first part of "America" is composed of six measures, divided into three two-measure phrases; the second consists of eight measures, divided into four two-measure phrases. (In the section on "Melody" below, the division and organization of melodies according to motives, phrases, and periods will be discussed.) The regularity of rhythm as the persistence of rhythmic patterns doubtless comes from the influence of the dance.

Suggestions for Study

1. Analyze any well-known tune for its basic rhythmic patterns and their measure groupings as in the example of "America," above.

2. Select examples of kinds of dances, and listen to the characteristic meter and other rhythmic accents. *For example:* the waltz, the minuet, the polka, the fox trot, the tango, the mazurka. Analyze the *blues,* noting the special twelve-measure phrase structure of three four-measure groups.

Dances selected from musical literature: Chopin's mazurkas and waltzes, *"Habanera"* from Bizet's *Carmen,* "Minuet" from Mozart's *Don Giovanni* or from Haydn's "Drum Roll" Symphony, the waltz rhythm in the "Ball Scene" from Berlioz's *Symphonie Fantastique.* For the typical dances of the seventeenth- and eighteenth-century suite (*allemande, courante, sarabande, gigue*), see pages 183–4.

Suggested Reading

Willi Apel, "Dance Music" in the *Harvard Dictionary of Music*. Cambridge, Mass.: Harvard University Press, 1944.

Émile Jacques-Dalcroze, *Rhythm, Music and Education,* trans. by Harold F. Rubinstein. London: Chatto & Windus, 1921.

Curt Sachs, *A World History of the Dance*. New York: W. W. Norton & Company, 1937.

———, *Rhythm and Tempo*. New York: W. W. Norton & Company, 1953.

For contemporary accounts of older dances, such as the *pavane* and the *galliard,* popular in the sixteenth century, see *Orchesography* by Thoinot Arbeau (1588). Translated by Mary S. Evans. New York: Kamin Dance Publishers, 1948.

MATERIAL FOR FURTHER STUDY

(1) *Irregular Accent.* Regularity of accent—music that you can stamp your foot to—is accepted as normal because of our common background in dances and marches. Irregularity of accent is commonplace in other cultures; furthermore, it is a common property of certain types of contemporary music (see p. 441).

(2) *Free Accent.* While the accents of much contemporary music are irregular, the note values are related in fairly exact ratios, in the sense that two half notes equal a whole note. In certain types of music, however, the rhythm is so irregular that even this relation breaks down, and the rhythm can only be described as free. This is true of certain types of primitive music, particularly of solo singers. According to certain theories, the same complete freedom of impulse characterizes Gregorian chant (see p. 138). There are also instrumental pieces in extremely free style, such as certain preludes and toccatas of rhapsodic and improvisatory character, that are notated without bar lines or signatures.

(3) *Accents of Duration or Position.* Accents derived from duration or position, as opposed to stress, are subtleties akin to the melodic accent. The durational accent is also proper to Greek and Latin poetry (modern poetry has accent of stress only). In music an accent of duration may result when a note is preceded and followed by shorter note values. It receives an impulse simply by being held longer. Leaping to or from a note also tends to give it accent (Ex. 9). Accents of duration or position are especially important in polyphony (see p. 44).

Ex. 9

(4) *Word Accent.* The accents of words are important in certain pieces. In general, however, the accented words receive a musical accent that either is metric or coincides with one of the rhythmic accents. The setting of the word accent to music is called *declamation* (see p. 121).

(5) *More on "Cross" Accents and Syncopation.* The idea of "cross" accent or syncopation may be applied not only to single notes but also to phrases and measures:

Ex. 10

In Example 10a the use of phrases of four eighths in measures two and three introduces a cross accent or even a new meter, depending on what happens in the other parts of the accompaniment. In Example 10b, the accents, coming on a subdivision of the beat in $\frac{3}{4}$ meter, technically constitute syncopation, but the actual effect here is a change of meter to $\frac{6}{8}$. In the following example from Beethoven's *Eroica* Symphony, what first sounds like a "cross" accent turns out to be a new meter (Ex. 11b):

Since the *sforzandi* (heavy reinforcements of tone) occur in all parts, the effect of this passage is not ONE two three, as it is barred, but ONE two, ONE two. The basic meter has been changed. (For "polyrhythm," see pp. 45 and 442.

3. *Melody, the Second Element*

> *We, with our elaborate harmonies have forgotten the charm of single notes. The African natives know it, and I remember a learned man once telling me that the Greeks had the same art.*
>
> JOHN BUCHAN in *Greenmantle*

PRELIMINARIES

THIS REMARK of JOHN BUCHAN points to an important feature of much of the music that we hear in the concert hall. Melody is heard in conjunction with harmony or even emerges from it as "the surface of the harmony." But this is true only of certain kinds of music, and one ought to examine melody for itself alone even though it may be much influenced by its harmony.

What is melody? This is one of those questions to which the simplest answer seems to be: "If you do not ask me, I know." Most people associate melody with a singable tune, something that starts, has a definite contour, and comes to a definite and satisfying conclusion. This conception of melody is good enough as far as it goes, but it must be broadened to suit the needs of music as a whole. The type of melody just described is quite satisfactory as a melody that is complete and self-contained, or, to put it differently, *important for what it is*. But there are other melodies that are important for *how they develop and for what they become* and that are not particularly satisfactory by themselves as tunes. "Complete" melodies are often flowing and singing (cantabile) in style; melodies that "become" often consist of motives or short phrases that contain rhythmic or melodic features capable of growth.

In the broadest sense a melody is any organized succession of tones. A short snatch of such tones may be qualified by speaking of it as a "melodic motive"; and one may speak of any succession of tones by the name *melodic line*. The term *voice part* is also used indiscriminately to identify a melodic line, whether sung or played by an instrument.

The word *melody* may be used in a broad sense to define a succession of tones, and this conception of melody embraces the most varied types. For example, a simple, singable folk tune has very little in common with the sophisticated complications of the "melody" that occurs at measure 6 of Schoenberg's Fourth String Quartet (1936), shown in Example 12. In the

Ex. 12 *

first place, the style of this passage is not grateful to the voice and is not intended for it. In fact, the skips at the end are physically impossible for the average singer. Example 13 shows the "subject" of Bach's Fourth

Ex. 13

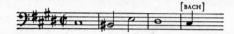

Fugue from Book I of *The Well-Tempered Clavier* (1722). As a tune, this "melody" is not impressive. Nevertheless, it is the main material out of which Bach creates a marvelous piece of instrumental music. The melody here is not important for what it *is,* but for its germinal power to *become.* Finally, the melody may be submerged in the harmony; it may not be heard as melody at all, but simply implied in the form of broken chords. Much of Gounod's famous melody *Ave Maria,* which he described as a "sacred melody adapted to the first prelude of J. S. Bach," is implicit in the broken chords of Bach's First Prelude from Book I of *The Well-Tempered Clavier.* Similarly, the melodies of a number of passages in Wagner may be heard as "the surface of the harmony." And there are some melodies that can be considered in terms of progressions of harmonies because the succession of tones falls into harmonic patterns.

RHYTHM. RANGE. INTERVALS. CONTOUR.

What determines the character of any melody? A number of factors, among them (1) rhythmic features, (2) range, (3) the interval arrangement of successive tones, and (4) general shape of contour.[1]

1. The rhythm of a melody has much to do with its character. Its basic meter, rhythmic accents, and phrasing all contribute. The *Blue Danube Waltz,* forced into the different meter and swing of a fox trot, is a different tune. The following example shows the theme of Beethoven's String Quartet, Op. 59, No. 2 (E minor), as it first appeared in his Notebook (Ex. 14a) and as it appeared in finished form (Ex. 14b). The second and

[1] This section concerns melodies in the abstract. However, the particular voice or instrument that performs a melody often determines the kind of melody used, its range, and sometimes other features. In short, the design of a melody may be determined to a marked degree by the opportunities and limitations that the composer sees in the voice or instrument. Later we will see how the limitations of instruments like the French horn determine the character of particular themes (p. 81). See also dynamics and expression with respect to melodies (p. 25).

final form is far superior both rhythmically and melodically because it has more variety and movement.

Ex. 14

Suggestions for Study

Select a familiar tune and try singing it with changed meter, with misplaced accents, or by changing the lengths of certain notes. Trying to improve a tune is an excellent exercise in "appreciating" why a tune is good and why it has persisted so long.

2. The range of a melody—how high and how low it goes—is frequently determined by whether the melody is intended for a particular voice or for an instrument. A folk song has a restricted range compared to many songs written for soloists; and a melody for the cello is not necessarily the same in range as a melody for the violin. As demonstrated in the Schoenberg example above (Ex. 12), the ordinary voice cannot cover the range of this "melody" at all. "The Star-Spangled Banner" is hard to sing because it exceeds the comfortable range of an untrained voice; and "America" is easy to sing because its range lies within comfortable limits.

3. To describe how a melody proceeds from one tone to the next—that is, whether it goes by step or by skip, and how much—musicians use the word "interval," which indicates the distance in pitch between two tones. The general name of an interval may be determined by counting the number of lines and spaces included by the two tones in question. The interval from one tone to its adjacent tone above or below is a second: a whole tone is a major second; a half tone is a minor second. In the opening of "The Star-Spangled Banner" (Ex. 15), the first interval is a third descending; in the third full measure, the first interval is a sixth descending, and in the same measure the step upward from D to E natural is a second.[2] Intervals

Ex. 15

---

[2] An interval less than an octave is a *simple* interval; one larger than an octave is *compound*. Sometimes compound intervals are reduced to simple form, a tenth being described as a third.

of this kind are called *melodic;* if two tones of an interval sound together, the interval is called *harmonic* (Ex. 16).

Ex. 16

Naturally a melody that proceeds mainly by steps gives a different impression from one that proceeds mainly by leaps; and a melodic progression by "consonant" intervals is different from one using "dissonant" intervals. In general, as leaps become harder to sing, they are regarded as less consonant and more dissonant. (For more on "consonance" and "dissonance," see the section on harmony, below.)

4. The general shape or contour of a melody is determined by the order, direction, and rhythmic pattern of the successive intervals. These factors combine to give a melody (especially one that is complete in itself) a definite contour. In addition, a melody often has a discernible high point or climax, just as a play has a climactic episode before the denouement. In graphic and simplified form a melody might look like any of the following:

Ex. 17

In Example 17a the high point comes at the beginning, in 17b in the middle, and in 17c toward the end. The position of the climactic point can be related to the type of emotional expression conveyed by the melody: ascending motion tends to give the impression of more energy, greater tension, and sometimes a lightening or brightening when played on certain instruments (e.g., the violin); descending motion suggests a relaxing of effort, and sometimes a darkening of color.

Few melodic contours are quite as simple as those shown above. To make this point clear, the contour of "America" is given in Example 18.

Ex. 18

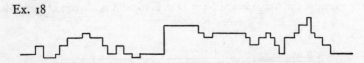

It does not conform simply and rigidly to any of the types shown in Example 17, but it comes closest to 17c in that the high point of the melody comes at the end. The graphic method used in Example 18 represents the pitch in relation to the rhythmic pattern.

EXPRESSION. DYNAMICS. MARKS OF EXPRESSION.

Up to this point we have considered melody in an abstract way as coherent patterns of rhythm and pitch. But no melody exists like that except on paper. Our "paper" melody is dead, simply a skeleton, a "black-and-white" version of the real thing. A melody, in short, implies the color and expression of a performance, and the emotional impact of a melody depends not merely on the intervals and rhythms of a melody in the abstract but just as much—perhaps more—on less tangible factors: the tone color of the voice or instrument, the nuances of loud and soft, the tempo, and deviations from tempo. The manner of performance, scoring, and marks of expression—more or less exactly indicated by the composer and interpreted by the performer—make the difference between a live and glowing performance and one that is dull and lifeless. Imagine the opening of the Tchaikovsky Sixth Symphony without the somber color of the deep instruments, without accent and swelling dynamic nuance to give it life and expression! (Cf. Ex. 20a.)

Expression is not an exclusive property of melody; it is an inseparable property of music as a whole. The term *expression* is extremely elusive. In a general way it means everything about the quality of a performance except pitch and rhythm. It includes the infinite shades of color and those of loud and soft; all the nuances of touch, subtleties of phrasing, and accent by the singer or player; the manner of attack, release, and connection of notes—everything that gives personality and individuality to the performance. The indications of expression are, at best, relative. Their execution must be entrusted to the ability and temperament of the individual artist. The subtlest shades of expression are impossible to indicate by the symbols of music. (For ornaments of expression, see the Glossary.)

However, there are well-defined terms and indications of expression, capable of varying degrees of precise meaning. *Dynamics* (the degrees of loudness and softness) are generally indicated by Italian terms such as *forte* or simply *f* (loud), *fortissimo* or *ff* (very loud), *mezzo forte* or *mf* (moderately loud), *piano* or *p* (soft), and so on. To increase loudness by degrees, one uses the term *crescendo* or *cresc.* (sign: $<$); to decrease, *decrescendo* or *diminuendo, decresc.* or *dim.* (sign: $>$).

There are also general indications of expression, a key to the character or style of a piece as a whole: *animato* (animated), *espressivo* (expressive), *sostenuto* (in sustained style). Notes that are to be smoothly connected to each other (*legato*) are included under the same slur (⌢). Disconnected notes (*staccato*) are distinguished by dots or strokes: for example,

♩̇   or   ♩̓

The Glossary includes a number of additional terms of expression.

Suggestion for Study

Make a contour of a familiar tune or melody in the fashion of Example 18.

THE ORGANIZATION OF MELODIES

Even with a few tones, some manner of organization is essential. It is not easy to describe how this is achieved, since in a complex organism like a piece of music the organization is carried out on various levels, so to speak, by the different elements of music mutually reacting on each other. A painting makes its visual effect by a complex and organic relation of color to the subject matter as it is represented in the dimensions of height, width, and, through perspective, depth. In music there is a similar complex relation between tone color and the musical material represented through the "dimensions" of pitch, duration, and harmony.

Duration and pitch are the two musical dimensions essential to melody considered alone. (The relation of harmony, the dimension of depth, will be considered later.) Such elements of simple rhythmic organization as the importance of persistent rhythmic patterns and the measure groupings of melodies have already been discussed.

Within the melodies themselves, considered as successions of intervals, two basic principles of organization may be observed: (1) melodic motives are stated, contrasted, and restated to create larger units of structure; (2) all the tones of the melody are related to a central tone as a kind of center of gravity (i.e., through tonality, see p. 30).

THROUGH MOTIVES, PHRASES, AND PERIODS. ANTECEDENT AND CONSEQUENT.

In most music a coherent design of some sort can be observed even in short melodies; at every stage of organization a need for unity and variety of material is felt. (For larger formal schemes, see Chapter 5.) Frequently, a rhythmic pattern serves not merely to animate the melody but to give it a unifying force. However, the growth of a melody through addition, contrast, and repetition of fragments of melody is more striking to the ear. The smallest unit in building a melody, its basic fragment, is the *motive,* consisting of at least one characteristic interval and one characteristic rhythm. Several of these may be combined in a *phrase;* and several phrases, in a *period*. The combination of two periods is called a *double period*. In such fashion complete melodies are constructed, just as sentences in language are composed of phrases and words.

The Irish folk song "Believe me if all those endearing young charms" (Ex. 19) will illustrate the point. The first line, "Believe me if all those endearing young charms," is set to three short motives. The third of these is essentially a repetition of the second, but it starts on a different tone. Together these three motives constitute musical phrase a. The sec-

Ex. 19

Believe me if all those endearing young charms

ond phrase, b, consists of two motives; both are rhythmically like the opening motive of the song but different melodically. Phrase a and phrase b combine to make a period, labeled period A.[3] With the line that starts "Were to change by tomorrow," a new period begins. Its music is similar to period A, and for this reason it is labeled period A′ (called A "prime"),

---

[3] There is a good deal of uncertainty about the terms "phrase," "period," and "double period"; "motive," however, has a relatively well-defined meaning. In some usage, the term "phrase" would be used to describe our period, above; and "period," our double period. If, however, we conformed to this usage in Example 19, there

implying that it is a varied, but quite recognizable version, of period A. Period A may also be called the "antecedent" and period A′ the "consequent," these terms referring, respectively, to two statements of like material, the first of which ends with a feeling of incompletion, the second with a feeling of finality.

Period A and period A′ together constitute a double period and comprise the whole first section of the song. At the words "Thou would'st" the middle part of the song begins. It starts with a new phrase, c. This too has its resemblances to motives already heard, but it is different enough to be distinguished by a new letter. This is followed by the music of phrase b.

The middle section of the song, then, consists of one period (phrase c and phrase b), labeled period B. At the words "And around" the song returns to music identical with period A′, which is used for the third and final section of the piece.

This song is a simple example of one kind of organization on a simple scale. It shows the hierarchy of motive, phrase, and period. It also furnishes an elementary example of a still larger organization: a "form" in three parts consisting of (1) the double-period (A and A′), (2) the period B, and (3) a return to period A′. (We will return to the question of form in a later chapter.)

Such methods of building melodies are typical of tunes complete in themselves, melodies that are, so to speak, "closed" in that they have a definite beginning, middle, and ending. Many folk songs and a number of "art" songs belong to this category.

It is worth noticing that the ends of some phrases give the impression of incompleteness, and others of completeness. In Example 19 period A ends with a feeling of incompleteness on the word "today." But period A′ ends on the word "away" with a melodic cadence (see p. 30) that gives the impression of completion. The reason is that it ends on D, the tonic (see p. 30) of the whole piece. In the same way, the song ends on D.

Suggestion for Study

Analyze a tune in the manner of Example 19. An example: "Home, Sweet Home."

As we have already seen, some melodies are not complete in themselves, but consist for the most part of a motive or motives that contain melodic or rhythmic features capable of considerable expansion and development.

---

would be only the term "motive" to describe both our phrase and motive; and there would be no proper term to describe our phrase a. Actually, another term is needed to complete the hierarchy of terminology. Up to a point the terms used are immaterial, provided that their meaning is clear in context.

There is no rule about how many motives constitute a phrase, or how many phrases, a period. But a double period is usually taken to mean two periods.

The opening of Beethoven's Fifth Symphony is motivic, and expands and develops in a dynamic way rather than being stated in a complete and relatively static manner. The Prelude to Wagner's music drama *Tristan and Isolde* also begins motivically. And all fugues are based on the idea of a "subject" (sometimes "subjects") in which are incorporated rhythmic and melodic "germs" of sufficient potential to be expanded into an entire piece of music.

Example 20a, taken from the opening of Tchaikovsky's Sixth (*Pathétique*) Symphony, shows how a motive can be expanded and transformed. The opening motive, heard in the deep register of the bassoon, consists of four notes played very slowly. The first phrase is constructed by a threefold statement of this motive, each time stated a step higher. This kind of repetition—when a melody or part of it is restated literally but at different level of pitch—is called a *sequence*.

Ex. 20

This motive furnishes the material for the introduction. It is used also at the beginning of the *allegro* that immediately follows. How this is done is shown in Example 20b. The motive of the introduction is transformed by being played rapidly, its first two notes are slightly disconnected, and a rest (silence) is now heard after the fourth note of the motive. The next statement of the motive is varied again. The first two eighth notes of the motive are made into four sixteenth notes. What follows, marked (3), is constructed from a fragment of the motive. Only the third and fourth notes of the motive are used, and they are played rapidly in sixteenth notes, but clearly preserve the interval of the descending second that is characteristic of the third and fourth notes of the original motive. (How Ex. 20b is transformed later is shown in Ex. 20c.)

Suggestions for Study

1. Listen to the opening movement of Tchaikovsky's Sixth Symphony. Note the use of motives and also the presence of lyrical, relatively "complete," melodies.

2. Listen to a Bach fugue for the play of motives and melodies. (The details of a fugue will be discussed later, see p. 61.) Examples: the "fugue" in the Overture of Bach's Orchestral Suite No. 1 in C major; Fugue No. 3 in Bach's *Art of the Fugue* (analyzed in detail, pp. 64–7).

ORGANIZATION BY TONALITY. CADENCE, SCALE, MODE, AND KEY

The relation of all tones of a melody (and also their harmonies) to some central tone is called *tonality*. The central tone used for any particular melody or piece is called the *tonic*. Many well-known tunes end on a tone that is felt as a point of final rest, a kind of home base, around which the other tones are grouped. Frequently a melody begins, as well as ends, on the tonic, as in "America." But this is not always true. "The Star-Spangled Banner" begins on the fifth above the tonic on which it ends.

Establishing this point of rest on the tonic is called a *cadence*. Cadence means "falling" and refers to the fact that originally a melody *descended* to the tonic. A melody doesn't have to "fall" to establish a cadence, but it does have to proceed in such a way that it establishes a point of rest, a relaxation of tension and movement comparable to the dropping of the voice at the end of a sentence. Cadence refers also to *chord* progressions that establish a tonic. A cadence that ends a piece is called the *final* cadence; and there are generally other cadences (melodic or harmonic), *intermediate* cadences, used in the course of a piece to establish a point of rest at the ends of phrases. While the melody may establish the cadence by falling, it often approaches the tonic in other ways, notably from the half tone below, a note called the *leading tone* because it establishes a strong tendency or "leading" to the tonic. The leading tone is equally important in establishing a tonic, whether it is found in the melody or in the harmony.

The order and relationship of tones to each other and to a central tone can be explained by using the terms *scale, mode,* and *key*. The word *scale* means ladder, and refers to a ladder-like succession of half and whole tones in some specified order. The *diatonic* scale, for instance, refers to the succession of half and whole tones that occurs when one plays from C to C on the piano (C, D, E, F, G, A, B, C; half tones occur between E and F and B and C, whole tones between the others; see below). Such octave (eight-note) scales can be duplicated in the octave(s) above and below, and one speaks of practicing a four-octave scale on the piano. The *chro-*

matic scale refers to a scale of successive half tones. On the piano this scale is produced by playing white and black keys one after the other as they occur on the keyboard. Within the C octave there are twelve half tones, and this chromatic scale can be duplicated in other octaves.

A scale is, so to speak, a statement of the half and/or whole tones used in any piece of music. In any scale we need to know the central tone, the tonic, to which the others are related and subordinate. In the C—C diatonic scale, if C is the tonic, we have established a relationship of tones called the *major* mode, starting on C (called C major). If A is the tonic, we have established a relationship called the *minor* mode, starting on A (called A minor). The relationship of the tonic to the other tones is, strictly speaking, called *mode,* although mode and scale are often used to mean the same thing (thus, major scale = major mode). The modes basic to the music commonly heard in the concert hall today are the major and minor just mentioned. (For other modes used in earlier times, see p. 35.) There are several forms of the minor, of which the most common, the *harmonic minor,* raises the seventh tone (to establish a leading tone, see p. 30), so that in the A—A progression of white keys, G sharp, not G, would be played.

The relationship of the whole and half tones in the major and minor modes is shown below (1 indicates a whole tone; ½, a half tone).

Major:	C		D		E		F		G		A		B		C
		1		1		½		1		1		1		½	

Minor: (pure)	A		B		C		D		E		F		G		A
		1		½		1		1		½		1		1	

Minor: (harmonic)	A		B		C		D		E		F		G♯		A
		1		½		1		1		½		1½		½	

The major and the harmonic minor are compared in graphic form below.

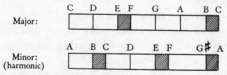

The important point here is not the mathematical relations of intervals, but their effect in expression. Sing or play the two modes. In the major the relationship of C to E gives quite a different impression from the comparable relationship of A to C in the minor. If one plays chords, the same is true. Compare the chord of C-E-G with chord of A-C-E. The impression is quite different. These differences can be perceived more vividly by comparing the effect of the major and minor mode based on the same tone, for example, C. The *harmonic* minor can be derived from the major of the same name by lowering the third and sixth degrees of the major by a half tone. For instance, C harmonic minor can be derived from C major by lowering the third degree (E) to E flat and the sixth degree (A) to A flat. The impression is immediately changed; the minor is darker and more somber in effect.[4]

The major and minor are not restricted to the notes C—C and A—A, but can be *transposed* to start on any other degree of the chromatic scale. For example, if the major mode starts on A flat, we say that the *key* is A-flat major. Thus *key* refers to the pitch of the central tone (tonic) and the mode concerned. Beethoven's Third Symphony is written in the key of E-flat major. This means that the central tone is E flat and that the other tones are related to it according to the scheme of the major mode. Similarly, in César Franck's Symphony in D minor the central tone is D and the other tones are related to D according to the scheme of the minor mode.

Suggestions for Study

1. Compare the effect of major and minor by listening to the slow movement of Haydn's "Drum Roll" Symphony. This begins in C minor, but at various points it goes to the major. After the first eight measures (which ought properly to be repeated), the music starts a new motive in the major (E-flat), and shortly after returns to C minor. At measure 27 the section begins in C major; notice the brilliant contrast to the opening. Try to distinguish the major and minor throughout this movement.

2. Compare the effect of changing modes by altering a tune, originally in major, to minor (e.g., "The Star-Spangled Banner").

3. Listen to the Schubert song *"Der Wegweiser"* ("The Guidepost") from *Die Winterreise* (*The Winter Journey*). It begins in minor; the middle part is the same tune transformed to major; after this the song returns to the minor form of the tune, as it began.

KEYS AND KEY SIGNATURES. MODULATION.

Since the major or the minor may start on any one of the twelve half steps of the chromatic octave, there are twelve major and twelve minor keys (actually there are a few more since C sharp can be taken in the sense of D flat, and so on). To preserve the proper relationships of the whole and half tones in the major and minor, certain sharps or flats have to be used if the major starts on a tone other than C, or if the minor starts on a tone other than A. Suppose the major mode starts on G (G major). To preserve the proper whole and half steps of the major (cf. p. 31), one

[4] The minor mode built on the same tone as a given major key is its *parallel* minor (C minor is the parallel minor to C major). A minor key that has the same key signature as a given major key is its *relative* minor (A minor is the relative minor to C major). In each case the tonic of the relative minor is a third below the tonic of the related major key.

change must be made: F must be played as F sharp. Similarly, D major must have two sharps (F and C), and F major must have one flat (B).[5]

These accidentals are put at the beginning of a piece in the form of a *key signature,* and throughout the piece the notes affected are played automatically sharp or flat, as the case may be, unless contradicted by an accidental. (For accidentals, see p. 534.)

The process of going from one key to another is called *modulation.* One may modulate in a purely melodic sense or, more elaborately, by harmony. The keys have close relationships which, in addition to the relationships between the tones of the major and minor, constitute tonality in a larger sense.[6]

MELODY AND SIMPLE FORMS

Above the organizing stage of motive, phrase, and period comes the level of addition and contrast of larger melodic segments. In "Believe me if all those endearing young charms" (Ex. 19) a double period and two single periods combined to make a three-part form. It is valuable to see the principles of coherence and design at work at every stage of musical composition, from the simple motive to the complexities of large-scale pieces like the symphony, which represents an elaborate evolution and mutual interaction of melody, rhythm, and harmony interrelated from the smallest to the largest component part. Rhythm has the power to organize, melodies evolve from small fragments of tone, and melodies in turn combine in simple forms. Larger forms depend on the resources of harmony, counterpoint, and tonality as well.

In all art works certain formal principles may be observed: *repetition of material, contrast of material, and repetition after contrast.* In this way the fundamental desire for unity, variety, and coherence is satisfied. Naturally, these basic aims are so general that they can and do manifest themselves in a very large number of individual works of art.

At the level of simple melodies, there are clearly recognized forms corresponding to these principles:

I. REPETITIVE SCHEMES

A familiar example is a hymn of several stanzas, each sung to the same music. This is called *stanzaic* or *strophic* form. "America" is an example. Sometimes songs with several verses have a clear form within the confines of the music that is repeated for each verse. "Believe me if all those endearing young charms" has several verses, each sung to the same music. At the same time the music of each verse is cast in a three-part form, as we

---

[5] All the key signatures are given for reference in Example 27.

[6] For more on tonality and modulation, including their importance for variety and expression, see Chapter 4.

have explained above. Sometimes a strophic form is modified, and the second of three verses is sung to a variant of the first and last. Schubert's song *"Der Wegweiser"* (see p. 294) is a good example of a *modified strophic* form. A theme and variations is also a repetitive scheme, but because of its complexity this form will be considered with the larger forms.

2. CONTRAST SCHEMES

A simple example of contrast is found in *two-part* or *binary* form, represented by the letter scheme, A B; a tune followed by a chorus that uses different music is one instance, as in "Good Night, Ladies." This scheme can be expanded to a scheme such as A A B. If the repetition of the A is exact, the form may be indicated as A :‖ B, sometimes called the *bar* form. The two dots before the bar mean to repeat. This form is a common one, and it has had a long lineage. It is a typical form of the songs of the minnesingers in the twelfth and thirteenth centuries, and it is found in many of the chorales set by J. S. Bach.

3. REPETITION AFTER CONTRAST

The principle of repetition after contrast is the most fundamental to the forms of music. A simple example of its generating power is one of the commonest of all formal schemes, A B A, called *ternary* or *three-part* form. It is also called *song* form because so many songs use this form (for a special type, the *da capo* aria, see p. 193). This form is amenable to several variations such as A A B A. The repetition of A or its return may be slightly varied, in which case it is indicated as A′. Another repetition-and-contrast scheme is the *rondo,* where a scheme such as A B A C A is employed. This scheme has a good many variants, but the essential point is the more or less regular recurrence of the refrain A. This form in its larger aspects will be discussed further in a later section.

Dances use a characteristic form called *dance* form, combining a binary division with a ternary form:

$$A :\|: B + A :\|$$
or written out: AA B + A B + A

The designation "B + A" is used to indicate that there is usually no break, as by a cadence, between B and A. Sometimes the B is really an A′. Almost any minuet in the works of Haydn and Mozart (e.g., Haydn's "Drum Roll" Symphony), or a dance from a Bach suite, or a number of the harpsichord sonatas of Domenico Scarlatti, illustrates this formal scheme.

It should be noted that the element of contrast in the forms described above is often emphasized by a contrast of tonality. In an A B A form, for instance, the melody may begin the contrasting section B at a tone level different from the beginning of the piece. In such cases tonality is also used as a unifying device, because the repetition of A is almost invariably in the key of the opening of the piece.

Suggested Listening

Chopin, "Raindrop" Prelude, Op. 28, No. 15 (ternary).

Mozart, "Turkish" Rondo (last movement of the A major Piano Sonata, K. 331).

Mozart, *"Dove sono"* (the Countess's aria in *Figaro:* A A B A).

Bach, Chorale *"Christ Lag in Todesbanden"* (bar form).

MATERIAL FOR FURTHER STUDY

(1) *Other Forms of the Minor.* There are three distinct forms of the minor: the *pure* minor, found by playing the white keys on the piano from A to A (see p. 31); the *harmonic* minor, already explained; and the *melodic* minor, shown in Example 21a. The latter exhibits a melodic

Ex. 21a

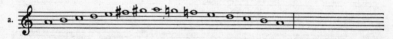

tendency to raise the sixth and seventh degrees of the pure minor in ascending, and to lower these degrees to the pure form in descending.

(2) *The "Old" or "Church" Modes.* In music before 1600, a *modal* system prevailed. The modern system uses two modes (major and minor) and the transposition of these two modes to any one of twelve half steps; the modal system used six modes and only one or two transpositions. The major was called the *Ionian* mode; and the minor, the *Aeolian.* There were in addition the *Dorian, Phrygian, Lydian,* and *Mixolydian* modes, which (as shown in Example 21b) can be derived by using the white keys

Ex. 21b

Dorian   Phrygian   Lydian   Mixolydian   Aeolian   Ionian

of the piano, starting respectively on D, E, F, and G. These modes are distinguished from the major and minor by certain specific interval differences. The most strikingly different mode is the Phrygian. Unlike any of the other modes, it has a half tone between its first and second degrees. The interval structure of the Dorian would be the same as pure minor if the B were flatted. The Lydian and Mixolydian are close to major. By flatting the B, the Lydian becomes F major; by sharping the F, the Mixolydian becomes G major.

The word *modality* refers to the old modes and their use in a contrapuntal-melodic system. *Tonality* is mainly concerned with the major and minor and with a complete system of keys related by harmonies. Tonality, in the modern sense, began to evolve in the seventeenth century. Prior to that time the system of modality was in force. A good example of a modal-sounding tune is "The Coast of High Barbary" (Ex. 22). It sounds

Ex. 22

The Coast of High Barbary

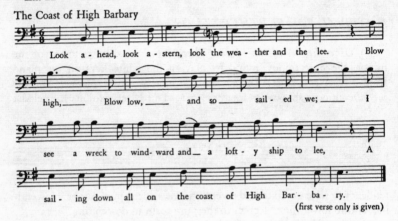

Look a - head, look a - stern, look the wea - ther and the lee. Blow

high,____ Blow low,____ and so____ sail - ed we;____ I

see a wreck to wind- ward and__ a loft - y ship to lee, A

sail - ing down all on the coast of High Bar - ba - ry.

(first verse only is given)

modal because it uses the D natural of the pure ("modal") E minor, not the D sharp of the harmonic minor. Vaughan Williams's *Fantasia on a Theme by Tallis* (for string orchestra) is a good example of the use of modes in contemporary music.

(3) *Other Scales.* Besides the scales already mentioned, there are others, actually quite a number. Among them are:

(a) The *whole-tone* scale. Since there are twelve half tones in the octave, it follows that there are six whole tones. Example 23 shows the

Ex. 23

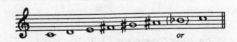

or

whole-tone scale. This scale (or something close to it) is found in some Oriental music; Debussy also used it for special effects.

(b) The *pentatonic* or *five-tone* scale (Ex. 24). This scale is very com-

Ex. 24

mon in folk and primitive music. It is sometimes called the "bagpipe" scale. Note that it has no half tones.

(c) Scales based on irrational intervals. There are a number of scales of primitive and Oriental people that employ scales with intervals that we call *irrational* because they do not fit our scheme of exact half and whole tones; and they cannot be written down with our system of notation. Scientists who have investigated such scales use a system in which an interval called the *cent* is basic. A cent is the hundredth part of a half tone as it sounds on the piano. Thus the octave comprises twelve hundred cents. Such minute divisions permit the scientist and the musician to describe exactly the irrational intervals found in systems other than our own.

(d) The so-called *Hungarian* scale. It is equivalent to the harmonic minor with the fourth degree raised (Ex. 25).

Ex. 25

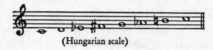

(Hungarian scale)

A number of contemporary composers have used various scales of the kind just mentioned; they have also experimented with tones less than a half tone (microtones). Ernest Bloch, for example, uses quarter tones in his Piano Quintet, and so does Bartók in his Violin Concerto. Other composers have used still smaller intervals. The Czechoslovakian composer Alois Hába used sixth tones, and the Mexican composer Julián Carrillo (b. 1875) used microtones as small as sixteenth tones.

Suggested Listening

A piece of Oriental Music (cf. the collection of phonograph records called *Music of the Orient*).

Hába, Duo in the sixth-tone system.

(4) *Overtones. The Harmonic Series. The Circle of Fifths and Key Signatures.* In musical instruments an individual tone is actually a combination of sounds consisting of the main pitch (or fundamental) and a certain number of additional tones called *overtones*. The latter are heard faintly or not at all, but nevertheless their presence contributes to the characteristic tone color of any particular instrument (cf. Chapter 6). If C

Ex. 26

(Harmonic series)

is the fundamental (Ex. 26), the overtones (also called *upper partials*) are those beginning with the C *an octave higher* (labeled 2), and the whole series, beginning with 1 (the fundamental), is called the *harmonic series*. (Ex. 26 shows the first sixteen notes of the harmonic series; the notes shown in black are out of tune.)

The production of different notes from pipes and strings is directly related to the relationships of the harmonic series. In simple tubes or pipes (that is, without valves or holes cut in the sides) only the notes of the harmonic series can be produced. If the deepest tone (fundamental) of a "natural" horn is the C labeled 1 in Example 26, the next tone that can be produced is the octave above, then the fifth above that, and so on. The number of frequency vibrations connected with each of these pitches is related also to the number of the harmonic series. For example, the octave above any note is always twice the frequency of the octave below (a = 220; a' = 440; for the meaning of a and a', see p. 535 and Ex. 182c).

The harmonic series establishes a hierarchy of intervals: the octave as the most "perfect," the fifth the next perfect, and so on. Since the octave can be viewed as a duplication, the fifth assumes a special importance, for instance in key relationships, as is shown below. The importance of the fifth is reflected in the terminology used. The fifth above a tonic is said to be the *dominant* and the chord built on the fifth is the dominant chord. In the same way, the chord built on the fifth below the tonic is the *subdominant*.

The keys most closely related are (1) the major and minor keys that share the same key signature (the relative major or minor) and (2) those whose key signatures differ by one sharp or by one flat. The keys of the latter group are also related by being a fifth above or below the other respectively. This relationship is responsible for the phrase "the circle of fifths."

This circle of fifths operates above a given note in sharps, and below the note in flats. Beginning with C, the major key of no sharps or flats, one counts a fifth above to reach G, the major key of one sharp; a fifth above G is D, the major key of two sharps. Again beginning with C, one counts a fifth below to reach F, the major key of one flat; a fifth below F is B flat, the major key of two flats. Example 27 shows all these keys. As the keys progress through the more numerous sharps and flats, they begin to over-

Ex. 27

a. Circle of fifths by sharps

b. Circle of fifths by flats

lap enharmonically (that is, the sound of the notes are the same but they are "spelled" differently). For example, seven sharps gives the key of C-sharp major. This is the *enharmonic* equivalent of D-flat major, the

Ex. 28

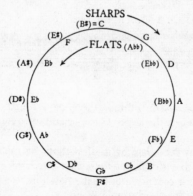

key of five flats, as shown in Example 28. All the relative minors are shown also in Example 27. Remember that the harmonic minor raises the seventh degree of the pure minor, as indicated in parentheses.

The complete circle of sharp and flat keys, derived by fifths, is of immense importance in the evolution of music. It is a complete system of tonality and harmonic relationships that affords through modulation the possibility of tremendous variety and unity. It is one of the chief means of building large-scale structures. The contrast of different keys also affords considerable variety of tone color, especially in the degree that certain instruments and voices are partial to certain keys and less suited to others.

(5) *Chromatic Alteration. Melodic Modulation.* A note altered by the addition of a sharp, flat, or natural not proper to the key signature is said to be *chromatically altered,* and the accidental involved is a *chromatic alteration.* The chromatic alteration is either ornamental or functional. It is ornamental when it is purely incidental and does not change the key, when it is simply for variety or color. In Example 29, the opening of the

Ex. 29

second movement of Haydn's "Drum Roll" Symphony, the chromatic alteration F sharp does not change the key (B natural is part of C-harmonic minor, the key of the piece). If, however, an alteration is used functionally, it becomes part of a new key and plays a part in modulating to it. In Example 30, taken from the first movement of Schubert's ("Un-

Ex. 30

finished") Symphony in B minor, the C natural actually effects a modulation from B minor to the key of G major and introduces the second theme, as shown.

A melody may modulate by itself without harmony. The melody proceeds to emphasize a different tonic as a center of gravity. This may be done by a melodic cadence around the new tonic or by introducing chromatic alterations that lead to new keys.

(6) *The General and Specific Names for Intervals.* The general names of intervals have already been given; they are found by counting the lines and spaces encompassed by the two notes of the interval. But intervals have a more specific character, each being either *perfect, major, minor, augmented,* or *diminished.* The following is one method of determining the specific character of an interval: use the lower note of the interval as the tonic and construct a major scale on it. If the upper note of the interval

falls on a note of this major scale, the interval in question is either *major* or *perfect*. It is a major interval if it is a second, third, sixth, or seventh. It is a perfect interval if it is a unison (also called prime), fourth, fifth, or eighth (octave). This distinction may be attributed to the Greeks, who considered the unison, octave, fifth, and fourth to be "perfect" intervals.

Example 31 illustrates the point. Consider the first (harmonic) interval,

Ex. 31

M = major; m = minor; D = diminished; P = perfect; A = augmented

D to F sharp. According to the rule, the major scale is constructed on D, as shown in Example 31b. Since the upper note of the interval, F sharp, coincides with a note of this major scale, it is a major third. In Example 31c the upper note G also coincides with a note of the scale and is a perfect fourth. In the same way, Example 31d is a major seventh.

But in Example 31e the upper note of the interval does not coincide with a note of the major scale of the lower note. When the upper note does not so coincide, it is either *minor, augmented,* or *diminished,* as follows:

(a) An interval a half tone greater than a major or perfect interval is called augmented. Example 31f is an augmented fourth.

(b) An interval a half tone smaller than a major interval is called minor. Example 31e is a minor seventh.

(c) An interval a half tone smaller than a minor or perfect interval is called diminished. Example 31h is a diminished fifth.

If the lower tone is sharped or flatted, as in Example 31i, it is sometimes easier to reckon the interval without using the sharp or flat and then restore the sharp or flat, proceeding according to the three rules above. In Example 31i the interval without the D sharp is a major sixth. Since the D sharp makes the interval a half tone smaller, the interval shown is a minor sixth.

4. Harmony, the Third Element

PRELIMINARIES

WHEN MELODIES ARE ACCOMPANIED by chords or by other melodies, the ear experiences the richness and subtlety of harmony, the dimension of depth in music. In Oriental and certain other cultures, both ancient and primitive, music has concentrated primarily on the development of melody and rhythm, frequently in a refined and subtle way. In the Occident the development has been directed toward harmony—using this term in its broadest sense, meaning several tones or melodies sounding simultaneously. Consequently, the vast majority of our Occidental music involves melody accompanied by chords, that is, harmony proper; or melody accompanied by other melody or melodies, that is, polyphony or counterpoint. In harmony proper the melody need not be in the top voice. The important point is that wherever the melody occurs, it is accompanied by chords rather than by melodies.

The manner in which the different parts of an ensemble are woven together is called the *texture*. If a piece is essentially a melody supported by chords, the texture is *harmonic;* if a melody is accompanied by other melodies, the texture is *contrapuntal* or *polyphonic*. Harmony is the vertical aspect of the texture, and polyphony or counterpoint, the horizontal aspect.

In graphic form harmony is represented at (a) and polyphony at (b):

(a) melody / supporting chords

(b) melody supported by / melody; vertical / regulation

The terminology used to distinguish the types of music described above is often quite confusing. For the purpose of this book, *monophonic* (one sound) music means music using melody only, such as a single unaccompanied tune. *Polyphonic* music refers to music of many sounds, that is, of more than one sound or more than one melody at the same time. *Contrapuntal* means the same thing as polyphonic, since *counterpoint* means "point against point" or, more generally, "melody against melody." Polyphony is the general term, counterpoint refers more specifically to the study of the subject, but the two terms may be used interchangeably. *Homophonic* means music of "the same sound," and is used to describe music in which a dominant melody is supported by chords. *Homophonic* is a synonym for *harmonic*.

To many music lovers there is some mystery about counterpoint. It is a closed book with seven seals. It sounds forbidding; and the word itself is a "contrapuntrocity"—to use an apt phrase of George Bernard Shaw. Actually, the mystery is principally in the name, not in the thing itself. Everyone who has sung rounds like "Three Blind Mice" or "Row Your Boat" has experienced counterpoint without being aware of it. In both these pieces melody is accompanied by melody, and in a particular way. In "Three Blind Mice" one voice begins the tune, and after a short interval of time the second voice begins with the *same* tune while the first voice continues on its way. Then the third voice enters in its turn with the *same* tune that began the round, while the first and second voices continue —and so on, depending on the number of voices taking part. In simplified form the procedure is

    1. Three Blind Mice, See how they run, They all run after . . .
           2. Three Blind Mice, See how they run, . . .
                    3. Three Blind Mice, . . .
                       etc.

When a melody accompanies or *imitates* itself in this strict note-for-note fashion, the polyphony or counterpoint is said to be in *strict imitation* or in *canon* (**not** cannon). A *round* is a special kind of canon that goes "round and round," over and over again, until by mutual agreement everyone stops. If the opening melody is imitated approximately but not exactly, the result is *free imitation,* or simply *imitation*. In practice, imitation of the "free" variety is more common than the "strict" sort. *Imitative counterpoint* is a general term used to designate the use of imitation.

But polyphony or counterpoint need not involve imitation at all; frequently the melodies combined are different. The counterpoint simply consists in giving melodic and rhythmic interest to each of the melodic parts of the ensemble. Sometimes two tunes that exist quite independently, like "Swanee River" and "Humoresque," can be combined. This kind of thing goes by the special name of *quodlibet* ("what you will"). The family gatherings of J. S. Bach were fond of singing *quodlibets,* and Bach used one in the last variation of his "Goldberg" Variations for harpsichord.

While it is true that counterpoint stresses the horizontal aspect of the ensemble and that harmony stresses the vertical aspect, counterpoint always has a vertical or harmonic aspect at any given point because the melodic parts have to be regulated according to some scheme of what sounds well together. In harmony the emphasis is on the appropriate chord to accompany the melody and on the progression from one chord to the next. At the same time the individual parts that make up the harmony may have varying degrees of melodic interest. In some pieces harmony and counterpoint are in nearly equal balance. A chorale harmonized by J. S. Bach illustrates this point well. The ensemble gives the impression of solid, varied, and most interesting chords; and each singer has a part that has some melodic interest as well.

THE RELATION OF RHYTHM TO POLYPHONY AND HARMONY

The role of melody in polyphony is obviously fundamental. Rhythm, however, is equally important in emphasizing the independence of the melodic lines. In the section dealing with rhythm (see pp. 19–20) we distinguished the various types of accents and their relation to the accent of meter. This same distinction between the accents of rhythm and meter is even more important in counterpoint, where two or more melodies are heard at the same time. The conflict of the different accents of the individual melodies with each other and with the "ensemble" accent of the meter gives life and interest to polyphonic music. Example 32 shows the rhythmic pattern (accent marks inserted) of the opening of the "development" section of Haydn's "Drum Roll" Symphony. The section opens with the

Ex. 32

motive of the first theme of the movement, imitated in various parts. Observe how much the rhythmic accent contributes to the passage.

A particular kind of rhythm called *polyrhythm* gives special independence to the rhythms. In polyrhythm two (or more) kinds of rhythm, such as duple in one part, triple in another, may be heard at the same time. In contemporary music, polyrhythms or "polymeters" of various sorts are especially liked. In the second movement of the Hindemith Third Quartet, for example, the basic meter is irregular, and the other parts impose other rhythms or meters on this irregularity. In Example 33, from the same Hindemith Quartet, a regular phrase of melody lasting for two eighth beats is imposed on the irregular meter indicated by the presence of the bar line.

Ex. 33 *

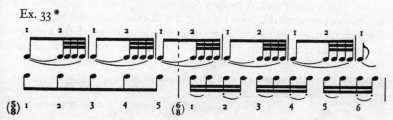

* Copyright 1923, B. Schott's Söhne, Mainz; by permission of Associated Music Publishers, Inc.

Harmony is inseparably connected with rhythm just as melody and counterpoint are. Progressions of chords inevitably set up series of tensions and relaxations, which have the effect of accented and unaccented points in the ensemble. Certain chords are felt as tendency chords in that they must be completed by other chords. This feeling of passing from *chords of movement* to *chords of repose* is similar to the impression given by accented and unaccented notes. Chords that contain dissonant notes are good examples of chords of movement, since the dissonance is felt to need resolution by moving to a consonance (for consonance and dissonance, see p. 46). Similarly, chords used in cadences establish the effect of passing from tension to repose. In Example 34 one passes from the relative dissonance of the first chord to the repose of the second chord; and the latter chord, a cadential chord, needs the last chord to complete the cadence The progression of these three chords is felt as a gradual attainment of repose through decreasing degrees of harmonic accent.

Ex. 34

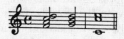

Ideas and terms derived from meter may be applied to harmony. One may speak of "upbeat" harmony to indicate unaccented chords that precede harmonically accented chords of movement or tension. The heavy accent of the harmony does not necessarily coincide with the heavy accent of the meter.

To summarize: Harmony consists of melody accompanied by chords. It may also consist of chords alone ("Chopsticks" is a primitive example), and the chords may be played in "broken" fashion, as in Bach's First Prelude from *The Well-Tempered Clavier.* In proportion as the accompanying parts that make up the chords acquire more melodic interest, the element of counterpoint enters. At a point where the main emphasis is clearly on melody accompanying melody, the texture becomes contrapuntal (i.e., polyphonic). A melody accompanying itself in strict imitation is a canon (or in some cases a round); if it does so freely, the music is in free imitation, or, more simply, imitation. On the other hand, the melodies in polyphony may be quite unrelated. The importance of rhythm in harmony and polyphony is often forgotten, but it must not be. Rhythm regulates the flow, the tensions, and relaxations—the "impulse, activity, and repose"—of everything in music.

Suggested Listening

Bach, Orchestral Suite No. 1 in C, *Passepied* II. The tune of this piece is played by the viola and violins I and II, and a different tune, played by the oboe, accompanies above.

The Overture to the same Suite consists of three sections: *adagio, allegro, adagio.* The *allegro* is a fugue (see p. 61). Listen to the way in which the melody, the "subject," is announced by itself and then imitated in the other voices.

Palestrina, *Kyrie* of the "Pope Marcellus" Mass. This piece begins in imitation and relies on imitation throughout. Here the imitation is harder to recognize than in the Bach fugue, because in the *Kyrie* the successive voices enter before the melody is completely heard.

Paul Hindemith, Third String Quartet. This contemporary piece begins in imitation. The dissonant style should not prevent the listener from recognizing the imitation.

CONSONANCE AND DISSONANCE

In a subjective sense consonance means simply that to any individual or to any era intervals or chords sound well, while dissonance means that they strike the ear harshly or disagreeably. Consonance is also related to feelings of stability and repose, while dissonance implies instability as well as motion toward a consonance as a point of repose. However, consonance and dissonance can be defined objectively in acoustical terms: the degree of consonance is relative to the simplicity of the ratios of the frequency vibrations of the tones that comprise the intervals of the chord. Example 26 shows certain notes in the first three octaves of the harmonic series. The numbers also indicate, for all practical purposes, the frequency relationships of the tones concerned. Thus the octave relationship is 2:1, the perfect fifth is 3:2, the perfect fourth is 4:3, and the major second is 9:8. The intervals just mentioned are less and less consonant in the order mentioned, because the relationships are less and less simple. Similarly, the major chord (for instance, C-E-G) has the relationship 4:5:6, and is more consonant than the minor (for instance E-G-B) which has the less simple relationship 10:12:15.

Scientifically speaking, consonance and dissonance are purely relative terms, and dissonance is simply less consonance. Schönberg, among recent composers, has emphasized this point. Where the line between them is drawn is an arbitrary matter, depending on the aesthetic taste of a particular time or individual. To the Greeks, the perfect fourths, fifths, and octaves were harmonically the "perfect" consonances, and the thirds and sixths were dissonances. This situation prevailed through the thirteenth century. At a later time, the thirds and the sixths were considered consonances along with the fifth and the octave, and the fourth was treated sometimes as a consonance and sometimes as a dissonance. In contemporary music it is fruitless to try to draw the line between consonance and dissonance. One can simply say that music is more or less consonant or, for that matter, more or less dissonant.

But one thing is quite clear. Certain periods established certain standards of consonance and dissonance. Thus if simple triads within the major and the minor were considered as the only consonant harmonies, a chord consisting of other notes was considered dissonant. To any established norm of consonance, anything else is dissonant.

The concept of consonance and dissonance is applied to the melodic as well as to the harmonic aspect of music. Here again melodies in different eras vary tremendously in the melodic intervals used, because the inherent feeling of two periods toward consonant and dissonant intervals may differ. In the sixteenth century, for instance, a melodic seventh was not usually employed, but today this interval is used freely.

A real distinction is felt between some melodic and harmonic dissonances of the same name. The interval of the harmonic second sounds relatively dissonant (i.e., less consonant), but the melodic second, that is, proceeding melodically by stepwise motion, is one of the commonest features of melody in general.

Suggested Listening

The following pieces are selected for their relative degrees of dissonance:
Palestrina, *Kyrie* of the "Pope Marcellus" Mass.
Haydn, Minuet from the "Drum Roll" Symphony.

Wagner, Prelude to *Tristan and Isolde*.
Hindemith, first movement of the Third String Quartet.
Schönberg, *Pierrot Lunaire* or Fourth String Quartet.

HARMONY

CHORDS: THEIR CONSTRUCTION AND INVERSION

The basic element of harmony is the chord, the simplest form of which
is the so-called triad. The triad consists of three notes imposed over each
other by thirds, or, to put it differently, of a third and a fifth imposed
above a given note, the *root*. The root is the lowest-sounding member of
a chord reduced to its simplest form of superimposed thirds. In Example
35a, F is considered the root of the triad, and the third and the fifth are the
notes A and C respectively. The chord may be *doubled* by adding other
voices sounding the same notes or notes of the same name in some higher
octave. (Ex. 35b.)

Ex. 35

Chords are said to be *inverted* or to occur *in inversion* when a chord
note other than the root serves as the lowest sounding voice. In Example
35c, the original root, F, is now the top voice, and the chord is said to be
in its *first inversion* (sometimes called the *six-three* chord or *chord of the
sixth,* because the intervals formed between the lowest and the upper parts
are a sixth and a third). Similarly, the chord in Example 35d is the *second
inversion* or *six-four* position of the chord.

The vocabulary of chords may be expanded by adding a third above the
triad in root position to form a seventh chord, so called because the interval between the root and the highest member is a seventh (Ex. 36a).
These chords can be doubled just as in the case of triads; and, similarly,
they may have inversions. However, the seventh chord has three inversions
instead of two (Ex. 36b, c, d).

Ex. 36

The idea of superimposing thirds on the triads may be carried still further to form ninth chords, eleventh chords, and even thirteenth chords (Ex.

Ex. 37

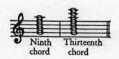

Ninth   Thirteenth
chord   chord

37). A fifteenth chord simply brings us back to the root two octaves higher. These elaborate chords are felt less and less as stable chords and begin to sound like other simpler chords on which dissonant notes have been imposed. Sometimes these chords are used more in the sense of sonority than as belonging to a key, as in Debussy's impressionistic music (e.g., *Pelléas et Mélisande,* see pp. 383–384).

The chord root, which is the lowest sounding note of the chord in its simplest form, defines the relationship of the chord to the key in which it occurs. Example 38a gives a chord reduced to simple form in Example 38b. The root of this chord is A, and it defines the relationship of the chord to the key in which the chord occurs. If the key were C major, the chord shown in Example 38b would be the chord on the sixth (VI) degree. Similarly, Example 38c gives a chord reduced to simple form in Example 38d, a seventh chord whose root is D. If this is in C major, the chord is on the second degree (II, the supertonic).

Ex. 38

The chords most important in establishing the tonality are those on the first degree (I, the tonic), the fourth degree (IV, the subdominant), and the fifth degree (V, the dominant). Example 39 shows these chords. One of the commonest chords is the dominant seventh (V7), the seventh chord built on the fifth degree of the scale (Ex. 39b).

Ex. 39

I   IV   V   V7

CADENCES

A melodic cadence was explained in the section on melody. In harmony the point of repose defined by the melodic cadence is confirmed by the chords of a harmonic cadence. The harmonic cadence confirms the tonality of the melody at the end of a phrase or point of repose. Cadences are very important to the feeling of flow and order in music through their power to regulate and define.

The most important harmonic cadences are those which use the following chord progressions:

1. Dominant—tonic (V—I): the *authentic* cadence. The most important cadence, and the one that defines the key in most decisive fashion (Ex. 40a).

2. Subdominant—tonic (IV—I): the *plagal* cadence; also called the *Amen* or *Church* cadence because it is frequently used for the "Amen" at the end of a hymn (Ex. 40b).

3. Tonic—dominant (I—V): a *half* cadence. The reverse, as it were, of the authentic cadence. It is used for a momentary pause in the course of a piece, but it creates an expectancy of what is to come. It is an intermediate cadence (see p. 30); by its very nature it cannot be a final cadence that ends a piece (Ex. 40c).

4. Dominant—submediant (V—VI): a *deceptive* cadence. The deception consists in substituting the submediant, the chord on the VI degree, for the tonic (I). Having avoided a final (authentic) cadence in this way, the music generally concludes with some form of the final cadence (Ex. 40d).

Ex. 40

| V | I | IV | I | I | V | V | VI |
| a. Authentic | | b. Plagal | | c. Half | | d. Deceptive | |

MODULATION

In its developed form, harmony comprises a complete system based on the chord progressions that define the tonality and on the concept of passing at will through any of the various major and minor keys. This process of changing key is called *modulation*. The entire development of music for the past three centuries has depended on the evolution of tonality and its complementary idea, modulation, not only for variety but also for the forms of music itself. All large-scale pieces that are structurally independent of a text depend on the resources of tonality and modulation, which, in the modern sense, began to evolve in the seventeenth century. It is significant that the variation enjoyed its greatest vogue in this period. The explanation lies in the fact that through variation an extended structure is possible with the *minimum* use of different keys and modulation.

The methods by which composers modulate from one key to another are very numerous, and they are beyond the scope of this discussion. But a simple way of modulating can be understood by an analogy. If two streets intersect, their point of intersection is common to both. If a man driving an automobile wishes to go from one street to another, he must first enter this common area before he can drive from one street to another. In the same way, a composer enters the area common to two keys before leaving one and going to another. He does not have to do this, but it is a common way of effecting a modulation.

A musical example may be helpful. In Example 41 the C major chord is established as the tonic (I) chord in C major by using the authentic cadence (V—I). By analogy, the automobile driver of the preceding paragraph has established his direction on, let us say, Main Street. In music, the C major chord can be considered as a chord common to C major and to G major. It is the tonic to C major and the subdominant (IV) to G major. The driver has now reached the common area where Elm Street (in G major) crosses Main Street (in C major). To reach Elm Street (G major), the driver no longer considers the common area as Main Street (C major) but as Elm Street (G major). He turns, and is soon driving on Elm Street. This is essentially all that happens in the kind of modulation illustrated in Example 41. The composer ceases to consider the C major chord in the key of C major; he treats it as if it belongs to G major, that is, as the subdominant, and confirms his new direction in G major by the authentic cadence (V—I) in the new key of G major. The composer is now happily driving along the Elm Street of G major.

Ex. 41

THE MELODIC DISSONANCES OF COUNTERPOINT

As a rule, the melodies of counterpoint are regulated vertically by the conception of the proper consonant intervals. Certain melodic notes that are considered dissonant (according to some particular notion of consonance and dissonance) are classified according to particular melodic conventions and allowed to exist among the consonances. Some of these dissonances are accented and others are unaccented.

The *passing note* and the *neighboring* (or *auxiliary*) *note* belong to the unaccented type. In Example 42a the note C on the second half of the first beat is an unaccented dissonance (a seventh) that "passes" by step-wise motion to fill the space between two consonant notes. On the second half of beat two (Ex. 42b) the C in the lower line is also an unaccented dissonance (a ninth), but it simply goes down one step to C and then returns to the consonant note—D—from which it came. Neighboring notes like this go to an upper or lower "neighbor" and return; passing tones "pass" to a note a third higher or lower.

Ex. 42

The *suspension* and the *appoggiatura* are two types of accented dissonances. In the suspension a note is rhythmically "suspended" by means of a tie, thus forming a dissonance on the strong beat of the meter as in Example 42c. At this point the basic harmony is A and F sharp, but the F sharp has been held back for one beat and is not heard until its "resolution" on beat two. In a suspension the dissonant note—in this case G—must be "prepared," that is, it must be sounding on the previous unaccented beat as a consonance; the dissonance of the suspension comes on the strong beat, and it is "resolved," that is, it goes to its real harmony on the following beat, usually by descending one step.

An appoggiatura is basically an unprepared dissonance that receives accent and then resolves to a consonance. The appoggiatura may be arranged so that it resolves either upward or downward (Ex. 42d).

These dissonances of counterpoint serve important artistic and expressive ends: they add variety to the harmony; they enlarge the possibilities of a more varied and interesting rhythmic and melodic pattern; and they give motion, since dissonance usually implies the movement from tension to repose.

Suggested Listening

Listen again to the pieces listed on pages 47–8, this time for the melodic dissonances of counterpoint.

MATERIAL FOR FURTHER STUDY

1. *Chord classification*. The chords are classified according to the scale degree on which the root of the chord falls: Tonic (I), supertonic (II), mediant (III), subdominant (IV), dominant (V), subtonic or leading-tone chord (VII). The subdominant should be considered as a relation

ship a *fifth below* the tonic, not as a tone below the dominant. It is basically the dominant "under" the tonic. The submediant is the mediant below the tonic, that is, the mediant between the tonic and the subdominant, in the same way that the mediant is between the tonic and the dominant.

Chords are also classified, just as intervals are, according to their particular qualities: *major, minor, augmented,* and *diminished* (there are no "perfect" chords). The major chord consists of a major third and a perfect fifth (Ex. 43a); the minor chord, of a minor third and a perfect fifth (Ex. 43b); the diminished chord, of a minor third and a diminished fifth (Ex. 43c); and the augmented chord, of a major third and an augmented fifth (Ex. 43d). Two of the important seventh chords are also shown in Example 43e and f: the dominant seventh (V7) and the diminished seventh (VII7). The latter is formed on the leading tone of the minor mode. Example 43e shows the dominant seventh of C major (or minor); Example 43f, the diminished seventh of C minor. These chords are illustrated in root position, but they can all be inverted.

Ex. 43

When chords are proper to the key concerned, they are *diatonic* to the key; but if accidentals must be added, the chord is *chromatic* to the key, and the chord is said to be "chromatically altered" or simply "an altered chord." The *same* chord may be either diatonic or chromatic (i.e., altered), depending on the context. The minor chord, shown in Example 43b, is diatonic to C minor, but it is an altered chord in C major. Similarly, the augmented chord of Example 43d is diatonic to A (harmonic) minor, but it is chromatic to C major. When the chords used in a piece of music stay mainly within the bounds of one key (or another to which it modulates), the harmony is called *diatonic;* when chromatic alterations are consistently used, the harmony is called *chromatic.*

All these names and terms are simply convenient labels for purposes of discussion. The important thing is the variety and color that the different chords and kinds of harmonies effect. The pieces of music already suggested for listening will illustrate the point; and reviewing them in terms of the chords and harmonies just discussed will open new vistas of interest.

2. *Polytonality.* This term refers to the simultaneous use of more than one key. Contemporary composers have used this device frequently (see p. 442).

3. *Harmonic rhythm.* This term is used to indicate the rhythmic pattern

of the *rate* of the changes in the harmony. In Example 44a, in spite of the
bustle of the broken chords (or arpeggios) of the first two measures, the
harmony does not change, as is shown in the reduction of this passage to
chords in Example 44b. In measure 3, however, there are two separate
harmonies, and in the last measure there is one. The harmonic rhythm of
this passage, that is, the *rate* or rhythmic pattern of the changing harmonies, is shown in Ex. 44c.

Ex. 44

The rate of harmonic change, not the speed of the notes themselves or
the liveliness of the tempo, determines the harmonic rhythm. In a lively
piece it often happens that the harmonies change less often *per measure*
than in a slow piece—where the changes may be relatively frequent.

5. *The Larger Forms*

The real problems of musical form are always, in the last resort, problems of movement.

DONALD FRANCIS TOVEY

FORM IN GENERAL

EVERY WORK OF ART must be organized to give it coherence. Painting must be more than a jumble of lines and colors, and music, more than a mere succession of sounds in which the ear can perceive no relation, continuity, or ordered movement. The patterns that serve to organize and give coherence to an art work are collectively its form. In a painting the form of a work may be perceived wholly and immediately. In music this is not so, because a characteristic of music is its existence in time. Consequently, musical form cannot be immediately perceived; it is the recollected sum of the individual moments of its whole life span or movement in time. This is why the listener, especially the beginner, has so much trouble with "form." He realizes intuitively the presence or absence of coherent organization—that there is or is not *a* form—but for the most part he lets the classifications fall as they will.

The story of the art of music is primarily that of composers seeking to express themselves in intelligible and appropriate form. The composer must have musical ideas and be able to cast them into appropriate form, "the form without which the music does not exist." No one can explain the mystery of the origin of musical ideas—who can say where a melody comes from? What the composer does with his material is easier to observe. It is inevitable that the style of expression and the form of expression will be related in some way, since style and form are two aspects of the same thing; or, as Louis Sullivan said with respect to architecture, "Form follows function." The type of organization in a Bach fugue is intimately conditioned by the imitative counterpoint in all voices of the texture, while a Mozart sonata form is a species of construction related to a particular style of melody supported by harmony.

When a composer is working only with sounds, his problem with respect to form is mainly one of musical design created from rhythm, melody, harmony, and timbre. However, when music is allied to words, as it is in songs and the opera, or when music is related to other factors, part of the unity of the work as a whole may be supplied in ways not primarily related to musical design. In dance music, for example, the form is determined primarily by the necessities of a particular dance step and the recurrence of its rhythmic patterns. For this reason, certain dance music may be very dull when played by itself. Likewise, movie music may be extremely effective in relation to the action on the screen, but it may be quite uninteresting and even incoherent as music by itself, since it may have no form of its own, being primarily used to reinforce the emotional effect of the drama at certain points. In certain sixteenth-century pieces such as motets and especially madrigals the most important element of coherence is the text, and sometimes the music would be nonsensical without it. Certain formal details of the organ chorale prelude cannot be understood without knowing the text attached to the original chorale tune on which the chorale prelude is based. Similarly, music that suggests a mood or story through its title or program cannot always be understood purely as musical design; one must know something of the program to appreciate the piece fully.[1]

The best example of musical forms conditioned by other factors is the opera. Its entire history might be written in terms of the struggle between those who advocated a primary coherence for the drama, and those who believed in a species of opera where the requirements of the music, as music, dominated the libretto. In the early seventeenth century Monteverdi said, "The text should be the master not the servant of the music." Gluck entertained similar ideas (see p. 265), and so did Wagner, who wrote copiously about them in his theoretical works (see p. 342). Ironically enough, Wagner often opposed his own theories in practice, because he overpowered the voice and the text of the drama with the symphony orchestra. Nevertheless, many of his observations are keen and just, and they concern the broadest musical considerations as well as formal details.

The problems of organizing music with texts or a program are different from those of "absolute" music. In the case of the latter the form is essentially a matter of the organization of the whole work by certain principles of musical design. In a very broad way, these principles are the universal ones of unity and variety, as already shown, but the application of such principles is so different from piece to piece as to result in an immense variety of individual forms in any particular art work.

In short, the architectural problem in music is less a matter of formal molds than of fluid shapes resulting from generating principles based on the need for variety and unity in the musical material. The forms of music are a result of the general application of the principles of variety and unity to the elements of rhythm, melody, harmony, and tone color as they concern a particular piece of music in a particular context. A piece may be unified by a persistent rhythmic pattern or by the return of a melody. A

[1] Form in relation to texts and program music is discussed more completely in Chapter 8.

single melody may be made the central factor in a piece of music, as it is in a fugue through the power of counterpoint, or as it is in an *ostinato* (q.v.) or a theme and variations. A reiterated harmonic progression may even be basic to the unity of a piece. In the same general manner, variety may be achieved by different and irregular rhythms, by tempo, by contrasting melodies, by contrast of tonality, harmony, texture, and even by the tone color of different voices and instruments.

Suggestion for Study

Listen to a piece of music, preferably one that you know. Write down in separate columns what contributes to its unity and what contributes to its variety. Do some things contribute to both?

THE LARGER FORMS

Emerson said that the world was globed in a drop of dew. In the same way, the principles of organization may be found in the smallest as well as the largest segments of a piece of music. Some of these stages, or levels, of organization have already been traced: the organizing power of simple rhythmic patterns, the function of the motive and phrase in melodies, and the co-ordination of these factors into the smaller forms, like binary, ternary, and dance form. Still larger forms often contain forms within forms, patterns within patterns; and these large forms are increasingly dependent on the power of harmony, counterpoint, and tonality to sustain them. The individual components of a large form may be complete in themselves, as in the minuet proper; or they may each be dependent on the larger, complete form, which only in its complete state gives meaning to each of the component parts. In a fugue, for example, the "subject" is insufficient by itself, and the coherence of the whole depends on how the dynamic potential of the fugue "subject" is realized.

The smaller forms described earlier have their counterparts at more complex levels of organization, where the constructive power of tonality is more important. For instance, the three-part (ternary) form may be very extended; it may be a large form in which subordinate parts have their own organization and may in turn be subdivided. The more complex the form, the more likelihood there is of form within form, pattern within pattern, and wheel within wheel. Each complex form must be considered on its own merits as an individual work. A good example for study is the *"Funeral March"* from Beethoven's *Eroica* Symphony.

MINUET. SCHERZO.

There is one excellent example of a form at the next level above the simple forms, namely, the minuet. Its scheme is relatively stereotyped;

and, although every minuet has its own particular characteristics, the general plan is repeated over and over again in hundreds of symphonies, chamber-music works, and piano sonatas.

The minuet, as it is used in works of this character, has three large subdivisions, each a complete form in itself: minuet, trio, minuet, thus making a large ternary form. Each of these parts is divided in turn into the subdivisions of the characteristic dance form:

$$\underset{\text{minuet}}{A:\|:B+A:\|} \qquad \underset{\text{trio}}{C:\|:D+C:\|} \qquad \underset{\text{minuet}}{A\ \ B+A}$$

The second minuet of this scheme is not usually written out as it is in the diagram above. At the end of the trio the abbreviation *"D.C."* (*da capo*) is usually placed, meaning to return to the opening minuet and play it again without repeats. The trio is often sharply distinguished in character, and sometimes in key or mode, from the minuet. Originally the word "trio" referred to a setting for *three* woodwind instruments, and a marked change of orchestration often occurs at the beginning of the trio. The scherzo, which later (with Beethoven) displaced the minuet, uses basically the same formal scheme.

THE RONDO

The rondo carried the principle of restatement-after-contrast further than ternary form, using such schemes as A B A C A. Its main feature is an indeterminate number of returns of the opening theme A (or even portions or variants of it) called *refrain,* while the contrasting sections are called *episodes* (or *couplets*) after the terminology of the old French *rondeau.* The sad facts about the rondo are that the relation of the details of the rondo to its large outlines is often very confusing, because the refrain A and the episodes may each be subdivided into schemes such as the dance form (see above). The *principle* of the rondo is much clearer than its application in practice. The regularity and symmetry suggested by the letter scheme above is frequently missing in actual music, and the only guiding principle that can be discerned in some cases is the more or less regular return of the refrain in whole or part. (For the sonata-rondo, see p. 73).

Suggested Listening
Couperin, *"La Favorite"* (*Chaconne-Rondeau*).
Mozart, D minor Piano Concerto (K. 466), last movement.
Mozart, String Quintet in G minor (K. 516), last movement.

THE THEME AND VARIATIONS

In a theme and variations, a melody, usually harmonized, is first stated and then followed by a number of varied restatements. The general principle is that of varying some feature (melody, rhythm, harmony) of the harmonized theme while retaining enough of its identity to preserve a relationship with the original statement, including the same number of measures. Up to the time of Beethoven, the same key, or its parallel minor or major, was usually retained as well. There are a number of ways by which a composer can vary a theme, for example:

1. Ornamenting the melody of the theme by adding notes or changing its rhythmic features, still retaining enough of the contour to keep some identity with the original. When the melody is being varied, the harmony often remains substantially unchanged, although there is no rule about this. Example 45 shows typical melodic variations, taken from the first phrase of the theme of Mozart's A major Piano Sonata (K. 331), and the corresponding measures of Variations I and II. In Variation III the melody is varied again, and the mode is changed to minor, a favorite device of variation.

Ex. 45

2. The melody may be subject to contrapuntal treatment. Beethoven, for instance, used a fugue in one of the variations of the last movement of the *Eroica* Symphony.

3. The accompaniment may be changed rhythmically or harmonically, as in Variation VI of the movement just mentioned.

4. Sometimes a variation is given a specific character, for instance that

of a dance. It is then called a *character* variation (for examples in Bach's "Goldberg" Variations, see p. 225).

Variation need not be limited to an instrumental theme and variations. Example 46 shows how Mozart repeats the melody of the aria *"Batti, batti"* (*Don Giovanni*) in varied form.

Ex. 46

(*Variation of melody of a.*)

The methods of variation mentioned above can be combined in various ways to produce individual variations quite remote from the original theme, such as those that occur in the course of Bach's "Goldberg" Variations for harpsichord or Beethoven's "Diabelli" Variations for piano.

Suggesed Listening

Handel, "Harmonious Blacksmith" Variations for harpsichord.

Mozart, A major Piano Sonata, mentioned above.

Haydn, "Drum Roll" Symphony, slow movement (a special type of variation; see pp. 78–9).

Haydn, "Kaiser" String Quartet (Op. 76, No. 3, in C major), second movement.

Beethoven, *Eroica* Symphony, last movement.

Brahms, *Variations on a Theme of Haydn* (Op. 56; Op. 56a is the orchestral version; Op. 56b is the version for two pianos).

Stravinsky, Wind Octet, second movement.

OSTINATO. CHACONNE. PASSACAGLIA.

There is another type of variation that depends not on variations on a stated theme, but on variations generated by recurrent harmonies, or, more characteristically, by a recurring melodic motive, called *ostinato* or *ground*. This recurrent motive is most frequently stated in the bass (hence the term *basso ostinato*) and recurs continuously as the generative motive to which all the variation elements are related. The *chaconne* and the *passacaglia* are examples of this type of variation. (For more details, see p. 187.)

Suggested Listening

Bach, *Passacaglia* in C minor for organ (*ostinato* largely in the bass).

Brahms, Fourth Symphony, last movement (based, for the most part, on an *ostinato* first stated in the top voices; see pp. 187 and 307–8).

Purcell, "When I am laid in earth," final aria from the opera *Dido and Aeneas* (for this *ostinato* and beginning of this aria, see p. 117).

Corelli, *La Follia,* for solo violin and harpsichord (Op. V, No. 12).

Monteverdi, *"Amor"* (*"Lamento della Ninfa"*), from his Eighth Book of Madrigals (1638); constructed on a *basso ostinato* of four descending notes. (For further discussion, see p. 169.)

THE FUGUE AND THE SONATA FORM AS COMPLEX EXPRESSIONS OF COUNTERPOINT AND HARMONY

Two other large-scale forms, the fugue and the sonata form, will be discussed here to illustrate elaborate types of construction and the relation between style and form.[2] The fugue and the sonata form are examples of achieving musical coherence in entirely different ways, reflecting their essentially different styles and textures. They are both good examples of the statement, quoted above, that "form follows function." The fugue is a formal procedure originating in imitative counterpoint (for this term, see p. 43). The sonata form is a manner of construction related to a texture whose main feature is a melody allied to harmony, tonality, and modulation.

THE FUGUE

The fugue is of a particular kind of texture, that of imitative counterpoint, within which a number of procedures are possible. Their combinations are so numerous that it is hardly possible to speak of the fugue as a form at all in the sense of contrasted and repeated sections. A fugue is composed with a certain number of voices (or melodic lines). Thus one speaks of a fugue for four voices. Another fugue may have three voices; still another, two; and yet another, five. But a fugue for more than five voices is not common. The most usual type of fugue uses a single subject, and that is the type described below. (For double, triple, or quadruple fugues, see p. 221). For purposes of comparison, one may think of a round like "Three Blind Mice" as analagous to a fugue. But a round can be considered only as a preliminary and elementary aid to understanding

[2] Other forms or formal types are discussed in Part II; see the Index for *prelude, toccata, chorale prelude, concert overture, symphonic poem,* and *"program" symphony.*

a fugue because after the initial entries the fugue continues on its own and much more complex way.

THE FUGAL EXPOSITION

The opening section of a fugue, where the individual voices enter one after the other, is called the *exposition.* That of a typical fugue for four voices is shown graphically below. A fugue begins with the statement of a melody called the *subject,* usually stated alone, although it may be accompanied.

Fugue exposition: fugato

```
              A              CS              FP
        II  ----------------------------------------------
    S       CS              FP              FP
 I  ------------------------------------------------------
              III  S              CS
              --------------------------------------------
                        IV  A
                        ------------------------------------
```

After the first voice (I) has stated the subject (S), the second voice (II) enters with the *answer* (A), which is simply the subject stated at the interval a fifth above or fourth below the note that began the subject. Subject and answer enter alternately as a rule, but the order of the voice entries is not specified. The top voice may begin, or the middle, or the lowest voice; nor is it specified which voice is to enter second. When the answer comes in for the first time, it is accompanied by the continuing music of the first voice, and if this accompanying material is regularly employed in the course of the fugue, it is called the *countersubject* (CS).

After the second voice has stated the answer, the third voice (III) states the subject in its original form. The second voice now has the countersubject (if there is one), and the first voice has a *free part* (FP). If there is a fourth voice, as there is in a four-voice fugue, it enters with the answer (usually identical with the second entry); the third voice now has the countersubject, and the other two voices have free parts. If there are more than four parts, this process continues until all the voices have entered.

When all the participating voices have entered in alternate subject-answer fashion, the *fugal exposition* is complete. Sometimes, however, additional entries occur in the tonic-dominant relation, and such a statement is called the *counterexposition.* A fugal texture that consists merely of a fugal exposition is called a *fugato.* (See Mozart's "Jupiter" Symphony, last movement; or Hindemith's Third String Quartet, opening.)

THE MIDDLE SECTION (DEVELOPMENT)

After the exposition, the fugue "develops," largely by means of statements of the subject (or answer) in different keys, or by *episodes.* In the usual episode a rhythmic or melodic motive of the subject or countersubject is developed contrapuntally, and sometimes sequentially, thus emphasizing the motive. Episodes are usually found in the middle part of the fugue, but they may be used elsewhere. Example 47 shows one type of episode, using a sequence. The characteristic melodic intervals of the opening subject with its repeated-note rhythmic pattern are the basis of the sequence. Only one voice of the episode is shown, but this is sufficient to make the point (Ex. 47b). Example 47a is the opening of the subject.

Ex. 47

Episode in sequence.

THE RETURN

Most fugues reach their climax at the return to the tonic key. The return is emphasized, as a rule, by one or more statements of the subject or answer. The number of statements used for the return is arbitrary, but it would be unusual to have a complete restatement of the exposition.

The climax is often intensified by various devices such as *stretto.* Stretto means simply that the entrances of subject or answer follow each other more closely in point of time than when first heard. If in the exposition the entries were four measures apart, subsequent entries less than four measures apart would constitute stretto. Stretto is a device of excitement and intensity. It may be used anywhere in the fugue but it is more common toward the end than at the beginning.

The fugue is sometimes completed by a *coda* (see p. 71); and the coda sometimes contains a *pedal.* The latter consists of a sustained long note on the dominant or tonic of the key, normally in the bass. Only the beginning and the end of the pedal need be consonant with the prevailing harmony. The pedal (also called *pedal point* or *organ point*), like many other features of the fugue, is merely a resource that can, but need not, be used by the composer.

The coda of a fugue must come at the end of the piece, just as the exposition must come at the beginning. But various other possibilities, including stretto and the so-called *devices of counterpoint,* may be used anywhere. The principal "devices" are *augmentation, diminution,* and *inversion.* Example 48a shows the opening of J. S. Bach's *The Art of the Fugue.* Example 48b shows the subject in inversion, that is, where the original subject goes up by a certain interval, the inverted form goes down by the same interval, and vice versa. Example 48c shows the original in augmented form, that is, the note values are twice as long as the original. In Example 48d the original is shown in diminution, the note values being halved.

Ex. 48

A fugue depends on the idea of the thorough exhaustion of a single idea (sometimes, ideas) by means of counterpoint. The emotional and psychological effect of a fugue is cumulative, and the final (tonic) statements of the subject or answer are the final emotional synthesis of an idea that has been subject to exhaustive exploitation.

Suggested Listening

Bach, *The Well-Tempered Clavier,* Book II: Fugue XII in F minor (three voices) and Fugue IX in E major (four voices). The latter uses stretto and diminution.

Bach, *The Art of the Fugue:* fourteen fugues on the subject stated in Example 48a. In this work Bach uses all the devices mentioned above and a number besides. Fugue III is analyzed below.

Handel, last movement of Suite No. 2 for harpsichord.

Bach, the "Great" G minor Fugue for organ.

There are many examples of vocal fugues in the Bach cantatas and the Handel oratorios (to mention two instances). For a very large vocal fugue (in eight parts), see the end of Verdi's *Falstaff.*

ANALYSIS OF FUGUE III FROM BACH'S THE ART OF THE FUGUE

Bach's *The Art of the Fugue* begins with so-called "simple" fugues, of which Fugue III, in four voices, is one.[3] Its "simplicity" is purely relative

[3] This fugue is easily accessible. For instance, it is printed in Carl Parrish and John F. Ohl, *Masterpieces of Music Before 1750* (New York: W. W. Norton & Company, Inc.; 1951, pp. 232-5). This entire anthology is recorded.

to the complications of later fugues in the same work. The subject of Fugue III (Ex. 49) is an inverted form [4] of the main subject of *The Art of the Fugue* (Ex. 48a).

Ex. 49

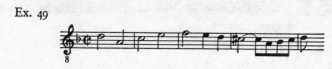

THE EXPOSITION

This fugue is in D minor, and the subject begins alone in the tenor (m. 1–4). Then the answer enters in the alto on a pitch a fifth above the subject. The answer (m. 5–8) actually has the original form of inversion (Ex. 48b). The first voice, the tenor, now accompanies the answer with the counter subject, and the two are shown together in Example 50.

Ex. 50

Compared with the answer, the countersubject is quite different rhythmically and melodically (notice its chromatic character), asserting in this way its individuality and integrity as a melodic line, and acting as a foil to the answer.

At measure 9 the subject enters, in the tonic again, and this time in the soprano. The alto now has the countersubject; and the tenor, a "free" part. At the end of the soprano's statement of the subject, we would expect the entry of the bass. Actually, Bach extends the material and delays the entry for two measures to break the symmetry of the four-measure phrase and to permit a heightened harmonic interest. The bass then enters with the answer at measure 15. The soprano now has the countersubject, and the tenor and alto both have free parts. The bass completes its statement in measure 18, and the exposition ends, still in the original key of D minor. The exposition of this fugue obligingly follows the procedure outlined above on p. 62.

[4] The subject is not the *literal* inversion shown in Example 48b, but what would *normally* be the "answer" form of inversion. To be specific, the subject of Fugue III uses a descending *fourth*, not *fifth*, for the opening interval. Changing the fifth to the fourth is often done, so that subject and answer will be in the *same* key (the first *in* the tonic, the second *in* the dominant, respectively). When an answer makes changes of this sort, it is called *tonal*; literal answers are called *real*.

THE MIDDLE SECTION

This section is devoted to episodes and to new entries of the subject and answer, but in highly individual ways, as will appear below. In graphic form the middle section looks like this (m. 19–54; Ep = episode, A′ = answer in decorated form, S = subject).

Ep I—A′—Ep II—A′—Ep III—A′—Ep IV—A—Ep V—S
19   23 26   29 33   35 39   43 47   51

The points of interest are so numerous that we must be selective. The purpose of the middle section of a fugue is well illustrated here: it modulates, there are re-entries of the subject or answer in the new keys, and the episodes emphasize and develop melodic or rhythmic features of the material of the exposition.

The first episode is devoted to developing two motives "a" and "b" (Ex. 50), both derived from the countersubject. Motive b is also common property of the subject and answer. The first episode is carried out in three voices, not four; in fact, all five episodes use three voices only, and the whole middle section is carried largely in the texture of three voices. The second episode uses b also, but in an inverted form. The third episode

Ex. 51

Episode III

uses motive "c" in inverted form, accompanied by a figure made of b and its inversion (Ex. 51).

The use of these motives is typical of the episode. However, what happens to the statements of the answer in this middle section is far from typical, the answer being stated in *decorated* form, a rare procedure in the fugue (m. 23). In addition, the decorated answer is syncopated (Ex. 52; the original notes of the answer are marked x.). This decorated

Ex. 52

answer form is used in different keys in the two following entries, separated by episodes as shown above. The next statement of the answer occurs in original form (Ex. 50), although in a different key (A minor). The fifth episode follows, and the middle section is concluded with a statement of the subject in the bass, leading to the return to the original key of D minor.

THE RETURN

The return is about the same length as the exposition, and it contains entries of the answer in the alto (m. 55), the subject in the soprano (m. 58), and a final entry of the answer in the tenor. The fugue is concluded with a coda of six bars, including a pedal on the tonic for the last four.

The return also has features of considerable interest. The first entry at measure 55 is in answer form, but it is the decorated form of the middle section. This time, however, it is not syncopated (Ex. 53). The counter-

Ex. 53

subject is also stated in decorated form. Similarly, the following entry (m. 58), that of the subject, is decorated; but it is not syncopated. Since the subject entry of measure 58 comes in *three* instead of *four* measures after the preceding entry, it is in stretto (shown at the end of Ex. 53). The final entry in the tenor brings us back to the original answer form of the beginning of the fugue. Then the coda, using the b motive and its inversion, pronounces, as it were, a benediction on the whole.

It is impossible, of course, to convey anything of the *effect* of this fugue by a structural analysis. The latter is primarily an aid to hearing what is there and to following the voice parts. Listening to all the parts in this way helps us to understand the fugue and to see how the strength, cohesive logic, and continuous unfolding of this fugue derive from the most economical and ingenious use of material by a great master of polyphony.

THE SONATA FORM

The fugue is a complex expression of polyphony in which the melody and the accompaniment are inseparable because the melody *is* the accompaniment. The sonata form is based on quite different premises. It developed in the later part of the eighteenth century, notably with Haydn and Mozart, and later with Beethoven, in response to the needs of a new type of texture, a harmonic-melodic one in which key and key change play a decisive part. In the fugue the texture and the melodic material are the unifying elements; variety is achieved by the interplay of the subject (or answer) in the different voices and by proceeding through different tonalities. A simple idea is thoroughly exploited by contrapuntal means. The sonata form, on the other hand, depends more fundamentally on harmony than on polyphony. For the most part, the melody clearly emerges from the accompanying harmonies, and the two elements of harmony and melody are distinctly heard, while in the polyphony of a fugue melodies accompany each other and consequently are heard in all parts. Contrast in the sonata form is achieved by the sharp juxtaposition of keys and melodies, by relatively clear sectional and period divisions within the themes themselves, and by the contrast of textures in the large divisions of the form. The whole structure of sonata form is unified by the formal principle of restatement after contrast.

Sonata form is closely identified with the internal arrangement of the material of the first movements of sonatas, as found in the symphony, chamber music, piano pieces, and other works after the middle of the eighteenth century. For this reason sonata form has been called *first-movement form;* or, because the first movement is most often an *allegro, sonata-allegro form*. Both these terms are misleading because sonata form need not be restricted to first or *allegro* movements. For example, all four movements of Beethoven's String Quartet, Op. 59, No. 1, including the *slow* movement, are basically in *sonata-allegro form*. Consequently, the term *sonata form* will be used here instead. The word *sonata* means the composite of the three or four movements that are usual in the instrumental sonata, the scheme that is common to the symphony, the string quartet, and to various other types of chamber and solo music.

The sonata form—that is, the structural scheme of a *single* movement —consists of three main divisions to which may be added an *introduction* at the beginning and a *coda* at the end. These main parts are called in order of appearance the *exposition,* the *development,* and the *recapitulation* (or *reprise*). In the Classic symphony (Haydn and Mozart) the exposition is usually repeated, as indicated by the double bar:

(Introduction) ‖: Exposition :‖ Development Recapitulation (coda)

The introduction is optional, and it is often slow, even though the first movement is invariably an *allegro*. The theme(s) of the introduction may be related to the rest of the movement, but this is not usual in Haydn and Mozart. Later, in the nineteenth century, introductions were sometimes expanded to great length, as in Schubert's ("Great") C major Symphony. In the sonata form the general purpose is to set out the thematic material in the exposition, to develop it in various ways in the development, and to restate it in the recapitulation.

THE EXPOSITION

In this section the composer sets out his materials. He achieves variety and interest (and also length) by contrasting two tonalities and, as a rule, two or more themes. Hence, the terms *first theme* and *second theme*. This thematic distinction is a rough and ready one, and is very helpful because differences in themes strike the ear of most listeners at once, whereas differences in tonalities are much less easily perceived.

There is actually something of a listening problem here. The fact is that the *number* of themes used in the exposition varies, so that only one theme, or three, four, or even five themes, might be used in the exposition. Haydn, for example, sometimes uses only one theme, but Mozart is usually more generous, often using more than two. The basic structural element of contrast is furnished in the exposition, *not* by two contrasting themes, but by contrasted keys of which there are invariably two: usually the tonic and the dominant in major keys, and the tonic and the relative major in minor keys. It is as though a speaker felt that the contrast of two

```
                                    II (dom. or rel.)            : (Dvl.)
Exposition: I (ton.)                   a            (b)
          a         (b)             bridge       (closing)
```

different pitch levels of his voice were more decisive and important than the number of ideas that he discussed.[5]

Happily, a number of pieces use one theme for each key so that the use of *first theme* and *second theme* coincides with *first key* and *second key*. If a distinct theme is heard at the end of the exposition, it is sometimes called a *closing theme* by virtue of its position. If there are several themes, they are usually contrasted in character, the opening theme frequently being forceful and motivic in nature, and the contrasting theme(s) being more songlike. Good examples of this contrast are the two principal themes in Haydn's "Drum Roll" Symphony, first movement; or those used in the first movement of Tchaikovsky's Sixth (*Pathétique*) Symphony.

In order to change from the first key to the second, a passage called the *bridge* is used. Its function is to modulate, that is, to change key—or in terms of the above diagram to change levels, from that of the first key to the second. Since the bridge serves to change key, it is by its very nature unstable, and this characteristic distinguishes it from the main themes.

[5] In the diagram used above, the Roman numerals I and II are used to distinguish the basic changes of key in the exposition. Sub-letters are used if there are two or more themes in the exposition. Thus I_a, I_b means that there are two themes in the first key; II_a, II_b, means that there are two themes in the second (contrasting) key. In this particular case, II_b is the "closing" theme. If there were but one theme common to both keys, the scheme would read: I----II (= I).

The bridge is represented graphically above. It is sometimes quite apparent where the bridge ends because the composer emphasizes this point with a cadence and even a pause before beginning the second key. Someone said about Mozart that at this point he is accustomed "to draw up and present arms." On the other hand, many bridge sections of Beethoven are organically joined to what follows so that the second key and its new material steal upon the listener almost before he is aware of it. The bridge may be long or short. A good example of a short and very easily heard bridge may be found in Schubert's ("Unfinished") Symphony in B minor. (See Ex. 30, quoted earlier.)

THE DEVELOPMENT

The second large section of sonata form is devoted essentially to developing the material already heard, although new material is sometimes introduced for the first time in the development (Beethoven's *Eroica,* first movement). The themes, and particularly the motives of the themes, are developed in various ways, especially by counterpoint (sometimes in imitation; sometimes even fugato), and by rapid and often numerous changes of key. In this connection *thematic motivation* means that motives of the themes, rather than entire themes, are used in different voices of the texture. The use of short motives taken from longer themes gives the composer more elasticity of movement, so to speak, and permits him to circulate these fragments from voice to voice of the texture. In this way considerable variety of texture, rhythm, and change of key can be achieved. (See the opening of the development of Haydn's "Drum Roll" Symphony for thematic motivation, Ex. 32.) The composer often takes great pains with the passage that connects the development with the recapitulation (Beethoven's *Eroica,* first movement).

THE RECAPITULATION

In this section the exposition is substantially restated, but now all the themes are stated (generally) in the tonic key, and the orchestration may be different. While the exposition stresses the fundamental contrast of two different key levels, the recapitulation emphasizes the stability and unity of a single key level. In the recapitulation, the bridge has the function of changing from the tonic to the tonic, which, surprisingly enough, is not as easy as it sounds, if monotony is to be avoided.

Recapitulation:

I			II	
a	(b)	bridge	a	(b)

In the exposition of a movement in a minor key the second contrasting key (II) and its theme(s) are usually in the relative major. When these theme(s) are restated in the recapitulation, they may be stated in tonic *major* (Haydn's "Rider" Quartet, Op. 74, No. 3, first movement); or the theme(s) may be transformed into tonic *minor* to preserve the prevailing mode of the piece (Mozart's G minor Symphony, first movement).

THE CODA

A *coda* may be added after the recapitulation proper. The coda serves as a kind of summing up, mostly using themes already heard. A coda to an exposition may even be used; if so, it may be distinguished by the term *codetta*.

In Haydn and Mozart the coda to the whole movement is relatively short; later, and in more ambitious works, the coda is sometimes expanded to very large dimensions so that in such pieces as Beethoven's *Eroica* Symphony, the coda of the first movement is nearly as long as the exposition itself. In the Schubert ("Great") C major Symphony, the "symphony of heavenly length" according to Robert Schumann, both the coda and the introduction are expanded to sections comparable in length to the exposition proper.

HOW TO "TELL" SONATA FORM

In the large-scale forms the inexperienced listener tends to lose perspective and to confuse details with the large outlines of a piece of music. The situation is similar to that of a man listening to a lengthy speech and trying to separate the main from the subordinate ideas. In music the problem is underlined by questions of this kind: "How do you 'tell' sonata form?" The best advice is to listen first to the large outlines of the music and only later to approach the details through repeated listenings.

Happily, the three large sections of sonata form have certain distinguishing features. Each section treats the themes successively but each time in a somewhat different way: specifically, the first section (the exposition) presents the themes in a contrasted but stable manner. The second section develops part or all of the themes, creating a feeling of change and instability by using fragments of the themes, by using counterpoint, and by passing through various keys. The third section (the recapitulation) repeats the thematic material of the exposition more or less in its original form but in an even more stable manner, that is, by using only one key, the tonic.

Of these sections, the most characteristic and striking to the ear in context is probably the development section. If one hears a piece of instrumental music in which melodies, accompanied by harmony, are presented and then developed, the piece is probably in some species of sonata form.

It is wise to proceed from clear-cut and relatively simple examples. An excellent piece with which to begin is Haydn's "Drum Roll" Symphony, analyzed below. Its first movement starts with an introduction; the movement proper (*allegro*) contains very clear divisions into the three typical sections. The divisions of the exposition itself are emphasized clearly by "first theme" and "second theme" of contrasted character; and Haydn makes a clear cadence at the end of the bridge before the beginning of the second theme. The problem of distinguishing the contrasting key levels is reduced to a minimum, as this contrast is emphasized with a new theme and only two themes are used in the exposition. The exposition proper (the *allegro*) is then repeated (or should be), and the development follows. The recapitulation is regular enough. There is also a coda: it recalls the introduction, a rather unusual procedure.

In the example below a "verbal" sonata form is used as an additional illustration. Short contrasting statements are used for the three main parts and for the two optional parts. The different keys are suggested by the different levels of the text.

(Introduction):
(A gloomy day)

Exposition: II: No, the sky is clearing.
          I: Maybe it's going to rain
                        (bridge)

Development:
  Maybe   maybe
    Maybe it's going   maybe,
      to rain. Or is it?   no,
        Is that a raindrop?   perhaps,
              No, maybe, no the sky is clearing

Recapitulation:
        I: Maybe it's going to rain . . . .II: No, the sky is clearing.

(Coda): (Yes, clearing)

  Suggested Listening
Haydn, "Drum Roll" Symphony, first movement.
Beethoven, *Eroica* Symphony, first movement.
Tchaikovsky, Sixth (*Pathétique*) Symphony, first movement.

MODIFICATIONS OF SONATA FORM

I. SONATA FORM WITHOUT DEVELOPMENT

Although the development section of the sonata form is one of its most characteristic features, composers frequently use a form that preserves all the features of the exposition and recapitulation, but that omits the development or simply uses a transition from the end of the exposition to the beginning of the recapitulation.

2. SONATA-RONDO FORM

There are a number of mixed forms which use features of several forms. A common instance of this is the sonata-rondo. A common procedure may be represented by the letter scheme: A B A (:||) C A B A. The A and B are comparable to I and II of sonata form. But the return to A is a feature of rondo. The C in this form is often a development, also a feature of sonata form.

3. THE SONATA FORM WITH FUGATO

It may happen that one of the main groups (usually the first) of the exposition of sonata form is cast in the form of a fugato. The main movement is in sonata form in all its important outlines, but in effect the texture of one of the sections of the exposition is imitative counterpoint, and the theme of this section is treated in fugato (i.e., fugal exposition). *Examples:* Mozart's String Quartet in G major (K. 387), last movement; Beethoven's String Quartet in C major (Op. 59, No. 3), last movement; Mozart's "Jupiter" Symphony, last movement.

THE COMPOSITE INSTRUMENTAL FORMS

The forms discussed so far, from the simplest folk song to the most complex fugue or sonata form, have one thing in common: they concern the internal structure of a *single* piece or movement. Most long pieces, however, consist of several movements, or at least sections, contrasted in mood and tempo. In this way the composer solves the problem of length and variety. It is extremely difficult to maintain the continuity and mood of a single movement or piece beyond a certain time limit.

A large piece of music consisting of more than one movement may be called a *composite* form. In instrumental music important examples are the sonata and the concerto. The sonata, for example, has generally three or four movements, although on occasions it may have more or less. With rare exceptions, the concerto has three movements. The sonata is basic to many types of instrumental music. A *symphony,* for instance, is a sonata for orchestra, and a *string quartet* is a sonata for string quartet. Most chamber music and a substantial amount of solo music depend, at least in part, on the composite scheme of the instrumental sonata.

These composite forms cannot be discussed to best advantage in one place because they change and evolve from one period to another. A sonata of Haydn is quite different from a sonata of Corelli, just as a concerto of Vivaldi depends on a totally different scheme from one of Brahms. For this reason the different types of sonatas and concertos are not considered here, but in Part II, where the repertory proper of music is grouped by styles and forms according to periods of like aims and sympathies.[6]

ANALYSIS OF HAYDN'S "DRUM ROLL" SYMPHONY

To illustrate a composite instrumental form, the "Drum Roll" Symphony of Haydn has been selected for extended discussion. This work (No. 103 in the Mandyczewski catalogue) is one of Haydn's last symphonies, No. 8 of the London symphonies, composed in 1795, four years after Mozart's death. This work shows many typical features of the Classic symphony (see p. 240); it also exhibits certain exceptional features peculiar to Haydn that give this symphony its special individuality.[7] The symphony is scored for woodwinds by twos, that is, two flutes, two oboes, two clarinets in B flat, and two bassoons; brasses: two horns and two trumpets; timpani, and the usual strings. (For information about the instruments, see Chapter 6.)

THE FIRST MOVEMENT

Haydn begins this work with an *adagio* of thirty-nine measures that functions as an introduction to the first *allegro* movement. The *adagio* commences with a mysterious roll of the kettledrums (timpani) which gives the nickname of "Drum Roll" to this particular piece. The roll on the timpani is followed by a slowly moving theme sounding in the deep register, and played in unison by the bassoons, cellos, and double basses. The end of the first and second phrase is harmonized by the woodwinds, which also furnish color contrast. The theme is then taken up by the violins and lightly harmonized; the *adagio* then continues (m. 25) in a fuller harmony using all the strings and some of the woodwinds, and finishes with unisons and octaves scored for strings and bassoons.

As the piece progresses, it becomes apparent that the main melody of the introduction is integrated into the *allegro* that follows, since it occurs in the development section and also in the coda. This "integrated" introduction was relatively rare at the time, but this happy idea of Haydn's was used by others who followed him in the nineteenth century (e.g., Schubert).

The *allegro*, the first movement proper, begins at measure 40. This movement is a concise example of sonata form. A diagram of this whole

---

[6] For the composite vocal forms, see p. 121, note 1.

[7] A recording (easily available) is essential to follow the analysis below. If possible, a miniature score should be used too. References to measure numbers are given in the discussion.

movement, showing the introduction, exposition, development, and re-capitulation is given here as an aid to grasping the general scheme. (br. = bridge.)

Introduction	Exposition	Development	Recapitulation	Coda
	II br. I		I br. II	
	m. 40	94	159	202

The Exposition. The exposition, the first section of the *allegro,* opens with a melody (the "first theme") in the first violins which illustrates very well the principles of the types of melody typical of the Classic period —a melody of short phrases repeated and balanced against each other. The melody is four measures long (see Ex. 54a), composed of two two-measure phrases that balance each other in length and complement each other musically. The first two measures end with the incompleteness of the dominant harmony, and the next two measures, with the finality of the tonic harmony. The next four measures repeat the melody just heard, also in the first violins, but with enough differences to give contrast: it is played an octave lower, and a little louder (*piano* instead of *pianissimo*); it is scored for all the strings, and the second violins add more movement with figuration in sixteenth notes.

A few other points may be added about the melody itself. First of all it is in rapid $\frac{6}{8}$, two beats to the measure, and begins on the upbeat. The details of the phrasing imposed on the basic two beats give special interest to the melody. The staccato notes (indicated by dots over the notes) are contrasted with the legato phrasing of other notes, indicated by slurs. The legato phrase does not coincide with the basic accent of the meter, but is set against it. For example, the last eighth note of the first measure is tied to the first eighth of the second measure. This is an example of the conflict of the accent of the meter (ONE two) and the accent of the phrase, because the metric accent comes on the first and fourth eighth, but the phrase accent comes on the sixth eighth note. Besides, the melody is limited in range and balanced around some of the principal notes of the key of E-flat major. To show this the "outline" notes of the melody are indicated in Example 54b. The other notes of the melody are largely melodic decoration around the notes shown (cf. also Ex. 55).

After the twofold statement of the melody, a pronounced contrast is introduced (m. 48) by bringing in the entire orchestra loudly, and giving it new thematic material. This material is not very significant as melody.

Ex. 54

Rather, it consists of animated scale figures or figuration outlining harmonies. The orchestration is also of interest. The function of the woodwinds is essentially to "double" the strings (some are simplified: the oboe part is a simplified form of that for violin II), and the brasses function as harmonic filler.

The Bridge. At measure 59 the full orchestra ceases, and two oboes emerge alone, softly, for a measure and a half, introducing a passage that serves as a bridge between the first large section in the tonic and the second large section in the dominant (m. 80). The bridge uses the first four or five notes of the first theme and begins at measure 60. Notice here again the use of short phrases and pronounced contrast. Measure 60 is followed by a measure of running sixteenth notes played loudly in unisons and octaves with strings and woodwinds—a marked contrast in all respects to the short, soft, and harmonized motive that just preceded it. The passage that follows is devoted to working out the modulation from tonic to dominant, and it closes with two heavy chords *fortissimo* in the new key of B-flat major at measure 79. This section, by the way, is enlivened by heavy accents indicated by *sf* (*sforzando*), some on the main beats of the measure (first and fourth eighth) and some giving off-beat accents (m. 67).

The "Second" Theme. The new ("second") theme at measure 80 is a delightful contrast (Ex. 55). Compared to the preceding, it is very lightly scored. It is played softly, and the bass now plays the harmony notes by

Ex. 55

plucking them (*pizzicato*). The melody itself is also a contrast to the first subject. It is more lilting and dancelike, and does not have the subtlety of phrasing of the first subject. Its phrase construction is also different. The first phrase is four measures long, not two as in the first theme, and it ends on the dominant; characteristically, the melody is repeated, but only the first three measures. The phrase is completed by repeating measure 3 and then using the motives of this measure to extend the phrase for four more measures. This section ends with two and a half measures of chords, used to define the cadence and to complete a notably short second section, with which the exposition concludes. The *allegro* (exposition proper) is then repeated, and after this repeat the development begins.

The Development. The development is based on principles of contrast different from those of the exposition. Whereas the latter depends on the fundamental contrast of two large areas in different keys and on the contrast of themes and subordinate details within these key areas, the development relies for contrast on different textures and the contrast of a number of keys. This difference reflects the varying functions of the exposition and the development. The former is devoted to "exposing" two fundamental and contrasted key areas and the thematic material used in them, and it does so in a way that impresses the listener with the stability of the material. The development, on the other hand, develops the material by fragmentary use of the thematic material of the exposition, and by using motives of the themes contrapuntally and to modulate to a number of keys; in short the material of the exposition is developed by being regarded from a number of different points of view.

Section I. The development starts characteristically (m. 94) with the opening motive of the first subject treated contrapuntally (Ex. 32). It begins in violin II and is imitated in turn by the viola, violin I, and finally by the cello and bass together. The advantage of such a short motive is its flexibility in going from one key to another. It also provides a rhythmic drive in this case. Haydn uses the motive to go rapidly from B-flat major to F minor (m. 98) and a few measures later (m. 104) to A-flat major, where a new counterpoint is added. The first section of the development comes to an end with the heavy chords of measures 111–12, followed by a hold over the rest, to indicate a brief pause.

Section II. The new section, starting at measure 112, uses the material of the introduction, but now it is played rapidly. It transforms the slow $\frac{3}{4}$ theme to rapid $\frac{6}{8}$. Played in this fashion, the slow theme sounds like a motive, but it is not used as such. It is heard for a single measure in the bass, and then it is swallowed up in the patterns of the lower voices. This section ends with two measures of a motive from the first subject. A general pause (rest in all parts) follows.

Section III. Section III (if it is a separate section) continues (m. 132) with the same motive. There are two new features that make for variety and interest. First, the motive played in the different choirs gives a color contrast in measures 138–43: the motive is heard (m. 138) in thirds in oboes; in the next measure horns are added with the motive also in thirds; in measure 140 the motive is shared between strings and clarinet; in measures 141–2 the motive is heard in woodwinds alone; and finally, the pure string tone is used in measure 143.

This passage also serves to modulate to D-flat major and to the passage that contains the second point of interest, namely, a complete statement of the second subject in this key, which is rather remote from the tonic and "dark" in color. For the moment (m. 144–50) the short motive and rapid key change are abandoned in favor of a complete and stable statement of the second subject. Following this, Haydn uses to advantage the motive of the second subject. Previously this motive extended the theme and closed the exposition. Here the motive is used to modulate (m. 150 and following), and the supporting harmony leads the development back to the dominant seventh chord of E flat with the full orchestra, *fortissimo*. This chord creates the expectancy of the return to the home key, and the tension is briefly heightened by a general pause.

The Recapitulation; the Coda. The recapitulation then begins. It is essentially a restatement of the exposition in the tonic key. We will be content with pointing out one arresting passage at the end of the recapitulation that has not been heard previously in the exposition. At measure 189 (where the string tremolos begin very loudly) one expects the chords of the cadence. But Haydn goes to A-flat major, not the tonic key, using *fortissimo* with full orchestra, and animates the chord structure by the use of tremolo (rapidly reiterated notes) in the strings. Two measures later the A-flat chord is darkened to A-flat minor, and then passes back to the dominant of E flat with E-flat minor also strongly suggested (m. 198– 201). Further interest is given by the *sf* on the off beat, by ending the passage with two measures of first violins alone, *diminuendo,* and by cadencing on a soft chord for the strings and clarinet. The ear does not know what to expect. If anything, it expects a dashing *allegro* as a coda to the movement, and an ordinary composer would certainly have written one, because, as a rule, the coda is in the same tempo as the movement proper. But Haydn, being no ordinary composer, does not do this. Instead he recalls the mysterious introduction with the roll of the timpani and follows it with the slow theme of the introduction in abbreviated form. Then, in a blaze of glory, the introduction theme is converted into a brilliant *allegro,* and the movement concludes with a dazzling summary of a few measures (m. 220–9), based on the opening motive of the first subject and the closing motive of the second.

THE SECOND MOVEMENT

In the second movement (*andante,* $\frac{2}{4}$ time) the key changes to C minor, the relative minor key to E-flat major, the basic key of the whole symphony. This movement is a theme and variations, and it is quite distinctive in character, inasmuch as the "theme" is really two distinct themes consecutively stated. As a whole, this movement may be considered a type of "double" variation.

Each of the main themes is constructed according to the *dance* form; and the second theme is set off in a pronounced way by being in C major as contrasted to the C minor of the first theme. To make this clear, a diagram is given below. "A" represents the first theme in its entirety; its subordinate themes are indicated by "a" and "b." "B" represents the second theme and its subordinate themes are shown by "c" and "d."

A:＿＿＿＿＿＿＿＿　　B:＿＿＿＿＿＿＿＿＿＿
　a :‖: b + a'　　　 :‖: c :‖: d + c' :‖
　‖ 8　　16　　‖ 26 ‖ 34　42　‖
Key: C min.　E flat　C min.　　C maj.　C/G　C maj.

Again, notice the thematic construction of short motives: $2 + 2 + 2 + 2$ for the eight-measure phrase of the opening. All these themes start with the upbeat. An imaginative touch: after the first double bar, the a returns not in the first violin, as it was heard at the beginning, but in the violas, cellos, and basses. For this reason and because of certain small changes, it is labeled a', indicating that it is substantially the same, but not identical.

Variation I; a complete variation of themes A and B, begins (m. 50) immediately after the statements of themes A and B. This variation is very simple in plan: a countermelody is added in the oboe. Why is there no repeat sign? Because Haydn wishes to change details in the repeat and to add the flute and the bassoon. This can be done only by writing out the repeat. The first variation of B begins at measure 84. Here the melodic line, played by a solo violin, is a decorated version of the original melody (Ex. 56). Note the double stops (see Glossary) in the last two measures

Ex. 56

of the violin solo part, and compare these two measures with the corresponding ones of the theme. In this variation the chief interest is concentrated in the solo part; the other instruments are purely for purposes of harmonic support.

Variation II begins at measure 108. It is full of interest, but we will not comment on it except to note the striking chord trill at measure 143.

The broad scheme of the entire movement is:

Theme A B; Variation I of A; Variation I of B; Variation II of A; Variation II of B; Coda.

The *coda* of this movement illustrates why Haydn's music far surpasses that of an ordinary composer. From a purely technical point of view, the movement could end without a coda at measure 158, since this measure corresponds to the end of the original B theme. Haydn, however, extends it for two more measures (m. 158-9), and then he adds a reference to the melody of section B. The next four measures are somewhat ambiguous with respect to the key of C major, since Haydn introduces a chord that more properly belongs to C minor. Nevertheless, he arrives back at C major in measure 170, and here he might have rested his case by the use of concluding chords. Consequently, we are not prepared for what actually happens (m. 171). The key changes abruptly without preparation, and the strings play tremolo on this chord for two measures. In the following measures (m. 173-4) Haydn goes to still another key (E flat). This change is accompanied by an increase in loudness by the addition of more instruments, and at the new key by the use of the whole orchestra playing *fortissimo.* At measure 176 a sudden contrast is achieved by giving the next three measures to the first violins alone, *pianissimo.* Now begins (m. 176) a remarkable passage, lightly scored, using the motive of the B theme (m. 179). The violins descend to become the *bass* of the passage, the motives are in the flutes and oboes. The harmony starting on E flat rapidly modulates back to C major for a triumphal final statement of the B theme in the full orchestra, emphasized by the timpani.

This is the kind of coda which embodies in it the idea of development. Later, other composers, for example Beethoven and Schubert, employ development technique in the codas of certain of their works, in some of which the coda is as long as the recapitulation itself. Such codas are sometimes called *terminal development.*

THE THIRD MOVEMENT

The third movement is the minuet. It has the pronounced triple time of the original dance. As in the previous movement, all the themes begin with an upbeat. Both the minuet and the trio are in the dance form, and have the corresponding melodic subdivisions. There are several points of special interest. The opening phrase is constructed of four measures, followed by an additional four measures, of which last measure is echoed twice to make two additional measures of a kind of whimsical afterthought—a humorous touch typical of Haydn. At measure 19 of the minuet the opening theme is stated, but with an interesting variation. The rhythmic pattern is retained, but the melodic intervals are changed, and the key is changed from major to minor. Furthermore, after two beats the melody heard in the violin I is imitated by the lower string parts. It turns out that this section is a kind of false return of the opening theme. The true return of the theme comes in its original form and key twelve measures later (m. 31, last beat).

As usual, the trio is markedly distinguished in style from the minuet. Whereas the minuet begins loudly, emphasizing the downbeats by heavy chords or by *sforzandi* in the full orchestra, the trio begins softly with the first violins on a legato melody. It is scored mainly for strings with a touch of the first bassoon and the horns, the latter to reinforce the cadences. After the trio the minuet is played again but without repeats (remember that the first minuet and the trio use the repeats as marked).

THE FOURTH MOVEMENT

The fourth and last movement is a highly interesting one (*allegro, alla breve,* two half-note beats to a measure). It begins with the two horns alone. The passage is typical, because the notes used are the only ones available to the horns in this register. In this case the limitations of technique on an instrument determine the limitations of the kind of musical passage played. Refer to Example 26 for the "harmonic" series. The natural horn can produce all the notes shown there except the lowest note (the fundamental), although it produces the notes shown in black considerably out of tune. Omitting the fundamental and the four "black" notes, the player of the natural horn (or trumpet) is left with eleven "good" notes. Cecil Forsyth in his standard work *Orchestration* [8] has put the situation very picturesquely: "A player on one of these 'natural' instruments was like a man continually hopping up and down a ladder, some of whose rungs were so shaky as to be a danger to life and limb. At the bottom they were far apart and badly spaced, while at the top they were set so close together that he had great difficulty in getting his feet on them at all."

Example 57 shows how Haydn adapted himself musically to the limita-

Ex. 57

tions of the horn and turned them to his advantage. The first horn plays the *written* notes C, D, and E (that is, harmonics 8, 9, and 10). It is accompanied by the second horn playing *written* notes E, G, and C (overtones 5, 6, and 8). Since these horns are in E flat and are transposing instruments (see p. 95), they sound as shown in Example 58.

Actually, it turns out that Haydn is using the horns as the harmonic

[8] Revised edition. New York: The Macmillan Co., 1935.

Ex. 58

foundation of the next phrase, where the violin introduces the main subject, and the horn passage just cited is repeated as the bass to it. It is noticeable that as the theme is extended (m. 9) the horns drop out, because the harmony requires certain notes not available to them. The clarinets are substituted.

This fourth movement is notable for a considerable amount of counterpoint, for the use of one principal subject, and for its unusual form. The details of these interesting features will be left to the curiosity of the reader. One rhythmic detail, however, should be pointed out. About half way through the movement (m. 208), all the woodwinds and strings are playing in quarter notes. *Sforzandos* occur in all parts on the second quarter note (Ex. 59). Since the *sforzandi* occur in this way for several

Ex. 59

consecutive measures, the effect is to change the beginning of the measure, to displace or syncopate it, as shown by brackets above the notes.

The Haydn "Drum Roll" Symphony is a work of great interest, and many more of its facets could be examined. It has been used here primarily as an illustration of a composite form. Consequently, relatively little has been said about its orchestration or its relation to the Classic period in which it was composed (for this, see pp. 240–2). A final point should be stressed: while Haydn's symphony illustrates certain principles of construction on which hundreds of works were composed, it retains its own special character—a pronounced individuality that distinguishes every masterwork and every creative genius.

Suggested Reading

D. F. Tovey, "Contrapuntal Forms" and "Sonata Forms" in *The Encyclopaedia Britannica* (Eleventh [1910] and subsequent editions). Cambridge, England: at the University Press.

Stewart Macpherson, *Form in Music* (Revised edition). London: Joseph Williams, 1935. (Original edition, 1908.)

Robert Erickson, *The Structure of Music*. New York: Noonday Press, 1955.

R. U. Nelson, *The Technique of Variation*. Berkeley and Los Angeles: University of California Press, 1948.

R. O. Morris, *The Structure of Music*. London: Oxford University Press, 1935.

6. Tone Color, the Fourth Element

TONE COLOR

TONE COLOR OR TIMBRE means the characteristic quality of sound of voices or instruments. A note of the same pitch sung by Marian Anderson is different in timbre when played by Jascha Heifetz on the violin. There are characteristic differences between voices and instruments in general and also between different individual voices and instruments of the same register. Two alto singers may have quite different qualities of voice; and the tonal characteristics of violins vary so greatly that a cheap violin can be bought for $35, and an important Stradivarius is valued at the fantastic sum of $100,000. Scientifically speaking, the timbre or quality of a tone is determined by the number and prominence of the harmonics it contains (for the "fundamental" and its harmonic series, see Ex. 26). In flute tone there are almost no harmonics. This accounts for its relatively "pure" sound. The tone of the oboe and of the violin is much more complicated because of the different and complex pattern of harmonics involved. (See p. 38.)

Whatever the scientific explanation may be, there is no doubt that the tone color of a voice or instrument is immediately perceived by the ear, and that it is one of the most expressive factors in the emotional impression made by a piece of music. Some voices, for instance, are so thrilling merely in themselves that the ear is fascinated and overcome by sheer physical beauty of sound at the expense of other musical values. The beauty of an individual voice or instrument tends to explain, at least in part, why certain performing artists always draw well at concerts, no matter what they sing or play. It is the physical excitement of their performance—a large part of which depends on beauty of tone—that attracts a large and faithful audience. This fact tends to show that of all the musical elements tone color is perhaps the most immediate and intuitive to most people; and treating tone color as the "fourth" element does not mean that it is fourth in importance. Rhythm, melody, and harmony are discussed before tone color because there has to be some compromise between the logic of presentation and an ordering of the elements of music as they seem most familiar and easily assimilated by the listener.

THE HUMAN VOICE

Of all the "instruments" the human voice is the most perfect, the most vivid in expressing human emotions, and the oldest—since music undoubtedly began with singing. At various times instruments such as the violin have paid the voice the sincerest form of flattery by imitating it. In eighteenth-century violin treatises one can read again and again statements like this: "The Art of playing the Violin consists in giving that Instrument a Tone that shall in a Manner rival the most perfect human Voice," and from that day to this, the singing style of the violin has been modeled on the voice.

A good voice is relatively rare, a fact that may account for the rise and widespread use of instruments. There have been many hymns of praise written to beautiful voices and singing in general. In the preface to his *Psalmes, Sonets, & Songs of sadnes and pietie* (1588), William Byrd, a famous English composer of the sixteenth century, had some remarkably interesting things to say about singing under the heading "Reasons briefly set downe by th' auctor, to perswade euery one to learne to sing." (sic!) Byrd says, in part:

It is the onely way to know where Nature hath bestowed the benefit of a good voyce: which guift is so rare, as there is not one in a thousand, that hath it: and in many, that excellent guift is lost, because they want Art to expresse Nature.

There is not any Musicke of Instruments whatsoeuer, comparable to that which is made of the voyces of Men, where the voyces are good, and the same well sorted and ordered.

The better the voyce is, the meeter it is to honour and serue God there-with: and the voyce of man is chiefely to be imployed to that ende. *Omnis spiritus laudet Dominum.*

> *Since singing is so good a thing,*
> *I wish all men would learne to sing.*

A "mixed" choir consists of men's and women's voices normally divided into four parts: soprano, alto, tenor, and bass. Sometimes these parts are subdivided into soprano I, soprano II, and so on. A women's chorus usually comprises soprano I and II and alto I and II; and a men's chorus, tenor I and II and bass I and II. Soprano II is sometimes called *mezzo-soprano;* and the high bass (basso I), the *baritone. Contralto* is used interchangeably for *alto.*

The typical ranges of the voices of the different parts of the choir are shown in Example 60. The black notes represent exceptional limits. Solo

Ex. 60

Soprano I   Soprano II   Alto   Tenor   Bass I   Bass II
            (Mezzo-soprano)   (baritone)

voices exceed these limits of course. Certain arias call for notes, either in written notes or in improvised cadenzas, beyond the ranges indicated. In Mozart's *Magic Flute* the Queen of Night is required to sing to the note f3, shown in Example 61. Even in the chorus exceptions occur. In Russian music particularly, the deepest register of the men's voices is exploited.

Ex. 61

e - wig dein

The tone color of voices cannot be, and need not be, described. Everyone is familiar with the sound of the human voice within the general divisions described above. Individual voices also vary greatly. A point that should be stressed, however, is the difference of tone colors of a note of the same pitch sung by different voices or by different registers of the same voice (chest, head, falsetto). "Middle" C (Ex. 181a) sounds quite different when sung by different parts of the vocal choir. For the bass part, this note is high in register; it requires the singer to tighten the vocal chords, and this straining tends to give a more brilliant effect than in singing notes lower down and more easily achieved. The same "middle" C sung by the soprano is a low note, and the vocal chords are slackened to achieve it. It could not give a brilliant effect, and it would not sound well sung *forte* by most soprano sections. Similarly, the C major chord shown in Example 62 is extremely brilliant sung *forte* by a men's chorus. But the effect of the

Ex. 62

same chord sung by a women's chorus is totally different; it would be sonorous and full, but it would be difficult, if not impossible, to achieve a brilliant sound in this register.

Considerations of this sort determine the vocal or choral color. Some composers—Brahms is a good example—are unusually sensitive to effects of this kind. The opening of his Requiem derives much of its choral color from the attention paid to the registers of the voices. In Example 63 the

Ex. 63

alto voice is relatively low and dark in sound; the tenor is brighter, and, indeed, it sings above the alto in two places. The brightness of the tenor juxtaposed with the darker shadings of the other three parts gives a special color to this passage.

Whether it is heard alone or in groups, the voice is sensitive to every nuance and inflection of color, mood, and feeling. In spite of the vast number of instruments and their immense capabilities and varieties of color, the voice still remains sovereign of them all, the focus and model of tone, the most personal and direct means of emotional expression.

INSTRUMENTS IN GENERAL

Instruments are so extremely numerous and varied in tone color that it is impossible to describe their timbres in general terms. The strings are nearest to the voice in sound, but they are quite different from the bright, dry colors of the woodwinds or the full rich voice of the brass. Similarly, there are pronounced differences within each of these groups, the clarinet being quite different in timbre from the oboe; and even within the same family of instruments, the higher and lower instruments have their marked differences of tone. The violin differs from the cello, the clarinet from the bass clarinet, the oboe from the English horn, and so on. From these immense color possibilities, the orchestra, the string quartet, and other instrumental groups draw a range of color and subtle tones of light and dark that defy description. Any attempt to convey, merely in words, the particular color or timbre of an instrument is bound to end in failure. One must listen to individual instruments by themselves and hear them in their orchestral or chamber-music combinations to appreciate their individual and collective tone characteristics. One other point should be emphasized about instruments in general. They have a generic life of evolution and change. Neither the violin, the oboe, nor the piano—to select three examples—is the same as in Mozart's time, and this point must be kept in mind, because the description that follows is devoted to modern instruments exclusively.[1]

Suggested Listening

There is a splendid short movie called *The Instruments of the Orchestra.* The music is composed by Benjamin Britten on a tune of Henry Purcell, and it is played by the London Symphony orchestra, conducted by Sir Malcolm Sargent. This movie will give a better idea of the sound of the instruments and of the orchestra in the twenty minutes that it takes than a book on the subject. The music is also available as a record called *The Young Person's Guide to the Orchestra.* (See Plate 1.)

Suggested Reading

Presser's Musical Instrument Pictures, Bryn Mawr, Pa.: Theodore Presser Co. A short, inexpensive pamphlet, giving pictures of the instruments and listing their characteristics.

THE CHOIRS OF THE ORCHESTRA

The orchestra is traditionally divided into four principal sections or *choirs:* the strings, the woodwinds, the brasses, and the percussion instruments. A full-sized orchestra has about a hundred and ten players, of whom approximately sixty are string players. In the brass and woodwind sections there is a single player to a part, and the parts are designated flute I, flute II, oboe I, oboe II, and so on. In the string sections, however, a number of players are used on the same part; in the first violin section (violin I), sixteen to eighteen men are playing the same notes.

The composition of the choirs and number of players usually allotted to each part follow:

Strings: violin I (16–18), violin II (16–18), viola (12), cello (10–12), and the double bass (8–10).

Woodwinds: 4 flutes (including piccolo), 3 oboes and English horn, 3 clarinets and bass clarinet, 3 bassoons and contrabassoon.

Brasses: 6–7 French horns, 3–4 trumpets, 3–4 trombones, a tuba (or similar deep-sounding brass instrument).

Percussion: 1 or 2 players of the kettledrums (timpani), and three other percussion players for the bass drum, snare drum, cymbals, and triangle.

There may be, in addition, two harpists, a pianist (who doubles on the celesta), and an organist.

THE SEATING OF THE SYMPHONY ORCHESTRA. THE SCORE.

When the members of an orchestra assemble on a stage, their arrangement and seating plan is far from casual. One of the "standard" plans used

---

[1] In Part II the instruments of earlier times will be described in the context of older music.

Ex. 64

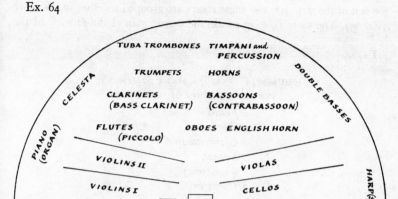

in seating a symphony orchestra is shown in Example 64. The disposition of the different instruments is the result of a combination of factors, such as the desire for maximum resonance, blending of the instruments, the particular acoustics of the hall, the pieces to be played, and the temperament of the conductor. Among various seating plans, the one fixed constant in a field of variables is the position of the first violin section, invariably located at the left of the conductor—probably because in this position the sound holes of the violins face the audience and the tone of their part, the most prominent in most scores, carries best to the audience.

The seating of the other sections may vary. The second violin section is sometimes placed where the cellos are shown in our plan, and, similarly, the violas, the cellos, and the double basses may be shifted; and correspondingly, other parts of the orchestra. As Leopold Stokowski has demonstrated, there are many different ways to seat an orchestra, and the corresponding changes in resonance are sometimes quite surprising.

Within the sections of the orchestra, seating of individual players is determined by a combination of excellence and seniority. Next to the conductor the most important position is held by the concert master, who sits in the "outside" chair (i.e., the chair nearest the audience) of the first stand (or "desk") of the first violin section (there are two players to a stand). He is responsible for carrying out the wishes of the conductor in all technical matters, such as seeing that the parts are properly marked for the players. In some respects he is even more important to the morale and discipline of an orchestra than the conductor. Each of the other string sections is headed by a leader called the *principal* who acts under the concert master. (For a picture of an orchestra, see Plate 1.)

As shown in Example 64, the players of each choir are grouped together on the stage (except that the double basses are sometimes separated from the rest of the strings), and these choirs are grouped together in the score (Ex. 65). The score is, so to speak, the master plan of the music and the

Ex. 65

SCHUBERT, ("GREAT") C MAJOR SYMPHONY

INSTRUMENTATION OF OPENING

2 *Flauti*

2 *Oboi*

2 *Clarinetti in C*

2 *Fagotti*
   (*bassoons*)

2 *Corni in C*
   (*French horns*)

2 *Trombe in C*
   (*trumpets*)

3 *Tromboni:*
   Alto
   Tenore
   Basso

Timpani in C and G

Violino I

Violino II

Viola

Violoncello

Contrabasso

set of directions from which the conductor transmits the composer's wishes into sound and to the audience. The player has only his particular part.

INDIVIDUAL CHOIRS AND INSTRUMENTS

THE STRINGS (SEE PLATE 2)

The strings are the backbone of the symphony orchestra, musically and quantitatively, since over half the members of the average symphony orchestra are string players. The stringed instruments of the orchestra all belong to the violin family, with the exception of some types of double basses which have certain features of the "viol" family such as sloping shoulders and flat backs (see Plate 15A).

The whole string choir embraces a very wide range in which all the chromatic tones are available. The first violins correspond to the sopranos in the vocal choir, except that they go much higher; the second violins, to the altos; the violas, to altos or tenors; the cellos, to basses or tenors (or even altos at times); and the double basses, to the deepest basses. The tuning and range of the various stringed instruments are shown in Example 66. All the strings except the double bass are tuned in fifths. The viola

Ex. 66

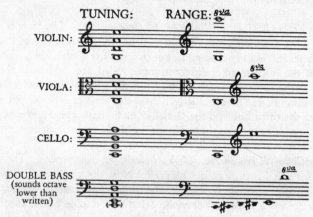

goes a fifth below the violin in range; the cello, an octave below the viola. The lowest note of the double bass sounds a sixth below that of the cello (or an octave for the five-stringed bass). The bass sounds an octave lower than written. (In the following I = Italian; G = German; F = French.)

1. *The Violin* (I: *violino*; G: *Violine* or *Geige*; F: *violon*). It has been said that more ingenuity and thought have been lavished upon perfecting the violin than has been spent upon the steam engine. If so, the labor has been well spent, because in this instrument ("the king of instruments") the art of instrument making has reached its highest point in terms of simplicity of materials and effect. The violin has the unique advantage of combining the emotional expressiveness and flexibility of the human voice, which it closely resembles, with a special brilliance and agility of its own in passage work. Unlike the human voice, the violin can also play chords to some extent. This instrument first emerged in the sixteenth century and evolved substantially to its present form in the eighteenth century with Antonius Stradivarius. Certain changes were made in the nineteenth century to increase the power and brilliance of the violin. The bow, "the soul of the instrument," is strung with horsehair, and it assumed its present form about 1780 in the hands of François Tourte, still considered the greatest of all bowmakers.

The violin is fully chromatic (that is, can play all the semitones) throughout its range. Originally the violin I part had more interesting and difficult things to do than the violin II. Since Wagner, however, the latter part has become increasingly difficult, and in some scores one part is as difficult as the other.

Almost any violin concerto will give an idea of the violin's capacity for singing tone and brilliant passage work. *An example:* the Mendelssohn Violin Concerto, first movement (see p. 313).

2. *The Viola* (*I: viola; G: Bratsche; F: viole or alto*). The viola is an alto violin. Like the violin, the viola is held under the chin, shares the same technique, and is fully chromatic, but in a register a fifth lower. The tone color of the instrument is different, more veiled and deeper, in the same way that the contralto voice differs from the soprano in tone color even on the same notes. To avoid ledger lines, the viola uses the C clef (see p. 533) on the third line and the G clef in its highest register. *An example:* the viola *obbligato* throughout Berlioz's *Harold en Italie* Symphony.

3. *The Cello* (*I: violoncello; G: Violoncell; F: violoncelle*). The proper name for this instrument is violoncello. Note the spelling. The word is derived from *violone*. In Italian, the suffix *"one"* means large, hence *violone* means a large viol or violin (that is, a double bass); the suffixes *"ino"* and *"cello"* mean small, hence *violino* means a little viol (violin) and *violoncello,* a small double bass. When one says "cello," it is equivalent to saying "little"—just a trifle more sensible than saying "bone" for "trombone."

Acoustically, the cello is about as perfect as the violin. Its four strings are tuned in fifths, an octave below the corresponding strings of the viola. The instrument is braced between the knees and held in place on the floor by an adjustable metal spike (or peg) that runs through a hole in the bottom of the cello. Like the violin and viola, each of the strings of the cello has its own particular tone color, the most striking being the top (A) string (which frequently has the moving quality of the baritone or tenor voice) and the second (D) string, which has a beautiful, softer quality. The cello is the bass of the string quartet but not of the strings in the orchestra. The latter requires the deeper bass tones of the double bass.

Examples: Saint-Saëns's Cello Concerto and Ernest Bloch's *Schelomo* (Hebrew rhapsody for cello and orchestra, 1916).

4. *The Double Bass* (*I: contrabasso* or *violone; G: Kontrabass; F: contrebasse*). This instrument, the deepest-sounding of the strings, is as tall as a man, and the player must stand to play it. In earlier times it was a three-stringed instrument tuned in fourths (the upper three notes shown in Ex. 66). The four-stringed instrument common in the nineteenth century added the lower fourth to E, and today many five-stringed instruments are used, adding the low C. Since the instrument sounds an octave below its written notes, the five-stringed bass takes the sounding register down a full

octave below the cello register. Incidentally, in early scores and up to early Beethoven (first two symphonies) the double bass played the same notes as the cello; the same printed part served for both, and the bass merely sounded an octave below the cello.

In construction, some double basses are true double-bass violins, whereas others have certain features of viols. This difference is also reflected in the bows, a few players still using the bow that is played with the underhand grip of the viol players, not the overhand grip of the rest of the string players. (For the viols, see p. 158 and Plate 15A.)

The double basses add greatly to the depth and resonance of the string choir. Through some mysterious alchemy, they solidify the sound and seem to give it an extra dimension. The double bass is not commonly used as a solo instrument. In orchestral literature the double basses are occasionally made to play in virtuoso fashion, a celebrated instance being the trio of the Scherzo of Beethoven's Fifth symphony.

SPECIAL EFFECTS IN STRINGS

The tone color is affected by the way the instruments are played and sometimes by the use of special devices like the *mute* (*con sordino* means "with the mute") which cuts out some of the harmonics, thinning and muting the sound. *Examples* of muted strings: Berlioz's *"Valse des Sylphes"* in his *Damnation de Faust;* Mozart's G minor String Quintet, slow movement (see p. 253). There are many special ways of playing that modify or change the color. *Pizzicato,* for instance, means to pluck the string instead of bowing it (*arco* means to return to bowing).[2] In the Scherzo of Tchaikovsky's Fourth Symphony all the strings play *pizzicato.*

String players distinguish a large number of kinds of bow strokes by which the *same* passage can be made to sound quite different in effect. The basic strokes are *legato* and *staccato* strokes and those in which the bow stays in contact with the string ("on-string") or bounding strokes ("off-string").[3] The important thing is the variety of expression attained by these different strokes. When listening to any of the pieces cited above, one can easily distinguish some of the different strokes (cf. especially in the Mendelssohn Violin Concerto).

Sometimes a section of the strings is subdivided. To make this division, called *divisi* (div.), part of the section (usually the "outside" chairs) plays the upper notes indicated on the staff, and the "inside" chairs play the lower notes (Ex. 67). If the section is divided into more than two parts, special arrangements have to be made.

In *double stops* the string player bows two strings at once; in triple stops, three; and in quadruple stops, four. Quadruple stops cannot be sus-

[2] See the Glossary for other terms: *sul ponticello, col legno, harmonics, portamento, glissando.*
[3] See the Glossary for more of these strokes: *détaché, martelé, sautillé, spiccato.*

Ex. 67

TCHAIKOVSKY, SIXTH SYMPHONY (THIRD MOVEMENT)

tained, and triple stops can be sustained only briefly and loudly (Ex. 68). In the orchestra these stops could be sustained by playing *divisi.* If the composer wants to be sure that they are played as double stops and not *divisi,* he writes *non-divisi.*

Ex. 68

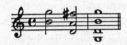

The *tremolo* refers to the same note rapidly repeated a number of times. There are several kinds of tremolos, but only two will be explained here. In the "measured" tremolo a note is repeated rapidly in a definitely measured rhythm (Ex. 69a). In unmeasured tremolo the notes are repeated as rapidly as possible, using very little movement at the point of the bow (Ex. 69b).

Ex. 69

Tremolo should not be confused with *vibrato.* Tremolo is a rapid repetition of a note of the same pitch. Vibrato is not a repetition, but an oscillation of tone in such a way that minute variations of pitch above and below the notated pitch occur. The string player does this by pressing the string with his finger and moving the wrist (or finger, sometimes, arm) back and forth to produce small deviations of pitch above and below the note concerned. The vibrato has become an organic part of string playing. It imparts an emotional and individual quality to the tone.

THE WIND INSTRUMENTS: PRELIMINARIES

The woodwinds and the brasses are all wind instruments. Originally the name *woodwind* was used to distinguish those made of wood from those made of *brass,* and although today not all the woodwinds are made of wood, the name still persists. In wind instruments the sound is produced by setting in motion a column of air in a tube or a pipe. This is done in various ways: in the woodwinds, by blowing across a lip or by using a reed; in the brass, by using a mouthpiece.

Wind instruments as a whole have suffered from great problems of intonation (playing in tune) and from incomplete scales. This is one reason why, since the seventeenth century, the string choir has been the most important section of the orchestra. In early woodwind instruments the small openings on the side of the instrument (which were stopped by the fingers and hence determined the pitch of a note) could not always be bored correctly and still be reached by the player's fingers. Producing half tones and the chromatic scale was another difficulty. These problems were not completely resolved until the nineteenth century, when the "Boehm" system of trackers and rollers (see instruments in Plates 3, 4A, and 5A) got around the problem of difficult stretches and correct pitch for the complete chromatic scale. Changes in temperature and humidity always have affected the intonation of wind instruments. With respect to the brasses, it was not until the nineteenth century that the old "natural" horns and trumpets could play more than the overtone series (see p. 344).

Some of the wind instruments are *transposing.* Among the woodwinds, the clarinet and the English horn are examples; among the brass, the horn and the trumpet. A transposing instrument is one that transposes the written note to another pitch. For example, the C major scale played by the A clarinet emerges a third lower in A major.

The system of transposition probably arose from the desire to notate the basic scale of the instrument in simplest form, that is, in C major. Furthermore, when instruments were built in families (and consequently with different basic scales), there were also fingering advantages, because a single fingering related to the written C scale would serve for several instruments of the same family. Thus the clarinet player could switch from a B-flat clarinet to an A clarinet without using a different fingering with respect to the written notes. This means that the B-flat clarinet part must be written a whole tone *above* its sound; and when reading a B-flat clarinet part, a conductor must think of the real sound a whole tone *below* the written note. Similarly, with horns in F, the written note is a fifth *above* the actual sound.

This system, evolved with the growth of instruments and for the convenience of certain players, is somewhat antiquated today, but so great is the force of tradition that little has been done about it until recently. Like Mark Twain's weather, everyone complains, but does nothing about it. The advantages to a few players are offset by the disadvantages to the conductor and to musicians in general who, while reading a score, must constantly keep in mind the various, numerous, and sometimes changing transpositions in the course of a piece of music. In rehearsal, too, a clear distinction must be made for transposing instruments between "written" and "sounding" notes.

THE WOODWINDS (SEE PLATES 3, 4A, 5A)

In the woodwind choir the flute and the oboe are the sopranos; the clarinet and the English horn, the altos (sometimes the tenors); the bassoon, the tenors or basses; and the double bassoon and the bass clarinet, the deep basses.

1. *The Flute* (*I: flauto; G: Flöte; F: flûte*). The type of flute that is commonly used today is held parallel to the floor and to the player's right. It is sometimes called the *transverse flute* to distinguish it from the older types of flutes like the recorder (see p. 158) which are held down toward the body—as are all the other woodwinds except the piccolo. The player directs the breath over the rim of a hole, the mouthpiece or embouchure, at the left of the instrument to produce the sound.[4] The usual range of the orchestral flute is three (chromatic) octaves upward from middle C (see Ex. 70a). The lowest register of the flute is somewhat "breathy," and in this register the flute cannot be played loudly. The flute is very easily "covered up" in the orchestra. The middle register is the most used; the upper register is light and brilliant in tone. (For "flutter tonguing," see the Glossary.)

The flute and the oboe (see below) "overblow" at the octave, that is, the fingering of the second (and third) octave largely duplicates the first, but the manner of blowing and tonguing are different.

An example: Bach's Second Orchestral Suite in B minor for flute and strings. The last movement (*Badinerie*) is a fine example of nimble passages in which the flute excels.

2. *The Alto Flute.* The alto flute (sometimes called the bass flute) sounds a fourth lower than the usual flute and is treated as a transposing instrument. Its tone is characteristically soft and rich. The lowest register is comparatively strong with qualities resembling the horn. The alto flute is seldom heard alone. *An example:* Ravel's *Daphnis et Chloé,* Suite II. A brief solo passage, using the low register, occurs a little more than half way through, directly after the directions in the score *"La danse s'anime de plus en plus et, dans un tournoiement éperdu, Chloé tombe dans les bras de Daphnis."*

3. *The Piccolo* (*I: flauto piccolo; G: kleine Flöte; F: petite flûte*). The piccolo is a small-sized flute. It is the highest soprano of the flute family. Its *written* range is shown in Example 70b, but it actually sounds an oc-

[4] The embouchure may refer to (1) the mouthpiece of an instrument or (2) the proper position of the lips and tongue in producing the sound. Today *embouchure* means the latter, except with reference to the flute, when it may mean either.

Ex. 70

tave higher. The tone of the piccolo is hard, bright, and shrill, especially in its upper registers. It gives a brilliant edge to the tone of an orchestra in loud passages. *An example:* Tchaikovsky's "Chinese Dance" from the *Nutcracker Suite.*

4. *The Oboe (I: oboe; G: Hoboe; F: hautbois).* The oboe is a double-reed instrument. The double reed consists of two thin pieces of cane tightly bound together with just enough space between them for the air from the player's lips to get through. The beating of these two reeds together sets the air in motion and produces the tone. The oboe has a conical tube terminating in a bell, and it "overblows" the octave. The usual range of the instrument is shown in Example 70c. It is entirely chromatic.

The oboe has a distinctive and penetrating tone color. Most of the solo passages for it are written in the middle of the register shown; the lowest fifth of the register (B flat to F) is quite reedy in sound and difficult to play softly.

The oboe traditionally sounds the A to which the whole orchestra tunes.

An example: the opening theme of the slow movement of Schubert's ("Great") Symphony in C major.

5. *The English Horn (I: corno Inglese; G: Englisches Horn; F: cor anglais).* This instrument is neither English nor a horn. It is essentially

an alto oboe to which the name *"cor anglais (anglé?)"* was applied when it took a curved or angular shape. Hence the possible derivation of the name "English horn." The modern English horn is straight (see Plate 3A); compared with the oboe, it is larger, and it has a pear-shaped bell. In order to facilitate playing, the double-reed mouthpiece is slightly extended and bent toward the player.

As shown in Example 70d, the English horn has about the same written range as the oboe. But, unlike the oboe, the English horn is a transposing instrument (in F), sounding a fifth lower than written. The fingering is practically the same as on the oboe. It stands in somewhat the same relation to the oboe as the viola to the violin, and has similar contralto tone characteristics.

An example: the celebrated passage at the beginning of the Third Act of Wagner's *Tristan.*

6. *The Bassoon (I: fagotto; G: Fagott; F: basson).* The bass of the double-reed family. Like the oboe and the flute, the bassoon is conically bored. Its length is reduced to about four feet by being doubled back on itself. The "Böhm" mechanism of trackers and rollers is of great value in the bassoon, since, prior to the nineteenth century, finger stretches and chromatic notes posed great problems for the player. The mouthpiece emerges from the instrument about two-thirds of the way up, and is carried to the player's lips by a bent tube. Its usual range is given in Example 70e. The bassoon has a dry, hollow tone, but it is capable of a variety of expression. It can suggest gravity and solemnity; it can also be used tellingly for humorous effect. *Examples:* Of the high register, the opening of Stravinsky's *Le Sacre du Printemps;* of the middle register, Dukas's *L'Apprenti Sorcier (Sorcerer's Apprentice) (Vif* section, m. 72–98); of the deep register, Tchaikovsky's Sixth Symphony, opening.

7. *The Double (Contra) Bassoon (I: contrafagotto; G: Kontrafagott; F: contrebasson).* This is the deepest-sounding of all the usual instruments of the orchestra. Its tube, about sixteen feet long, is doubled back on itself four times; it emerges over the head of the player, and is bent back once more with the bell pointing downward. In other respects it shares the qualities and mechanism of the bassoon. It is seldom used as a solo instrument. *Examples:* Haydn's *Creation;* Beethoven's Ninth Symphony, last movement; Debussy's *La Mer.*

8. *The Clarinet (I: clarinetto; G: Klarinette; F: clarinette).* Among the wind instruments, the clarinet has the largest range, the greatest control of dynamics from the softest to the loudest tone, and the most diverse tone colors in the different parts of its registers. The distinctive tone color of its deepest notes, the *chalumeau* register, is particularly characteristic. The

clarinet is a single reed instrument, and it is a relatively late addition to the
orchestra, having been introduced in the last part of the eighteenth century. Its written range is shown in Example 70f; it is a transposing instrument. The most common clarinets are those in B flat and A. While there
are some differences of tone, the selection of one or the other depends, for
the most part, on the ease of playing in a particular key. The clarinet has
a cylindrical bore and overblows the twelfth, that is, the fingering is duplicated, not at the octave (as in the oboe), but at the twelfth.

Examples: The clarinet is a favorite instrument for chamber music, and
some of the finest examples of clarinet music are found in chamber music.
Mozart (K. 581) and Brahms (Op. 115) each wrote a wonderful quintet
for clarinet and strings. Other examples of clarinet music are numerous:
the opening of Schubert's ("Unfinished") Symphony in B minor uses the
oboe and the A clarinet in unison to play the theme; Weber's opera *Der
Freischütz* (see p. 339) assigns the clarinet to prominent solos representing
one of the chief characters (Max).

9. *The Bass Clarinet (I: clarinetto basso; G: Bassklarinette; F: clarinette
basse).* The bass clarinet sounds an octave below the regular clarinet. It is
usually in B flat. The lower part ends in an upward bell, and the upper
end is curved backward and downward to the player. *Examples:* Wagner's
Tristan (Act II in the "King Mark Scene"; Act III at the beginning of the
"Liebestod").

Effects comparable to various string bowings (see p. 93) are produced
by the woodwinds and brass by different tonguings and slurrings. The
differences between sharp attacks on individual notes and legato slurrings
are quite marked. The woodwinds can also produce a pronounced vibrato,
but, unlike the strings and brass, they do not use mutes.

THE BRASS INSTRUMENTS (SEE PLATE 6)

Until the nineteenth century the only brass instrument that could produce the semitones through its entire compass was the trombone. It did
so by means of a slide which in effect extended and shortened the tubing
as necessary. Until that time the horns and trumpets were "natural" instruments, that is, they were limited to producing the notes of the harmonic series of the fundamental tone of the instrument (for the harmonic
series, see Ex. 26). The fundamental, being very hard to produce, was
practically useless. Within the two octaves bounded by tones No. 2 and No.
8, there were only six good notes; in the next octave, six were available
(counting both No. 8 and No. 16). This fact explains why horn and trumpet melodies were so limited, why they followed certain melodic patterns
rigidly, and why these instruments were used more harmonically than
melodically.

Some improvement in this situation was effected by the use of "crooks" (pieces of tubing) which could be inserted into the instrument to give it a different key—but only one crook could be used at a time. The use of a number of crooks also explains how the system of transposition came into vogue, since without one standard fingering, the horn or trumpet player would be forced to learn a new fingering for each crook and to remember which he was using.

Even with the crooks, the natural instruments were limited to a single key at a time and to the diatonic scale. Furthermore, the whole of the diatonic scale could be played only in the upper register, starting at the beginning of the third octave.

In the late eighteenth century it was found that placing the hand in the bell of the horn lowered the pitch by a semitone. This discovery was not of tremendous help, because the tone color resulting from hand stopping was different from the tone color of notes produced in the usual way.

In the first quarter of the nineteenth century, however, a revolution in playing brass instruments took place when it was discovered that valves could be added to the horn and trumpet to make them fully chromatic throughout their registers. In effect these valves (three or four in number) added varying lengths of tubing to the original length of the instrument, so that new fundamentals and their corresponding harmonic series were added a semitone, a whole tone, and three semitones below the original series of the natural instrument. Moreover, by pressing down these valves in combinations, three additional fundamentals and their series could be added by semitones below the first three. Thus seven different harmonic series arranged by descending semitones were made possible by the valves; and by selecting the proper note from any series the brass player could sound the entire chromatic scale.

By 1850 the superiority of the valved instruments had been clearly proved, and from that time on the brass section of the orchestra (as in Wagner) was complete in its melodic and harmonic possibilities. The musical repercussions of this revolutionary change will be discussed in Part II of this book (see p. 344).

1. *The Valve Trumpet* (*I: tromba clarino; G: Trompete; F: trompette*). The modern orchestral trumpet is the brilliant soprano of the brasses. It is a transposing instrument, usually in B flat, capable of playing all the semitones within the *written* range shown in Example 71a. By a slide mechanism, the B-flat trumpet may be changed to one in A. In the woodwinds the tone is dependent on the type of reed used; in the brasses the tone and the ease of tone production are related to the type of mouthpiece employed. The trumpet uses one that is cup-shaped. The old F trumpet is now little used, although it has more power and, according to some musicians, a more "noble" tone. *Examples:* Haydn's Trumpet Concerto; Stravinsky's

Ex. 71

a. B-flat
TRUMPET:
(written)

b. F-HORN
(written)

c. TENOR
TROMBONE:
(B-flat)

d. TUBA:

Octet. The old "natural" trumpet parts go very high. Listen, for example, to the recording of the last movement of Bach's Second "Brandenburg" Concerto.

2. THE VALVE CORNET (*I: cornetto or cornetta; G: Cornett; F: cornet-à-pistons*). The valve cornet is usually in B flat, has the same range as the valve trumpet, and is somewhat more agile. It is seldom used in the orchestra.

3. *The French Horn* (*I: corno; G: Horn; F: cor*). This instrument, the true horn, is the alto or tenor of the brass choir. It is actually a conical tube about twelve feet long, coiled up in compact form. It ends in a wide bell about twelve inches across. The mouthpiece is funnel-shaped. Built in F, it is a transposing instrument. Example 71b shows the written range, the sound of which is a fifth lower on the F horn. The French horn is notable for its mellow, blending tone. Certain shadings of tone and pitch may be obtained by placing the hand in the bell, as explained earlier. *Examples:* the opening of Strauss's *Till Eulenspiegel* has a fine horn solo; three horns are used in the trio of the Scherzo movement of Beethoven's *Eroica* Symphony; in Weber's Overture to *Der Freischütz,* four horns are used with beautiful and telling effect. Schubert's Symphony in C major begins with two horns alone. In Brahms's First Symphony the introduction to the last movement has a beautiful horn call.

4. *The Trombone* (*I: trombone; G: Posaune; F: trombone*). The trombone is the tenor or bass of the brasses. When the slide is fully extended, the trombone produces its deepest note (the range is shown in Ex. 71c). As the slide is brought closer to the player, the effect is the same as that produced by the valves of the horn and trumpet, that is, a new fundamental and a new harmonic series are introduced, so that all the chromatic tones are produced by using a succession of different positions of the slide. The common trombone is the tenor trombone in B flat, but it is treated as a nontransposing instrument. On this instrument, very wide gradations of tone are possible, from a very soft and mellow tone to a tremendously loud blare. *Examples:* Wagner's Overture to *Tannhaüser;* Berlioz's *Symphonie Funèbre et Triomphale* (the second movement contains an elaborate trombone solo).

5. *The Tuba* (*the same word is used in other languages*). The tuba is the double bass of the brass choir. It is a nontransposing instrument (its range is shown in Ex. 71d). The tuba is used prominently by Wagner in his *Ring* operas (The dragon Fafner is depicted by the tuba in *Siegfried*).

As in the strings, the brass may be muted. Brass mutes are pear-shaped pieces of wood or metal inserted into the bell of the instrument. The mute is especially effective in the horn and trumpet.

THE PERCUSSION IN GENERAL (SEE PLATE 5B)

There are a number of percussion instruments, but relatively few of them appear with the same regularity as the instruments discussed above. Percussion instruments may have definite pitch, as in the case of the kettledrums, bells, chimes, celesta, and xylophone; or indefinite pitch, as in the case of the side drum, the bass drum, the cymbals, the tambourine, the triangle, and the gong. Of these various instruments only the kettledrums and the celesta will be discussed further. However, some of the others are included on Plate 5B.

The Kettledrums (*I: timpani; G: Pauken; F: timbales*). The kettledrums are the indispensable part of the percussion and one of the most important parts of the entire orchestra. In the old type of kettledrum, the skin covering the head of the kettle was tightened (and hence tuned) by means of screws with T-heads along the side of the top of the drum. Today the tuning is usually done by means of a pedal (pedal-timpani) which permits rapid tuning and even *glissandi* (see Glossary) on the kettledrums.

Before 1850 two kettledrums were used; after this time, three are often found and sometimes even four. Until the advent of Beethoven (1770-1827) the smaller of the two drums was tuned to play the tonic note of the key of the piece; the larger drum was tuned to the dominant a fourth lower. The ranges within which the small and the large drum could be tuned are shown in Example 72. Beethoven changed this arrangement (when he wished) by tuning the larger drum to the tonic and the smaller drum to the dominant a fifth *above*. Beethoven also used other intervals besides the tonic and dominant, for instance the octave in the Eighth and Ninth Symphonies. Later more complex, and also chromatic, intervals were used (e.g., by Berlioz).

Ex. 72

The tone of the drum is affected by the kind of drum sticks used. The usual type of stick is made of hard wood covered by piano felting. There are also sticks covered with much softer spongelike material. The kettledrums may be muffled or muted. There are many types of drum rolls, including those which strike the drum skin in various ways and places.

Examples: The kettledrum can be heard in almost any symphony. Listen especially to the opening of Haydn's "Drum Roll" Symphony. For a timpani solo and the use of the "octave" tuning, listen to the Scherzo of Beethoven's Ninth Symphony. A really spectacular example of kettledrums occurs in Berlioz's Requiem (in the *"Tuba Mirum"*), in which eight pairs of kettledrums play the background harmony.

The Celesta. The celesta looks like a small upright piano. The keyboard controls hammers that strike small steel bars, thus producing a pure bell-like tone. The celesta part is written an octave below sounding pitch, and the instrument has a range of four octaves (Ex. 73). The celesta has the

Ex. 73

distinction of being one of the few instruments that cannot play out of tune. *Example:* Tchaikovsky's "Dance of the Sugar-Plum Fairy" from the *Nutcracker Suite.*

THE HARP. THE PIANO. THE ORGAN.
The Harp (I: arpa; G: Harfe; F: harpe). See Plate 4B. The "double-action" harp used in the orchestra today was introduced about 1810. Its range is shown in Example 74. At the base of the harp are seven

Ex. 74

pedals, one each for the seven strings of the octave. These pedals can be depressed through two notches (hence the name "double-

action"). When in normal position, the harp is tuned to C flat.
By depressing the pedal one notch, the tone "C" is produced; by
depressing two notches, C sharp. If all the pedals were depressed
by one notch, the C major scale would result. By the proper use
of the pedals, all the major and minor keys are possible. Rapid glissandos
and harmonics are particularly effective. *Examples:* Berlioz's *Symphonie
Fantastique* (the second movement, "A Ball," uses two harps); Debussy's
L'Après-midi d'un Faune.

The Piano (I: *pianoforte;* G: *Klavier;* F: *piano*). The piano (properly,
the pianoforte) dates from the early eighteenth century, and came into
common usage after 1750. It is arranged in octaves of white and black
keys, the latter playing the sharps and flats. The range of the modern piano,
slightly over seven octaves (Ex. 75), is greater than that of any other instru-

Ex. 75

Range of the Modern Piano.

ment (except the organ). Today there are two principal shapes: the *grand*
in which the body of the instrument, containing the soundboard and
strings, is parallel to the floor; and the *upright* in which the body is upright, as it were, to the floor and parallel to the player's body. The grand
is capable of greater resonance and power, and is invariably used in the
concert hall. A small species of upright is sometimes called *spinet,* although the word "spinet" refers more properly to a species of harpsichord.
The upright and spinet are cheaper than the grand. They also occupy less
space, but they have neither the power nor the sonority of the grand.

As the name implies, the pianoforte plays both loud and soft; it can also
play the gradations in between. This is accomplished entirely by the degree of pressure applied to the piano key by the player's finger. The touch
of the player is of great importance in producing gradations of power and
also varieties of tone, expression, and special styles of execution such as
legato and staccato (see Glossary). On the piano a *crescendo* or *diminuendo* is achieved by degree of pressure on the keys; this distinguishes the
piano from other keyboard instruments like the organ and the harpsichord
(the organ can, however, make a *crescendo* by other means; see p. 106).
The piano cannot produce a vibrato—the clavichord is the only keyboard

instrument that can—although some pianists try to create the impression of a vibrato by "vibrating" the finger on the keys.

When the piano key is depressed, it sets in motion a complicated mechanism that results in a felt-covered hammer striking the strings, usually three to each note. After the key has been released, the strings are dampened by a felt-covered piece of wood that is normally raised from the string only at the moment of the impact of the hammer.

The pedals of the piano. Each of the three pedals which the pianist manipulates with his feet has a special function.

1. The pedal to the player's right is called the *damper* pedal, or less accurately, the *loud* pedal. By depressing this pedal, the player raises all the dampers from the strings, allowing any strings struck by the felt hammers to vibrate freely instead of being dampened as normally occurs after the player lifts his finger from the key.

2. The pedal on the left side is called the *soft* pedal. In the modern piano each note is normally produced by the hammer striking on three strings tuned in unison. The soft pedal shifts the action so that the hammer strikes only two (sometimes only one) of these strings. The term *una corda* (one string) refers to the shifting to one string, as was commonly done by the soft pedal in older pianos (e.g., Beethoven). By using the soft pedal, the player produces a more muted and softer tone.

3. The *sostenuto* (middle) pedal raises only such of the dampers as belong to those notes that are being held down by the player when this pedal is depressed. This pedal permits the sustaining of single notes or chords while other notes are being dampened as usual.

The piano has one disadvantage: its limited sustaining ability. On the other hand, its advantages are manifold. It combines in one instrument the ability to play melodies and to accompany them as well. It can play melodically, harmonically, and contrapuntally. It has a tremendous range in pitch, dynamics, and expression; and these numerous advantages explain its great popularity and the immense literature of music written for it.

The Organ (I: organo; G: Orgel; F: orgue). The organ is the most elaborate of all instruments. It is really a combination of a number of instruments controlled by several keyboards (or manuals) played by the hands and feet. The basic principle is that wind is forced from a wind chest through various kinds of pipes. Each of these has a valve mechanism to control the wind supply so that the pipe will sound or be silent as the player regulates it at the keyboard. What the keyboard plays is in turn dependent on what ranks (or stops) the player is using. A stop is a set of pipes of a particular tone color, and the whole set is made ready to sound by drawing out a knob or by pressing a tab, whereupon the pipes in this stop will "speak" when the keys of the proper keyboard are depressed. The combination of stops used by the organist is called the *registration*.

The types of construction of the pipes determine their tone quality, which may range from the characteristic organ tone (*diapason*) to sounds that imitate all the other instruments, such as the flute, the strings, and other woodwind and brass instruments. In a most general way, the shorter the pipe the higher the sound, and vice versa. This helps explain the terminology of the stops. An 8′ (eight-foot) pipe means that the pipe sounds at written pitch. A 4′ pipe sounds an octave above written pitch, a 2′ pipe, two octaves above written pitch, and so on. Similarly, a 16′ pipe sounds an octave below written pitch, a 32′ pipe, two octaves below.

A large organ is a combination of several different organs, each separately housed and each containing a certain number of stops. Thus a big organ might consist of the *great* organ, the *swell* organ, the *choir* organ, and the *pedal* organ, each of which has a manual proper to it. These organs can usually be *coupled,* that is, two (or more) organs may be played from one manual.

When the organist sits on the bench before a large organ, he may be confronted with four manuals on which the hands play. Below will be a set of pedals played by the feet. Ranged around the manuals are various *stops.* If the organist wishes to play on the *great* organ, he must first draw stops that belong to it and then play on the manual of that organ. If he wishes to draw a stop that belongs to the *choir* organ but wishes to play it on the *great* manual, the organist must draw the stop in question on the *choir* organ, and also a stop that couples the *choir* to the *great*. On the organ the mechanical possibilities of this kind are very numerous. For example, by pressing a single button whole combinations of stops, or even the resources of the entire organ, may be engaged.

The organist increases the volume of sound by adding more stops (this may be done mechanically by depressing a pedal called the *crescendo* pedal). Or he may give the psychological impression of playing louder by playing more notes without adding any new stops. The organ can also produce a *crescendo* by means of the *swell* shutter, a mechanism found in the *swell* organ whose pipes are enclosed in what is, in effect, a large wooden box with shutters that open and close. These shutters are controlled by a pedal called the *swell* pedal. When the organist depresses this pedal, the shutters gradually open, increasing the sound in proportion to the degree the pedal is depressed, and vice versa.

INSTRUMENTATION AND ORCHESTRATION

The terms *instrumentation* and *orchestration* are frequently used to mean the same thing. They may also have more specific meanings: instrumentation means the kinds and numbers of instruments employed, while orchestration refers to the art of combining the instruments in different ways and for different effects. The information supplied above comes largely under the category of instrumentation. In Part II of this book, where specific pieces of music are discussed at greater length, details of orchestration will be mentioned from time to time.

One should keep constantly in mind that the history of instruments is a story of change from one period to another. Similarly, the disposition of the orchestra and its combinations has seen many changes in the past three hundred years. For instance, until the middle of the eighteenth century, the orchestra was dependent on a keyboard instrument (organ or harpsichord) to furnish the basic harmonies. It was also much smaller than our symphony orchestra today, and only the strings were relatively complete as a choir.

The modern orchestra dates from the late eighteenth century, and came into its own in the nineteenth century. In the late eighteenth century the woodwind choir became complete with the addition of the clarinets, although this choir did not realize its full chromatic possibilities until the addition of the so-called "Boehm" mechanism in the nineteenth century. The brass choir did not assume its present place in the orchestra until the nineteenth century with the invention of the valves.

Suggested Reading

Willi Apel, articles on individual instruments in the *Harvard Dictionary of Music*. Cambridge, Mass.: Harvard University Press, 1944.

James Blades, *Percussion Instruments and their History*. London: Faber & Faber, 1971.

Adam Carse, *The History of Orchestration*. New York: E. P. Dutton & Co., 1925.

Cecil Forsyth, *Orchestration* (Revised edition). New York: The Macmillan Co., 1935.

Walter Piston, *Orchestration*. New York: W. W. Norton & Company, 1955.

Gardner Read, *Thesaurus of Orchestral Devices*. New York: Pitman Publishing Corp., 1953.

Curt Sachs, *The History of Musical Instruments*. New York: W. W. Norton & Company, 1940.

Percy A. Scholes, *The Oxford Companion to Music* (Ninth edition). London: Oxford University Press, 1955 (First edition, 1938). See articles, "Orchestra and Orchestration," and those on individual instruments. The illustrations in this work are excellent and copious.

7. Aspects of Performance

WHAT THE CONDUCTOR DOES

CERTAIN NATURAL QUESTIONS occur to anyone who sees a conductor and orchestra for the first time. "What does the conductor do?" "Is he really necessary?" "Why is he paid so much for waving a stick?" In the first place, the conductor has many more responsibilities than conducting the concert. He is responsible for selecting the music and determining the soloists; he must be a diplomat when conflicts arise within the orchestra or between it and the many kinds of people who support it; and, ideally, he should be the focus of the community's musical life. As far as the orchestra is concerned, the conductor's greatest responsibilities are discharged behind the scenes at rehearsal.

It is not easy for the layman to appreciate what the conductor does for the orchestra behind the musical scene and on the concert platform. Actually, a modern orchestra without a conductor would be like an army composed of generals with no one in command. Without a single guiding spirit to act as interpreter of the composer's intentions and to carry them out by a specialized technical discipline, the performance of music involving over one hundred players would range from the passable at best to an impossible chaos. In the 1920's a conductorless orchestra (called *Persymphans*) did exist for a time in Russia, but such a situation is so exceptional that it confirms the remarks just made.

"But," someone will object, "each player has his part. Why can't he play it?" This is a logical question, but insoluble problems would result from a *laissez faire* of this sort. Even if the hundred or more players in an orchestra were in agreement about the numerous questions of tempo and interpretation in a piece of music, they would have trouble starting and stopping together, not to mention making retards and changes of tempo. There would be problems of ensemble, because all the players could not see each other; and individual players, surrounded by such a mass of sound, simply could not tell whether they were playing too loud or too soft in context. Without a conductor, there would be no one to "cue" (i.e., signal) difficult entries to the player or rescue him when lost. The lack of a conductor would be especially serious in the performance of new works and in the case of inexperienced orchestras.[1] Finally, the conductorless orchestra would have no one with final authority to assert the discipline essential to the production of a unified conception of the musical work itself.

What is the actual relationship between a piece of music, the orchestra, and the conductor? When a work is scheduled for performance, the conductor first masters the score so that he knows the music completely. Then he determines how he wants it to sound: the proper tempo, the expression, the balance of the choirs, the details of bowing and tonguing, and so on.

The conductor's most important job is done at rehearsal, where he meets his most important test as a conductor and musician. He is on trial before a jury of professional specialists who can detect at once whether he knows his score, knows what he wants from the orchestra, and knows technically how to get it. An orchestra is also impressed by efficient rehearsing and by considerate treatment on the part of the conductor.

In rehearsal the conductor works out the technical details of the music so that the performance will be letter-perfect; he must see that the correct notes are played in time and in tune, and according to the proper expression. He indicates entrances to individual players or sections by giving a cue. Similarly, he must bring out a part here and subdue another there, so that the important melodic material will be heard in the right dynamic balance to its accompaniment. Traditionally, the conductor leads with a *baton* in the right hand, and with this he sets the tempo and beats the time. The left hand is used to cue and to indicate shades of loud and soft and various types of expression. A most important means of communication is with the eyes and by facial expression. A conductor whose head is buried in the score has little communication with the orchestra. Beyond his qualifications as a musician and master of the art of the baton, the conductor is distinguished in proportion to his stature as a person and his enthusiasm for the music he conducts. These intangible qualities transmit themselves to the members of the orchestra and through them to the audience.

The public performance is the final test. Ideally, the performance should be the sum of all that has been learned at rehearsal, raised to the *nth* power. The extra something is supplied partly by the extra nervous energy that playing in public summons up and partly by the conductor, who must extract technical perfection from his players and be able to project

[1] Famous orchestras have been known to experience difficulties of ensemble even under a conductor. Pierre Monteux, one of the most celebrated conductors of the present day, stopped a renowned orchestra in rehearsal and remarked: "Gentlemen, I know that you know this piece backward, but please don't play it that way."

his feelings about the music to the audience in a convincing way. In short, the conductor should inspire both the players and the audience by the greatness of music which he feels deeply himself.

One of the truest and most eloquent passages ever written about performance was printed over two hundred years ago in *The Art of Playing on the Violin* (1751) by the Italian composer and violinist, Francesco Geminiani. This passage applies to all performers, and, since the conductor focuses the energies and talents of all the musicians of the orchestra, it is a good answer, in the broadest and most general terms, to the question of what a conductor does musically. Geminiani said:

> I would besides advise . . . the Performer, who is ambitious to inspire his Audience, to be first inspired himself; which he cannot fail to be if he chuses a work of genius, if he makes himself thoroughly acquainted with all its Beauties; and if while his Imagination is warm and glowing he pours the same exalted Spirit into his own Performance.

Suggestion: Attend a rehearsal of a professional (or amateur) orchestra. See for yourself what the conductor really does.

THE IMPORTANCE OF PERFORMANCE AND INTERPRETATION

> Poor composers, learn to conduct, and conduct yourselves well! (Take the pun, if you please.) For the most dangerous of your interpreters is the conductor. Don't forget this.
>
> BERLIOZ in his *Mémoires*

Berlioz had good reasons for his irony and even bitterness toward conductors and performers, and his comment underlines a fact little appreciated by the audience: the importance of the performer in the interpretation of a piece of music. The composer preserves his ideas through a system of written musical symbols, but the only significant moments in the life of music—when it is heard again as sound—depend on an act of re-creation in which the performer interprets the intentions of the composer to the listener. Unlike the painter, whose work is directly perceived, the composer must preserve his music in a written record called the *score,* which in turn is interpreted by editors and performers before it reaches the ear of the listener. This is why the score, its edited forms, and its interpretation by the performer, all play such an important part in the life of music. In fact, a central and difficult problem of music is its recovery from the inaudible realm of the printed page or the composer's manuscript.

There is something to be said for the variety with which different performers interpret the same piece of music. At the same time, many composers have suffered from performances that represent their intentions incompletely, poorly, or not at all. The more remote in time music becomes from its point of origin and living tradition, the more this is likely to be so.

The dependence of music on a system of notation and on performers explains why cultural historians have recorded so little until recently about the role of music in civilization, in spite of abundant literary and pictorial evidence of the importance of music in the culture and society of the past. For one thing, it is only in the last fifty years that real progress has been made in understanding the meaning of musical notation before 1500. In this respect music is still in a position that would be comparable to that of English literature if such works as *Beowulf* and *The Canterbury Tales* were still "untranslated" from the English of an earlier day into the English of our own. Even when deciphered, early music manuscripts tell us only the relative pitch of the notes and their duration. To this must somehow be added the proper tempo, the proper instruments, and the appropriate kind of emotional expression before the music can become the living thing visualized by the composer. The manner of singing or playing is often more important than the notes themselves. Even in printed music, which dates from about 1500, there are relatively few marks of expression in music before the time of Bach's death in 1750.

Under these conditions it is not surprising that so little music of early times has been "translated" and performed until recently; and cultural historians cannot be blamed for the fact that for every hundred persons who have heard the names of Giotto and Dante, and perhaps even read Dante's *Divine Comedy,* there is hardly one who has heard the name— not to mention the music—of Francesco Landini, the most famous Italian composer of the same time.

Suppose a situation analogous to that of music existed in painting. Under such circumstances, whenever one wished to look at a painting of Leonardo da Vinci, the picture would have to be repainted by a modern "brush-performer" from technical notes that Leonardo had left concerning the size, the composition of the objects to be represented, and possibly, with luck, the kind of brush strokes, the colors, and the methods of mixing the pigments. Upon completion, the painting would fade away, and each subsequent viewing would be dependent on a similar process, but one often endowed with quite different end results because of the differences in knowledge, skill, and interpretation of each "brush-performer."

In music, this perpetual problem of the re-creation of a composition is not limited to remote times. There is still considerable obscurity regarding a substantial number of details in the performance of eighteenth-century music, for example, the Bach sonatas for solo violin. Besides, even with a complete knowledge of the performance of any work, it might be impractical or even impossible to recover a performance as the composer heard it. The instruments used in the performance of a symphony in Haydn's time and the technique of playing them differed in substantial details from those of today; and it is debatable whether a conductor should try to recapture these conditions even if he could. A minimum requirement is that the performer try to recapture the spirit of the original to the best of his ability under present conditions. In the twentieth century, musical scholarship has devoted considerable attention to solving the problems of performance, especially with regard to older music.

With respect to any musical performance certain questions may legitimately be asked: Is the performer a responsible, as well as a gifted, artist? Is he playing the music from an edition that preserves the composer's intentions, or from one in which the changes of an editor stand between the composer and the audience? The last question does not imply that editing a work is necessarily undesirable—quite the contrary. Editing for performance is frequently desirable and sometimes indispensable, especially in the case of "old" music, where the performer often needs specialized and expert directions about the details of phrasing, dynamics, tempo, the accompaniment, and so on. The key to editing is, of course, the editor; and how he edits depends on his skill, attitude, and expert knowledge. This is why there are such discrepancies in different editions of the same piece of music.

It goes without saying that in a performance the manner of playing or singing with respect to tempo, tone color, and expression can make an enormous difference in the musical result as the listener hears it. Under the bow of the great violinist Ysaÿe, for example, passages that were empty and meaningless when played by others became extraordinary. Considerations of performance are always important, and they become increasingly so for music more than a hundred years old. If a piece of sixteenth-century music is performed at half the tempo intended by its composer, the result is comparable to looking through the wrong end of a telescope. Then, too, instruments have changed. If a Bach organ fugue is performed on a nineteenth-century organ, the color of the sound is almost certain to be different from that of Bach's organ, and in all likelihood the counterpoint of the fugue will be less distinctly heard. When played on the piano, few of the sonatas of Domenico Scarlatti give the crisp and brilliant effect of the harpsichord, for which Scarlatti wrote them. In the whole field of expression, such as dynamics, phrasing, vibrato, and *tempo rubato,* the attitude of two performers can be so dissimilar that two individual performances from the same printed page may differ immensely.

One must remember that the score is a collection of symbols that indicate, with varying degrees of precision, what a soloist or a group of performers is to sing or play. The human equation accounts for the surprisingly diverse interpretations of the same score. This is especially true of earlier music, for which composers indicated relatively few marks of expression, relying heavily on the musicianship and the taste of the performer. Today the score tells quite exactly what the performer should do. But no matter how precisely the score is marked, each performance differs from all others in some way, reflecting the individuality, attitudes, and abilities of the performing artist. In the last resort, the score is merely the starting place for a trained musician imbued with the traditions and conventions of his time and inspired by his own feeling for beauty.

Suggestions for Study

The whole point of the problem of performance is best understood by examining a few pieces in their several stages, from printed score or manuscript, through an edited version, to actual performance.

1. The first example is "Sumer is icumen in," a famous piece of English music written about 1250. It is the first known composition for six voices and the "first specimen of canon as a form in its own right" (Manfred Bukofzer). Plate 7 shows a photograph of the original manuscript (music printing did not begin until about 1500), and beside it the first few bars in modern notation. The upper four parts of this music are in canon—the cross about a third of the way through the first line shows where the first voice is when the second voice of the canon starts—and the lower two lines (also the lower two lines of the manuscript) are marked "Pes," reiterated bass motives that furnish harmonic interest and fullness. Even with the modern score the performer must somehow add the tempo, the marks of expression, and so on, according to his knowledge, experience, and musical feeling.

Now listen to a recording of this piece. Note that "Sumer is icumen in" is usually given in triple time. The duple time shown in our example is now thought to be the original version.

2. The second example is Bach's unaccompanied *Chaconne* for solo violin from his *Partita* in D minor. The first line of Plate 8 shows a portion of this piece as it occurs in Bach's own hand (known as the "autograph"). The second line shows part of the same music as it occurs in an edited version. Presumably the changes have been made by the editor because he believes either (1) that the music cannot be performed as it is written or (2) that it sounds better with his additions or changes, especially under present conditions. The fact that there are widely varying interpretations of this piece can be seen further by comparing certain different phonograph versions that are currently available. (See particularly the Schroeder version, the Heifetz version, and the Segovia version played on the guitar.)

3. Examine a score of the Tchaikovsky Sixth (*Pathétique*) Symphony. Note how elaborate the markings are by comparison with the first two examples. Nevertheless, this complex and relatively exact system of markings does not prevent the occurrence of a number of quite different interpretations of this work, as the various performances in the concert hall or on phonograph records prove.

8. *Music and Description*

THE UNEQUALED POWER of music to move the emotions has long been recognized. Sometimes music achieves its effects by pure design and color; sometimes it reinforces the general emotional mood or event suggested by a text, as in songs or the opera; and sometimes it depicts or suggests the idea or story conveyed by the titles of "program" music. Music is not a language in the ordinary sense of the word. It lacks the precision of meaning that words and pictures have; and, unlike language, music cannot *by itself* convey a precise meaning or tell a story. But it can reinforce stories, titles, and pictures with an intensity that is often far greater than the original. Indeed music sometimes succeeds in creating a mood or emotional "meaning"—even by itself—where both pictures and words have failed. Above all, it can awaken the most powerful and universal emotions, and in this sense music *is* a language—the language of the emotions and passions.

Music that depends entirely on musical tones is called *pure* or *absolute* music—unfortunate terms that somehow imply that all other music is slightly tainted, impure, or less absolute. For its coherence and emotional effect, absolute music depends on rhythm, melody, harmony, and tone color and on the formal designs that these elements engender. The listener responds to this music in the degree that his emotions are stirred by music as tone.

When music is accompanied by a text, the composer may seek to underline and emphasize his text by music that is deliberately aimed at illustration. In general, the more particular and concrete the musical illustration, the more obvious and naïve—and often delightful—is the effect, and vice versa. In certain madrigals, chansons, and even motets of the sixteenth century, individual words that suggested physical movement were set realistically. A madrigal by the English composer Thomas Weelkes (d. 1623) entitled "As Vesta was from Latmos hill descending" contains

6

Ex. 76

examples of this type of realism (Ex. 76). At one point the text says, "came running down a-main," and the music obligingly and realistically comes "running down." In the same piece, at the words "two by two" two voices are used; at "all alone," a single voice; and at "altogether," all the voices. In the early sixteenth century the Jannequin chanson *"Le Chant des Oiseaux"* ("The Song of the Birds") portrays bird songs with a semblance of physical reality. Many other examples could be found in the history of music, where composers seek to make the listener hear "the crowing of the cock," "the sound of the trumpet," and other sounds of the physical world, like the barking of the dog Cerberus who guards the entrance to the opening of the underworld in Gluck's *Orpheus.*

Not all descriptive music is so naïve as the physical realism just described. In a motet *"Absalon, fili mi"* the great composer Josquin des Prez (c. 1450–1521) is concerned with King David's lament over the death of his treacherous son Absalom (see II Samuel 18). David's grief for his son is emphasized by the dissonant harmony on the word *"plorans"* (weeping):

Ex. 77

Melodies sometimes suggest the text by a "gesture in sound," as someone has said. Schubert has used a "gesture" of this kind in his song *"Die Krähe"* ("The Raven") from the song cycle *Die Winterreise (The Winter Journey).* In this song Schubert describes the raven that flies vulturelike over the rejected lover, waiting for him to die in the snow. The circling motion of this sinister bird is depicted in a singularly menacing way by simple undulations of the melody which begins in the piano as follows:

Ex. 78

Sometimes the underlying mood of a whole section of text is created by reiterated figures or by rhythmic patterns. In many pieces by Bach and his contemporaries the most important word or idea of a whole section is set to an appropriate pattern of intervals or rhythms, and this pattern is used in pervasive fashion throughout the entire section dominated by the idea in question. A good example of this kind of thing may be found at the end of Purcell's opera *Dido and Aeneas* in Dido's final aria. Dido, about to die, bids Aeneas farewell:

> When I am laid in earth, may my wrongs create
> No trouble in thy breast.
> Remember me, but ah! forget my fate.

The poignancy of the occasion is suggested and intensified by a chromatic bass line reiterated over and over again (i.e., a *basso ostinato*). Its chromatic character also renders the harmony more expressive.

Ex. 79

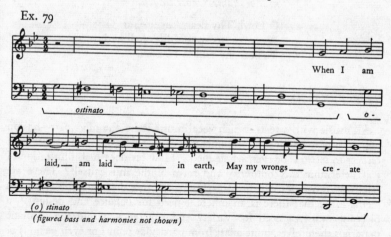

In some music the profundity of the thought expressed in the text is matched by the nobility of the music, with little help from word painting. The music transmutes into sound the feelings inherent in the text, wedding the text and the music into one. When Handel sets "I know that my Redeemer liveth" in the *Messiah,* there is no obvious word painting, but the listener is moved by Handel's music to the words of Job's affirmation of faith in his adversity.

It happens frequently that the greatest moments of text fused with music are those concerned with love or with religious convictions, set with apparent simplicity by the greatest composers. The more powerful and universal the emotion, the less particular and realistic the setting is likely to be, and the more mysterious the reason for the effect. In this area the indefinite character of music is its greatest strength, and its effects are impossible to explain. The music does not depict a story in any concrete detail; instead, the intangibles of universal emotion are conveyed to the listener by an organic fusion of text and music, often in the context of a continuity of increasing emotion. A case in point, as regards a love story, is the end of Wagner's opera *Tristan and Isolde* where the cry "Tristan" bursts from the heart of Isolde as she rushes to her dying lover. And more universally moving perhaps, in the case of sacred music, are passages from Bach's Mass in B minor (such as the *Qui tollis peccata mundi*—Who bearest the sins of the world), or the extraordinary ending of his *St. John Passion,* which ends simply and as if pronouncing a benediction with the most beautiful and moving of all Bach's chorales, beginning:

Ach Herr, lass dein lieb' Engelein
am letzten End' die Seele mein
in Abrahams Schoss tragen.

O Lord, Thy dear Angel send
Where'er my mortal life shall end
To bear my soul to Heaven.

THE TEXT AND VOCAL FORMS

All music with a text—which vocal music is for the most part—has an opportunity to be illustrative, sometimes of specific words, sometimes with respect to sections or even whole pieces. How far does such illustration of text determine the continuity and form of the music itself? There are relatively few cases in which the text is the *sole* determinant. The truth seems to be that there is an inherent need for balance and design in a piece of music, a need for variety and coherence within the thematic materials themselves, quite apart from particular points or even sections of text that have obviously inspired the music and with which it has a more or less apparent relationship. Sometimes a verse form plays an important part in determining the manner of the musical setting of the text. A verse refrain, for instance, is often retained as a corresponding musical refrain.

In the complete scheme of a piece of music with text, the words affect the musical setting most when the text itself has a strong continuity or dramatic cohesion that cannot be broken without destroying the effect and meaning of the whole. This kind of thing happens in certain types of operas, or even songs, the text of which involves a dramatic story. In Mozart's opera. *The Marriage of Figaro* (see p. 270) the dramatic text is set to music that is often continuous and is continuously changing in order to reflect the dramatic changes of situation (see especially, the Finale of Act II). In other types of opera, however, this continuous kind of setting is not necessarily appropriate. For instance, in Handel's opera *Giulio Cesare* (*Julius Caesar;* see p. 196) which may be taken as a typical example, the basic ideals are quite different from those of Mozart's *Figaro*. In *Giulio Cesare* the dramatic parts of the story are musically recited (*recitativo*) and at intervals the singers comment on the action by means of an aria (i.e., a song), which is in effect an emotional reflection on the dramatic action related in the preceding recitative. In such situations the aria seldom advances the action dramatically. It highlights what has taken place by commenting lyrically and perhaps psychologically on the action; and the music of the aria usually is composed not according to the needs of dramatic continuity but according to inherent laws of coherence and repetition. This explains why so many arias and songs, essentially lyrical in character, follow the pattern of repetition-after-contrast as in the ternary form (A B A) or in the *da capo* aria (see p. 193).

Many vocal pieces, while illustrating particular words or intensifying the mood of the text, depend for their fundamental musical design on forms that could stand alone, without text, and that by virtue of their use of the principles of variety and coherence are common to all music, vocal as well as instrumental. In Schubert's well-known song *"Gretchen am Spinnrade"* ("Gretchen at the Spinning Wheel"), the accompaniment provides the spinning figure which pervades the entire piece, and this figure could have no special meaning apart from the text (Ex. 80). However, the *form* of

Ex. 80

the whole song is not determined by this particular text but by the verse form, which embodies a refrain; and the form would be coherent as a formal design without *any* text. On the other hand, Schubert's *"Erlkönig"* (text by Goethe) would be completely unsatisfactory without the text, because the music closely follows the unfolding of a drama between the Erl King (i.e., Death), the father, and the dying child; and the continuous music is far more dependent on the text at every point than on inherent laws of coherence and variety simply in musical terms.

Schubert's *"Erlkönig"* is a masterly organic fusion of text and music. The text has become so saturated and intensified with music that, having heard the song, one cannot read Goethe's text without thinking of the music. Music with a text must either achieve this organic relationship or it must have coherence in musical terms. If neither is the case, the music becomes incidental to the forms of literature or the theater. The earliest operas are a case in point. The settings of the libretto *Euridice* (for the story, see Gluck's *Orpheus,* p. 267) by both Caccini and Peri (1600) are more literary than musical works. These musicians were inspired by the idea of the declamation of drama to music, and to a large extent the music remained incidental to the drama.

On the other hand, texts are sometimes set to music that is cast in molds derived from instrumental music. The sonata forms doubtless had an impact on the large forms of choral music of the late eighteenth and nineteenth centuries; and the operas of Wagner, especially his music dramas after *Lohengrin,* would not have been possible without the kind of development technique implicit in the development sections of the sonata forms of Beethoven.

Historically speaking, the desire to illustrate a text by appropriate music is a very old one. A number of examples of early music could be cited: for example, Dufay's fifteenth-century *Gloria in the Manner of the Trumpet* (recorded in *Two Thousand Years of Music*) has musical figures that are clearly intended to imitate the trumpet (if indeed they were not played on the trumpet); and in the vocal music of the Renaissance (fifteenth and sixteenth centuries) there are numerous examples of word painting of various sorts, as explained above, in chansons, madrigals, and even in motets and Masses.

In such pieces the problem of the importance of texts in their relation to music is also apparent. The chanson and similar forms of secular music, which delighted in illustrating particular words in the text, often used formal schemes like ternary, rondo, stanza forms, or those with refrains. These forms were partly dictated by the inherent artistic necessity for coherence, partly by a natural tendency to reflect the verse forms. In some cases the decisive factor was the requirements of the dance to which certain secular pieces were intimately related, as they were sung *and* danced. In these, the return of musical sections simply meant that the music reflected the return of certain sections of the dance.

Secular music like the chanson was rhythmic, sprightly, and repetitive in form. By comparison, the madrigal (the most sophisticated of the secular forms of the Renaissance), the motet, and Mass settings present quite a different picture with respect to the relation of words and music. The texts of madrigals, motets, and Masses were invariably composed without repeating sections of music. The individual sections of text were set musically one after the other, each to its particular music, so that these pieces were composed straight through ("through-composed"), without repetitions of music or text.

The fact that these pieces were "through-composed" would seem to show that in them the text completely dominated the music, especially when individual words were portrayed musically in a realistic way. But this was not really the case. The rich texture of the polyphony provided great variety in itself, and often actually *obscured* the words. Indeed, the Council of Trent, the great Church Council of the mid-sixteenth century (ended 1563), seriously considered abolishing polyphonic Masses and motets in the church service precisely for the reason that the texts could not be heard because of the polyphony. Similar complaints came from composers of songs and opera at the beginning of the seventeenth century. To them the texts had to be rescued from Renaissance polyphony, which obscured the words and their meaning. Much later, Wagner expressed a determination to rescue the drama from the dominance of music; and it is ironical that the power of his orchestra and the richness of his harmony often obscured the texts just as effectively as Renaissance polyphony ever had.

After the sixteenth century sacred music exhibited to a marked degree the same problems with respect to words and music as the opera of the same time, many of whose forms it adopted. The cantatas of Bach and the oratorios of Handel made extensive use of the recitatives and arias of the early eighteenth-century opera. In addition, these sacred works used types of music more characteristic of their own genre: the imposing chorus and, in the case of Bach, the Lutheran chorale in its various forms.

From all this emerges the fact that music and text must arrive at some organic relationship based on a reconciliation of their different demands. Individual words may be vividly illustrated, the mood of whole sections may be consciously underlined by persistent and suggestive figures, or music may follow the form suggested by the text. In the total design, however, music has more often a binding and co-ordinating role to play through the individual forms common to *all* music or through the unifying textures of polyphony.[1]

DECLAMATION

Whether words are set realistically to music or not, the composer is always faced with the problem of declamation if he has a text. The latter

[1] These remarks apply also to the individual pieces of the large-scale "composite" vocal forms. For the most part the latter use both vocal *and* instrumental forces, and special problems arise which are better treated in Part II of this book. See the Index for *oratorio, cantata, Mass, Passion, opera,* and *song cycle.*

term simply refers to the manner of "declaiming" the words: how the word accents correspond to the accents of the music, and how the length of the spoken syllable corresponds to the duration of the music set to it. Except for deliberate effect, setting an *accented* syllable to an *unaccented* note of music, or vice versa, is *faulty* declamation and a kind of musical *faux pas* rarely found among composers worthy of the name. The duration of the music on any particular syllable is quite another matter. While the *accent* of the music invariably coincides with the speech accent, the *duration* of music for any syllable is often quite arbitrary. In short, individual notes may be set relatively long or short as regards the length of the spoken syllable. The duration of a single syllable is related to the number of notes set to it. If a syllable is set to a single note of music, the setting is called *syllabic*, but if there is more than one note to a syllable, the music is said to be *melismatic*. In certain cases, several syllables are set to the same (repeated) note.

The following example from Purcell's opera *Dido and Aeneas* shows several styles of declamation (Ex. 81). Some of it is syllabic, some melis-

Ex. 81

matic. It is noticeable, too, that while the word accents are invariably set to corresponding musical accents, the setting of the words is highly stylized as regards the natural *quantities* of speech. Intoning the words to the rhythms given by Purcell makes an interesting rhythmic pattern, but it is not the way the words would ordinarily be spoken, especially at the words "prest with torment."

Sometimes the composer wishes the words to be more important than the music, and consequently he uses music simply as a means of intoning the text. In operatic recitative the words are given musical pitch and accent, but the "melody" of the recitative, while it helps to support the text musically, is subordinate to the text in interest and importance. The recitative is not necessarily intended to be interesting as music, but to serve as a vehicle for the text and its meaning.

PROGRAM MUSIC—MUSIC THAT TELLS A STORY

The term *program music* refers, as a rule, to *instrumental* music that depicts the mood or tells the story that is suggested by the title or program attached to a piece of music. Well-known examples are *Till Eulenspiegel* of Richard Strauss, *Les Préludes* of Liszt, and on a small scale, the piano piece "Soaring" from the *Fantasy Pieces* of Robert Schumann.[2] Vocal music with a title is often frankly descriptive (Jannequin's chanson *"Le Chant des Oiseaux,"* mentioned above), but program music is usually associated with instrumental music that does not have a text to tell the story or to relate the program.

How essential is the program to the music? Must the listener know the program before he can enjoy the music? Obviously if the composer arouses the listener's curiosity or disturbs his attention by a title suggesting a program, he must either (1) make the title general enough in mood so that the listener need not expect a story, as in "Soaring" of Schumann or in *La Mer* (*The Sea*) of Debussy; (2) furnish a relatively detailed account of his program, as in Berlioz's *Symphonie Fantastique;* or (3) make his piece intelligible in musical terms over and above the program. These categories are not mutually exclusive. The fact is that Schumann's "Soaring," Debussy's *La Mer,* and Berlioz's *Symphonie Fantastique* are enjoyable as music without programs, although, particularly in the case of the Berlioz symphony, knowing the program increases our enjoyment of the piece as a whole by explaining certain details or directing our imagination to the contemplation of large moods or pictures. If a piece of instrumental music is completely dominated by its program, it becomes incidental music, in the way that the average movie score is incidental to the picture. Most pieces of program music, however, have a solid base of musical coherence.

Just as some composers of vocal music were eager, even in early times, to illustrate the text by corresponding music, other composers of instrumental music showed interest in depicting a mood or subject. Some pieces of this character existed by the sixteenth century (the lute piece, *Der Judentanz* of Neusiedler) and even earlier, but it was really in the seventeenth century, when independent instrumental music began to flourish, that interest in program music developed. The harpsichordists and early violinists delighted in imitations of birds—the cuckoo being a favorite—hunting scenes, the ringing of changes of bells, and even catfights. These pieces, a number of them short, had spiritual descendants in the eighteenth century (Rameau's *Le Rappel des Oiseaux—The Call of the Birds*). There were many short pieces of like character in the nineteenth and twentieth centuries, those of Schumann and Mendelssohn, for example, and the charmingly vague, impressionistic pieces of Debussy (*Ce qu'a vu le vent de l'Ouest—What the West Wind Saw—*1910).

In many pieces the problem of sustaining a mood or depicting a situation is solved neatly by writing a short piece. Besides, pieces that are supported by solid musical construction can sustain a mood for some time

[2] The program music of the nineteenth century is discussed more fully in Part II.

provided that the mood is somewhat general and indefinite in character. This accounts for the fact that certain pieces, both short and long, composed originally as absolute music, suggest titles at a later time either to the composer or to someone else. Schumann is said to have added titles to some of his pieces after the works were completed (his *Fantasy Pieces*); and there are a number of pieces to which titles have been added, not by the composer, but by general acclaim. The titles of Handel's "Harmonious Blacksmith" Variations, Haydn's "Lark" String Quartet, and Beethoven's "Moonlight" Sonata were not bestowed by their composers.

Not all early pieces of program music were short. The idea suggested by the program or title could be expanded by purely musical means. In some cases cuckoo calls became fugue subjects, and the theme of *The King's Hunt* of John Bull (early seventeenth century) was extended by treating it as a series of variations, each of which could be imagined as a stage in the "King's Hunt." Similarly, in *The Bells* of William Byrd (d. 1623) the variation form is particularly adapted to a dissertation on large, medium, and small bells, ringing their manifold and varied changes.

Thus program music is not limited to short pieces; but in the longer pieces the basic structure is that of musical forms independent of the program. The program idea had a wide influence. Vivaldi's *Seasons* (the first four concertos of his Op. VIII) are program concertos of sorts. Programs are attached, too, to pieces that are basically sonatas, symphonies, or overtures. A classic example is Beethoven's Sixth ("Pastoral") Symphony. Its construction is perfectly clear as "pure" music, but the titles of individual parts—the "Tempest," "The Scene by the Brook"—aid us in understanding and enjoying all its details, including the musical depiction of the cuckoo and the nightingale. Earlier, Beethoven's Third (*Eroica*) Symphony was devoted to depicting a hero, including, in the slow movement, his burial (*"Funeral March"*). This symphony uses the forms of the sonata, but the music is so "heroic" and grand as to leave no doubt about the relation between the mood of the title *Eroica* and the music. Beethoven's own remark well summarizes his dominant attitude toward program music, expressed in connection with the "Pastoral" Symphony: "more the expression of feeling than of painting." [3]

Program music invaded orchestral music more extensively in the program symphonies of Berlioz and Mahler and in the symphonic poems of Liszt and Richard Strauss. The important thing about the symphonies of Berlioz and Mahler was not that they deviated from traditional forms but that they managed to solve the problems of a form in which the program element had become more significant.[4] However, the most important innovation in the nineteenth century with respect to program

[3] For Mendelssohn's attitude toward program music, see *concert overture.*
[4] For more details, see *Berlioz, Mahler, program music.*

music was doubtless the symphonic poem invented by Liszt. He succeeded in creating this new type of large-scale symphonic music by using a few themes suggested by various aspects of the program and extended by thematic variants called *thematic transformations*. Within the framework of this continuous one-movement scheme, Liszt constructed forms that were inspired by a program but that were also coherent and logical as music.

Suggestions for Study

1. Listen to a song (or a selection from opera) that you do not know, purely for its musical design, harmonies, rhythms, and melodies. Then listen again, following the text closely. How does a knowledge of the text increase your enjoyment and understanding of the music?

2. Repeat the process just suggested, using a piece of program music that you have not heard before. Compare your impressions of the piece heard primarily as music and those after knowing the title and the program on which the piece is based.

3. Look first at the text of a song or aria. Then listen to the music, observing how the composer has set the accented and unaccented words of the text to notes that are correspondingly accented or unaccented, or relatively long or short.

4. Listen for the various manners of illustrating individual words or sections of text in the pieces mentioned in the course of this chapter.

Suggested Reading

Willi Apel, "Program Music," "Word Painting," and "Text and Music" in the *Harvard Dictionary of Music*. Cambridge, Mass.: Harvard University Press, 1944 and later editions.

Aaron Copland, *Music and Imagination*. Cambridge, Mass.: Harvard University Press, 1952.

Paul Hindemith, *A Composer's World, Horizons, and Limitations* (The Charles Eliot Norton Lectures, 1949–50). Cambridge, Mass.: Harvard University Press, 1952.

D. F. Tovey, *Essays in Musical Analysis,* Vol. IV (Illustrative Music). London: Oxford University Press, 1937.

9. Beauty and Related Questions

W HEN WE SAY that a thing is beautiful, what do we mean? We can only mean that it is beautiful according to some *personal* notion of beauty. St. Augustine said in effect: I like what I like, and what I like is to *me* beauty. Similarly, as the author of this book, I have said that such and such a piece is beautiful, and I can only mean that I think (or, more accurately, feel) that it is. And what is the nature of beauty? Plato identified the good with the beautiful, but that does not necessarily seem to be so. Most musicians would agree that the first movement of Beethoven's Ninth Symphony is a "good" piece but not necessarily that it is beautiful. At the present day much art is felt to be good while being far from beautiful. From all this we may conclude that the criterion of beauty is an entirely personal matter.

On the question of quality in art—what is good or bad—we are on somewhat firmer ground, but not much. It is not difficult to show that objective standards of goodness and badness in art *for all times and places* are almost impossible to achieve. The prevailing taste of any age affects its judgment. The Romantic period was unsympathetic to the rationalism of the preceding age, and the early twentieth century reacted strongly against the music of Wagner and Tchaikovsky. Some music appeals greatly to one nationality but leaves another cold (for example, the music of Elgar). Oriental music and its tone production are quite foreign to the ideals of the West.

At the same time there are certain standards of judgment within limited spheres. The so-called "classics" constitute a body of music that represents a collective judgment as to what is "good," and the current repertory of the opera house and concert hall is a monument to the collective judgment of the present day. But this judgment has pronounced limitations: it does not tell us if or why Beethoven is a better composer than Tchaikovsky; it does not help us determine the quality of old, new, or unfamiliar music; it does not remove prejudice against the merely strange and unfamiliar; and it tends to deny the validity of individual judgment.

What is good taste or judgment, and can it be cultivated? In the first place, is there a difference between taste and judgment? If so, the difference is a small one. On the whole, judgment implies a keenness of discrimination or discernment in which a certain intellectual character enters; taste is a somewhat larger term including sensitivity of feeling as well. For our purposes, however, these two words will be used interchangeably. Taste implies powers of selection, and this in turn implies selection according to some standard. When we say that someone has good taste, we must mean that it is "good" according to some accepted standard of prevailing taste. According to this, some persons have "good" taste instinctively, and others must acquire it if they would have it at all. Good taste thus implies a point of reference, and the latter can degenerate to a personal issue embodied in the saying: "Good taste is what I like, and bad taste is what you like." For the beginner in music there can be only one standard: that represented by the classics; and through them he must try to perceive values that have stood the test of time according to the collective judgment of the age of which he is a part.

This is only a point of departure, and the individual listener can and should ask questions of his own. It seems to me that these questions have to take some form such as: "Is the basic material of a piece of music interesting?"—that is to say, are the melodies, harmonies, rhythms, and tone colors arresting and striking in themselves. "Are these basic materials cast in an appropriate form?" (using "form" in a broad sense of movement and coherence). And above all: "Is the music emotionally or intellectually significant to me?" The answers to these questions depend on native instinct, background, training, and experience. Taste or judgment is the collective result of these factors and changes with training and experience.

Training and experience are the key to the cultivation of taste, which is a continuous process. Musical training is a responsibility of this book, and experience is a natural function of time. At the outset, the listener who knows what he likes should have respect for his own judgments while trying to learn from collective judgments or those of individuals of greater training and experience. There is nothing that dismays a listener more than to admire or be moved by a work that is not approved by critics, theorists, or "musical authorities." Ernest Newman has commented on this situation in a way that may be comforting to the music-lover:

Stendhal has an amusing story of a spectator at a new Italian opera saying to the man next to him, "Will you be so kind as to tell me, sir, whether I am enjoying myself?" In these more advanced days, when he has been duly harried and fuddled by the theorists and the pedagogues, his question would probably take the form of "Will you kindly tell me, sir, whether I am enjoying myself so hugely for the right reasons?" Is it not possible for a music-lover to get to the heart of the right thing sometimes for the wrong reasons—or what the theorist would regard as such—and conversely for the theorist to admire the wrong thing for the right reasons—or what he has persuaded himself to be such?[1]

The quality of a performance is often confused with the quality of the piece played; and, in a brilliant performance, an inferior work may be judged better than a superior work that has been badly played. Most criticism of music discusses the performance of music far more than the musical qualities of the composition itself. And this is natural enough, because the standards of criticism of performance are comparatively objective. It is relatively easy for a musical person, even without special training, to detect whether the performer is playing in time and in tune, and whether the ensemble is good or bad. Beauty of tone of a voice or instrument is immediately apparent, and so are indefinable qualities of personality like stage presence, poise, and temperament. Criticizing the *interpretation* of a piece of music is more difficult, because it implies enough knowledge and training to establish a standard by which any individual performance may be judged. But, on the whole, criticizing a performance is far easier than judging musical quality, because the latter depends on far more intangible and indefinable factors.

Finally, what does music mean? In the sense of language, it doesn't "mean" anything; and any analogies between rhythm, harmony, and melody on the one hand and the grammar and the precision of language on the other are faulty and without significance. Like language, however, music is a means of communication. But what is the nature of the thing communicated? Is it the composer's feelings? Is it a tonal organization in time—which Stravinsky presupposes "before all else"—or a moral stimulus to the receiving mind—as Hindemith maintains? What is communicated depends not only on the individual work of art, but also on the listener's capacities, background, and training to receive what a composer has to communicate. Music transcends language in that it can communicate emotion more directly, and sometimes it can transmit emotions and intensities of emotion of which language is incapable.

Wagner spoke of the orchestra's "power of uttering the unspeakable," and this power of music permits it to transcend the function of language. (For music with words, see Chapter 8.) For this reason, those who feel obliged to supply a story to music when none exists succeed only in undermining the unique power of music to give expression to the unutterable. What the emotional character of this utterance is must remain the private

---

[1] In an article "Doctors and Patients" in *The Sunday Times* (London), November 21, 1954. Quoted by permission.

business of each listener; and it is a presumption for anyone to assume that the music-lover is devoid of imagination and emotional receptiveness in the presence of great art.

With respect to the "unutterable," there is not so great a cleavage between absolute and descriptive music as one might imagine. As we have tried to show (in Chapter 8; see also Chapter 19), the "program" often inspires the themes and certain external details of a piece of music, but musical considerations are usually primary, and the unique powers of music are not necessarily lost because a piece of music is garbed in a descriptive title. Only when music becomes incidental to the forms of literature or the theater does this cease to be so.

In short, music "means" in the sense that it has a unique and indefinable power to communicate or stimulate broad emotional states that cannot be expressed otherwise. This view of the meaning of music lies somewhere between the extreme views of those who hold that all music tells a story or has an inner program and those who are convinced that music means nothing more than musical design (cf. Hanslick: *"Musik ist tönend bewegte Form"*—Music is form animated by sound). Upholders of these two views have carried on an age-old controversy which has inspired a large and sometimes acrimonious literature. Those who have protested against descriptive music have been responsible for many eloquent passages, sometimes not without humor. An eighteenth-century critic wrote in protest against the literal representation of the sounds of nature: "Our intermezzi . . . are full of fantastic imitations and silly tricks. There one can hear clocks striking, ducks jabbering, frogs quacking [sic!], and pretty soon one will be able to hear fleas sneezing and grass growing."[2]

To the questions "What is beauty? What is good and bad in art?" there are no final answers. While the collective judgment of the present day concerning works of art is embodied in the classics, music has unique properties, and the meaning, beauty, and quality of any particular work are unique for each individual. As the listener examines the repertory of music—the subject of the remainder of this book—he will have ample opportunity to test for himself the meaning, beauty, and quality of music.

Suggestions for Study

1. Criticize the quality of two pieces, one already familiar, one heard for the first time.

2. Criticize a piece of music now. Write another criticism of the same piece at the end of your course in music and compare the two criticisms.

3. Read a professional critic's review of a concert that you have attended yourself. Observe the proportion of criticism devoted to details of perform-

[2] J. A. Hüller (1754). Quoted in Susanne K. Langer, *Philosophy in a New Key* (Cambridge, Mass.: Harvard University Press, 1951), p. 220.

ance ("Miss Zilch played with fire but with faulty rhythm") and to the
value of the work itself.

4. Write a critical report on a performance *as a performance*.

Suggested Reading

Aaron Copland, *Music and Imagination.* Cambridge, Mass.: Harvard
University Press, 1952.

Benedetto Croce, "Aesthetics" in *The Encyclopaedia Britannica* (Fourteenth edition).

Alfred Einstein, *Greatness in Music,* trans. by César Saerchinger. New
York: Oxford University Press, 1941.

Eduard Hanslick, *The Beautiful in Music,* trans. by Gustav Cohen. New
York: H. W. Gray, 1891. (Original German edition, 1874.) Also in
paperback, revised and edited by Morris Weitz, New York: Bobbs-
Merrill, Library of the Liberal Arts, 1957.

Paul Hindemith, *A Composer's World, Horizons, and Limitations.* Cambridge, Mass.: Harvard University Press, 1952.

Susanne K. Langer, *Philosophy in a New Key.* Cambridge, Mass.: Harvard University Press, 1951. (Original edition, 1942.)

James L. Mursell, *The Psychology of Music.* New York: W. W. Norton &
Company, 1937.

Roger Sessions, *The Musical Experience of Composer, Performer, Listener.* Princeton, N.J.: Princeton University Press, 1950.

Igor Stravinsky, *Poetics of Music,* trans. by Arthur Knodel and Ingolf
Dahl. Cambridge, Mass.: Harvard University Press, 1947.

Oscar Thompson, *Practical Music Criticism.* New York: M. Witmark &
Sons, 1934.

Part Two:

THE DEVELOPMENT AND REPERTORY OF MUSIC

10. *The Development of Music to 1600*

THE ORIGINS OF MUSIC

Exactly how music began is a fascinating question that cannot be answered with certainty. It probably began with singing, but today we can come no closer to the origins of music than by studying the music of primitive tribes and the babble songs of small children. Music arose because of some need for expression—it is possible, but less likely, that it began in imitation of birds or sounds of nature or instruments—and in primitive society music served the need of the community as something inseparable from worship, ritual, dancing, working, love-making, and drinking. It is thought today that some of the music of primitive tribes in Africa or among the American Indians approximates a style not far removed from the first music that ever existed. Characteristics of this music are persistent and irregular rhythms, intervals whose limits are not precisely defined (as they are on the piano, for example), restricted range of melody, and lack of harmony. The drum is an important accompanying factor, and sometimes other instruments are used, but instruments probably developed later than singing itself. In all this, the manner of performance is more important than the notes sung. A nasal delivery, yelling, or even squawking may be primary ingredients of the music and inseparable from its proper expression.

In the high civilizations of ancient times, as, for example, those of Egypt, Sumeria, Greece, and Rome, music was intimately related to religious, court, or community life. It was connected with dancing and poetry, and with national and religious festivals, as in Greece. The development of instruments at an early stage in these cultures may be clearly demonstrated by their appearance in works of art and by various references to them in literature and in sacred writings, for example in the Bible. In centers of wealth and talent, court "orchestras" existed.

Under the conditions obtaining in sophisticated societies such as Egypt and Greece, music was bound to attain system, order, and logic. Fixed tunings and scales were invented, particularly with the advent of instruments such as the lyre (harplike instrument) and wind instruments such as the aulos (resembling the oboe) and the flute. The Greeks discovered the principles of acoustics and the properties of strings, and their speculations about the nature of music, its aesthetic value, and its role in education dominated much of the later thinking about music. As far as we know, the music of these high civilizations had no harmony in the modern sense; but subtleties of rhythm, melody, and scale patterns (i.e., modes) were extensively explored. The various scales—or possibly different regions of the vocal range—were considered to have a special ethical significance in that one scale was especially appropriate to war, another to love, and so on. A similar attitude toward music persists in the Orient today.

Suggested Listening

American Indian music. (Album 6 of the Library of Congress collection contains eighteen Indian pieces.)

Greek music: "Hymn to the Sun." *Seikilos*—Epitaph. (Recorded in *Two Thousand Years of Music.*)

Suggested Reading

Curt Sachs, *The Rise of Music in the Ancient World, East and West.* New York: W. W. Norton & Company, 1943.

FOLK MUSIC

Folk music occurs in every time and place. It comprises songs and dances that have attained common currency among the mass of people in communities, regions, or nations. Who composed the music may or may not be known; and even when the composer is known, a tune often attains the status of being of a community origin by virtue of changes and adaptations over the years in folk usage.

Most of the folk songs we hear today are of relatively recent origin. Many German folk songs, for example, date from the nineteenth century. Folk songs were handed down for years by oral tradition, and in this process many early folk songs were lost. The earliest known folk songs are not older than the twelfth century, and there are very few of these. Some old folk songs are still sung among the "folk,"—for instance, *"Christ ist erstanden"* (Christ is arisen), a tune that probably originated in the practice whereby the laity was permitted to sing the *Kyrie* of the church service. Most early folk songs that we know now survived by being incorporated into sacred and secular music. The tune *"L'Homme armé"* (The armed man) was used in the tenors (see p. 140) of Masses in the fifteenth and sixteenth centuries, and a number of folk songs were arranged in polyphonic settings (e.g., the *Lochheimer Liederbuch* about 1450). Luther found the folk song a treasure chest of tunes for adaptation to the music of the new Lutheran service in the sixteenth century, and a number of instrumental composers preserved folk songs by using them in their pieces, especially in theme and variations (see the *Fitzwilliam Virginal Book* c. 1600). From such sources, Rochus von Liliencron was able to compile nearly a hundred and fifty folk melodies and their texts giving a picture of German life about 1530.[1]

Folk songs and dances owe their long life to the simplicity and beauty of their melodies and to the fact that they express the emotions and sentiments deeply and intuitively felt by regional and national groups of peoples. The emotional hold of a nation's songs over its people is attested by the remark: "I care not who writes the laws of a people if I may write its songs." Folk songs reflect such varied but universal themes as love, death, work, play, drinking, and dancing.

The character of folk music varies as widely as the nationalities or communities from which it comes. The truth of this is evident if we compare German folk songs of fairly regular rhythm and harmonic background (e.g., *"Tannenbaum," "Die Lorelei"*) with a Hungarian folk song of irregular rhythm and unusual intervals (including chromatic tones), such as those found in collections of tunes gathered by Béla Bartók (see also his collection of piano pieces, *Microkosmos*). Similarly, compare the modal and rhythmic character of the English folk song "The Coast of High Barbary" (Ex. 22) with the more melodious Irish folk song, cast in the major, "Believe me if all those endearing young charms" (Ex. 19). Spanish folk songs and dances are entirely different from those of Russia, and the immense number of the latter exhibits in itself a great variety. In the United States the many regional types of folk songs reflect the variety of occupations and cultures of the country: songs of the Negroes, songs of lumberjacks, cowboys, mountaineers, rivermen, and so on.[2] The musical variety of folk music is emphasized still more by recent investigations through the phonograph, which show that many folk songs use intervals of less than a half tone or intervals that do not correspond exactly to our half and whole tones (as defined by the piano). The addition of many ornamental tones is also a feature of folk songs. In spite of such wide variety, however, most folk songs have in common singable qualities and the use of refrains or stanza forms.

Folk music has always been a treasury of melody for composers. It was used by medieval and Renaissance composers for secular and sacred music. In more recent times, the use of folk music was intimately connected with musical nationalism in the nineteenth and twentieth centuries (see Chapter 23), and many other composers, such as Brahms, have used folk music

[1] In his book *Deutsches Leben in Volkslied um 1530.* (Berlin and Stuttgart: W. Spemann, 1885.)

[2] For an easily accessible collection of American songs, see *The Burl Ives Song Book* (New York: Ballantine Books, 1953) or *The American Songbag,* edited by Carl Sandburg (New York: Harcourt, Brace & Co., 1927).

in their compositions. Rather than quote folk music, some composers, for example Bartók, have preferred to create a style based on rhythmic and melodic features derived from folk music.

At the same time, folk music has sometimes been influenced by composed music. There is a theory that most folk music is derived by a process of "seepage" from composed music. Good examples of seepage can be seen in many modern German and Austrian folk songs which have undoubtedly been influenced by the melodic, harmonic, and rhythmic traits of German and Austrian music in general. But in many other folk musics, as, for example, the folk music of Bulgaria, Hungary, and Russia, this is not true. In American folk music some relationships have been established between Negro spirituals and regular composed hymns, but this influence is paralleled by that of African tribal music. And the seepage theory does not seem to be true in the case of Negro secular music, such as the original "blues" or of music of culturally isolated areas.

Discussions of folk music often stop with folk songs. However there is also a large repertory of folk dances, such as ritual dances (Morris and Sword dances in England), processional dances, and country dances (Austrian *Ländler*). Folk instruments are also a fascinating adjunct to folk music; and sometimes the instruments determine certain features of the music itself. The characteristic scale of the Alpine horn includes the augmented fourth (sharped fourth degree), which in turn affects the character of a melody. There are numerous wind, percussion, and stringed instruments associated with dancing (for example, the flute, bagpipe, fiddle). While these instruments may be familiar types, the actual physical instruments used may be relatively crude homemade specimens, and the manner of playing them is often distinctive. "Fiddling," for instance, is not the same as "violinning"; the fiddle is usually held against the chest with corresponding changes in the bowing.

Folk music constitutes an immense treasury of music. That so much attention is paid to collecting it is a tribute to its innate fascination and emotional attraction not only for the race from which it sprang but for people everywhere.

Suggested Listening

There are many recordings of folk music by folk singers (e.g., in the United States: Burl Ives, Carl Sandburg, John Jacob Niles, "Leadbelly," Pete Seeger), as well as collections of authentic folk music that have been recorded in the field (e.g., those issued by the Library of Congress, Washington, D.C.).

Suggested Reading

Grove's Dictionary of Music and Musicians (Fifth edition, 1954) has an exhaustive article (240 pages) on folk music by nationalities. Extensive lists of books are included.

Collections of folk songs are exceedingly numerous. Besides those mentioned above (see note, p. 135), see John A. and Alan Lomax, *Our Singing Country* (New York: The Macmillan Co., 1941; second edition, 1948). In England, the collections of Cecil Sharp are excellent. For folk songs in general, see Florence H. Botsford, *Folk Songs of Many Peoples* (3 vols.; New York: The Woman's Press, 1921–2).

GREGORIAN CHANT

The early Christian Church used music from various sources, and its liturgy (service) for Mass and Office (see below) was sung (i.e., chanted) to different types of music, some resembling hymns, and some, a more elaborate type of song. Parts of the service were intoned musically by the priest to various kinds of reciting formulas. An important body of music for the Christian service was assembled by St. Ambrose of Milan in the fourth century—hence the name "Ambrosian" chant. A more important and extensive collection was made under the supervision of Pope Gregory "the Great" about 600. Pope Gregory did not compose this music; he—or those under him—acted as collector and editor. From this time on, "Gregorian" chant and its later additions dominated all other types of chant, and it is the official chant used today in the Roman Catholic Church.[3]

Gregorian chant (or plainsong, as it came to be called later) has two aspects: a musical and a liturgical one. The latter concerns the relation of Gregorian chant to the service. There are chants for the Office, the eight hours of the day at which service is held (Matins, Vespers, Compline, etc.); and chants for the Mass (the commemoration of Christ's sacrifice on the Cross). Only the latter service will be considered here. When the Mass is sung, part of it is intoned by the priest (for example, prayers, Epistle, Gospel) and part is sung by the choir. The latter part includes parts of the Proper and of the Ordinary. The Ordinary, the most important for our purposes, includes those parts of the Mass whose texts are unchanging: *Kyrie, Gloria, Credo, Sanctus,* and *Agnus Dei.*[4] The Proper means "proper to the time or season," and its texts change from Mass to Mass, containing references to the particular time. Thus an *Introit* (the entrance music) for Christmas uses a text different from the one for Easter. The Proper texts that are sung by the choir include the *Introit,* the *Gradual,* the *Alleluia,* the *Offertory,* and the *Communion.* All the Gregorian texts are Latin, and most of them are prose.

Musically, the Gregorian chant is purely melodic, traditionally unac-

---

[3] The service does not have to use music. In low Mass, it can be spoken instead of sung.

[4] The Appendix contains a complete outline of the parts of the Mass and the complete text of the Ordinary.

companied, free and irregular rhythmically.[5] At first, Gregorian music sounds strange to our ears because it is modal: that is, it is in the "old" modes. There are eight of these modes, as is shown in Example 82. The

Ex. 82

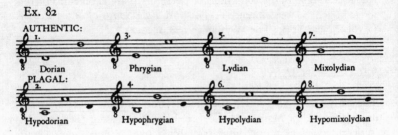

modes determine the melodic limits of the chant and the relationship of the tones within it. There are four "authentic" modes (Dorian, Phrygian, Lydian, and Mixolydian), and each has a related ("plagal") version (Hypodorian, Hypophrygian, Hypolydian, Hypomixolydian) that shares the same tonic or *final* on which the mode ends. The music is distinguished by different styles. The hymn type uses mostly a note of music to a syllable of text, called a *syllabic* setting. When more than one note is set to a syllable, the setting is called *melismatic;* this is used for chants more elaborate musically. In the intoning style of the priest, a number of syllables may be set to notes of the same pitch, a kind of "reciting" style. The chants differ widely in their forms: some are composed without repetitions of music; others repeat short phrases, motives, or even sections; and still others, such as the hymn types, use the same music for successive verses (strophic form).

No description, however, can give an idea of the calm, impressive beauty of plainsong, its aura of prayer and devotion. For this we must listen meditatively to the music itself. Of the two pieces suggested below, one is taken from the Ordinary and one from the Proper. The latter, a Gradual, is more elaborate musically than the *Kyrie* because the Gradual was traditionally sung by the soloists of the choir. (For the relation of soloist(s) and choir(s) in performance, see *Antiphonal* and *Responsorial* in the Glossary.)

Suggested Listening
Kyrie ("*Lux et Origo*").
Gradual "*Qui Sedes*."

The music of these two chants is given below. It is found in the *Liber Usualis* (the most convenient of the collections of the chant), page 16 and

[5] The rhythm of the chant is a subject of debate. For a fine article on the chant, see "Gregorian Chant" by Willi Apel in the *Harvard Dictionary of Music* (Cambridge, Mass.: Harvard University Press, 1944).

Ex. 83 *(for the number of the mode, see Ex. 82)*

Kyrie (Lux et origo)   Mode 8.

Ky - - ri - e   e - - le - i - son. iij. Chri - ste

e - - - - le - i - son. iij. Ky - - - ri - e

e - - - - le - i - son. ij. Ky - ri - e

e - - - - le - - i son.

Gradual "Qui Sedes." Mode 7 (actually both 7 and 8).

Qui se - des, _____ Do - mi - ne, • su - - -

per _ Che - ru - bim, _____ ex - ci - ta _ po -

ten - ti - am _ tu - am, _____ et _____

_____ ve - ni.

℣ Versus: Qui re - - - - -

- - - - - gis Is - ra - el, _ in - ten - de: ___ qui de -

du - - - - - - - - - - - - cis - ve - lut o - - vem •

Jo - - - seph _____

page 335, respectively. The chants mentioned have been recorded by (among others) the monks of the Solesmes Monastery in northeastern France.

THE MIDDLE AGES

In the Middle Ages (ninth through thirteenth centuries) the chant had an elaborate development. To the original words and music of the official chant were sometimes added new words or new music or both. This process was tolerated on the grounds that these additions were pious and illuminating commentary on the original authoritative version. From a purely musical point of view, this process, called *troping,* was an important one because in this way whole new compositions could be produced; and to this process the development of music owed new forms such as liturgical dramas celebrating important events like the birth of Christ and the Resurrection. Since some of these elaborations can be traced (at least by tradition) to specific persons, the earliest known composers of Western music date from these tropes. After centuries of tolerating additions of this kind, the Church became more and more alarmed as the tropes threatened to drive out the original versions of the texts and the chants; and finally, in the Council of Trent (ended 1563) these pieces (except for a few specific exceptions) were banned from the official service.

A more important development for music as a whole began in the addition of another melody or melodies to the chant as countermelody(ies) that sounded at the same time. From these additions grew slowly the whole process of polyphony and harmony, the most characteristic and lasting development of Western music. Nearly all the sacred forms of medieval polyphony take their point of departure from the chant which was incorporated in some form or other, usually in a lower voice and usually called the *tenor*.[6] Early forms that incorporated the plainsong include the *organum, descant,* and *motet*—the last mentioned quite different from the motet of the sixteenth century.

In *strict* organum the original chant was duplicated rigidly at intervals of the fourth or fifth when two parts were used; and when there were more parts, the octave was employed as well. This organum was parallel and improvised, following the rhythm of the Gregorian chant on which it was based. Example 84 shows the beginning of a strict organum in four voices. In the nineteenth and twentieth centuries parallel organum was used on occasion to give "modern" music the special flavor of the modes and the sonorities of chords moving in open fourths and fifths. Debussy's *Pelléas et Mélisande* opens with chords moving in this way (see Ex. 144a).

---

[6] That is, the "holding" voice. Later, the term *cantus firmus* was used as a general term ("the fixed melody" or song) for *any* pre-existent melody.

Ex. 84

Sit glo—ri—a Do—mi—ni in se—cu—la:

lae—ta—bi—tur Do—mi—nus in o—pe—ri—bus su—is.

However—to return to medieval polyphony—the parallel and rigid character of strict organum (ninth and tenth centuries) disappeared later in free organum (eleventh and twelfth centuries), where the voice accompanying the plainsong began to move in contrary motion and to enjoy a melodic life of its own. (For *descant* or *discantus*, see the Glossary.)

The most complex and highly organized type of medieval polyphony was the thirteenth-century motet, closely associated with the new cathedral of Notre Dame in Paris. This school of composition coincided in time with the high point of the political power of the Papacy and the medieval Church. The construction of the motet was especially interesting. A fragment of chant in the tenor was regulated by an ordered scheme of rhythmic patterns. Above this, a second voice, called the *motetus,* was composed. The words of its text ("word" in French = *mot;* hence, *motetus* or *motet*) were different from the text from which the tenor was drawn, but presumably they commented on or illuminated the latter. If a third voice was added (the *triplum*), it used still another text, although again theoretically related in meaning to the other voices. Each of the voices was deliberately distinguished from the others by its own text, melody, and, to some extent, rhythm. At first the upper two voices were Latin, but later French texts were used; and the French motet became secular in character. Example 85 shows a Latin motet.

The motet, especially the Latin motet, illustrates aspects of medieval life. Just as St. Thomas Aquinas reordered scholastic theology in the thirteenth century within the confines of a given mold, the motet ordered music on the authority of plainsong, relating the other parts to it. The deliberate horizontal organization of the motet is also characteristic of the horizontal social organization of the time, more international than national, dominated by the Church, by Latin, the universal language, and by the stratified structure of feudal society. Then, too, the interplay of the architectural

Ex. 85

O mi-tis-si-ma vir-go Ma-ri-a, po-sce—

Vir-go vir-gi-num, lu-men lu-mi-num, re-for-

[Hec Dies]

tu-um fi-li-um ut no-bis au-xi-li-um

ma-trix ho-mi-num, que por-ta-sti do-mi-num,

det— et re-me-di-um con-tra de-mo-num fal-li-bi-

per te Ma-ri-a de-tur ve-ni-a; an-ge-

les-as-tu-ci-as et ho-rum ne-qui-ci-as.

lo nun-ci-an-te, vir-go— es post et an-te.

forces and the supporting flying buttresses of Notre Dame itself—the Gothic cathedral in which this polyphony was heard—have a counterpart in the interplay of the voices of the *motetus* and their relation to the supporting tenor. (See Plate 10A.)

Suggested Listening

Parrish and Ohl, *Masterpieces of Music Before 1750* (New York: W. W.
  Norton & Company, 1951), contains conveniently accessible examples of
  the kinds of music mentioned above. This anthology is also recorded. In
  particular, see:

No. 6, for two-part strict organum.

No. 7, for free organum.

No. 10, for a French motet.

For a Latin motet, see *Hec Dies,* Example 85 above. It is recorded.

For other types of medieval polyphony, see Parrish and Ohl:

No. 8, for *melismatic organum* (not discussed above).

No. 9, for *discantus = descant* (within the organum of No. 9).

No. 11, for *conductus* (not discussed above).

Suggested Reading

Henry Adams, *Mont-Saint-Michel and Chartres.* Boston and New York:
  Houghton Mifflin Co., 1904. For an interesting account of medieval life
  and art.

For the most part the sacred music of early times is better known than
the secular music. Church music was carefully preserved by oral tradition,
and after music could be written down (from about the eleventh century)
the manuscripts containing this music were carefully safeguarded by
churches and monasteries. But folk and secular music in general had no
such all-powerful agency interested in its preservation, and relatively little
of it survived. A number of secular tunes owe their existence entirely to
the fact that they were used in sacred music. In some cases, too, there is no
really sharp distinction between sacred and secular music. In medieval life
the Church played a far more extensive role in the general life of the community than it does now: its edifice was not only the center of worship,
but also served as the local theater which represented the liturgical drama,
the Passion story, and perhaps other spectacles of more secular character.

However, there are various instances of secular music that did survive.
Some examples of medieval dances, at least from the thirteenth century,
are extant. In one case, a considerable body of secular music has come
down to us, namely, the songs of the troubadours and the trouvères in
France and of the minnesingers in Germany (the *Meistersinger* made
famous by Wagner are a much later and much less important movement).
These pieces, preserved only as melodies and in a notation that has led to
endless controversy about the rhythm, are in the native tongue, not the
prevailing Latin of the sacred music, and celebrate the cult and code of
chivalric love. The impulse for these songs came, in part at least, from the
Crusades, and the best examples of the troubadours and trouvères coincide
in date with the early Crusades (late eleventh to early thirteenth centu-

ries). The preservation of this secular music may be due to the fact that the troubadours, trouvères, and minnesingers were a princely and knightly class. Their music was not popular or folk music, but aristocratic songs composed for the entertainment of those who could afford to write the music down and look to its preservation. Traditionally, it was sung by a professional class of musicians called *jongleurs,* who probably accompanied the songs in an improvised way on some species of stringed instrument. (See Plate 9A.) Among the troubadours were Count William IX of Poitiers (1087–1127), Bertran de Born (died before 1215), and Bernard de Ventadour. Even kings like Richard "the Lion-Hearted" were included among the trouvères.[7]

The music of the troubadours and trouvères was cast in the modes (some also in the major and minor). The rhythm was that of the rhythmic patterns derived from classical poetry such as trochaic (long short) and iambic (short long). In theory, at least, the long was twice as long as the short, so that musically a trochaic foot was represented by ♩ ♪ and an iambic by ♪ ♩ rhythm. These basic patterns were not rigidly applied, and it is probable that the rhythm of these songs was freely interpreted. The chief forms of poetry used were the *virelai,* the *rondeau,* and the *ballade.* The musical forms did not follow the verse forms exactly. In the virelai *"Or la truix"* (see under Listening), a typical example,

the verse pattern is	ab cd ef ab
but the musical form is	ab cc ab ab

The verse refrain (ab) is used at the beginning and the end; the music that is used for this refrain is used also for part of the verse. The typical form of the minnesingers consisted of two verses (*Stollen*) and a conclusion (*Abgesang*). Musically this comprised the "bar" form: A:‖B. Taken as a whole, the songs of the troubadours, trouvères, and minnesingers showed a considerable variety of content: love songs, laments, funeral dirges, songs to nature, and others political or moralizing in intent.

Suggested Listening
Parrish and Ohl:
No. 4, Trouvère song (*"Or la truix"*).
No. 5, Minnelied (*"Willekommen Mayenschein"*).
No. 12, Instrumental dance (*"Estampie"*).
The recorded anthology *L'Anthologie Sonore,* No. 18, has both trouvère

[7] Richard's mother was Eleanor of Aquitaine, as powerful, fascinating, and musical a woman as the times produced. Brought up in the Troubadour atmosphere of the court of Aquitaine, she married Louis VII of France (1137), and in so doing contributed to merging the currents of the troubadours in the south of France with those of the trouvères in the north. Upon the annulment of her marriage to Louis (1152), Eleanor married Henry, Duke of Normandy (crowned Henry II of England, 1154), an important political marriage, to which was born Richard "the Lion-Hearted" and John "Lackland" (who signed the Magna Carta).

and minnesinger melodies, including one by Richard "the Lion-Hearted."

Suggested Reading

George W. Cronyn, *The Fool of Venus.* New York: Covici–Friede, 1934. A fascinating historical novel dealing with the troubadours and trouvères, and the historical milieu of their art.

In the development of polyphony, France was the most important country till the end of the thirteenth century. England must also have contributed considerably to this development, to judge by the famous canon "Sumer is icumen in," dating from about 1250, a piece in six parts of which four are in canon.[8] For the most part, the idea of consonance was based on the intervals considered perfect by the Greeks: the fourths, fifths, octaves, and unisons. The primary consideration in medieval polyphony was the addition of line to line, as in the motet. The idea of thinking in chords was quite foreign to this music; and just as depth of perspective in painting was limited, the element of harmony was subordinate to considerations of combining melodies and rhythms. In sacred music the rhythm was limited to triple time—possibly in symbolic reference to the Holy Trinity—and the rhythmic patterns of the polyphony were applied in a relatively rigid way.

The severity and almost scholastic logic of sacred polyphony is a product of one side of medieval life; but another is reflected in its dances, folk songs, and the aristocratic songs, charming and moving by turns, produced by the troubadours, trouvères, and minnesingers, the flower of medieval and musical chivalry. (For the dances *estampie* and *stantipes,* see the Glossary.)

THE FOURTEENTH CENTURY: ARS NOVA. MACHAUT. LANDINI.

A remarkable development characterized world literature in the fourteenth century, a development that had less-appreciated counterparts in music. In the world of belles-lettres, Dante, Boccaccio, and Chaucer broke away from Latin as an international language and began using the language of their own countries for literary expression. From this time onward the languages of the principal European countries developed rapidly. Their literatures increased in bulk and range of expression; and language became an important vehicle in national communication and political aspiration. Dante, basically a medieval figure, wrote his greatest work, *The Divine Comedy,* in his mother tongue. Boccaccio's lively and some-

[8] For this term see the Index. See Plate 7 for a facsimile of this piece; for additional comment, see p. 113.

times bawdy stories of contemporary life, *The Decameron,* are written in Italian, and, similarly, the stories of Chaucer's *Canterbury Tales,* in plan and tone modeled on Boccaccio, are written in English.

A reaction against the dominance of the Church, Latin its international language, and the solemnity of church music was especially noticeable in French and Italian music of the fourteenth century, first of all in the person of the Frenchman, Guillaume de Machaut (d. 1377), equally distinguished as a poet and as a musician. His polyphonic chansons (mostly in two and three parts) celebrate secular, especially love, themes, using the French tongue so appropriate to their expression.

In his secular works Machaut puts into practice certain new ideas suggested by an important theoretical work called *Ars Nova* (the New Art), written earlier (about 1325) by Philippe de Vitry. This work advocated the use of duple as well as triple time and more rapid note values; other treatises recommended thirds and sixths as harmonic consonances. The importance of *Ars Nova* may be judged by the fact that the whole musical era of the fourteenth century is sometimes called by this name to distinguish it from the *Ars Antiqua,* the old art of the preceding century.

Compared with that of the thirteenth century, the style of Machaut's secular music is more flexible to our ears, partly because it is more varied melodically and rhythmically, including numerous syncopations, and because the harmony sounds more consonant. Most of Machaut's secular music (i.e., chansons) used forms related to medieval French poetry: the *virelai* (see p. 144 and plate 11A), the *ballade,* and the *rondeau* (for the last two, see the Glossary; for *chace,* see below).

A similar development took place in Italy centering around the figure of the blind organist Francesco Landini (1325–1397). His forms are similar to those used in France (e.g., *ballata = virelai*), but there was one distinctive new one, the *madrigal* (see the Glossary; not to be confused with the sixteenth-century madrigal: see p. 156). The *caccia* (English: *chace*), which has a parallel in the French *chace,* is a hunting song, a musical feature of which is the use of the canon.

The sacred music of the fourteenth century takes its point of departure from the previous century, especially in the case of the medieval motet, but the rhythmic complications are greater. For the first time one encounters in the fourteenth century the polyphonic setting of a complete Mass,[9] including one by Machaut himself. As a matter of fact, a vivid contrast between the secular and sacred music of this period is furnished by the study of Machaut's music as a whole.

During the fourteenth century important changes took place. The new possibilities with respect to rhythm alone made music much more flexible and capable of infinite complication; in point of fact, the end of the four-

---

[9] The Ordinary only. About 1300, polyphonic settings of the Proper practically died out, although this eclipse was temporary.

1 The London Symphony Orchestra making the film *Instruments of the Orchestra* (Sir Malcolm Sargent, conductor).

2A The Griller Quartet (left to right: Griller, violin; Hampton, cello; Burton, viola; O'Brien, violin).

B The double-bass section, BBC Symphony Orchestra.

3A Oboes and English horn, BBC Symphony Orchestra.

B Bassoons and double bassoon, BBC Symphony Orchestra (background: French horns).

4A The clarinets and the bass clarinet, BBC Symphony Orchestra.

B The harp, London Symphony Orchestra.

5A The flutes (center), San Francisco Symphony Orchestra.

B The percussion section, BBC Symphony Orchestra (right to left: timpani, large drum, cymbals, small drum).

6A French horn section, BBC Symphony Orchestra.

B Brasses, San Francisco Symphony Orchestra (left to right: tuba, trombones, trumpets; in background: timpani, cymbals).

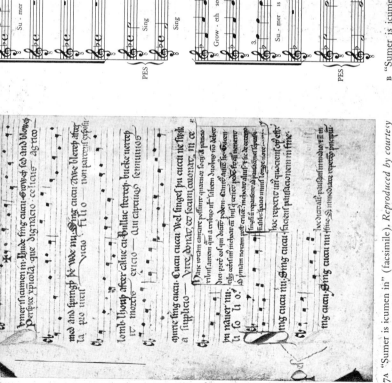

B "Sumer is icumen in" in modern notation (original version). *Quoted from Manfred Bukofzer, Sumer Is Icumen In: A Revision, University of California Publications in Music, Vol. 2, No. 2 (1944).*

7A "Sumer is icumen in" (facsimile). *Reproduced by courtesy of the Trustees of the British Museum.*

8A Bach's Chaconne for unaccompanied violin (facsimile of the autograph). *From Johann Sebastian Bach, Solosonaten für Violine, Bärenreiter-Verlag, Kassel and Basel.*

B Bach's Chaconne in an edited version. *From J. S. Bach's Six Sonatas and Partitas for Violin Solo, J. Joachim and A. Moser, eds. Courtesy of International Music Company, New York.*

The minnesinger Herr Reinmar playing the vielle. From a collection of minnesinger melodies about 1300.

B Performing the chanson *"Jouyssance vous donneray"* of Sermisy. Flemish painting about 1531 (left to right: singer, flutist, lutanist).

A Notre-Dame in Paris, showing the flying buttresses.

Italian State Tourist Off

1A Singing and dancing Machaut's *virelai*, "*Dame, a vous sans retollir.*" From his *Remède de Fortune*, late fourteenth century.

B Baude Cordier's chanson "*Belle bonne*" (about 1400). Notation in the form of a heart. In the manuscript some of the notes, as well as the outline of the small heart in the center, are drawn in red. *From Willi Apel,* The Notation of Polyphonic Music, 900–1600. *With the permission of Mediaeval Academy of America.*

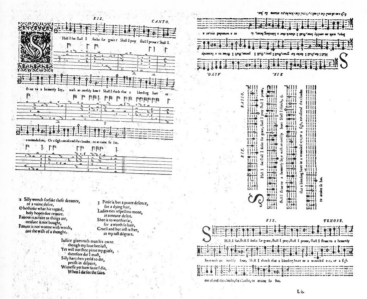

12A Dowland's song "Shall I sue" (1600). The notation indicates at least two kinds of performance: the singer and lute accompaniment, as shown on the left; or the addition or substitution of three other singers for the lute, as shown on the right. These parts were printed in the manner shown so that individual singers seated around a table could perform from a single score.

B Detail from Jan Brueghel's painting "Hearing" (about 1620), showing a large number of contemporary instruments. Grouped about the table are three of the six part books of a six-part madrigal by the Englishman Peter Philips (about 1600). By implication, the players used the same music.

3A Jan van Hemessen's "Clavichord Player" (about 1534).

B A harpsichord made by Jean Couchet in Flanders (about 1650). The four buttons on the right side of the case serve to regulate the number and kind of strings engaged by the playing manuals. In a modern harpsichord, buttons are replaced by a number of pedals regulated by the feet in the manner of the piano.

e Metropolitan Museum of Art. The Crosby Brown llection of Musical Instruments, 1889.

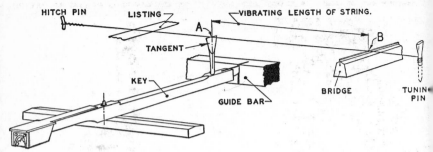

14A The clavichord mechanism. The pressure of the player's finger causes the metal tangent to strike the string. By a series of up and down impulses of the finger on the key, the player can make the string move up and down slightly, producing vibrato.

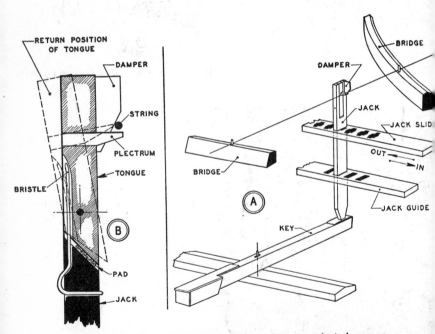

B The harpsichord mechanism. Depressing the key causes the jack to move up, and the plectrum strikes and moves past the string. The jack then slides back by its own weight, and the plectrum clears the string by virtue of the hinge shown at the left.

How the Viol is Tuned and Applyed to the Scale of Musick.
...t is supposed you understand *time*, and consequently the *Scale of Musick*;
...ch known, the Tuning of your *Viol* appears in such order as you see the Six
Semitones to.

The viol from Simpson's "The
Division-Violist" (1659).

B The recorder from Hotteterre's *"Principes de la
Flute traversière . . ."* (1708).

produced by permission of the Museum of Fine Arts, Boston.

C The lute as played by Charles Mouton
(flourished in the seventeenth century).

16A A French painting depicting the dance *"La Volta"* at the wedding of the Duke de Joyeuse and Princess Margarethe of Lorraine (1581). Musicians at upper left.

B "The Concert," an engraving by Picart after a painting Domenichino (early seventeen century).

teenth century was one of the most fascinating and complicated periods with respect to rhythm in the whole development of music, not excepting the present day.[10] The use of both duple and triple time, and the introduction of more and more syncopations made for flexibility of melody.

The concept of what was consonant and what was dissonant had undergone a revolutionary change although its effects were not immediately apparent. The harmony, although based on "modern" thirds and sixths, sounds strange, even experimental and wandering, to modern ears because it is still dominated and largely determined by the movement of the individual parts. For like reasons, the cadences often sound unfamiliar.

Secular music achieved a new stature. Its text was cast in the vernacular, not in Latin. The melody was put in the highest part, and none of the parts was derived from the liturgical chant of the Church. In sacred music, on the other hand, the chant (usually in the tenor) was invariably imbedded in the polyphony. In this way the polyphony for the church service was tied to the tradition and authority of the official chant. But secular music was freer and more progressive in its outlook and its musical processes.

Suggested Listening
Parrish and Ohl:
  No. 13, Machaut, Mass (*Agnus Dei* I).
  No. 14, Landini, Ballata *"Chi più le vuol sapere."*
Machaut, *Ballade "Plourés, Dames"* (recorded in *"Sacred & Secular Music of XII–XVIIth Centuries"* by Yves Tinayre).

Suggested Reading
Clive S. Lewis, *The Allegory of Love. A Study in Medieval Tradition.* Oxford: The Clarendon Press, 1936.
Oliver Strunk, *Source Readings in Music History.* New York: W. W. Norton & Company, 1950. For text of the *Ars Nova.*
Henry O. Taylor, *The Mediaeval Mind* (Fourth edition, 2 vols.). Cambridge, Mass.: Harvard University Press, 1949.

THE EARLY FIFTEENTH CENTURY: DUNSTABLE. BINCHOIS. DUFAY.

Musically, the fifteenth century was divided into two parts. The first half continued the musical currents common to the fourteenth century. The later part showed the invention of new textures and forms that made pos-

[10] In this connection, it is not entirely accidental that modern composers such as Hindemith have been fascinated by the fourteenth century not merely for its harmony but also for its rhythm. For notation c. 1400, see Plate 11B.

sible a whole new musical world, that of the Renaissance—the general European movement marked by the revival of classical art and learning. The music of the fourteenth and early fifteenth centuries served as a bridge between the music of the Middle Ages and the Renaissance, periods quite different in their musical idioms and aesthetic conceptions.

Three composers dominated the early fifteenth century, John Dunstable (d. 1453) in England, and Gilles Binchois (d. 1460) and Guillaume Dufay (d. 1474) in France. The activity of the latter two was centered in the Burgundian Court at Dijon. Many of Dunstable's manuscripts were found

Ex. 86   [JOHANNES DE LYMBURGIA—FIFTEENTH CENTURY]

The above reduced to simplest form:

on the Continent, a fact explained by political events. During this period England was involved with France in a long and costly war, the Hundred Years' War, which required the presence of English troops, their commanders and retainers, of whom Dunstable was one, on French soil.

The chansons (literally, songs), mostly in three parts, and the sacred music of this time covered a remarkable range of expression and indicated a harmonic advance by attaining sureness and clarity of harmonic progressions, especially at the cadences. The new emphasis on harmony (that is, on the vertical regulation of voice parts) is shown by the emphasis on parallel thirds and sixths and on one special style called *faux bourdon.* In this style, using three voices, the upper two parts sound in parallel thirds and sixths to the lowest voice, an arrangement that stresses the progression of the music as *chords.* As Example 86 shows, this manner of composing, conceived in parallel construction, also existed in ornamented forms.

While whole sections were sometimes composed in this way, its use was more often limited to short portions of music.

Sacred music also showed a far less austere style than formerly. The tenor itself might even be derived from secular music. Dufay's four-part polyphonic Mass *Se la face ay pale* uses a secular tenor taken from a song of that name; and a comparison of this work with Machaut's polyphonic setting of the Mass a century earlier illustrates vividly the change that had taken place in sacred music.

The attention paid to the regulation of consonance and dissonance between voice parts is a sign of harmonic (i.e., vertical) thinking. From the point of view of musical expression, the texture of music gained an added dimension of depth, which is comparable to the greater interest in perspective that painting of the fourteenth and fifteenth centuries showed by comparison with earlier times. A painting of Giotto (1276?–1337?) achieved its effect primarily in two dimensions, and in this regard is somewhat similar in emotional projection to the thirteenth-century ("Paris") motet. The interest in depth and perspective that occurred in painting and music in the following centuries was perhaps inevitable in a society more and more preoccupied with human values, secular subjects, and their portrayal.

Suggested Listening

Parrish and Ohl:

No. 15, Dufay. *Kyrie* (I) from the Mass *Se la face ay pale.*
No. 16, Binchois, Chanson *"Adieu m'amour."*

L'Anthologie Sonore has recorded the complete *Kyrie* of the Dufay Mass above.

Dunstable, *"Quam pulchra es"* is recorded in "Medieval and Renaissance Choral Music" (Stevens; Victor 13555/60).

THE LATE FIFTEENTH CENTURY: JOSQUIN DES PREZ

In the late fifteenth century occurred those changes in the fabric of music which formed the basis of the style of the late Renaissance in which such famous figures as Palestrina composed. The chief of these changes was fundamental to the essence of all later polyphony: the equalizing of the voice parts in function and musical interest. Prior to this time, typical voice parts such as the *tenor,* the *descant* (soprano), and the *contratenor* were composed by addition: the tenor first, the descant as countermelody, and the contratenor as something of a filler part. The top part often had the chief melodic interest; all the parts were different musically, fulfilled a different musical function, and sometimes they had different texts as well.

The fundamental change that took place in the late fifteenth century involved equalizing the voice parts by retaining the same text in all parts and by having each part imitate the music of the other. This style of *imitation* was already inherent in canon, its strictest manifestation. Canon had already been used for whole pieces (cf. "Sumer is icumen in"), and sporadic attempts at short sections in imitation occurred before the middle of the fifteenth century in the works of Dunstable and Dufay, among others. But the late fifteenth century exploited this means as an essential resource. In the following example (Ex. 87), taken from the opening of Josquin des Prez's Motet *Ave Maria* (Parrish and Ohl, No. 19), the imitation between the parts is clearly seen. Each part has the same text and the same music.

A desire for greater sonority led to the use of four (and occasionally

Ex. 87*

* Printed from Parrish and Ohl, *Masterpieces of Music.* By permission of W. W. Norton & Company.

more) parts as a typical number, instead of three, and the greater number of parts in turn necessitated a greater attention to their harmonic regulation, that is, the clear distinction as to what was consonant and dissonant as regards the sound of the whole ensemble. A chordal style, in which the voice parts proceeded together in the form of chords (as opposed to the polyphony of imitation) served as relief and variety to the style of imitation; it pointed also to an increased interest in harmonic considerations. The chordal style represented a balanced blend of harmony and polyphony, inasmuch as the individual voice parts were treated as melodies (i.e., polyphonically), but the progression of parts moved in the manner of chords.

The polyphonic Masses and motets of the late fifteenth and sixteenth centuries were composed in a blend of imitation, ordinary (non-imitative) polyphony, and chordal styles. The music was typically divided into sections that followed the natural divisions of the Latin text; and each of these sections was composed successively to different music. The text and, to some extent, the imitative polyphony were the unifying elements, inasmuch as there were generally no repetitions of music (hence, one speaks of a "through-composed" form). The polyphonic texture also afforded composers immense opportunities for variety. In both form and texture the new motet and Mass differed from the earlier motet and Mass.[11]

The new style of the late fifteenth century was gradually effected through the work of many composers, for the most part in France and the Low Countries (what is now the Netherlands; hence the term "French-Netherland" style). Among them were Ockeghem, Busnois, Obrecht, and, particularly, Josquin des Prez (c. 1450–1521), regarded by many musicians as the first great composer.[12] Universally admired in his own time—"the notes do what he wills," said a contemporary—Josquin employed a perfect command of the technique of composition in the interests of a profound emotional expression of the texts of sacred and secular music. In some cases a conscious relationship seems to exist between words and his musical realization of them (see Ex. 77).

The new style of polyphony also penetrated the chanson, but here the "through-composed" style was not used, and sections of music were repeated. Some of the chanson settings of Josquin are relatively somber for secular music (see, for instance, his "*Déploration de Jehan Okeghem*"). By way of contrast, the later "program" chansons of Clement Jannequin (c. 1475–1560) are sprightly, amusing, and lengthy. Their titles suggest a natural opportunity for word painting in such pieces as "*La Bataille*,"

[11] However, the plainsong and sometimes secular melodies were still used as *cantus firmus.* Sometimes the pre-existent tune was put in the tenor in relatively long notes; sometimes it formed the basis of the melody that was used in all the voices.

[12] The German scholar, A. W. Ambros (1816–76), one of the first modern writers to appreciate Josquin, wrote, "In Josquin we have the first musician who impresses us as having genius."

(16 – polyphony mastered.

commemorating the Battle of Marignano, and *"Le Chant des Oiseaux"*; and Jannequin makes the most of his texts to create music suggestive of battle sounds and bird songs. The new style was also applied to polyphonic settings of secular songs (Lieder) in Germany, for example, by Heinrich Isaak (c. 1450–1517).

By the early sixteenth century the new technique of imitative counterpoint (polyphony) had been mastered. The sonority of the additional voice parts and the clarity of their harmonic regulation permitted a variety and intensity of expression that had not been known hitherto. This music, still little known to the general musical public, deserves to be heard as the cultural and artistic counterpart of the great schools of painting of the same time. Josquin, for instance, is a figure of importance comparable to Leonardo and Raphael in cultural history; and the artistic development of the Renaissance as a whole cannot be fully appreciated without a knowledge of its music.

Suggested Listening

Parrish and Ohl:

No. 19, Josquin des Prez, Motet *Ave Maria.*

Josquin, Mass *Pange Lingua.*

Jannequin, chanson *"Le Chant des Oiseaux"* (*L'Anthologie Sonore,* No. 6).

Heinrich Isaak, Lied *"Innsbruck, ich muss dich lassen"* (recorded by Trapp family chorus).

Suggested Reading

Charles Reade, *The Cloister and the Hearth* (1861). A study of the transition from the Middle Ages to the Renaissance. A recent edition—New York: Dodd, Mead & Co., 1944.

Gustave Reese, *Music in the Renaissance.* New York: W. W. Norton & Company, 1954.

Walter Scott, *Quentin Durward* (1823). A recent edition—New York: Modern Library, 1933.

THE SIXTEENTH CENTURY: THE LATE RENAISSANCE

SACRED MUSIC: PALESTRINA. LASSO. BYRD.

The sixteenth century was crowded with activity in almost every field of endeavor: exploration in the New World, the growth of modern nations, the rise of Protestantism, the Counter-Reformation formed to combat it, and similar expressions of the human spirit in painting, literature, architecture, and music.

An intense activity in music may be explained in part by the general tempo of the time, in part by the increased centers of wealth and population and by the invention of music printing. Chapels connected with church or court vied for the services of professional musicians and composers, and the concentration of musicians under these advantageous conditions produced a huge amount of music essential for the consumption at these centers. Examples are the chapel of the Burgundian Dukes at Dijon, the Papal Chapel at Rome, and the Chapel in St. Mark's in Venice. Music printing began in the late fifteenth century, and accelerated the spread of music throughout Europe. One of the earliest, and still one of the most beautiful, examples of music printing was a collection of secular music of the late fifteenth century, called *Odhecaton* (literally, a hundred songs), printed by Petrucci in Venice in 1501.

From a purely musical point of view, one of the most important events of the early sixteenth century was the spread of the French-Netherland style to other countries of Europe, notably to Italy. Composers from Flanders, Burgundy, and the Low Countries occupied important posts in Italian music centers, and the new style of imitative polyphony spread rapidly. Josquin, for instance, lived and worked for a time in Italy; and Adrian Willaert (1490–1562), born in Flanders and educated there, went to Italy and served in the influential position of *maestro di cappella* at St. Mark's (see Plate 10B) from 1527 to his death in 1562. Taking advantage of the divided choir and the two organs at St. Mark's, Willaert experimented with large ensembles divided into two (and sometimes more) choirs. From these experiments came a double-chorus style (*chori spezzati*). (For examples of double-chorus style of writing, see under Gabrieli, below).

In the first part of the sixteenth century a most important event occurred in Germany, the Protestant Reformation under Luther. Luther preserved much of the traditional music in the new Protestant service, but he also felt the need for a distinctive music for the new service, the Protestant chorale in German.[13] Luther devoted much attention to assembling a body of music of this sort, some of it adapted to congregational use and some to the choir. These pieces resembled hymns, and their texts were in German so that the congregation could readily understand them. Some were newly composed—for example, *"Ein' feste Burg"* ("A Mighty Fortress") probably by Luther himself—and some drew their melodies from older sources such as Latin hymns, folk songs, the old German Lied, and even dances. In justifying the origin of some of these melodies, Luther remarked that the devil should not have all the good tunes for himself. It is a tribute to the vitality of these tunes and texts that Bach used and harmonized many of them again and again in the eighteenth century.

The Reformation spread to other countries, especially to France and

[13] In German, the word "choral" may mean either the Protestant chorale or the Gregorian chant of the Catholic Church.

England; and, inspired by Luther's example, reformers in these countries created special musical forms to suit their needs. In France metrical versions of the psalms, translated into French, were set to music (e.g., Goudimel's settings of the metrical texts of Marot and Béza). In England the *anthem* and the *service* with English texts gradually developed as counterparts of the motet and Mass respectively. The English *verse anthem* of the late sixteenth century indicates the presence of a solo part or parts (i.e., the verse) in the anthem.

Alarmed by the spread of Protestantism, the Church called one of its most important Councils, the Council of Trent (ended 1563), from which stemmed the so-called Counter-Reformation, aimed at internal reform as well as at combating heresy through the Inquisition. The deliberations at Trent also included music, and there were some churchmen who wished to ban polyphonic music from the church service because they thought that such settings obscured the words. One of the cardinals, who later reigned briefly as Pope Marcellus, was influential in preventing such drastic measures. However, it is possible that the Council of Trent, as a result of its critical attitude toward church music, influenced it toward a somewhat simpler style of polyphony.

At any rate, some of the most famous composers of the sixteenth century wrote for the Catholic Church service in the second part of the century, and so came under the legislation of Trent. Among them were Giovanni Pierluigi da Palestrina (1525–94) in Rome, Orlando di Lasso (1532–94) in Munich, William Byrd (1543–1623) in England (as far as he composed for the Catholic service, which the English permitted in certain specified places), the Spaniards, Cristóbal de Morales (c. 1500–1553) and Tomás Luis de Victoria (c. 1548–1611), and in Venice, Andrea Gabrieli (c. 1520–86) and his nephew Giovanni (1557–1612). Their motets and Masses were based on a combination of chordal and imitative polyphony perfected by earlier composers like Josquin, but the style was refined, particularly with regard to the clarity of the harmony and the treatment of dissonance. The old modes persisted, but there was greater and greater use of the major and minor, called *Ionian* and *Aeolian,* respectively. The old *cantus firmus* (derived from Gregorian chant or other sources) was then seldom found in the motet, but a number of Masses used a *cantus firmus* in the tenor or drew on pre-existent melodies for the melodic material (*cantus-firmus Mass*). Sometimes whole pre-existent *compositions* served as the basis of a Mass; Palestrina's *Dies Sanctificatus* Mass is based on his motet of the same name, and hence the term *parody* or *transcription Mass.*

In general, the polyphonic style was most transparent and carefully regulated in the works of Palestrina, and in this regard the Palestrina style was not the most typical of the time, but the most carefully refined. In other composers polyphony was subject to the most disparate individual treatment, harmonically and rhythmically, as one would expect of great masters such as Byrd and Lasso, to select two. The rhythms of the individual parts were frequently so irregular and powerful that they modified the rhythm of the whole; and modern editions sometimes use irregular measures to reflect this fact. Harmonically, Byrd and Lasso were far freer than Palestrina. Byrd in particular specialized in the "cross relation," a device by which a note in its diatonic form appeared close to (or together with) a note in its chromatic form in another voice. In his motet *Ave Verum*, the F sharp in the soprano (Ex. 88) is contradicted by the F natural in the tenor. In Venice, the Gabrielis continued to specialize in the double-chorus style made famous by Willaert.

Ex. 88

Suggested Listening

Byrd, *The Great Service*.

Byrd, motet *Ave Verum*. See also Parish and Ohl, No. 25.

Palestrina, "Pope Marcellus" Mass (*Kyrie* only).

Morales, *Lamentabatur Jacob*.

Victoria, *Jesu, dulcis memoria*.

Lasso, motet *Tristis est anima mea* (Parrish and Ohl, No. 23).

G. Gabrieli, *Processional and Ceremonial Music* (double chorus with instruments; that is, in *concertato* style, see below).

Suggested Reading

See the end of the chapter.

SECULAR MUSIC: MARENZIO. MORLEY. WEELKES. WILBYE. DOWLAND.

Secular music enjoyed a vogue commensurate with the intensity and brilliance of contemporary social life. Secular pieces were naturally quite different from the solemn Masses and motets. The French *chanson*, for instance, continuing from the preceding century, specialized in witty and often erotic texts set to a rhythmically animated music that emphasized chordal style and the repetitive forms of music (such as ternary and rondo forms). Claude de Sermisy (c. 1490–1562), Guillaume Costeley (1531–1606), and Lassus (Lasso) as a young man composed in this style (see Plate 9B). Late in the century, poets and musicians tried to achieve a natural union of poetry and music in imitation of classical antiquity. Their *vers mesurés,* as they were called, attempted to capture the natural length of the French syllables in corresponding lengths of musiĉ. The musician Claude Le Jeune, under the influence of Ronsard and the circle known as the *Pléiade,* set poems of Baïf and Ronsard in *vers mesurés.*

More important than the French chanson, especially after the middle of the century, was the Italian *madrigal.* The Italian humanists, inspired by the poet (and Cardinal) Pietro Bembo (1470–1547), revived the old madrigal poetry. (The poet most often set by the madrigalists was Petrarch.) The madrigal—the term means a rustic song in the mother tongue—is somewhat indefinite in form, but it has one distinctive feature: the last two lines generally rhyme and convey a pointed moral to the whole poem, as in "The Silver Swan," set as a madrigal by Orlando Gibbons (1583–1625):

> The silver swan, who living had no note,
> When death approached unlocked her silent throat.
> Leaning her breast against the reedy shore
> Thus sung her first and last, and sung no more:
> Farewell all joys; O death, come close mine eyes:
> More geese than swans now live, more fools than wise.

The sentiments expressed by madrigal poetry as a whole were extremely varied, ranging from the typical lover's lament to philosophical disquisitions ("What is our life"). Musically, the madrigal was composed in a style similar to the motet, although usually much less somber in tone—the mood of individual madrigals varied as much as the mood of their texts. The musical texture was a combination of imitation, non-imitative polyphony, and chordal style, just as in the motet, and the madrigal was also "through-composed" as a rule. A typical feature of the madrigal was so-called *madrigalisms,* a term used to denote illustrative music set to suggestive words (for an example in Weelkes, see p. 116). The classical madrigal reached a high point in Italy in Luca Marenzio (1553–99). Later Claudio Monteverdi (1567–1643) brought a dramatic element and sometimes independent instrumental parts into the madrigal, thus completely transforming its forms and styles in the early seventeenth century.

The Italian madrigal was imported into England in the last dozen years of the sixteenth century, and, being rapidly acclimatized, enjoyed a short but extraordinarily intense favor among English composers in the late sixteenth and early seventeenth centuries. Among a galaxy of madrigal composers, Thomas Morley (c. 1557–c. 1603), Thomas Weelkes (d. 1623), and John Wilbye (1574–1638) were perhaps the most celebrated. With the latter two especially, the English madrigal attained an emotional expressiveness and technical finish that marked the peak of its achievement. The texts themselves were of a particularly high literary order, and it is worth remarking that a high point of literature at the end of the reign of Elizabeth (Shakespeare) coincided with a similar period in English music.

Thomas Morley, who wrote an important treatise, *A Plain and Easy Introduction to Practical Music* (1597), from which a good picture of English music of the time can be obtained, also specialized in the so-called *ballett,* modeled on the Italian *balletto.* This form was characterized by "fa-la" refrains, by strong, dancelike rhythms (*"ballare"* means to dance), and by stanza schemes.

A certain pronounced interest in individual expression may be observed in the songs for solo voice with lute accompaniment that appeared at the end of the sixteenth century. John Dowland (1563–1626), the greatest of these lutanist song composers, as well as the greatest lute virtuoso of his time, had a marked lyrical gift, and his best songs are as inspired melodically as those of Franz Schubert over two hundred years later (see Plate 12A).

Suggested Listening

Parrish and Ohl:

No. 20, Crequillon, French chanson *"Pour ung plaisir."*

No. 27, Marenzio, Madrigal *"S'io parto, i' moro."*

Weelkes, Madrigal *"As Vesta was from Latmos hill descending."* (From *The Triumphs of Oriana,* a collection of twenty-nine madrigals in honor of Queen Elizabeth, the "Oriana" of the title. Edited by Morley, it was published in 1603. This entire collection has been recorded.)

Morley, ballet *"Now is the month of Maying."*

Dowland, lute ayre *"In Darkness let me dwell"* (from *A Musicall Banquet,* 1610).

INSTRUMENTAL MUSIC

Instrumental music now began to break away from a position subordinate to vocal music. Instruments had been used extensively in the Middle Ages and in the early Renaissance, but largely in the role of playing the same music as the voice parts (called "doubling"). Only in exceptional cases, as in some dances and in a few instrumental interludes, were instruments expressly called for before the sixteenth century. However, paintings of the time, sculptures, and references in literature show that instruments were used far more than was explicitly designated in the music *as written.* From the theorists, too, we know that the performance of many pieces was a fluid matter, often depending, somewhat casually, on the instruments at hand. Typical instruments were the recorders (wooden flutes, held vertically downward, unlike the modern flute that is held parallel to the floor), the lute (a guitarlike instrument with a pear-shaped body), and the viols (see Plate 15). The latter, a family of stringed instruments, were played with a bow, and even the smallest were held at the knee or between the legs. Hence the Italians called the viol *viola da gamba* (viol or viola of the leg). All these instruments typically came in families, from the small treble to the large bass instruments. In construction, the viol family was distinguished from the violin family by flat backs, sloping shoulders, relatively deep ribs, six strings (usually) instead of four, and frets (pieces of gut tied around the fingerboard to guide the player's fingers).

The keyboard instruments in common use were: (1) the organ, from small portable organs to the very large instruments in churches; (2) the harpsichord, whose keyboard activated a mechanism that plucked the string (similar instruments: the spinet, the virginal); and (3) the clavichord, in which the string was struck by a small piece of metal called a "tangent." The harpsichord came in various sizes, sometimes with several keyboards like the organ. The clavichord was a small house instrument. Its silvery tone was beautiful, but it could not be heard beyond the confines of a room (see Plates 13 and 14).

In the sixteenth century instruments were used to double voice parts as they had done previously. But there was also more independent playing of instruments. To transcribe vocal pieces for instruments was a natural step. Thus motets were transferred to single instruments like the organ or to ensembles of instruments, and called *ricercar(e)*. The instrumental adaptation of the chanson went by its Italian name, *canzona,* and was a piece lighter in tone as a rule, just as the chanson was lighter than the motet. It was a common practice in vocal music of the time to add improvised ornamentation and figuration in performance, and this custom was doubtless adopted in instrumental music, with the probable difference that improvised additions were specifically suited to the character of the instrument. In this way, pieces derived from vocal music may have sounded far more instrumental in character than is suggested by the written score as it has come down to us.

There was also a large body of lute music, not merely as accompaniment, but also for solo players. Many of these pieces were dances, two favorite ones being the *pavane* (usually in duple time) and the *galliard* (in triple time).[14]

The lute was the common instrument of the sixteenth century, enjoying a position comparable to that of the pianoforte today. The literature writ-

---

[14] For contemporary dances see Thoinot Arbeau, *Orchésographie* (1589). (Translated by Mary S. Evans. New York: Kamin Dance Publishers, 1948.) See also Plate 16A.

ten for the lute was immense, and it was used throughout Europe: in Italy, Spain, France, Germany, and England.

The lute, the bass viol, and the keyboard instruments began to achieve an idiomatic style specifically different from that of vocal music. Players of the viols, especially the bass viol, must have attained a considerable technical facility, to judge by contemporary instruction books. The organists and harpsichordists were busy running up and down the keyboard, often in somewhat arid figurations; but they also composed many beautiful pieces such as variations, toccatas,[15] dances, and pieces based on vocal models. Several important collections of keyboard music attest to a flourishing activity of this kind in Elizabethan England. The *Fitzwilliam Virginal Book* (c. 1600) contains nearly three hundred pieces for keyboard, among them many dances, variations, pieces with fanciful or descriptive titles ("The Fall of the Leaf"), and still others drawn from vocal models. Incidentally, instrumental music began to have a reciprocal influence on vocal music—as indeed, it probably had from earliest times. The rhythm of dance music in particular influenced the rhythm and phrases of vocal pieces.

A great deal of the so-called *a cappella* (unaccompanied) music of the sixteenth century only appeared to be such. In actual practice it was mostly accompanied,[16] but there were no separate parts for the instruments, which simply doubled the vocal parts as a matter of course. Toward the end of the sixteenth century, however, the addition of instrumental parts or the presence of instrumental forces in a piece of vocal music was designated by the specific term *concerto* or *concertato*. This term simply emphasized the presence of instrumental forces, although it sometimes implied that the instrumental parts were something distinct from the part sung. This style was especially noticeable in the music of Giovanni Gabrieli at Venice, and later in Monteverdi.

The sixteenth century added vast treasures to music. The great motets and Masses of the Church were not more solid and impressive than the secular music: the chansons, madrigals, dances, and instrumental music. The tremendous variety and emotional range of life of this era, as portrayed in contemporary literature, painting, architecture, and sculpture, was reflected just as surely in the solemn tone of church music, the sprightly chanson, the urbane and aristocratic madrigal, and in the measure of the dance, now restrained and sedate in the *pavane,* now animated with leaping steps and abandoned gaiety in the *galliard.* Nor was the palette of the Renaissance painters more varied or colorful than the choirs of voices in all their variety, the timbres of the organs, the brilliantly

---

[15] Preludelike pieces of no special form, often used to show off the range of the instrument and the capabilities of the player.

[16] The Sistine Chapel at Rome was the only specific place where accompaniment to vocal music was forbidden.

etched sounds of harpsichords, and the characteristic tones of lutes, recorders, and viols.

Suggested Listening

Parrish and Ohl:

No. 21, Andrea Gabrieli, *"Canzona francese"* (based on the Crequillon chanson, Parrish and Ohl, No. 20, referred to above).

No. 22, Lute Dances.

Byrd, *Earl of Salisbury's Pavane & Galliard* (for virginal).

John Bull, *The King's Hunt* (theme and variations for virginal).

Luis Milan, Three *pavanes* for vihuela (Spanish lute).

Suggested Reading

Thomas Morley, *Plain and Easy Introduction to Practical Music* (1597). Modern edition by R. Alec Harman. London: J. M. Dent & Sons, 1952. Excerpts are given in Oliver Strunk, *Source Readings in Music History.* New York: W. W. Norton & Company, 1950.

Reginald O. Morris, *Contrapuntal Technique in the 16th Century.* Oxford: The Clarendon Press, 1922. The best discussion of sixteenth-century style ever written.

Gustave Reese, *Music in the Renaissance.* New York: W. W. Norton & Company, 1954.

II. *The Seventeenth Century: Opera and Related Forms. Sacred Music.*

THE BAROQUE (*1600–1750*)

LIKE ALL THE ARTS, music affords a number of intellectual pleasures. One of them is the contemplation of the rich panorama of music and its recurring life cycles: the birth of new ideas, their fruition, and decay. The time span of the longest of these cycles is about three centuries, marked in each case by vigorous reaction to the artistic ideas of the past and by the substitution of new ideas and their appropriate forms of expression. The *Ars Nova* of the fourteenth century represented a reaction of this sort, consciously expressed in the title "The New Art", as opposed to "The Old Art" of the music of the thirteenth century. Similarly, three hundred years later the early seventeenth century reacted strongly against the Renaissance, and the break with the past was indicated by the title of Caccini's *Le Nuove Musiche (The New Music)*. In the twentieth century, again three centuries later, a reaction against the Romanticism of the preceding century is apparent in a number of "New Musics."

The length of these life cycles breaks again into subordinate divisions of about one hundred and fifty years. A natural division of this kind occurred in the middle of the fifteenth century, beginning with Josquin des Prez and ending with Palestrina about 1600. In the middle of the eighteenth century, a century and a half later, there was a marked reaction to the music of the so-called *baroque* period. Bach and Handel came to be considered old-fashioned; the sons of Bach, followed by Haydn and Mozart, set a new fashion, and the types of music they inaugurated continued, to a considerable degree, through the nineteenth century.

Today it is fashionable to divide music—and for that matter, the fine arts in general—into neat pigeonholes for purposes of description. This tendency is more or less inevitable, but there is always the danger of "the hardening of the categories," as someone has aptly said. Each period has its overlaps and recessive characteristics from the past as well as the seeds of the future; and any attempt to describe movements in art and music in general terms can be helpful and illuminating only in the degree that labels and generalities are regarded as the norms of a bewildering variety of individual works. This is so because the art works of any time, taken collectively, exhibit a range of excellence and manner of expression as different as the talents and backgrounds of the individuals who created them. However, every period does have its peculiar *Zeitgeist,* its special spiritual characteristics, no matter how tenuous; and knowing what these are helps us to understand and appreciate each work of art in terms of the problems and aesthetic ideals of the individual creator.

The difficulties of generalizing are especially acute in the case of the seventeenth and early eighteenth centuries, the so-called *baroque.*[1] This era is difficult to treat as one artistic unit because of the many inconsistencies and contradictions in the period as a whole—so much so that substantial objections have been raised to the use of this term to describe music as different as that of Monteverdi at the beginning of the seventeenth century and Bach in the early eighteenth. To minimize this difficulty, we will discuss first the seventeenth century as a whole, and then the early eighteenth century, most of whose music falls within the orbit of Bach and Handel.

Compared to the music of the Renaissance or the eighteenth century, that of the seventeenth century appears less impressive, not in invention, but in its quality as a whole. The reasons lie partly in the condition and evolution of music itself. For one thing, a marked change in composing habits required time to solidify new technique. The inexplicable appearance or nonappearance of first-rate composing talents had something to do with it. In addition, political and other external conditions of the time played a part in the quantity and quality of artistic expression. Germany and England in the seventeenth century were two good examples of countries basically unfavorable to the welfare of music. The terrible religious wars (the Thirty Years' War) in seventeenth-century Germany and the Civil War in England weakened both countries politically and economically, reduced musical production, and in some cases worked great hardships on individual composers (for example, Heinrich Schütz in Germany). In England the restoration of Charles II to the throne (1660–85) and the reigns of those who followed him were not especially favorable to music. Charles, for instance, had neither the taste nor the money to encourage music in the grand manner of the Tudor monarchs Henry VIII and Elizabeth, who were themselves musicians and did much to encour-

---

[1] The word *"baroque"* was presumably derived from the Portuguese word *"barroco,"* an irregular or deformed pearl; or it may come from a word meaning a faulty syllogism in logic. Until the twentieth century, the term *"baroque"* was used largely to depreciate art of extravagant and corrupt taste. In modern times, the attainments of the baroque as a period of art have been reconsidered in relation to its defects.

age the music of the English Renaissance. The dramatic flair of Henry Purcell (1659–95), the most gifted composer in seventeenth-century England, would doubtless have found better and more productive expression in Italy or France, countries far more sympathetic to opera than his native land.

In seventeenth-century France the political and social climate favored the growth of music, especially the opera. Under Louis XIV, the most powerful of French kings, France rose in the seventeenth century to the dominating position among European nations. Wealthy and powerful, Louis was willing to encourage art, literature (Molière), and music, if only as an adjunct to the brilliance and splendor of his court. The perfection of the French court opera in the seventeenth century would have been quite impossible without the active support of the King, who bestowed dictatorial powers on Lully, his court composer, in order to create spectacles worthy of the court at Versailles and his own august personage. Louis was rewarded by magnificent opera—possibly the most perfect dramatic productions of all time—and by many thinly veiled references to his own glorious virtues. *See Plate* 19B.

Italy, which dominated music in Europe for the next century and a half, stood somewhat apart from the main political streams of the time. It owed its musical pre-eminence to a long and continuing musical tradition, a natural inclination toward music, and a number of patrons and local centers of wealth and culture that were able and anxious to encourage music and to support talent. Among the latter were the Popes at Rome, the Jesuits as an order (who used music partly to impress and to propagandize), civic centers such as Venice and Naples, and various petty courts and wealthy families.

The art of the seventeenth century was dominated by a new spirit, an interest in a more personal kind of expression that sometimes bordered on the spectacular and the flamboyant. It took the form of elaborate decoration, exaggerated and sometimes distorted forms. The human figure, for instance, was sometimes represented not in its natural form but as a creature half man and half animal. In extreme cases an artificial and even bizarre quality permeated painting, sculpture, decoration, and opera sets; and in formal gardens the forces of nature itself were subjected to contrived forms and designs. Allegory and symbolism were tools in this removal from actuality. *See Plates* 17 *and* 19A.

Compared to the relatively static representation in Renaissance painting and sculpture, baroque art, especially in its early phases, was emotionally restless, and its lines and figures specialized in writhing movements or movement arrested in space. The altar in St. Peter's achieved its effect not merely by the sumptuous colors of its marble but also by the sense of movement and torsion conveyed to the eye by its twisted columns. The sculptures of Bernini, to take another case, were often remarkable studies in motion, frozen, as it were, as an action was taking place. Paintings, in an excess of exuberance, tended to overflow their borders.

In architecture, the well-defined planes and right angles of the Renaissance gave way to curved and elongated lines. In many baroque forms the individual parts themselves were not self-sufficient as structures, but existed only in relation to a central and unified plan (e.g., the final plan of St. Peter's; the whole layout of Versailles; also the one-subject Bach fugue). Such works of art present to the viewer (or listener) an almost unlimited perspective, since the curves and irregular lines appear quite different from different points of view.

Baroque art took varied forms in different times and different countries, and a common denominator of its manifestations in Italy, Germany, Spain, France, and England, even in the seventeenth century, is not easy to find. In general, the baroque tended to seek the ornamental or the monumental in which mass was stressed at the expense of line; the early baroque often sacrificed continuity for momentary effect. The very magnificence of baroque color and decoration is frequently overpowering. The defects of such an art are implicit in its qualities. The technical virtuosity needed for its expression became at times an end in itself and more important than the thing expressed (cf. the *prima donna* of the seventeenth- and early eighteenth-century opera). *See Plate* 21A.

NB   In music, composers began to seek a more personal manner of expression and tried to represent more intense and more varied emotional states (the so-called *affections*). One of the first signs of this change was a revolt against Renaissance polyphony, which, in the view of the early baroque, obscured the all-important text. For polyphony, musicians of the early seventeenth century substituted a solo part supported by a subordinate harmony. At the same time, the new texts themselves expressed more violent emotions than formerly; or the same kinds of emotions were expressed in a more personal way by a far more dissonant and chromatic style (i.e., using half steps of the scale). To represent the capricious mood of the text, composers used arbitrary and changing rhythms (cf. the poetic rhythms of John Donne) and an expressive and more widely graduated range of louds and softs. An elaborate, although frequently unwritten, ornamentation characterized the melodic lines. The restless style of this music is analogous to other art of the time.

The Preface to Caccini's *Le Nuove Musiche* was an important expression of the new philosophy, style, and musical practice. One aspect of the latter is worth emphasizing. Caccini's work (1602) makes clear that the score *as written* was only a skeleton of what was actually performed. The individual performer was expected to play a considerable creative role by ornamenting and improvising on the written notes within certain limits of contemporary taste and judgment.

~~consequence~~

A natural corollary to an expressive and dominant melody was a supporting harmony; and, consequently, the growth of the harmonic process was implicit in seventeenth-century music. This harmonic growth was accompanied by more and more reliance on the major and minor and by the gradual emergence of tonality, in which melodies and chords defined a tonal center or "tonic." A new and special manner of indicating the harmony, the *figured bass,* implied that the supporting parts of the accompaniment were vertically (that is, harmonically) regulated. A melody with an accompanying bass and figures is shown in Example 89. The bass line

Ex. 89

La Follia
(Adagio)   [Corelli]

(*basso continuo; thorough bass*) and the figures below it constituted the figured bass. The figures indicated the proper harmonies or harmonic intervals to be played above the bass; and from them the player, usually an organist, harpsichordist, or lutanist, composed the harmonic accompaniment. Technically, this was called *realizing* the figured bass.

The figured bass was such a universal phenomenon in the *ensemble* music of the seventeenth and early eighteenth centuries (as opposed to certain pieces for soloists) that the whole period has been called the *Thorough-Bass Period,* a reasonably accurate description as far as purely musical phenomena go. The *basso continuo* was characteristic of the times in several respects. It exhibited the same never-ceasing movement observed in seventeenth-century painting and sculpture; and it stressed the new emphasis on harmony as opposed to polyphony.

The growth of harmony was thus closely connected with the new expressive style of the seventeenth century. At the same time, the old polyphonic style of the Renaissance did not die out, but continued to exist side by side with the new style, especially in connection with the surviving forms of imitative counterpoint.

The seventeenth century thought of music as a function either of the theater, the church, or the chamber. Theoretically, either the old or the new style could be used in music serving any of these three functions. In practice, the new style was associated first of all with the opera in connection with the theater; but it penetrated the forms of church music as well. Traditionally, polyphony had been used most extensively in the church, and the development of vocal polyphony in seventeenth-century church music was a natural evolution from the past.[2]

An important phenomenon of the baroque period was the gradual emergence of the orchestra as such. The Renaissance had used a number of instruments grouped largely in families, the wind instruments being dominant. Typically, Renaissance instruments doubled the parts of the singers, and the selection of particular instruments was a somewhat casual matter. In these instrumental ensembles there was no arrangement into the functional choirs of the modern orchestra (see Chapter 6).

In the baroque era the string choir gradually became the backbone of the orchestra, but there was still no standard division into choirs of strings, woodwinds, and brasses—a division which dates from the later eighteenth century. Unlike the modern orchestra, that of the seventeenth century was supported by the figured bass from which the fundamental harmonies were supplied by the harpsichord or organ, the *basso continuo* being doubled by various instruments such as the cello, double bass, or bass viola da gamba. Besides the strings, typical baroque instrumentation included pairs of oboes, flutes (or recorders), and, later, horns. The bassoon sometimes complemented the two oboes in trio fashion, and on occasion it served also to double the *basso continuo* part. The clarinet was a late-comer and figures hardly at all in the baroque orchestra. Added power and brilliance were furnished, as required, by trumpets and timpani, and sometimes other instruments were used as well. But the one really constant element was the string choir plus the figured bass. In short, by modern standards the orchestra was unstandardized and small; and it is significant that the most famous orchestra of the seventeenth century was the string band of twenty-four players maintained by Louis XIV.

From time to time individual composers showed considerable interest in the capabilities or color effects of particular instruments (noticeable as early as Monteverdi's *Orfeo;* see below). In general, however, the seventeenth-century musician was content to double the melodic lines of polyphony with several instruments indiscriminately or to contrast sonority and dynamics rather than to exploit the particular timbre and idiom of a single choir or instrument. (Individual instruments were, however, developed rapidly in solo sonatas and, later, concertos.)

In the early eighteenth century this situation began to change. A newer progressive school sought to use individual instruments more prominently, to establish a clearer distinction between the choirs, and to separate the melodic instrument(s) from the accompanying choir(s) used as harmonic support. These tendencies may be distinguished in certain works of Handel and more especially Rameau, among others. The completion of the process of establishing clearly defined choirs and distinguishing be-

[2] The functions of music with respect to instrumental forms are discussed on p. 180.

tween solo and accompanying instruments took place at the same time that polyphonic textures and the figured bass disintegrated after 1750. The final phase, involving the addition and perfection of certain instruments, notably the brasses, did not occur until the nineteenth century. *See Plates 12B, 15, and 16B.*

OPERA AND RELATED FORMS: MONTEVERDI. LULLY. PURCELL.

In the music of the seventeenth century, the two most important *new* developments were (1) the origin, growth, and dissemination of opera, and (2) the development of the styles and forms of instrumental music. The opera began as an offshoot of Italian humanism intent on reviving the artistic ideals of classical antiquity—a purpose already evident on the French *Pléiade* (see p. 156). In Italy, an intellectual circle of poets, musicians, philosophers, and scholars, meeting in the house of Count Bardi in Florence, pondered the problem of representing words with appropriate music. They rejected polyphony, concluding that a *dramma per musica* (drama through music) could be realized most effectively by *declaiming* the text to music in a style of reciting called *stile recitativo*. Thus operatic recitative was born. The first important effort to put these theories into practice was a setting of the Orpheus and Eurydice myth (for the story, see p. 267), under the title *Euridice,* composed by Jacopo Peri for the occasion of the festivities in connection with the important political marriage of Henry IV of France and Maria de' Medici (1600). At the same time the identical story was set by another member of the Florentine circle, Giulio Caccini. These new works in the theatrical style (*stile rappresentativo*) were essentially recitative, declaimed to the accompaniment of a figured bass and punctuated with a few moments of song. A beautiful one, Peri's *"Gioite al canto mio"* ("Rejoice in my song") is still occasionally performed (it is recorded).

The new expressive style was used also in songs, or *monodies,* as they were called, accompanied by the figured bass. Caccini's *Le Nuove Musiche* of 1602 contained a number of these monodies, and the Preface tells us something about Caccini's musical purpose in these songs. It was, he says, "to bring in a kind of Musick by which men might as it were talk in harmony. . . . Certain it is, that an *Ayre* composed in this manner upon the conceit of the words, by one that hath a good fashion of singing, will work a better effect and delight, more than another made with all the art of descant [i.e., polyphony] where the humour or Conceit of the words is not minded." [3]

[3] This English translation appeared without acknowledgment in John Playford's *Introduction to the Skill of Music* (Enlarged First edition, 1655). For the full text, see Oliver Strunk, *Source Readings in Music History* (New York: W. W. Norton & Company, 1950), pp. 377–92.

MONTEVERDI

In the hands of Peri and Caccini the opera was more a literary than a musical form, and its future would have been problematical indeed without a musician of genius to rescue it from its literary friends. Happily, such a man, Claudio Monteverdi (1567–1643), the greatest composer of the seventeenth century, was at hand. Monteverdi was as important to the development of music in the seventeenth century as Beethoven was to that of the nineteenth; and, like Beethoven, Monteverdi bridged the composing styles of two different periods. While Monteverdi never composed in purely instrumental forms, his influence on the development of instrumental style (through the use of accompanying instruments in the *concertato* style and in the opera) was widely felt. His influence on the development of the opera, sacred music, secular vocal forms, and the expressive style in general, was enormous. *See Plate* 22A.

Monteverdi's first opera was written (1607) for the court at Mantua. Like Peri's, it was concerned with the legend of Orpheus and Eurydice, but it was called *Orfeo* (not *Euridice*) and used a different libretto. Monteverdi's *Orfeo* combined the new style with other musical forms inherited from the Renaissance: the new reciting and song style of the baroque with the orchestral instruments and chorus characteristic of the Renaissance. *Orfeo* was notable for a musical variety, interest, and continuity that the earlier efforts of Peri and Caccini had lacked. And, most important, it demonstrated Monteverdi's remarkable insight into dramatic situations and his understanding of deep emotion. To take an example: when Orfeo is informed of the death of his wife Euridice, he is too overcome with disbelief to grasp his tragedy. But it must be so; and with this realization, Orfeo begins a recitative *"Tu se' morta"* ("Thou art dead") that becomes more and more impassioned as his loss becomes real to him and as he sings of his resolve to enter the dread underworld and rescue Euridice.

Monteverdi's last opera was written thirty-five years later (1642) for Venice, where he had gone in 1613 as *maestro di cappella* to St. Mark's. This work, *L'Incoronazione di Poppea* (*The Coronation of Poppea*), a thoroughly immoral story, concerned Poppea, the mistress of Nero, and her successful attempt to depose his wife, the Empress Octavia. The change in the operatic form since the beginning of the seventeenth century may be noted in connection with *Poppea*. For one thing, the old mythological type of libretto was replaced by one drawn from actual history. Genuine historical figures are in themselves more believable as real persons than the Orfeos and Euridices of legend, and from the splendid libretto that Busenello wrote for *Poppea* Monteverdi made the most of portraying the characters of Nero, Poppea, Octavia, and Seneca. In his last opera Monteverdi brought to musical characterization a vivid reality of which only the greatest opera composers like Mozart and Verdi have been capable.

The dramatic story of *Poppea* unfolds musically through a combination of recitative, aria, and arioso (more lyrical in character than the recitative but not in a set form like the aria). Monteverdi made little use of the chorus, and the instrumental forces are reduced to the minimum of a string orchestra. In short, compared with *Orfeo, Poppea* showed a marked economy of musical forces, possibly because in this opera everything but the singers is redundant to the realization of the drama. It is possible, too, that Monteverdi had more elaborate forces in mind and that what remains is only a sketch. Possibly the advent of the commercial opera had its influence. In 1637 the first public opera house opened in Venice, and, like all such commercial operatic ventures since, the management doubtless pampered its "stars" and skimped on everything else, in this case, the chorus and the orchestra.

One of the most remarkable moments in *Poppea* is the death scene of Seneca. The latter, tutor and adviser to Nero, will not consent to the plans of Nero and Poppea to depose Octavia, and as a result his death is ordered by Nero. In the scene in question, Seneca is urged by his friends to escape, but he will have none of it (this scene bears a striking family resemblance to the last hours of Socrates as related in the *Phaedo* of Plato). The time has come, says Seneca, to put into practice and deeds the virtues for which he stands, and his arioso *"Amici, amici, e junta l'hora"* ("My friends, the hour has come") is a remarkable musical portrait of Seneca's dignity and persistent virtue in the face of certain death (Ex. 90).

After the first years of the seventeenth century Monteverdi employed the new expressive style in his other secular vocal forms. His earlier madrigals fall in the sixteenth century, and are composed in Renaissance style. But after 1614 the madrigals employ the figured bass and frequently use instruments in the *concertato* style. The individual melodic lines of many of the later madrigals are more harmonic in character, and the old idea of the polyphonic madrigal is abandoned for forms more clearly inspired by soloists and a dramatic text. To achieve greater agitation of expression in his dramatic texts, Monteverdi claimed to have invented a new style, a style of excitement (*stile concitato*); and his chief manner of exciting his listeners turned out to be the string tremolo, an indispensable adjunct of all opera ever since. (For tremolo, see Ex. 69a.)

Some of his last "madrigals" were more like scenes from opera. The title of his Eighth Book of Madrigals (1638) indicated the change: *Madrigals of War and Love with some pieces in the theatrical manner* (*Madrigali guerrieri et amorosi con alcuni opusculi in genere rappresentativo*). One of these pieces, *"Non havea Febo ancora,"* is set for three men's voices and soprano solo with figured *continuo,* and falls into three parts. The first, sung by the three men, describes the setting; the second, a soprano solo aria (*"Lamento della Ninfa"*) is accompanied by the men's parts sympathizing with the solo *Ninfa* as "she laments for the lover she has

Ex. 90

SENECA

A-mi-ci, a-mi-ci, è giun-ta, è giun-ta l'ho-ra di pra-ti-

ca-re in fat-ti quel-la vir-tù che tan-to ce-le-bra-i.

Bre-ve an-go-scia è la mor-te,— un so-spir pe-re-gri-no e-sce dal

co-re, o-ve è sta-to mol-t'an-ni qua-si in ho-spi-tio, co-me fo-ra-

stie-ro; e se ne vo - - - - - - - la al-l'O-

lim-po del-la fe-li-ci-tà sog-gior-no____ ve-ro.

lost"; in the third part, the men briefly conclude. In the "*Lamento,*" the singers are accompanied only by a figured bass, the bass itself being a four-note *ostinato* figure (for *ostinato,* see p. 187). In this piece we hardly know which to admire more: the extraordinary emotional impact of the music or the technical virtuosity of the composer that made it possible. With this aria (and an earlier one in his opera *Arianna,* 1608) Monteverdi created a definite *genre* called the *lamento aria* devoted to the lamentings of the deserted or despairing lover. The *lamento aria* was widely imitated throughout the seventeenth century, a famous example being Purcell's *Dido* aria, "When I am laid in earth" (see p. 117).

After the death of Monteverdi, the dramatic opera was carried on by his pupil Pietro Cavalli (1602–76). But it was not long before the ideals of the Italian opera began to change. The pre-eminence of the drama was undermined by a more lyric concept of opera, and the formal aria became increasingly important (e.g., in the works of Marc'Antonio Cesti, 1618–69). In the later seventeenth century the lyrical opera developed rapidly in Naples. Its chief representative was Alessandro Scarlatti, whose role in eighteenth-century opera will be described later.

The opera began in Italy, but it spread rapidly through Europe. Not only was the opera something new, but it was attractive in other respects. It allied a number of the arts, and it was a spectacle expensive and impressive enough to appeal to the vanity of a sovereign or local potentate rich enough to be interested in adding splendor to his court. Of all forms of music, opera has always been the most expensive, the most glamorous, and the best attended for the least musical reasons, and its support as an adjunct of court life should not surprise anyone who has observed the diamond tiaras in any of the great opera houses of the world.

Suggested Listening

Parrish and Ohl:

  No. 30, Caccini, Madrigal *"Dovrò dunque morire"* (from *Le Nuove Musiche*).

  No. 31, Monteverdi, *"Tu se' morta"* (from *Orfeo*).

Monteverdi's *Orfeo* and his *Coronation of Poppea* have both been completely recorded.

Monteverdi, *"Lamento della Ninfa"* (from his Eighth Book of Madrigals).

Suggested Reading

Denis Arnold and Nigel Fortune (ed.), *The Monteverdi Companion.* London: Faber & Faber, 1968.

Manfred F. Bukofzer, *Music in the Baroque Era.* New York: W. W. Norton & Company, 1947.

D. J. Grout, *A Short History of Opera.* New York: Columbia University Press, 1947.

Leo Schrade, *Monteverdi, Creator of Modern Music.* New York: W. W. Norton & Company, 1950.

Oliver Strunk, *Source Readings in Music History.* London: Faber & Faber, 1952. For Caccini's Preface to *Le Nuove Musiche*.

THE FRENCH COURT OPERA: LULLY

Of all the court opera, the most impressive was unquestionably that of Louis XIV under Jean-Baptiste Lully (1632–87). Born an Italian, Lully went to Paris as a child, and through good fortune and sheer talent for music and intrigue he ingratiated himself with the King. Unhandicapped by any personal regard for ethics or moral values, Lully rose higher and higher in a court whose machinations he thoroughly understood and whose monarch he succeeded in amusing. As a result, Lully died a wealthy and honored man.

But the King's judgment with respect to Lully as an artist was not misplaced, and the monopolistic authority granted to Lully by Louis XIV, making him the absolute artistic dictator of French opera, was precisely the power needed to create a first-class production. Any impresario might well envy Lully. In the whole history of the musical stage it is doubtful if anyone has ever had a more complete control of the details of the production of an opera. In modern times the only musician who has approached the degree of authority enjoyed by Lully is Arturo Toscanini, and even he could not boast the support of a French king.

The opera of Lully was inspired by the Italian opera, notably that of Cavalli (the pupil of Monteverdi), whose operas had been represented on important occasions in Paris, but the final product was markedly different from the Italian model. The French opera must be understood in connection with two dominant traits of the French: their love of the theater and their passion for dancing, expressed especially in the ballet. Prior to the composition of his serious operas (or *tragédies lyriques,* as they were called), Lully had written extensively for the court ballet, in which he and even the King himself had participated as dancers. Except in the recitative, the rhythms of the dance are seldom absent from the Lully opera. Even the arias are permeated with a feeling of dance rhythm. *See Plate 18.*

An exceptional literary standard, expected in the French theater, was maintained in the librettos of Lully's operas, largely as a result of his collaboration with Philippe Quinault, a poet of marked talent, who worked with Lully on twenty operas over a period of fourteen years. The variety and kinds of subjects treated—classical, heroic, allegorical, and pastoral—were an indication of the abilities of both Quinault and Lully in dealing with a wide range of emotional representation. The clarity of expression of these texts was a prime concern to Lully, and he modeled his recitative on the accent, length, and musical pitch of French syllables as they were declaimed by the best actors in the contemporary French theater. As a result, the recitative was more carefully regulated than the Italian recitative. Lully notated it with special care, and it is sometimes called *measured* recitative (*récitatif mesuré*) (See Ex. 91). Sometimes these recitatives were accompanied not merely by the harpsichord but in a more dramatic style by the orchestra. The text of the recitative con-

Ex. 91

ARMIDE (Act I, sc.1)

Je ne tri - om - phe pas du plus vai - llant de tous, Re - naud, pour qui ma haine a tant de vi - o - len - ce, L'In-domp-ta - ble Re - naud é - cha - pe à mon cou - roux.

tained the heart of the drama. The arias were lyrical and decorative but less interesting than the Italian arias, being somewhat simpler and more rhythmic in character. On the other hand, Lully made extensive use of the chorus, a feature less common in Italian opera.

In several respects the orchestra played an important role. It sometimes accompanied the recitatives as well as the arias, and it played for the chorus and the ballet. The orchestral texture was notably sonorous, being scored as a rule in five (not four) string parts. Lully's skill with the orchestra was not a matter of chance, for he first made his reputation as a violinist of remarkable talent. In the *French overture,* Lully created an orchestral form that inaugurated a vogue lasting for years afterward all over Europe. Used in his later works, this species of overture (i.e., the piece played to raise the curtain) opened in a slow, ponderous style characterized by dotted-note rhythms, followed by a rapid section of fugal texture and animated rhythms, and sometimes terminated by a return or reference to the opening section. The character of this overture was suited to the ponderous dignity of the occasion: the assembly of the court for the opening of the opera. The French overture lasted until the middle of the eighteenth century and was used far beyond the confines of French opera. Handel began certain of his Italian operas and English oratorios with it; and, as an independent form, many composers saw its advantages as an instrumental piece for orchestra or solo players. Bach, for example, wrote four orchestral overtures, actually French overtures plus dances.

In 1687 Lully died somewhat prematurely as a result of poor medical care of a wound incurred by—of all things—striking his toe with a stick used to beat time. But his operas continued to dominate the musical stage in France for years, even acting as a dead hand on the dramatic efforts of Rameau after the middle of the eighteenth century.

Suggested Listening
Parrish and Ohl:
   No. 36, Lully, Overture to *Armide.*
Lully, aria *"Plus j'observe"* (*Armide*).
Lully, Minuet (*Amadis*); Gavotte (*Atys*).

ENGLISH OPERA: HENRY PURCELL (1659–95)

Compared with the position enjoyed by Lully in France, Purcell's situation and opportunity for composing opera in Restoration England were quite different. In the first place, the English had never accepted opera. The only comparable form was the *masque,* which resembled the court ballet in France. The central fact of the masque was its dances and related spectacles in which the "masquers" usually wore an exotic disguise (hence the term). The masque was, as a rule, related to some specific occasion, and it was limited to the court, which usually participated actively in its production. Not until the early years of the eighteenth century did England succumb to the rage of Italian opera, and then only as an exotic product of Handel, an imported foreigner.

A large part of English music for the stage in the seventeenth century was precisely that: incidental music for the public theater; and various composers such as Matthew Locke (1675) and Purcell himself compared their unfavorable position with that of opera composers in Italy and France. It is significant that Purcell's *Dido and Aeneas,* his only true opera (that is, a drama represented on the stage and composed to music from beginning to end), was produced in a girls' boarding school, despite the fact that Purcell was connected for most of his life with the Restoration court. Purcell composed an astonishing amount of incidental music for the theater, some of which was so extensive that it might be called "semi-opera." The music for *King Arthur, Diocletian,* and *The Fairy Queen* (which includes a full-scale masque) was as lengthy, ironically enough, as that for *Dido and Aeneas,* but the music of these "semi-operas" (all the above-mentioned composed after *Dido*) was incidental to a play and was not conceived as an organic whole.

Purcell composed *Dido and Aeneas* about 1689, toward the end of his short life. As in so much of the art of the English Restoration, the influence of the French was strong. The Lully operas, all of which preceded Purcell's opera, furnished the external model. Thus the recitative was carefully measured, the arias betrayed the influence of dance rhythms, the ballet was featured, and the chorus and French overture were used with telling effect. But Purcell was a composer of such marked individual genius that he transcended his model. He excelled at setting English texts, and while his recitative is measured in the manner of Lully, its musical effect is quite different. The variety of his rather mannered rhythms is as astonishing as effective, and by the manipulation of the relative lengths of English syllables in his arias and recitatives, Purcell gave special emphasis—more than was possible in ordinary speech—to what he wished to bring out. (For an example of Purcell's declamation, see p. 122.) The choruses, as monumental and sonorous as those of Lully, are somewhat more interesting musically and more closely related to the action, often following an aria without a break and sometimes being related to it thematically. It is not surprising that Handel took Purcell's choruses as a point of departure for his chorus style in the oratorios. A favorite device of Purcell's, the *ostinato,* is used with remarkable success in some of the arias of *Dido*. The *ostinato* was common also in the works of Lully, but Purcell's use of it is especially distinguished and personal to him. In the last aria of this opera, Dido, abandoned by Aeneas, sings of her approaching death in a wonderfully expressive song, "When I am laid in earth, remember me, but ah, forget my fate," accompanied by strings over a chromatic *ostinato*. (For the music of this aria, see p. 117.) *Dido and Aeneas* has the lasting attraction of solid dramatic qualities and beautiful music; and one can only imagine what other masterpieces of opera Purcell might have written under different conditions, or if, like Schubert, he had not died while still a young man. *See Plates 20 and 22B.*

Suggested Listening

Purcell, *Dido and Aeneas* (it is recorded complete).

Suggested Reading

Edward J. Dent, *Foundations of English Opera*. Cambridge: The University Press, 1928.

Jack A. Westrup, *Purcell*. New York: E. P. Dutton & Co., 1937.

SACRED MUSIC: GABRIELI. MONTEVERDI. CARISSIMI. SCHÜTZ.

The sacred music of the seventeenth century was a stronghold of polyphony, but it was also markedly affected by the addition of instruments (*concertato* style) and by the new expressive style and forms of the opera. On the one hand, Masses and motets were still cast in the style of sixteenth-century polyphony (for example, by Felice Anerio, Palestrina's successor as composer to the Papal chapel). On the other, some sacred music adopted the recitative and aria of the musical theater; or it employed all sorts of instrumental combinations and vocal resources, from a solo voice to a multichorus style resembling the "colossal" architecture of certain contemporary baroque buildings.

Giovanni Gabrieli (d. 1612) was a pioneer in the *concertato* style. In his motet *In Ecclesiis* (included in the *Processional and Ceremonial;* see p. 155) he combined the double-chorus effects traditional to Venice with instrumental accompaniment, especially the organ and the brass, using the new dissonances and sonorities more characteristic of the early baroque.

In Monteverdi, too, we may see this Janus-like face of sacred music. Some of his sacred music was archaic in imitation of the strict polyphony of the sixteenth century; but there were other pieces of revolutionary character with solo, chorus, and instruments, much closer to the expressive style of his operas—an instance being the extended "Vespers" in twelve sections, *Vespro della Beata Virgine da concerto.* A good example of the "colossal" style, and something of a musical curiosity, was written by a compatriot of Monteverdi: Benevoli's Mass for voices and instruments, fifty-three voice parts in all, arranged in a number of choirs, and written for the dedication of the Salzburg Cathedral in 1628.

The most direct imitation of the opera in sacred music in the seventeenth century is found in the oratorios of Giacomo Carissimi (1605–74). By their very nature these pieces, sacred but not liturgical (i.e., not for the service), lent themselves to dramatic representation, and the contemporary style of the opera was logically adopted. The oratorio proper began in the sixteenth century as a dramatic presentation of edifying and uplifting themes mostly drawn from Bible stories. In Rome, St. Philip Neri encouraged this type of music in the late sixteenth century, and it was performed in the Oratory (*oratorio:* hence the name) of his newly built church, Santa Maria in Vallicella. St. Philip died in 1595, but the oratorios continued, after 1600 set mainly in the new style in imitation of the opera, although not staged.[4] The best of these pieces are the oratorios of Carissimi, and his masterpiece, *Jephthah,* contains moments of impressive beauty. Set in Latin, it is comparable in its musical characteristics to the contemporary opera, using recitative (sung by the *Historicus,* that is, the narrator), arias, ariosos, and choruses. Unlike the opera, these oratorios commonly used an opening and closing chorus.

In Germany, the most important composer of sacred music was Heinrich Schütz (1585–1672). The favorite pupil of Giovanni Gabrieli (and later, a pupil of Monteverdi), Schütz brought the Italian *concertato* style of his master back to Germany, thus combining the currents of German and Italian music. He composed a variety of pieces in the *concertato*

---

[4] Cavalieri's *Representation of the Body and Soul,* 1600, is typical of the subject matter of the oratorio. But since this work was actually represented on the stage, it is sometimes called a sacred opera.

style, some of them simply scored for one or two voices with figured *continuo,* some for large ensembles of a number of voices and instruments, such as trombones, "cornetts," strings, and organ. In his *Seven Words of Christ on the Cross* (1645) Schütz used the oratorio style: choruses to open and close the work, independent instrumental pieces (in this case called *sinfonia*), and dramatic action related by the recitative. The reflective moments are set in aria or arioso style accompanied by the figured bass. The voice of Christ is singled out for the special accompaniment of three instruments, a distinction that foreshadows a similar style of accompaniment by Bach in his *St. Matthew Passion*. Schütz also left motets in an archaic style; and his last works, four settings of the Passion story (according to Matthew, Mark, Luke, and John), revert to a severe, unaccompanied polyphony in which choruses alternate with an unaccompanied chantlike recitation.

Schütz did not set German chorale tunes, although he composed music for the psalms in simple hymn style. But Hermann Schein (1586–1630) adapted the *concertato* style to chorale settings; and many other composers used the chorale in various ways in the service of the Protestant Church. Their use in the church cantata will be discussed briefly in connection with Bach.

The most characteristic and successful use of the chorale occurred not in vocal but in instrumental music, the organ chorale prelude. The German organists of the seventeenth century began to treat the chorale in various ways: sometimes it was set out simply in relatively long notes and accompanied with figurations; sometimes the chorale itself was broken up into sections, and each treated in imitation somewhat in the manner of a motet. Among the best composers of chorale preludes at this time were Samuel Scheidt (1587–1654) at the beginning of the century, and Johann Pachelbel (1653–1706) and Dietrich Buxtehude (1637–1707) at its end. Some of these settings served the purpose of accompanying the congregational singing of the chorale; and others were used by the organist for *solo* instrumental preludizing upon the chorale melody. The pieces of Pachelbel and Buxtehude represent the immediate background for the most beautiful and profound of all the organ chorale preludes, those of J. S. Bach in the early eighteenth century (see p. 207).

French sacred music was partly modeled on the Italian—witness the influence of Carissimi on the oratorios of Marc-Antoine Charpentier—but this was less so in the case of sacred music in England. The secularized church music of the Restoration was typically the anthem or verse anthem of John Blow and Purcell. The verse anthems in particular were similar in style to Purcell's dramatic music, comprising choruses and solos (the verse) for one, two, and occasionally more soloists. These anthems were sometimes accompanied by the organ from the figured bass, and sometimes by the orchestra (including orchestral interludes in some of

Purcell's anthems). They often concluded with a short "Hallelujah" chorus, a type that Handel adopted in a number of choruses. An especially beautiful anthem of Purcell, "Thou knowest, Lord, the secrets of our hearts," was composed for the funeral of Queen Mary (1695). A moving piece of music set in simple style, this anthem was used at his own funeral later in the same year.

The sacred music of the seventeenth century is still relatively little heard compared with the motets and Masses of the late sixteenth century or the Bach cantatas and Handel oratorios of the eighteenth. There are doubtless good reasons for this neglect, one being that many pieces are simply not interesting enough. But this excuse will not serve in the case of the best music of the time, that of Gabrieli, Monteverdi, Schütz, Carissimi, and Purcell. The neglect of their masterpieces may be laid partly to lack of easily accessible performing editions and to the difficulties of assembling the large forces of voices and instruments often required. In recent years, however, more and more of this music has been performed in concert, occasionally in churches, and on phonograph records. To this pioneering we owe the restoration of an important if little-known repertory of music, the best of which strikes us with the freshness of its invention, the brilliance and richness of its vocal and instrumental coloring, and the emotional depths of the religious convictions that gave it life.

Suggested Listening

Parrish and Ohl:

No. 32, Carissimi, Scene from *The Judgment of Solomon.*

No. 33, Schütz, sacred cantata (Concerto), *"O Herr, hilf."*

Carissimi, *Jephthah* has been recorded complete.

Schütz, *Seven Last Words* has been recorded. For a selection of the music, see Willi Apel and Archibald T. Davidson (eds.), *Historical Anthology of Music: Baroque, Rococo, and Pre-Classical Music* (Cambridge, Mass.: Harvard University Press, 1950) No. 201.

Buxtehude, chorale prelude *"Wie schön leuchtet der Morgenstern."*

Purcell, verse anthem *"Rejoice in the Lord alway."*

Suggested Reading

Manfred F. Bukofzer, *Music in the Baroque Era.* New York: W. W. Norton & Company, 1947.

12. *The Instrumental Music of the Seventeenth Century*

BESIDES THE OPERA, the most characteristic new development in seventeenth-century music was the flowering of instrumental music. Composers originated new forms suited to instrumental music *per se* and new styles appropriate to individual instruments, especially the newly invented violin. Unsupported by a text, instrumental music had to create in abstract design; and in the case of existing forms, especially those based on vocal models, it had to find methods of expansion more suited to a new idiom and to the ambitions of creative minds. In this respect the composers of the seventeenth century were no different from artists of every time and place, who can never be satisfied merely with the *status quo*, but must constantly search for new means of expression appropriate to themselves, the times in which they live, and the means at hand.

Apart from accompanying vocal music, instrumental music as an independent art was faced with two main problems: developing an idiomatic style and achieving length. The latter, being a problem common to all the forms of instrumental music, was the more general one, and, on the whole, the more difficult to solve. It is fascinating to observe how composers of the time solved the problem of length in terms of what they had and what they lacked. The early seventeenth-century composer inherited a modal system (for the modes, see p. 35) grounded in vocal polyphony. He had relatively few harmonic resources because harmony *as chord progressions* was in an experimental stage and the variety inherent in modulation (going from one key to another) was strictly limited to a few keys closely related to the main key of the piece. As a typical result, composers tried to achieve length by a number of statements of the same idea without modulating, or by combining relatively short sections into some kind of a whole. This explains the seventeenth-century vogue of the theme and variations, which did not require the resource of modulation, but which restated the same idea in a number of varied ways while staying in the same key. In addition, the variation was an excellent testing ground for exploiting different figurations suited to a particular instrument. The lack of a developed harmony also explains the growth of types of music consisting of a number of relatively short movements, for example, the suite and the sonata. The "free" forms, such as the prelude and the toccata, achieved length only by incorporating other forms and textures within them; and the forms of polyphony, for instance, the fugal types, often borrowed certain techniques of variation to expand their normal limitations. At the very end of the seventeenth century the situation changed as the harmonic process became clarified and as the scope of modulation expanded. At that time the variety inherent in an expanded scheme of key change permitted composers to achieve a far greater length than before. In the case of the fugue, for instance, a single subject could be developed at great length by means of modulating from one key to another while using the manifold devices of polyphony already known.

Like music with texts, instrumental music served different functions. In the theater it was used largely as accompaniment or for certain forms essential to the opera, for example, the overture. Instrumental music for the church was related, first of all, to the organ, which was physically centered there; the chorale prelude, certain types of functional toccatas, and various fugal forms were intimately connected with the organ. Finally, one type of sonata, the "church" sonata (*sonata da chiesa*) was performed in church.

By way of contrast, the other type of seventeenth-century sonata, the "chamber" sonata (*sonata da camera*) was chamber music, as indicated by the title. The *sonata da camera,* originally an Italian form of chamber music, consisted of dances similar to those of the dance suite, another species of chamber music. A more traditional form, the *fantasia* or *fancy,* persisted for a long time in England. It was inseparably connected with the ensembles of viols, the amateurs who cherished them, and an archaic polyphony. Other pieces, such as the keyboard variations, fall in the category of chamber music; and, surprisingly enough from a modern point of view, certain pieces for the orchestra, such as the early *concerto grosso,* should be classified as chamber music, since they were so intended. The modern concert hall did not yet exist.

The styles that existed side by side in the seventeenth century naturally made themselves felt in instrumental as well as in vocal music. The old polyphony continued in such fugal forms as the *ricercar, canzona,* and *fancy,* modified by new structural devices and presented in the idioms and typical figurations of contemporary instruments. Some of the old dances continued, but new ones rapidly displaced them. The new expressive style had its closest instrumental parallel in such "free" forms as the toccata; while the purely instrumental designs and idioms were worked out most thoroughly in the variation and the sonata.

It was in the last two that the new violins found their most characteristic expression. In the same way, the lute and the harpsichord developed idioms peculiar to themselves in suites of dances, variations, and sometimes polyphonic pieces. But polyphony is more congenial to the sustained tone of the organ or to ensembles of melodic instruments. Actually, a number of the forms were exploited by all sorts of instruments. Still, some types are more suited than others to a particular form. Dance music is not especially suited to the organ; and, on the other hand, the chorale prelude cannot be imagined on the lute.

RICERCAR. CANZONA. FANTASIA.

The types of polyphonic imitation, especially the *ricercar, canzona,* and *fantasia,* were developed in a remarkable way by the seventeenth-century keyboard players, particularly the organists. At the beginning of the century these forms resembled the sixteenth-century motet or chanson; at the end of the century they had been transformed to fugal types that served as immediate models for J. S. Bach. The composers most closely connected with this change were the organists J. P. Sweelinck (c. 1562–1621) in Amsterdam, Girolamo Frescobaldi (1583–1643) in Rome, J. J. Froberger (1616–67) in Vienna, and two others already discussed, Pachelbel and Buxtehude in Germany. Bach was most influenced by the two last mentioned, particularly by Buxtehude's dramatic style of figuration. To a lesser degree, the polyphonic forms were developed also in certain types of ensemble music, notably the fancies for viols and the *sonata da chiesa* (see below). The English music for viols, already archaic by mid-seventeenth century, came to an end with the Purcell *Fantasias* of 1680.

Suggested Listening
Parrish and Ohl:
   No. 34, Frescobaldi, *Ricercar dopo il Credo* for organ.
Buxtehude, Prelude and Fugue in E minor.
Purcell, *Fantasia* No. 9 (four voices).

PRELUDE AND TOCCATA. FRESCOBALDI.

The prelude and the toccata, later associated with the fugue as "prelude and fugue" or "toccata and fugue," began as independent types. The prelude and the toccata were called "free" forms because no special form was associated with them. In early times a certain type of prelude originated in the need to try an instrument with a few chords and running passages after it had been tuned—no unnecessary thing in the case of a complicated lute tuning. Later, the prelude became a prelude to another piece, in the sense of "prelude and fugue," and in this functional capacity the prelude might assume any one of a number of forms.

The toccata, originating in the sixteenth century, had an elaborate development in the seventeenth. Ordinarily it was more ambitious than the prelude, and often implied a certain degree of elaborate figuration and virtuoso technique (as in Buxtehude). Actually, there were a number of toccata types. A functional significance is implied by the title of Frescobaldi's *Toccata for the Elevation of the Host,* indicating its role in the Mass. This particular toccata illustrates the quiet, almost aimless, wandering from chord to chord that characterizes the typical organ preludizing; and the somewhat chromatic harmony is reminiscent of the expressive style of the early seventeenth century from which Frescobaldi's *Toccata* comes. The structural elaboration of the toccata is seen in another type: after a first section in preludelike style, the toccata continues without pause with a second section, actually a fugal type like the *ricercar,* and then returns (optionally) to the music of the first preludelike section. This species of toccata illustrates how the composer succeeded in attaining length by combining two forms in a continuous whole. An interesting survival of this kind of toccata is Bach's celebrated Toccata and Fugue in D minor. Bach originally labeled this piece "Toccata," a correct title for a traditional form; but certain later editors, knowing better than Bach, gave it the double title by which it is known today.

One final point about the prelude and toccata: they were free forms, and many of them had a rhapsodic character realized best by a certain freedom of time and spontaneity on the part of the performer. François Couperin, the greatest French harpsichordist of the early eighteenth century, expressed the point perfectly when he wrote about his own preludes:

> While these Preludes are written in measured time, there is a conventional style to be observed. A Prelude is a free composition, in which the imagination follows all that occurs to it. But since geniuses capable of spontaneous invention are rarely found, those who use these set Preludes must play them freely without binding themselves to strict time, unless I have specifically indicated it by the term *mesuré.*
>
> *L'Art de toucher le clavecin,* Paris, 1716.

Suggested Listening
Parrish and Ohl:
  No. 37, Pachelbel, Toccata in E minor, for Organ.
Frescobaldi, *Toccata for the Elevation of the Host.*

THE DANCE SUITE

The dance suite did not come into being *as such* until the late seventeenth century. Prior to that time dances were grouped together for purposes of dancing, but largely in pairs, such as the *pavane* and *galliard,* so characteristic of the sixteenth century. At first most of this music served the purpose of actual dancing, and collections of dance music of early times typically grouped a number of the same kinds of dances together. The particular dances required were then selected and played as the occasion demanded. In the course of the seventeenth century this situation changed; new dances came into fashion, and dances were grouped together as art forms of instrumental music no longer intended for dancing.

Elementary groupings of this kind occurred in French lute and harpsichord music after 1650. Composers put together dances such as the *allemande, courante, sarabande,* and *gigue.* These dances were all in the same tonality, but no fixed order prevailed, and the number of dances varied from piece to piece. As a matter of fact, the make-up of the suite has never been really fixed except in textbooks; and although the dances named above might be called the "key" dances, especially in the eighteenth century, many other kinds of dances were used, among them the *gavotte,* the *minuet,* the *passepied,* and the *bourrée.* But to return to the French: the lutanists and harpsichordists (e.g., Gaultier, Chambonnières) lightened the texture by defining the melody better and by accompanying it with a relatively simple and transparent harmony; and they added certain specific ornaments, such as trills (see the Glossary) that gave a stylized elegance to their pieces. This French dance style spread all over Europe in the late seventeenth and early eighteenth centuries. Froberger was much influenced by the French style after his visit to Paris (c. 1660).[1]

It is impossible to describe the character of all these dances. For one thing, many of them have a long life and history of change. The *sarabande,* for example, officially defined as "slow and stately," was originally a wild dance so suggestive and abandoned that its participants and even onlookers, if apprehended by the wrong people, were punished by death. However, a discussion of general characteristics may be helpful, and below, the rhythms of certain dances from a *sonata da camera* of Corelli are given (see p. 186). The old custom of pairing dances as in the *pavane* and *galliard* persisted in many suites of the seventeenth century. The suite often began with an *allemande* and *courante* (or the Italian type, *corrente*). The *allemande* was in moderate duple time, the *courante,* in a faster triple time. This arrangement originated in the custom whereby all the dancers, including those of ripe age, danced a moderate measure first,

---

[1] The term *partita* is used to describe the dance suite in some instances. This is confusing, especially since the same term is occasionally used to mean the variation.

followed by a more strenuous dance that featured leaping movements and the retirement of all but the young and athletic. The *sarabande* in triple time reverted to a slow tempo as a rule, and the *gigue* concluded in sprightly $\frac{6}{8}$ or $\frac{12}{8}$ time,—compound triple time with two or four basic beats to the measure.

The internal construction of each dance was conditioned by the requirements of the dance, and as a result phrase structures of four measures plus four measures and similar symmetrical schemes were common. Furthermore, the dance was ordinarily broken in the middle by a double bar with repeat marks, thus:

———————————— : ‖ : ———————————— : ‖

At the first double bar the music arrived at a cadence and generally at a contrasted key; and in the second part it worked back to the original key. This form, called the *dance* form for the obvious reason of its origin, had a long development, and from it a number of later forms took their departure (cf. p. 34).

Suggested Listening
Parrish and Ohl:
   No. 35, Froberger, Suite in E minor, for clavichord.

THE SONATA: THE CHURCH SONATA, THE CHAMBER SONATA. CORELLI.

One of the most important formal and idiomatic developments of seventeenth-century instrumental music took place in the evolution of the sonata, chiefly worked out in ensembles involving the violin family. The violin, which originated in the sixteenth century, was the new instrument par excellence of the seventeenth century, and the violin family rapidly displaced the older family of viols. In general, the idiomatic development of the violin took the form of two different styles: first, a *cantabile* (song) style modeled on the voice; and second, and more peculiar to the instrument, a style of figuration and running passages based on its technical capabilities. The point is illustrated by two passages taken from a piece by Corelli: the first shows the vocal style (Ex. 92a), at least in principle; the second, the figuration (Ex. 92c). It should be noted that the cantabile imitation of the voice was sometimes more apparent than real, since this bare outline of slow cantabile movement was ornamented in performance (just as it was in the voice), as shown in Example 92b.

The problem of abstract design was inherent in the sonata, especially the "church" sonata, from the beginning. Its complicated evolution from

Ex. 92

earlier forms (such as certain types of *canzonas*) cannot be discussed here. Instead we will describe the end result: the sonata as it appeared in its first clearly established form in the music of Arcangelo Corelli (1653–1713) during the last twenty years of the seventeenth century. Typically, the sonata existed in two basic types: (1) the *sonata da chiesa* (church sonata) and (2) the *sonata da camera* (chamber sonata). Each of these types could be expressed in one of two kinds of instrumentation: (1) the *trio sonata* with two solo parts accompanied by the figured bass; and (2) the *solo sonata,* accompanied by the figured bass.[2] Ideally, the latter was played by the *continuo* player (on the cello, viola da gamba, or string bass) and "realized" by the keyboard player. Consequently, the figured bass implied the services of two players in performance; and hence the trio sonata (the trio referring to the three melodic lines of the score) was ideally performed by four players, and, even more curious, the solo sonata by three (soloist, *continuo* player, and keyboard player). While strings were by far the most common medium, other instruments, such as the flute and oboe, were used increasingly in the late seventeenth and early eighteenth centuries.

The *sonata da camera* is closely related to the suite. The typical Corelli sonata of this sort begins with a prelude of undefined character and is followed by three dances as a rule. In Sonata No. 8 of Corelli's solo sonatas (Op. V) the order of movements is as follows: *Preludio—Allemanda—Sarabanda—Giga.* The opening of each of these dance movements is given in Example 93 to indicate the different character of typical dances. Each of these pieces is divided by the usual double bar in the middle.

---

[2] A "solo" sonata, in the modern sense of a single player, was relatively rare; so rare, in fact, that the absence of a figured bass was usually indicated by a specific title such as *senza basso* (without bass).

Ex. 93

The church sonata is more abstract. A typical piece of this kind has four movements: *slow—fast—slow—fast.* All these movements are relatively short compared with sonata movements with which we are more familiar today (e.g., Beethoven's piano sonatas). The first slow movement often has something of the character of an introduction. The second movement is typically a species of fugue. The third movement, again slow, is often cantabile in nature; and the last is usually a *gigue,* or it maintains a *gigue*-like rhythm.

Many composers contributed to the sonata in the seventeenth century. Purcell, for instance, wrote twenty-two. But the most influential of all was Corelli. His forty-eight trio sonatas and twelve solo sonatas enjoyed an immense popularity in their own time and for years afterward. They were considered the indispensable equipment for the violinist. And no wonder: they were so perfectly written for the violin that they almost played themselves, and at the same time they were full of inventive fancy as regards the thematic material and the sonorous capabilities of the instrument.

Suggested Listening
Parrish and Ohl:
No. 39, Corelli, *Sonata da chiesa* (trio) in E minor (Op. III, No. 7).
Corelli, *Sonata da camera* (solo) in E minor (Op. V, No. 8).

THE VARIATION. THE OSTINATO. CHACONNE *AND* PASSACAGLIA.

As we have already seen, the theme and variations was especially favored in the seventeenth century for two reasons: it offered one logical way to solve the problem of length, and the individual variations were ideal for exploiting the new instrumental figurations. Starting with the English virginalists in the early seventeenth century, one could mention many instances of the variation. But it is more fruitful to consider other aspects of the variation, chiefly two: the *ostinato* and related forms, and the principle of thematic variants.

The word *ostinato* refers to the continuous repetition of a melodic line in such a way that it has structural significance—individual *ostinatos* vary in length from four or five notes to more than eight measures. In this scheme, the *ostinato* figure is the central element to which all else is related, and it serves the same function, although in a different technical way, as a theme serves in a theme and variations. The *ostinato* is most often stated in the bass. Several examples of this *basso ostinato* have already been cited: the *"Lamento della Ninfa"* of Monteverdi (four-note *ostinato*) and the final aria of Purcell's opera *Dido and Aeneas* (a five-measure *ostinato;* see p. 117).

Another type, related in spirit to the *ostinato,* is a variation created by the repetition of a set scheme of harmonies. The harmonic progression is constant, but in each successive variation the figuration or some other feature changes to produce the variation. The proper terminology for the *ostinato* and the fixed harmonic scheme has been the subject of much debate. Today the *ostinato* type is most frequently called the *passacaglia;* while the fixed-scheme type is called a *chaconne.* But, as a matter of fact, it is almost impossible to make hard and fast distinctions between what is proper to each.[3] Another common type, depending on such repetitive schemes, is the *folia* (or *follia*).

Apart from the variation proper, the *principle* of variation served the seventeenth-century composer well, especially in the role of thematic variants. Just as the theme of the *Blue Danube Waltz* can be turned into the *Blue Danube Fox Trot,* the theme of a *pavane* can be used in the different rhythm of the *galliard.* It sometimes happened, too, that the several movements of a sonata were thematic variants of each other (Ex. 94), and this idea was even applied to the different sections of pieces in imitation, as sometimes happened in the *ricercar.*

Ex. 94

movement II   *movement V*

All in all, the idea of variation played an important part in the development of instrumental music of the seventeenth century. It is a manner of extending and developing music that will always have its attractions; and,

[3] On this point, see the different opinions of Apel, in the *Harvard Dictionary of Music,* and Bukofzer, in *Music in the Baroque Era.*

as Bach, Beethoven, and Brahms, among others, showed, it had possibilities far beyond the wildest dreams of the seventeenth century. After 1700, however, a more developed harmony and a complete system of modulation opened up new vistas of composition, and the role of the variation became relatively less important among musical forms.

Suggested Listening
Parrish and Ohl:
No. 38, Purcell, Ground for Harpsichord, *A New Ground* ("ground" means *ostinato*).
Corelli, *La Follia* (solo sonata, Op. V, No. 12).

Suggested Reading
Robert U. Nelson, *The Technique of Variation.* Berkeley and Los Angeles: University of California Press, 1948.

In music, the seventeenth century was something of a transitional period, studded with individual works of great beauty and interest. That it did not produce, with any consistency, works comparable in quality to the best of the sixteenth and eighteenth centuries is understandable in view of its intense preoccupation with invention and experiment. However, an examination of any substantial body of art, literature, or music should afford various pleasures, derived partly from the individual pieces themselves and partly from relating them to other points of reference more or less familiar. The music of the seventeenth century is an apt illustration of the point. The individual masterpieces of Monteverdi, Purcell, Corelli, and others give us pleasure in themselves as music, and we respond to them emotionally according to individual taste and capacity. At the same time, we relate these pieces with heightened satisfaction to the whole musical development of the time and to later pieces with which we are more familiar. The resulting expansion of knowledge and the cultivation of taste that knowledge implies are central to the main problem of the listener and this book, namely, the fullest possible enjoyment and appreciation of the individual masterpiece.

13. *The Early Eighteenth Century: Opera and Secular Cantata. Sacred Music.*

PRELIMINARIES

THE EXTRAVAGANCE, exuberance, and restlessness that characterized much of the youthful art of the early baroque were greatly tempered by time and the evolving conventions of music itself in the course of the seventeenth century. Many characteristic forms continued into the eighteenth century, but inevitably they became different in spirit, and, as frequently happens in the later stages of any movement, there was a tendency to formalize inherited styles and forms. This is not at all surprising in an age of formal gardens, painting, architecture, and manners—an age that specialized in highly elaborate and conventionalized dress complete with powdered wigs and beauty patches, and in verse forms like the heroic couplet, whose maximum of refined order could conceal, even if it was not meant to, the minimum of inspiration. If manner was not everything, at least the form of expression frequently became more important than the thing expressed.[1]

In the eighteenth century Reason was held to be capable of solving every problem—the self-confidence of an age that had not yet heard of Schopenhauer or Freud! After the middle of the century the French Encyclopedists started to codify all knowledge as a guide for human experience, and even religion became a rational subject.

Formalism and rationalism have specific counterparts in music, and the

---

[1] A good deal of nonsense has been said and written about the form and content of works of art, about their inspiration and emotion on the one hand and their forms on the other. The fact is that in *any masterpiece* inspiration extends to form as well as content: that is to say, form and content are two aspects of the same thing; and, by the same token, a masterpiece might be defined in terms of its inspired oneness. Still, there is a point in talking about form *and* content, if only for the reason that the later stages of any style of expression tend to develop formulas in which lesser artists take refuge. A high degree of technical and formal competence may characterize a work of art otherwise empty.

opera is a good example of a formalized style of expression in a traditional form. In the early seventeenth century, composers of the opera were dominated by a dramatic spirit which held that the text should be "the master not the servant of the music." In the late seventeenth century this attitude was replaced by a lyric concept of opera in which music was the master. Consequently, set forms, such as the *da capo* aria (see p. 193), which were highly organized in purely musical terms, replaced the earlier type of setting, which was more continuous dramatically and more responsive to each change of word and mood of the drama.

Actually, a new formalism in music resulted partly from increased technical capacity, especially with respect to harmony and modulation. These resources gave music far greater possibilities of length and coherence in purely musical terms, not only in instrumental music—to whose abstract patterns and designs these musical means had been most essential—but in vocal music as well. Most of the old forms were retained at least in name, but the types of figuration were conditioned by the more clearly defined chord progressions of the harmony, still within the figured-bass system. Music, in short, clarified, amplified, and formalized its own designs in terms of its own technical advances. In ornamentation, a similar formal order was introduced: certain ornaments became conventional and stereotyped, and specific signs to indicate them became more numerous.[2]

To a considerable extent, the formal designs and figurations of music were musical in origin, but they were derived partly from ideas of rational procedure. A unity of mood within whole sections or even whole pieces was one artistic goal. Another, closely related to and even conditioned by the first, aimed at the achievement of this mood or emotional state by means of appropriate figures, rhythms, or harmonies. The latter idea, already inherent in seventeenth-century music, became codified in the writings of eighteenth-century theorists, especially toward the end of the baroque period (c. 1750). It is known as the "Doctrine of the Affections," an "affection" (Italian: *affetto*) meaning roughly an emotional state.

According to this musical rationalism, any emotional state could be conjured up by the use of the proper musical ingredients in the same way as $2 + 2 = 4$ or as $H_2 + O =$ water. Thus, love, hate, or fear each had its specific rhythmic, melodic, and harmonic formulas. In somewhat the same manner Erno Rapée's *Motion Picture Moods* codified musical clichés for the movie pianist in the early days of the films. In this book are all the formulas for representing love, hate, fear, as well as custard pie, train smash, fat man, and so on. Reflections of this theory of representing emotion, which had been in the air for decades, can be found in the works of many composers.[3] The mood of sorrow and pain is often expressed in the

---

[2] See the Glossary for *trill, mordent,* and *turn.*

[3] Marc-Antoine Charpentier's *Rules of Composition* (c. 1690) explain the use of different keys "for the expression of the different passions." He lists eighteen different

cantatas and larger vocal works of Bach by chromatic figures that persist
through whole sections (as in the *Crucifixus* in the B minor Mass). In
Purcell's aria "When I am laid in earth" (see p. 117), the chromatic *ostinato* is appropriate to the emotion and tragic fate of Dido. Bach's vocal
or vocally inspired pieces often illustrate a related or collateral principle in
that a typically consistent figuration persists through whole sections,
stresses unity of mood, and is derived from a more or less realistic representation of a *single* word or idea fundamental to the whole thought expressed. In his chorale prelude *Durch Adams Fall ist ganz verderbt*
(*Through Adam's Fall all is lost*), the pedal part of this organ work has a
reiterated figure of a descending interval (diminished 7th), clearly representing *the fall* over and over again [4] (Ex. 95).

Ex. 95

Durch Adams Fall

(PEDAL PART)

The tendency toward concrete representation of texts and specific things
was especially strong in French music because the latter was closely committed to representation in the theater and to the idea of imitation of
nature. This attitude on the part of the French made the progress of instrumental music, especially that which depended largely on abstract design, relatively slow in France. It is significant that the French excelled
in instrumental dance music, but not in the sonata, during the seventeenth
century. The Italian sonata had developed for nearly a century before the
French accepted it and began to contribute to its development early in the
eighteenth century (e.g., with Leclair). Even then the French were somewhat bewildered by an abstract form that had no text and represented

---

"Key-feelings," among them: C major, "Gay and warlike"; E-flat major, "Cruel and
harsh"; E-flat minor, "Horrible, frightful"; A minor, "Tender and plaintive." (See
H. Wiley Hitchcock, "The Latin Oratorios of Marc-Antoine Charpentier" in *The
Musical Quarterly* for January, 1955, p. 58).

[4] Albert Schweitzer, in his book on Bach, first published in 1905, startled the
musical world with his discovery that Bach represented emotional states by certain
corresponding rhythms, melodies, and harmonies. By brilliant intuition and induc-
tion, Schweitzer had discovered Bach's application of the old theory of the affections.

nothing but pure patterns of tone, which they likened to the coldness and inexpressiveness of marble. Fontenelle's question *"Sonate, que me veux-tu?"* (O sonata, what do you want of me?) is typical of the attitude held by many French musicians of the time.

As a matter of fact, the music of France and Italy represented musical attitudes poles apart and as widely divergent as the national temperaments of these two countries. Many amusing passages contrasting these two national types of music occur in eighteenth-century writings. The following is a fair example, taken from Rousseau's article "Genius" in his *Dictionnaire de Musique* (First edition, 1767–8; English translation, c. 1770).

> Would you then wish to know if any spark of this devouring flame inspires you? Be quick, haste to Naples, listen to the masterpieces of Leo, Durante, Jommelli, and Pergolesi. If your eyes are filled with tears, if you feel your heart palpitate, if gaiety agitates you, if sorrow involves you in transports, take Metastasio and labour; his genius will enflame yours. . . . But if the charms of this grand art leave you calm, if you feel no ravishing transports, if you discover nothing beautiful but what barely pleases, dare you demand what genius is? Vulgar mortal, dare not profane that heavenly appellation. What would it avail to thee to know it? Thou canst not feel it. Compose French music, and peaceably retire.

Just as in the seventeenth century, music of the early eighteenth century was classified according to its use for theater, church, or chamber. But the two basic styles of the seventeenth century had changed. To be sure, the old style of polyphony continued, although more conditioned by harmony than formerly, and it was used especially in the instrumental fugue and in church music. But the expressive style of the early seventeenth century, inspired by the immediate realization of text by music, ceased to be so essential. It was displaced by a style more homogeneous musically, and the melody was dictated by purely musical considerations, not by the expressive representation of a text. At the same time, the melodies were distinguished either by a cantabile character or by the addition of figurations and unflagging rhythms, derived from the new style of concerto writing. The latter permeated not only instrumental music, but also the aria, especially the virtuoso aria in the opera. The relatively long arch of melody and the figured bass were the twin magnets of the texture; the inner parts, if they existed, were less important.[5] In some cases the new harmonic style of the comic opera introduced a short-phrased melody and a simple, thin harmony.

[5] The style mentioned here does not include the fugue in which all parts are equally important.

OPERA AND SECULAR CANTATA: ALESSANDRO SCARLATTI. HANDEL. RAMEAU. PERGOLESI. THE BEGGAR'S OPERA.

THE NEAPOLITAN OPERA: ALESSANDRO SCARLATTI

After the middle of the seventeenth century interest in the aria as beautiful music, complete in itself, became more pronounced. In the old dramatic opera, the recitative often passed imperceptibly and continuously to the arioso or the aria, conforming to the continuous changes of the drama. In the lyric opera, the aria was sharply separated from the recitative, and their function and style were quite clearly distinguished. By the end of the seventeenth century Alessandro Scarlatti (1660–1725) had established this new opera as a distinct type in Naples, hence the name "Neapolitan opera." It sharply discriminated between the dramatic and lyrical elements, dividing them into separate compartments, as it were. At any point the story of the drama was related in the recitative, immediately followed by the aria (or sometimes other musical forms), whose purpose was to comment lyrically and reflectively on the action that had just been described in the recitative. In simplest terms, the core of this operatic scheme was a series of short scenes consisting of:

(1) What happened; (2) How someone felt about it.

The recitative took two basic forms: (1) *recitativo secco* or *dry recitative* accompanied by the harpsichord (later, the piano); (2) *recitativo accompagnato* or *accompanied recitative* accompanied by the orchestra. The musical heart of the Neapolitan opera was the aria, and the most characteristic type of aria was the so-called *da capo* aria. Its formal scheme looked like this:

A _____ ⌒ B _____
                    Fine   D.C. (D.S.)

The first section (A) ended on the tonic. The following section (B) was often contrasted in key, character, and sometimes in tempo and the manner of accompaniment. The letters *D.C.* or *da capo* meant to return to the beginning, repeating the first section, the end of which was indicated by a fermata (⌒) or the word *Fine* (end). In practice, the singer was expected to improvise an elaboration of the repeat of the A section. *D.S.* (*dal segno*) meant simply to return "to the sign," a device used if the repeat did not go back to the very beginning.

The *da capo* aria became extremely popular. It is not surprising that it did, and in purely musical terms the *da capo* aria deserved its popularity. The form is eminently satisfactory musically because it is symmetrical, coherent, and varied. Furthermore, the composer, if he was lazy or busy, did not have to write out the first part again; and, at the same time, the singer was allowed liberties in repeating the first section with improvisations, thus giving further variety, and affording an outlet for the singer's vanity and flights of vocal fancy. Modern singers still have plenty of vanity, but they seldom take advantage of the opportunity to improvise in the repeated first part. Times have changed, we no longer improvise freely, and we have forgotten the traditions of the eighteenth century.

The *da capo* aria worked extremely well in a lyrical setting and in a context where it was not required to advance the dramatic action. For the latter it would have been unsatisfactory or even ridiculous. If, for instance, in section A the singer had the lines: "Hercule, I am going to shoot you," followed in B by: "Bang, bang, you are dead," it is ridiculous to repeat A, even with variations. On the other hand, if the above texts were relegated to the recitative, the singer, having shot "Hercule" in a *recitativo,* could reflect lyrically on the situation in a *da capo* aria as follows: A "I'm glad he's dead," followed by B "It should have been done long ago" and then by A, profitably repeated, with improvisations.

There is obviously no point in a beautiful aria unless it is going to be beautifully sung, and the emphasis on the aria was accompanied by a craze for beautiful voices and for beautiful singing as an end in itself (*bel canto*).[6] The result was sometimes the cultivation of virtuosity for its own sake, especially among the *castrati* (male sopranos and altos). The curse of the best composers and poets was the demands of the singers and the public for music, especially arias, that would serve as a vehicle for brilliant individual performance rather than for music and poetry that would together fulfill the demands of the whole opera. Mozart's operetta *Der Schauspieldirektor (The Impresario)* is an amusing commentary on this state of things.

The libretto of a typical Neapolitan opera was drawn from classical history (less often from mythology), and it was arranged in three acts. Of the librettists, Zeno (d. 1750) and Metastasio (d. 1782), who understood the special requirements of the lyrical opera very well, were the most successful. Metastasio's twenty-seven librettos were set over a thousand times in the eighteenth century.

Besides the important recitative and aria, the Neapolitan opera used ensembles of soloists (duets, trios; less often, quartets), but rarely the chorus. Of the purely instrumental pieces, the overture was most usual and most important. This *Italian overture,* or *sinfonia,* as it was sometimes called, differed in arrangement and spirit from the *French overture.* Usually both had three sections, but the Italian overture followed the tempo order

---

[6] Who can say exactly what *bel canto* is? It literally means "beautiful song" or "beautiful singing" and is most closely associated with the Italian style of singing from the seventeenth to the nineteenth centuries.

fast—slow—fast, and in general it was more sprightly, more harmonic in texture, and less pompous than the French overture. While the French overture became obsolete after 1750, the Italian overture or *sinfonia* (i.e., symphony) became important later in the early history of the symphony.

The abuses of the Neapolitan opera were all too evident. The self-sufficiency of the music of the aria was in itself a temptation to disregard the text and to treat the aria with little regard to its context in the opera as a whole. There are amusing contemporary accounts of gentlemen in the boxes of the opera theater who played cards during the recitatives and stopped only to listen to the aria of their particular favorites. Actually, the faults and abuses of the Neapolitan opera were clearly recognized by numerous critics in the early eighteenth century, among them Benedetto Marcello (1686–1739), a composer as well as critic, who wrote (1720) an amusing and penetrating satire *Il Teatro alla Modo* (*Theater à la mode*) on the foibles of singers, their "patrons," the *castrati,* the machinery used to lower gods and goddesses, and, in general, the manifold problems of the composer, librettist, and performers in creating what must have been at its best a splendid, although mannered and highly stylized, musical spectacle.

The whole scheme of the Neapolitan *opera seria* (serious opera) was a highly stylized, even artificial, one, far less realistic than the dramatic opera. Still, the basic idea of separating the narrative and the reflective elements into recitative and aria was a rational solution to what was essentially a musical problem. Hence, there is no use in criticizing this species of opera for lacking a dramatic continuity to which it never pretended. We may criticize the scheme, but once having accepted it we can only comment on its successful realization in individual works. That there were a number of beautiful and successful examples of the Neapolitan opera is shown by a study of the works of Alessandro Scarlatti and especially Handel, whose forty-odd Italian operas are printed and fairly accessible.

THE ITALIAN OPERAS OF HANDEL

To understand George Frideric Handel (1685–1759), we must understand him first of all as a composer of Italian opera, for it was in this capacity that he wrote his first major works and made his reputation. Furthermore, his oratorios reflect his training in the opera. Handel began to compose operas as a young man in Hamburg. Then, after a brilliant success in Italy, he was engaged by the Elector of Hanover (afterwards George I of England) and almost immediately given a leave of absence to visit England.

In London Handel composed his *Rinaldo* (1711), possibly the first really successful Italian opera heard in England. Even with its success, the Italian opera was more of a fashionable spectacle than something for which the

English felt a need or a basic artistic sympathy. For one thing, who could understand a reasonably complicated plot sung entirely in Italian? In the case of *Rinaldo* a remarkably ironic procedure took place: the text, originally in English, had to be translated into Italian so that the English audience could not understand it, or, for that matter, realize that "what is too silly to be said is sung"—to quote an eighteenth-century witticism. Actually, *Rinaldo* was a promising, or rather brilliant, beginning for Handel in England. Addison and Steele wrote satirically about this opera in their *Spectator Papers.* But this should deceive no one, for Addison, in particular, was not a disinterested party. His opera *Rosamund* (music by Clayton) had been a dismal failure four years earlier. *Rinaldo,* on the other hand, sumptuously produced, was an immediate success, and proved to be the foundation of Handel's reputation and the beginning of his long career in England. But this is not the place to trace the complications, fortunes, and misfortunes of the various opera companies with which Handel was associated, or the vicissitudes he suffered at the hands of his royal, aristocratic, or other supporters.[7]

Within the last forty years there has been something of a revival of the Handel operas. A number of these works were performed in Germany, especially in the 1920's and 1930's, and in the United States; and, most recently, substantial parts of single works (*Giulio Cesare,* see below) have been recorded. The problems of reviving a Handel opera are considerable. For one thing, the scheme of writing seems old-fashioned to a modern audience accustomed to Wagner and Verdi. The texts also have to be translated, and the roles originally intended for *castrati* present another difficulty. Since *castrati* no longer exist, the roles assigned to them have to be sung by tenors and basses, and consequently the pitch is lowered by an octave. Unfortunately this change disturbs the sonority and balance of the original with respect to the accompaniment and the other voices. It would be possible to retain the pitch if the *castrati* roles were assigned to women. But this is merely to trade one problem for another. A statuesque female strutting about the stage as Julius Caesar, a role for a *castrato,* would look very strange indeed.

The Handel operas took their point of departure from the Neapolitan model of Alessandro Scarlatti, to which Handel added many individual features of his own. His operas, taken as a whole, reveal many beauties in individual scenes and arias; and sometimes a surprising dramatic tension is achieved quite apart from the lyricism of the arias. In the opening scene of *Giulio Cesare,* for example, one could not ask for a more dramatic or gory scene than that in which Cornelia, the wife of Pompey, is unexpectedly presented with the head of her murdered husband. In this same work, as in others, it is obvious that Handel was thinking in terms of

---

[7] For such interesting matters, see, among others, Newman Flower, *George Frideric Handel* (London: Cassell & Company, 1922; revised edition, 1947).

continuity of scene when he linked several arias together. While the recitatives and arias serve their basic function of narration and lyrical reflection, there is a great variety in the mood and in the accompaniment of the individual aria and accompanied recitative. In the latter, Handel sometimes achieved an extraordinary expression of text, largely through the resources of a most imaginative and fluctuating harmony (e.g., *"Alma del gran Pompeo"* from *Giulio Cesare*). The orchestration and staging are often quite elaborate; and although the recitative and aria system is not conspicuously favorable for characterization, some of the characters in his operas stand out with vivid reality.

Among the most interesting of these Handel works are *Giulio Cesare,* 1724; *Tamerlano,* 1724; *Rodelinda,* 1725; and *Orlando,* 1733.

Suggested Listening

Parrish and Ohl:

No. 44, Handel, Recitative, Sinfonia, and Aria from *Rinaldo.*

Handel, *Giulio Cesare:*

"Presti omai" (virtuoso aria of Caesar).

"Alma del gran Pompeo" (accompanied recitative sung by Caesar).

"Piangerò la sorte mia" (*da capo* aria of Cleopatra).

Suggested Reading

Charles Burney, *A General History of Music.* London, 1776–89. Reprint in modern edition by Frank Mercer; New York: Harcourt, Brace & Co., 1935. Extensive accounts of opera in the eighteenth century by a contemporary.

Edward J. Dent, *Alessandro Scarlatti.* London: E. Arnold & Co., 1905.

D. J. Grout, *A Short History of Opera.* New York: Columbia University Press, 1947.

Oliver Strunk, *Source Readings in Music History.* London: Faber & Faber, 1952. For the text of Marcello's *Il teatro.*

THE FRENCH OPERA: RAMEAU

The other important opera of the time was French, and the most important composer, Jean-Philippe Rameau (1683–1764). Rameau's operas were the products of his later years; he did not write his first opera until he was about fifty years old. One of the first of his operas, *Les Indes Galantes,* was recently revived with great success in Paris. Even with the change and lapse of time since the death of Lully, Rameau still spoke of himself as Lully's successor. Nevertheless, his operas were influenced somewhat by the Italian *bel canto* style and *da capo* form.

By trying to preserve tradition, Rameau pleased few of his critics, but his operas were well received by the public. The Lully adherents, the old guard, criticized his operas with respect to their recitative and librettos (which, in point of fact, were not up to the level of Lully's), and the new progressive Italian adherents of Pergolesi (see p. 199), like Rousseau and the Encyclopedists, criticized Rameau for not following the lead of the Italians.

In general, Rameau preserved the main features of the Lully opera, at least with respect to the externals of the recitative, aria, chorus, and ballet. But like Handel, Rameau began to experiment with the continuous scene. Rameau's orchestration is also far more elaborate and relatively "modern" than Lully's, and certain of Rameau's pieces for instruments alone, depicting earthquakes, thunderstorms, or even monsters (*Dardanus*), are impressive pieces of instrumental program music. At his best, Rameau achieved a monumental and simple grandeur that is comparable to Handel's and that anticipated Gluck's. Compared with Lully's, Rameau's music is more sustained and more grandiose, his ornamentation more elaborate (like the contemporary Rococo decoration), and his melodies and figurations are more inspired by the harmonies that accompany them. The latter is not surprising in a man who first formulated the modern theory of harmony.

Suggested Listening
Parrish and Ohl:
  No. 41, Rameau, Scene from *Castor et Pollux* ("*Séjour de l'éternelle. paix*").
See also the aria "*Tristes apprêts*" from the same opera (1737).

THE SECULAR CANTATA

The opera had a pronounced impact on the forms of vocal chamber music in the early seventeenth century. Precisely the same thing happened in the eighteenth century, for the Neapolitan opera had a marked impact on the chamber cantata. Alessandro Scarlatti wrote an enormous number of chamber cantatas (at least six hundred), which consisted basically of two pairs of recitatives and arias, thus:

Recitative—Aria; Recitative—Aria.

This was one standard scheme of the chamber cantata, in essence an unstaged portion of the contemporary opera, accompanied by the harpsichord or small orchestra. Since these pieces were intended primarily for gatherings of highly sophisticated people, certain cantatas (Scarlatti's in particular) were composed with far more daring harmonies than was the opera. In France, the secular cantata also reflected the opera, using the paired scheme of recitative—aria. But those of Rameau generally used three pairs, not two as in Scarlatti.

THE COMIC OPERA: PERGOLESI. THE BEGGAR'S OPERA.

The comic opera of the eighteenth century was a complete antithesis of the *opera seria*. The plots of the comic opera were relatively simple, intelligible, sometimes sentimental, and, above all, amusing. They concerned themselves with middle-class or even peasant figures familiar to everyday life, not the remote heroes of history or mythology, characteristic of the *opera seria*. In some cases the lyric elements so dominated the *opera seria* that it might as well have been presented as a concert, while the comic opera specialized in dramatic episodes and the sharp delineation of individual character. Moreover, the comic opera was sung in the language of its country, and, except in the Italian *opera buffa* (Italian comic opera), the recitative was replaced by spoken dialogue. Musically, the songs or little arias of the comic opera might be compared to "hit" tunes. In at least one instance, the comic opera made a special and important innovation, the *ensemble finale*. In this, the various characters were assembled on the stage by dramatic means, effectively ending the act by a large ensemble piece that rang down the curtain.

In Italy the comic opera evolved from the *intermezzo*. The latter consisted of a short piece sandwiched between the acts of the serious opera. Thus for a serious opera in the customary three acts, two intermezzi would be essential. An important step was taken when two such intermezzi were made continuous, and, still later, detached from the serious opera and used independently as a two-act comic opera. This is what happened in the case of G. B. Pergolesi's (1710–36) famous *La Serva Padrona* (*The Servant-Mistress*), first performed in Naples (1733). Originally it was played as an intermezzo between the acts of Pergolesi's serious opera *Il Prigionier Superbo,* but it proved so popular that it was detached and played as an independent piece, becoming in this way the first of a long line of *opere buffe*.

Seldom has the musical world surrendered so completely to such an unpretentious piece. The operatic audience welcomed with huzzas a piece that consisted of the simplest of everything: three characters (of whom one is silent!), half a dozen tunes and the necessary recitative to hold them together, and a plot that concerns a scheming maidservant who induces her master to marry her. The secret lay in the catchy and simple tunes and rhythms, the simplicity and interest of the subject matter, and the manner in which the music characterized the situation. In composers like Pergolesi, music found a new voice. The transparent scoring and the clearly defined melodies of short phrases, conditioned by the simple harmony, anticipated a later time, that of the rococo and early Classic period. Needless to say, Pergolesi's work was the signal for the composition of many works of this kind, and, as we shall see, the comic opera had a vigorous development in the late eighteenth century.

In France the comic element was introduced into the *Théâtre de la foire* (Theater of the fair) at the end of the seventeenth century in the form of satire or parody of the serious opera. Characteristic were the folksong-like tunes or *vaudevilles* whose words often mocked the serious opera. For example, the text of a famous song from Lully's *Armide* beginning "The more I observe these places, the more I admire them" became in the parodied version: "The more I observe this roast, the more I desire it." As a mature art form, the French comic opera dates from a later time (see p. 269).

In England, as in France, comic opera began as a parody of the serious opera. A brilliant case of this kind was *The Beggar's Opera* (1728), the libretto by John Gay and music arranged from ballad and other sources by J. C. Pepusch. This comedy was essentially a play with incidental music. The songs, interspersed at appropriate moments in the action, were based on ballad tunes or on popular works of other composers (the stirring song "Let us take the road," which all the highwaymen sing together, was a blatant steal from Handel's *Rinaldo*). *The Beggar's Opera* was excellent theater, marvelous fun, and appealed to a wide audience because it managed to represent a number of things to a number of people. It was a scene from the low life of contemporary London; it was an effective political satire; and it was a parody of Italian opera.[8] It was also a thorn in Handel's flesh, for its great success contributed to the failure of his Italian-opera ventures in London. Because of the ballad origin of many of the tunes, the comic opera in England is properly described as *ballad opera*.

Suggested Listening
The Beggar's Opera and Pergolesi's *La Serva Padrona* have both been recorded complete.

SACRED MUSIC: HANDEL. BACH.

THE ENGLISH ORATORIOS OF HANDEL

Handel began to write oratorios almost by accident. When the Bishop of London refused to allow the Biblical story of *Esther* to be staged, Handel put it on in concert form, and its success naturally suggested that he write other oratorios, especially in view of the low fortunes of his Italian-opera company at that time (1732). Handel's English oratorios had earlier antecedents in the oratorios of Carissimi (see p. 176), and, as a very young man, Handel wrote one or two oratorios on the Italian model. But without Carissimi, Handel would have had no trouble constructing his oratorios from Biblical texts, the musical machinery of his Italian opera,

[8] For details, see the article "Beggar's Opera" in *Grove's Dictionary of Music* (Fifth edition, 1954).

and the English chorus. The infinite variation of these last-mentioned ingredients, rather than the Carissimi model of a century earlier, explains the external elements of the mature Handel oratorio.[9]

The fact is that the mature oratorios, all in English, varied greatly from work to work in tone and technical realization. There were dramatic or "operatic" oratorios which could be staged with little rearranging (e.g., *Samson*) since, besides the expected choruses, they included specific characters assigned to recitative and aria, and were divided into acts.[10] Other oratorios consisted largely of choruses (*Israel in Egypt* is mostly for double chorus); and, at another extreme, there were works of epic character, related in the third person with little dramatic conflict. The *Messiah* is an example of the latter type, and, for that reason, it is one of the least representative of the Handel oratorios, although musically it is undoubtedly the best.

The Handel arias and ariosi, and the "dry" and "accompanied" recitatives in the oratorios are similar to those in his operas. But the large-scale choruses, quite foreign to the Italian opera, are typical of the oratorio. These tremendous choral frescoes, now massive and chordal, now based on imitative polyphony, show Handel at his best. In many of these works Handel's majestic and elemental power is expressed in melodies, rhythms, and figurations that anticipate Gluck and especially Beethoven. It is significant that Handel is one of the few composers whom Beethoven admired besides himself.[11] Handel, too, paid close attention to the words and, when he wished, conjured up musical pictures to match his text, especially delighting in the musical representation of texts that speak of light or darkness (Ex. 96). In these oratorios the orchestra functioned as a powerful supporting accompaniment to the individual voice or chorus. To the orchestra also were assigned pieces of purely instrumental music, especially the overture (usually French) with which Handel opened his oratorios.

The Messiah. The *Messiah* contains some of Handel's best music; and this fact and the character of the subject account for its immense popularity. Composed (1741) on texts drawn for the most part from the prophetic books of the Bible and the psalms, it is divided into three parts:

I. The prophecy of Christ's coming; His nativity; rejoicing and comfort in the Saviour.

[9] The Handel oratorio may be explained on still other grounds as a social phenomenon. After the comparative failure of the Italian opera, associated with the court and the aristocracy, Handel discovered that the middle class would attend and warmly support oratorios because of the Biblical subjects and English texts.

[10] Another example is *Semele,* which might be classed as a "secular" oratorio because of the text. It was originally written by the dramatist Congreve with an operatic performance in mind. *Semele* contains the famous aria "Where'er you walk."

[11] Apart from the oratorios, an excellent example of Handel's power to evoke a mood of monumental grandeur is his Overture to *Music for the Royal Fireworks* (1749), written to celebrate the Peace of Aix-la-Chapelle (1748).

Ex. 96

[ISRAEL IN EGYPT]

II. Emotions inspired by the Passion, concluding with the "Hallelujah" chorus.

III. Belief in the Resurrection, beginning with "I know that my Redeemer liveth," and ending with reference to "the Lamb that was slain" and an "Amen" chorus.

Accompanied by a fairly small orchestra (strings mainly), the *Messiah* has two independent instrumental pieces: the French Overture with which it begins and the "Pastoral Symphony" (using a *siciliano* rhythm), which celebrates the nativity of Christ in Part I. The epic of the *Messiah* is unfolded, as we would expect, by means of recitatives, arias, and choruses. The accompanied recitatives are remarkably interesting, as they are in Handel's works as a whole, and the arias exhibit all the variety of the Italian opera on which they are modeled. The operatic virtuoso aria, for instance, occurs on various occasions (the bass aria "Why do the Nations so furiously rage together"). The choruses show a great variety. This is true in the contrast between those primarily in chordal style and those that emphasize various degrees of polyphony ("And the Glory of the Lord" or "And with his Stripes"). Perhaps it is more accurate to say that the variety extends to almost every chorus, for it is characteristic of Handel to contrast massive sonorities of chords with polyphonic textures or with the relatively transparent sound of single lines or pairs of voices.

In his settings of words, Handel's intent and power to depict his text vividly are everywhere evident, ranging from literal description ("The Trumpet shall sound") to the sustained mood of triumphant exaltation in the "Hallelujah" chorus (text from Revelations). In this chorus—the most exciting as well as the most famous piece in the *Messiah*—Handel achieves an emotional intensity of which only the greatest composers are capable. It is an electrifying piece from beginning to end; and it is not surprising that King George II of England, on first hearing it, rose to his feet as an act of homage, followed by his courtiers—an example that has been followed by audiences ever since. From a musical point of view the "Hallelujah" chorus combines in one piece the most typical choral effects of Handel, one of the most skillful writers for chorus that ever lived. Here the massive sounds of full chords are contrasted with imitative counterpoint or with the whole ensemble in unisons and octaves. Sometimes, a single voice part proclaims a short phrase, holding its final note, while the other voices join in ("And Lord of Lords"). The exciting contrast of textures and rhythms, the masterly combination of themes, and the *adagio* ending are all typical of Handel.

Handel doubtless reached his greatest heights in the *Messiah,* and parts of this work will always remain moving experiences, even if one has heard them to the point of exhaustion. But Handel was the composer of more than one oratorio—actually he was one of the most prolific composers of all time—and the wonderful treasures of his other oratorios await those who will perform or listen to them.

Suggested Listening
Parrish and Ohl:
    No. 45, Handel, *Solomon:* chorus "Draw the tear from hopeless love."
Handel, *Messiah* (complete recording).
    Israel in Egypt ("Hailstones" chorus).
    Samson ("Let their celestial concerts all unite").
    Acis and Galatea. This charming pastoral work cannot really be called an "oratorio." Described as a "serenata," it is operatic in intent.

Suggested Reading
Winton Dean, *Handel's Dramatic Oratorios and Masques*. London: Oxford University Press, 1959.
J. P. Larsen, *Handel's Messiah*. New York: W. W. Norton, 1957.

Romain Rolland, *Handel,* trans. by A. Eaglefield Hull. London: Kegan Paul, Trench, Trubner & Co., 1926.

Robert A. Streatfeild, *Handel.* London: Methuen & Co., 1909.

Paul Henry Lang, *George Frederic Handel.* London: Faber & Faber, 1967.

BACH AS A CHURCH MUSICIAN

Unlike Handel, Johann Sebastian Bach (1685–1750) spent much of his life in the service of the Lutheran Church. Bach was first a church organist at Arnstadt and then at Mühlhausen. He became successively court organist and chamber musician to the Duke of Weimar (from 1708–17), and then (1717–23) chapelmaster and director of chamber music for Prince Leopold of Anhalt at Cöthen. In 1723 Bach was appointed cantor of the Thomasschule in Leipzig and also organist and director of music at the two principal Leipzig churches, the Thomaskirche and the Nicolaikirche. Bach spent the remaining twenty-seven years of his life in Leipzig, and it is there that he composed much of his sacred music. At Leipzig Bach was required to compose and produce music for the Lutheran service every week, and from these requirements came his most extensive body of music, approximately three hundred church cantatas, of which about two hundred have survived.

The Church Cantatas. The church cantatas were substantial pieces of music, lasting about twenty-five minutes. The cantata [12] was the main music of the lengthy Sunday service, and as such it was composed about a text suitable for a particular Sunday of the year. A cantata for Advent (the period including the four Sundays before Christmas) naturally used a text different from one for Christmas Day or for Easter. The music of the cantata was fairly elaborate, using various combinations of choruses (which might or might not use some form of the chorale), simple congregational settings of the chorale, recitatives, arias, and duets. As a rule the cantata was accompanied by the orchestra in addition to the organ playing the figured bass; and sometimes the cantata began with an independent piece for orchestra.

The actual composition of the cantata depended on the text, the occasion, and the vocal and instrumental forces at hand. There was no set form for the cantata, the musical resources mentioned above being used in a variety of combinations. Some cantatas were almost entirely for soloists; others, mainly for chorus. Thus, it is hardly possible to speak of a *typical* Bach cantata, but there were certain commonly used schemes. In one of these an elaborate chorus, often based on a chorale, opened the work. One or several pair of recitative and aria might follow, perhaps another chorus, and, frequently, a simple four-part congregational setting of a chorale closed the cantata.

[12] The cantata was usually called *Stück, Hauptstück,* or *Concerto.* The actual term cantata was less usual. *Hauptstück* (principal or main piece) indicated its dominating musical position in the service.

Even with the chorale, however, there was no set procedure. Sometimes a chorale was not used in the cantata at all, and sometimes a chorale (or chorales) dominated it, as in the so-called *chorale cantata* in whose composition Bach specialized during one short period (probably 1724–25) in the early Leipzig years. A few cantatas were based entirely on a chorale, for instance, *Christ Lag in Todesbanden* (*Christ Lay in the Bonds of Death*), Cantata No. 4.[13] The chorale itself was used in certain basic ways (of which there are numerous varieties) in the cantatas: (1) in simple four-part congregational setting, resembling a hymn; or the same with ornamented melody; (2) set in relatively long notes, either for voices or instruments, so that the melody predominated; (3) as the basis of a piece in imitative counterpoint like a motet or fugue.

How did the cantata evolve? During the seventeenth century the chorale had been used in simple and ornamented form in church music, and in combination with the new forms of the *concertato* (e.g., by Schein). A species of chorale cantata was also exploited by Franz Tunder (d. 1667) and, among others, by Johann Kuhnau, Bach's immediate predecessor at Leipzig. Toward the end of the seventeenth century the recitative and the aria were incorporated into the cantata. About 1700, contemporary poets (Erdmann Neumeister) began to write cycles of verses in free poetic forms (as compared to the stiffness of the chorale texts) suited for the recitative and aria, usually paraphrasing Biblical texts and episodes, and related to the proper themes of the Church year. Bach combined these new elements of recitative and aria with the traditional chorus and chorale in the various forms of the church cantata by which we know Bach today.

Of the theological ideas that permeated Bach's works, the most important and central to his thought were the ideas of *atonement* and *redemption*. According to theology, mankind was eternally cursed with the original sin of Adam's Fall (cf. Bach's chorale prelude *Through Adam's Fall all is lost*). But man was saved from eternal damnation by Christ's supreme sacrifice on the Cross, which atoned for Man's original sin, and literally redeemed each Christian believer from the torture of hell-fire. Again and again, aspects of these ideas occur in the sacred music of Bach; and the depth and reality of these ideas are obvious from the fervor of their setting. Bach's special predilection for setting texts involving "death," "eternal sleep," and others of like nature is explained by the idea of atonement. To Bach, death held no terrors; on the contrary, it held out to him the promise of eternal salvation, a heavenly reunion with his Saviour in Paradise, where all sin had been washed away by the sacrifice of the Lamb of God.

These ideas may be seen in miniature in one of the most famous of the cantatas, *Christ Lag in Todesbanden* (mentioned above), written for

[13] The numbering of the Bach cantatas was determined by their order of publication by the Bach-Gesellschaft, and has nothing to do with their order of composition.

Easter Day, 1724. The text of this work relates Christ's sacrifice, His struggle with the Devil, His triumph over Death, and the joyful celebration of the Christian soul, redeemed from Hell and promised eternal salvation. Based *entirely* on various settings of the chorale of the same name, *Christ Lag* is remarkable for the somber magnificence of its music and the extraordinary fertility of Bach's imagination in creating such varied forms of the chorale.

In its musical plan, however, *Christ Lag* was less characteristic of the cantatas as a whole than another equally famous cantata, *Wachet Auf* (*Sleepers Wake,* Cantata No. 140) for the twenty-seventh Sunday after Trinity (1731). The latter cantata was based on the familiar parable of the wise and foolish virgins (Matt. 25: 1-13), awaiting the coming of Christ as a bridegroom to whom the Christian Soul (or Christendom) would be united. Bach arranged this cantata as follows:

(1) *A large-scale chorus* using the chorale *Wachet Auf* in long notes in the soprano while the other voices and the orchestra accompany with appropriate figurations. For the orchestra, Bach used three oboes, strings, organ; and a horn reinforced the chorale (verse 1) in the soprano.

(2) *A recitative* announcing the coming of Christ, the bridegroom.

(3) *Aria in the form of a duet* between Christ and the Soul, represented as the bride of Christ. This aria is accompanied by the figured bass and a solo *violino piccolo* (a smaller, higher-pitched violin) playing an *obbligato* (i.e., an independent accompanying part).

(4) *Verse 2 of the chorale,* set for tenor, figured bass, and a unison *obbligato* for strings (violins I and II, viola).

(5) *An accompanied recitative* (Christ welcomes his bride).

(6) *Aria in the form of a duet* between Christ and the Soul, joyously celebrating their marriage union; accompanied by the figured bass and a solo oboe, *obbligato.*

(7) *Verse 3 of the chorale* in a congregational four-part setting, accompanied by the orchestra.

Wachet Auf is more typical than *Christ Lag* because it contains a mixture of the old traditional chorale tunes and texts and the new texts of Biblical paraphrase, using operatic forms. Needless to say, these elements are fused into a unified whole by the splendor of Bach's music.

Suggested Listening
Parrish and Ohl:
  No. 46, Bach, chorale *Christ Lag in Todesbanden* (from Cantata No. 4).
  No. 48, chorus *Es war ein wunderlicher Krieg,* from the same cantata, showing how the chorale is used as the basis of a chorale motet (imitative counterpoint).
Bach, *Wachet Auf* (recorded complete).

Suggested Reading
See the end of the chapter.

The Organ Chorale Preludes.   The organ chorale preludes utilized the chorale in ways similar to the cantata, that is to say, in relatively long notes, or elaborated by ornamentation, or in the imitative manner of the motet or the fugue. There were many subdivisions and variations of these methods. The figurations accompanying the chorale were characteristically based on some stylized representation of the most striking idea of the text of the chorale concerned, for example in *Durch Adams Fall* (see p. 191) or *In Dir ist Freude* (*In Thee is Joy*), where a repeated figure suggested a joyful peal of bells (Ex. 97). Of the many chorale preludes set by Bach

Ex. 97

In Dir ist Freude

during his career, those found in two collections are most familiar: (1) the *Orgelbüchlein* (*Little Organ Book*) of 1717, forty-six preludes planned for different Sundays of the Church year, and (2) the "Great Eighteen," a collection made by Bach at the end of his life, representing his most mature, elaborate, and, in some cases, revised treatments of the chorale prelude.

Suggested Listening
From the *Orgelbüchlein:*
  Christ Lag in Todesbanden. Chorale in top voice, unadorned, with accompanying figurations. Parrish and Ohl, No. 47.
  O Mensch, bewein' dein' Sünde gross (*O Man, bewail thy grievous sin*). Ornamented melody.
  Durch Adams Fall.
  In Dir ist Freude.
From the "Great Eighteen":
  O Lamm Gottes unschuldig (*O guiltless Lamb of God*).

The St. Matthew Passion.   In addition to the cantatas, Bach composed other pieces of sacred music on a far larger scale for extraordinary or special occasions. Among these works (largely oratorios, Passions, and Masses), the *St. Matthew Passion* and the Mass in B minor stand out above all others. The first of these depicts the Passion story according to the gospel of St. Matthew: the story of Christ's last hours, the last supper, His arrest, trial, and crucifixion. Prior to Bach's time, the Passion story had been celebrated in the musical idiom of the day. There were settings of the Passion in Gregorian chant, others in motet fashion; and in the late seventeenth century, settings in oratorio style, the immediate background for the Passions of Bach. In the *St. Matthew Passion* Bach represents scenes from the life of Christ, mostly by means of the large chorus (with or without chorale), the simple four-part setting of the chorale, and the recitative, arioso,[14] and aria forms. Some of the forces required are exceptionally large. The opening chorus ("Come, Ye Daughters, share my anguish") and the closing chorus both use two choirs and two orchestras; and the opening chorus requires, in addition, a third unison choir of boys' voices for the chorale. Bach's setting of the voice of Christ is remarkably appropriate. The narrative of the other persons of the drama is, for the most part, contained in *recitativo secco.* But Christ speaks in accompanied recitative, his voice surrounded with a halo of strings, except in the final moments of His agony where the accompanied recitative is abandoned— an extraordinary touch.

Basically, the *St. Matthew Passion* relies on a plan not unlike that of the Neapolitan opera: a series of scenes each comprised of a narrative and a lyrical reflection on it. Some scenes are simple recitative and aria, permitting the *individual* to express an emotional reaction to what has taken place. In other scenes the reflective and emotional commentary takes the form of a chorale setting in which the *collective* emotion of the whole Christian congregation, as it were, is expressed with respect to the unfolding drama ("O dearest Jesus, what crime hast Thou committed, so harsh a judgment to receive?"). Sometimes the individual and collective elements combine in extraordinary ways. While Christ is praying in the Garden of Gethsemane, a tenor sings, "I would beside my Lord be watching," and the chorus interrupts the aria periodically to alternate its emotional commentary with that of the soloist.

In a work full of the touch of genius, Bach's most remarkable achievement is the selection, location, and harmonization of the chorales used in the *St. Matthew Passion.* The chorale most frequently appearing and most central to the drama is the properly named "Passion" chorale *O Sacred Head now wounded,*[15] and Bach's five different settings of this chorale show how a great master can depict the increasingly somber tones of his

---

[14] The Bach arioso, like the earlier arioso, is a combination of the recitative and the aria, but it is distinguished by distinct rhythms, especially in the accompaniment.

[15] Also known by other names. Many chorales had a number of verses, and a single chorale tune might be known by the different titles derived from the beginnings of its several verses.

text through the increasingly somber settings of the same chorale. Set first in the relative brightness of E major, *O Sacred Head* is harmonized in each appearance by more and more solemn keys and harmonies, reserving the darkest of them and the most deeply placed registers of the voices for the last setting, which immediately follows the death of Christ on the cross. This setting is surely one of the most moving in the whole range of Bach's sacred music.

The Mass in B minor.   The Mass in B minor does not belong to the main stream of Bach's activities as a church musician. The Latin text of the Catholic Mass still survived in abbreviated form (*Kyrie, Gloria*) in the Lutheran liturgy, but the origin of the Mass in B minor was personal to Bach. In 1733 Bach, beset by troubles in Leipzig, sought "the powerful protection" of the Catholic sovereign Augustus III, the King-Elector of Poland-Saxony, who had his court at Dresden. To accompany his petition, Bach composed and sent to Augustus the *Kyrie* and *Gloria* of the Mass in B minor. Later Bach completed the other parts of this Mass (*Credo, Sanctus, Agnus Dei*). Although its text is liturgical, this Mass is unsuitable for the service, if only because of its length; it requires over three hours to perform.

The Mass in B minor is quite different from the cantatas,[16] not only in its origin but in the forms employed. It consists of choruses and arias, but there are no chorales or recitatives. It is Bach's grandest and most monumental work, not necessarily in forces, but in the vastness of its conception. From the opening chords of the *Kyrie* (chorus and orchestra), we are in the presence of music of overpowering magnitude. The dynamic energy of its rhythms carries us forward with a never-ceasing movement, and the extended long arch of the vocal lines sustains the tremendous span of sound (see the tenor entrance in the *Cum Sancto Spiritu*, Ex. 98).

Bach is faithful to his texts, for he is always musically responsive to the

Ex. 98

(Tenor) Cum san-cto spi - - - ri-tu in glo - - -

- - - - - - ri-a De-i Pa-tris, A - - men

(rapid notes follow)

[16] However, the Mass borrows some of its music from certain cantatas. The *Crucifixus*, for instance, comes from an earlier cantata (No. 12, *Weinen, Klagen, Sorgen, Zagen*). Musical cannibalism of this kind was common in the eighteenth century. Bach practiced it to some extent, and Handel was a flagrant example, borrowing extensively from himself and others. In fact, Handel has been described as "the most successful musical burglar that ever lived."

great variety of moods inherent in the collective texts that comprise the Ordinary. Some of these texts are set to traditional music, the opening theme of the *Credo* being derived from a Gregorian *Credo*. Other texts are set in a manner suggested by theology: the *Et in unum Dominum* ("And I believe in one Lord") is composed for soprano and alto in free canon (two voices using essentially the same music), symbolizing the one-ness of Christ and God. A subtlety of this kind could easily escape the listener, but not the contrasts of mood in the large choruses. The second *Kyrie,* for example, is based on the following somber, chromatic subject

Ex. 99

Ky - ri - e   e - lei - - - son, e - le - i - son,   e -

(Ex. 99); while the opening of the *Gloria* that immediately follows is a marked contrast, an outburst of praise and adulation "Glory to God in the Highest." The high trumpet appropriately proclaims the diatonic fugal subject in its own brilliant image and key (D major; see Ex. 100).

Ex. 100

Gloria

[D Trumpet: sounding pitch]

In the *Cum Sancto Spiritu in Gloria Dei Patris,* the final movement of the entire *Gloria* (altogether there are eight separate and distinct pieces), Bach returns to the brilliance of D major. For sheer musical excitement, this is the high point of the entire Mass. The "open" sound of the theme, the dazzling sonorities of its setting in a high register, the inexhaustible energy of its rhythm, and the massive span of its sustained-chord sections open a shining vista *in Gloria Dei Patris.*

From this nothing could be farther removed than the hushed tones of the middle of the *Credo:* the *Et incarnatus* and particularly the *Crucifixus* ("He was crucified also for us, suffered under Pontius Pilate, and was buried"). The *Crucifixus* is set in E minor to a chromatic *ostinato,* the voices mourning in turn to the words *Crucifixus, Crucifixus.* At the final phrase *et sepultus* ("and was buried") Bach effects a remarkable change to G major, and the voices sink lower and lower, concluding in the darkness of their deepest registers.

But again, the following *Et resurrexit tertia die* ("and on the third day He rose again") changes completely as the text requires, and the jubilation of the Resurrection is portrayed. No musical joy could be more unbounded than the electrifying solo Bach has given to the bass section at the words *Et iterum venturus* ("And He shall come again with glory to judge the living and the dead").

The *Sanctus* begins in sustained chordal style and then uses a fugue for the *Pleni sunt coeli*. The opening of the *Agnus Dei* is assigned to an alto solo, and the final supplication *Dona nobis pacem* ("Give us peace") is entrusted to the chorus once again, using the music already heard in the *Gratias agimus* from the *Gloria*.

The Mass in B minor is Bach at his greatest. In this one work he has distilled all the joys and sorrows of Christendom, and only a musician of genius, moved by the profoundest convictions, could have written this tremendous affirmation of universal faith.

Suggested Listening

Bach's *St. Matthew Passion* and the Mass in B minor are both recorded complete. For a selection from the former, see Parrish and Ohl, No. 49 (Arioso for Alto, *Ach Golgatha*).

Suggested Reading

Hans T. David and Arthur Mendel, *The Bach Reader*. New York: W. W. Norton & Company, 1945 (revised edition, 1966).

Karl Geiringer, *Johann Sebastian Bach*. London: Oxford University Press, 1966.

Albert Schweitzer, *J. S. Bach,* trans. by Ernest Newman. New York: The Macmillan Co., 1950.

Philipp Spitta, *Johann Sebastian Bach,* trans. by Clara Bell and J. A. Fuller-Maitland. New York: Dover Publications, 1951.

Charles S. Terry, *The Music of Bach*. London: Oxford University Press, 1933.

——, *Bach: The Mass in B minor* (Second edition). London: Oxford University Press, 1947.

——, *The Cantatas and Oratorios* (2 vols.). London: Oxford University Press, 1925.

14. *The Instrumental Music of the Early Eighteenth Century*

THE CONCERTO GROSSO: *CORELLI. TORELLI. VIVALDI. BACH. HANDEL.*

FOR THE MOST PART, composers in the first part of the eighteenth century perfected the instrumental forms that had already been developed during the previous century. But the concerto, as a purely instrumental form, was relatively new; even the older of the concerto types, the *concerto grosso,* did not appear until the last part of the seventeenth century, and Corelli was among the first to compose *concerti grossi.* In *form,* these "Grand Concertos"—as translated into English—were essentially trio sonatas (see p. 185 and below) accompanied by string orchestra, and the word *concerto* in the title suggested the competing and contrast of the two unequal and opposing masses of tone. One of these bodies, the trio of two soloists (usually violins) and the figured bass, was called the *concertino* (i.e., the little concerto), while the larger orchestral body of two violins, viola, string bass, and keyboard was called the *ripieno* (literally, "filling," or "chock-full") or the *concerto grosso.* Since the latter term was sometimes used to specify the whole ensemble of *concertino* plus *ripieno,* we have one of those nice confusions in terminology, all too usual in music. At the beginning of the eighteenth century the score of a typical *concerto grosso* looked like this:

Concertino:	Violin I _____
	Violin II _____
	Cello or _____
	Gamba (figured)
Ripieno:	Violin I _____
	Violin II _____
	Viola _____
	Bass (figured) _____

With regard to the number and character of its movements, the *concerto grosso* of Corelli resembles his trio sonatas. In the "chamber" form (*concerto da camera*), dances predominate; in the "church" form (*concerto da chiesa*), the forms are relatively abstract, using the basic order of the trio sonata: slow—allegro (usually fugal)—slow—fast (often a *gigue*). Actually, the concerto was more experimental than the trio sonata; the number of movements was more often five than four, and the concerto as a whole showed somewhat more freedom and less uniform treatment than the older sonata.

The really important innovation of the *concerti grossi* was the application of the older concerto idea to instrumental music by contrasting the body of tone of the soloists in the *concertino* with the greater mass of the orchestra.[1] In the Corelli concertos the principle of contrasting mass of tone was carried out in a relatively primitive way, the orchestra being used largely to reinforce the *concertino* at various points, thus:

Concertino:				
	added *ripieno* tone		added *ripieno* tone	

Giuseppe Torelli (1658–1709) and especially Antonio Vivaldi (c. 1675–1741) made the contrast between these two bodies of tone more vivid by distinguishing their thematic content, assigning the *concertino* different, and sometimes more difficult, music to play. In this way the concerto retained the traditional principle of contrasting masses of sound; at the same time, thematic contrast made the music more interesting, and the soloists were set apart from the orchestra by the character and difficulty of their music. Vivaldi also reduced the number of movements to three or four. Furthermore, in the three-movement form Vivaldi often adopted the tempo order of the solo concerto (fast—slow—fast), already initiated by Tomaso Albinoni (see p. 215).

Recently, the name of Vivaldi has become something of a household word. This is as it should be; but the fact is that Vivaldi remains still an imperfectly appreciated genius. In his fertility of invention and in the variety of his forms he deserves to rank as the most prolific and influential concerto composer of his time. Vivaldi experimented constantly with the concerto; and the *concerto grosso* forms are mixed in many ways with those of the solo concerto. Vivaldi's experiments included instrumentation, and he introduced other instruments, notably wind, into the string ensemble. Vivaldi's ingenious and restless mind was stimulated also by

[1] A *ripieno* (orchestral) part might be played by a single player, but, more likely, by two or more.

the idea of a "program" concerto (*The Seasons* and *The Sea Storm* in Op. VIII). *See Plate* 22C.

Vivaldi's inspired melodies and his advanced writing for the stringed instruments were those of an eminent composer and violinist of the first rank. By comparison, his harmonies are less interesting and varied. They tend to become static, and Vivaldi sometimes relied on his driving rhythms rather than on harmony to give flow and life to his ensemble. Vivaldi's occasional lack of harmonic enterprise is a striking contrast to the consistently inspired harmonies of Bach—a point tacitly made by Bach himself in his transcription of certain Vivaldi concertos. In them Bach seldom altered the original melodies, but he transformed the harmony by copious additions to the inner parts of the ensemble, enlivening the harmony and incidentally increasing the rhythmic animation of the texture as a whole.

Bach's "Brandenburg" Concertos (dedicated to the Margrave of Brandenburg, 1721), a set of six *concerti grossi,* are, like Vivaldi's, touched with genius and invention. Bach used a varied instrumentation from one concerto to the next, mixing string and wind instruments in various combinations. He progressed beyond Vivaldi with respect to the keyboard, elevating it to solo rank in the fifth of these concertos. Bach did not do things by halves. In this concerto he wrote out an independent part for the harpsichord and in addition gave it a difficult and lengthy cadenza (see Index, and below). Like Vivaldi, Bach adopted the number and order of movements of the solo concerto; and while the principle of the *concerto grosso* is apparent in the "Brandenburgs," Bach specialized in mixing the *concertino* and *ripieno* instruments in a polyphonic texture so that the two bodies of tone were less sharply differentiated. Each of these concertos has a pronounced individuality, and their astonishing variety is a measure of the fluidity of the concerto form, created by means of varied instrumentation, texture, and the number and kinds of instruments used in the *concertino* (cf. his Second "Brandenburg").

Handel's concertos are more conventional—insofar as a great composer can be conventional. As a whole, his best known concertos are the twelve *Grand Concertos* of Opus 6, close to the Vivaldi model and entirely for strings (there are also oboe concertos). But, as is frequently the case in Handel's music, his concertos are unpredictable, and they show mixtures of the church and chamber forms common to the early eighteenth century.

Suggested Listening
Corelli, *Concerto Grosso* Op. 6, No. 3; or Op. 6, No. 8 (The "Christmas" Concerto).
Vivaldi, Concerto in G minor (Pincherle No. 407).[2] This concerto is a

[2] There are several numbering schemes for the Vivaldi works. The most sensible

good example of a mixture of the *concerto grosso* with solo concerto elements. The first two movements are characteristic of the former, an *adagio* followed by a fugal *allegro*. The breadth of the *adagio* and the fiery drive of the fugue are superb examples of Vivaldi's style.

Bach "Brandenburg" Concerto No. 2. Note the *concertino* of violin, flute, oboe, and trumpet; and the orchestral body of strings and figured *continuo*.

Handel, Grand Concerto in F major (Op. 6, No. 9). Of the six movements, the first four are "abstract"; the last two are dances: minuet and *gigue*.

Handel, Concerto Grosso in C major (first movement), for oboes, strings, and *continuo* (Parrish and Ohl, No. 43).

THE SOLO CONCERTO: VIVALDI. BACH.

In the *concerto grosso* the timbres and unequal volume of sound of the *concertino* and *ripieno* are opposed; in the solo concerto the timbre of a single instrument and the virtuosity of a soloist are contrasted with the color, massive tone, and less agile technique of the orchestra. The solo concerto was probably originated by Tomaso Albinoni at the end of the seventeenth century; at any rate, the first solo concertos were for violin, and the first important composers were Vivaldi and Bach. The Vivaldi solo concerto had three movements: *fast—slow—fast* or *very fast*. The slow movement was sometimes transitional in character. Sometimes it resembled a lightly accompanied solo aria inspired by the long line of Italian vocal melody. However, it was in the fast (*allegro*) movements, especially the first movement, that the important new development took place. The scheme of this movement may be called the *ritornello* form.[3] The *ritornello* refers to a section of music assigned to the orchestra and recurring like a refrain. In this form, the orchestra (*tutti*), usually strings, begins the concerto by stating the *ritornello*. The soloist follows in a new section, dominated by him and accompanied lightly by the orchestra. Basically, the *ritornello* form alternates sections of *tutti* and *solo*. The following diagram represents one of Vivaldi's schemes (T = *tutti;* S = *solo;* the different levels indicate possible changes of key):

$$T_2 \qquad S_2$$

$$T_1 \qquad S_1 \qquad\qquad\qquad\qquad\qquad T_4$$
(Tonic key) (Tonic key)

$$T_3 \qquad S_3$$

is that of Marc Pincherle. Unfortunately, his scheme is restricted to the instrumental works (see Marc Pincherle, *Antonio Vivaldi,* 2 vols. Paris, 1948; volume 2 contains the catalogue).

[3] Originally a *ritornello* was the *returning* orchestral passage played between sections of arias in the opera.

In the *ritornello* form, a good deal of variety was possible through modulation and, in the solo passages, by the contrast of lighter texture, solo figuration, and the particular tone color of a single, superior instrument. The opening *solo* might use the same theme as the *tutti,* but this was by no means essential. Typically, the *solo* used the opening phrase of the preceding *tutti,* and then modulated by passage work such as figurations and arpeggios.

Any soloist worth his salt wants to show off his musical and technical capacities, and hence a feature of most solo concertos was a passage devoted to satisfying this yearning on the part of the soloist. In principle, such passages, called *cadenzas,* were justified on the theory that the soloist heightened the musical effect and expanded the thematic material by technical flights of fancy, improvised on the spot or otherwise composed for the occasion. Early examples of the cadenza already occur in Vivaldi and Bach, and it is exceptionally interesting that both (unlike Handel) wrote out certain cadenzas, contrary to the general practice of the later eighteenth century (Mozart). In the nineteenth century the abuse of the improvised cadenza induced composers, Mendelssohn and Schumann, among others, to write it out, just as Bach and Vivaldi had done in a few pieces early in the eighteenth century.

Bach uses the *ritornello* as a scheme, but not precisely in the manner of Vivaldi; just as in the *concerto grosso,* he tends to blur the distinctions between the sections of *tutti* and *solo.* Bach composed a number of violin concertos of which there survive two for solo violin (E major, A minor) and the celebrated one for two solo violins (in D minor). By adapting the solo violin concerto to the harpsichord, Bach invented the harpsichord concerto, and most of his concertos for harpsichord were arranged from his own "lost" violin concertos. Bach also transcribed a number of the concertos of Vivaldi, among others, as concertos for harpsichord or organ alone. In the case of his famous *Italian Concerto* Bach wrote an original work that transferred the concerto form to the solo harpsichord.

Similarly, Handel transferred the concerto form to the organ, and his organ concertos are mixtures of concerto, sonata, and dance elements. Their rather loose, and especially improvised, character is suggested by the frequent direction *organo ad libitum,* which implied that Handel inserted a cadenza or improvised freely as fancy seized him.

The concerto of the early eighteenth century was a new and exciting form constantly evolving. It is a serious mistake to think of it other than as a scheme capable of numerous individual applications. The same thing could be said, incidentally, about the majority of the forms of music. The concerto embodied the principles of contrasted masses of tone, instrumental color, and technique. A large repertory of music quickly mushroomed as composers realized the implication of these principles and began to appreciate the inviting prospect before them. The variety of treatment from work to work was often quite amazing, and the sharp distinctions made between the *concerto grosso* and the *solo concerto*—which have to be made for purposes of general discussion—were often quite blurred in actual practice. These varieties and gradations, including concertos for more than one soloist, cannot be mentioned here in spite of their great interest. (But see Vivaldi's Concerto for four solo violins; also its transcription by Bach for four harpsichords).

A measure of the success of the concerto was its popularity, long life, and effect on other kinds of music. The concerto had immense possibilities for the composer and great attractions for the performer and the public. It was flexible and it was capable of great variety. It also challenged the composer and performer to exploit the tone color and technical capacity of the individual instrument, especially the violin. The virtuoso operatic aria paid the concerto the obvious tribute of imitating its instrumental figurations, just as instrumental music had imitated the cantabile style of the voice. Finally, the chamber audiences that listened to these concertos found them to their taste, partly because the variety inherent in the new form held their interest, and partly because the soloist excited and dazzled them, now with showers of notes, now with an emotional outpouring of melody in a way that has never failed to attract an audience from that day to this.

Suggested Listening

Vivaldi, Violin Concerto in A minor (Op. 3, No. 6). This solo concerto uses, basically, the *ritornello* scheme discussed above. The second movement (*largo*) is an ornamented solo aria, accompanied very softly by three violins and viola (no figured *continuo*).

Bach, Violin Concerto in A minor; compare this solo concerto with the Vivaldi, especially with respect to the much greater mixture of *solo* and *tutti* elements in the texture.

THE SONATA: BACH. DOMENICO SCARLATTI.

In the seventeenth century the trio sonata for two violins and figured bass was the favorite form of chamber music. In the eighteenth century it lost something of its favored position to the solo sonata (soloist and figured bass). Changes of this kind are seldom accidental, and in this particular case the solo sonata owed its popularity to the fact that it was a more brilliant vehicle for performers and more attractive to a public interested in the new concerto style. Consequently, the trio sonata was somewhat pushed aside; while a number of pieces were written in this form and show the stylistic advances of the time, the trio sonata had essentially reached a dead end as a form. Apart from this, the eighteenth-century trio sonata differed from earlier pieces in two basic respects: (1) the church sonata and the chamber sonata mixed their respective abstract and dance elements freely so that in many cases individual sonatas no longer differentiated sharply between the church and chamber types; (2) at the same time, the instrumentation became more varied; instead of the typical two violins of the seventeenth century, other instruments became more common (e.g., two oboes, flutes, violin and flute, violin and viola da gamba).

THE TRANSFORMATION OF THE TRIO SONATA

After 1700, the trend to solo playing often transformed the trio sonata into the solo sonata. The paradox was that the three-voiced texture of the music remained but was performed differently. Biblically speaking, the voice was the voice of Jacob but the hand was the hand of Esau. To be specific, the three parts of the old trio sonata were now distributed as follows: one of the solo parts was retained by a solo instrument, while the harpsichordist played the other solo part in the right hand, accompanying in the left with the harmonies that had previously been realized from the figured bass. Bach's six sonatas for cembalo (harpsichord) and violin are striking examples of the old trio texture performed in the manner just described. A diagram will help to clarify the point:

Trio sonata	Sonata for harpsichord and violin
Violin I	Violin
Violin II	⎤ Harpsichord
Figured continuo	⎦

This change had certain important advantages: it contrasted the timbres of the solo violin and the harpsichord; the violinist was cast in a solo role, and, at the same time, the harpsichordist ceased to accompany by improvising from the figured bass, for he now played from a written-out part equal in importance to the part for violin. Indeed, in some sonatas the harpsichordist became even more important than the violinist, and the order of Bach's title, *cembalo and violin,* is significant.

As we should expect, these sonatas of Bach's are full of musical interest. They show, among other things, his musical ingenuity in transferring the trio texture to a new medium. From Bach, Rameau, and others [4] dates the modern attitude toward the sonata for violin and keyboard, in which the two are equal partners. Bach's equally beautiful sonatas for viola da gamba and harpsichord and his six trio sonatas for organ may be mentioned in passing. In the latter the texture is transferred to a single

[4] Such as the French composer Mondonville, who emphasized the harpsichord part still more.

instrument, and the brilliance and technical difficulties of these "trio sonatas" are legendary among organists.

THE SOLO SONATA

The traditional form of the solo sonata, a soloist accompanied by the figured bass, had one great advantage over the trio sonata, at least in the eyes of a virtuoso: the soloist could pursue the primrose path of virtuosity alone. Consequently, the demands made on the soloist were considerably greater in the solo sonata than in the trio; and the solo sonatas of the eighteenth century, in particular the violin sonatas of a long line of violinist-composers (Vivaldi, Geminiani, Leclair, Veracini, Handel, and Tartini) [5] were filled with arpeggios, double stops, and other technical devices that added variety and brilliance, while maintaining a high standard of musical interest.

Beyond a doubt, the early eighteenth-century sonata reached its peak of difficulty in Bach and Domenico Scarlatti (1685–1757), the former in his six solo violin sonatas *senza basso* and the latter in his harpsichord sonatas.[6]

THE SONATA *senza basso*

Bach's violin sonatas *senza basso* comprise three church sonatas and three dance sonatas (called *partitas,* the old word for suite). They are solo sonatas in the modern sense of a single player without accompaniment, a species of violin music little cultivated for the obvious reason of the violin's limitations with respect to furnishing harmony as well as melody. Bach tried to suggest a way to transcend this limitation by using double stops (i.e., more than one string played at the same time) and by treating the instrument contrapuntally not only in fugues but in other movements. Only those who possess the greatest virtuosity and musicianship can give convincing performances of these remarkable and enigmatic works.

THE HARPSICHORD SONATAS OF DOMENICO SCARLATTI

While the solo sonatas represent only one of the many phases of Bach's work, the main efforts of Domenico Scarlatti were concentrated in the sonata for solo harpsichord—just as later Chopin was a specialist in piano music. Scarlatti composed about five hundred and fifty of these sonatas,

---

[5] Handel is the exception in this group. Although he played the violin, he was really an organist and harpsichordist.

[6] Bach's Suites for cello alone (*senza basso*) are dances and can be considered sonatas only in the sense that the dances of a *sonata da camera* constitute a sonata. Considered absolutely, the suites do not contain as many difficulties for the cellist as the solo violin sonatas pose for the violinist. But relative to the cello technique of the time, which was much more primitive than that of the violin, these cello pieces are just as astonishing as the solo violin sonatas.

mostly toward the end of his life. Unlike other sonatas of the time, these sonatas are single movements, although Scarlatti intended a large number of his pieces to be grouped in pairs. Composed for the Spanish court (Scarlatti was chamber musician to the Spanish Queen, Maria Barbara), these sonatas have many original features; indeed, they are perhaps the most original music for solo keyboard in the entire eighteenth century. Their harmonies and rhythms reflect the particular flavor of Spanish music, its dances and its instruments, especially the guitar. They explore the true possibilities of the harpsichord from its quietest to its most brilliant idioms. In the latter Scarlatti assaults the ear with torrents of notes and dazzles the eye with great leaps from one note to the next, or he makes the performer cross hands in a manner that requires the accurate grace and agility of a ballet dancer. The texture and figuration of these pieces are essentially harmonic, and the forms also utilize the resources of harmony for contrast and extension. The chief external framework is the dance form, but within it Scarlatti invented a number of types of formal arrangements, some of which anticipate those of the later eighteenth century.

Suggested Listening

Bach, Sonata No. 3 in E major for harpsichord and violin.

Bach, *Chaconne* for solo violin (from the *Partita* in D minor).

Tartini, "The Devil's Trill" Sonata in G minor (solo sonata).

D. Scarlatti, Sonata in C minor for harpsichord (Kirkpatrick, 115; Longo, 407).

Suggested Reading

Ralph Kirkpatrick, *Domenico Scarlatti*. Princeton, N. J.: Princeton University Press, 1953.

THE EVOLUTION OF OLDER FORMS: BACH. HANDEL. COUPERIN.

THE TOCCATA. THE PRELUDE

The remaining types of instrumental music were all deeply rooted in the past. The preludes and toccatas still show the same variety of treatment and mood as those of the seventeenth century: on the one hand, the completely free forms that consisted mainly of broken chords; and, on the other, the rhapsodic virtuoso toccatas that were sometimes expanded by middle sections based on imitative counterpoint (e.g., Bach's Toccata in D minor, known as Toccata and Fugue in D minor). The eighteenth-century toccata, however, tended to a more dramatic style of figuration, echoing short motives back and forth in the texture. Buxtehude first specialized in this style, and it was copied by Bach (Ex. 101).

Ex. 101

THE FUGUE

By the early eighteenth century the older types of imitative polyphony, such as the *ricercar* and *canzona,* had merged into the fugue. The older *ricercar* and *canzona* used several sections, each with its own thematic material. By the time of Bach a fugue consisted typically of a single subject elaborated in one continuous section. This new procedure was possible because a single subject could be greatly extended by treating it in different keys and by the use of a device called the *episode*. The purpose of the episode was to isolate and devote special attention to some characteristic rhythmic or melodic motive inherent in the subject or the countersubject (for a discussion of the fugue and the episode, see pp. 61–4). Through the episode and the possibilities of modulation, the eighteenth-century fugue created an elaborate polyphonic structure using only one subject.[7]

While the older *ricercar* and *canzona* gradually became obsolete, the kinds of subjects that characterized them survived in many fugue subjects which bear a family resemblance to their ancestor forms. The following subject, that of the Ninth Fugue in Book II of Bach's *The Well-Tempered Clavier,* is similar to the vocal (motet-derived) style of the typical *ricercar* subject (Ex. 102).

Ex. 102

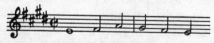

The fugue was developed to its highest point by Bach. Imitative polyphony was his mother tongue, and he spoke this language in countless keyboard and vocal fugues. The two books of his *The Well-Tempered Clavier*[8] each contained twenty-four preludes and fugues. These two

---

[7] The one-subject fugue was the most common type, but others were more elaborate. A double fugue, for instance, is a fugue on two subjects that are either (1) developed together or (2) developed separately and then combined. Triple and quadruple fugues elaborate the same procedures.

[8] The original title is *Das Wohltemperierte Clavier* (Book I, 1722; Book II, 1744). Since the word *Clavier* (*Klavier*) meant either harpsichord or clavichord, the usual English title *The Well-Tempered Clavichord* is somewhat misleading.

collections are a monument to the modern tuning system, which permits a "well-tempered" keyboard instrument to play in *all* keys without re-tuning. In both of these books Bach demonstrated his "Well-Tempered Clavier" by composing a prelude and fugue in the major and in the minor key on each of the twelve half steps of the chromatic octave (i.e., in twelve major and twelve minor keys). From this time onward, the key system was complete, since all the keys (or their enharmonic equivalents) were available. The preludes were not related thematically to the fugues; they served the function of "prelude" to a fugue. The forms used in individual preludes varied greatly; and the different procedures in the fugues, taken as a whole, summarized most of the previous devices and types of imitative counterpoint.

The organ fugues were larger in scale, more monumental in conception and impression, as befitted the noble and sustaining character of the organ and the large buildings in which it was generally housed.[9] In this regard, the difference between the harpsichord and organ fugues is similar to that which exists between chamber and orchestral music.

At the end of his life Bach wrote *The Art of the Fugue* (*Die Kunst der Fuge*) as a demonstration of all fugal procedures, starting from a single central subject. In the fourteen fugues of this work Bach summarized everything that is worth knowing about the fugue, including such types as the double, triple, and even quadruple fugue, and such devices as inversion, augmentation, and diminution (see p. 63). The work starts with "simple" fugues and works up to the crescendo of the final fugue, a gigantic and unfinished torso of a quadruple fugue. But Bach was never to complete it, for after working his musical autograph [10] into the final stages of this fugue, he laid down his pen, never to write another note. (Fugue No. 3 is analyzed on pp. 64–7.)

The fugue was used by many others, and it was not restricted to instrumental music. The Bach cantatas and Handel oratorios are full of fugues, worked out by the forces of voices and instruments. Handel's fugues are generally more loosely organized than Bach's. He uses the fugal texture more casually, less extensively and systematically than Bach;

[9] The organ of the time of Bach specialized in bright tone colors. The sharply edged tone of these organs was better suited to polyphony than is that of the average modern organ.

[10] In German, B = B flat and H = B natural. Hence "Bach" is spelled musically as follows:

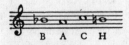

B   A   C   H

Musical autographs and similar devices were favorite parlor tricks of many composers. In recent times, Vaughan Williams used the above Bach autograph as the opening theme of his Fourth Symphony (1935), and numerous other modern composers have also used this autograph.

and it is not unusual for him to abandon the fugue after the completion of the exposition.

Suggested Listening

Bach, Toccata in F major for organ (virtuoso toccata).

Bach, Prelude and Fugue No. 9 in E major from Book II of *The Well-Tempered Clavier.*

Handel: for free treatment in a vocal piece, see Parrish and Ohl, No. 45.

Handel, *Concerto Grosso* Op. 6, No. 9 in F major, fourth movement. See also the last movement of his Suite No. 2 for harpsichord, mentioned below.

THE SUITE

The main principles of the suite and its "key" dances have already been described (see p. 183). The key dances (*allemande, courante, sarabande, gigue*) still survived in the eighteenth century, but other dances and other pieces (such as *rondeaux*) were added. The number of dances included in the suite was considerably increased, especially in France, the home of the dance suite. Some of François Couperin's suites (or *Ordres*, as he called them) have over twenty separate pieces.

The *Ordres* of Couperin were notable for the refinement and elegance of ornamentation, either written out or notated with specific signs (Ex. 103). The French fondness for representing something in music also

Ex. 103

(manner of performing the signs)   [COUPERIN, LA GALANTE]

(mordent)   *(trill)*   *(turn)*

showed itself in these suites. Besides the dances proper, there were other pieces with titles having nothing to do with any dance. Some but not all of these titles had program significance. Couperin's Eleventh Suite is particularly interesting. Entitled *Les Fastes de la grande et ancienne Mxnxstrxndxsx* (The pompous display of the grand and ancient order of Ménestrandise), this suite was intended to satirize the Ménestrandise, the Paris corporation of musicians that had a monopoly on playing for dancing. Couperin had suffered from this monopoly, and in this suite he took his revenge. He ends the suite, for example, with a realistic portrayal of the discomfiture of the Ménestrandise ("Disorder and rout of the whole troupe caused by the drunkards, the monkeys, and the bears").

Rameau's pieces for harpsichord were not called *Ordres,* but his collections, like the Couperin *Ordres,* mixed dances and pieces with descriptive titles. In his *Pièces de Clavecin* (1724) Rameau included twenty-four pieces, among them a *minuet, allemande, courante, gigue,* two *rigaudons,* one with a *double,*[11] and some highly descriptive pieces such as the famous *Le Rappel des Oiseaux* (The Call of the Birds).

Both the "English" and the "French" suites of Bach (each containing six suites) are based on the dances and style of ornamentation of the French models, but there are no descriptive pieces. Some of these suites have preludes of great interest, such as that to his English Suite in G minor, cast in the form of a *concerto grosso.*

The so-called suites of Handel are sometimes suites and sometimes mixtures of the church and chamber (i.e., dance) sonata, transferred to the keyboard. For a number of these "suites" Handel used the title *Lesson,* and the fact that a number of dances occurred in them persuaded editors that they must be "suites." This was not always the case; the presence of dances mixed with fugues and other "abstract" movements simply pointed to an origin, not in the French dance suite, but in the two types of the Italian ensemble sonata.

Suggested Listening
Parrish and Ohl:
  No. 40, François Couperin, *La Galante* for clavecin (harpsichord). Note the ornaments and their written-out versions by Parrish and Ohl (cf. Ex. 103).
Rameau, *Le Rappel des Oiseaux* (from *Premier Livre de pièces de clavecin,* 1706).
Handel, Suite No. 2 in F major. This piece is a mixture of church and chamber-sonata elements. The last two movements consist of an aria-like *adagio,* followed by a fugue.

THE VARIATION

The impetus that the variation received in the seventeenth century continued into the eighteenth, and some of the most extraordinary variations date from that time. In the works of Bach and Handel there are famous examples: the Bach *Chaconne* for solo violin, his *Passacaglia* for organ, and Handel's *Passacaglia* in G minor for harpsichord (Suite No. 7). In the cantatas of Bach and the oratorios of Handel there are less well

[11] In the suites a dance was sometimes followed by another called "double." The "double" was essentially a variation of the preceding dance.

known but equally beautiful *ostinato* pieces: the magnificent choral piece that opens Bach's *Jesu, der du meine Seele* (Cantata No. 78); and the wonderfully expressive chorus "How long, O Lord, shall Israel groan" with which Handel begins his oratorio *Susanna,* a chorus and work almost unknown.

Of the theme and variations, the most remarkable are certainly Bach's "Goldberg" Variations, a set of thirty variations on a *sarabande*-like theme. In these pieces Bach showed a modern attitude toward the variation that was not resumed until Beethoven. The different variations of the "Goldbergs" take on a much more specific individuality and character than do other variations of the time. Compare, for instance, Handel's "Harmonious Blacksmith" Variations (Suite No. 5). In the latter the theme is followed by variations that systematically explore different figurations, using eighth notes, sixteenths, triplets, and so on. In the "Goldberg" Variations a more pronounced character is achieved in various ways, for example, by setting every third variation in canon or by giving a definite formal character to a variation—the sixteenth variation is a French overture. Thus each variation is a variation of the original theme, but it has in addition a marked individuality in its own right.

Suggested Listening
Bach, "Goldberg" Variations for harpsichord.
Bach, *Passacaglia* in C minor for organ.
Handel, *Passacaglia* in G minor for harpsichord (Suite No. 7).

Suggested Reading
Robert U. Nelson, *The Technique of Variation.* Berkeley and Los Angeles: University of California Press, 1948.
Ralph Kirkpatrick, edition of the "Goldberg" Variations (New York: G. Schirmer, 1938) contains a valuable preface discussing these variations at length.

BACH AND HANDEL COMPARED

With the discussion of the variation, we come to the end of the panorama of the baroque era, and in retrospect we see that with few exceptions the forms and styles of the early eighteenth century were summarized by Bach and Handel. In this sense, most of the music of the time fell within their orbit; and for this reason the discussion of the early eighteenth century has centered on these two composers. At the same time we have tried to emphasize the stature of others, such as Vivaldi, Alessandro and Domenico Scarlatti, Rameau, and Couperin, whose virtues have sometimes been obscured by the attention paid to

Bach and Handel, two of the greatest figures of that or any other time.

The selection of a mere handful of famous composers to illustrate the development of music has the advantage of presenting the main outlines in relatively sharp and simple focus; but it has the marked disadvantage of omitting many others, some of whom enjoyed equal or even greater reputations in their own lifetimes. G. P. Telemann (1681–1767) was far better known than Bach, a relatively obscure, provincial musician, celebrated mainly as an organ virtuoso. Actually, Bach secured his post at Leipzig after the first two choices—Telemann and Graupner—could not or would not accept it; Bach was selected because the authorities felt that since the best was not available they must be satisfied with what they could get! Bach's reputation today dates from Mendelssohn's performance of the *St. Matthew Passion* in 1829 and from the subsequent publication of his works, begun by the Bach-Gesellschaft in 1850 and completed in 1900.[12]

The name of Handel, on the other hand, would have topped any eighteenth-century list of famous composers. Handel was a glamorous international figure from the beginning of his career as an opera composer in Germany, Italy, and England. In the latter country, as court composer and an impresario of the Italian opera, he was connected with the highest personages in a brilliant society. His checkered career of fortune and bankruptcy, associated with theater and court, was a profound contrast to that of Bach, most of whose life centered in the church and home. Bach's musical orbit was the church and the chamber, and his most characteristic music was his chamber music, organ works, chorale settings, and church cantatas. Handel's life centered in a fashionable society, and his music was most closely connected with the forms of the theater and chamber music, the most characteristic of which were the opera and its related forms. Only in the later part of their lives, when Handel turned to the oratorio, did Bach and Handel have much in common, and even then there was only a superficial resemblance. Bach's church music, written specifically for the church service, was thoroughly permeated with a German spirit and with the sixteenth-century theology of Luther. Handel's oratorios were not intended for the church service at all, but, like the earlier oratorios of Carissimi, they aimed at moral edification largely through the depicting of Biblical scenes and stories. Handel's oratorios were really large tableaux or frescoes devoted for the most part to sacred subjects, and musically they drew their forms from the Italian opera and from the long-established choral tradition of England (e.g., Purcell). It was something of an accident that Handel was drawn to the oratorio; and, in view of his glittering career as an Italian opera composer to a fashionable and aristocratic world, it is ironic indeed that the English oratorios, supported

[12] Brahms claimed that the two most important events of the nineteenth century were the founding of the German Empire and the publication of the works of Bach.

by the middle class, succeeded in perpetuating his reputation, while his operas vanished like dust and were forgotten for two hundred years.

Thus in their lives Bach and Handel represent two divergent worlds, and it is the representation of these diversities in musical terms that makes their music summarize the time in which they lived. These differences are evident not only in the kinds of music characteristic of their respective milieus, but also in their personal styles of expression. Bach was more consistent than Handel in almost every respect. He established a unity of mood by the continuous elaboration of an idea through his prodigious resource of polyphonic invention and by the perpetual and driving rhythms that welled from him, effortless and inspired. Handel's music is less continuous and less animated by polyphony. It is even less consistent in quality than Bach's. There is no other great composer who wrote so much run-of-the-mill music as did Handel; he was too busy to write always as he could, and much of what he wrote represented only a sketch of what he himself played. And then, too, Handel's music needs a sympathetic performance, and it must be served up "piping hot," almost as if it were being improvised on the spot in the heat of musical enthusiasm.

Bach's music was rooted in traditional theology and counterpoint. But while Bach drew from the past, he faced toward the future, and his inventive genius was always present in whatever he touched. Bach's harmony is characteristic. Why is it so varied and expressive? It is founded on the figured bass, but it drew on all the resources of polyphony as well as on those of diatonic and chromatic harmony. Bach's harmonization of the chorales is a simple example of the extraordinary variety and expressiveness of his complex harmony. It is no wonder that the generation immediately following Bach—a generation that longed for a simple "return to nature"—reacted against what Bach stood for: the complexities of a harmony inspired and enriched by polyphony; or that the nineteenth and twentieth centuries rediscovered Bach with delight, each for different reasons.

Bach lived and worked in the eighteenth century, but Handel was more of it, not only as a person, but also as a famous composer of a most characteristic kind of eighteenth-century music, the Italian *opera seria.* His harmony, too, is more characteristic of the eighteenth century than is that of Bach; it is less rooted in polyphony, more chordal and more brilliant in effect. The logic of continuous polyphony appealed less to Handel than it did to Bach, and his music sometimes resembles a series of brilliantly improvised pieces. While Handel's music is more typical of his own time than is that of Bach, it is prophetic in certain respects. Like Rameau's harmony, Handel's is inspired by the chord, less by moving lines as in Bach and Couperin. At the same time, Handel's oratorios set a model for the future.

No matter what the similarities and dissimilarities of Bach and Handel may be, our reaction to their music must be based, as with the music of every composer, on the emotions aroused by the individual masterpiece. As we listen to the moving *Crucifixus* from the B minor Mass, the great fugues, or the "Hallelujah" Chorus, we forget all considerations but the music itself, heeding only those emotions which transcend time and place. *See Plates 20, 22D, and 23.*

15. *Instrumental Music of the Classic Period*

THE CLASSIC PERIOD (*1750–c. 1820*)

WHEN BACH AND HANDEL DIED in the middle of the eighteenth century, an era in music came to an end. New currents, which had been evident for some time, swept away the old style, substituting others. The baroque dissolved into the rococo, and this in turn was absorbed into the main stream of the Classic style of Haydn and Mozart.

There were new currents everywhere. In the late eighteenth century the old system of monarchy which had dominated European politics for centuries was seriously undermined. In France the Bourbons, who had attained an absolute power under Louis XIV in the seventeenth century, fell with a resounding crash, and the nation passed through the ordeal and terror of the French Revolution (began 1789), which succeeded in executing Louis XVI, a substantial part of the aristocrats, and some of the citizenry. At this same time, other European states combined against France, and the subsequent Napoleonic Wars convulsed Europe until 1814.

These political events were not unheralded. Existing institutions had long been the subject of severe criticism, and French writers such as Voltaire and Rousseau had attacked the church and the state with a view to long-overdue reform. Rousseau exerted an immense influence with his ideas of the rights of the common man and his slogans of simplicity and "return to nature." In short, everyone recognized the inequalities of privilege except the few who benefited from them. The middle class, the *bourgeoisie,* had gained rapidly in wealth and influence, and they had become increasingly restless under an unwieldy, inefficient and irresponsible government in which they had little say. Their restlessness was heightened by reading and listening to the philosophers who advocated systems of reform that would permit a government to function by the consent of the governed. Ironically enough, this ideal was first realized in practice, not in

Europe, but in the New World; and the political ideals embodied in the new American constitution had their effect on the French Revolution. Modern economic theory, essential to the working of a society proposed by the philosophers, also dates from the late eighteenth century, for in 1776 Adam Smith published his *Wealth of Nations,* the most influential economic treatise ever written.

In view of the violence that characterized the French Revolution, it may seem a contradiction in terms to call the eighteenth century the *Age of Reason.* But this contradiction was more apparent than real. A rational spirit did characterize the times, and the belief was general that reason could solve any problem. The philosophers and intellectuals sought rational answers for the difficulties that confronted them in politics, religion, social life, and art. It was a historical accident that the government of Louis XVI was too unwieldy, too stupid, and too nearsighted to see the handwriting on the wall, and the bloody revolution that ensued was typical of the way nature fills a vacuum. By way of contrast, the same ideas permeated the English government by a slow process of evolution, partly because of the political genius of the English and the flexibility of their political institutions, which were more representative of the social order; partly because of a national disinclination to change; and partly, no doubt, because they had cut off a King's head a century and a half earlier.

An important monument to the spirit of rationalism was the French *Encyclopedia* (1751–76), edited by Diderot.[1] This great work was based on the premise that universal knowledge could be made available in accessible form, and that its substance should serve as a guide to human conduct and a philosophical outlook. The Encyclopedists believed that men could attain absolute knowledge and that every question might be answered by a combination of reason and knowledge. This attitude was characteristic of the whole "Enlightenment" (German: *Aufklärung*), a term used to describe the belief of the eighteenth century in the role of reason in all life. The Enlightenment was opposed to absolutism of any kind in thought or politics; its rationalism was based on systems such as those of Descartes, tempered by the belief in the importance of experience (as expressed by Locke) and by the reconciliation of both rationalism and experience in the works of Kant.

The events and spirit of the times made themselves felt in arts and letters. The growth of the middle class was reflected in various ways: in the English novels of Richardson, the French bourgeois drama, and the comic opera. An increasing bitterness against social and political conditions took the form of biting satires, such as Voltaire's *Candide* and particularly Beaumarchais's *The Marriage of Figaro,* a play that actually furnished one of the sparks that ignited the French Revolution (cf. Mozart's opera *The Marriage of Figaro*).

[1] *The Encyclopaedia Britannica* also appeared at this time (1768–71).

In music, the prevalent rationalism codified the musical representation of the emotions by set rhythms, intervals, and harmonies in the "Doctrine of the Affections" (see p. 190), and, significantly, these theories persisted longest in France. The operas of Gluck actually fulfilled the ideal hopes of the Encyclopedists; and Gluck's classical subjects reflected a revived interest in antiquity. The rationalism of the French, however, was opposed and undermined by the relatively simple, natural, and impassioned style of the Italians, and the continuing conflict between French and Italian music centered in these opposing points of view, which were amalgamated in the German and particularly the Austrian style of the Viennese (Haydn, Mozart). The mature art of the late eighteenth century fulfilled a rational ideal of balance, order, and emotional restraint.

From a sociological standpoint certain new developments may be observed. The rise of the middle class and an increase in wealth and leisure prompted the advent of the musical amateur. And an emphasis on simplicity put music within his technical capabilities; C. P. E. Bach's collection of keyboard sonatas entitled *Für Kenner und Liebhaber* (For Connoisseurs and Amateurs, 1779) is an example. At the same time, a large number of methods devoted to teaching the amateur to play or sing in "ten easy lessons" crowded the market.

The French Revolution had a direct impact on music. It produced music for the "masses" and at least one notable piece, the *"Marseillaise,"* the French national anthem. The horrors of the French Revolution also furnished the plots of various operas with themes of "horror and rescue" (e.g., Cherubini's *Medea, 1797*). Furthermore, the French Revolution reversed the prevailing system of patronage under which artists and composers (including Haydn and Mozart) had been dependent on the largess of the court or wealthy patrons. In the new French state musicians became state employees, and music became an instrument of public policy and a national concern. Cherubini wrote a "Hymn to the Dead of the Revolution"; and the National Conservatory of Music was founded in Paris at this time.

STYLES IN ART AND MUSIC: THE ROCOCO. THE MATURE CLASSIC STYLE.

As we have already noted, the signs of a new style in art and music were apparent before the middle of the eighteenth century. In music, the decorative ornaments of Couperin, the catchy melodies and thin harmonies of Pergolesi, and the harmonic textures of Domenico Scarlatti pointed to something new. The sons of J. S. Bach furthered the new, lighter type of melody and the chordal harmony already apparent in Pergolesi. This "early Classic" style resembled the prevailing rococo style in the fine arts and served as a bridge from the baroque to the Classic period of the late eighteenth century, whose most celebrated musical representatives were Gluck, Haydn, and Mozart.

What is the rococo style? In the fine arts it was a French style of sophisticated simplicity and delicate ornamentation, typically composed of rockwork, shells, scrolls, and flowers. It flourished in the France of Louis XV. As a reaction to the earlier style, the rococo substituted small structures for the grandeur and heaviness of the baroque. The miniatures of Watteau replaced large canvases; and, by way of contrast with the baroque, rococo figures were thin and slender. The slogan "return to nature" induced a studied naïveté in art and music. The simplicity of the pastoral scene, so characteristic of the rococo, was a marked contrast to the heroes and mythological scenes characteristic of the baroque. The object of rococo art was to amuse. Its chief subject was love, which was both sophisticated and sentimental. The grand passions were replaced by refined wit, elegance, and touching sentiments. Specific elements of the rococo were described by the phrase *"style galant et touchant"* (gallant and moving style) and by the word *sensibilité* (German: *Empfindsamkeit*)—the latter used to describe sensitivity to emotional nuance, to detail, and to elegance. *Cf. Plates 21*A and B.

These styles were transitional developments between the baroque and the Classicism of the late eighteenth century. France dominated the culture of the time, but the spirit of rationalism and the French rococo were challenged in the North Germany of Frederick the Great (himself a Francophile in art), where the *Sturm und Drang*[2] movement wished to shake off the influence of the French. It sought to express more untrammelled emotion, emotion not according to a correct but often empty and frivolous elegance, but according to passionate feeling. The *Sturm und Drang,* however, was less characteristic of the fundamental mood of the late eighteenth century than of the nineteenth, and the rococo was displaced less by the *Sturm und Drang* than by a Classicism that absorbed both styles into an art more solid and sober than either. This Classicism of the late eighteenth century aimed rather at "a noble simplicity and a quiet greatness," as Winckelmann (1717–68) characterized Greek art in his influential *History of the Art of Antiquity* (1764). To this art belong the works of Goethe, the paintings of David, and the operas of Gluck. The works of Haydn and Mozart are excellent examples of the changes that took place in the last fifty years of the eighteenth century. Their early works are filled with the melodic ornaments and harmonic mannerisms analogous to the spirit of the rococo. Their last works exhibit the maturity of Classic art: a purified melody, an enriched harmonic texture, and forms that are amplified and perfected.

The Classicism of the late eighteenth century was actually influenced by

[2] *Storm and stress.* This term comes from the title of a drama by Klinger (1776).

the study of Classical antiquity.[3] But the term "Classic," used originally in literature, dates from the early nineteenth century. It was used by the Romantic movement to differentiate its art of freedom and inspiration from the art of established rules of the eighteenth century. These distinctions were adopted by musicians, for example, Robert Schumann, to distinguish the "old" music of the immediate past from the "new" music. But nothing is new. The *Ars Nova* of the fourteenth century (see p. 146) spoke in analogous terms about the *Ars Antiqua,* the "classical" music of established rules that had preceded it in the thirteenth century.

In music, the rococo style originated in a reaction against counterpoint and the comparatively austere style of earlier composers like Bach and Handel. The sons of J. S. Bach thought their father's music was old-fashioned, although they greatly respected it. Rousseau thought counterpoint was as absurd as several people talking at once; to him Pergolesi's simple, catchy tunes and transparent harmonies were the ideal. In spite of this attitude, counterpoint ("the learned" style) persisted in certain types of music, notably church music. The new fashion encouraged a vogue of harmony and melody that was simplicity itself. Compared to the long arch of melody that had been characteristic of Bach, the "new" melody was short-breathed and repetitive. Typical were short phrases of two or four measures balanced against each other either by repetition or by contrast of different short melodies.

The rococo melodies were basically ornamental and expressive in character. Just as works of art were decorated with rockwork and shells, the music was elaborated by musical ornamentation—a style anticipated by François Couperin and continued in composers like C. P. E. Bach and Nardini. An expressive style, sometimes bordering on sentimentality, was based on a delicate, chromatic harmony and on the appoggiatura. The latter was like a musical "sigh," in that an accented dissonant note was followed by an unaccented consonance, usually accompanied by a change of dynamics (in Ex. 104, the appoggiaturas are marked "x"). In contrast to this rather sentimental lyricism, there was also a type of bold and robust passage work, almost, it would seem, inspired by the spirit of the *Sturm und Drang,* and based on scale passages (cf. end of Ex. 104) and broken chords (Ex. 105). A number of composers combined the lyric and robust style, among them C. P. E. Bach, most characteristically, and in their early works, Gluck, Haydn, and Mozart. A special type of melody, *the singing allegro,* was typical of J. C. (the "London") Bach, and after him, of Mozart. In *the singing allegro,* a songlike element was introduced into a

[3] The term "Classic" or "Classical" is subject to a number of interpretations. It may refer (1) to the Classical antiquity of Greece or Rome, (2) to a work of the first rank, as a standard classic, or (3) to something that emphasizes a formal manner rather than "free" inspiration.

Ex. 104

Ex. 105

fast movement by setting a lyrical theme to notes of comparatively long duration in an otherwise rapid movement (Ex. 106). These elements were all amalgamated in the Classic style of Haydn and Mozart. In them the same general attitude toward balanced and contrasted phrase structure prevailed, but their mature works exhibit a kind of melody purified of the

Ex. 106

excess of extravagant decoration, empty scale passages, and sentimentality.

With the chief interest concentrated in the melody, the other voices were often pushed into the background merely as accompaniment. This was especially true of the rococo of the early Classic period. In order to enliven the harmonic support, composers resorted to various devices. Among these was the *Alberti bass* (so called after the composer, Alberti), in which the chords of the harmony were broken up into figures and rhythmically animated (Ex. 107).

Ex. 107

[Alberti bass]

One of the chief problems of the new style was to replace the old figured bass with an appropriate substitute. In the figured-bass system (common to most music from 1600 to 1750 and even later), the basic harmonies were played from a bass underneath which were figures to indicate the harmonies; the other instruments played the parts containing the melodic interest (see diagram, p. 236). After 1750, the figured bass was gradually rendered obsolete by the new style, and the basic harmonies had to be supplied in other ways. On the harpsichord, for example, the melody was assigned to the right hand and the harmonies to the left. To animate them the Alberti bass was frequently used. In the orchestra, the fundamental harmonies were delegated to certain groups of instruments, notably the brasses and woodwinds; in fact, the whole orchestra became more clearly divided into melodic and harmonic instruments. However, a texture or style of orchestration that assigned all the melodic interest to one part or to one type of instrument and relegated the subordinate harmonies to the rest was inherently limited in perspective and monotonous to the audience and to the player. This impoverished harmonic style was characteristic of the rococo, and it presented a serious problem for composers. Somehow the texture had to be enriched harmonically and enlivened rhythmically. Haydn was the first to see how this could be done (in the String Quartets of Op. 33, 1783). In effect he retained the chordal harmony of his time but permeated this harmonic texture with melodic motives derived from the principal melodies. Thus the texture ceased to be merely a dominant melody supported by subordinate chords. All the voice parts shared in the melodic interest, at least periodically, because snatches of melody in the form of motives were assigned to various voices in turn. Haydn had really imposed a kind of motivic polyphony on a melodic-harmonic texture, and he had solved the problem of monotony inherent in pure harmony. As we will see later, the use of thematic motives was particularly helpful in the development sections of sonata form because short motives lent themselves readily to a polyphonic texture and modulation. In the following diagram the changes that took place in the figured bass, rococo, and Classic textures are shown: at A in the figured bass, at B in the early Classic or rococo, and at C in Haydn's thematic motives.

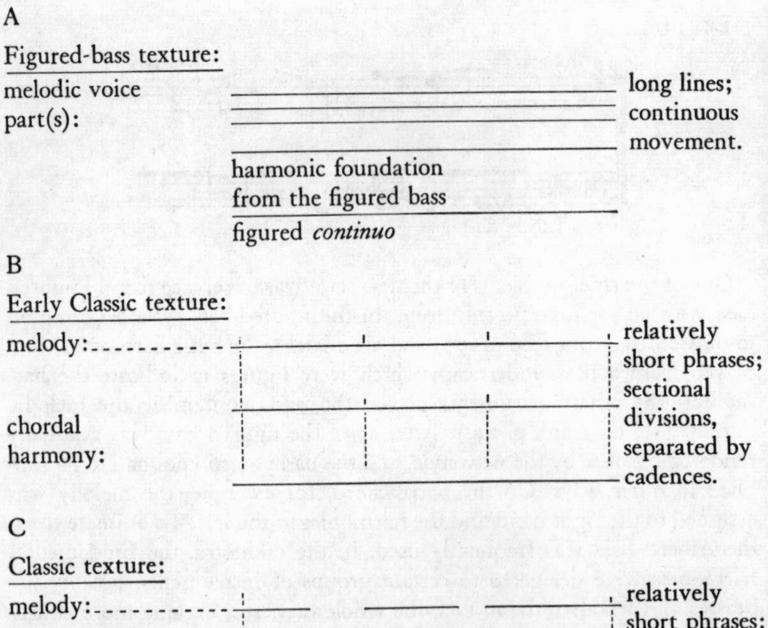

A

Figured-bass texture:

| melodic voice part(s): | ——————————————— | long lines; continuous movement. |

harmonic foundation
from the figured bass

figured *continuo*

B

Early Classic texture:

melody:-   relatively short phrases; sectional divisions, separated by cadences.

chordal harmony:

C

Classic texture:

melody:- - - - - - - - - -   relatively short phrases; sectional divisions, separated by cadences.

chordal harmony with thematic motives:

To gain greater contrast and increased expressiveness, the composers of the whole Classic period used a wider gradation of dynamics (louds and softs) than was used previously. Furthermore, their attitude toward dynamics was somewhat different from that of their predecessors. With *dynamics* (margin annotation)

Bach and Handel, the *crescendo* and *diminuendo* was usually limited to single notes or parts of measures. Classic composers began to use a *continuous crescendo* that lasted several measures or more—a device exploited first by the celebrated orchestra at the Mannheim court under J. W. A. Stamitz (1717–57). Other dynamic effects that characterized the new style were the *sforzando* (a sudden forcing of tone) and sudden contrasts of the extremes of loud and soft.

Changes in instrument (margin annotation)

To meet the requirements of a new style, changes in the instruments occurred. The typical keyboard instruments that remained from the preceding period were adapted to the new conditions or they yielded to new substitutes. The organ, for example, was made capable of producing *crescendo* and *diminuendo* by means of the so-called *swell* shutter (see p. 106); and the harpsichord, which is incapable of any appreciable gradation between louds and softs, gradually became obsolete, yielding its place to the pianoforte. The latter could produce a great range of *crescendo* and *diminuendo* as well as the smallest nuance of tone, and its gradations of tone and color were admirably suited to an expressive and personal style of music and performance. Although an instrument of ancient origin, the clavichord, with its possibility of nuance, expression, and bell-like tone, was in some respects the ideal instrument of the rococo. But the dynamic range of the clavichord was so small that for all practical purposes the pianoforte became the principal keyboard instrument outside the church. However, the pianoforte of Mozart's time was quite different from the pianoforte today. The tone was weaker and also clearer, particularly in the bass. The tension of the strings was far less, and the frame was much less reinforced. As compared with the modern pianoforte, the tone of the instrument of Mozart's time resembled that of the stringed instruments more closely and blended with them much better. *Cf. Plates 13A, 14A.*

In the orchestra new instruments were added. The clarinet, for example, proved a valuable addition because of its wide range and the contrasted tone colors of different parts of its register (see p. 98). More important than the introduction of single new instruments was the change in the way all the instruments were used, that is, in orchestration. The modern divisions of the orchestra and their function were established at this time. A clear division was made between the instruments that were to play melodic passages and those which were to sustain the harmonies. The different instruments of the orchestra were more clearly divided into choirs of like instruments: the strings, woodwinds, brasses, and percussion. The Mannheim orchestra, one of the most progressive of the day, standardized the arrangement at about fifty players (the modern symphony orchestra has about a hundred), and the following subdivisions:

(1) the *strings:* violin I, violin II, viola, cello–bass (the cello and the bass used the same written part until Beethoven's time, but the bass sounded an octave below the cello).

(2) the *woodwinds:* flute I and II, oboe (and/or clarinet) I and II, bassoon I and II.

(3) the *brasses:* trumpet I and II, horn I and II.

(4) the *percussion:* timpani (kettledrums) tuned to the tonic and the dominant.

Generally speaking, the higher strings and the woodwinds were used melodically, and as occasion demanded, harmonically. The other instruments were used harmonically, or sometimes for special effects, such as fanfare figures played by the trumpets. The woodwinds and the brasses were used more to hold harmony notes than to play melodies because of the limited number of notes at their disposal.

The string choir was complete both harmonically and melodically, that is, this choir could sound all the parts of the harmony, and each stringed instrument was able to play all the half steps through its range. The woodwind choir was also relatively complete, particularly with the advent of the clarinet, which could serve as tenor, alto, or soprano instrument. The flutes functioned mainly as soprano instruments, the oboes as sopranos or altos, and the bassoons as basses or tenors. There were still some difficulties in the woodwinds with respect to playing all the half steps in tune.

The brasses were incomplete both harmonically and melodically, partly because as a rule only horns and trumpets were used, and more particularly because these "natural" (no valves) horns and trumpets were capable of producing only the natural notes of the overtone series. Only in the high register were consecutive notes of the scale available, and even then the chromatic notes could not be produced except by a technique of "hand stopping," which changed the tone color of the note (for the limitations of the horns and trumpets, see pp. 99–101).

Suggested Reading

Adam Carse, *The Orchestra in the XVIIIth Century.* Cambridge, England: W. Heffer & Sons, 1940.

Paul Henry Lang, *Music in Western Civilization.* New York: W. W. Norton & Company, 1941. See particularly Chapters 12 and 13.

THE SONATA

All changes of style imply changes in form; new forms are invented, and old ones are adapted to new conditions. The Classic period was no exception. The sonata underwent a series of drastic revisions, the concerto incorporated certain elements of the sonata, the serious opera was "reformed," and the comic opera was expanded.

In the early seventeenth century the most characteristic and important development of the early baroque was the opera of Monteverdi. In the late eighteenth century, with Haydn, Mozart, and early Beethoven, the most significant efforts in the new style were devoted to instrumental music, especially the sonata, and, to a lesser extent, the concerto. The sonata, as a scheme of construction, was common to a number of performing mediums as different as the symphony and the piano solo. The term "sonata" does not always appear in the title of every piece that is in fact a sonata. A sonata for a string quartet was called simply String Quartet, or Quartet, using the name of the performing medium or indicating the number of players rather than the name of the basic type of piece involved. A similar situation obtained in other types of chamber music, such as the trio, duo, quintet, and so on. The concerto, which differs from the sonata, will be considered elsewhere.

The sonata of Haydn and Mozart was quite different from that of Corelli, Bach, and Handel. The "new" sonata of the late eighteenth century was dependent on the resources of harmony and tonality, and it was based on the idea of a dominating melody and a supporting harmony— on the contrast and repetitions of sections rather than the continuous expansion typical of the older sonata. The Classic sonata began to develop about 1750. Its pioneers were the sons of J. S. Bach (especially C. P. E. Bach and J. C. Bach), J. W. A. Stamitz at the Mannheim court, and others. Haydn and Mozart between them brought this type of sonata to its first real maturity. Beethoven's early works were modeled after those of Haydn and Mozart, and his last works opened new vistas that inspired the Romantic musicians of the nineteenth century.

Like the earlier sonata, that of Haydn and Mozart was a composite of three or four movements. The Classic sonata, however, used a different order of movements (*fast—slow—minuet—fast*), and the internal character of the movements was quite different. Sometimes the position of the slow movement and the minuet was reversed. The piano sonatas of Haydn and Mozart had typically three movements, starting with a fast movement and omitting one of the other three. For the most part, the symphony and the various types of chamber music used the four movements described above.

Each of the different movements had its characteristic plan of construction,[4] as follows:

The first movement: fast, typically *allegro*. This movement, sometimes preceded by a slow introduction, was usually in sonata form, the most characteristic and significant formal solution of the Classic period. Infrequently, the first movement was cast in the form of theme and variations (e.g., Mozart's well-known Piano Sonata in A major, K. 331).

The second movement: usually slow, typically *andante* or *adagio*. The forms used in the slow movement varied greatly from sonata to sonata. Characteristic were: three-part song form on a large scale, a theme and

---

[4] All these forms have been described in Part I, see pp. 57–64, 67–74.

variations, some type of rondo, sonata form, or sonata form without development (abridged sonata form). Sometimes the minuet—trio was used as the second movement; in which case the slow movement became the third movement. The slow movement was often composed in a related key (in the subdominant, dominant, or the relative major), rather than in the tonic.

The third movement: generally the minuet—trio—minuet. If the minuet was omitted, the third movement was a fast movement having the characteristics described under the fourth movement.

The fourth movement: fast or very fast, typically *allegro, allegro assai,* or *presto.* Characteristic forms were: sonata form, rondo, or a combination of sonata form and rondo, called *sonata-rondo* form. Some sonatas whose first movement was cast in the minor mode concluded with a fourth movement in the parallel major. (The last movement of Mozart's Quintet in G minor is in G major.) Sometimes, in such cases, only a part of the last movement was in major. Less commonly, a sonata that began in the major concluded with a last movement in the minor.

1861

THE SYMPHONY: HAYDN'S "DRUM ROLL." MOZART'S "JUPITER." BEETHOVEN'S EROICA.

Like many forms, the symphony had mixed origins. It owed its external plan to the Italian operatic *sinfonia (fast—slow—fast),* later detached for concert purposes, and then developed as an independent form (for example, in G. B. Sammartini, 1701–75). The symphony also had its adherents in France (Gossec) and England (J. C. Bach, Boyce), but the real home of the symphony from its inception was Germany and Austria. The North Germans (C. P. E. Bach), the Mannheim composers, and the Viennese experimented ceaselessly with the symphony. Among the latter, Haydn and Mozart brought the symphony to its first peak of perfection: Mozart in his last three or four symphonies and Haydn in his last symphonies written for London. Significantly, these works of Haydn and Mozart were influenced by each other: Mozart by the thematic motivation of Haydn, and Haydn by the lyricism of Mozart. The most essential problem of the symphony was summed up in the quest that led to this mutual influence: the search for thematic material that had in itself lyric beauty and genuine personality and for material that would furnish motives or some characteristic feature for development. The lyric and the motivic were the perfect complement and counterfoil to each other. From them the symphony (and all the sonata forms) derived its basic contrast of themes and textures and its possibility of amplified development.

An excellent example of the mature Classic symphony, and yet one possessing many individual features of its own, is Haydn's "Drum Roll"

Symphony, so called because it opens with a roll of the kettledrum. Composed in 1795 for London, it is No. 103 of the 104 symphonies listed by Mandyczewski.[5]

The first movement is highly unified, yet full of variety; and it shows a number of features of Classical art in general. In its dynamics, the piece is marked by restraint, for while it is not lacking in volume of sound, the contrast of louds and softs is subordinate to a broad scheme of balances in melodies and tonalities. The themes are characteristically limited in range and carefully balanced in phrase structure. A personal type of emotional expression is markedly absent. There are no elaborate retards or nuances indicated, and they would seem out of place in this music. In general, the first movement is notable for balance, clarity, and a certain impersonality. It is delightful, economical in use of material, and, in retrospect, strikes one as having neither a note too much nor too little. In short, without being stereotyped, this movement achieves a perfect "classical" balance of thematic material and mode of expression.

Haydn begins the symphony with an *adagio* introduction. An introduction is not unusual *per se,* but this one has exceptional features. It is "integrated" with the main body of the movement, as the thematic material of the introduction is used later in the development section and the coda. Furthermore, the rather mysterious opening is a perfect foil for the lightness and gaiety of the *allegro* of the first movement proper. The latter is a clear example of what sonata form is supposed to be. The main divisions of exposition, development, and recapitulation are clearly set forth. In the exposition there are two clearly defined melodies, one for each of the two principal keys, and the two melodies are connected by a bridge passage. The first theme furnishes motives for the texture and for the development, and the second is more lyrical in character. The development extends the material of the exposition by admirable polyphonic use of motives, mostly from the first theme, and by the use of new keys. By a particularly happy touch of inspiration, Haydn transforms the second theme of the exposition by restating it in the development in a darker key, a lower register, and with a different sonority. As is customary, the recapitulation repeats the main material of the exposition, but now entirely in the tonic. An arresting feature of the recapitulation is the way Haydn extends it (for details, see p. 78). The coda to the movement is unusual, imaginative, and brilliant.

Finally, the instruments are used with originality. To begin the work with the roll of the kettledrum alone is an arresting idea. Haydn also uses the color contrast of different choirs of the orchestra to repeat and thus extend the material without monotony. While the brasses, because of their melodic limitations, are used mainly to reinforce the harmonies, Haydn

---

[5] This work has already been analyzed in minute detail in Part I of this book (see pp. 74–82). Consequently, only those special features that summarize characteristic traits of the Classic symphony or Haydn as a composer will be stressed here.

takes advantage of the character of the first theme to use its opening motive in the horns where possible (e.g., measure 139 in the development and measure 220 in the coda). Indeed, the subject itself may have been created with the notion of the limitation of the horns in mind.

The second (slow) movement is a theme and variations in C minor—the relative minor to the main key of the symphony (E-flat major). It has two notable traits: the treatment of the variation itself, which is a species of "double variation"; and the quite extraordinary coda (for details, see p. 80). The third movement is the typical minuet, in the triple time of the dance. As in most minuets, the trio is sharply contrasted in character to the minuet proper. The fourth (*allegro*) movement shows in its opening horn motive how a skillful composer can turn limitations to advantage. Haydn uses the limited notes available to him to create a short (four-measure) motive. Then he repeats this as a bass to a countersubject played by the strings. Two other points about this movement are worth noting: the form is exceptionally interesting; and about half way through (m. 208) *sforzandi* occur in all parts on the second quarter note of the measure (see p. 82), thus introducing a syncopation that actually displaces the measure accent.

The Haydn "Drum Roll" Symphony has served as an admirable model for analysis; it is one in which the genius of Haydn is frequently evident. A large number of pieces embody the same general principles as the "Drum Roll," and show in addition specific traits of interest and originality. In these, in the typical first movement, the principles of the sonata form are used with great variety by individual composers, and even by the same composer from one work to another. A common denominator of the exposition of a Haydn or Mozart sonata form is its basic contrast of two keys; but within this scheme, Mozart often used more than two themes, while Haydn sometimes limited himself to one for the entire exposition. In certain "archaic" types of earlier sonata forms, the recapitulation begins with the *second* subject in the tonic key (Domenico Scarlatti, C. P. E. Bach). The sonata as a whole is also characterized by numerous mixtures of such forms as (1) the sonata-rondo in which elements of the rondo and the sonata form are combined (see p. 73), and (2) the sonata form using elements of the fugue (see Mozart's "Jupiter" Symphony).

The change that took place in the symphony during the last years of the eighteenth century and the early years of the nineteenth can be illustrated by commenting briefly on two additional symphonies, the "Jupiter" Symphony of Mozart (K. 551) and the Third (*Eroica*) Symphony of Beethoven (Op. 55).[6] The "Jupiter" is the last of Mozart's forty-one symphonies. Composed in 1788, before the "Drum Roll" Symphony of Haydn, it was one of a set of three, the other two being the E-flat Symphony (No.

[6] We urge the reader to follow the records of these two works with score in hand.

39) and the famous and somber G minor Symphony (No. 40). Compared with the "Drum Roll," the "Jupiter" shows many differences of detail, although it embodies the same principles of construction. It has a far greater amount of thematic material, as is generally characteristic of Mozart, and, furthermore, the themes are basically more lyrical (cf. the lovely aria-like slow movement). The harmonies of the "Jupiter" are also richer and fuller because Mozart gave the inside parts of the texture more to do and because his harmony is somewhat more chromatic than is that of Haydn. The last movement is a tremendous tour de force in which the sonata form is infiltrated with fugal textures. The first section of the exposition is actually a fugal exposition and the whole last movement uses, all told, five subjects that are combined in various ways. The final pages of this symphony are a dazzling exhibition of Mozart's contrapuntal skill in combining themes, including inversions and exciting strettos (see p. 63 for meaning of stretto).

It seems hardly credible that Beethoven's *Eroica* (1803; first performance, 1805) was composed less than ten years after Haydn's "Drum Roll." The first two Beethoven symphonies still owe a considerable allegiance to the symphonies of Haydn and Mozart; the Third Symphony predicts a new world. The thematic material is less suave, but it is more monumental and more capable of development. The opening theme is a good example of a grand simplicity that is capable of much development. Its first statement ends in a kind of question that has to be answered (Ex. 108a); and later in the first movement this ending is transformed to another kind of question (Ex. 108b) which seems both question and a triumphant answer.

Ex. 108

The whole symphony is distinguished from its predecessors by its dramatic qualities and insistence on personal expression. The two short chords that begin the work call the audience dramatically to attention. Throughout the symphony, the drama is sharply underlined by the clashing dissonances, far more intense than those used by Haydn or Mozart, by powerful figurations, by rhythmic syncopation of individual notes or even measures, and by dynamic outbursts in the form of numerous and characteristic *sforzandi* that are like ejaculations of pent-up emotion. At these moments we hear a more personal note than in the symphonies of Haydn and Mozart. (Cf. Ex. 116, p. 289.)

In almost every way, the *Eroica* is an expansion with respect to previous models. The dimensions of the forms are considerably expanded. A key to this change is Beethoven's attitude toward the development of material; the most vivid instance is the development section of the sonata form. The latter now becomes the heart of the movement. Beethoven obviously has chosen much of the thematic material of the exposition with an eye to its possibility of development, and in the development proper he expands the material by the most varied devices of polyphony and by extensive modulations, including those to remote keys. Beethoven even extends the development of the first movement of the *Eroica* by introducing a new theme; and he turns the coda into another development—this "terminal" development being nearly as long as the exposition itself. This continual spinning out sometimes invades the exposition, and, consequently, in some works there is a less sharp division between the two main tonal sections of the exposition.

The second movement of the *Eroica* is entitled "Funeral March." Its tone is the profound seriousness appropriate to the occasion; and it is typical of the mood of many Beethoven slow movements that reflect the quiet depth of the German folk song and chorale. The slow movement, too, shows Beethoven's powers of expansion; starting with the basic three-part song form—the first part of which shows its origin in the dance form —Beethoven extends this simple germinal form to a work of immense length.

The third movement substitutes the scherzo (literally, "joke") for the old minuet. Formally, the structure is the same: scherzo—trio—scherzo, each part being based on the dance form. But the tempo is now much faster; there is only one (conductor's) beat to the measure, and the impression is no longer that of the court dance in three distinct beats. If Beethoven had a joke in mind for this movement, it is not obvious; in fact, the brilliant trio is "no joke" at all for the three horn players who perform its opening. Note, incidentally, that Beethoven adds a third horn to the instrumentation of the *Eroica*.

The last movement is a set of truly remarkable variations on a theme of his own (ballet music from *Prometheus*). Characteristically, Beethoven sticks to few of the rules. The bass that accompanies the original theme is stated first and developed for two variations; not until the third variation does the principal theme make its appearance. In subsequent variations Beethoven departs further from the traditional practice of variations. He does not restrict himself to the same number of measures as the original theme contained; he modulates, he develops, and in general shows his great gifts for improvisation and development of all sorts, including the fugato. The pronounced individuality of certain variations may be observed by comparing the opening variations with the sixth. The latter is cast in the new key of G minor and is entirely different in character from what precedes it. In one of the later variations the theme is transformed by being played *andante*. The last movement is a fitting close to a symphony that opens new vistas in dramatic expression and overflowing personal sentiment.

Suggested Listening
Haydn, "Drum Roll" Symphony.
Mozart, "Jupiter" Symphony.
Beethoven, Third (*Eroica*) Symphony.

Suggested Reading
See the end of the chapter.

THE SOLO SONATA: C. P. E. BACH. HAYDN. MOZART. BEETHOVEN.

The solo sonata and chamber music of the Classic period shared the same kind of construction and design as the symphony. They differed in the peculiar demands and opportunities of the performing medium, especially in chamber music.

The chief type of sonata for a single player was the keyboard sonata for clavichord, harpsichord, or piano. The clavichord was particularly well suited to the ornamental and expressive style of early Classic music, but it was very limited in volume of tone. The harpsichord became obsolete about 1775, and most pieces for solo keyboard (except the organ) after this time are primarily for the piano.[7] Mozart's pieces, for example, including the concertos, are, after this date, for the piano, not the harpsichord.

The most characteristic examples of the early Classic sonata (about 1750–75) are those of C. P. E. Bach, the most influential instrumental composer between Handel and Haydn.[8] His keyboard sonatas are a perfect combination of the chief elements of the early Classic style: thin harmony, the decorative and expressive style of the rococo, and the robust passage work and fantasy of the *Sturm und Drang* (cf. Ex. 104 and 105).

In spite of the interest of certain of their piano sonatas, the contributions of Haydn and Mozart to the sonata are more impressive in other types of instrumental music, particularly the symphony and chamber music. The pianoforte sonatas of Mozart, taken as a whole, do not represent him at his most interesting and best; and two of his best-known works for piano

[7] The fact that a number of pieces are entitled "for pianoforte or harpsichord" can be regarded as a device to attract the largest possible number of purchasers.

[8] His book *Versuch über die wahre Art das Klavier zu spielen*, 1753 (*Essay on the True Art of Playing Keyboard Instruments*, trans. by W. J. Mitchell; New York: W. W. Norton & Company, 1949) had a tremendous influence in his own time and for years afterward. Beethoven knew it well.

solo are not especially representative of the sonata. The A major Sonata is a delightful work, but it has no movement in sonata form—the first being a variation and the last a rondo (the "Turkish" Rondo). The C minor *Fantasia* is an instance of Mozart at his best, but it is not a sonata at all.[9]

Unlike the piano sonatas of Haydn and Mozart, those of Beethoven cover all periods of his music and are representative of his whole development, from his first sonata in F minor (Op. 2, No. 1, the opening theme probably inspired by one of C. P. E. Bach) to the great sonatas of the last period, Op. 106 (the "Hammerklavier"), Op. 109, Op. 110, and Op. 111, the last. For the purpose of comparison with the Haydn and Mozart sonatas, we suggest listening to two Beethoven piano sonatas from his "middle" period, the famous C-sharp minor "Moonlight" Sonata (Op. 27, No. 2, probably 1801) and his D minor Sonata (Op. 31, No. 2). Both of these have unusually interesting opening movements. The "Moonlight" begins with a slow movement,—Beethoven labeled the piece *Sonata quasi una fantasia*—whose dreamlike character doubtless suggested the title by which this sonata is now universally known. The other sonata begins with the usual *allegro*, but there is nothing conventional about the piece itself. Its remarkable opening alternates slow recitative-like passages with the stirring and animated subject.

Suggested Listening

C. P. E. Bach, Piano Sonata No. 3 (*Für Kenner und Liebhaber,* Third Collection). Compare the first movement with the first movement of Beethoven's first piano sonata, Op. 2, No. 1.

C. P. E. Bach, Symphony No. 3 in C major. The slow movement is a good example of Bach's lyric, chromatic style.

Mozart, Piano Sonata in A major (K. 331).

Mozart, Fantasy in C minor (K. 475).

Beethoven, "Moonlight" Sonata (Op. 27, No. 2).

Beethoven, Piano Sonata, Op. 31, No. 2.

CHAMBER MUSIC

Chamber music of the time involved the most varied combinations. Consequently, the problems and opportunities centering around the instrumental combinations employed were very numerous. Perhaps it was the opportunities and challenges inherent in chamber music that prompted

[9] The *fantasia* (fantasy) is a rhapsodic piece of large dimensions like the sonata, but without any formal key scheme. The sections are usually strongly contrasted as in *fantasias* by C. P. E. Bach.

Haydn, Mozart, and Beethoven to produce some of their best work.

First of all, what is chamber music? As we have already seen, baroque music was classified according to its function for the theater, church, or chamber. Therefore a number of pieces, such as the early symphony, vocal music, chamber sonatas, and chamber concertos, all intended for the chamber, would have been called "chamber music" at that time. But that would not be true today because, among other things, the modern conception of chamber music involves the idea of a single player to a part, thus ruling out orchestral music. The concept of a single player to each part in chamber music became general sometime after 1750; and since that time chamber music has meant instrumental music (vocal music is usually excluded) suitable for playing in a room, using a single player to a part, and composed for combinations ranging from two to nine players. This definition must be applied somewhat elastically. In the first place, the minimum number of two players is specified because music for a single soloist (for example, a piano sonata) is generally ruled out of the category of chamber music. The maximum limitation to nine players might be challenged, for example, in the case of Mozart's *Serenade* for thirteen wind instruments (K. 361). While the number nine is admittedly somewhat arbitrary, this number is selected for practical reasons. Chamber music has traditionally been composed to be played by friends at home or, on a more elegant scale, in the drawing rooms of private houses for the entertainment of guests. Few houses can accommodate the sound of more than nine players (even if they could be assembled), and beyond this number the sound tends to become orchestral. It is probably for this reason that so few chamber works involving more than nine parts have been composed. The *Serenade* of Mozart, mentioned above, was probably intended as music for out of doors.

It is true that chamber music today is often played in concert halls by professional players, but this fact need not disturb the fundamental concept of chamber music or alter the definition. The character of chamber music tends to differ in certain respects from orchestral music. Music that is played for the love of it, and by individual players in a room, is composed with more elaborate detail for the individual parts than music for large bodies of players in a large hall. In a Mozart quartet, for example, the second violin and viola parts usually have far more interesting detail for the player than the same parts in a Mozart symphony. This explains why the average musician prefers to play chamber music for his own pleasure.

The difference between chamber music and orchestral music has a parallel in the fine arts. Paintings or frescoes that have to be seen from a distance must be conceived in large-scale terms; details are simply not perceived by the eye. On the other hand, miniatures or etchings have far more detail. Similarly, the symphony is conceived on broad lines, and the finer and more elaborate details of texture are more characteristic of chamber music.

TYPES OF CHAMBER MUSIC

It is impossible to discuss here all the combinations of chamber music, but some of the possibilities will be suggested. A *duo* most often involves the piano for the reason that with it a harmonic fullness is possible. This is the case in the sonata for violin and piano, for flute and piano, and so on. One of the problems of this type of chamber music is to equalize the musical and sonorous balance of the two instruments taking parts, since the piano is more powerful and has more harmonic potential than its partner.[10] While this problem does not arise in the same degree when the duo does not involve the piano, there are other difficulties, largely harmonic. In the case of two stringed instruments, the thin harmony can be rectified in part by playing in double stops. Another way is to suggest harmonies by figuration in the accompanying part (as in Mozart's duos for violin and viola).

The same problem arises, although to a lesser extent, in the case of a *trio.* A common type is the "piano trio," meaning a trio for piano, violin, and cello. In the case of string trios (violin, viola, cello), the harmonic problem is already solved in theory, although the sonority is not as full as in the case of a quartet or quintet (cf. Mozart's wonderful string trio, the *Divertimento* in E-flat major, K. 563).[11] The use of markedly contrasted instruments also afforded the composer many opportunities for variety of color. In the Mozart Trio for piano, viola, and clarinet (K. 498) there are many remarkable color contrasts; the minuet, in particular, contrasts the various colors of the different registers of the viola and the clarinet, including the *chalumeau* (lowest) register of the latter.

The perfect medium for chamber music is the *string quartet* of two violins, viola, and cello.[12] It is the most popular with composers and players because in it the minimum number of players produces the maximum musical effect. The string quartet can produce a harmony of four parts, corresponding to soprano, alto, tenor, and bass. It also permits a solo

[10] With the disappearance of the figured bass, J. S. Bach's "progressive" type of sonata that equalized the solo and the keyboard parts (see p. 218) became the only one. In the early Classic period the keyboard often dominated the melodic instrument (cf. Mozart's early sonatas for violin and harpsichord).

[11] The *divertimento* was a piece comprising a varying number of movements, usually four to seven, of which some had sonata characteristics and others, those of a dance. Certain *divertimentos* had two minuets (cf. the Mozart trio just mentioned). The *divertimento* was beloved of the Viennese, and there are numerous examples in the works of Haydn and Mozart. Similar forms were the *cassation* and *serenade.*

[12] The evolution of the string quartet from older types of chamber music is a complicated story. See the article "Quartet" in Walter W. Cobbett, *Cyclopedic Survey of Chamber Music* (2 vols.; London: Oxford University Press, 1929–30). See also Tovey's article "Haydn" in the same work.

melody to be accompanied by a full harmony of the three additional parts. Each of the instruments can function either melodically or harmonically throughout a wide chromatic range, and the complete register from the lowest cello C to the highest violin note is well over five octaves. In addition, the color possibilities from combinations of different registers of the instruments are very great. It is no mistake that the repertory for string quartet is greater than that for any other single combination of chamber music, and includes some of the finest works by the greatest composers. Haydn wrote eighty-three string quartets (if the *Seven Last Words* is included); Mozart, twenty-six (plus an *Adagio and Fugue*); and Beethoven, sixteen in addition to the *Great Fugue*.

To extol the virtues of the string quartet is not to say that a *quintet* is less perfect musically. The string quartet is simply the most efficient and flexible combination in terms of the number of players involved. Certain added sonority and color that are obtained by the larger number of parts have to be weighed against the difficulty of getting a fifth player, a very important practical consideration in chamber-music circles. From a musical point of view, the composer has to consider the problem of handling the extra forces so that the individuality of the single part does not become lost in the harmonic web.

On the other hand, there are marked advantages in the string quintet, among them the added sonority of the fifth part and the darker and richer colors of a second viola or cello. Mozart, and after him Schubert and Brahms, handled this combination in a beautiful and imaginative way. The string quintet may be set for two violins, two violas, and a cello (as in Mozart and Brahms), or for two violins, viola, and two cellos (as in Schubert). Mozart's String Quintet in G minor, one of his greatest works, illustrates the advantages of the quintet. Because of the added part, the first viola can serve a dual harmonic purpose: it can be the bass of a string trio of two violins and viola; it can be the soprano of a string trio of two violas and cello. The color contrasts of light and dark are considerable, and Mozart takes advantage of this possibility at the opening of the first movement. In the slow movement the first viola is used in duet with the first violin, while the other three voices furnish the harmonic foundation (see also the slow movement of his C major String Quintet).

When the piano combines with three or more instruments in chamber music, there are always problems, and they are somewhat different from those that occur in smaller combinations. In a *piano quartet* (piano and three other instruments) the ensemble tends to break into two opposing bodies of tone, the three melodic instruments on the one hand and the piano on the other. The melodic instruments are capable of a complete three-part harmony, and their tone color does not always blend well with the keyboard instrument. In the case of strings particularly, there are sometimes problems of intonation, because the piano is rigidly tuned and

the strings are capable of shades of difference that the piano cannot dupli-
cate. These factors tend to set the piano apart from the other instruments.
Consequently, it is frequently treated as a concerto instrument, and chamber music combinations of this sort are, with certain conspicuous exceptions (for example, the piano quintets of Schubert, Schumann, and
Brahms), less often attempted and less liked by players than the string
quartet. Still, any musician loves to make music in the middle of a sonorous body of sound, and perhaps this explains why some of the best piano
quartets and quintets have been written by composers who were themselves pianists.[13]

THE CHAMBER MUSIC OF HAYDN, MOZART, AND BEETHOVEN

Between them, Haydn, Mozart, and Beethoven composed a substantial
body of chamber music. Of Mozart's extensive and varied output in this
genre, the musical center of gravity rests in his string quartets and quintets
(including his Quintet for Clarinet and Strings). Haydn's most important
chamber works are his string quartets and, to a lesser extent, his piano
trios. Beethoven's chamber music includes the ten sonatas for violin and
piano, the piano trios (e.g., the "Archduke Trio," Op. 97), and the string
quartets—to name the most important. Each of these composers wrote
string quartets throughout his lifetime, and the musical evolution of each
is mirrored in his quartets as a whole. Beethoven's development, for instance, is reflected in the change from his six early quartets of Op. 18 to
the quartets of his last years (Op. 127, Op. 130, Op. 131, Op. 132, Op. 135).
As a matter of fact, the whole development of the Classic sonata and its
forms can be traced from Haydn's first quartet (c. 1755) through the last
quartets of Beethoven.

Suggested Listening
Beethoven, the "Spring" Sonata for Violin and Piano, No. 5 (Op. 24).
Haydn, the "Sunrise" String Quartet (Op. 76, No. 4).
Mozart, Trio for Piano, Viola, and Clarinet (K. 498).
Mozart, String Quartet in G major (K. 387).
Mozart, String Quintet in G minor (K. 516).
Beethoven, String Quartet in F major (Op. 59, No. 1).

(For Beethoven's last quartets, see Chapter 17).

---

[13] There are many other chamber-music combinations involving wind and brass,
notably the clarinet and the French horn, but they cannot be discussed here. Cobbett's
Cyclopedia (see above, p. 248, note 12) furnishes details concerning all the major
works of chamber music, by types and by composers.

These six works all belong in the first rank of chamber music or, for that matter, music as a whole. The last three have been singled out for additional comment.

The Mozart String Quartet in G major is the first of the mature Mozart quartets; it is also the first of a set of six dedicated to Haydn—the so-called "Haydn" quartets of Mozart. These quartets (1782–85) were modeled directly on the Op. 33 quartets (1781) of Haydn, in which he speaks of a "new and special manner" of composing (that is, the use of thematic motives). Indeed, as Alfred Einstein says in his book on Mozart, "The impression made by these quartets of Haydn's was one of the profoundest Mozart experienced in his artistic life."

Mozart's debt to Haydn and Haydn's appreciation of his young friend are shown vividly by a story connected with the dedication of these quartets to Haydn. In February, 1785, Leopold Mozart, the father of Wolfgang, reported on an evening of music when three of these quartets were played for Haydn: "Herr Haydn said to me, 'I declare to you before God as a man of honor, that your son is the greatest composer that I know, either personally or by reputation; he has taste, and beyond that the most consummate knowledge of the art of composition.'" Shortly afterward (September 1785), Mozart, then twenty-nine years old, published these six quartets with an affectionate dedication in Italian to Haydn, at that time in middle age (fifty-three):

To my dear friend Haydn! A father who had concluded to send his children into the world at large thought best to entrust them to the protection and guidance of a famous man who fortunately happened to be his best friend as well. Behold here, famous man and dearest friend, my six children. They are, to be sure, the fruit of long and arduous work, yet some friends have encouraged me to assume that I shall see this work rewarded to some extent at least, and this flatters me into believing that these children shall one day offer me some comfort. You yourself, dearest friend, have shown me your approval of them during your last sojourn in this capital. Your praise, above all, encourages me to recommend them to you, and makes me hope that they shall not be entirely unworthy of your goodwill. May it please you therefore, to receive them kindly and to be their father, their guide and their friend. From this moment I surrender to you all my rights on them, but beg you to regard with leniency the faults which may have remained hidden to the partial eye of their father, and notwithstanding their shortcomings to preserve your noble friendship for him who loves you so dearly. Meanwhile I am, from all my heart, etc. W. A. Mozart. Vienna, September 1, 1785.

The opening of the G major Quartet shows from the outset the influence of the idea of thematic motivation. The short phrase given the viola (m. 5) is taken up successively by the second violin (m. 6) and the first violin (m. 7). The accompanying parts are not merely static harmony; they have considerable interest melodically, even if subordinate to the chief melody. The parts themselves are more equal in interest than in the earlier Haydn and Mozart quartets. While these earlier works neglected the viola and cello, this quartet of Mozart's gives far more to the lower two strings. In particular, the viola has a solo in the development section of the first movement (m. 67). With the increased activity of the lower voices, the harmony becomes fuller and richer.

Mozart follows the first movement (in sonata form) with the minuet, not the slow movement. The former is in G major, while the trio is in G minor—one of several ways in which this particular trio is set off from the minuet proper. The following slow movement (C major, $\frac{3}{4}$ time), a sonata form without development, is remarkable for its profundity of feeling and lyrical beauty. The fourth and last movement anticipates the fugal procedures of the "Jupiter" Symphony. Mozart begins the exposition of this movement with a fugato. Another fugato is used to begin the second key, and Mozart then combines the subjects of both fugatos in a kind of double fugue. The latter is used again in the fascinatingly compressed recapitulation. A coda concludes the movement and the work.

Mozart's String Quintet in G minor is a somewhat later and more profound work. The contrasted trio textures of the two statements of the first theme have already been mentioned (p. 249). The first movement is notable for the fullness of the sonority of its five voices and for the beauty of the first two themes (Ex. 109a,b). The opening theme has striking possibilities for development: it is chromatic and contains a number of small motives. The second theme is a haunting one, particularly in its third phrase, which leaps upward a minor ninth from D to E flat.

Ex. 109

The minuet has several points of interest. First of all, beginning at measure 4, the phrasing is such that duple time is actually heard instead of the triple time in which the minuet is written. The four measures following measure 4 are written in $\frac{3}{4}$ time; they actually sound like six measures of $\frac{2}{4}$ (Ex. 110a). Secondly, the reverse of the key situation in the

Ex. 110a

minuet of the G major Quartet occurs in the Quintet, where the minuet is in G minor and the trio, in G major. The G major trio of the Quintet steals suddenly upon the listener. The first violin emerges alone from the cadence of the minuet, playing a B natural, a decisive note that distinguishes G major from G minor (Ex. 110b). The other parts immediately

Ex. 110b

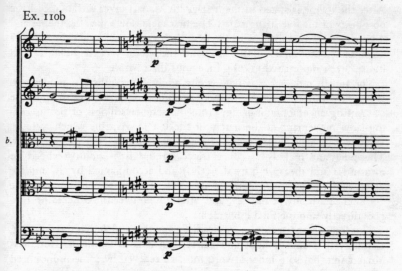

join in and play the legato melody softly. At measure 14 Mozart makes good use of the dark colors of his lowest three instruments. The two violas play the melody in thirds and are accompanied by the cello.

The slow movement that follows is an extraordinary example of emotional profundity and technical perfection. The piece is full of color contrasts and shades of light and dark. Mozart calls for mutes on all the instruments; this gives a peculiar sheen to the music. The sonority of the opening chords is deepened and darkened by the choice of key, E-flat major, the key a third below the tonic of G minor (rather than the more usual key of B flat, the relative major, a third above). After the opening four measures there is a duet between the violin I and the cello.

At first these two instruments are heard alone, then with all the other parts.

A bridge section modulates to B flat. But it is in B-flat minor, not the B-flat major that the ear expects (m. 18). The *sforzando* with which the passage begins is also unexpected. The darkness of the remote key of this passage is intensified as the instruments descend, hushed to a *piano;* and at the end of this phrase (m. 19) the second viola emerges to declaim dramatically a brief motive from its deepest register. Then begins a modulation, full of harmonic ingenuity, from the tonic minor back to the tonic major (m. 26), accomplished in a miraculous way. The first violin soars into the octave above to sound the D natural, *sf-p* (*sforzando-piano*), to emphasize the major. Here all is light—a complete contrast to what has preceded. The character of the accompaniment is also changed. It is completely harmonic, but the three inside voices animate the passage rhythmically by playing "off the beat" with rests between their chords. After the theme is stated in the first violin Mozart takes advantage of the possibility of his five string parts. The first viola now takes the theme and it is echoed in duet form with the first violin, while the other three voices accompany, the cello on the beat and the violin II and viola II with figures even more rhythmically ingenious than before.

The fourth movement is not, as one might expect, the last movement. It is a slow movement (in G minor) of some length, serving the purpose of creating an emotional bridge from the somber stillness of the preceding slow movement to the gaiety of the last movement, which follows. Whatever its artistic purpose, it is a complete and moving piece in itself. The poignant melody is concentrated in the first violin (echoed in measure 4 and measure 9 by the cello) and accompanied by the middle voices and the *pizzicato* notes of the cello. The movement ends on the dominant harmony of the key, and, after a hold over the concluding rest, goes directly into the final movement.

This movement seems to contradict everything that has preceded it. Certainly it is full of light and gaiety, and it is in G major. Doubtless Mozart felt that so somber a work must be relieved by some pronounced contrast at the end. At any rate, the opening of the last movement is a welcome contrast. This movement has an interesting and complicated formal structure: essentially a rondo, but with elements of sonata form and imitative counterpoint. Like many rondos of Haydn and Mozart, the main opening statement (twenty measures), as well as several other of the main parts, are cast in the dance form: A:‖:B+A:‖. Thus the large parts of the structure are themselves subdivided into smaller and repeated parts. The movement ends in the brightness of G major, concluding with strains of gaiety a work that opened in dark and somber mood.

Beethoven's String Quartet in F major is the seventh of his string quartets. It is also the first of the three "Rasoumovsky" quartets of Op. 59, commissioned by Count Rasoumovsky, the Russian ambassador to Vienna. Formally, this quartet is unusual because all the movements are in sonata form, including the second movement, a particularly interesting scherzo in B-flat major. Compared with Mozart's G major Quartet, there is more equality of interest among all the string parts; the second violin and the viola have more to do. The dimensions of the forms themselves are more ample, particularly the extended development sections and codas. In the first movement, for example, the development includes a fugato. There are also more distant modulations and greater contrasts of all sorts including those of range and color (Ex. 111).

Ex. 111

Besides the interest of its form, the second movement impresses us with its reiterated rhythmic patterns (Ex. 7) and its harmonic changes. The third movement (*adagio molto*), in F minor, is typical of Beethoven in a mood of profundity. Note especially the extraordinary development section with its full harmonies, motives shared among all voices, elaborate harmonic changes, and *pizzicato* running figures in the cello (m. 59) and viola (m. 67). The coda ends with a kind of accompanied cadenza for the first violin, leading directly into the last movement (*allegro,* F major). This movement, based on a *Thème Russe,* poses difficult ensemble problems for the players, largely because of the syncopated and conflicting rhythms, carried out by the two violins as one pair, pitted against the viola and cello as the other.

The true measure of these works cannot be merely their popularity in the concert hall. The reaction of the player is of great importance too, for, after all, chamber music is for him as much as for the audience. Furthermore, the player hears the work in a different way from the listener; his perspective cannot help but differ. The same person often receives different impressions of a piece of music when he listens and when he plays it. To the writer of these lines, the first movement of Beethoven's A minor Quartet (Op. 132) is a different and even greater experience when played. At any rate, these pieces of chamber music can be heard and played again and again with a pleasure that never diminishes.

Suggested Reading

See articles on the chamber music of Haydn, Mozart, and Beethoven in
Walter W. Cobbett, *Cyclopedic Survey of Chamber Music* (2 vols.).
London: Oxford University Press, 1929–30.

THE SOLO CONCERTO

The beginnings of the concerto, the *concerto grosso* and the solo concerto of the early eighteenth century, have already been discussed (see
Chapter 14). Since the *concerto grosso* became obsolete after 1750, our
remarks relate primarily to the solo concerto. To recapitulate briefly: The
idea of a solo concerto is basically a musical "competing" between a
soloist and the orchestra. In this competition there are basic contrasts
between the soloist and the orchestra with respect to technical ability, mass
of sound, and instrumental timbre. The most typical solo concertos are
the violin concerto and the piano concerto; concertos for other instruments are less frequent (cello, clarinet, flute, bassoon, horn, and so on).
Occasionally a composer writes a concerto for more than one instrument.
Examples are Vivaldi's concertos for four solo violins; Mozart's *Sinfonie
Concertante* for violin and viola; Beethoven's Concerto for piano, violin,
and cello; Brahms's Concerto for violin and cello.

The concerto of the Classic period has at least three typical features that
taken together set it apart from other forms of the time: (1) its three
movements, (2) a "double" exposition in the *first* movement, and (3) a
cadenza.

The first and last of these features are easily described. The three-
movement form resembles the scheme of the symphony without the
minuet: *fast—slow—very fast.* The cadenza is a musical flight of fancy
used to exhibit the technical capabilities of the solo instrument in the
hands of a virtuoso player. Most typically, the cadenza occurs at the end
of the first movement, but it may occur elsewhere in this movement or in
any of the other movements. The cadenza of the Classic concerto was not
written out, but left to the performer to write out or even to improvise in
the concert, the latter being the original idea. This practice was a natural
and normal one as long as the composer was the performer (for example,
Mozart). In this case, the cadenza was more than a vehicle for the display
of technical virtuosity. It also served the purpose of a special kind of
musical coda in which the principal ideas of the movement were presented
once more in a new light of virtuoso display. The musical value of the
cadenza tended to decrease when the composer and the performer were
no longer the same person. In the nineteenth century many composers,
such as Schumann and Mendelssohn, wrote out their cadenzas in full to
avoid the musical abuses that had arisen in cadenzas written by per-

formers more interested in virtuosity than in musical ends. On the other hand, excellent cadenzas uniting musical ends and technical skill have been written by some great virtuosi, for instance, Joachim and Kreisler.

The position of the eighteenth-century cadenza is generally indicated merely by a *fermata* ($\frown$), meaning to hold at will. The *fermata* occurs for the most part on a chord which produces the feeling of expectancy or incompleteness (most often a I^6_4 chord; see under *harmony*). This chord creates the appropriate atmosphere for the entrance of the soloist—like the carefully staged entrance of a beautifully gowned woman at a ball. The end of the cadenza invariably leads to the dominant (V) of the home key, thus resolving the harmonic expectancy created at the *fermata*. The cadenza usually terminates with a more or less elaborate trill (see Glossary), and the orchestra comes in triumphantly on the tonic. In the case of the most typical cadenza, that at the end of the first movement, the orchestra concludes with a final *tutti* statement.

The third feature of the Classic concerto is the "double" exposition of the first movement: the first exposition played by the orchestra alone, the second by the soloist and the orchestra. In graphic form the double exposition of a typical concerto looks like this (T = *tutti* or orchestra; S = soloist; Exp. I (II) = exposition I (II); I = themes in first key; II = themes in second key):

Double Exposition:

Exp. I	(T)	Exp. II (S)	
I	(II)	I	II
Tonic	Tonic	Tonic	Dominant or relative major

Development: S and T concerting; modulations; development of I and II.

Recapitulation:

Mainly repeat of			
Exp.	II (S and T)	Cadenza	Coda
I	II	(S)	(T)
Tonic	Tonic		Tonic

In this scheme the second exposition has certain features of sonata form, such as the two contrasting keys. The opening *tutti* of the first exposition, however, is by no means a musical duplication of the more elaborate, main (second) exposition. The two expositions generally start with the same thematic material. But the first exposition is usually entirely in the tonic, and frequently only part of the thematic material of the second exposition is used. Compared with the second exposition, the first exposition lacks the contrast of key, the contrast of solo and orchestra, and often the contrast of thematic material.

It is conventional to say that the typical first movement of the Classic concerto is an offspring of the sonata form, but it is not true; and the often-stated idea that the double exposition of the concerto is merely the written out repeat of the exposition of sonata form is completely misleading and entirely erroneous.

For some time the best critics, among them Donald Francis Tovey, have been uneasy about the discrepancy between the "textbook" definition of the first-movement concerto form and its treatment by masters like Mozart and Beethoven. Therefore, the evolution of the first movement of the concerto from the time of Vivaldi to Mozart will be demonstrated below for those who care to follow it.

MATERIAL FOR FURTHER STUDY

The evolution of the first-movement form of the Classic concerto. Actually, as recent studies have shown, the sonata and the concerto had parallel, but somewhat different developments. The requirements of the concerto differed from those of the sonata, because in the latter there was no "competition" between the performing instruments. As described earlier in this book, the sonata principles of earlier times were replaced during the Classic period by the new phrase structure and by the melodic and harmonic style of the time. In the symphony, chamber music, and solo sonata, the sonata form was the most characteristic and successful solution. But in the case of the concerto, the principles of the earlier solo concerto of Vivaldi, especially as regards the first movement, carried over into the new style of composing and were blended with it. Thus the development of the sonata form took place *at the same time* as the development of the Classic concerto. *But the principles of the baroque concerto determined certain features of the Classic concerto to a much greater extent than the baroque sonata determined the features of the Classic sonata.* The typical first-movement form of the Classic concerto is not an offspring of the Classic sonata form. It is the principles of the former that are derived from an earlier type of concerto and grafted to the melody, supporting harmony, and typical phrase and key structure of the Classic style.

To clarify this further, let us review briefly the earlier solo concerto of Vivaldi (d. 1741). In his solo concertos the prevailing scheme of the first movement was the *ritornello* form (see p. 215). In this scheme the orchestra, basically strings, stated the opening section of the concerto and then alternated with sections in which the soloist dominated and was accompanied by the orchestra. A typical scheme of a Vivaldi first movement looks like this (T = *tutti* = orchestra; S = soloist):

$$T_1—S_1—T_2—S_2—T_3—S_3—T_4$$

This scheme consisted, in short, of four *tutti* (*ritornelli*) with which three solo statements alternated. A picture being worth a thousand words, we give another diagram that shows at a glance the basic evolution of the concerto from Vivaldi to Mozart.

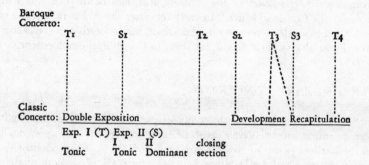

The double exposition of the first movement of the Classic concerto is actually an adaptation of the first three sections (T_1-S_1-T_2) of the *ritornello* form described above. The first *tutti* of the *ritornello* form becomes the first exposition of the Classic concerto. It begins and ends in the tonic key, and is mainly in the tonic throughout. It may contain the melodic material of the following second (*solo*) exposition, but it usually does so in abbreviated form. The S_1 of the *ritornello* form becomes the second (main) exposition of the Classic concerto. It begins typically with the *solo* version of the main *tutti* subject. It may be preceded by an entry of the solo instrument before the second exposition proper. The two contrasting tonalities of this exposition correspond to the exposition of sonata form. Hence it ends in the new key. T_2 of the *ritornello* form *becomes the third and final section of the double exposition.* This is one of the features of the concerto that has been little understood in the past. In the Classic concerto this section is called the *closing tutti,* and it belongs to the double exposition, *not* to the development. The repetition of the double exposition is extremely rare, and repeat signs are always suspect as additions of an editor.

The middle sections of the *ritornello* form become a development: S_2 for instance. T_3 may become absorbed in the development *or* in the recapitulation. The development section is modulatory or rhapsodic. The orchestra and the solo are competing musically.

The recapitulation is basically another solo section, and, as in sonata form, the material of the exposition is restated basically in the tonic. The movement is completed by a final *tutti* section. The usual position of the cadenza is at the end of the recapitulation or in the final *tutti*. In any case, the movement is customarily ended with a *tutti* coda.

The other movements of the Classic concerto present no special problems but share the forms typical of the sonata.

The development of the Classic concerto can be studied in its earlier phases in J. C. Bach (the "London" Bach). It reaches its full maturity in the numerous concertos of Mozart. With Beethoven the concerto is a complete amalgamation of the contrast principles of the concerto with those of the Classic style itself. In early concertos the orchestra tends to be relegated to a role accompanying the soloist, but in Beethoven the orchestra almost always has a significant share in the musical development.

TWO MOZART CONCERTOS

Since Mozart is the concerto composer par excellence of the late eighteenth century—just as Vivaldi is of the earlier part of the century—we will discuss salient points of two Mozart concertos: the A major Violin Concerto (K. 219) and the D minor Piano Concerto (K. 466). Both of these well-known concertos show marked individuality and somewhat unusual features.

The Violin Concerto (No. 5) is the earlier work (1775). Mozart wrote relatively few violin concertos—five that are undoubtedly genuine—and those only in his early years. The Piano Concerto, on the other hand, is No. 20 of 25 piano concertos, and it was composed in 1785, ten years later, a long time in Mozart's short life.

The Violin Concerto consists of the usual three movements, but it has several exceptional features. After the first exposition—thirty-nine measures of *allegro* presented in the tonic by the orchestra—the soloist surprises us by entering with a songlike *adagio* of six measures, the thematic material being quite different from that of the opening *tutti*. The *adagio* actually serves as a transition between expositions I and II. After the *adagio* the soloist continues, now in the original tempo (*allegro aperto*). But again a surprise: the soloist does not have the theme of the opening. Instead, the soloist is given a new theme (Ex. 112a) which soars above the accompaniment of the main theme of the first exposition (Ex. 112b), played by the orchestra.

The relative importance of the first and second exposition can be judged by their length; the first has thirty-nine measures, the second, seventy. The development is more of an episode in a related key; there is no genuine development of material already heard. A splendid transitional passage leads back to the recapitulation, which basically repeats the second exposition, but this time entirely in the home (tonic) key. The

Ex. 112

solo part is more exciting, and there is a fermata (see p. 257) indicating the free cadenza. The first movement then closes with the orchestra playing a section corresponding to the closing section of the second exposition.

The second movement is an *adagio* in a closely related key (E major). An unusual feature is the form, which is analagous to that used in the first movement of a concerto. There is also a *fermata* for a cadenza. The return to the recapitulation is beautifully done, heard first in the orchestra and then echoed by the soloist.

The last movement is marked *Rondeau Tempo di Minuetto*.[14] There are several short cadenzas indicated in this movement. A surprising middle section provides a dramatic change. It is cast in $\frac{2}{4}$ time and the mode is changed to minor (A minor). This is the same kind of "Turkish" music as in the "Turkish" Rondo of the finale of the A major piano Sonata already mentioned. This is sprightly and sparkling music. The return to the minuet proper is varied in ornamental fashion.

The D minor Piano Concerto is a more mature and far more dramatic work. The drama is partly inherent in the character of the thematic materials, partly in the contrast of the motivic themes and those more lyric in character. There is also drama in the sharp juxtaposition of the

[14] The use of different dances in *rondeau* form goes back much earlier. In the early eighteenth century, for example, a common title in French dance suites is *Gavotte en Rondeau.*

soloist and the orchestra, now grown to the proportion of a symphony orchestra. In this respect and in the important part the orchestra plays in the musical development, the D minor Concerto approaches Beethoven's concept of the concerto more than do the majority of the Mozart concertos. It is significant that in the A major Violin Concerto, Mozart uses only two oboes, two horns, and strings, while in the D minor Piano Concerto he specifies flute, two oboes, two bassoons, two horns, two trumpets, timpani, and strings—in fact, precisely the same instruments that comprise the orchestra for the "Jupiter" Symphony.

The Piano Concerto is also a marked contrast in mood and in dimension to the Violin Concerto. The latter is not without its forceful moments, but it is basically graceful, polished, and brilliant. In the former, however, the motivic and forceful themes are far more stormy and agitated, especially in the opening *tutti* of the first movement. The Piano Concerto is longer by virtue of more thematic material and greater expansion of it. Both the orchestra and the soloist have more to do with the development of the material, thus balancing each other in musical interest. Characteristic of the greater responsibilities of the solo part are the passages played without accompaniment—the first entrance of the piano is unaccompanied—and the increased amount of scale and passage work assigned to the soloist, particularly in the extended closing passage of the second exposition. A cadenza is indicated in the usual place at the end of the recapitulation, and an orchestral coda, drawn from the material of the first exposition, ends the movement.

In the slow movement (*Romanza*) in B-flat major a lovely lyrical opening and closing part is in complete contrast with a middle section in minor, devoted not to singing style but to figuration in the solo piano part.

The last movement (D minor) begins in sprightly, vigorous fashion. Formally, it is a rondo with one section devoted to development of the material, thus combining elements of the rondo and the sonata. In this movement there is a particularly marked contrast between the dramatic type of theme with which the piece begins and the gaiety of the most important contrasting theme in F major (Ex. 113). A notable feature is the coda, of exceptional length for Mozart, and based on the theme just mentioned. The concerto ends with this joyful theme in the brilliant key of D major, not in the minor in which the movement (and the concerto itself) opens. Just as in the G minor String Quintet, the somber tone of the first movement is dissolved in the joyful triumph of the finale.

Like his chamber music, Mozart's concertos are numerous (about forty) and for a number of different instruments. In addition to the violin and the piano concertos, there are four concertos for horn, two for flute, and one each for clarinet, bassoon, violin and viola, and flute and

Ex. 113

harp. In this brilliant concerto-company the large number of different, individual solutions to the concerto problem is striking. That these solutions are all based essentially on the same principles is a tribute to Mozart's ingenuity and economy in his eternal search for new varieties of expression.

Suggested Listening

Mozart, Violin Concerto in A major (No. 5).
Mozart, Piano Concerto in D minor (No. 20).

Suggested Reading

Denis Arnold and Nigel Fortune (ed.), *The Beethoven Companion*. London: Faber & Faber, 1971.

Cuthbert M. Girdlestone, *Mozart and His Piano Concertos*. Norman: University of Oklahoma Press, 1952.

Arthur Hutchings, *A Companion to Mozart's Piano Concertos* (Second edition). New York: Oxford University Press, 1950.

Donald Mitchell and H. C. Robbins Landon (ed.), *The Mozart Companion*. London: Faber & Faber, 1956.

Rudolph Réti, *Thematic Patterns in Sonatas by Beethoven*. London: Faber & Faber, 1967.

Charles Rosen, *The Classical Style: Haydn, Mozart, Beethoven*. London: Faber & Faber, 1971.

Donald F. Tovey, *Essays in Musical Analysis* (6 vols.). London: Oxford University Press, 1935-9. Volume III is devoted to concertos.

16. *Opera and Sacred Music of the Classic Period*

OPERA DIFFERS FROM ONE PERIOD TO ANOTHER, but there are certain general points about it that should always be kept in mind. In the first place, an opera is a drama realized in music, and, in its strictest sense, it is composed to music from beginning to end. There are recognized exceptions, especially in the comic opera, where spoken dialogue may be used under certain conditions (see *Fidelio* and *Der Freischütz*). In the second place, opera is a combination of different arts: music, poetry, acting, dancing, staging, and costuming. Of these, music is not always or necessarily the most important. Frequently the librettist and the stage architect are considered at least as important as the composer. A third point is that opera is the most expensive kind of music to perform, and it has always operated at a deficit, by subsidy, or by court, state, or private support. In earlier times opera was most frequently a court function used to glorify the monarch, local court, or potentate. A fourth factor, and one that is most important to opera as music, is that there is an eternal conflict between the demands of the music on the one hand and those of the drama on the other. When music and drama are linked together, neither can follow its own dictates completely. There must be some compromises. When the words are sung, the drama cannot unfold as rapidly as when the words are spoken. On the other hand, if music is to have any interest at all *as music,* the various devices employed to make music interesting may slow down the drama and even obscure it. Music for its part must not carry its requirements too far or the words will cease to have coherence and the dramatic continuity will be lost; or the drama may be replaced by a text that is merely an excuse on which to hang the music. Most of the writings about opera are concerned with the fundamental problem of reconciling the demands of the music and the drama. In effect, the ideal opera is not the dramatist's opera, in which the drama overshadows the music (cf. Peri's *Euridice*); or the musician's opera, in which the music overshadows the drama (cf. the Neapolitan opera of the early eighteenth century); but a blend of the two where music and drama act as partners in a project which is greater than the sum of its parts (cf. Mozart's *Figaro*).

THE OPERA SERIA. *THE GLUCK "REFORM."*

The old Neapolitan *opera seria* continued into the late eighteenth century. Mozart wrote in this form (e.g., *Idomeneo*, 1781) as well as in the forms of the comic opera. Other celebrated composers who continued the traditions of the *opera seria* into the Classic period were J. A. Hasse, Jommelli, and Piccini (the rival of Gluck; *not* spelled Puccini). But the important thing was not the continuation of the *opera seria*, but its reform by Gluck (1714–87).

As we have already noted, the abuses of the *opera seria* were by no means unrecognized by critics of the opera or by composers themselves. Benedetto Marcello (see p. 195) and Count Algarotti (1712–64) both wrote satires exposing the weaknesses of the serious opera. The later works of composers like Jommelli and Traëtta show a renewed interest in the libretto, the continuity of the form, and the use of the chorus.

The virtue of Gluck lay in uniting the reform ideas and giving them practical form in works of genius. As a young man he wrote Italian *opera seria*, as well as comic operas in the French style for Vienna. Convinced of the validity of the ideas of the reformers, Gluck wrote two Italian operas for Vienna which exhibited the proposed reforms: *Orfeo ed Euridice*, 1762, and *Alceste*, 1767. Much credit for these works must go to his librettist, Calzabigi.

Gluck enumerated his ideas in a famous document, the Preface to the opera *Alceste*. In it, he stressed the following points: [1]

1. Music should not dominate the poetry, but should enforce the expression of the sentiment of the text.

2. The continuity of the action should be maintained and not interrupted by display of ornamental pieces merely to satisfy the demands of the singers [a slap at the *da capo* aria and its ornamented return].

3. The overture should prepare the listener for the mood of the piece.

4. The instruments should be chosen and used to suit the situation described in the text.

5. There should be less sharp distinction between the recitative and the aria.

6. The chief endeavor should be to "attain a beautiful simplicity."

7. Mere display of difficulty or novelties not inherent in the dramatic situation should be avoided.

[1] For the complete text, see Oliver Strunk, *Source Readings in Music History* (New York: W. W. Norton & Company, 1950).

8. Any rule should be sacrificed for the sake of the total effect.

Actually, the principal work of the reform was carried on in French, not Italian opera, and the clash between the reform credo of Gluck and the traditional school of Italian *opera seria* came to a head in Paris in the operatic "war" between Gluck and the Italian opera composer, Piccini. For Paris, Gluck wrote all the later reform operas: *Iphigénie en Aulide* (1772), *Armide* (1777), *Iphigénie en Tauride* (1779). In addition, both the earlier Italian reform operas were rewritten for Paris: *Orphée et Eurydice* (1774) and *Alceste* (1776). In the case of the French reform opera, Gluck's ideas enumerated in the Preface to *Alceste* were already characteristic of French opera in the tradition of Lully and Rameau. Gluck also employed several features of the French opera not common in *opera seria* and not specifically mentioned in the *Alceste* Preface, for example, big chorus scenes and the ballet. In Gluck the ballet is related to the dramatic action (not inserted merely to have dancing for decorative purposes or to relieve the tedium). At times, as in *Orphée* (see below), the ballet music is thematically related to its musical context. This type of "integrated" ballet was inspired in part by the reforms proposed by the French ballet master, Noverre. Finally, the ideas of Rousseau and the Encyclopedists had already anticipated in general the reforms of Gluck, and in him the French intellectuals found the genius who put their ideas into practice.

As with many reformers, there was some discrepancy between Gluck's reform credo and his practice. Like Wagner after him, Gluck was more of a musician than a poet, and while he created musical moods to emphasize the text, music was not relegated to a secondary position in the scheme of the opera. In addition, particularly in the early work, *Orfeo,* important remnants of the old *opera seria* remained. The character Orfeo is a male contralto (later changed to tenor in the Paris version), and the old device of the *deus ex machina* (a device used in Greek drama to unravel the complications of the plot by the intervention of a god) is necessary in the person of the god Amor to bring the opera to its desired conclusion.

However, after *Orfeo* Gluck followed in the main his principal idea. The action is simple and monumental. The music is continuous where the drama demands it. There is less distinction between recitative and aria, and the former is accompanied by the orchestra in dramatic style. The old stylized overture is abandoned, and in its place is substituted a single movement or one that flows directly into the action (*Iphigénie en Aulide*). The instruments of the orchestra are chosen for their effectiveness in depicting a situation. In Gluck's hands, the characterization of individuals may be observed in certain operas, as is shown in the representation of the passions of such figures as Alceste, Orestes, Iphigenia, and Achilles.

ORPHEUS AND EURYDICE (ORPHÉE ET EURYDICE)

We suggest listening to Gluck's *Orpheus and Eurydice,* keeping the particulars of his reform ideas in mind. Notice especially (1) the use of the instruments of the orchestra, including the exceptional trombones; (2) the simplicity and grandeur of the choruses; (3) the ballet related to the action; (4) the combination of expressive style (in several of Orpheus's arias) and style related to the *Sturm und Drang* (see p. 232) with its forceful string figuration, leaping figures, and tremolos; and (5) the extended scenes.

The story of the opera is given with reference to material pertinent to the above five points. Orpheus, a legendary figure famous for the beauty and moving power of his playing on the lyre, has just married Eurydice. The joy of Orpheus soon turns to grief, however, because Eurydice perishes from the bite of a serpent.

Act I. After the overture, the curtain rises to disclose Orpheus and a chorus, clustered around the tomb of Eurydice, solemnly bewailing her death ("If here where all is dark and silent"). Orpheus is inconsolable and resolves to descend to the underworld to reclaim Eurydice from the relentless gods. He is supported in his purpose by Amor, the God of love, who tells Orpheus that he shall see Eurydice again, but that he must lead her back to earth without looking at her. Orpheus prepares to descend to the underworld.

Act II. After a brief orchestral introduction, Orpheus, playing the lyre, is seen threading his way among the Furies of the underworld who acknowledge his presence by a chorus ("Who is this mortal one"). The chorus refers to the barking of the dread dog Cerberus, who guards the path, and the musical barking is heard in the orchestra. In an aria, accompanied by harp (a modern substitute for the lyre, and quite appropriate in the context), Orpheus pleads for sympathy and help from the underworld spirits. At first they reject his pleas with a monumental NO (in unisons, and octaves, reinforced in the orchestra by trombones). But, gradually mollified by the power of his playing, they permit him to pass. This continuous scene, shared between Orpheus and the chorus, is followed by a ballet, the celebrated "Dance of the Furies." It is integrated into the action in that the Furies of the underworld give vent to their emotions in this way; and it is integrated musically because the ballet uses some of the music previously heard in the chorus. The "Ballet of the Elysian Fields" introduces Eurydice who sings of the abode of "the Blessed ones." Her sentiments are echoed by the chorus. The spirits promise to lead Orpheus to Eurydice.

Act III. Orpheus is calling to Eurydice to follow him. But Eurydice cannot understand why he will not look at her. Orpheus urges haste, but Eurydice demands "a single glance." Orpheus begs Eurydice to trust him.

But she reproaches him bitterly for what she thinks is his silent disdain. Orpheus cannot bear her reproaches and turns to gaze on her. As she dies, he sings, "I have lost my Eurydice." Orpheus then resolves on death in order to rejoin Eurydice. But Amor stays his hand, and, as a reward for his constancy and faith, awakens Eurydice and permits her to return to earth with him. (For the purposes of a happy ending, Gluck changed the Greek myth, according to which Orpheus, overcome with grief by the loss of Eurydice, treated the Thracian women with contempt. In revenge, they tore him to pieces.)

THE COMIC OPERA: PERGOLESI. MOZART.

The vogue of *opera seria* in the early eighteenth century had been undermined by the comic opera. Pergolesi's comic operas started a rage in Italy after his initial success with *La Serva Padrona* (1733; see p. 199); and *The Beggar's Opera* contributed to Handel's failure as an impresario of serious opera. The comic opera was successful because it could always be understood (being sung in the language of its country), because it had genuine dramatic values, and because it was amusing.

It was also typical of the reaction to the baroque, and in many ways it was characteristic of the new spirit of the later eighteenth century. Musically, it sought simplicity in its emphasis on short-breathed, lively melodies, supported by transparent harmony. The plots represented a "return to nature," by abandoning the old mythological and historical heroes for pastoral, peasant, and middle-class figures. The subjects of the plots emphasized everyday affairs and sometimes themes of current political interest. Pergolesi's opera is an example of the former. Dominant political themes of the time are seen in Monsigny's *Le Roi et le Fermier* (*The King and the Farmer;* 1762), in which the shepherd foils the noble villain; and in Mozart's *Le Nozze di Figaro* (*The Marriage of Figaro;* 1786), in which the designs of a philandering nobleman are thwarted by his own servants and wife.

Pergolesi created a distinct new genre, and it was subsequently imitated by other composers who amplified the unpretentious scheme of *La Serva Padrona.* The number of characters was increased, and sometimes three (or even four) acts were used. Some features of the *opera seria* were borrowed, for instance, the more elaborate orchestra and independent orchestral pieces such as the overture. In certain operas like Mozart's *Don Giovanni* elements of both the comic and the serious opera may be found. In Italy important composers of *opera buffa* after Pergolesi were Logroscino, Galuppi, Piccini, and Cimarosa. But the greatest was Mozart, an Austrian brought up in the tradition of Italian opera.

THE FRENCH COMIC OPERA

In France the comic opera (*opéra comique*) was modeled directly on Pergolesi, whose music precipitated the so-called "war of the *bouffons*" (i.e., the players of Italian *opera buffa*) in which the adherents of French music in the grand tradition of Lully and Rameau were opposed by the adherents of the Italian *opera buffa* of Pergolesi and his followers. In all this, philosophy and politics were intimately enmeshed. Pergolesi's opera, being simple and natural in plot and music, greatly appealed to J. J. Rousseau, who himself wrote a little comic opera *Le Devin du village* (*The Village Soothsayer;* 1752), directly modeled on Pergolesi. Rousseau also roundly condemned French music in a celebrated *Letter on French Music,* 1753 (for text, see Oliver Strunk, *Source Readings in Music History*). Rousseau's *Letter* may be considered part of the *"bouffon* war," in which the King and the aristocrats supported the traditional French opera, while the Queen and the intellectuals like Rousseau and the Encyclopedists supported the cause of Italian music.

Just as in the case of Italian *opera buffa,* later French comic opera became more complex and less naïve. The subject matter, however, continued to be basically the same, being concerned with pastoral, peasant, middle-class, and everyday life. A frequent topic was the rescue of the village maid from the base schemer of high station. The bourgeois drama, introduced by Diderot, created good librettos for the comic opera. The best poets were Favart, Sedaine, and Marmontel. Examples of middle-class subjects are Philidor's *Tom Jones* (1765; on Fielding's novel of the same name) and Monsigny's *Le Déserteur* (*The Deserter;* 1769, libretto by Sedaine). A change from these topics is indicated by still later works: Grétry's *Richard Cœur de Lion* (1784) and Cherubini's *Les Deux Journées* (1800), produced in London as *The Water-Carrier* (1801).

The *opéra comique* had a vogue outside of France, notably in Vienna. Gluck, for instance, wrote several comic operas for Vienna (*La Rencontre Imprévue—The Chance Encounter;* 1764). As with the *opera buffa,* the later history of the French comic opera witnessed the blending of comic and serious elements. The *opéra comique* in the nineteenth century is distinguished from the *grand opera* only in its use of spoken dialogues.

THE GERMAN COMIC OPERA

The German form of the comic opera, the *Singspiel,* resembled the English ballad opera (cf. *The Beggar's Opera;* see p. 200), and was actually founded on it. As in England, spoken dialogues were interspersed with simple songs and dances of ballad or folk-song nature. Later, the German *Singspiel,* centered in Vienna, was based on the French *opéra comique,* and was consequently more elaborate in its settings. J. A. Hiller's *Die Jagd* (*The Hunt;* 1770), for example, was based on the libretto of Monsigny's

Le Roi et le Fermier. Other examples of the developed Singspiel are Mozart's two operas *Die Entführung aus dem Serail* (*The Abduction from the Seraglio;* 1782) and *Die Zauberflöte* (*The Magic Flute;* 1791). In the nineteenth century, Beethoven's *Fidelio* (1805; revised, 1814) and Weber's *Der Freischütz* (1821) were later manifestations of the *Singspiel;* the characteristic spoken dialogue occurs in both.

THE COMIC OPERAS OF MOZART

Mozart's extraordinary versatility has already been amply demonstrated. It can be shown again in his operas, for he wrote in the various prevailing styles: the Italian *opera seria,* the *Singspiel,* and the Italian *opera buffa.* To the latter he contributed three of his greatest works: *Le Nozze di Figaro* (1786), *Don Giovanni* (1787)—called by Mozart a *dramma giocoso* in spite of its serious elements—and *Così Fan Tutte* (Thus Do All Women; 1790), Mozart's last comic opera.

The serious opera and the comic opera have already been described in general. Certain particulars about the comic opera, notably its forms, remain to be mentioned:

(1) The *cavatina,* a form simpler than the arias (i.e., without *da capo*). Similar forms are the *arietta,* the *air,* and the *canzona.*

(2) The aria in rondo or free rondo form. In *The Marriage of Figaro,* Figaro's aria *"Non più andrai"* is an aria in rondo form.

(3) "Composite" arias. The composite aria comprises two or three sections, all in the same key but different in character and in speed (for example, *andante, allegro, presto*). The last section often has the characteristics of a *stretta,* that is, a concluding or coda-like section performed at increased speed.

(4) The ensemble. In an ensemble a number of characters are included in one piece, for climactic and often dramatic effect. If the ensemble comes at the end of the act, as it often does, it is called an *ensemble finale.* Most of Mozart's *ensemble finales* are also composite finales. They consist of a number of different pieces, each with its own tempo, character, and form; and each corresponds to the dramatic necessities of the plot. All the individual pieces or sections are performed continuously to make up the complete finale—see the Finale in Act II of *The Marriage of Figaro*—and most finales end with a *stretta.*

THE MARRIAGE OF FIGARO

Just as Gluck's *Orpheus* was suggested as an illustration of the "reform" opera, so Mozart's *The Marriage of Figaro* will be discussed as an example of the *opera buffa.* One could hardly ask for a work in which musical and dramatic elements are better balanced, one that better illustrates the mature *opera buffa*—or an opera that is more delightful.

The librettist Lorenzo da Ponte, a figure of great importance in the creation of the Mozart opera, adapted the text from Beaumarchais' famous comedy *Le Mariage de Figaro* (1784). The latter stressed the conflict between the oppressive aristocracy and the lower classes, and because of its political implications, it was banned in Vienna. All the political skill and intrigue of Da Ponte was essential to secure a hearing for Mozart's work. Happily, the first performance of *Figaro* was a success in Vienna, and the subsequent Prague performances, a triumph.

The most striking single feature of this opera is the creation and portrayal of individual characters. One can never forget the individualities of Susanna, Figaro, Cherubino, and the Count—to mention only four—nor the way in which Mozart's music depicts them. The subtlety and deftness of Mozart's orchestra in characterization cannot be sufficiently praised. As in all *opera buffa,* the narrative unfolds by means of recitative. Furthermore, in *Figaro* the finales and composite arias carry the action swiftly along with the continuous dramatic unfolding of the rapidly changing situation.

The delineation of character begins with the libretto. From Da Ponte's text alone one can receive a clear impression of the characters involved. But Mozart succeeds marvelously in adding depth and subtlety to these characters by musical means, and he stresses certain facets of the situation and makes them more vivid through all the resources of music. Mozart characterizes individuals and situations by appropriate melodies, striking rhythms, and harmonic intensity and suggestion. With the greatest skill, he uses the orchestra to depict; and in his hands dynamics are a powerful tool for emotional change. In large ensembles, Mozart portrays individual character by individualizing the melodies used for each.

Since the text is the heart of the drama, one should listen to *Figaro* with a libretto in hand.[2] The plot, being extremely complex, cannot be summarized completely, so we will choose certain scenes for comment. The comedy concerns the events leading to the marriage of Figaro and Susanna, against the background of the philanderings of Count Almaviva, a member of the nobility. Figaro, the valet of the Count, is about to marry Susanna, the personal maid of the Countess Almaviva; and the marriage takes place in spite of the Count's determined efforts to keep Susanna himself.

After an overture full of sparkle and gaiety (in sonata form without development), the curtain rises on the first scene, which is between Susanna and Figaro. Susanna is trying on a hat in front of the mirror, and Figaro is pacing out measurements on the floor. Notice how accurately the orchestra reflects first Figaro's ponderous and measured pacings, and then the coquettish vanity of Susanna. (Ex. 114).

In this scene Susanna reveals to Figaro that the Count has been trying to make love to her. Figaro, full of indignation, resolves to thwart the

[2] Good English translations are available, that of E. J. Dent, for instance.

Ex. 114

Count and Don Basilio, the Count's go-between. This resolve is related to the audience in an aria in three-part form, *"Se vuol ballare,"* in which Figaro sings, "If you want to dance, dear Count, I shall call the tune." The text of his aria gives Mozart many opportunities for word painting, and he makes the most of them through the orchestra. The aria is also a composite aria using a *presto* section in the middle.

The trio *"Cosa sento,"* in the middle of this act, is an excellent example of how Mozart differentiates the sentiments of three different persons with respect to a situation. One is made to see Don Basilio as a sly and oily intriguer enjoying the discomfiture of the Count and Susanna. At the same time, the agitation of Susanna is reflected in Mozart's music to the text "Oh, how dreadful! I am ruined."

At the end of the act there is a piece that is brilliant and characteristic of Mozart. Cherubino, the adolescent page of Count Almaviva, has a passion for ladies—for all ladies, in fact. Cherubino's adventures have become altogether too numerous to suit the Count, and, as a disciplinary measure, the Count in effect banishes Cherubino, ironically bestowing on him a commission in the army. Figaro concludes the first act with an amusing satirical song (*"Non più andrai"*), contrasting Cherubino's gay life as an "amorous butterfly" with what he may expect among warriors marching through mud and snow. This basic contrast in the mood of the text gives Mozart the opportunities for musical characterization, of which he is a great master. The brilliant close of this aria is built on the text *"Cherubino alla vittoria, alla gloria militar"* ("Cherubino off to victory, to military glory"), and it is a marvel of "military glory." In the marchlike music of this passage the trumpets are used with great effect to underline Figaro's satirical words as he regards with great amusement the discomfort of the dandified Cherubino.

Michael Kelly, a friend of Mozart's (and in the original cast as "Ochelly") wrote a fascinating eyewitness account of the first performance of this aria at the first orchestral rehearsal of *Figaro:*

> I shall never forget Mozart's little animated countenance, when lighted up with the glowing rays of genius; it is impossible to describe it as it would be to paint sunbeams. I remember at the first rehearsal of the full band, Mozart was on the stage with his crimson pelisse and gold-laced cocked hat, giving the time of the music to the orchestra. Figaro's song *Non più andrai* Benucci [singer] gave with the greatest animation and power of voice. I was standing close to Mozart, who, *sotto voce,* was repeating: "Bravo, bravo, Benucci" and when Benucci came to the fine passage, *Cherubino alla vittoria, alla gloria militar,* which he gave out with stentorian lungs, the effect was electricity itself, for the whole of the performers on the stage, and those in the orchestra, as if actuated by one feeling of delight, vociferated: *"Bravo, bravo, maestro, viva, viva, grande Mozart."* Those in the orchestra, I thought, would never have ceased applauding, by beating the bows of their violins against the music-desks. The little man acknowledged by repeated obeisances his thanks for the distinguished mark of enthusiastic applause bestowed upon him.[3]

In the beginning of Act II the Count, a gay Lothario himself, is greatly agitated by an anonymous letter (actually written by Figaro) implying that the Countess has a lover. Going to her rooms, the Count is enraged to find her door locked. Actually, Susanna and the Countess are quite innocently dressing Cherubino for an intended intrigue against the Count. What happens as a result of this is the subject of the lengthy *ensemble finale* (beginning *"Esci omai"*), in which one situation rapidly gives way

[3] Michael Kelly, *Reminiscences* (2 vols.; London: H. Colburn, 1826).

to another as unexpected as it is delightful and amusing. The reaction of different persons and groups to the same situation is characterized by Mozart in masterly fashion in the large ensembles. (It is impossible to follow this here—and it *must* be followed completely and in detail in order to understand the whole pageant of situation and character.)

The third and fourth acts continue the marvelous interplay of plot and counterplot, but the details must be left to the curiosity of the reader. However, a subtlety of characterization in the fourth and last act should not escape attention. Figaro, misinterpreting Susanna's actions, thinks that she is unfaithful to him, and he bitterly contemplates his situation, upbraiding Susanna and all women in the recitative *"Tutto è disposto"* ("All is ready") and the following aria *"Aprite un po' quegl' occhi"* ("Open those eyes a little"). The orchestration of this aria refers pointedly to the situation. According to old belief, a man whose wife was unfaithful grew horns on his head. When Figaro speaks bitterly about the infidelity of women, the passage "the rest we'll pass over in silence; you all know what happens" is heavily underscored with horns, emphasizing the text with a kind of musical pun that everyone in the eighteenth century understood only too well.

In the end Figaro and Susanna are united, the Countess forgives the Count once more, and the opera closes with the sentiment "forget and forgive who contented and happy would be."

Suggested Reading

Edward J. Dent, *Mozart's Operas.* New York: Oxford University Press, 1947.

Alfred Einstein, *Gluck,* trans. by Eric Blom. New York: E. P. Dutton & Co., 1936.

Donald J. Grout, *A Short History of Opera.* New York: Columbia University Press, 1947.

SACRED MUSIC: HAYDN. MOZART.

Sacred music is a broad term that includes music used for the church service and music on sacred subjects used for special occasions. Examples of types of music connected with the service are Masses, motets, litanies, hymns, offertories, vespers, and cantatas. The Requiem is a special type of church service, a Mass for the dead used at the funeral service. The oratorio is the best instance of a piece of sacred music that is not used in the church service.

In the late eighteenth century the oratorio and the Mass settings were the most elaborate and important musically. Haydn composed twelve polyphonic settings of the Mass; Mozart, nineteen, including a Requiem;

and Beethoven, two.[4] A feature of the eighteenth-century Mass is the increased dimensions of the musical setting of each of the five parts of the Ordinary (*Kyrie, Gloria, Credo, Sanctus, Agnus Dei*) that comprise the polyphonic Mass.[5] There is a tendency to subdivide the text of the lengthiest sections, the *Gloria* and *Credo* in particular, into separate and distinct parts. We have already mentioned earlier that the *Gloria* of Bach's B minor Mass is subdivided into some eight distinct pieces. Similarly, in Beethoven's *Missa Solemnis,* the *Gloria* has at least seven sections. To be sure, Bach and Beethoven are extreme cases.

The Requiem Mass differs in certain respects from the usual Mass. The *Kyrie* is prefaced by the text *"Requiem aeternam"* (hence the name of the Mass), which starts "O Lord, give them eternal rest." The *Gloria* and *Credo* are not appropriate to the burial service, and are displaced by a lengthy Latin hymn *"Dies Irae"* ("O Day of Wrath"), a thirteenth-century poem attributed to Thomas of Celano. This is followed in order by an Offertory *"Domine Jesu Christe"* ("O Lord, Jesus Christ"), the *Sanctus* and *Benedictus,* the *Agnus Dei,* and the Communion *"Lux aeterna luceat eis"* ("Let eternal light shine on them"). This sequence of texts is followed in such celebrated pieces as the Mozart Requiem and those of Berlioz and Verdi (Brahms uses a special text for his Requiem; see p. 331).

Sacred music of the time of Haydn and Mozart exhibits a duality of musical style in which the new harmonic-melodic way of composing is contrasted with the more archaic polyphony ("learned") style of imitation and fugue. There is also an emphasis on the chorus and the orchestra. Solo parts or ensembles of soloists occur for the most part as episodes in the choruses. The influence of the opera is noticeable in Italian church music, but in sacred music as a whole, the recitative and aria are largely restricted to the oratorio (cf. Haydn's *Creation*).

The influence of the orchestra and the forms of instrumental music made themselves felt in sacred music, especially in Germany. Some Masses may even be called "instrumental," as the orchestra plays a predominant part in them with respect to the voices, and because the musical coherence of the whole work is achieved by schemes of repetition and contrast, derived from such instrumental music as the sonata and rondo. In the mature Masses of Haydn and Mozart there is a blend of the old vocal polyphony and symphonic development.

Mozart's Requiem Mass (unfinished at his death in 1791; his pupil Süssmayer completed it) leans heavily on the symphony orchestra for its effects. Vocally, the Requiem is set mostly for chorus with solo episodes or ensembles of soloists (there are no solo arias). The old style of counter-

---

[4] Beethoven's Masses will be discussed later (pp. 329-30).

[5] Remember that only the text of the Ordinary is set polyphonically (but see p. 146, note 9). For the complete text of the Ordinary, see the Appendix.

point may be seen in the opening *"Requiem"* and particularly in the following *Kyrie,* which is a fugue on two subjects (a species of "double" fugue). The two subjects, one set to *Kyrie,* the other to *Christe,* are shown as they are first heard (Ex. 115). In the *"Dies Irae"* the orchestra adds tremendously to the excitement suggested by the text "Day of Wrath."

Ex. 115

An oratorio is an elaborate musical piece of considerable length, set, usually, to a sacred text from the Bible or related sources (e.g., the Apocrypha). Since the oratorio is an occasional piece aimed at moral edification, it may be performed in the concert hall or in the church, but it is not part of the church service proper. A special type of oratorio is concerned with the "Passion" story (see p. 208), and to this the term *Passion-Oratorio* is applied. A good example of the latter is Graun's *The Death of Jesus* (1755).

The best-known oratorios of the time, however, are those of Haydn. His models for *The Creation* (1799) and *The Seasons* (1801) are the oratorios of Handel, with which Haydn became familiar during his visits to England. Like Handel, Haydn uses recitative and arias, duets, trios (and even larger ensembles), chorus, and orchestra. The style and texture is that of the Classic period, except that the "learned" style of imitation and polyphony is stressed in the choruses. The orchestration is also typical of Haydn's time. A special characteristic is the musical care with which Haydn depicts the scenes of nature in his oratorios.

  Suggested Listening
Mozart, Requiem (opening *Kyrie* and *"Dies Irae"*).
Haydn, *The Creation.*

  Suggested Reading
See the end of the chapter.

HAYDN AND MOZART COMPARED

  It is natural to compare Franz Josef Haydn (1732–1809) and Wolfgang Amadeus Mozart (1756–91), just as it is to compare Bach and Handel;

and in the same way it is easy to emphasize them at the expense of a host of other composers. Nevertheless, in their lives and music Haydn and Mozart summarize much of the style and condition of music in the late eighteenth century, and in this sense they are together a mirror of the musical life and times.

They lived at the same time, in the same region of Vienna, and under the same system of patronage; but their lives were very different. Haydn's life was relatively uneventful, and his extremely productive career with the Esterhazy family shows patronage at its best. Only at the end of his long career, when he was famous, did he venture outside his own country for the two English visits. On the other hand, Mozart's phenomenal artistic success as a child prodigy took him all over Europe and to England before his maturity; and into his tragically short life he packed the joys and sorrow, the travels and experiences of many ordinary lifetimes. Mozart was more a victim than a beneficiary of the patronage system, and he never had a regular patron. After his marriage to Constanze Weber, he was never free of financial worry. The last two years of his life were filled with unprofitable honors, intense activity, and dire poverty. His last letters to his friends, especially Michael Puchsberg, begging for money, are pitiful and tragic, a sad commentary on the wasteful cruelty with which society sometimes treats those it can least afford to lose.[6] *See Plate 24A.*

Haydn and Mozart enjoyed a perfect friendship and mutual esteem, as is evident from the passage in which Mozart dedicates his first mature quartets to Haydn (see p. 251). Because Haydn was born some twenty years before Mozart and also because of the disparity in the length of their lives—Mozart lived to be thirty-five, Haydn, seventy-seven—Mozart was influenced as a young man by Haydn, but Haydn, when already over fifty, was influenced by the still young but mature Mozart toward greater clarity of form and a more cantabile (singing) style. The majority of the Haydn works heard today, a number of which were composed after Mozart's death, were influenced by Mozart; and all Mozart's mature instrumental works fell under the influence of Haydn.

The stature of Haydn as a composer may be measured by comparing his early quartets and symphonies of the 1750's with the symphonies and quartets composed forty years later in the 1790's. The change of style that took place in this time reflects not only the maturity of an individual composer, but also the change in composing styles to which Haydn contributed so much. Haydn inherited the homophonic style of the sonata, but his special genius brought great changes to it. This is especially evident in his last symphonies (the "London" Symphonies) and in his last twenty string quartets. The remarkable individuality of these last works has often been

---

[6] Mozart's letters are a wonderful commentary on musical conditions of the late eighteenth century and his relation to it—his autobiography, in fact. See the excellent translation of all the letters by Emily Anderson (ed.), *The Letters of Mozart and His Family* (3 vols.; London: Macmillan and Co., 1938).

commented on, and it cannot fail to impress those who hear them. Haydn's composing career was one long experiment in improving the forms and styles of expression, particularly in instrumental music, in which he excelled. He is the "father" of the symphony and the string quartet in that these forms reached their first maturity in him.

In earlier discussions, various elements of Haydn's style have been mentioned, for example the motivic melodies and the dancelike rhythms of the "Drum Roll" Symphony. Other melodies are characterized by a cheerful and playful gaiety, particularly in the rondos found in the last movements of the symphonies or chamber music. A deep quiet, spiritually at one with the German Lied, often permeates the slow movements (cf. the slow movement of the String Quartet Op. 76, No. 5).

Haydn's harmonies and rhythms are often surprisingly daring, for although he uses a relatively restricted range of keys, his modulations and choice of keys are sometimes quite remarkable. Haydn is frequently unconventional in rhythm. For instance, an eight-measure phrase may be constructed of five measures plus three measures, not of four measures plus four measures, as one might expect. The way in which Haydn uses the *sforzando* to change the bar line and the meter has been pointed out in connection with the discussion of the "Drum Roll" Symphony (see p. 82).

The division of the orchestra into well-defined choirs, and the function of individual instruments or choirs as melodic or harmonic instruments, took place in the late eighteenth century. Haydn and Mozart freed the viola from dependence on the cello part; they subdivided the string parts (*divisi*) on occasion; and by adding the clarinets they achieved a more complete woodwind choir, melodically and harmonically.

Haydn's character, as one knows it from his biography, is reflected to a considerable extent in his music. It reveals a lively character, a kindly man —"Papa" Haydn was a title of affection, not ridicule—with moments of great force and profundity in which he anticipates Beethoven. There is nothing in his life, perhaps, that gives a clue to one of his most essential traits: his true originality, to which all his music is a monument. On the other hand, his pronounced love of a joke has many musical counterparts, and this characteristic of Haydn's has endeared him to music lovers of all times.[7] His humor ranges from subtleties, understood primarily by professional musicians, to a broad jesting that has become legendary. To the latter category belongs the "Surprise" Symphony in which Haydn inserted a sudden, very loud chord in the middle of an apparently innocuous slow movement, with the supposed intent of awakening all the sleepy and inattentive courtiers in the audience. A number of other instances could be cited, such as the "Farewell" Symphony and the "Joke" Quartet.

Until recently, Haydn was one of the great composers forgotten by the

[7] Perhaps too much so. Haydn's gaiety and humor have been stressed at the expense of his originality and profundity.

general public. Only a handful of his symphonies (numbering over a hundred) were played, and his chamber music was known largely by those who played it. There is no complete edition of Haydn's works, although a Haydn Society has been formed recently to rectify this situation. With the advent of the phonograph and especially of the long-playing record, Haydn is coming into his own. This is as it should be, for Haydn, together with Mozart, perfected the characteristic means of expression for the symphony and sonata of the late eighteenth century.

Mozart was one of the greatest creators of spontaneous melody. Singing melody is more characteristic of Mozart than of Haydn, and even penetrates certain of his *allegro* movements (i.e., his *singing allegro*). At the same time, Mozart inclines to introduce chromatic elements into his subjects (cf. the opening of his G minor Quintet; see Ex. 109a).

Mozart was so full of melody that his forms are overflowing with song and thematic material. In the sonata form, for instance, Mozart may have three, four, or even more, distinct melodies in the exposition, while Haydn has far fewer; in fact, a single melody may serve Haydn for a whole exposition. These differences of procedure are partly rooted in the different character of the typical themes of Haydn and Mozart. Since Mozart's melodies tend to be complete in themselves, Mozart is more inclined to contrast several of them. On the other hand, Haydn's themes are more often constructed motivically with a view to what they will become. These differences help to account for Haydn's greater economy with respect to melody in the expositions and also for his relative prodigality with respect to the development sections. As a rule, his development sections are longer than Mozart's for the reason that his thematic materials, more motivic in character, are capable of a longer development than are Mozart's more stable and more lyrical subjects.

The richness of Mozart's harmony comes partly from the chromatic elements mentioned above, partly from the fact that the inner parts of the texture are fuller and more interesting than those of Haydn. This may be seen by comparing the second violin and the viola parts of the Mozart string quartets with those of Haydn. In fact, in Mozart one may find an almost perfect balance of the forces of harmony and counterpoint. There is a wonderful equilibrium between the demands of the ensemble as a whole and the demands of the individual part, which naturally prefers not to be mere accompaniment, but to share motives and melodies with the other parts.

By use of certain devices Mozart achieves dramatic effectiveness in his instrumental music. For example, the dramatic contrast of the major and the minor in his G minor Quintet is a case in point; or his use of dissonance for special effect at the entry of the first violin in the introduction of the String Quartet in C major (the "Dissonance" Quartet, K. 465).

Mozart's forms are distinguished by both clarity and individuality. He separates one section clearly from another; and the individuality with which he treats a large number of forms is one of the signs of his genius, as we have tried to demonstrate in previous discussions of opera, concerto, symphony, and chamber music. Mozart also contributed a number of special solutions to the problem of combining forms, for instance the rondo and the sonata form, and incorporating fugal elements into the sonata.

In one of his letters, Mozart has indicated his way of composing. When he was entirely alone and in good spirits (he wrote), his ideas flowed best and most abundantly. Where they came from or how "I know not; nor can I force them." Mozart doubtless had a tremendous facility in composing. Yet on at least one occasion, he must have worked hard at improving his first thoughts. The autograph of the quartets dedicated to Haydn shows that Mozart revised considerably, and the preface (cited above, p. 251) speaks of the loving care that Mozart had lavished on these works.

Mozart possessed musical gifts of the highest order as a performer and as a composer. But more than that, his gifts were almost universal in scope.[8] There is hardly a type of composition that Mozart did not try and, trying, transform into something of individual beauty. In addition, his range of emotional expression encompasses the most brilliant gaiety and the intensely tragic. Mozart's life shows a similar scale of emotional intensity, but it would be difficult to trace any direct relation between his moments of despair and the character of his music composed at these times. Still, to express emotion most convincingly one must first have experienced it; and the music to the brilliant comedy of *Figaro* could only have been written by a man who thoroughly understood at first hand the sorrow and joy of life. The same kind of joy in life is found in his instrumental music, in the last movements especially. The intensively sad, even tragic, may be found in his *Don Giovanni*. The latter has its comedy just as *Figaro* has its moments of poignancy (the Countess's aria *"Dove sono"*). Certain of the instrumental pieces are likewise touched with deep shadows and suffering. The G minor Quintet is a good study in deepening intensity of emotion, finally relieved in the last movement by lightness and gaiety.

Above all, Mozart's understanding of the human heart and his insight into the deep wells of individual character lie at the background of his power to create the vivid personalities that crowd his operas. One can never forget the vivid individuality of Figaro and Susanna or Don

[8] The attractions of Mozart's music for a universal audience are seldom admitted. The finish and perfection of his music are supposed to be attractive only to relatively sophisticated audiences. In this connection it is worth noting that a recent explorer among the Indians in territory between Venezuela and Brazil found that a Mozart Symphony played on a portable phonograph was an *open sesame* to them. The Indians were indifferent to Sousa's *Stars and Stripes Forever* and to Louis Armstrong, but they were mad about Mozart.

Giovanni, Leporello, Donna Anna, or Osmin. In these sharply defined individuals, one can see reflected in a far more universal way the foibles, triumphs, and tragedies of men and women everywhere. For this reason it is not surprising that so many interpretations can be read into the relationships of the main characters in *Don Giovanni,* in much the same way that Hamlet is a mysterious individual whose basic character can be variously interpreted.

In certain ways Mozart is a child of his times, but in others he looks forward to a later day. It is significant that the nineteenth century thought of him, but not of Haydn, as belonging to certain currents of the Romantic movement. This ambivalence in Mozart's position may be summarized by recalling his revolt against the Archbishop in Salzburg, at the same time having to rely in Vienna on the patronage of an emperor who failed him. The cult of lyricism and expressiveness in the nineteenth century saw in Mozart's melodic prodigality and dramatic power a kind of personal expression close to its own aesthetic values. In addition, *Don Giovanni* and *Figaro* may be viewed as social documents, commenting on the abuses of the old system against which the French Revolution was aimed. It is doubtful, however, if the political significance in these works appealed to Mozart as much as the dramatic possibilities of the libretto. The animating force in Mozart's life from first to last was music.

Suggested Reading

Alfred Einstein, *Mozart, His Character, His Work,* trans. by Arthur Mendel and Nathan Broder. New York: Oxford University Press, 1945.

Karl Geiringer, *Haydn, A Creative Life in Music.* New York: W. W. Norton & Company, 1946.

Donald Mitchell and H. C. Robbins Landon (ed.), *The Mozart Companion.* London: Faber & Faber, 1956.

László Somfai, *Joseph Haydn: his Life in Pictures.* London: Faber & Faber, 1969.

17. *The Early Nineteenth Century*

ROMANTICISM

THE NINETEENTH CENTURY was one of the great centuries of human thought and activity. It was also a century of great contradictions: between freedom and oppression, science and faith, capitalism and socialism. The Napoleonic Wars, born of the French Revolution, succeeded in creating a new tyranny, that of Napoleon. After his fall in 1814, a reaction against the new liberal currents of the time was personified in Prince von Metternich, the Austrian chancellor and one of the chief supporters of the Holy Alliance (Austria, Russia, Prussia). The liberal movement for constitutional changes and reforms led to European revolutions in 1830 and particularly in 1848, when Louis Philippe abdicated in France and Metternich resigned. Other important political events were the unification of Germany and Italy into modern states and the founding of the German Empire (1871). At the same time, the defeat of France by Germany established the latter as a great power.

The liberalism and democracy of the nineteenth century were predicated on individualism, and freedom was the slogan: free speech, free press, and individual liberty. These ideals took other forms, especially that of humanitarianism (for example, the foundation of the International Red Cross), toleration, and kindliness. The brotherhood of man and similar aspirations led to writings like those of Tolstoi in Russia, to the freeing of the Russian serfs (1861) under Alexander II, and the abolition of slavery in the United States (1863).

At the same time, political and social thinkers could not overlook the everyday miseries of masses of people as a result of the Industrial Revolution and the factory system. The struggle was now one of "liberation" of the working class. Capitalism came under serious attack in the writings of the socialists, at first those of the "Utopian" socialists like Robert Owen in England, and more effectively later those of Karl Marx, whose "scientific" socialism was embodied in his *Das Kapital* (1867-94). "Utopian" socialism was tinged with humanitarianism and liberalism, but the "scientific" system of Marx and especially the political system that it engendered were antithetical to humanitarianism, and the collectivism of his socialism could not be reconciled with the individuality of liberal democracy.

The tremendous advance of scientific thought and experiment in the nineteenth century was bound to bring about various conflicts with the established order. The theory of evolution of Spencer and Darwin challenged the notion of man's divine origin, and consequently science and faith collided. Established dogmas and the comfortable rationalism of the eighteenth century were challenged and often overthrown. At the end of the century the modern psychology of Freud (already anticipated by Schopenhauer and others) showed the vast power of fantasy and the dream world in shaping human conduct, and completely discredited the old idea of behavior regulated solely by reason. The scientific discoveries of the time were incorporated in many practical applications, such as the telegraph (1832) and telephone (1884), the electric light (1840), the automobile (1887), and the radio (1895).

While the natural sciences were trying to explain the universe in mechanistic terms, music and literature were adding mystery, strangeness, and romance to beauty—a reaction of art to the rationalism of the previous century. In literature, there was a tremendous outpouring of love lyrics (Heine, Shelley) and the fanciful and historic (Byron, Scott). Poems were dedicated to the ideals and brotherhood of man (Schiller's *Ode to Joy* used by Beethoven in the Ninth Symphony). The myth, folklore, and themes of nature pervaded literature (Wordsworth, Coleridge). Later a realistic reaction marked the decline of these sentiments. The novels of Flaubert and Zola specialized in portrayal of conditions as they existed; and in opera, *verismo* (truth) indulged in scenes of realistic brutality (Bizet's *Carmen,* Puccini's *Tosca*).

The new sentiments in nineteenth-century art were known loosely as *Romanticism*. The Romantic movement started in the late eighteenth century as a literary movement in Germany.[1] Such writers as Tieck and Novalis turned to the culture of the Middle Ages in a reaction against the supposed shallowness and arid formalism of the eighteenth century. The term "Romantic" was used to express the spirit of the age of the Romanesque or of the medieval *roman.* The imagination of writers of this time was awakened by medieval romances, by the spirit of chivalric adventure, by the picturesque and suggestive in nature, and by folklore and magic. Thus Romanticism furnished some new subjects for art works, but above all it brought to their expression the fanciful and naïve, the emotional, passionate, and exotic. Romanticism represented the "addition of strangeness to beauty" (Walter Pater). The movement spread from Germany throughout Europe, especially to France and England. An interesting by-

[1] For an excellent extended account, see Paul Henry Lang, *Music in Western Civilization* (New York: W. W. Norton & Company, 1941).

product of Romanticism was a renewed zeal for old music; and the desire for authentic source material led to the publication of critical editions of older composers (among them Bach, Handel, and Palestrina).

While Romanticism as a term and as a movement was first of all literary in origin (Goethe and Schiller), its choice of subjects and especially its rather indefinite emotional character suggested music as a particularly appropriate medium of expression. In music, the early Romantic movement is represented by Schubert and Mendelssohn, and more characteristically by Schumann, Chopin, and Weber.[2] Later stages of the Romantic movement are reflected in the works of Berlioz, Liszt, and Wagner, among many others.

FORMS AND STYLES OF ROMANTIC MUSIC

A number of the characteristic themes of the Romantic movement, such as those of love or longing for nature, found their appropriate expression in an intense lyricism embodied in short pieces: the songs of Schubert and Schumann, the mood or "character" piece for the piano (such as *bagatelle, impromptu, moment musical, capriccio*), and other pieces with special titles suggesting a program. Schumann's *Fantasy Pieces* suggest moods rather than pictures, and poetic references of various kinds emphasize the literary sympathies of much Romantic music. A number of composers in the nineteenth century were highly cultivated in literature, sometimes themselves gifted as writers, and they often looked to literature for inspiration. Schumann is a good example. He was inspired by poetry, especially that of Jean Paul Richter. At the same time, Schumann's own literary gifts enabled him to write penetrating musical criticism of a high order, for which he was first known, and he contributed greatly to the encouragement of young musicians, notably Chopin and Brahms, through articles in *The New Magazine for Music,* which he founded in 1834. The best example, however, is Berlioz. His writings show an immense talent for literary expression, and there was no composer in the nineteenth century more susceptible than he to the inspiration of literature, particularly of Shakespeare.

The song and the one-movement piano piece were excellent vehicles for Romantic lyricism; the traditional forms, such as the sonata form, were less so. The lyrical subject was not at home in a development section of sonata form, and counterpoint, necessary for development of thematic material, was less natural to many of the composers of this period than

---

[2] Indeed from Weber's *Freischütz* (1821) one can date the beginning of musical Romanticism. The case of Beethoven is a special one, and will be discussed in the next section.

were the resources of harmony. In addition, in works of large dimensions, the Romantic musicians were seeking a synthesis of their material into a unified whole. Wagner sought this in an alliance of all the arts in the music drama; and Liszt was animated by similar ideas of continuous unity in creating the symphonic poem and the sonata in one movement. The old formal distinctions between the different movements of the symphony began to break down, and individual movements (sometimes all the movements) were linked together. Sections or themes from one movement were recalled in later movements to give a cohesive unity to the entire work, and the weight of the symphony sometimes shifted to the last movement.

The emotional effect came into its own in Romantic music because the desire for individual expression prompted a search for the unusual. Rich and strange harmonies or distant keys were used for beautiful colors or sonorities. The melody itself became more expressive in its curves, its chromatic coloring, and its wealth of expressive dynamic nuance. Special attention was paid to the orchestration and the clear definition of melodies, not only by the use of striking solo instruments, but also by the rich and sometimes unexploited registers of the instruments. The cello, for instance, was often used for expressive *tenor* melodies sounding the main melodic material in the middle of the surrounding texture; and analogous effects were achieved on the piano. In rhythm, greater flexibility or even ambiguity of accent was exploited (for example, by Chopin), and combinations of different rhythms and syncopations were effectively used by composers like Brahms.

Significantly, the range and power of the piano were increased. Its great range of pitch and dynamics and its almost infinite possibility of nuance made the piano an ideal instrument for an emotional style. The greatly increased use of the piano pedals permitted new effects of sonority approaching those of the orchestra (e.g., Liszt).

The manner of playing an instrument or the "interpretation" of a conductor sometimes added an emotional and personal element that was "Romantic" in itself. Hence the special importance of the virtuoso soloist and conductor. Emotional and subjective interpretations were characteristic of the nineteenth century—appropriately so with regard to much Romantic music, but less so with regard to older music of quite different aesthetic aims.

Of the social changes related to musical life, the most important was the gradual death of the old patronage system. In some cases it was replaced by the free market, and in others, by state support (the opera in Germany). The commercial concert and the commercial opera began to flourish, and, with them, the traveling virtuoso. The appearance of the music journalist or critic also dates from this time, because music had to be interpreted and explained to a new, middle-class public through newspapers and magazines.[3] Education in music became more widespread as the number of schools of music and conservatories increased and as printed music became cheaper and more abundant. The free economic market for the composer was a natural result of the spirit of the time and a *laissez-faire* economy. But it had the unfortunate effect of making it harder for new music to be heard, and it widened the gap between the composer and his public—a gap that has been widening ever since (see p. 382 ff).

Suggested Reading

Alfred Einstein, *Music in the Romantic Era.* New York: W. W. Norton & Company, 1947.

LUDWIG VAN BEETHOVEN (1770–1827)

Any discussion of music in the nineteenth century must begin with Beethoven, for, like Monteverdi two centuries earlier, he bridges two eras. While the music of the eighteenth century played a formative role in Beethoven's early style, his last works are separated from those of Haydn and Mozart by a wide gulf—a gulf as pronounced as that which the rise of the middle class, the French Revolution, and Romanticism produced between the eighteenth and nineteenth centuries. Beethoven's greatness manifests itself in a force and intellect that required new styles and expanded forms to contain his ideas and emotions, and his example profoundly influenced all subsequent music. *See Plate 24B.*

Beethoven exhibited a new attitude toward society, and his position in contemporary Viennese society was quite different from that of Haydn and Mozart. A prouder and bolder spirit by nature than either of them, and imbued with the new ideas of the rights of man and the revolutionary idea of the pre-eminence of the artist, he treated the highest personages in society as equals from the beginning. Bettina Brentano, who numbered Goethe and Beethoven among her friends, suggested that Beethoven treated God as an equal. Although this gifted lady was a notoriously unreliable witness, the fact remains that Beethoven was on terms of friendship with the highest members of society, including Archduke Rudolf; and several of them, fearing that Beethoven might leave Vienna, settled on him an annuity of four thousand florins. Unlike Mozart, whose funeral was practically unattended and who was buried in a pauper's grave, Bee-

[3] However, the music critic as an institution has always been the subject of criticism. George Bernard Shaw, himself a brilliant music critic in his early years (under the pseudonym Corno di Bassetto), wrote, ". . . the middle-class music critic is the most ridiculous of human institutions. I do not take my function seriously because it is impossible for an intelligent man to do so, and I am an eminently intelligent man." See his *London Music in 1888–89* (published in book form, 1937).

thoven's funeral was attended by twenty thousand people from all ranks of Viennese society.

Like the music of many composers, that of Beethoven can be divided into three styles; in his case, however, this division has special significance because of his position between two centuries. The threefold division was made more than a hundred years ago (1852) by Wilhelm von Lenz, according to whom Beethoven's first style imitated Haydn and Mozart, the second showed his complete freedom from his models, and the third was a new, personal, and somewhat introspective style. These distinctions are useful if they are not taken too seriously. As a matter of fact, the distinctions are not strictly chronological, and Beethoven's works present special difficulties of classification because he worked with such care and concentration that each production is an individual and particular organism.

First period: to 1800, until Beethoven was thirty years old. Among the works in this period are the first six string quartets (Op. 18), the first eleven piano sonatas, and the first two symphonies.

Second period: 1800–15. This period includes the Third through the Eighth Symphonies, his only opera *Fidelio,* five string quartets (Op. 59, Op. 78, and Op. 95), the Violin Concerto, the Third, Fourth, and Fifth Piano Concertos, and Piano Sonatas No. 12 (Op. 26) to No. 27 (Op. 90).

Third period: 1815–27. This period embraces the greatest works of Beethoven: the last piano sonatas, the last five string quartets (starting with Op. 127), the Ninth Symphony, and the *Missa Solemnis.*

Did Beethoven really belong to the Romantic period? The Romantic period thought so, and almost every subsequent composer paid him tribute. Perhaps the situation is similar to that of Goethe, who thought of himself as a Classicist until Schiller attempted to prove that his *Iphigenie* put him with the Romanticists. Beethoven was imbued with the ideals of the time, the brotherhood of man, the heroic, and the rights of the individual. His very character was attune to the stuff of the early nineteenth century, and his personal style of music was suited to the general expression of these sentiments. On the other hand, Beethoven was not basically inspired by the typical lyrical expression of Romanticism; he shared its literary penchant only in part; and his music does not really represent the "addition of strangeness to beauty." All these things can be found in Beethoven's music, but fundamentally they are peripheral to a hard core of musical logic applied, for the most part, to the instrumental forms of the Classic period expanded to their elastic limit and, in his last works, sometimes beyond.

Still, Beethoven's works contained the seeds of the Romantic spirit; and while he brought the Classic era to an end, he helped inspire Romanticism. Beethoven actually had far more influence on the Romantic composers than they on him; and those that followed tended to isolate phases of his work for their point of departure. In this sense Beethoven was a Romantic composer and the fountainhead of much of the instrumental music of Romanticism.

The symphonies are a case in point. Mendelssohn and Schumann were particularly influenced by the Fourth Symphony. The Sixth ("Pastoral") was most influential in the orchestral program music of Berlioz and Liszt, although Beethoven himself considered this symphony "more the expression of feeling than painting," and the programmatic elements, though prominent, are subordinate to the symphonic development. Schubert, and later Brahms, followed the general plan of the Third, Fifth, and Seventh Symphonies. The germs of a unified synthesis of an art work, the ideal of Liszt and Wagner, are found in Beethoven's Fifth and Ninth Symphonies. In the former the third and last movements are connected, and a substantial section from the third movement is quoted in the last. The final movement of the Ninth ("Choral") Symphony attempts another synthesis, that of soloists, chorus, and orchestra in an instrumental work. Beethoven begins this movement with quotations from the preceding movements, and then, having summarized and apparently rejected them, he proceeds to *incorporate* the vocal elements into the framework of the symphony itself. A number of other choral symphonies followed the advent of the Ninth Symphony, and Berlioz used the same procedure of summary and rejection in the last movement of his *Harold* Symphony, a purely instrumental work.

Beethoven was such a universal figure that he inspired whole generations, and not merely through the forms of the symphony. His fertility in development of material, so noticeable in his development sections in sonata form or in his variations, inspired Wagner; and the mature operas of the latter would not have been possible without Beethoven's technique of development. In a general way, his dramatic and dynamic style inspired those around him, and his imaginative and individual solutions bewildered as well as attracted a generation whose watchword was individuality. But his last and most profound works, the last five string quartets, have no direct descendants. It was not possible, for they are the most individual and personal expression of a great artist, withdrawn from life and tapping the deepest springs of his noblest thought and inexorable logic.[4]

Beethoven brought to music a greater emotional intensity than did either Haydn or Mozart. His heroic and dynamic style depends on the magnitude of his conceptions and on the driving power and elemental force with which they are executed. To achieve his ends, Beethoven expanded the previous range of louds and softs. The *sforzando* is used for

---

[4] Beethoven's withdrawal from life was undoubtedly occasioned by the total deafness of his last years. See Beethoven's own pathetic comments on his condition in the *Heiligenstadt Testament* of 1802. His deafness and family difficulties with his brothers and nephew were the great trials of his life.

various effects, some rhythmic, some harmonic, some dynamic, but always with the impression of a strong personal insistence on the point at issue. He took advantage of sharper dissonances for great harmonic contrast and for emotional intensity; and it is no mistake that some of these dissonances

Ex. 116 (*Eroica,* first movement)

new theme of the development follows

are emphasized by *sforzandi* to make the point even stronger (Ex. 116). His modulations into more remote keys also give him the opportunity for greater contrast and for musical architecture on a grander scale. The listener is immediately impressed with the strength of the themes themselves and with the sheer power of the figuration of the accompanying parts. The rhythm, particularly, is always a driving force. It is one of the most interesting features of Beethoven's music; and in this respect Beethoven is one of the most imaginative composers. Rhythm is the single most dominating trait of certain works (the Seventh Symphony); and throughout his music the drive of the rhythm, the shifting of accent and meter, and the force of his syncopations are central to its titanic strength, its relentless movement, and its inexhaustible variety.

Compared with his models, Beethoven's music is more continuously and organically conceived. Compared with Mozart's music, his is less sectional; rather, each new section or theme is fused with what has already been heard. The process of development took on new significance with Beethoven, for the expansion of a musical idea was at the heart of his method and especially congenial to one of his imagination and flair for improvisation. Hence the development sections became central to the sonata form and the codas are frequently closing developments.

Beethoven's whole method of composition, as shown by his notebooks, was a relatively slow and painful one: a continuous search for melodic material of a hard gemlike core, which in turn could serve as germinal motives to develop a whole structure. This process was quite different from that of Mozart, who spoke of themes coming to him "from he knew not where," and "being able to see how to develop them." Such spontaneity of melodic inspiration is also characteristic of Schubert, but not of Beethoven.

Ernest Newman says of the Beethoven themes: "To assume that it was out of the themes that the movement grew is probably to see the process from the wrong end . . . the long and painful search for the themes was simply an effort, not to find workable atoms out of which he could construct a musical edifice according to the conventions of symphonic form, but to reduce an already existing nebula . . . to the atom, and then, by the orderly arrangement of these atoms, to make the implicit explicit. The themes are not the generators of the mass of music but are themselves rather the condensation of this." [5]

The inherited forms of the eighteenth century were gradually changed by Beethoven so that his later works are far removed from his models. He completely changed the old minuet, substituting the scherzo, so different in mood and rhythm.[6] While Beethoven retained the outlines of the old concerto form of Mozart, there were important changes. The orchestra became a dominant force, and in his last concertos certain traditional features were abandoned. In his Fourth Piano Concerto (G major) the solo-

[5] *The Unconscious Beethoven* (New York: Alfred A. Knopf, 1927). In a somewhat similar way the English poet Coleridge jotted down ideas and notions in his notebook, and out of this chaos his imagination created such great poems as *The Rime of the Ancient Mariner*. The creative methods of Coleridge have been brilliantly described by John Livingston Lowes in his book *The Road to Xanadu* (Boston and New York: Houghton Mifflin Co., 1927).

[6] The scherzo, meaning "joke," is symbolic of Beethoven's love of humor. Beethoven was himself a practial joker, and there are many examples of prankish rhythms and jokelike surprises in his music.

ist, not the orchestra, opens the work; and in the Fifth ("Emperor") Concerto, the cadenza is written out—a practice that was generally followed thereafter.

The works of the last period in particular exhibit the most fanciful use of inherited forms, especially the fugue and the variation. The "Great" Fugue (Op. 133), originally the last movement of the B-flat Quartet (Op. 130), is so extended and overpowering, that it was detached from the quartet and played as a separate piece. In his variations Beethoven displayed his enormous powers of fantasy and improvisation.[7] A fondness for the variation was characteristic of him throughout his life (see the last movement of the *Eroica;* or the F major Variations which use different keys for the individual variations); however, in the variations of the last period—the "Diabelli" Variations for piano, those in the E-flat Quartet (Op. 127) and A minor Quartet (Op. 132), and in the last piano sonata—Beethoven proceeded beyond the previous limits established by Bach's "Goldberg" Variations and reached a point of achievement that is not likely to be surpassed.

Beethoven's continual search for new means of expression took many forms. He experimented with mixtures of forms (for instance, the sonata with the rondo), and he introduced voices into the Ninth Symphony and recitative-like passages into the piano sonata (Op. 31, No. 2; Op. 110) and string quartet (Op. 132, transition to the last movement). In the C-sharp Minor Quartet (Op. 131) Beethoven combined seven movements, of which the first is a fugue, into a continuous whole.

Beethoven also increased the size of the orchestra. In the *Eroica* he added a third horn, and in the Ninth Symphony four horns are required. In the Fifth and Ninth Symphonies Beethoven achieves additional power and sonority with three trombones. The double bassoon is sometimes used, and in the Ninth Symphony, triangle, bass drum, and cymbals are added to the percussion. In his orchestration Beethoven gave the timpani increased prominence, assigning them thematic material in the Ninth Symphony. He emancipated the cello from the double bass, and treated it as a tenor as well as a bass. In this connection, one may cite the use of two solo celli in the second movement of the "Pastoral" Symphony.[8]

Beethoven's importance in music cannot be overestimated. In his music, the listener feels the greatness of an elemental force, a composer of the very first magnitude. This is true in the sense that his music appeals

[7] In this connection, it should not be forgotten that before his deafness Beethoven appeared constantly as a piano virtuoso, and was particularly renowned as an improviser at the keyboard. Mozart, who heard him improvise at the piano, remarked, "Pay attention to him; he will make a noise in the world some day."

[8] Beethoven was primarily an instrumental composer. His two most important large-scale works involving the voice are the opera *Fidelio* and the *Missa Solemnis.* They will be discussed later.

directly to the listener because of its extraordinary power, intensity, and variety of emotional expression. It is also true in the historical sense. Some composers are born at the wrong time and place for the full realization of their potentialities (e.g., Purcell). Others, like Beethoven, come at precisely the right time. He lived when a new spirit of individuality and a spirit of revolt against the established order of things had permeated arts, letters, and politics. Temperamentally, he was in tune with the spirit of his era, and he possessed the supreme ability to articulate the deepest thoughts and aspirations of people everywhere. Beethoven brought to logical fruition the models he had inherited from Haydn and Mozart. But he also reflected a new spirit, especially in his late works, and his music is the portal through which one must approach the nineteenth century and the Romantic movement in music. For similar reasons, Beethoven had an immense influence on the future course of music in the nineteenth century. Above all, whatever Beethoven's historical importance may have been, he has never become old-fashioned; and that in itself is the supreme tribute to the universality of genius.

Suggested Listening

The following works of the "middle" period have already been analyzed and suggested for listening:

The *Eroica* Symphony (see pp. 243–5).

The String Quartet, Op. 59, No. 1 (see pp. 254–5).

For works of the "last" period:

Piano Sonata in A-flat major (Op. 110).

String Quartet in A minor (Op. 132).

For individual movements:

The "Great" Fugue (Op. 133).

String Quartet in E-flat major (Op. 127), slow movement (variation).

Ninth Symphony, first movement.

Suggested Reading

Denis Arnold and Nigel Fortune (ed.), *The Beethoven Companion*. London: Faber & Faber, 1971.

Paul Bekker, *Beethoven,* trans. by M. M. Bozman. New York: E. P. Dutton & Co., 1925.

A. W. Thayer, *The Life of Beethoven* (2 vols.), revised and edited by Elliot Forbes. Princeton: Princeton University Press, 1964. Includes the text of the *Heiligenstadt Testament.*

J. W. N. Sullivan, *Beethoven, His Spiritual Development.* London: Jonathan Cape, 1927.

Romain Rolland, *Jean Christophe* (1904–12), a novel in which the hero is a musician who obviously resembles Beethoven—a work for which Rolland received the Nobel Prize in 1916. Available in a reprint edition —New York: Modern Library, 1938.

*THE SONG. THE SHORT PIANO PIECE. SCHUBERT. SCHU-
MANN. CHOPIN.*

The vast number of songs composed in the early Romantic period was typical of its lyric side. Another body of music, similar in character and devoted to establishing brief moods, was written for the piano using short forms, sometimes dances like waltzes and *Ländler,* sometimes short mood or descriptive pieces with titles, and sometimes short "character" pieces like nocturnes or preludes. These tendencies are characteristic of the music of Franz Schubert (1797–1828), Robert Schumann (1810–56), and Frédéric Chopin (1810–49).

Schubert's spontaneous melodies grace over six hundred songs, inspired by many different subjects from a number of the best-known poets of the time, among them, Goethe, Schiller, Schlegel, Ossian, Heine, and Mayrhofer. The last-named, a friend of Schubert's in Vienna, paid an extraordinary tribute to the composer. He confessed that he did not understand the full force of his own poems until he had heard Schubert's setting of them. Similarly, the singer Vogl, who was instrumental in introducing Schubert's songs to the Viennese public, spoke of a special quality of Schubert's genius: his "clairvoyance" in penetrating the heart of the poem and giving it vivid expression through music.

The poetic mood of a Schubert song is established by both the melody and the piano accompaniment. Schubert brought into greater prominence the role of the latter: for instance, in *"Gretchen am Spinnrade"* ("Gretchen at the Spinning Wheel"), the whole song is unified by the continuous whirring motives in the piano (see Ex. 80), which are entirely different from those heard in the voice; nevertheless they establish the mood and serve to unify diverse elements in the voice part. This is the general function of the piano in the Schubert song. Sometimes the piano part plays a more direct role in the structure. In the song *"Auf dem Flusse"* ("On the River") from *Die Winterreise* (*The Winter Journey*) the return of the first section is accomplished by stating the melody in the piano part while the voice sings a kind of *obbligato* recitative. In the extraordinary song *"Der Doppelgänger"* ("The Phantom Double") the climax of the song is actually achieved by harmony. Thus in many songs the melody and the accompaniment cannot be separated.

In realizing the meaning of a text in music, Schubert is not bound by any one type of representation. Sometimes he attempts to depict actual sound as in *"Die junge Nonne"* ("The Young Nun"), where the convent bell is heard repeatedly tolling. Sometimes the musical setting consists of suggestive figures. In *"Die Krähe"* ("The Raven") from *Die Winterreise* the musical figuration creates a mood approaching the physical motion of the slow-circling bird of prey (see p. 116–7).

A feature of the Schubert Lieder is the setting of whole groups of poems, all concerning the same general subject, in song cycles. For example, *Die Winterreise* (1827) consists of twenty-four songs all devoted to the emotions of a rejected lover as he contemplates the twenty-four scenes of his "winter journey." The texts of these songs (by Wilhelm Müller) are rather sentimental and not especially distinguished. Schubert, however, transforms them into something quite extraordinary, each poem with its own mood, yet each related to the central mood of the cycle. *Die Winterreise* combines certain typical traits of the early Romantic movement: the love theme, longing for nature, and youthful naïveté.

Individually, the Schubert songs fall into various formal types. The strophic song, for example, uses the same music for all verses, like a hymn. The modified strophic song does the same, but with some contrasting element. In *"Der Wegweiser"* ("The Sign Post"), also from *Die Winterreise,* the form is A A' A, the middle section being the same melody as in the other two sections but cast in the major instead of the minor. In the regular "song" or ternary form a complete contrast is used in the middle section (A B A). Other types of Schubert songs have almost no musical repetition; they are unified by the text. This type of setting is often employed in ballades. In some cases, as in the celebrated *"Erlkönig,"* recurrent phrases of music are identified with characters in the drama and recur as needed. Finally, there is a special type of song that may be called the "declamatory" song. The best single example is *"Der Doppelgänger."* Here the voice declaims the text more in the form of a recitative than in melody, while the unity and continuity are furnished by the accompaniment.

In his songs Schubert arrives at a "classical" balance between form and content. But many of the sentiments expressed are characteristic of the Romantic movement. The same is true of Schubert's colorful harmony and his use of the small "character" forms in his piano music. During his short life, Schubert was extremely profilic; and later (see p. 300 ff) we will speak briefly of his symphonies, chamber music, and piano sonatas. But had Schubert written only the songs we know today, he would still be regarded as one of the world's great musicians.

Suggested Listening
"Gretchen am Spinnrade."
"Der Erlkönig."
"Der Doppelgänger."
The song cycle *Die Winterreise.*

The vogue of song writing that Schubert inaugurated continued, especially in Germany. Schumann, Brahms, and later Hugo Wolf, all wrote first-class songs. Schumann's two hundred songs date from about 1840, and their quality is exceptionally high. Like Schubert, Schumann used the song cycle (e.g., *Dichterliebe, Frauenliebe und Leben*), and these cycles are even more continuous and organized as a whole than are Schubert's.

It is characteristic of Schumann and his times that he should transfer the song cycle to the piano, thus combining the short lyric forms into a larger whole. Typical cycles are *Papillons, Carnival,* and the *Fantasy Pieces*. These titles reflect the literary and imaginative side of Schumann's nature. In some cases the moods and titles are probably suggested directly by literary models. In others we know that the music was already existent and that Schumann added the titles later. But this does not make any real difference. The titles simply summarize a mood that was doubtless in Schumann's mind when he composed the piece.

The piano was well suited to the expression of these pieces, and Schumann, who had a special inclination for this instrument, explored its possibilities far more than did Schubert. Schumann's use of the pedals, his chord doublings, his peculiar positions of chords, the effect of chords and figurations using new contractions and expansions of the player's hand, all result in a richness of sonority that is almost orchestral. The harmony is often related to the effect or mood suggested by the title. Poetic effects of vagueness or questioning may be achieved by starting or ending on an incomplete chord (cf. the ending of "Why" in the *Fantasy Pieces*). His piano writing is full of rhythmic interest, and subtle cross-rhythms and syncopations distinguish his style, to which Brahms was much indebted. Schumann's great originality is especially evident in his songs and piano works.

Suggested Listening
The song cycle *Frauenliebe und Leben* (*A Woman's Love and Life*).
The *Fantasy Pieces* for piano.

Chopin was above all a specialist in writing for the piano. He composed in many of the smaller forms as well as in the forms of the concerto and longer forms that he himself invented (for example, the four *Ballades*). Chopin represents a somewhat different kind of Romanticism than does Schumann or Schubert. His music is typical of French *salon* society in contrast to the German Romanticism of Schumann. It belongs in the drawing room; and his melodies, tinged with melancholy, lack the robustness of Schumann's. Furthermore, there is in Chopin's music little trace of the love of nature that is so typical of German Romanticism. But it has qualities directly related to Poland, the land where he was born, and the numerous settings of Polish national dances such as the mazurka and the polonaise are characteristic expressions of Chopin's nationalistic feelings.

Chopin is at his best and most typical in the short dances, "character" pieces, and in the longer forms of his own inventions. Of the former, the *nocturne* is a type particularly associated with Chopin, although the form was actually established by John Field. The nocturne is dominated by a melancholy, sometimes languid melody, a singing style for which Chopin is famous.[9] Chopin's *Berceuse* and *Barcarolle* are basically types of nocturnes. His *preludes* range over a variety of moods. The *impromptus* suggest the importance attached to inspiration and the mood-of-the-moment among Romantic musicians. The *études* are devoted to working out special problems of piano technique. In them, Chopin brings the piano style to its highest point of virtuosity before Liszt. Typical is the use of double thirds and sixths, arpeggios, and passage work of all kinds, frequently dazzling in effect, and entirely different from the melodies of the typical nocturne. Besides the nationalist Polish dances, there are a number of *valses* more closely related to French society of the time.

Chopin made distinguished contributions in the field of harmony and in developing the piano idiom. In general terms, he managed to give his harmony a richness and shimmer by fleeting modulations. His piano style was quite new. It was a marked contrast to that of the contemporary German school, which specialized in rivaling the orchestra in range and dynamics (cf. Liszt). In Chopin's style, touch and variety of touch were of great importance. He insisted on a pure legato and singing style of playing, and contemporaries spoke of his hands gliding over the keys (the piano action, incidentally, was much easier than it is now). Playing passages and figuration in this way produced a kind of irridescent rippling effect. Moscheles confessed in his diary that certain Chopin passages involving "awkward and harsh modulation" no longer shocked him, because of the gliding method of playing them. Chopin's use of dynamics was often noted by his contemporaries; his soft passages were so soft that no strong *forte* was necessary to produce a contrast. Chopin employed the pedals to sustain and to bring out the harmonic implications of his elaborate figuration. His playing was especially renowned for its *rubato*. But this does not mean that Chopin did not keep strict time. Chopin said, "The singing hand may deviate from strict time, but the accompanying hand must keep strict time."

Chopin made his greatest contributions in harmony, in the expanded possibilities of the piano idiom, and in the characteristic types of the shorter musical forms. A poetic imagination, which cannot be described, permeates his best works.

[9] The Italian opera composer Bellini (see p. 336) is said to have influenced Chopin toward this style after Chopin's arrival in Paris. This opinion is open to question. See the article "Chopin" in *Grove's Dictionary of Music and Musicians* (Fifth edition, 1954).

Suggested Listening

Nocturne in E-flat major (Op. 55).

Prelude in D-flat major ("Raindrop") (Op. 28, No. 15).

Mazurka in C minor (Op. 56, No. 3).

Ballade in G minor (Op. 23).

Suggested Reading

Richard Capell, *Schubert's Songs* (Second edition). London: Gerald Duckworth & Company, 1957.

Joan Chissell, *Schumann*. London: J. M. Dent & Sons, 1948.

"Chopin" in *Grove's Dictionary of Music and Musicians* (Fifth edition, 1954). In this article will be found a good summary of Chopin's life, his love affair with George Sand, a summary account of his music, and an elaborate bibliography.

18. *The Sonata, Symphony, and Concerto After Beethoven*

THE SONATA AND SYMPHONY IN GENERAL

THE EARLY ROMANTIC MOVEMENT stressed lyrical expression. In music, the song and the short piano piece were typical. At the same time there was no sign of slackening fertility in the traditional forms of the symphony, chamber music, and piano sonatas. But the "traditional" forms were not the same. The old organic logic of Mozart and Beethoven was replaced by other ways of organizing the material; the dominance of the lyric theme, a new and more colorful harmony, elements from program music, and a desire to unify the individual movements all played their part in the course of musical development in the nineteenth century.

The sonata of the Romantic composers clearly took its point of departure from Beethoven, but, having departed, it was never to return. This was inevitable. The best of the Romantic composers were immensely gifted—consider the lyric spontaneity of Schubert or Tchaikovsky—but their gifts were quite different from Beethoven's, and they were influenced by the new musical currents that surrounded them. While they retained the traditional *outward* forms of the symphony, chamber music, and piano sonata, they transformed these forms internally in the image of themselves and their own times. The Classic scheme of logically balanced statement and development of material in closely related keys was disturbed by the influx of lyrical themes and by a more chromatic harmony. A new effusiveness of melodies—beautiful, emotional, sometimes gushing and sentimental—disturbed the old balance between the motivic and lyric. It was almost as if a flowery language were imposed on a foundation of concise logic, sometimes obscuring and sometimes obliterating it. Different keys were chosen less for their close relationship than for their contrasts; and, similarly, the themes themselves were highly contrasted, and these thematic contrasts became more decisive in the scheme of the sonata form than the relationships of keys. The result was a far more sectional scheme than the Classic symphony. In the sonata form, the counterpoint basic to the Beethoven development section was replaced by such devices as reharmonizing the thematic material or substituting harmonic color for genuine development of melodic material. Furthermore, the preponderance of lyrical subjects left less to develop motivically. Consequently, repetition of material, repetition of rhythmic patterns, and reliance on the variety and color of an enlarged orchestra became characteristic. Nothing could be more instructive in this respect than a comparison of typical movements of a Beethoven symphony on the one hand, with those of a symphony of Bruckner or Mahler on the other (see below).

Any creative artist realizes, of course, that a form disturbed must mean a new form created; and the Romantic composers, having loosened the structural underpinning of the Classic sonata, had to put something in its place. Consequently, they strove to unify whole pieces whose *individual* movements or divisions were more sectional in character than those of their Classic predecessors. The idea of unity in a whole composite of movements was typical of the time; indeed, Beethoven had already experimented with schemes of this character, and Wagner sought an alliance of all the arts in the continuous music drama. This striving for large-scale unification took such forms as linking whole sections or movements by using variant forms of the same theme or restating whole sections in later movements, as Beethoven had done in the Fifth and Ninth Symphonies. This *cyclic* principle may be seen in various composers. Schumann, for example, used it in his song cycle *Frauenliebe und Leben,* in which the opening piano introduction is repeated at the end of the cycle; or, more strikingly, in his Quintet for Piano and Strings. In the latter, the opening subject is used as the subject of a fugue in the last movement, acting as a unifying device for the whole work. César Franck is another composer who used the cyclic principle in a number of works, including the famous Symphony in D minor. Other manifestations were the symphony and sonata played without a break—an idea also inspired by Beethoven, who adapted this procedure for one of his last quartets (Op. 131, C-sharp minor). Subsequent examples are Mendelssohn's "Scotch" Symphony and Schumann's Fourth Symphony. Liszt, to whom such ideas were attractive, produced a piano sonata (the B minor Sonata) all in one movement [1] and later the symphonic poem. Finally, a whole genre of symphonic and other pieces owed their inspiration to Beethoven's "Pastoral" and Ninth Symphonies: the "program" symphony of Berlioz and the various pieces that employed texts and voices (cf. Mahler; for the "program" symphony and symphonic poem, see Chapter 19).

This is not to claim that the sonata of the nineteenth century was necessarily less successful than its Classic predecessor; but it was different, and

---

[1] Liszt was probably influenced in this direction by Schubert's *Wanderer Fantasie,* not a sonata, but a single movement whose sections are cyclically related.

it must be judged in terms of what it tried to accomplish. A result of the new attitude was a somewhat more effusive statement of ideas and a greater length of individual movements and works. The restatement of themes from early movements toward the end of large pieces tended to shift the emphasis to the last movement, where previously the chief interest had centered in the first. An accompanying phenomenon to all this was a bigger symphony orchestra and a larger, more powerful pianoforte that could rival the orchestra in volume and color. In chamber music, a more sonorous, even orchestral, kind of scoring became the rule.

INDIVIDUAL WORKS: SCHUBERT. BRAHMS. TCHAIKOVSKY. BRUCKNER AND MAHLER.

Since the proof of the pudding is in the eating, it seems best to select important representative works for comment. Only a few pieces can be singled out; and we have chosen to follow, for the most part, certain typical works of *one* kind, namely symphonies, thus being forced to neglect many beautiful examples of chamber music and piano sonatas of the nineteenth century.

SCHUBERT, THE ("GREAT") C MAJOR SYMPHONY

The first movement of the ("Great") C major Symphony (No. 9; 1828), composed a year after Beethoven's death, is typical of certain new directions. There are five large sections, approximately of equal length: an introduction, exposition, development, recapitulation, and coda. The chief theme of the opening is used in the course of the movement, thus integrating the introduction with the rest of the movement. The first theme of the movement proper is motivic and straightforward, and it is cast in a rhythmic pattern that Schubert uses throughout the movement (Ex. 117a).

Ex. 117a

The second theme is a dancelike subject that reminds us of Schubert's many attractive dances and his interest in dance rhythms in his music as a whole. While the second theme of a Classic symphony in a major key is invariably in the dominant key, Schubert puts his second theme in E minor (not G major, the dominant), a distinct departure (Ex. 117b). Compared with Beethoven's organic bridge sections and his developments, Schubert's procedure in this symphony is very illuminating. As shown in Example 117b, Schubert's bridge is essentially nonexistent: in place of a section leading organically from one section to another, Schubert con-

Ex. 117b

nects the first and second theme by a joint of quick modulation occupying a single measure (see the same procedure in the C major Quintet described below). Schubert's change is by no means unconvincing, but it emphasizes the sectional character of his work. The development of Schubert's work is also sectional rather than organic. Schumann described this symphony as the "Symphony of heavenly length," but the adjective "heavenly" should be applied to *symphony* rather than *length,* especially as regards the development. In the latter, Schubert relies on harmonic richness and coloring to vary the restatement of thematic material, and for further variety, the color and power possibilities of an enlarged orchestra, including three horns and three trombones that are used with excellent, sometimes electrifying, effect. A unifying device that is exploited almost to exhaustion is the constant reiteration of the same rhythmic patterns. The coda, like many of Beethoven's, functions as a terminal development.

This symphony is a great masterpiece, but it achieves its effect in a manner different from that of the Beethoven symphonies. Less concise and less organic than the latter, the C major Symphony is an overpowering work in the power and grandeur of its themes (some of which are reminiscent of Beethoven), its lyric beauty, and the magnitude of its conception.

SCHUBERT, QUINTET FOR STRINGS

The Quintet for Strings (C major; Op. 163; 1828) is one of the greatest of all Schubert's voluminous works. Like the C major Symphony just described, it was composed in the last year of his short life, and these two works represent his most powerful expression as an instrumental composer. The scoring is typical of a new sonority in chamber music. Instead of the two violas which Mozart used (see pp. 249, 253), Schubert uses two cellos (besides two violins and viola). In this way, he achieves a greater sonority and also a deeper and darker color in the lower and middle registers of the texture.

The first movement shows the same kind of bridge and development as in the C major symphony. The bridge is ingenious, naïve, and successful (Ex. 118), and it leads to a wonderful second theme that only Schubert could have written. Not less wonderful than the theme itself is its coloring in the lower instruments of the ensemble. The development is still sectional, but it is more powerful, more dramatic, and better organized than that of the C major Symphony. Compared with the developments of Mozart and Beethoven, the development of this Quintet is somewhat looser in texture—a fact that can be made apparent by comparing the inside voices. The rhythms too are over-reiterated. But we forget all this as we listen to the marvelous lyric and harmonic ideas that permeate this movement.

If Schubert could rise above himself, he did so in the slow movement that follows. The choice of key (E major) is in itself interesting, stressing a mediant relation instead of the subdominant more characteristic of the Classic model. The lower instruments furnish a background of quiet depth so characteristic of the slow movements of Schubert and Beethoven,

Ex. 118

while above this the first violin pours out its song. But this mood does not last. With a sudden harmonic wrench, Schubert plunges into a new world. The key is changed to F minor (not a related key, but a semitone higher), everything is darkened in color, and the mood becomes dramatic and stormy; the cellos rumble in the bass. The emotional impact of this movement cannot be described; it must be heard and experienced. At any rate, the contrast of this middle section is a striking example of Schubert's dramatic use of material.

Perhaps it is fruitless to speculate on what Schubert might have composed had he lived to old age. Nevertheless, in estimating Schubert critically, we must consider the fact of Schubert's early death. Our opinion of Beethoven, for instance, would be quite different if we knew only the works he had composed up to the age of thirty-one, the age at which Schubert died. At that age Beethoven had written only one symphony (Brahms, none) and relatively few other works. Beethoven's greatness is based upon the works of his middle and late period. On the other hand, Schubert composed an enormous number of works in his short life: ten symphonies and other orchestral pieces; seventeen operas, mostly fragments; fourteen string quartets and other chamber music; twenty-two piano sonatas, many "character" pieces for piano, and over six hundred songs. Schubert's early death is one of the tragedies of music. Toward the end of his life, rather than any slackening of productive capacity, there was evidence only of increased maturity. The tragedy lies in the untimely death of one of the greatest natural musicians in the full possession of his powers and doubtless before his greatest potential had been realized. And this in a composer whose gifts for spontaneous melody and insatiable desire and capacity for composing have never been surpassed. Schubert's life was in itself a striking contrast between his external condition of poverty and continual want and his inner life of poetry and music. At his death the musical world lost, in Liszt's telling phrase, "the most poetical musician that ever was."

Suggested Listening
The ("Great") C major Symphony.
String Quintet in C major.

Suggested Reading
Gerald Abraham (ed.), *Schubert: A Symposium.* London: Lindsay Drummond, 1946.
Otto E. Deutsch (ed.), *The Schubert Reader.* New York: W. W. Norton & Company, 1947.

JOHANNES BRAHMS (1833–97)

Brahms belongs to another generation, having been born about thirty-five years later than Schubert and some twenty years after Mendelssohn, Schumann, and Chopin. In the formative years of his life the course of German music was much influenced by the "New German School of the Future," dominated by the ideas and personalities of Liszt and Wagner. Brahms opposed the programmatic tendencies of this school, and he and the famous violinist Joachim published an open letter (1860) attacking its aims. Brahms's opposition to the Wagner school was strongly supported by the influential Viennese critic and aesthetician Eduard Hanslick, who took the stand that music is a phenomenon complete in itself, obeying its own laws (see his important book *Concerning Beauty in Music,* 1854). Hanslick said, "Music is form animated by sound," thus opposing the programmatic and the poetic-intuitive concept of music. However, the real influences in Brahms's life were Beethoven and Robert and Clara Schumann. After meeting the twenty-year-old Brahms, Schumann wrote a famous article "New Paths," hailing the young man as a kind of messiah of German music. Brahms practically became a member of the Schumann family, for whom he entertained the deepest affection.

Brahms's music is an excellent refutation of the idea that Romantic music is all emotion and no form, while Classic music is the reverse. Within his disciplined forms, Brahms assimilated into his style the typical Romantic richness of harmony, remote and colorful modulations, contrast of sonority, and complex rhythmic combinations. It is significant of Brahms's discipline that he threw away as much as he composed—or so we surmise from letters and other sources. He did not make a habit of retaining sketches, in the manner of Beethoven. Brahms evolved an individual style in which vigorous and intricate rhythmic patterns, inspired by those of

Schumann, are especially prominent. Typical of Brahms are polyrhythms of two notes against three, three against four, and so on. The syncopations in Brahms's music are particularly striking: he syncopates not merely individual notes but even whole measures and phrases. His scoring is relatively thick, the melodic lines being often doubled in thirds or sixths (Ex. 119). This is true in both his piano writing and orchestral scoring.

Ex. 119

Brahms, Fourth Symphony (last movement, m. 25-8)

The harmonies are sonorous but relatively thick and dark in sound. Similarly, in the orchestra Brahms was sparing in his use of the bright colors of unimpeded solo instruments, although he was more generous in this respect with regard to the horn and clarinet, his two favorite instruments. A famous conductor remarked about Brahms's scores: "The sun never shines there."

Brahms used a number of the cyclic devices already mentioned. The Finale of the First Symphony uses the horn-call motive heard in the introduction to the movement. In the Third String Quartet (B-flat; Op. 67) the thematic material that opens the first movement is worked into the last variation of the Finale. In the Third Symphony a kind of motto is used to unify: F—A/A-flat—F, a motto supposed to mean *"Frei aber Froh"* (free but happy).

Brahms is the best example of the continuation of certain Classic traditions in the Romantic style; he is the most direct descendant of Beethoven. Brahms adapted the Classic forms to his individual style in his four symphonies, his extensive chamber music, piano sonatas, and concertos. At the same time, he is closer to the typical lyrical expression of Romanticism in his numerous and beautiful songs (about two hundred) and short pieces for the piano. Unfortunately, we must limit our specific comments to a single work, the Fourth Symphony (but see below for Suggested Listening).

BRAHMS, FOURTH SYMPHONY

The sweep of the opening theme of the Fourth Symphony (Op. 98; 1885) is characteristic of Brahms, as are the vigor of the rhythm, the syncopations (often accentuated by the *sforzando*), and the variety of figuration. The second main theme emerges from the cello, a beautiful lyric subject rich with the color of the middle register of the instrument. The exposition, compared with that of Schubert's C major Symphony, establishes a more organic relation between sections and a more closely knit transition from one theme to another. The development, however, begins as if it were a restatement of the opening of the exposition. Two other features are especially striking: the remarkably effective return to the recapitulation with an augmented form of the opening theme (Ex. 120); and the brilliant coda that climaxes the movement, restating the opening themes in a new garb.

Ex. 120

[opening theme]

[Augmented form]

The second movement (*andante moderato*) has unusual features. The movement is in E major, but it is not a simple E major. The movement begins with one measure for two horns, playing the following theme in unison (Ex. 121); it is then taken up by the woodwinds. This opening is

Ex. 121

Andante moderato

HORNS IN C.

characteristic of an ambiguity often used in Romantic music as a color device or one of effect and surprise. By itself, the opening measure might be heard as C major. With the entry of the strings, however, it becomes apparent that the main tonality is E major (Ex. 122), and the horn theme is in an "old" mode, the Phrygian (equivalent to playing the white keys

17 Baroque opera sets from Cesti's *Il Pomo d'Oro* (1667), performed as part of the festivities at the wedding of Emperor Leopold I of Austria and the Infanta Margherita of Spain. Designs by Burnacino.

A "The Garden of Joy" (Act I, Scene 15). The central figures are (left to right) Paris, Venus, and Momo. Note the typical baroque decoration, receding planes in space, figures in arrested movement, and the general effect of monumental grandeur.

B "The Mouth of Hell" (Act II, Scene 6). The set is cast in the form of a mouth with eyes above and teeth below.

18A French court ballet (1625) during the youth of Louis XIV and Lully. Detail taken from a water color of Daniel Rabel (1578?–1637).

B Dancing the minuet accompanied by the strings (see in background). French engraving (1682). Music of the minuet, lower left.

19A The opera house in Vienna where Cesti's *Il Pomo d'Oro* was first performed (cf. Plate 17).

B Louis XIV and his family. Painting by Largillière (about 1710).

20 Composers' autographs. From upper left to right: Purcell, Handel, Bach, Arne ("God bless our noble King"), Berlioz, Liszt.

21A Architecture of the late baroque: interior of the "Wies" Church in Bavaria, built by Zimmermann (1757).

B The Rococo Theater, Schwetzingen, Baden (built in 1715).

22A Claudio Monteverdi (1644).

B Henry Purcell. Painting by Closterman.

EFFIGIES ANTONII VIVALDI

C Antonio Vivaldi, from an engraving by
I. Caldwall (1725).

D Johann Sebastian Bach. Painted in 1748 by
Elias Gottlieb Hausmann.

A A painting by Denner.

The National Portrait Gallery, London.

B A caricature by a disgruntled contemporary (1754).

24A The Young Mozart (1767).

B Beethoven in 1815. Portrait
by Christopher Heckel.

C Niccolò Paganini. Lithograph by Begas
(before 1831).

25A The "Wolf Glen" Scene from Weber's opera *Der Freischütz*. Drawn by Moritz von Schwind.

B Wagner's plan for the Festival Theater in Bayreuth (1876).

26A French *contredanse* (1805).

B Monet: "Impression: Sunrise" (1872).

27A The waltz, Vienna. A mid-nineteenth-century engraving.

B A scene from a performance of Wagner's *Tannhäuser* at Bayreuth (1954).

28A Richard and Cosima Wagner (1872).

B Giuseppe Verdi. Portrait by Boldini (1886)
Galleria Nazionale d'Arte Moderna, Rome.

C Franz Liszt playing to his friends in Vienna, by Kriehuber (1846).
Left to right: Kriehuber, Berlioz, Czerny, Liszt, and the violinist Ernst.

Brown Brothers.

9A Claude Debussy as a Young
Man (1884). Painting by Marcel
Baschet.

B Detail of Georges Seurat's painting "The Parade" (1889). An
example of pointillism.

Collection, Stephen C. Clark.

30A Jean Cocteau at the piano with "The Six." Left to right: Milhaud, Auric, Honegger, Tailleferre, Poulenc, and Durey.

B Scene from Martha Graham's ballet "Appalachian Spring" (1944).
Music by Aaron Copland.

31A Portrait of Igor Stravinsky by Edward Weston. *From* Stravinsky *by Merle Armitage, G. Schirmer, 1936.*

B "The Three Musicians" by Pablo Picasso (1881–). An example of "synthetic cubism" (1921).

32A Arnold Schoenberg (1947).

B Berlin Philharmonic Hall (1963).
New type of construction.

Ex. 122

of the piano from E to E).² The fluctuation between E major and the chords and tones borrowed from the Phrygian mode (D natural, C natural) is characteristic of a striving for color and unusual effect, and in other works, for similar reasons, Brahms often deliberately leaves the harmony momentarily undefined.

The long-arched and lyrical second theme is assigned to the cello, again in its tenor register. There is no regular development; or rather, a development is placed irregularly, coming after the first theme in the recapitulation and being devoted to the first theme. In the last measures the Phrygian mode is again reiterated in essence (Ex. 123).

Ex. 123

(skeleton of melodic parts in wood winds only)

The third movement is also interesting for various reasons. In the first place, it is not a scherzo, either in meter or in form. To be sure, something of the joking spirit of the scherzo is retained, and Brahms labeled this movement *allegro giocoso*. But he cast it in $\frac{2}{4}$ time instead of the typical triple meter of the scherzo. Internally, the interest comes from the syncopations of the subject, the breaking up of the subject into fragments, and their ingenious treatment and arrangement. There is a development, placed in a position analagous to that noted in the second movement. The coda begins with a pedal in the timpani and includes a terminal development.

The fourth and final movement (*allegro energico e passionato*) is universally called a *chaconne* or a *passacaglia*—except by Brahms who did not label it. It is a masterly set of thirty variations, worthy to take their

² There has been some confusion about this opening. One author confidently wrote, "The horn introduces the theme in the *foreign* key of C, the clarinets and pizzicato violins take it over in the *proper* key of E major" (italics mine). Of course this is nonsense. The opening is not in C major any more than *read* is *reed* because it happens to sound that way by itself.

place beside those of Bach and Beethoven. The common factor most consistent to the variations is not the harmonic scheme of the opening statement, but the melodic line of the soprano, which assumes the importance of an *ostinato,* now in the bass, now stated in decorated or disguised form. The scheme of the opening, as well as the opening of several variations, is shown in Example 124. Again it is obvious that

Ex. 124

Brahms's harmonization of the opening has borrowed from the Phrygian mode; but in this case it is not so much for reasons of color and variety as for those of harmonic flexibility in successive variations. The coda once again states the soprano *ostinato,* and then, in Tovey's words, "storms to its tragic close."

Suggested Listening
The Fourth Symphony.
Quintet for Clarinet and Strings (one of Brahms's most impressive works).
Intermezzo for piano, E-flat minor (Op. 118, No. 6).
Songs: *"Wie Melodien," "Immer leiser"* (Op. 105, No. 1 and 2).

Suggested Reading
Karl Geiringer, *Brahms, His Life and Work,* trans. by H. B. Weiner and Bernard Miall. New York: Oxford University Press, 1947.

TCHAIKOVSKY, SIXTH (PATHÉTIQUE) SYMPHONY IN B MINOR

The Sixth (*Pathétique*) Symphony in B minor (Op. 74; 1893) is the last and best of the symphonies of Peter Ilyitch Tchaikovsky (1840–93). It was first performed only weeks before his death, and it is possible that the last movement, an *adagio* filled with the spirit of tragic resignation, was composed by Tchaikovsky in a mood of premonition. Tchaikovsky said that this symphony had a program—"a program which shall remain a mystery to everyone." But we can guess at the mystery: surely, the program was Tchaikovsky's own nature, for his music is the autobiography of a man cursed with an unhappy and introspective temperament. (For details of his life, see Suggested Reading.)

Part of the brilliance and power of Tchaikovsky's instrumental works depends on his skill and method of orchestration. Essentially he is a follower of the French (i.e., Berlioz), with his emphasis on the pure colors of single instruments and choirs of like instruments rather than on mixtures of many instruments. Thus there are brilliant solos for individual instruments. In the strings, tremolos, rapid passages, and virtuoso figurations are particularly notable. In the *Pathétique* Symphony, Tchaikovsky uses a large orchestra (three flutes, two oboes, two bassoons, two trumpets, three trombones and tuba, three timpani, strings with cello and double bass separated); and the heavy brass and special use of the deep instruments are not unrelated to the somber effect. In the opening, for example, the double basses play *divisi*. Very characteristic of Tchaikovsky is the rapid alternation of choirs or solo instruments in short phrases. In this symphony, for instance, pure woodwind groups are frequently contrasted with pure string groups.

The musical construction of the opening themes of this symphony have been discussed earlier (see pp. 29–30). The first movement, basically in sonata form, is a good example of the sectional character of the Romantic symphony. In Tchaikovsky's music this fundamental character is accentuated by the pronounced contrasts in his music: the most fiery and passionate themes are frequently followed by melancholy and even sentimental, lyric melodies, thus emphasizing the different sections. This is true in the first movement of the *Pathétique* Symphony (a name used by the composer himself). In addition, the changes of tempo, essential to the contrasted moods, stress the sectional divisions still more. The thematic material of the *adagio* introduction is used again and is transformed in the following *allegro non troppo*. An animated statement of the material follows, the music gradually quiets, and the section ends in a solo for the cello, *adagio*. A complete silence; and the second theme begins, *andante*. This melody is a complete antithesis to what has preceded it, proclaiming a new, lyrical mood, characteristic of Tchaikovsky. This new theme, a type of melody doubtless influenced by the Italian opera composer Bellini, derives its effect less from sheer beauty of outline than from the emotional manner of performing it. Marked "muted" and to be played *teneramente, molto cantabile, con espansione,* the theme is also marked with the most minute gradations of louds and softs (Ex. 125).

The rest of the first movement shows the same kind of sectional character; the music is essentially very powerful and impressive, but it is

Ex. 125

dynamic
markings of bass

arranged more as a series of pictures on contrasting phases of a subject
than as a single picture in which all the elements are organically fused
in one framework.

In the second movement Tchaikovsky has preserved the dance structure
of the traditional minuet or scherzo (i.e., with trio in the middle), but the
dance itself is in $\frac{5}{4}$ time (see p. 13), probably derived from the meters of
Russian folk music or dance. The third movement is basically a march in
$\frac{4}{4}\left(\frac{12}{8}\right)$ time. It is dominated by a single theme, which gradually gathers
strength and bursts out with full momentum in the final pages (Ex. 126).

Ex. 126

(m. 229)

The fourth and last movement is the *adagio,* an example of how the
weight of the Romantic symphony gravitates toward the end. The *adagio*
completes the cycle of the *Pathétique,* announced in the first measures of
the opening movement; it closes the symphony and epitomizes Tchaikovsky's music and life.

Suggested Listening
The Sixth Symphony.

Suggested Reading

Gerald Abraham (ed.), *The Music of Tchaikovsky.* New York: W. W.
Norton & Company, 1946.
Herbert Weinstock, *Tchaikovsky.* New York: Alfred A. Knopf, 1943.

BRUCKNER AND MAHLER

The symphony took other directions in the works of Anton Bruckner
(1824–96) and especially in those of Gustav Mahler (1860–1911).[3] Both

[3] It is impossible to note here all the currents of the nineteenth-century symphony.
However, certain other symphonies are considered in their special context. See
Berlioz, Dvořák, Borodin, and César Franck.

left nine symphonies of monumental proportions. Bruckner, the older man (actually older than Brahms), stems from Schubert and resembles him in lyric melody. He still adheres to the four-movement form of the symphony but the dimensions are expanded to epic proportions. A Bruckner symphony resembles somewhat a series of large canvases in a gallery. Bruckner was thoroughly permeated with the Romantic spirit with respect to his melodies, to his chromatic harmony, which was modeled in part on Wagner, and to the characteristic horn or trumpet calls of his orchestration. The structures of Bruckner are broadly conceived. The adagios go back to the ample proportions of the *adagio* of the Ninth Symphony of Beethoven. Bruckner's special interest in the slow movement and its devout chorale-like themes earned for him the title of *adagio-composer.* The finales are typically cyclic, using material from previous movements (e.g., the Fifth Symphony), and the weight of interest becomes centered in the finale. Bruckner actually stands somewhat apart from the other composers of his time. While he was undoubtedly influenced by Wagner, he was something of a solitary figure. The naïve piety of his own character is the emotional key to his music.

Mahler's activity was divided between his work as a great conductor and as a composer of symphonies and songs. Mahler stems from Schubert and particularly from Bruckner (whose friend he was), but his confessed gods were Beethoven and Wagner. The breadth and spirit of the *adagio* movement and the epic style of his early works derives from Bruckner. But he has a broader kinship to the choral idea of Beethoven's Ninth Symphony and to the ideas and music of Wagner. Unlike Bruckner, Mahler had a strong literary side. In the Mahler symphonies, one finds the intermingling of symphonic elements with those of poetry, song, and philosophical ideas (Schopenhauer and Nietzsche) that reflect his own personal conflicts. Mahler was preoccupied with the soul of man and its identification with the nature of the infinite. This preoccupation injected an ecstatic element into his music at the expense of *traditional* formal structure. It resulted in the use of greater and greater orchestral as well as vocal forces to depict his world-encompassing ideas. The greatest of forces is required in the Eighth Symphony, "the Symphony of a Thousand," so called because its multiple orchestral and vocal requirements of male, female, and children's choirs, in addition to the special brass and regular orchestras, demand about a thousand persons for its performance.

It has often been remarked that Mahler was basically a song composer. At any rate, his symphonic pieces overflow with song elements. Some of these themes are in folk-song style or that of Austrian folk dances (e.g., the *Ländler* in the *scherzi*). A special feature is the introduction of earlier song material of his own into later symphonic pieces, sometimes simply played by instruments, sometimes with vocal resources as well.

Mahler demands a gigantic orchestra, but he uses it with the utmost effect. Probably no one, not even Berlioz or Richard Strauss, knew the orchestra better than he. In addition to the monumental effects possible with a large body of players, Mahler produced many pages of really delicate scoring. It is in this latter respect that his work was important for the future of orchestration. Passages which employ soloistic orchestration *in the manner of chamber music* are characteristic of Mahler, and were something quite new at the time.

Mahler went beyond anyone in his conception of the symphony as a continuous journey, a point of no return. The weight of interest is pushed to the end. In his use of keys, too, he is continually progressing to new ones; he does not necessarily return to the home key of the piece at all. Used first in his song cycles and later in his symphonies (cf. the Ninth Symphony), Mahler's "progressive" tonality is the final departure from the Classic model of Mozart and Beethoven.

With Mahler the last vestige of the Classic symphony disappeared. For the essentially dramatic character of the latter was substituted a heroic narrative of lyrical elements, symbolically and philosophically conceived. Mahler's enormous structures must be supported by musical flying buttresses: the song theme and text as structural devices, the cyclic reference, and even a kind of cyclic relationship (as in Wagner's *Ring*) between the themes of the first four symphonies. The Classic symphony was replaced by a gigantic orchestral song.

Suggested Listening

Bruckner, Fourth ("Romantic") Symphony in E flat (1874).
Mahler, Ninth Symphony in D minor (1909).

Suggested Reading

Alma Mahler, *Gustav Mahler: Memories and Letters*, edited by Donald Mitchell. London: John Murray, 1968.
Dika Newlin, *Bruckner, Mahler, Schönberg*. New York: King's Crown Press, 1947.
Bruno Walter, *Gustav Mahler,* trans, by James Galston. New York: Greystone Corp., 1941.

THE CONCERTO IN THE NINETEENTH CENTURY

The nineteenth-century concerto took several directions: one inevitably followed Beethoven; another was more related to the new idea of continuous movements and thematic variants *à la Liszt*. Still another factor transformed the concerto, namely, the new technical demands of spectacular virtuosi like Paganini and Liszt, who were themselves composers.

One thing, however, is certain; the eighteenth-century idea of the concerto completely disintegrated in the nineteenth century. The chief factor in the change was the symphony and the symphony orchestra; in effect, the distinctive concerto form of the eighteenth century was swallowed up by the nineteenth-century symphony. After Beethoven, the double exposition gradually ceased to exist, except sporadically, and the cadenza was usually written out by the composer and sometimes put in a different place than formerly. The old idea of competition between the soloist and the orchestra remained, but it took place basically within the framework of the symphony. It is significant, too, that the piano and the violin had to be made more powerful to rival the power of the ever-growing symphony orchestra.

Even in Mozart one can see signs of a change in the concerto form. The D minor piano concerto (see p. 261) is already more dependent on the orchestra for musical development. In Beethoven the symphony orchestra is the complete musical equal of the soloist, and while the old double exposition is still preserved, certain hints at its breakdown may be observed (see p. 290).

MENDELSSOHN, VIOLIN CONCERTO IN E MINOR

The Violin Concerto in E minor (Op. 64; 1844) is a classic example of the change that took place. As the brilliant English critic, Donald Tovey, pointed out years ago, this concerto is a revolutionary piece—as strange as that may seem to us now. It is also the perfect violin concerto: perfect musically, flawlessly written, and from the performer's point of view, ideal because it sounds much harder than it is.[4] This concerto extinguishes the old concept of the Classic concerto form. No longer is there a double exposition. The soloist begins and shares the exposition with the orchestra. It is in regular sonata form with an elaborate coda. The cadenza is written out and forms a remarkable linking passage between the development and the recapitulation. The movements are also linked in a continuous whole, although the tenuous connecting link between movement I and II (a single note held in the bassoon) is sometimes drowned out if frenzied applause ensues at the end of the first movement.

This concerto has always been a favorite of performers and the public. It is not hard to see why. The themes themselves are fresh and varied, the workmanship is solid, and the interest is shared between the soloist and the orchestra. The solo part is no empty display but a musical working out of the music, now in swift and vigorous figuration, now in tender and Romantic song style. Finally, the skill of Mendelssohn as an orchestrator cannot be overlooked. His magic touch and thorough understanding

[4] Although Mendelssohn was not a violinist but a pianist—and a remarkably good one—he had excellent technical advice from one of the most celebrated violinists and teachers of the day: Ferdinand David, head of the violin department at the Leipzig Conservatory (of which Mendelssohn was director). Unlike Brahms, who sought the advice of the even more famous Joachim, Mendelssohn took David's advice to heart.

of the orchestra are reflected in numerous spots in this concerto, for example, in the opening of the main second subject, as explained below.

The three principal themes of the exposition are revealing: the first (Ex. 127a), a theme composed of rhythmic motives outlining the chord of the main key of E minor; the second (Ex. 127b), a contrasted theme distinguished by chromatic notes; and the main second subject (Ex. 127c), remarkable for the orchestral coloring of its beginning. In the latter, the solo violin is actually used as the bass (holding the open G string), the flute plays the middle of the harmony, and the two clarinets serve as soprano and alto.

Ex. 127

The second (slow) movement is typically Romantic. The lyrical tranquillity of the opening (in C major) is followed by the impassioned song of the middle section (in minor), in which the violin sometimes plays in octaves and sometimes combines the melody and its own accompaniments in double stops. A transition of a few measures (*allegretto non troppo*) leads to the last movement *allegro molto vivace,* in sonata form with rondo elements, a sprightly fast movement typical of Mendelssohn. It is set in E major (not E minor), and the change of mode contributes to the gaiety and brilliance of the conclusion.

PAGANINI AND LISZT

The essential evolution of the symphonic concerto can be traced in German music through Beethoven, Weber, Mendelssohn, Schumann, and Brahms. But a more spectacular development was connected with the names of Paganini and Liszt. Niccolò Paganini (1782–1840), presumably the greatest, and certainly the most famous violinist that ever lived, literally burst like a meteor on the musical horizon. No one had ever seen or heard anything quite like him. It is no secret that Liszt ("the greatest pianist") was fired by the spectacle of Paganini's success, and with these two the musical world of the early nineteenth century was dazzled by a kind of violin and piano playing of which it had not previously dreamed.[5] The result was a tremendous impulse to the purely virtuoso concerto in which the musical factors were frequently secondary. Paganini's two violin concertos are perhaps less interesting musically than the piano concertos of Liszt. The latter applied the principles of his symphonic poem to the piano concertos, especially the second in A major (1839; revised 1849–61), which is played without break. *Cf. Plates* 24c and 28c.

THE VIRTUOSO CONCERTO

It is impossible to speak of the many other concertos of the time, even of those of Brahms and Tchaikovsky—not to mention the virtuoso violin concertos of Viotti, Spohr, Vieuxtemps, Wieniawski, Bruch, Joachim, and Lalo, or the piano concertos of Chopin, Schumann, Grieg, and Saint-Saëns. In the main these concertos illustrate in one way or another the principal directions mentioned above. But one more thing must be said. The enormous increase in the technical capacity of instruments in general led to the increase in the number and difficulty of concertos for the traditional instruments such as the violin and the piano. In addition, other instruments came to be played by soloists. The most conspicuous of these instruments was the cello, until the nineteenth century relatively backward compared with the violin and the piano. In the nineteenth century it took a new lease on life, its technique rapidly expanded, and important concertos (especially those of Schumann, Dvořák, and Saint-Saëns) were written to incorporate its new technical and expressive capacity.

In the concertos of the nineteenth century as a whole the two most striking developments were the adoption of the forms of the symphony and the enormously increased technical capacity of the instruments and the fabulous virtuosos who played them.

Suggested Listening
Mendelssohn, Violin Concerto in E minor.
Liszt, Piano Concerto No. 2 in A major.

Suggested Reading
For Liszt, see p. 328.
Eric Werner, *Mendelssohn: A New Image of the Composer and His Age.* New York: The Free Press, 1963.

[5] The "new" pianism of Liszt combined the previous advances of Chopin and the possibilities suggested by the pyrotechnics of Paganini and his own considerable technical imagination. Liszt's *Transcendental Études on the Model of Paganini* are a clue; they include studies in the tremolo, octaves, arpeggios, and so on.

19. *Orchestral Program Music*

THE FUNDAMENTAL CHANGES in the symphony and the sonata, discussed in the previous chapter, were largely concerned with musical design. But there were other changes in form and procedure, associated in some degree with a "program"—some kind of story or title attached to the piece. It is by no means easy to make sharp distinctions between "absolute" and "program" music. If Tchaikovsky's *Pathétique* Symphony is program music—and a title does not necessarily constitute a program—we can only guess what the program is; and, at any rate, the music needs no further explanation. This brings us to the main questions: Must we know the details of a program to understand a piece of program music? If so, how is the music influenced by the program? The rest of this chapter contains a detailed answer, the gist of which is: most pieces of instrumental program music have a musical intelligibility of their own quite apart from the program; *but* a knowledge of the program is helpful and sometimes essential in understanding and enjoying many details of a work. Individual pieces of music vary greatly in this regard.

THE CONCERT OVERTURE

The concert overture is included in this chapter because it is a symphonic form (without being *a* symphony), more or less related to program music. The overture was originally written as a curtain raiser for the opening of the opera. A number of opera overtures, however, can be and are detached from their original operatic setting and played in concert. Beethoven is a case in point. For his only opera *Fidelio,* Beethoven wrote four overtures. For dramatic reasons, three of these were unsuitable for the opera, and are used independently as concert overtures, although only the so-called *Leonore No. 3* is regularly played. Similarly, overtures written for plays are often performed independently: Beethoven's Overture to *Coriolanus,* his Overture to Goethe's *Egmont,* and Mendelssohn's Overture to the *Midsummer Night's Dream* (the music of this overture actually existed before it was used as incidental music).

In the strict sense of the word, a concert overture is one written for a concert, not in connection with an opera or a play. A good example is Mendelssohn's *Hebrides* Overture, also known as *Fingal's Cave.* Most concert overtures (including those mentioned above) are connected with a program in some manner. The program influence is felt most frequently in the character or mood of the subject itself, sometimes in the incorporation of specific details related to the title or the story suggested by it. In Mendelssohn's *Midsummer Night's Dream* the "fairy music" of the opening is inspired by the play, yet it would be quite understandable as thematic material even if we lacked the title and did not appreciate the connection. But the braying of the ass in the same work does not by itself make musical sense; it is understandable as a detail explained by an episode in the play which is indicated by the title. For the most part, such details as the last are incidental, and the typical form of the concert overture is essentially musical in conception.

Mendelssohn's *Hebrides* Overture (1832) is typical in this respect. In 1829 Mendelssohn visited Scotland and the outer Hebrides, and was much impressed by what he saw; so much so, that he noted down the main themes of the *Hebrides* as a musical impression of what he had experienced. Doubtless the opening subject of the overture (Ex. 128) suggests a

Ex. 128

(Allegro Moderato)

p

swelling and running of the sea, particularly if we are looking for music suggestive of the title. All the same, it is an excellent theme for purely musical development, and the overture turns out to be in sonata form. Mendelssohn's attitude toward program music was similar to that of Beethoven: he was more interested in "the expression of feeling than painting." Mendelssohn said of the *Hebrides* Overture: "I wanted to express how queer I felt when on the Islands," but this did not prevent him from writing a piece as clear and solid in structure as it is rich and suggestive in melody and orchestration.

As a matter of fact, the majority of concert overtures are in some species of sonata form; otherwise, it becomes difficult to distinguish them from the symphonic poem.

Suggested Listening
Beethoven, Overture, *Leonore No. 3.*
Mendelssohn, *Hebrides* Overture.

THE PROGRAM SYMPHONY: BERLIOZ

There had been program symphonies before Hector Berlioz (1803–69) —using the word "program" in the broadest sense—but the program was relatively incidental. In the Berlioz symphony the situation changed because the program intruded itself on the listener. Berlioz furnished the symphony with a cast of characters; and although we might not always be aware of them, Berlioz often insists that we shall be, particularly in the *Symphonie Fantastique* (1829).

In this work, the first of his symphonies, Berlioz expects his audience to share the despair of his unhappy love for the Shakespearean actress, Harriet Smithson. This autobiographical compulsion was something new in music, and with Berlioz—as with everything that he did as a young man—it took an extreme form. This is the program, a bit abbreviated (and only the titles need be used for a purely symphonic performance):

"A young musician of extraordinary sensibility and overflowing imagination in a paroxysm of despair caused by unhappy love has poisoned himself with opium. The drug is too feeble to kill him, but plunges him into a heavy sleep accompanied by the weirdest visions. His sensations, emotions, and memories, as they pass through his diseased brain, are transformed into musical images and ideas. The beloved one herself becomes to him a melody, a recurrent theme (*idée fixe*) which haunts him everywhere.

(1) *Reveries, Passion* . . .

(2) *A Ball:* At a ball, in the midst of a noisy, brilliant fête, he finds the loved one again.

(3) *In the Country:* On a summer's evening in the country he hears two herders. . . . The pastoral duet in such surroundings, the gentle rustle of the trees . . . fill his heart with long-missed tranquillity. . . . But she appears anew. . . . What if she proved faithless? . . .

(4) *March to the Scaffold:* He dreams that he has killed his loved one, that he is condemned to death and led to execution. A march . . . accompanies the procession. . . . Finally, the *idée fixe* . . . appears for a moment, to be cut off by the fall of the axe.

(5) *Dream of a Witches' Sabbath:* He sees himself at a Witches' Sabbath. . . . Unearthly sounds, groans, shrieks of laughter. . . . The melody of his beloved is heard, but it has lost its character of nobleness and timidity. . . . It is **she** who comes to the Sabbath! . . . She

joins the diabolical orgy. The funeral knell, burlesque of the *Dies Irae*. Dance of the Witches. The dance and *Dies Irae* combined.

The irony is that a good deal of the *Symphonie Fantastique* could be heard and understood in unprogrammized form, and some of the music had already been composed before Berlioz used it in this symphony. The *Symphonie Fantastique* would not do for a Classic symphony, but with the exception of the last movement and the fall of the axe in the fourth, it would pass without difficulty as a Romantic symphony by an extremely talented young man who was not troubled about such things as reversing the order of the themes in a recapitulation if it suited him.

The *idée fixe* theme, associated with the "beloved," had psychological value for Berlioz, especially in its transformation—and, as Berlioz intended, his "beloved" could not have been much pleased with the caricature of the theme in the last movement. But since the theme is used as part of the thematic material and is structurally necessary to the musical development, an audience, not knowing the program, could understand the theme (Ex. 129) purely as a musical device, employed and transformed in the same way as was done later by Liszt.

Ex. 129

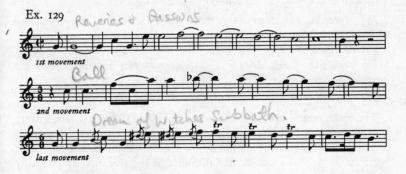

1st movement

2nd movement

last movement

The program explains a number of things that would not be clear without it: notably the presence of a brilliant waltz, which represents the *Ball,* in the second movement instead of a scherzo; the ending of the fourth movement with the axe stroke; and, especially, the significance of the fifth and last movement. Among other things, the presence in the latter of the *Dies Irae,* a melody most closely associated with the Requiem Mass, would not be understandable without the program.

The *Symphonie Fantastique* created a furor. It was something new; it was the essence of the fantastic in Romanticism;[1] it had genuine musical

[1] One must remember that this was the age of De Quincey's *Confessions of an English Opium Eater* (which Berlioz had been reading), Victor Hugo, and Edgar Allan Poe (1809–49).

qualities, and even the most virulent detractors of Berlioz—and there were plenty—admitted that the orchestration exhibited genius.

In some respects, it is too bad that the *Symphonie Fantastique* was ever performed. It had little impact on the history of the symphony apart from orchestration, and it gave Berlioz a reputation as a musical wild man—which he was at twenty-six. As he grew older, Berlioz became relatively conservative; and he was perfectly capable of composing, under an assumed name, a piece that fooled everybody with its Classic style (*L'Enfance du Christ*). Even today Berlioz has not lived down the *Symphonie Fantastique*. Still, it is a fascinating work of great originality.

Berlioz composed three more "symphonies," each quite individual in character: *Harold en Italie* (1834), *Roméo et Juliette* (1839), and *Symphonie Funèbre et Triomphale* (for military band, chorus, and strings; 1840). *Harold en Italie,* requested, although never played, by Paganini, shows the progress that we might expect in five years from a man of Berlioz's gifts. It is a less spectacular work than the *Symphonie Fantastique,* but it is better musically. All the old autobiographical underbrush of the former has vanished. There is a title and the individual movements have titles, but there are the conventional four movements, roughly corresponding to the usual symphony:

(1) *Harold in the Mountains. Scenes of Melancholy, of Happiness, and of Joy* (*adagio, allegro*).

(2) *March of the Pilgrims Singing the Evening Prayer* (*allegretto*).

(3) *Serenade of an Abruzzi Mountaineer to His Sweetheart* (*allegro assai, allegretto*); taking the place of the scherzo.

(4) *Orgy of Brigands; Remembrances of Preceding Scenes.*

. The viola, which represents the person of Harold (there is no apparent relation between Berlioz's symphony and the celebrated poem of Byron), is treated in *obbligato* fashion; and the "Harold" theme, one of the most beautiful of Berlioz's long-arched melodies, is the *idée fixe,* substantially unchanged throughout the symphony. *Harold* is quite comprehensible without any program, but certain details in it are explained by the titles. The dynamic scheme of the Pilgrim's March takes on a new meaning in view of the title. It begins very softly, becomes gradually louder and then dies away—obviously calculated in terms of the approaching pilgrims and their passing away in the distance. Other details are inspired not by the program but by Beethoven, particularly in the last movement, which begins with the recollection of themes from the preceding movement in the manner of Beethoven's Ninth Symphony. However, the last movement is the most bombastic and least interesting musically.

Roméo et Juliette (1839) is full of wonderful music—for example, the "Love Scene" (Berlioz's favorite) and the "Queen Mab" Scherzo—but it is not really a symphony. It is more of a "dramatic cantata with a symphonic heart." Nevertheless, Berlioz insisted that it was a "dramatic symphony with chorus, solo singing, and prologue in choral recitative, composed after Shakespeare's tragedy." At any rate, Berlioz did not write another "dramatic symphony," and it is significant that his next work, inspired by literature, was styled a "dramatic legend" (*La Damnation de Faust*). Still later, Berlioz's dramatic efforts were siphoned into the opera (*Les Troyens,* 1856–9; *Béatrice et Bénédict,* 1860–2). The importance of the literary element in the works of Berlioz has been exaggerated, but there is no doubt that his imagination was greatly stimulated by literary situations, and particularly by the possibility of injecting dramatic elements akin to the opera into instrumental music.

Berlioz's symphonies were more or less isolated phenomena. Liszt's *Faust* (1854–7) and *Dante* (1855–6) Symphonies, for instance, may be viewed more as the extension of Liszt's own principles developed in the symphonic poem. Perhaps the only real successor to Berlioz was Mahler.

Berlioz has always been a highly controversial figure. But there is general agreement on one point: he was the father of modern orchestration. Berlioz imagined and often achieved colossal effects and combinations never realized before. And he was able to produce just as extraordinary effects with four as with four hundred instruments. This was possible because of his great knowledge of the instruments and his intuitive grasp of balance, register, and color; and no composer had ever notated his score with more care, including the exact number of performers. In his *Treatise of Modern Instrumentation and Orchestration* (1844), Berlioz described the ideal orchestra: 242 strings, of which four play an octave below the present double bass, thirty pianos, thirty harps, the wind and brass doubled, trebled, and even quadrupled, and tremendous percussion resources. While Berlioz never achieved an orchestra of this size, his ideal was not as fantastic as it seems. Berlioz believed, with truth, that a true *pppp* of beautiful tone and in perfect pitch could not be achieved in the strings without a large number of players to cancel out individual imperfections.

With large orchestral resources, Berlioz produced startling effects, an example being the use of eight pairs of kettledrums to play chords for the basic harmony in the *Tuba Mirum* of the Requiem. He also used conventional resources imaginatively. He subdivided the strings still further; he made brilliant use of effects such as *pizzicato, ponticello, col legno,* and the mutes. He used the pure colors of solo instruments or homogeneous groups (i.e., all string, all woodwind tone, and so on), but there are in his music many mixtures of colors as well. He loved the antiphonal effects of large sound masses, such as the four brass choirs in the Requiem. In the more conventional orchestra he contrasted one orchestral choir with another, especially to echo the same phrase in a different color. A special feature of Berlioz's scores is the large number of unison, octave, or even several-octave doublings, partly for balance, partly for effects of color and spacing. Certain passages with instruments doubling a line in octaves give the impression of a kind of musical halo.

There is hardly a composer in the whole panorama of music who has been more misunderstood or maligned than Berlioz. Perhaps it could not be otherwise. A highly sensitive artist, full of contradictions, flamboyant in appearance and personality, he was a gold mine for the sob sister and yellow journalist of his day. Unconventional, aware of his great gifts, sharp-tongued, and living a life full of bizarre episodes, Berlioz was himself to blame for the fantastic legend that grew up about him. Actually, he was more naturally gifted than any other French composer of the nineteenth century. It is a mystery how Berlioz could have been so severely criticized for lacking melody and for imperfect harmony. His melodies, it is true, are varied in character and sometimes commonplace and vulgar, but we have only to listen to the "Harold" theme or especially to the melody of the wonderful song (accompanied by orchestra), *Le Spectre de la Rose,* to realize Berlioz's natural melodic capabilities. Everyone recognized his abilities with the orchestra, but not the fact that his harmony was conceived in terms of the instruments, voice leading, and colors of the orchestra. Berlioz's harmony sometimes suffers from lack of variety; it is sometimes banal. But it is difficult to understand the charge that his harmonies were "incorrect." Berlioz's most noticeable weakness was the sectional character of his music, accentuated by sudden and sometimes violent contrasts of mood, basically inspired by the literary or dramatic origin of his works. *See Plates 20 and 28c.*

Berlioz's literary sensibilities and his love of great literature were ingrained in him. He himself had literary talents; indeed, he was one of the few musicians who might have been an equally great writer. His musical criticism is penetrating in judgment and couched in the language of a high stylist. Actually, to this day no one has written a better criticism of Berlioz's music than Berlioz himself. The following just and revealing estimate is found in his *Mémoires* (1870), an autobiography of the greatest musical and literary interest. The passage in question is quoted for its intrinsic interest and for its literary quality, which is apparent even in translation:

I have never dreamt of making music *without melody,* as so many in France are stupid enough to say. . . .

The prevailing characteristics of my music are passionate expression, intense ardour, rhythmical animation, and unexpected turns. When I say passionate expression, I mean an expression determined on enforcing the inner meaning of its subject, even when that subject is the contrary of passion, and when the feeling to be expressed is gentle and tender, or even profoundly calm. This is the sort of expression that has been discovered in *The Infancy of Christ,* the *Heaven* scene in *The Damnation of Faust,* and the *Sanctus* of the *Requiem.*

A propos to the *Requiem,* I will mention a class of ideas which I have been almost the only modern composer to deal with, and the mere import of which has entirely escaped the older writers. I refer to the enormous compositions which some critics have called architectural or monumental music . . .

The musical problems I have tried to solve in these works . . . are exceptional, and require exceptional methods. In the *Requiem,* for example, I employ four distinct brass orchestras, answering each other at certain distances round the main orchestra and chorus. In the *Te Deum,* the organ at one end of the church answers the orchestra and two choirs at the other, while a third large choir represents the mass of the people, taking part from time to time in a vast sacred concert. But it is more especially the form of the pieces, the breadth of style, and the deliberateness of certain progressions, the goal of which is not at once perceived, that give those works their strange gigantic physiognomy and colossal aspect. The result of this immensity of form is, that either one entirely misses the drift of the whole, or is crushed by a tremendous emotion. . . .

My "architectural" works are the *Mourning and Triumphal Symphony,* for two orchestras and chorus [Berlioz seems to have gone astray here, as this work is for military band, chorus, and strings]; the *Te Deum,* the *Judex Crederis* of which is, without doubt, my most grandiose creation; the cantata for two choirs *L'Imperiale,* . . . and above all, the *Requiem.* As for such of my compositions as are conceived on an ordinary scale, and require no exceptional means of execution, it is just their inward fire, their expression, and their rhythmical originality, that have been most injurious to them, on account of the kind of execution they demand. To render them properly, the performers, and especially the conductor, ought to *feel* as I do. They require a combination of extreme precision and irresistible *verve,* regulated vehemence, a dreamy tenderness, and an almost morbid melancholy, without which the principal features of my figures are either altered or completely effaced. . . .

If you ask me which of my pieces I prefer, my answer is that of most artists: the love-scene in *Romeo and Juliet.*[2]

Suggested Listening
Harold in Italy.
Romeo and Juliet, "Love Scene."

[2] Hector Berlioz, *Memoirs;* translation by Rachel and Eleanor Holmes, annotated and revised by Ernest Newman. (New York: Alfred A. Knopf, 1932), p. 487 *ff.* Quoted by permission of Alfred A. Knopf, Inc.

Suggested Reading

Jacques Barzun, *Berlioz and the Romantic Century* (2 vols.). Boston: Little, Brown & Co., 1950.

Hector Berlioz, *Memoirs.* Translation by Rachel and Eleanor Holmes, annotated and revised by Ernest Newman. New York: Alfred A. Knopf, 1932.

Tom S. Wotton, *Berlioz.* London: Oxford University Press, 1929.

THE SYMPHONIC POEM. LISZT, LES PRÉLUDES. RICHARD STRAUSS.

The symphonic poem represents the application of the idea of thematic variation to a form in which the themes are inspired wholly or in part by a program. It is in one continuous movement and more closely related to the overture than to the symphony. The symphonic poem was invented by Franz Liszt (1811–86), and his first venture of this kind was entitled *Ce qu'on entend sur la montagne* (What one hears on the mountain; 1848) based on a poem of Victor Hugo. *Les Préludes* is by far the best known of Liszt's symphonic poems, and it will be analyzed below. As we have already shown, the idea of relating thematic materials was much in the air, and it is quite probable that Liszt was indebted to Schubert (especially to his *Wanderer Fantasie*) for the impulse that suggested applying the principle of thematic variants to a symphonic piece of large dimensions.

The procedure of varying the theme in the Lisztian manner was called *transformation of theme,* and it served two principal purposes: musically, it extended the material; and psychologically, it was capable of depicting different aspects of the subject or idea suggested by the program. Later, this device was used by Wagner; and in a more developed form it became the *leitmotiv* (leading motive) that was to be so central to Wagner's mature operas.

Les Préludes is a good example of how Liszt transformed his main subjects, how musical themes can correspond to poetic ideas or moods, and how a musical form succeeds in binding these elements together. This symphonic poem requires a large orchestra [3] and uses a chromatic harmony that influenced other composers, particularly Wagner.

Les Préludes falls into four clearly defined parts, corresponding roughly to moods implicit in one of Lamartine's poems (from his *Méditations poétiques*) which Liszt paraphrased and included as a preface to the printed score. However, the themes of *Les Préludes* are derived from an earlier work, revised about 1850, so that the music existed before Liszt ap-

[3] Two flutes, piccolo, two oboes, two clarinets, two bassoons, four horns, two trumpets, three trombones, tuba, three timpani, side drum, cymbals, bass drum, harp, and strings.

pended the title *Les Préludes* to it. From this we can only surmise that
Liszt saw in Lamartine's poem a general summary of the moods of his
music. The relation between Liszt's music and the Lamartine poem is
purely fortuitous, and the main feature of *Les Préludes* is the manner in
which Liszt manipulates, "transforms," and combines his themes for an
extended structure.

This is not to say that the themes themselves were not inspired by *any*
program. The music was composed (1848) as an overture to a group of
pieces for male chorus (*Les Quatre Elémens—The Four Elements*), and
the themes of the overture are all taken from the choruses. The fact that
Liszt went to some pains to give a title to his revised overture shows that
he thought of it as program music, at least in general terms.

Even if we did not know that Liszt's music was not inspired by Lamartine's poem, we could show that there is only a loose correspondence between the poem and the music, and that the most decisive considerations
are musical rather than literary. To demonstrate this, we will quote the
poem and analyze the music. The poem runs as follows in translation:

> What is our life but a series of preludes to that unknown song of
> which death strikes the first solemn note? Love is the magic dawn of
> every existence, but where is the life in which the first enjoyment of
> bliss is not dispelled by some tempest? . . . Yet no man is content to
> resign himself for long to the mild beneficent charms of Nature; when
> the trumpet gives the alarm, he hastens to the post of danger so that
> he may find in action full consciousness of himself, and the possession
> of all his powers.

This poem is extremely suggestive—in fact obvious—in its series of
images. The most characteristic suggestions are (1) A series of preludes,
(2) Love, (3) Tempest, (4) Nature, (5) The trumpet. Liszt's themes are
broadly suggestive of the moods outlined above—obviously why Liszt was
attracted to the poem. The themes themselves are manipulated by thematic
transformation; they are partly developed for variety and then repeated for
musical coherence. In Example 130 the principal themes are given in the
order of occurrence. (In this scheme *a1, a2*, etc., are thematic transformations of *a*).

Section I. The preludes; love. The tempo is basically *andante*. Theme *a*,
somewhat in the nature of an introduction, is followed by two successive
sections based on the transformation of *a:* measure 35, *a1;* measure 47, *a2*.
A contrasted theme, *b*, is heard in a new key (E major) at measure 70.
The latter is obviously a love theme.

Section II. A tempest. The tempo is basically *allegro* (beginning m.
109). This section begins with the development of a motive of *a;* bombastic scale passages, chromatic harmony, the power of the full orchestra,
and various keys are used for the tempest. A kind of trumpet motive (dis-

Ex. 130

tantly related to *a*) is heard at measure 160, and an incomplete statement of *a3* (m. 182) concludes the section.

Section III. Nature and love, appropriately in the tempo *allegretto pastorale* (beginning m. 200). A new pastoral theme, *c,* is given to "pastoral" instruments, the horn and the oboe, aided by the flute and clarinet; at measure 260, it is combined with the love theme, *b,* from measure 70. This is natural enough, for love and nature are presumably twins. Besides, combining these two themes gives more musical interest. The combination of these two themes is heard again at measure 296, this time in a different key, the home key of C major.

Section IV. Basically *allegro* (beginning m. 344). This section is not related to Lamartine's order of ideas at all, and even if the music had been inspired by the poem, this section would show how music asserts itself. Logically, according to Lamartine's poem, we should go on to "the trumpet gives the alarm, etc."; but Liszt turns on more orchestral power and returns to the opening themes in new transformations: at measure 346, *a3;* the love theme *b1* at measure 370; and a coda *a1* at measure 405. In effect, Liszt has restated his opening section in a varied form.

Liszt's solution in *Les Préludes* is a satisfactory blend of programmatic mood and solid musical construction. Attempts to show that the form of this piece is really a three-part form or even a modified sonata form seem quite futile and not really central to the question. Why not accept the work for what it is: four tableaux, of which the first, second, and last are essentially musical transformations of the same material; and all of which is an organic blend of themes, perhaps inspired by a program, and musically related and ordered? The really important thing is not what the form is, but that there is a form and that it works.

Liszt's ideas were a source of inspiration to many others, and his symphonic poems became the model for a host of imitators who saw in this new form an excellent vehicle for translating their poetic ideas into musical terms. Numerous examples could be cited, among them: Smetana, *My Fatherland;* Tchaikovsky, *Romeo and Juliet;* Saint-Saëns, *Danse Macabre;* Debussy, *L'Après-midi d'un Faune;* Dukas, *L'Apprenti Sorcier;* and many others. *See Plates 20 and 28c.*

After Liszt, the most successful composer of symphonic poems was Richard Strauss (1864-1949), at the end of the nineteenth century. The "tone poems" of Strauss are based on the Liszt model, but they are somewhat more dependent on a program or literary element, pay more realistic attention to detail, and show a great variety of forms. Strauss did not always furnish a program himself; pertinent and confidential information had a way of emanating from his friends. In some cases Strauss carried musical realism to extremes. A case in point is the realistic portrayal of the details of family life in *Sinfonia domestica* (*The Domestic Symphony*). However, the descriptive music used to portray the chief character in *Till Eulenspiegel* is convincing and delightful. *Till Eulenspiegel* and *Tod und Verklärung* (*Death and Transfiguration*) are probably his best efforts in this form. Strauss's sense of humor and satire is often evident in the selection and delineation of the subjects in these works, although it is markedly absent in the frankly autobiographical work *Ein Heldenleben* (*A Hero's Life*).

Technically, Strauss used the transformation of themes which Liszt had developed, but in certain ways he advanced beyond his model. The leading motives, associated with character, incidents, or moods, are apt to be combined polyphonically in the style of Wagner. The tone poems are usually cast in well-defined forms, such as the rondo in *Till Eulenspiegel* or the variation in *Don Quixote*.

The tone poems of Strauss are worthy successors to those of Liszt. The suggestive themes, their ingenious transformations, the solid musical construction, and brilliant orchestration assure these works a permanent place in the repertory of every symphony orchestra worthy of the name.

Suggested Listening

Liszt, *Les Préludes.*

Richard Strauss, *Till Eulenspiegel.*

Suggested Reading

Ernest Newman, *The Man Liszt.* New York: Charles Scribner's Sons, 1935.

Humphrey Searle, *The Music of Liszt.* London: Williams & Norgate, 1954.

Alan Walker, *Liszt* (Great Composers series). London: Faber & Faber, 1971.

20. *Sacred Music and Opera in the Nineteenth Century*

SACRED MUSIC

AN IMPORTANT CHARACTERISTIC of the Romantic movement was its anti-quarian interest. Certain church musicians turned from the rather elaborate and florid style of eighteenth-century sacred music to the ideals of the sixteenth century, in particular to Palestrina. In Germany, a group of musicians in the Catholic church wished to reform church music and formed the Cäcilienverein (1867), a society named after St. Cecilia, the patron saint of music. Members of the group were instrumental in the publication of scholarly editions of Palestrina and other collections; they revived Masses and motets of the old masters, and also composed in six-teenth-century style. In Germany and France, interest in Gregorian chant increased, and at Solesmes, a monastery in northeastern France, important work on old manuscripts led to new versions of the chant. Today the fruits of the labors of the Solesmes monks are incorporated in the official chant books of the Church. In France, too, there was interest in the revival of sixteenth-century ideals in sacred music: Alexandre Choron founded the Royal Institute for Classic and Religious Music (1817); and Louis Niedermeyer, the Niedermeyer School (1835). The latter had an impor-tant influence on certain French composers, for example, Gabriel Fauré. Late in the nineteenth century (1894) Alexandre Guilmant and Vincent D'Indy founded the Schola Cantorum for the purpose of singing old music.

In contrast to music in unworldly and ancient style, sung without ac-companiment, a great deal of music for the Mass was produced in typical nineteenth-century idiom, using the full resources of the voice and orches-tra. The Masses of Mozart and Haydn served as models for the early nine-teenth century. Beethoven, however, showed a somewhat changed attitude toward the text. Whereas older composers were more interested in setting whole sections according to the prevailing mood of the text, Beethoven was inclined to a minute verbal interpretation of each phrase. He said with respect to his first Mass (C major, Op. 86), "I believe that I have treated the text in a manner rarely practiced before." This remark is still truer with regard to his other and greater Mass in D, the *Missa Solemnis* (Op. 123),[1] a work difficult to sing and to interpret. Composed in his last period, this Mass was considered by Beethoven as his greatest and most successful work. On the score he wrote, "It comes from the heart, may it reach the heart." Both of the Beethoven Masses use four solo singers, four-part chorus, and orchestra.

The *Gloria* of the *Missa Solemnis* is a good example of Beethoven's "minute verbal interpretation" of changes of text. The *Gloria* opens brilliantly with full orchestra and chorus, reaching a climax on the phrase *in excelsis Deo* (to God on high), set appropriately in a high register, *fortissimo*. The following text *et in terra pax* (and on earth, peace) naturally suggested to Beethoven a sudden change. The music becomes soft at once, the words are set for a single voice part (the bass) in a deep register, and the size of the orchestra is reduced. The rest of the *Gloria* shows similar attention to detail. At *Gratias agimus* (we give thanks), the character, key, and tempo of the music change. In the *Quoniam,* at the words *Tu solus altissimus, Jesu Christe* (Thou alone are highest, Jesus Christ), the chorus soars to high A in the soprano, doubled in octaves below and held for six measures on the word *highest.* This soaring quality and holding of notes is characteristic of Beethoven's treatment of the voice in the *Missa Solemnis.* The orchestra at this point is typical also in that it has independent musical interest. Only Beethoven could have written the end of the *Gloria.* The fugue that begins with the text *in gloria Dei Patris* (in the glory of God, the Father) gradually embraces all the voices, including the four soloists, and ends with a coda, played *presto,* on the text and music with which the *Gloria* began.

As a whole, the settings of the Mass in the nineteenth century exhibit a bewildering array of all combinations of forms and harmonic styles. Charles-François Gounod (1818–93) is an example of this variety. His fifteen Masses include *a cappella* Masses as well as those in orchestral and chromatic style. Some Masses in the nineteenth century are intended for church use and others are not; and some are unacceptable to the Church. In the Schubert Masses in A flat and E flat, for instance, parts of the *Credo* are omitted.

As one might expect, the music of Liszt and the "New German" school

---

[1] This work is an "occasional" work. It was intended originally for the official installation of Archduke Rudolph (who had been Beethoven's pupil) as Archbishop of Olmütz in 1818. The work was not finished until 1823, and the first performance took place in St. Petersburg in 1824. The terms *"Missa Solemnis"* (Solemn Mass) and *"Missa Brevis"* (Short Mass) cannot be exactly defined. The latter implies either that only a part of the Ordinary text is set, or that the piece is in simpler style. The former usually denotes a special occasion, or a more elaborate style.

reflects their orchestral practices. Liszt wished to lead men back to an appropriate observance of the divine service by uniting the means of the theater and the church, and to do this he used the full vocal and orchestral resources at his command for what he called "humanistic" music. Examples of this tendency are Liszt's *Missa Solemnis* for the Cathedral at Gran (1855) and, later, Bruckner's Mass in F minor (1871).

Liszt also established a new Catholic oratorio based on his theories about the church music of the future. His two important works are *The Legend of Saint Elizabeth* (1862) and *Christus* (1865). The former uses leading motives. *Christus,* a more important work, is an amalgamation of different styles: Gregorian chant, unaccompanied song, and, at the same time, pieces using the possibilities of the modern orchestra.

A more conventional kind of oratorio was inspired by Handel. Haydn's oratorios (already mentioned) and Mendelssohn's *Elijah* (1846) are based on the Handel model, using the recitative and aria system, solo voices, chorus, and orchestra. Compared with Handel, these composers are somewhat more flexible in the use of forms, specifically, the recitative. In *Elijah* the recitative is sometimes shared consecutively among all four solo parts. Mendelssohn's excellence as a writer for the chorus was not lost on England, where he exerted a profound influence.

The Requiem Mass needs to be sharply distinguished from other Masses. The text is different, and in the nineteenth century it was sometimes used to commemorate a special occasion with pieces of extraordinary magnitude. Such is the case in the Requiem settings of Berlioz, Verdi, and Brahms. The Brahms Requiem is a Requiem only in the sense that it was composed in commemoration of the death of his mother. Otherwise it has no relation to church music. It does not use the liturgical text, being composed of seven pieces on texts chosen from Biblical sources by Brahms. The Berlioz Requiem [2] and the "Manzoni" Requiem of Verdi both use the liturgical text, but it is hard to imagine either work in church, even though the Verdi Requiem was first performed in St. Mark's in Venice. These extraordinary and moving settings carry Beethoven's dramatic attitude toward the text to the farthest imaginable point. For instance, the *Dies Irae,* whose vivid text possibilities attracted many composers to the Requiem, gave Verdi and Berlioz an opportunity to terrify their listeners with the prospects of hell fire. Both of their Requiems are distinguished by their magnitude of conception and by large performing forces, especially the Berlioz, an astounding, supercolossal, and magnificent "architectural" work (see Berlioz's own remarks, p. 323). The Fauré Requiem (1887) is totally different. In contrast to the settings of Verdi and Berlioz, Fauré's setting is brief, quiet, and contemplative, almost ascetic. It has the purity

[2] Originally commissioned by the French Government for those who died in the July Revolution of 1830, but actually performed for the burial service of General Damrémont, 1837.

of vocal line that Fauré learned from his studies of old music at the Niedermeyer School. Yet it is colored by a subtle and complex harmony that marks all Fauré's works. The same is true of the choruses. The whole is quietly accompanied by organ and orchestra.

The liturgical music for the Russian Church service differed in several respects from the church music of Western Europe. It was for a different liturgy, its Russian style was distinctive, and it was sung unaccompanied. The use of organ or instruments was actually forbidden in the church, and Russian composers and choir directors tried to achieve the utmost range and sonority from the forces at their disposal. The range of the voices was extended, especially downward, and the Russian basses were specially trained to sing in their deepest register. Furthermore, Russian composers discovered that they could produce an additional sonority in the chorus by extensive octave-doublings of the voices (for example, soprano and tenor) and by *divisi* in the orchestral sense. In the lower register, for instance, the voice parts were subdivided for somber effects of darkness reminiscent of the orchestral scoring of Tchaikovsky. Other conspicuous features of these choral settings were moving voices over static harmonies and parallel chord structure. The general harmonic and melodic style was naturally similar to the Russian idiom of the time (see pp. 363–4). The best-known composers of Russian liturgical music were Bortniansky (1751–1825), Tchaikovsky, Rimsky-Korsakov, Gretchaninov (1864–1956), Rachmaninov (1873–1943), and Tchesnokov (1877–1944).

Suggested Listening
Beethoven, *Gloria* from the *Missa Solemnis.*
Berlioz, *Dies Irae* from the Requiem.
Verdi, *Dies Irae* from the Requiem.
Brahms, Requiem (No. 1, "Blessed are they that Mourn"; and No. 4, "How lovely is thy dwelling-place").
Fauré, Requiem (opening).
Gretchaninov, *Credo* (Op. 29, No. 8).

OPERA

In the eighteenth century, Italian and, to a lesser extent, French opera dominated Europe. They continued to do so in the first part of the nineteenth century, although their manner and style of expression gradually changed. A significant new development, however, took place in Germany. The Romantic movement suggested a new type of subject centering on folklore and myth; the forms and technique of instrumental music, such as thematic development and transformation of themes, made new procedures possible; and in Weber, and particularly in Wagner, German opera found musical champions who brought it to the forefront as a world influence. After Beethoven, Wagner was easily the most important single influence in the music of the nineteenth century, and his operatic methods and personal genius made a deep impression on all branches of music. At the same time, French and Italian opera, devoted to quite different ideals from those of Wagner, continued to evolve, and achieved a new intensity and beauty of expression in the last works of Verdi. The political and social events of the nineteenth century encouraged national aspirations and corresponding artistic efforts in Russia, Bohemia, and elsewhere; and from these countries emerged opera composers such as Mussorgsky and Smetana, whose chief operatic interest lay in the depicting of national themes.

OPERA IN FRANCE: MEYERBEER. AUBER. GOUNOD. BIZET. OFFENBACH.

The type of opera prevalent in France in the first part of the nineteenth century is seldom, if ever, heard today. Gluck's influence was still felt in the serious operas of Cherubini and Spontini. Spontini's *La Vestale* (1807), for instance, was a combination of Gluck's lyric tragedy, Italian *opera seria,* and a "horror" subject, dear to the hearts of those who had experienced the French Revolution.

The so-called French *grand opera* (beginning about 1830) is somewhat more characteristic of the times. Under the impact of the French bourgeois drama, the opera abandoned the subjects of mythology (in the tradition of Gluck) for historical subjects. These operas, of which the most important composer was Giacomo Meyerbeer (1791–1864), were a curious mixture of the musical and the decorative (for example, the virtuoso "tinsel" aria), genuine dramatic moments, including continuous scenes, spectacular stage effects, and colossal orchestral resource. Musically, the French grand opera used the recitative and aria for individual "numbers," love duets and other ensembles, large choruses, and the inevitable ballet. The overture was usually a potpourri (a medley) of tunes, sometimes drawn from the opera itself. Dramatic effects were made possible by generally good librettos, especially those of Scribe.

The best of these grand operas was undoubtedly *The Huguenots* (1836) of Meyerbeer, an opera calling for huge tableaux, on a historical and gruesome subject (the massacre of the French Huguenots on St. Bartholomew's Day, 1572). To portray the text properly, Meyerbeer used a very large orchestra for tremendous effect. In spite of the grandiose and bombastic in this opera, its popularity was not undeserved. There are continuous scenes of great dramatic force; and, in Act 4, the "Consecration of the Swords" and the duet that follows border on genius, as even Wagner, who hated Meyerbeer, admitted. While the virtuoso elements in the arias are frequently tiresome, Meyerbeer possessed a real lyrical power. Other notable elements are the ballet and the recurrent use of the Luther

Chorale *Ein' Feste Burg* as a motive representing the faith of the Huguenots.

Two other operas belonging to the grand opera genre may be mentioned here: Rossini's *William Tell* (1829), written for Paris and really a grand opera, although the style was naturally marked by characteristic Rossini traits of rhythm and orchestral brilliance; and Berlioz's *Les Troyens* (1863).

In the nineteenth century the French comic opera was transformed from farce to bourgeois drama. Consequently, the comic opera was not necessarily funny, and *opéra comique* and the grand opera were at times indistinguishable except for one thing: the *opéra comique* always used spoken dialogues. Typical composers were Boieldieu (*La Dame Blanche,* 1825) and Auber (*Fra Diavolo,* 1830). The continuing rise of the *bourgeoisie* was accompanied by a greater emphasis on the lyric and the sentimental in opera. As a result, the *opéra comique* after the middle of the century had the outward forms of the grand opera combined with a lyric-sentimental tone. The following well-known operas are examples of this trend: Gounod's *Faust* (1859), Thomas's *Mignon* (1866), Delibes's *Lakmé* (1885), and Massenet's *Manon* (1884). Late in the century Wagner had an influence on French opera (e.g., Chabrier's *Gwendoline,* 1886).

A new school was created by Georges Bizet's *Carmen* (1875). While this work was called an *opéra comique,* and exhibits the general outward traits of the grand opera, its realistic subject matter distinguished it sharply from the Gounod-Massenet school. In his naturalism, Bizet may be compared to the French novelist Zola. Bizet's treatment of gypsies and bandits with true-to-life brutality created a type of realistic opera that gave impetus to the *verismo* ("true-to-life") school of Mascagni, Puccini, and certain French writers like Charpentier (*Louise,* 1900).

The opera *Carmen* itself is full of life and color, including Spanish local color, suggested by castanets and typical dances. The tunes and dances are animated by the utmost rhythmic verve and spirit, and serve to delineate the principals as flesh-and-blood individuals. The tunes and rhythms are matched by a brilliant orchestration with various special effects. The striking contrasts and the emotional range are reflected in the overture, in which a martial opening is followed by an ominous *andante.* It is characteristic of the realistic plot that the opera ends tragically with a passionate scene in which Don José brutally murders Carmen, his faithless mistress.

The comic and farcical tone of French opera returned in the delicious operettas of Jacques Offenbach (1819–80). His pieces are full of wit and satire of Greek mythology with topical allusions to the contemporary French political scene. Basically, his operettas consist of "hit" tunes interspersed with dialogues. Catchy, amusing, and unpretentious musically, these operettas enjoyed a great popularity. Examples are *Orphée aux*

Enfers (*Orpheus in the Underworld;* 1858) and *La Belle Hélène* (*The Beautiful Helen;* 1865).

OPERA IN ENGLAND: GILBERT AND SULLIVAN

The English lyric stage produced few works of note. Those of exceptional interest are *The Bohemian Girl* of William Balfe (1808–70), very popular in its time, and particularly the operettas of Arthur Sullivan (1842–1900) and the librettist W. S. Gilbert. These operettas made Sullivan the most popular English composer of his time. Victorian England was vastly entertained by Gilbert's satire of grand opera and contemporary institutions and fads. "Gilbert and Sullivan" became a household word in the English-speaking world; the operettas owe their continuing popularity to wit (sometimes ponderous), catchy tunes and choruses, brilliant orchestration, and their suitability for amateur theatrical productions. The well-constructed librettos of Gilbert gave Sullivan excellent musical opportunities, and the staging of these operettas by the original D'Oyly Carte Company contributed to their success. Among the best-known operettas are *Trial by Jury* (1875), *H.M.S. Pinafore* (1878), *The Pirates of Penzance* (1879), *The Mikado* (1885), and *The Yeomen of the Guard* (1888).

Suggested Listening

Meyerbeer, *The Huguenots* (Act IV: "Consecration of the Swords").
Bizet, *Carmen* (Overture; Act II: "Chanson du Toreador"; Act IV: Finale).
Gilbert and Sullivan, *The Mikado.*

OPERA IN ITALY: ROSSINI. BELLINI. DONIZETTI.

The Italian opera of the first part of the nineteenth century was primarily a "number" opera. There were relatively few continuous dramatic scenes. The center of interest was the voice, and the coloratura soprano and the heroic tenor were especially favored. The aria, *bel canto* singing, and vocal display were typical. Nevertheless, the dramatic recitative accompanied by the orchestra, and the love duets, choruses, and *ensemble finales* were often finely treated. In Italian opera the overture was usually a free piece or a potpourri of melodies. Compared with the French opera, the orchestra was smaller, the ballet rarely used, and the librettos were generally inferior. It is noticeable that the Italian librettists leaned heavily on such English Romanticists as Scott and Byron for their plot material and, after 1820, on such French literary sources as Hugo and Dumas.

The most important figures of the Italian opera in the early nineteenth century were Rossini, Bellini, and Donizetti. Gioacchino Rossini (1792–1868) continued the old traditions of *opera seria* (*Otello,* 1816) and *opera buffa* (*Il barbiere di Siviglia—The Barber of Seville*—1816). He rapidly became the most successful composer of Italian opera. Spontaneous melodies of catchy and vivacious rhythms were natural to Rossini, and he used the orchestra in a particularly brilliant way. The solo instruments stand out in their primary colors, and the whole texture is animated by the most lively string figuration. Rossini became famous for his extensive use of horns and a continuous crescendo.

Il barbiere marks the real end of the *opera buffa* except for isolated examples in Donizetti and Verdi. It is a worthy companion piece to Mozart's *Figaro,* not only in style and treatment but in the subject matter, which furnishes the plot background for Mozart's opera. In itself *Il barbiere* abounds in comedy, wit and satire, good characterization, good theater, ensembles, and brilliant orchestration. The *parlando* (speaking) style of some of the arias adds to the animation (for instance, *Largo al factotum*).

For some reason, Rossini ceased to write operas at the height of his fame and popularity. Although he lived until 1868, Rossini abandoned opera after *William Tell* was produced in Paris in 1829. Perhaps the popularity of the Meyerbeer style discouraged him. At any rate, after 1829 the French opera was dominated by Meyerbeer, and the Italian opera by Bellini, Donizetti, and the still greater talents of Verdi.

Bellini and Donizetti occupied the operatic stage between Rossini and Verdi. The best and most famous of Bellini's operas is *Norma* (1831), written before the composer was thirty years old. In Vincenzo Bellini (1801–35) may be seen a high point in the cult of melody, especially in the aria and the love duet. He created a type of melancholy, elegiac melody important for the opera and for its influence on Liszt, Wagner, Tchaikovsky, and possibly Chopin (see note p. 296).

With Bellini, the voice and the beautiful melody were the first consideration. Lovely arias, typically cast in three-part forms, abound in his scores. But they are seldom unadorned, being ornamented by turns, figuration, and ornamented phrase endings (Ex. 131). Vocal cadenzas are featured, interspersed throughout the arias. Sometimes, the cadenzas are

Ex. 131

Bellini, *Norma* (Act I, No. 4)

accompanied by an *obbligato,* instrumental part (e.g., the flute). The cadenza-technique consists of scales, trills, and arpeggios; and while it makes very exciting display pieces, it also interferes with the unfolding of the beautiful melody and particularly with the continuity of the opera. Singing had become an end in itself, and the singer also took many liberties with the score. But we must not forget how the arias were transformed by the beautiful voices that Bellini had at his disposal. Hearing great arias like *"Casta Diva"* from *Norma,* sung by a truly great voice, is an unforgettable experience.

Although the melody is the single dominant factor in the Bellini operas, there is considerably more to them than that. Bellini knew how to handle the chorus, the ensemble, and the dramatic recitative that served for rapid exchange of sentiment between the leading figures of an opera. The finales, too, are often much extended in scope (although roughly divided into numbers), and the harmonies are rich with chromatic and enharmonic chords, colorfully used. Besides, Bellini's librettos rise above the general mediocre level of those of his contemporaries. Of special interest, in view of the methods of Weber and Wagner, is the occasional use of "remembrance" motives or tunes. By this device the same tune is used later in an opera to recall dramatically an earlier situation. In Act I of *Norma,* the melody and orchestral accompaniment of the duet between Pollione and Adalgisa are recalled in the finale between Norma and Adalgisa.

Bellini has been criticized for certain dramatic weaknesses, but there is no doubt of his marked lyric talents or the influence of his beautiful melodies on European music.

Gaetano Donizetti (1797-1848) wrote in the various operatic styles of his time: *opera seria* (*Lucia di Lammermoor,* 1835), *opéra comique* (*La Fille du Régiment,* 1840), and *opera buffa* (*Don Pasquale,* 1843)—the last two operas written for Paris. Donizetti began as an imitator of Rossini, but after Rossini stopped writing operas, Donizetti's style became more independent; he anticipates Verdi by a more extensive use of the orchestra and in the way he develops his musical material.

Donizetti resembles Bellini in certain ways. His harmony is rich in chromatic and enharmonic effects. He also employs "remembrance" tunes (in *Lucia,* the melody of the love duet which closes Act I is used as an orchestral interlude in the "Mad Scene" in Act III). And, like Bellini, Donizetti had melodic gifts. There are the same kinds of melodic turns, ornaments, and virtuoso cadenzas. An extreme example of the latter occurs at the end of the "Mad Scene"—a virtuoso nightmare for soprano and *obbligato* flute.

The librettos of the Donizetti operas are generally mediocre. In some cases, however, Donizetti, who possessed literary ability, rewrote passages and improved them (the last act of *Lucia*). In spite of the low literary level of his texts, Donizetti frequently rises to heights of dramatic power. Scenes of melodrama or horror are powerfully set, as in Act II of *Lucia* when Lucia reads the forged letter.

Donizetti's orchestra is a powerful tool, playing an increasing part in the musical development and emphasizing the situation in dramatic recitative. Instruments appropriate to the occasion are selected: low brass to underline somber themes, for instance.

The chorus, too, is effective in commenting on the action or the emotional situation. Typically, Donizetti sets significant passages in unisons or octaves, and the resulting clarity of effect permits the chorus to perform a function not unlike that of the chorus in Greek drama. The ensembles are well handled, although the conception is often dominated more by musical than dramatic considerations. The characters in these ensembles are sometimes differentiated, but not sharply in the sense of the usual Mozart ensemble.

In certain respects, both Bellini and Donizetti are dated as opera composers. Their "number" operas were calculated in terms of the virtuoso aria suited to the singer in a tradition that specialized in a type of old-fashioned vocal virtuosity. Nevertheless, there are numerous individual arias and dramatic scenes that reveal the natural abilities of these composers and explain their enduring position in the operatic repertory.

Suggested Listening

Rossini, *The Barber of Seville* (Overture; "*Largo al factotum*").

Bellini, *Norma* (Act I: "*Casta Diva*"; "*Ah! bello a me ritorna*").

Donizetti, *Lucia di Lammermoor* (Act II: "Letter Scene"; Act III: "Mad Scene").

OPERA IN GERMANY: BEETHOVEN. WEBER.

In the first part of the nineteenth century, Italian opera dominated the German theater. German opera, a comparatively recent development, was mainly a sideline, and the opera composer in Germany who wished to be successful went to Italy to learn to compose in the Italian manner. In addition, French opera had important repercussions in Germany. The *opéra comique* altered the character of the *Singspiel,* Cherubini influenced Beethoven as an opera composer, and the Italian composer Spontini, so successful in Paris as a composer of French Opera (*La Vestale*), was invited and went to Berlin (1820). Until the middle of the century the repertory of the German opera house was composed largely of Italian and French operas. German opera was performed mainly in those centers where the composer happened to be the local conductor as well. In spite of the great importance of the German opera as a Romantic phenomenon, it remained, with few exceptions, an unexported national product until the international vogue of Wagner became synonymous with German opera.

Beethoven's only opera *Fidelio* belongs to the first decade of the century. Written in 1805, it was revised in 1806, and received a third and final form in 1814. The plot came from a French libretto of Bouilly, adapted and put into German by Sonnleithner. *Fidelio* is a rescue opera on the theme of conjugal love, and it is related to the *Singspiel* in the sense that Mozart's *Magic Flute* is a *Singspiel:* that is, there are spoken dialogues. Its high seriousness, however, lifts it far above the popular tone of the early form. Unlike the *Magic Flute,* it has little comic relief, but the rescue of Florestan achieves a happy ending.

From the beginning of the overture [3] we hear Beethoven's powerful voice, whether in arias dominated by figuration (e.g., the "Revenge" aria in Act II) or those reminiscent of the slow movements of his symphonies (opening of *"Komm, Hoffnung,"* Act I). In this opera the demands of music sometimes conflict with those of the drama. In the Quartet *"Mir ist so wunderbar"* (Act I), Beethoven's interest in the imitative counterpoint of the ensemble clearly has the upper hand of the text situation. However, dramatic sentiments are powerfully underlined in the dramatic recitative accompanied by the orchestra and in the tremendous climax scene where the off-stage trumpet indicates that the Minister of State has arrived and rescue is at hand. A special type of dramatic setting, the *melodrama,*[4] already exploited in the eighteenth-century *Singspiel,* is used in the "Grave-digging Scene" in Act II. Finally, the orchestra is very important in the musical development and it is relatively large.

The German Romantic opera really began with *Der Freischütz* [5] of Carl Maria von Weber (1786–1826). This work (1821) also marked the emancipation of the German opera from Italian and French models. Significantly, Weber had been called to Dresden in 1815 to found a German opera. In many ways *Der Freischütz* embodies the ideals of German Romanticism. The basic idea of the plot is significant: magic bullets which never fail to hit their mark are furnished by Zamiel, the black huntsman (i.e., the devil), in return for the soul of the one who receives them. In addition to the magic and supernatural elements, the opera specializes in local color of the forest, peasants, rustic love, hunting, and hunting horns. Other typically Romantic elements are the folk tale, the folk-song type of melody, and folk dances. These elements are rather naïve and nationalist in emphasis.

---

[3] The overture commonly used is called the *Fidelio* Overture, in E major (No. 4). There are three others, all in C. No. 3 (*Leonore No. 3*), as we have already pointed out, is frequently used as a concert overture.

[4] In this particular sense, the word "melodrama" means that a *spoken* text is accompanied by instruments.

[5] Literally, "free-shooter." In this opera it means a marksman who receives seven "free" (magic) bullets, six of which do as he wills, but the seventh, as the devil wills.

Like the *Singspiel, Der Freischütz* uses spoken dialogues, but emotionally this opera goes much further. Sentiments concerned with magic, incantations, the gruesome, and the horrible are expressed more vividly than ever before, especially in the continuous finale of Act II, where the magic bullets are cast by Max and Caspar in the Wolf's Glen. In this scene the speaking or declaiming technique of melodrama is used, but the effect is greatly intensified by the really extraordinary use of the orchestra to depict the situation and by the most lurid sound effects of birds, boars, rattling of wheels, and so on. Opposed to this kind of sensationalism are the typical sentimentality of the love scenes and the pious sentiments of forgiveness expressed at the end of the opera. *See Plate 25A.*

To Weber, German opera owes a larger and more effective orchestra and the use of unifying motives—"remembrance" motives. The remembrance motives are used both in the voice and in the orchestra, in which particular instruments are assigned to characterize certain individuals; and the overture forecasts the mood and action by using melodies drawn from the main motives of the opera. The brilliant orchestration and the dramatic effect to which it is put are striking in Weber's score, and had a considerable influence on his contemporaries. The string figuration, for instance, is brilliant and extended in range. The solo instruments are very clearly delineated. Weber uses the *pizzicato* for dramatic effect in the overture where the plucking of the double basses on beats two and four is reinforced by the timpani to produce a singularly sinister effect. The brass instruments, the horns in particular, convey the mood of hunting and forest scenes. Orchestral color is achieved by contrasting the high and low registers of instruments and by exploiting certain special registers (for instance, the low *chalumeau* register of the clarinet).

Dramatically, Weber gains his greatest intensity of effect from the dramatic recitative, certain continuous scenes, large ensembles, and the use of the orchestra and remembrance motives to characterize and unify. Musically, his works are impressive for their colorful chromatic harmony, persistent rhythmic motives, and their melodies, some of folk-song character or outlining harmonies, others dashing and brilliant in the *perpetuum mobile* manner. German to the core, Weber wrote music, particularly in *Der Freischütz*, that summarized the special qualities of German Romanticism, a fact thoroughly appreciated by Wagner.

Suggested Listening

Beethoven, *Fidelio* (Act I: Recitative *"Abscheulicher! Wo eilst du hin?"* and the aria *"Komm, Hoffnung"* that follows).

Weber, *Der Freischütz* (Overture; Finale of Act II: "Wolf-Glen Scene").

Suggested Reading

D. J. Grout, *A Short History of Opera*. New York: Columbia University Press, 1947.

James Harding, *Rossini* (Great Composers series). London: Faber & Faber, 1971.

21. The Operas of Wagner and Richard Strauss

RICHARD WAGNER (1813–83)

RICHARD WAGNER was one of the giants of music; he was also an important representative of the culture of the nineteenth century. In some respects the philosophical ideas of Schopenhauer and Nietzsche are reflected in Wagner's music. Nietzsche saw in *Tristan* the ideal Dionysiac drama, but he later broke with Wagner because he believed that *Parsifal* was a hypocritical renunciation of Wagner's ideals. The search for the universal and all-embracing that characterized the Romantic movement had a counterpart in Wagner's theory of the music drama which sought to embrace all the arts in one complete art work (*Das Gesamtkunstwerk*) striving for a common dramatic end. In his use of mythology for subjects involving passion, redemption, and renunciation, Wagner was also a child of the Romantic movement. Wagner's life was in itself a Romantic drama; and it is symbolic that he and Liszt, two of the most Romantic and complex musical personalities of the time, should be united by Wagner's marriage to Cosima, the estranged wife of Von Bülow and the daughter of Liszt. *See Plate 28A.* (For Suggested Reading, see the end of this chapter.)

Wagner influenced music everywhere; moreover, the subjects of his operas had a national political significance. His glorification of German heroes through mythology struck a responsive chord in the new German Empire, and although Wagner was a political progressive as a young man, and consequently a political exile from Germany in 1848, he enthusiastically hailed the Empire in 1870. The significance of Wagner's work was not lost on Emperor William II, who struck a famous pose as Lohengrin emerging from the swan boat.

The early operas of Wagner reflect the types and subject matter of the times. *Rienzi* (1840) is a French grand opera in Meyerbeer style. Following this, Wagner wrote Romantic operas in the style of Weber, whose work he continued and expanded in *Der fliegende Holländer* (*The Flying Dutchman;* 1843), *Tannhäuser* (1845), and *Lohengrin* (1850). In method and operatic attitude Wagner owed much to Weber in the "remembrance" motives, in certain melodic turns of phrase, in the emphasis on the orchestra, and in considering the opera as a union of all the arts, an idea already formulated in embryo by Weber. *See Plate* 27B.

In the three Wagner operas just mentioned, the subject matter includes mythology, elements of magic, and the supernatural. Furthermore, themes characteristic of much of Wagner's later thought are evident: the struggle of good and evil, the conflict between the spiritual and the sensual, and redemption through love. Technically, the remembrance motives became more important as Wagner sought to achieve a more continuous whole. The orchestra assumed greater and greater importance, and at times became almost magical in its imaginative depicting of situations. The recitative and aria of his earlier works gradually fused into what later became the *Sprechgesang* (see below). In short, while *The Flying Dutchman* and *Tannhäuser* were still "number" operas, *Lohengrin* had become a practically continuous music drama in which the motives representing the chief ideas and characters were developed symphonically.

After the cold reception of *Tannhäuser* in Dresden (1845), Wagner said, "I must induce the public to understand and participate in my aims as an artist." Consequently, theoretical writings occupied his attention before the composition of his mature opera. The most important of these writings were *Art and Revolution* (1849), *The Art Work of the Future* (1850), and, the most significant, *Opera and Drama* (1850-1). In the opening section of the latter, Wagner said, "The error in the art-genre of opera consists in the fact that a Means of Expression (Music) has been made the object, while the Object of Expression (the Drama) has been made a means." Wagner sought to relieve the drama from the tyranny of music (cf. Gluck). Thus the poet and the musician should be as one. Wagner proposed the myth as the ideal subject matter, since it appealed directly to the emotion, and his ideal type of poetry was the old *Stabreim,* an alliterative form of ancient Germany poetry, for example:

> Die Liebe bringt Lust und Leid
> Doch in ihr Weh auch webt sie Wonne.

> (Thus love doth lighten loss,
> For 'tis from woe she weaves her wonder.)

Musically, the drama should be depicted, according to Wagner, through "tone-speech" and by the power of the modern orchestra. The latter can make plain the harmony and characterize the melody in a way far superior to that of the vocal mass (i.e., the chorus and ensembles). The great value of the orchestra lies in its power of uttering the unspeakable by its organic alliance with gesture, by bringing up the remembrance of an emotion by motives when the singer is not giving voice to it.

After the theoretical works mentioned above, which also helped to clarify his own ideas and plan for *Der Ring des Nibelungen* (*The Ring of the Nibelung*), Wagner completed the musical composition of this gigantic poem, written 1848–52 (in the reverse order of the composition). *The Ring* consists of four complete operas which taken together form one continuous whole: *Das Rheingold* (*The Rhinegold;* 1854), *Die Walküre* (*The Valkyrie;* 1856), *Siegfried* (1856–7 and 1865–71), and *Götterdämmerung* (*The Twilight of the Gods;* 1869–74). During the writing of *Siegfried,* Wagner laid aside *The Ring* and composed *Tristan und Isolde* (1859) and his only "comic" opera, *Die Meistersinger von Nürnberg* (1867). *Parsifal,* his last opera, was finished in 1882.

Wagner was his own poet. He drew his themes from mythology, and he was fond of abstract themes of renunciation, redemption through love, and fulfillment through passion. The mature Wagner opera represented the reform of opera in accordance with the ideas already mentioned and by the application of Beethoven's symphonic technique, especially that of development. The symphonic motives that make the continuous unfolding possible are described as *leading motives* (*Leitmotiv;* plural: *Leitmotive*), although Wagner himself did not use this term. These motives, usually short, are capable of modification with respect to rhythm, intervals, and accompanying harmony, and they were selected to depict individuals, situations, and principal ideas. (For an example, see the discussion of *Tristan,* below.) The motives are shared indiscriminately between the orchestra and the voices, although the orchestra has, as a rule, a greater part in working them out; and they are modified or transformed to reflect other facets of personality, to characterize a new situation, or to change the perspective. This system made possible such a gigantic creation as *The Ring,* in which four complete operas are joined by common motives.

The voice half sings, half declaims the text in *Sprechgesang* (speechsong), a kind of fluid recitative which represents a merging of the recitative and the aria into an "unending melody." The *Sprechgesang* was meant to underscore the text meaning by appropriate music. Thus expressive texts should be emphasized by expressive intervals, and consequently the *Sprechgesang* is often marked by large or chromatic intervals (Ex. 132). It is a mistake to imagine that Wagner ruled out arias from his operas (e.g., *"Du bist der Lenz"* from *The Valkyrie*); or, for that matter, "love" duets (see *Tristan*) or ensembles. Actually, the lyrical moments are cemented into a continuous whole by the *Sprechgesang* and the symphonic texture of the orchestra. The mood of the action is forecast by the overture (*Vorspiel*) a free and variable one-movement form, usually employing the chief leading motives that are to come.

Ex. 132

Wagner, *The Valkyrie* (Act II, scene 2)

In spite of Wagner's theories, the music, especially the music of the orchestra, is of the greatest importance in his operas. In one sense, the voice and the poetry are imposed on the symphonic web; and it is significant that certain selections of the music are used alone as concert pieces for orchestra. As Gluck said earlier, "The orchestra never lies," and through the dramatic unfolding and combining of the leading motives by symphonic means, every situation can be accurately depicted. Thus in certain works (e.g., *Tristan*) the music dominates the poetry.

In this continuous music, the motives weave polyphonically over a base of highly chromatic and expressive harmony. The music avoids cadences or uses deceptive cadences to emphasize the continuity, and sequences spin out the phrases. Wagner is fond of set rhythmic patterns, and he is in fact more reliant on harmony than on rhythm for variety. The dynamics are fluctuating constantly, and are used for climactic effect. Typically, Wagner's dynamic climaxes consist of a series of *crescendo-diminuendo* passages increasing in intensity.

Wagner's orchestra was an instrument of fabulous power, and he was its absolute master. Even in his early works, he displayed a complete knowledge of the contemporary orchestra. In the hands of Berlioz, Liszt, and Wagner, the orchestra had become complete in all divisions. The number of instruments had been vastly increased, the woodwinds greatly improved, and the brass made chromatic by the addition of valves. *The Ring* requires a complete family of tubas, eight horns, three trumpets, bass trumpet, and four trombones, including a contrabass trombone. Comparable expansion had taken place in the rest of the orchestra. The whole orchestra could furnish some seventeen choirs and about one hundred voice parts! With such variety and range of pitch and dynamics, magical effects related to the situation could be produced almost entirely by orchestral means. As in all great orchestrators, Wagner's demands from the orchestra were directly related to the orchestral effects he wished to create. No one before or since has created such effects of brilliant light (*Lohengrin*) or dark cavernous sounds (*The Ring*). The opulence and variety of his instrumental colors are surely the most extraordinary in opera.

Wagner's directions with respect to the orchestra are as precise as those of Berlioz. He marks exactly all tempi, nuances, and even the number of players required. The same thing is true of his stage directions. The special ideas of Wagner led logically to a unique orchestra and unique equipment to give expression to his art works. The visible monument is the Wagner theater at Bayreuth, built for the production of *The Ring*. In this theater the orchestra and conductor are invisible to the audience. The auditorium itself is shaped like a wedge, the thin edge touching the stage, the thick end being the back of the auditorium. All the seats face the stage directly; there are no side boxes or galleries, nor is there a prompter's box. *See Plate 25B.*

Wagner was undoubtedly one of the greatest musicians that ever lived. Compared with his musical gifts, however, his powers as a poet and dramatist were of a lesser order. The validity of his theories on the importance of the poetry and allied arts cannot be sustained by his practice in the operas. In fact, the music of the orchestra carries everything before it, and by its power and musical self-sufficiency often relegates the voice and the text to a secondary position. Wagner the musician supported at times Wagner, the insecure poet or dramatist. The long discursive and repetitive episodes in *The Ring* would not be tolerated in a poem. Their presence can be justified only because they are essential to a tetralogy, each one of whose units must be more or less self-sufficient, and whose artistic unity and success are dependent on music. The magic of the music, its textures, and orchestral colors transcend and transform much that is ridiculous, ponderous, and dramatically uncertain. Finally, the *Stabreim* itself is eminently suited to the flexibility of the leading motives, and it fulfills a musical rather than a poetic demand. Wagner had to resuscitate an ancient poetic form to meet the needs of his music dramas.

From the point of view of the traditional opera, Wagner produced a crisis that threatened to engulf the lyric stage by overwhelming the voice in the flood of music of the symphony orchestra. In content, also, Wagner was at variance with past tradition. With the exception of *Die Meistersinger,* which deals with characters who are felt to be genuine people, the mature works of Wagner do not deal with traditional drama or with the characterization of individuals in the sense of the Mozart opera. Mythology is the means toward the expression of philosophy and the psychological interplay of the ideas of fate, redemption, and renunciation. The personages in *Tristan* and *The Ring* are less real to us as *people* than as symbols of deep psychological forces, passions, or ideas. From this threatening impasse, the traditional opera was rescued mainly by the mature efforts and greatness of Verdi.

TRISTAN AND ISOLDE

Tristan and Isolde is typical of Wagner's fondness for myth, legend, and medieval epic, which he adapts for his own use. The main outlines of the plot are these:

Act I. After the impressive overture, the curtain rises on a scene aboard a ship journeying from Ireland to Cornwall in England. Tristan, the nephew and heir apparent of King Mark of Cornwall, is bringing Isolde, an Irish princess, to be King Mark's bride. Isolde is raging against Tristan, partly because he has slain a previous lover of hers and partly because she is in love with him. She resolves to give him a death potion (her mother, a sorceress, had given her this and a love potion for emergencies), which she instructs her maid Brangäne to prepare. Brangäne secretly substitutes the love potion. Tristan, at Isolde's command, drinks the potion, fully expecting to die. Isolde snatches the cup from him, and she, too, drinks, thinking to die with him. Instead, the magic love potion does its work, and Tristan and Isolde, after gazing longingly into each other's eyes, embrace with wild ecstasy just as the ship approaches the Cornish shore. They are separated by their retinue just in time to preserve the amenities before Mark welcomes his bride.

Act II. The marriage of King Mark and Isolde has taken place. The King has gone hunting, and Isolde is impatiently awaiting her lover, Tristan (the overture indicates motives of longing and distant sounds of hunting horns off stage). Brangäne is uneasy. She fears treachery on the part of Melot, one of the knights of the court who she believes is suspicious of the relation of Tristan and Isolde. But Isolde persists in giving the prearranged signal to Tristan. The lovers meet, their ardor mounts, they sing rapturously of their love and their erotic love-death. They identify night with their joy, and they dread the coming of the hateful day. Just as they approach the climax of their love, in the most intense orchestral and vocal musical eroticism ever written and staged, Melot and King Mark burst in. It is just as Brangäne had feared. The hunt had been arranged by Melot as a trap to surprise the lovers. Tristan shields Isolde, Mark is sorrowful and reproachful, and Melot furious with righteous anger. Tristan is bewildered but shows no remorse. He vows he will leave and asks Isolde to accompany him. This is too much for Melot who attacks Tristan. They fight, and Tristan is seriously wounded.

Act III. The most melancholy strains are heard. Tristan has been carried to his ancestral home across the sea in Brittany by Kurwenal, his trusty aide. Tristan awaits impatiently the expected arrival of Isolde's ship. The watchman plays a sad tune. Tristan is delirious. He reminisces about his past and calls continually for Isolde. Finally, a ship is sighted. At the news, Tristan grows wild with excitement. He staggers to his feet and tears off his bandages. As Tristan is dying, Isolde comes on the scene, and in one of the most heart-rending of all operatic scenes, she approaches Tristan just as he dies. Meanwhile, another ship is sighted, bringing King Mark, to whom Brangäne has confessed, and who is coming to forgive. Kurwenal, not knowing Mark's real intentions, tries to repulse the King's party as invaders. He kills Melot and is himself slain. King Mark and Brangäne hasten to Isolde, but it is too late. Isolde sings the strains of the *Liebestod* (love-death) and expires; and as Tristan and Isolde were united in love, they are united in death. Deeply moved, King Mark and Brangäne contemplate the tragic scene as the curtain falls.

Tristan and Isolde is one of Wagner's best music dramas. It is also one of the most chromatic and symphonic. The short motives with which the opera begins (in the overture) are characteristic of the chromaticism that prevails (Ex. 133). The motives themselves (a and b), those of Tristan

Ex. 133

(The Glance)   *(Fulfillment)*

and Isolde, are opposed as well as united musically, symbolic of the course of opposition and union of the two principals of the drama. These two motives, being short, are extremely flexible for development and modulation; being chromatic, they are expressive, and give rise to many expressive harmonies.[1] Two other motives (c and d) are given to show their motivic musical character and their presumed meaning for the drama. The whole is bound together by the *Sprechgesang* and by the symphonic motives into which is woven the lyricism of such moments as those in the *Liebesnacht* in Act II (Ex. 134). The expressive power of chromatic harmony, modulating by half steps, the dynamic fluctuation of the voices and the orchestra, the color and the power of the latter, all are used masterfully by Wagner to wring the last drop of emotion from a drama of fulfillment

[1] In the course of this opera the extensive use of these half tones tends at certain points to loosen the tonality to such a degree that it is difficult to say which key it is in—if indeed in *any* specific key. Wagner himself pointed out that the opera composer may partially dissolve the tonality where he is supported by the drama, whereas an "abstract" symphonist cannot do this. By his extensive use of half-tone melodies and chromatic harmonies, Wagner actually pointed the way to non-tonality and to the twelve-tone technique of Schoenberg (see p. 409).

through passion and redemption through love—a drama to which Wagners' own life and music were monuments.

Ex. 134

RICHARD STRAUSS (1864–1949)

After Wagner, Strauss was the most gifted and versatile of German composers of his generation. He was also a first-class conductor and one of the greatest orchestrators. His early musical education was along strictly traditional lines under the watchful eye of his conservative father. Modern music for him was Mendelssohn and Brahms. In 1886, however, he became converted to the Wagner school and the philosophy of "music as

expression." The period immediately after this was devoted to the composition of his best-known symphonic poems, which have already been
described. The operas were written in the early years of the twentieth
century, but their point of departure was the Wagner music drama of the
nineteenth century. The best of these are *Salome* (1905), on a libretto
from Oscar Wilde's play; *Elektra* (1909); and *Der Rosenkavalier* (1911).
The latter two, as well as others, were based on librettos by his chief
collaborator, Hugo von Hofmannsthal. His later operas were less successful.

The operas of Richard Strauss are based on the Wagner textures and
mechanics. The leading-motive system is the unifying principle, and the
Sprechgesang with its expressive contours and intervals is used throughout. The conception is a symphonic one, and the orchestra carries the
principal burden of unfolding the continuous music. Unlike Wagner,
however, Strauss was not his own librettist; but he depended on librettos,
the best of which could have stood alone as plays. In Hofmannsthal,
Strauss found a collaborator as important to his works as Da Ponte was
to Mozart, and for much the same reasons. In both cases, the poet furnished librettos notable for clearcut dramatic situations and clearly drawn
characters with the requirements of the operatic medium in mind. *Der
Rosenkavalier* (The Cavalier of the Rose) bears the significant subtitle
"A Comedy for Music." In the Strauss opera, characterization is already
inherent, as a rule, in good librettos. Strauss underlines what is already
there and makes it more vivid by music, especially through the orchestra.
In *Der Rosenkavalier* he comes closest to Mozart's spirit. In this work
occur also "love" duets and ensemble pieces (as in both Wagner and
Mozart). In other works he goes back for his subjects to classical antiquity
(*Elektra*) or to figures from Biblical times (*Salome*). In Salome, Strauss
created one of the most controversial and amoral creatures in operatic
history.

Strauss shared many characteristics with Wagner, and, to a lesser extent,
with his contemporaries. His melodies and harmonies are based on
Wagner, but sometimes extend the Wagner idiom. His *Sprechgesang* may
be even more expressive, the leaps more extreme, and the dissonances
sharper. Like every great composer, he has a style that is individual. In
general, it fluctuates between two extremes. His fiery nature reveals itself
in music of tumultuous power and brilliance. A highly contrasted side is a
type of sweet, almost cloying music, that relies on such devices as thirds
and sixths and a kind of sentimental harmony (for example, the waltz
music in *Der Rosenkavalier*). Dance rhythms, particularly that of the
Viennese waltz, are frequent. *Cf. Plate* 27A.

Strauss's mastery of the orchestra is legendary. In his own time, only
Mahler, and perhaps Rimsky-Korsakov, knew the orchestra as well as he,
and no one demanded more from his players. The tremendous advance

of instrumental technique in the twentieth-century orchestra takes its departure from Strauss who asked the seemingly impossible from his players. He extended the range of all instruments and made unheard-of demands, especially on the brass. The result was a dazzling orchestral palette, capable of every possible orchestral shade of expression.

With Strauss, the Wagner ideal of music drama came to an end. The twentieth-century composer reacted against the Romantic themes, the emotionalism, the chromatic harmony, and the grandiose which it represented. This was natural enough. Still, any fair-minded musician recognizes the operas of Wagner and Strauss for the works of genius that they are, based on the ideals and culture of another time.

Suggested Listening

Wagner, *Tristan and Isolde* (Act I: Prelude; Act II: *"Liebesnacht"*; Act III: *"Liebestod"*).

Strauss, *Rosenkavalier* (Act I: Prelude; *"Kann mich auch an ein Mädel erinnern":* monologue of the Marschallin; Act II: waltz music; Act III: *"Ist ein Traum,"* finale).

Suggested Reading

Robert Donington, *Wagner's 'Ring' and its Symbols.* London: Faber & Faber, 1969.

Ernest Newman, *The Life of Wagner* (4 vols.). New York: Alfred A. Knopf, 1933–46.

Correspondence between Richard Strauss and Hugo von Hofmannsthal, 1907–1918, trans. by Paul England. New York: Alfred A. Knopf, 1927. A complete edition in German appeared in 1952.

For the Strauss operas as a whole, see D. J. Grout, *A Short History of Opera.* New York: Columbia University Press, 1947.

William Mann, *Richard Strauss: A Critical Study of the Operas.* London: Cassell, 1964, and New York: Oxford University Press, 1966.

22. *Verdi*

THE CAREER OF GIUSEPPE VERDI (1813–1901) was an intensely interesting one, musically and politically. Verdi identified himself with the Italian movement for liberation from Austrian rule, and some of his operas, particularly the early ones, were interpreted by Italian audiences as patriotic expressions. Consequently, Verdi was in frequent conflict with political censors. His passionate admiration for Cavour and Mazzini, who led the fight for Italian liberation, was the cause of an important event in Verdi's life. At the urging of Cavour, Verdi became a deputy to the first Italian Parliament in 1861, where he served until 1865. At the death of Manzoni, Verdi composed the "Manzoni" Requiem (1874) as a monument to that Italian novelist and poet. Verdi's political feelings were also responsible for the rancor he entertained toward Wagner at the time of the defeat of France by Germany (1871). Wagner represented to him the triumph of Germany ("those damned Goths") at the expense of Latin culture. Later, Verdi's feelings toward Wagner changed, but he never approved of the influence that Wagner had on some of the younger Italian composers. *See Plate 28B.*

Any list of the greatest opera composers would have to include Verdi. His twenty-six operas include *Otello* and *Falstaff,* perhaps the two finest operas that have come from Italy, the home of opera. Verdi's career was not only an immensely distinguished one; it was one of the longest in music history. In his old age, Verdi could look back upon fifty-four years of writing opera; his last (*Falstaff*) was completed at the age of seventy-nine. During this long span, Verdi devoted himself continually to solving the problems of opera and to the evolution of a style in which the drama and the music were entirely complementary. Little influenced by Wagner, Verdi proceeded along lines of the traditional opera, following the path that his own gifts and inclinations indicated. It is a tribute to the strength and integrity of Verdi that he was one of the few who managed to avoid speaking Wagner's language.

In the long period between the first opera (*Oberto,* 1839) and the last, more than a half century later, Verdi's work naturally exhibited evolution and change.[1] The early works of Verdi were influenced by the ensembles of Donizetti and the lyricism of Bellini. He greatly admired Rossini throughout his life, and learned from the orchestration of Berlioz. In later life, Meyerbeer's style influenced the operas written for Paris. There is also a Beethoven flavor to some of his works (*Macbeth,* 1847; *Falstaff*). Verdi's evolution, however, is best explained in terms of two controlling factors: the primary importance of the voice and the necessity of a good libretto.

Verdi never lost sight of either consideration. In the texture of his music, the voice, either alone or in ensemble, preserves its identity, and is supported and intensified by the orchestra. In the early Verdi operas, there is more melodic than harmonic interest, and the accompaniment is rather thin. Later, there is less emphasis on pure melody; the recitative and aria tend to merge, and the orchestra gradually becomes more important in characterizing the text. Still, the orchestra never overwhelms the voice. The use of recurrent motives in *Aïda*—the reason Verdi was accused of aping Wagner, a charge much resented by Verdi—was only a phase of Verdi's development, since the use of such motives may be found in his early works before he knew any of the Wagner works that use leading motives. As we have seen, these motives may also be found occasionally in the works of Bellini and Donizetti. It is striking that most Italian critics in the nineteenth century commented on the use of such motives as being evolutionary and not imitative, an opinion shared by critics at the present day.

To Verdi, the first and central problem was a good libretto. His letters [2] show his concern with this matter and his insistence on a good libretto from his collaborators. His part in actually shaping librettos, particularly that of *Aïda,* is not as well known as it should be. Verdi, like Mozart and Rossini, looked for a libretto that would make possible a real *dramma per musica* in which there were sharp contrasts of flesh-and-blood characters and the opposing conflicts of dramatic situations. As his letters show, he

---

[1] The early operas are seldom heard today. The present repertory includes *Rigoletto* (1851), *Il Trovatore* (1853), *La Traviata* (1853), *Un Ballo in Maschera* (*A Masked Ball;* 1859), *La Forza del Destino* (*The Force of Destiny;* for St. Petersburg, 1862), *Aïda* (for Cairo, 1871), *Otello* (1887), and *Falstaff* (1893). Verdi also wrote several operas for Paris, including *I Vespri Siciliani* (*The Sicilian Vespers; 1855*) and *Don Carlos* (1867).

[2] It was Verdi's habit to make copies of all his letters (1844–1900). From them one makes the acquaintance of Verdi, the man and the artist. They give a detailed and extraordinary idea of the man, his ideas about the Italian theater, the preparation of libretti and operatic setting, and his correspondence with the poets who fashioned the libretti.

wished to avoid boredom and excessive length in his operas, a desire that sometimes led him to overcompression of material. The prime qualities that Verdi sought in a libretto were dramatic effectiveness in the theater, imagination, directness, and simplicity.

The principal sources from which the librettos as a whole were drawn include Schiller, Victor Hugo, Dumas, and Shakespeare. On the whole, the level of the Verdi libretto is high, especially in *Rigoletto* and in the later works, *Aïda, Otello,* and *Falstaff*.[3] Verdi's best-known librettists were Piave (who did *Rigoletto* and *La Traviata*) and particularly Boito, a well-known composer and poet. His librettos for *Otello* and *Falstaff* are first-class and contribute no small part to the excellence of these works. In subject matter, Verdi's plots range from the melodramatic, theatrical, and gory to dramas from Shakespeare with characters and situations of universal scope. The fact that humor and comedy are relatively rare in Verdi sets his last and only comic opera, *Falstaff,* somewhat apart from his other works. Verdi was not impressed with the "true-to-life" subject matter of the *verismo* school (see p. 370). He said, "It is better to invent reality than to copy it," and pointed to Shakespeare's characters as proof. *Verismo* was influenced by Verdi, but not he by it.

Typical mechanics of the Verdi opera taken as a whole are: the aria including the *cabaletta;*[4] recitatives, either dramatic or arioso-like; duets, particularly "love" duets; and choruses, ensembles of trios, quartets, and ensemble finales (an eight-part fugue closes *Falstaff*). In *Aïda* and in the operas written for Paris there are also ballets and dances. The ballet, however, is not a feature of the operas played in Italy.

Melodic invention was one of Verdi's most pronounced gifts. His lyric "hit" tunes are often combined with "catchy" rhythm (*"La donna è mobile"* from *Rigoletto*). The virtuoso "tinsel" aria tends to disappear in the later works. In these, a simpler type of lyric expression with fewer ornaments is characteristic; the vocal line becomes less formal and rigid, and the recitative and aria frequently blend in a kind of arioso type, reminiscent of a similar process in the last works of Monteverdi (see p. 168). The melodies themselves tend to become more expressive by using larger leaps and by covering a large range in the same direction (Ex. 135).

Verdi's orchestration emphasizes the clear colors of solo instruments. The lavish use of brass is a notable feature of many scores. The parts of the orchestra are harmonically widespread to give clarity and sonority, and the doublings are likely to be spaced out over several octaves, as in Berlioz.

[3] After initial hostility, Victor Hugo admitted that *Rigoletto* actually represented an improvement of his play (*Le Roi s'amuse*) in several scenes (Act I, scene 2; the Quartet).
[4] Verdi uses the term for the final *stretta* close of arias or duets, where elaborate treatment gives way to quick uniform rhythm; that is, the *cabaletta* is the fast section following the slow cavatina, a two-section form typical of early nineteenth-century opera.

Ex. 135

Verdi, *Aida* (Act III)

Verdi continually experimented with new instruments and new combinations to achieve his desired effects. In *Aida,* he uses special long trumpets, and the orchestration of the last scene is a particularly striking instance of novel orchestral combinations.

In the last analysis, Verdi's problem came down to achieving dramatic continuity and characterizing events and persons. Toward these ends, he insisted on a good drama, modified where necessary to the peculiar demands of the musical theater. In his scheme he wished to heighten the effect through the voice intensified by the orchestra. The dramatic continuity starts from the libretto, and the music characterizes and intensifies the drama. It is striking that a number of the best Verdi operas are based on plays that belonged to world literature. In contrast to Verdi's method, the continuity in the Wagner operas comes primarily from the weaving of the motives by the symphony orchestra, and Wagner had to compose his own librettos to meet this need.

Since characterization is so central to Verdi's operas, it is fitting to show the methods by which it was achieved:

(1) By the character of the melodies and recitatives themselves. In *Aida* local color is suggested by exotic intervals (such as the augmented fourth or diminished third). In later works, the fusion between the words and the melodies used to depict them is remarkable. In *Falstaff,* for example, a rapierlike lightness and grace of music matches similar texts (the laughter scenes, the *"Pizzica, pizzica"* chorus). In *Rigoletto* the dramatic recitative in the scene between Rigoletto and the cutthroat Sparafucile is carried on in a kind of *parlante* above the somber melody given to the *obbligato* solo cello and double bass.

(2) By striking rhythms (for example, the martial rhythms of trumpets).

(3) By harmonic intensity and suggestion. In Example 136, from *Falstaff,* the bewilderment of Ford is suggested harmonically, as follows: "Is it a dream" (unstable, augmented chord) "or reality" (stable "real" major chord).

(4) By suggestive use of the orchestra: the storm at the beginning of

Otello; the wine ascending to the head of Falstaff; the timpani after each accusation of Rhadames by the priests in *Aïda;* overtures to prepare the mood, or descriptive interludes.

(5) By dynamics for emotional change. Verdi insisted on a wide range

Ex. 136 *

Verdi, *Falstaff* (Act II, part I)

* Printed by courtesy of G. Ricordi & Co.

of dynamics from the softest piano (*pppppp*) to the loudest sounds of the full orchestra. Many nuances are called for to underline the many shades of emotion in the text.

(6) By individualizing the kind of melody in large ensembles. Iago is usually sharply differentiated in the ensembles in *Otello.*

(7) By dramatic ensembles; ensembles brought together naturally by dramatic means, combining different viewpoints and reactions to a situation (Quartet in *Rigoletto*).

(8) By "remembrance" motives. Used relatively little, most copiously in *Aïda,* these motives are sometimes very effective in the setting. In *Rigoletto,* for example, the use of the aria *"La donna è mobile"* at the end dramatically impresses Rigoletto (and the audience) with the fact that it is not the Duke that has been murdered. In *Falstaff* the motive accompanying the words *"dalle due alle tre"* ("from two to three") is used vividly to recall the situation.

FALSTAFF

Falstaff is not Verdi's most representative opera. A comedy could not be. But, with the exception of *Otello,* it is his best, the most perfectly balanced in drama and music, the gayest, and most brilliant. The libretto (by Boito), based on Shakespeare's *Merry Wives of Windsor* and *Henry IV,* is a masterpiece. The central character is that fat old rogue, Sir John Falstaff.

Act I. The opera opens with a rush. There is a tumultuous sweep of strings, and Dr. Caius bursts into the Garter Inn where Falstaff is sitting with his rascally servants, Bardolph and Pistol. Caius complains that he has been robbed by Bardolph and Pistol. He receives small comfort from Falstaff, who rapidly gets rid of him. Caius angrily goes off, vowing vengeance, and Falstaff berates his servants—for being clumsy.

Falstaff has a project afoot. He has noticed two fine ladies in the town, Mrs. Ford and Mrs. Page, and he proposes to send them each a love note, dispatched by Bardolph and Pistol. But they will have none of this "pandering." They sing of their "honor." Falstaff turns on them angrily with heavy satire, brushes them out the door, and sends the notes by a page.

The next scene is in the house of Mrs. Ford, who is visited by Mrs. Page. They have both received Falstaff's identical letters, and they compare notes. Highly amused and also outraged, they determine to punish him, and hatch a plot to get him to the Ford house with the idea of humiliating him. Accordingly, Dame Quickly is sent to Falstaff with a "confidential" message from Mrs. Ford that she is dying of love for him and that her husband is out every day *"from two to three."*

Act II. Dame Quickly delivers the message to Falstaff, who preens himself on his way with the ladies. The obsequious and faintly ironic motive *"Reverenza"* ("Your Reverence") with which Quickly greets Falstaff, and the *"dalle due alle tre"* ("from two to three") motive are perfect for the situation, and they are among the few motives that recur in the opera (Ex. 137).

Ex. 137 *

* Printed by courtesy of G. Ricordi & Co.

In the meantime, Caius has enlisted the aid of Ford against Falstaff, and they are joined by Bardolph and Pistol, who now have a grievance against him too. Like the ladies, they plot, and Ford, who is unknown to Falstaff, volunteers to approach him. Ford, using the assumed name of Fontana ("Brook" in Shakespeare: good for several puns), reaches Falstaff just after the departure of Quickly. Ford pretends he is a wealthy townsman secretly in love with Mrs. Ford, and he makes the proposal that Falstaff seduce her, on the novel theory that it will then be easier for him. Falstaff replies, in effect: nothing easier; I have an appointment with the very lady today from two to three. Her blockhead of a husband is away and I will manage it for you (the actual wording of Falstaff's remarks is suggestive to the point of indecency). And now, continues Falstaff, I must go and change for my appointment. Ford, startled out of his complacency, is beside himself. "Is this a dream? Or is it reality?" (see Ex. 136) he exclaims. "Awake, awake, Master Ford," he rages. And then, in a famous monologue, he gives vent to the bitter and savage anger of an outraged husband. Falstaff returns, a miracle of beauty in brilliant attire. They go out together: Falstaff to his rendezvous; Ford to round up his friends to hunt down Falstaff.

Knowing none of this, Mrs. Ford receives Falstaff, whose immediate advances she gently and firmly repulses. Mrs. Page arrives breathless to announce the hot pursuit of Ford and his friends. With great haste, Falstaff is concealed behind a screen. Ford enters, and then begins a furious hunt for Falstaff all over the house. They do not find him. In the meantime, Falstaff is hidden away in a basket of dirty clothes. The furious bustle is mingled with the stifled groans of Falstaff. Meanwhile, another subdrama is taking place. Nanetta, the daughter of Ford, loves Fenton against her father's wishes. Taking advantage of the confusion in the house, they are making love behind a screen. A loud kiss is heard, and Ford believes that he has found Falstaff at last. He dashes aside the screen to find his daughter with Fenton. This only adds to his anger and disappointment. But he must still find Falstaff, and he dashes out. Again, confusion everywhere. This time, Mrs. Ford quickly summons her servants. They hoist the dirty-clothes basket with Falstaff groaning inside. And then, with a one-two-three, the servants topple the basket and all its contents out the window and into the river below. The ladies shriek with delight, the men return, and hear the explanation of their ladies. The wonderful and continuous ensemble of this scene, packed with action and change, can only be compared with the *ensemble finale* of Act II of Mozart's *Figaro*.

Act III. The next act opens with an extraordinary scene. Falstaff is sitting dejectedly in front of the Garter Inn, pondering bitterly on what he has just experienced. "O wicked world," he mutters, and he thinks of the treachery of women and how he nearly drowned. But as he drinks his mulled wine, his spirits rise, and he describes the effect of the wine as it ascends to his head, while the orchestra accompanies him with a delicious orchestral trill. With a stroke of genius, Boito makes Dame Quickly return. *"Reverenza"* she intones. It is absurdly funny. Falstaff can hardly bear the sight of her. But she has another message. It was all a mistake, she says; and if Falstaff will come to Herne's Oak, in Windsor Park, at the stroke of midnight, wearing a pair of antlers, Mrs. Ford will make amends. That Falstaff agrees to this new trap (baited by the Fords and all their friends) is a tribute to the enticement of women and the eternal gullibility of men.

The final scene in Windsor Park is full of orchestral magic. It is night, the Fords and the rest of the company are all disguised as fairies, elves, and other assorted night-folk. The appearance of Falstaff in his weird pair of horns is incredibly incongruous. Poor Falstaff. He is pinched (*"Pizzica"* chorus) black and blue by the fairies and pixies, who scare him half to death. He is ready to repent and agree to anything, but in the midst of this Falstaff recognizes one of his servants, and the jig is up. The opera closes with Nanetta united to Fenton, and the principals combine in singing a gigantic eight-part fugue, "All the world's a jest," with which the opera ends.

It is impossible to describe the intensity, pace, and vivacity of this opera. It is alive with drama and music from beginning to end. The texture is continuous, but always musically interesting in itself. There is a rapid unfolding from one event to another, and the old idea of set pieces (i.e., "numbers") hardly exists. The aria is there in spirit with its lyric moments, and so are the recitatives and ensembles that are scattered throughout, but they are all so organic to the drama that one scarcely feels them as separate entities at all. Even Nanetta and Fenton are barely able to squeeze in a love duet; they are always interrupted by the action flowing about them. Only in the final ensemble is a formal set piece, the eight-part fugue, thoroughly worked out.

Above all, the wonderful musical portraits of the chief characters can never fade from our minds. Whether it is Dame Quickly with her characteristic *"Reverenza"* and *"dalle due alle tre,"* or Ford, or the lovers, or Falstaff—the greatest of them all—we hear their voices and we see them as we do our friends. *Falstaff* was written by Verdi in his old age, but the opera itself will never grow old, for its youth will be perpetually renewed by its own eternal springs of gaiety and jest.

Suggested Listening
Rigoletto. Act III: *"La donna è mobile";* Quartet (*"Bella figlia dell'amore"*).
Falstaff (it is recorded complete).

Suggested Reading
Francis Toye, *Giuseppe Verdi, His Life and Works.* New York: Alfred A. Knopf, 1946.
Franz Werfel and P. Stefan (eds.), *Verdi. The Man in His Letters,* trans. by Edward Downes. New York: L. B. Fischer, 1942.

23. *Nationalism in Music*

IN ITSELF, the term *nationalism* is rather vague, but it has a relatively precise meaning in music. *Musical nationalism* refers specifically to a nineteenth-century movement, particularly in Russia, Bohemia (Czechoslovakia), and Scandinavia, that sought to put an end to the domination of foreign importations, especially from Germany and Italy, to encourage native composers and native folk music, and to emphasize themes drawn from national history and legend. The impetus for these developments came partly from the Romantic movement that idealized the importance of folk materials and partly from political events in the nineteenth century that encouraged national aspirations everywhere. The influence of Romanticism was more consistent than that of political events. The Czechs were struggling against Austria, but there was no similar struggle in Scandinavia; and in Russia the struggles were entirely those of internal reform. These reforms were not unimportant, and we can see a typical theme of the aspirations and despair of an oppressed people reflected in Mussorgsky's *Boris Godunov*. It is also true that political ferment in Russia, particularly in the 1860's under the hopeful reforms of Tsar Alexander II, who freed the serfs in 1861, had important counterparts in literature (Tolstoi) and music.

The term *musical nationalism* is restricted to the three countries mentioned mainly because prior to the nineteenth century they had very little native *art* (as opposed to *folk*) music of their own. Certainly it is quite possible to find national characteristics in other countries. German Romantic music, for instance, specialized in native themes, folk songs, and national myth and legend (e.g., Weber and Wagner). Even in Italy, the source of an international style especially in opera, there was some musical evidence of Italian political and national aspirations to be free of Austria (cf. Verdi's operas). In a broad sense, national characteristics in European music had been obvious for centuries and the subject of bitter acrimony. In the eighteenth century, there were musical "wars" between the adher-

ents of French and Italian music, and the distinction between the music
of different nations was the subject of numerous contemporary books and
pamphlets (for instance, Rousseau's *Letter on French Music*).

The specific meaning attached to *musical nationalism* is, for the most
part, the result of a rather self-conscious attitude. The national schools of
the nineteenth century were somewhat self-conscious in their intent to
throw off foreign domination, to use native folk materials, and to cultivate
a native opera and school of composers. By comparison, the other leading
musical nations took for granted the development of native musical resources by their own composers because this development had been going
on for a long time, not necessarily through the use of folk themes, but
by developing features of style natural to themselves. In some cases, of
course, they used folk material and subjects drawn from national history
and legend.[1]

NATIONALISM IN RUSSIA: GLINKA. "THE FIVE." RUBINSTEIN. TCHAIKOVSKY.

The most important of the national movements in the nineteenth century occurred in Russia. In the eighteenth century, Russian music was
dominated by Italian and French opera and the French ballet. Catherine
the Great (ruled 1762–96) invited such well-known Italian opera composers as Galuppi, Traëtta, and Paisiello to her court. The first important
native composers were Michail Glinka (1804–57), "the father of Russian
music," and Alexander Dargomijsky (1813–69). Both were important
chiefly for their operas. Glinka was first successful with the patriotic opera
A Life for the Tsar (1836). A more important work, *Russlan and Lud-
milla* (1842), on a subject by Pushkin, may be regarded as the beginning
of distinctly Russian music. Dargomijsky's best work was the opera *The
Stone Guest* (1869), also on a Pushkin subject taken from the story of
Don Juan.

A more important group of national composers were those known variously as the "Balakirev group," "The Five," or "the mighty handful." The
latter phrase came from Vladimir Stassov, the influential critic and apologist for the group. The "Five" composers were: Mily Balakirev (1837–
1910), César Cui (1835–1918), Alexander Borodin (1833–87), Modest
Mussorgsky (1839–81), and Nikolai Rimsky-Korsakov (1844–1908). Over

[1] In the late nineteenth and twentieth centuries, the impact of "self-conscious" nationalism can be seen in Spain, where composers like Albeniz, Granados, and Falla
emphasized native rhythms and dance melodies. Similar movements, using national
themes and folk songs occurred in England (Vaughan Williams), Hungary (Kodály,
Bartók), Finland (Sibelius), the United States (Roy Harris), and Latin America
(Villa-Lobos, Chavez). Certain aspects of nationalism in the twentieth century will
be discussed later in relation to individual composers (see Chapter 26).

a period of time these composers came under the influence and inspiration of Balakirev, and, loosely united in their common tie with him, they gradually evolved a common direction and belief. "The Five" opposed the international influence of German and Italian music, especially with respect to the opera, although they were much interested in the advanced school represented by Liszt and Berlioz. Their primary interest, however, lay in evoking Russian history and legend and in using native Russian idioms.

At first, "The Five" were all amateurs. Balakirev was self-taught as a pianist and composer. Cui was a military engineer by profession, and Borodin was a celebrated chemist. At the beginning of his career, Mussorgsky was in the army, and later (from 1863) in the engineering department of the government as a clerk. Rimsky-Korsakov was a naval officer. Much has been made of the fact that, except for Rimsky-Korsakov who later had training along traditional lines, these men were amateurs. The implication is that they were not capable of giving their ideas technical expression. This was not the case; rather, their technical idiom emanated from the character of their ideas and musical materials—a fact that accounts for the distinctive flavor of their music. The so-called "crudities" of Mussorgsky, for instance, were more the result of a desire to represent his Russian subject matter realistically and directly by appropriate means than the result of insufficient technique. Rimsky-Korsakov, however, thought otherwise, and having received a traditional training, set out to "correct" the works of Mussorgsky and others.[2]

Undoubtedly the most important and characteristic form of expression of the Russian nationalists was the opera, in which are found subjects drawn from Russian history and those based on fantasy and legend, frequently of Oriental character. The opera afforded a natural medium for the use of folk-song and folk-dance material and for the expression of a naturalistic (i.e., realistic) attitude toward music, expressed in phrases like "art must strive to represent life" and "truth before beauty." In addition to the operas of Glinka and Dargomijsky mentioned above, the most important are: Borodin's *Prince Igor* (1869), Mussorgsky's *Boris Godunov* (1874), and Rimsky-Korsakov's operas *The Snow Maiden* (1882) and *The Golden Cockerel* (posthumously performed 1909).[3]

Boris Godunov, on a libretto after Pushkin, is undoubtedly the finest Russian opera, one of the great operas of the world repertory, and an important phenomenon in the national school of Russia. In reality this work is a kind of folk drama in which the chief protagonist, represented by the

---

[2] In recent times, a number of Mussorgsky's scores have been restored to their "un-Rimskyed" version. In these restorations, one can see the power and expression of the "crude" Mussorgsky in a new light. A number of Mussorgsky's works, however, are still presented in the Rimsky-Korsakov revisions.

[3] This list is only a small sampling. There are, for instance, fourteen operas of Rimsky-Korsakov alone, which represent his most important work and which, incidentally, are virtually unknown in the United States.

chorus, is the suffering Russian people. The opera also contains powerful studies of character, especially that of Tsar Boris (ruled 1598–1605) during the "time of troubles" (1604–13) in Russian history. His guilt-ridden character is reminiscent of the theme and power of Shakespeare's *Macbeth.* The "Monologue" and "Death Scene" of Boris are justly famous. In *Boris,* Mussorgsky fuses the melody and the recitative into an expressive and continuous melodic recitative. There is some use of the leading-motive technique and also of folk song. The chorus in the powerful "Coronation Scene" near the beginning of the opera is based on a Russian folk song. In this scene, too, Mussorgsky's "crude" harmonies (see Ex. 138) and his

Ex. 138

distinctive orchestration, including the clangor of various bells of all sizes and the color of the other instruments, produce an unforgettable effect.

We can only hint at the considerable amount of music composed by the Russian nationalists. Glinka, Borodin, and Cui all composed songs (the latter over two hundred), but we can take those of Mussorgsky as representative. His songs are not similar to the German Lieder, which are characteristically lyrical; they are dramatic sketches almost like moments from opera. His unconventional songs include several song cycles, among them, *Without Sun* and *Songs and Dances of Death.* Humor and especially satire are evident in certain songs like "The Song of the Flea" and "The Seminarist." The folk song collection of Balakirev (1866) and the two collections of Rimsky-Korsakov witness the interest in native folk song.

The instrumental music includes symphonies such as the Symphony in B minor (No. 2) of Borodin, the best symphonist of the group. The opening movement of this work is dominated by a single impressive theme which is shown and commented on below. A number of other pieces for orchestra are, roughly, symphonic poems: Balakirev's *Russia;* Mussorgsky's *A Night on the Bare Mountain* (called a "symphonic fantasy"), and Rimsky-Korsakov's *Scheherezade* (1888). The chamber music is best represented by the two string quartets of Borodin; and the piano music by Balakirev's *Islamey* (a fantasy) and Mussorgsky's *Pictures from an Exhibition* (later orchestrated by Ravel, among others).[4]

---

[4] The liturgical music has already been discussed, see p. 332.

While it is difficult to generalize about an entire group of composers, their music has, broadly speaking, many elements in common, so that one feels that this music is specifically Russian and not anything else. A distinctive feature is the melodic material. This may be genuine folk song or melody of the folk-song type. Borodin, for example, while using a folk-song style, uses very few genuine folk songs. Typical of Russian folk song (and therefore of Russian folk-song style) are phrases which end with the descending fourth (see Ex. 139). These melodies often have a small range and are somewhat static in movement, going over the same phrase or centering around the same note. The phrases are seldom symmetrical in length, and frequent metric changes are common (i.e., from $\frac{4}{4}$ to $\frac{3}{4}$ to $\frac{5}{4}$, and so on), and so are irregular accents and syncopations. Thus the melodies are flexible and varied in their phrasing and accent; and this is true, too, of the scale patterns on which they are based. There is a mixing of major and minor, the whole-tone scale, the pentatonic scale, and the old modes. To achieve certain specific exotic "Eastern" or "Oriental" effects of melody, "The Five" resorted to characteristic intervals (such as the augmented second) as well as to other devices of harmony and orchestration. In the following examples (Ex. 139a and 139b), two melodies are given to illustrate certain of these characteristics. The first

Ex. 139

(the beginning of Mussorgsky's *Boris*) shows the static centering of the melody and the drop of the fourth at the end of the phrase. The second (the opening theme of Borodin's B minor Symphony) shows the fluctuation of both the major third (D sharp) and the minor third (D natural), as well as the modal A natural and C natural (Phrygian). This flexibility permits all sorts of variety and colorful harmony.

It is not possible to do justice to harmony without a technical analysis. Still, one can convey some idea of it in general terms. Many chords are used for their sonorities with less attention to their "correct" grammatical usage. Various modulation possibilities are explored, a typical one being by semitones. A harmonic feature of *Boris*—especially in the "Coronation Scene"—is the contrast and juxtaposition of chords, related, although remotely, by the use of enharmonic relationships (see Ex. 138). The same kind of chord relationships are used in Rimsky-Korsakov's *Scheherazade*. Another trait of the harmony is parallel chord structures such as organum and *faux bourdon,* a kind of chord construction so evident in Debussy (*La Cathédrale Engloutie*).

Beginning with Glinka, the Russian orchestration followed generally the lead of the French school by using the clear colors of solo instruments and the homogeneous color of the specific choirs of the orchestra. In addition, special instruments like the bells and gongs in *Boris* distinguish the Russian instrumentation. The most extraordinary Russian figure in the field of orchestration is Rimsky-Korsakov, who ranks with Berlioz in his use of the orchestra. The brilliance of Rimsky-Korsakov's orchestral coloring and his remarkable use of solo wind instruments permeate all his works. In addition, his love of Oriental, fantastic, and fairy themes led him into all sorts of orchestral experiments to achieve unusual colors and effects. Like Berlioz, Rimsky-Korsakov wrote a book on orchestration, *Principles of Orchestration* (1896–1908), which became a standard work.

Anton Rubinstein (1829–94) and Tchaikovsky were contemporaries of "The Five," but they did not belong to this group. Both these men were traditionalists and considered reactionaries by the group around Balakirev. Rubinstein, more than Tchaikovsky, was an adversary of national music. Nevertheless, he was an important figure as a pianist, and exercised a considerable influence on Russian musical life. In 1862, for instance, he founded the Imperial Conservatory at St. Petersburg, the first such institution in Russia. It was supported by the court and by official circles, as compared to Balakirev's "Free School," founded about the same time. Rubinstein was director of the Conservatory until 1867 as well as director (from 1859) of the important Russian Musical Society.

Tchaikovsky is much more important musically, as we have already seen. While not one of "The Five," he was somewhat influenced by Balakirev and was friendly with him at one time. His music also shows some Russian nationalist traits, notably the use of the folk song (Fourth Symphony, last movement; "1812" Overture), violent contrasts of mood, and the use of operatic material from Pushkin (*Eugen Onegin,* 1879).

Suggested Listening

Mussorgsky, *Boris Godunov* (Prologue, Scene 2: "Coronation Scene"; Act IV, Scene 1: "Death of Boris").

Borodin, Symphony in B minor (No. 2), first movement.

Rimsky-Korsakov, *Scheherezade* (symphonic poem).

Suggested Reading

Gerald Abraham, *Studies in Russian Music.* New York: Charles Scribner's Sons, 1936.

Michel D. Calvocoressi, *Mussorgsky.* New York: E. P. Dutton & Co., 1946.

NATIONALISM IN BOHEMIA: SMETANA. DVOŘÁK.

The national school of Bohemia (Czechoslovakia), centering around Prague, was founded by Bedřich Smetana (1824–86) and continued by Antonín Dvořák (1841–1904). For centuries Bohemia had produced a large number of musicians; but under the political domination of the Austrian (Hapsburg) Empire, they had been absorbed into the stream of Austro-German (especially Viennese) musical life. The literary and political movements for national independence came to a head in the general European revolutions of 1848. While the political movements for constitutional government (Slavic Congress, 1848) had been overthrown by 1849 by Austrian countermeasures, national aspirations had some outlet, especially after 1860, in the literary revival of the Bohemian language and in the music of Smetana and others.

Smetana's most important work is connected with the stage. He was instrumental in establishing a native theater for opera and a national operatic repertory, and in inspiring musical life in general. His eight patriotic operas (e.g., *The Brandenburgers in Bohemia,* 1863) are little known outside his own country, where they are (or were) an intimate part of musical life. However, his comic opera, *The Bartered Bride* (1866), is given performances in every large opera house in the world because the humor and satire, the sharp delineation of character, the brilliance of the orchestration, and the lilt and syncopation of the rhythms and melodies transform a work full of Bohemian local color into a masterpiece that has a universal appeal. Smetana's best-known orchestral music, the cycle of six symphonic poems with the collective title *My Country,* also celebrates national themes. The favorite single work from this cycle is the second of these pieces, *The Moldau* (1874), a title referring to the river that runs through Prague. His piano music (influenced by the style of Liszt) exhibits an interest in national dances such as polkas.

In his own country Smetana is regarded as the father of Czech musical nationalism. Outside Bohemia, the musical world admires his music for its universal traits: lyric melodies, piquant rhythms, brilliance of orchestration, and fine scoring for chorus in his operas and other choral works.

Antonín Dvořák is best known as an instrumental composer; he himself played in an orchestra (as violinist and violist) for some time before he became world-famous. His works had a much wider audience than did those of Smetana. Early in his life he became well known in Germany, and received enthusiastic help from Brahms, Bülow, and Hanslick. Later, his fame spread and he visited England and the United States where he wrote some of his best-known works, in particular, Symphony No. 5 ("From the New World") and the "American" Quartet.

Dvořák completed the work of Smetana in establishing the Bohemian school (cf. his operas, such as *Russalka,* 1900). While his instrumental style has affinities with Beethoven and Schubert, the use of national themes, native dances, and melodies based on folk-song style gives his music a specific national character. There is a striking affinity between the melodies of Dvořák and those of Schubert; they have the same spontaneity and naïveté. More than Schubert, however, Dvořák makes use of melodies that contain phrases or modal effects typical of folk song. The great rhythmic drive in Dvořák is based partly on the folk-dance rhythms of his country, and partly on his inherent musical instincts for rhythm, in which he somewhat resembles Beethoven. Instances of his use of dance rhythms are abundant. The *Slavonic Dances* for orchestra are good examples. The dance called *Furiant* is substituted for the scherzo in some of his instrumental works that otherwise use the traditional sonata forms. Another example is the use of the *Dumka* (plural: *Dumky*), a dance that is sometimes melancholy and slow, and sometimes passionate and emotional (see his *Dumky* Trio). Besides the specific dances, the rhythmic patterns are frequently vigorous without any dance connotation. Especially notable is the use of dotted rhythms.

Ironically enough, Dvořák's best-known work, the "New World" Symphony (1893), has nothing to do with Bohemian nationalism. Although the themes, especially that of the slow movement, are often cited in connection with American nationalism, Dvořák himself said that the melodies were not taken from existing melodies, but were his own and simply represented his impression of "The New World." At any rate, the "New World" Symphony is a fine work, interesting formally for its use of the cyclic principle in the last two movements. More important, its powerful rhythms, distinctive themes, and colorful harmonies and orchestration have made it a popular favorite among Dvořák's works and one of the most-played symphonies of the entire world repertory.

Suggested Listening

Smetana, *Bartered Bride* (overture and opening scene).
Smetana, *The Moldau.*
Dvořák, Symphony No. 5 (E minor, "From the New World").

Suggested Reading

Rosa Newmarch, *The Music of Czechoslovakia.* New York: Oxford, 1942.
John Clapham, *Antonin Dvořák.* London: Faber & Faber Ltd., 1966.

NATIONALISM IN SCANDINAVIA: GRIEG

The music of the Scandinavian school is less important than that of Russia and Bohemia. The most important composers are: the Dane, Niels Gade (1817–90), and the Norwegians Edvard Grieg (1843–1907) and

Christian Sinding (1856–1941). The Finnish composer, Jean Sibelius, may also be considered part of this movement, but he will be discussed elsewhere (see p. 416).

The nationalism of Scandinavia is partly colored by German Romanticism. It is significant in this connection that the Scandinavians received their early training in Germany, particularly in Leipzig. However, the use of melodies based on native folk songs or similar idioms and on strong, distinctive rhythms of native dances gave a special character to their music. This is the case of Gade, the oldest of the composers mentioned, who may be considered the founder of the Scandinavian school and the leading Danish composer.

The most important composer of this group, however, was the Norwegian, Edvard Grieg. Educated at the Leipzig Conservatory, Grieg returned to Norway with an enthusiasm for Schumann's music and a lasting distaste for the training and methods of Leipzig. About 1864, Ole Bull (the great Norwegian violinist) and Rikard Nordraak (a young man in whom were centered the chief hopes of the Norwegian nationalists) opened Grieg's eyes to the folk culture of Norway, and this was a turning point in Grieg's life. Thereafter he was dedicated to the cause of Norwegian nationalism, which he furthered by his own music and other activities. In 1867 he founded the Norwegian Academy of Music, and in 1871 he helped to found the Christiana Musical Society to promote orchestral music.

Grieg is known best for his *Peer Gynt* Suite (1876) and his Piano Concerto (A minor, 1868). He was, however, a distinguished composer of short pieces for the piano (ten books of "Lyric Pieces"), and his numerous songs show him to particular advantage. As one might expect, he used folk-song-like melodies and distinctive dance rhythms. While some of Grieg's music is overcolored by chromatic harmonies, his harmony as a whole is quite subtle and individual; and certain aspects of it forecast the impressionism of Debussy (cf. the Grieg Quartet in G minor, Op. 27, 1877–8, with Debussy's G minor Quartet, 1893). Few of Grieg's songs and piano works are played today. Nevertheless, they contain many beauties, and Grieg's originality as a harmonist deserves to be appreciated beyond the confines of Norway, for whose music he did so much.

Suggested Listening
Grieg, *Peer Gynt* Suite.
  Haugtussa, Song Cycle (Op. 67, 1896–8).
  Bridal Procession (Op. 19, No. 2) for piano.

Suggested Reading
Gerald Abraham (ed.), *Grieg, A Symposium.* London: Lindsay Drummond, 1948.

24. *After Wagner and Between Two Wars*

W AGNER EXERTED A PROFOUND INFLUENCE on European music during his lifetime, and even after his death (1883) his musical presence was powerfully felt until the first World War. Consequently, it is convenient to discuss certain developments late in the Romantic period in terms of "after Wagner"—or more broadly between the Franco-Prussian War (1870–1) and the advent of the first World War (1914), which brought the Romantic era to a close.[1]

Wagner had the most pronounced impact on those who followed him in Germany and Austria; and others in Italy, France, and England are indebted to him in greater or less degree. In Germany the most important composers who came within Wagner's orbit were Bruckner, Strauss, Mahler, Reger, and Wolf. The first three have already been discussed.

REGER. WOLF.

Max Reger (1873–1916) was a gifted musician of great versatility, whose music was received coldly by the critics and recognized rather belatedly by the public. He admired Bach greatly, and like Bach he possessed prodigious contrapuntal skill. His pervasive chromaticism is witness to his love of Wagner. In some ways he resembled Brahms in his avoidance of program music, his penchant for chamber music, and cultivation of forms from times past. It is characteristic that his best works are variations,

[1] We have deliberately avoided the term *post-Romantic* because it is ambiguous and confusing. Does it imply that the music concerned is not Romantic? If so, it is misleading. Furthermore, all music to the present day is, chronologically speaking, post-Romantic. Similarly, the term *pre-Classic* refers vaguely to music before the Classic period. More satisfactory terms are *early Classic, late Romantic,* and so on.

fugues, and organ chorale preludes. Reger suffered somewhat from the defect of his virtues. Some of his music has a certain monotony from overthickening of the texture and from excessive use of the tremendous technical resources of which he was master. His voluminous music includes pieces for the orchestra, vocal works with orchestra, extensive chamber music, organ and piano music, choruses, sacred music, and a large number of songs.

The considerable reputation of Hugo Wolf (1860–1903) rests almost exclusively on his songs (about three hundred). His main creative activity was limited to about ten years of his life (1886–96), during which time he set texts by some of the best German poets (e.g., Mörike, Eichendorff, Goethe). In his songs he fulfills on a small scale Wagner's ideal of the union of the arts of poetry and music, for he demonstrates his extraordinary ability to set German verse in such a way that the text and music seem to be as one. Furthermore, the voice and the piano accompaniment are highly unified, and Wolf emphasizes their unity of conception by the title *Songs for Voice and Piano.* The piano part creates the mood of the poem but it is also intertwined with the voice in the texture. For example, a phrase begun by the voice may be completed by the accompaniment, and a dissonance in the voice may be resolved in the piano part. In some respects, the function of the piano is analogous to that of Wagner's orchestra, but, unlike Wagner, Wolf wrote parts for the voice that are essentially vocal in conception. The influence of Wagner is also evident in the chromatic harmony, the chromatic melodies themselves, and to some extent in the avoidance of intermediary cadences. However, some of Wolf's melodies are relatively simple and straightforward, a number are declamatory, and occasionally the old modes are used for special effects (for instance, "*Auf ein altes Bild*").

Wolf was a fanatic admirer of Wagner. He strongly supported Bruckner and attacked Brahms. Historically, Wolf's importance lies in the transference of the Wagner idiom and ideals to the song, and musically, in his unique power to saturate the text with music in a setting in which the voice and the piano are inseparably united as musical partners.

Suggested Listening

Reger, *Variations on a Theme of Mozart* (Op. 132).

Wolf, Songs: "*Anakreons Grab*" (Goethe); "*Auf ein altes Bild*" (Mörike); "*Nachtzauber*" (Eichendorff); "*Peregrina I*" (Mörike).

Suggested Reading

Frank Walker, *Hugo Wolf: a Biography* (Second edition). New York: Alfred A. Knopf, 1968.

VERISMO: *PUCCINI*

The Italian *verismo* (realistic) school of opera dates from Pietro Mascagni's *Cavalleria Rusticana,* a one-act opera of peasant life (1890). It created a furor and was enormously successful. Two years later, Ruggiero Leoncavallo's *Pagliacci,* an opera of circus life, appeared. The real leader of *verismo,* however, was Giacomo Puccini, whose operas are briefly discussed below.

Musically, *verismo* was influenced by certain of Wagner's procedures, and more particularly by Verdi and by Bizet's *Carmen* (1875). Following the ideals of literary figures like Zola, Flaubert, and Ibsen, *verismo* drew material from everyday life as opposed to the "heroic," exalted operatic themes from history or mythology; realism to the point of brutality is characteristic. In these operas the coloratura aria is abandoned for the short air, flexible recitative, and dramatic ensembles. The arias are full of warm, luscious, and rather sentimental melodies, somewhat shallow in expression; and pathos is more typical than real tragedy, even when the brutality is shocking. Recurrent motives, chromatic harmonies, and the orchestra are used somewhat in the manner of Wagner to suggest the dramatic situation. From Verdi, *verismo* borrowed the pliable arioso and certain melodic turns of phrase and harmonic idioms. A rather thin harmonic texture results from the typical unison or octave passages (sometimes double or even triple octave doublings, as in the duet between Rodolfo and Mimi, Act I of *La Bohème*). The harmonies themselves are colorful, chromatic, and sometimes modal. Occasionally, *verismo* has features in common with impressionism (see p. 376), as for instance (1) exoticism (*Madame Butterfly* of Puccini), (2) chords used primarily for sonorities, and (3) parallel chord structures such as the old *faux bourdon* or organum (Puccini's *Tosca* where Cavaradossi begins to paint).

Of the veristic composers, Puccini (1858–1924) was by far the most successful. His undoubted lyric gifts and his theater and orchestral sense are amply demonstrated by his four best-known operas. Puccini first came into real prominence with *La Bohème* (1896), a picture of Bohemian life in Paris about 1830 (adapted from a novel by Murger). This was followed by *Tosca* (1900), *Madame Butterfly* (1904), laid in Japan, and among others, by *Turandot* (1924), a return to fairyland Romanticism, though composed in relatively modern style. *Turandot* was not quite finished at the time of Puccini's death, and it was completed by Alfano. Of these operas, the most interesting musically are *Butterfly* (which uses authentic Japanese melodies) and *Turandot*. *Tosca* is the most realistic as well as the crudest dramatically. *La Bohème* is possibly the best loved and most popular. Its combination of the gaiety of the Bohemians and the pathetic in the character of Mimi, and the lyricism of such moments as the love

duet of Rodolfo and Mimi, endow this opera with exceptional attractions
for the public.

Suggested Listening

Mascagni, *Cavalleria Rusticana* (Intermezzo).

Leoncavallo, *Pagliacci* (Prologue).

Puccini, *La Bohème* (Act I: Mimi's aria, *"Si, mi chiamano Mimi";* Duet:
    Mimi–Rodolfo: *"O soave fanciulla"*).

Puccini, *Madame Butterfly.* Act II, Scene 1: *"Un bel di."*

Suggested Reading

Richard Specht, *Giacomo Puccini,* trans. by Catherine A. Phillips. New
    York: Alfred A. Knopf, 1933.

Mosco Carner, "The Exotic Element in Puccini" in *The Musical Quar-
    terly,* January, 1936. This article, with others, including "In Defence of
    Puccini," appeared again in the same author's *Of Men and Music* (Lon-
    don: Joseph Williams, 1944), p. 66.

ENGLAND: ELGAR

In the late nineteenth century the most prominent English composers
were Arthur Sullivan (see p. 335), C. H. H. Parry, Charles Stanford (a
native Irishman), and Edward Elgar. A kind of renaissance of native
English music, which was to flower in the twentieth century, began with
the work of the last three mentioned. In addition, a special feature of
English music in the nineteenth century was the attention paid to collecting and editing folk songs of England, Scotland, Ireland, and Wales (e.g.,
by Cecil Sharp).

Elgar (1857–1934) appeals enormously to Englishmen, but his works
have been less successful elsewhere. In the United States he is known principally as the composer of the "Enigma" Variations and *Pomp and Circumstance* (No. 1 of a set of military marches of the same title). Elgar is
something like Fauré and Mahler; they are all true national composers in
that their works say something special to listeners of their own nation but
are less appealing to others. Elgar possessed excellent technical equipment,
although he was largely self-taught. A well-trained violinist, he composed
naturally and even brilliantly in terms of the orchestra.

His work is sometimes influenced by Wagner. The oratorios are a combination of the older oratorio and the Wagner music drama; a leading-
motive system gives the basis of coherence. One can also see traces of the
influence of Brahms, Richard Strauss, and Wagner's chromatic vocabulary.
Elgar's music is by turns vigorous and somewhat sentimental. His ex-
uberant melodic leaps and his virtuoso figuration for the orchestra, in

14

which he recalls Richard Strauss, give his music moments of great virility. His opulent and colorful harmonies and use of thirds and sixths add richness to his scores. A special fondness for sequences and leaps in the melodic lines is shown in Example 140.

Ex. 140 *

Elgar, *Falstaff* **(beginning)**

Allegro

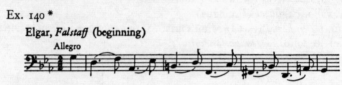

* By permission of Novello & Co., Ltd.

Some of Elgar's music is weakened by a patchwork of styles. Nevertheless, in certain works he achieves an individuality that shows his distinction as a composer (the "Enigma" Variations, 1899; *The Dream of Gerontius,* 1900; the Violin Concerto in B minor, 1910; and the "symphonic study," *Falstaff,* 1913).

Suggested Listening
Elgar, *Falstaff.*

Suggested Reading
The article "Elgar" in *Grove's Dictionary of Music and Musicians.* Fifth edition, 1954.
Michael Hurd, *Elgar* (Great Composers series). London: Faber & Faber, 1969.

FRENCH INSTRUMENTAL MUSIC: FRANCK. FAURÉ AND THE FRENCH SONG.

After the Franco-Prussian War, the French entered a period of political decline, and, strangely enough, one of artistic resurgence. This was especially true in instrumental music. Prior to that time, musical life had been dominated by the opera. In 1871 a group of composers, intent on reviving instrumental music in France, formed a society called Société Nationale de Musique, the prime movers being Saint-Saëns, Lalo, Fauré, César Franck, and his pupils. There were others, too, who took part in this renaissance of French instrumental music, among them the conductor Jules Pasdeloup, Bizet, Chabrier, Chausson, Dukas, Debussy, and Ravel. Instrumental music was not their sole concern, but with them the main forms of instrumental music returned to the French scene. Thus we have symphonies by Bizet, D'Indy, and César Franck, to name a few.

While some French music in this period came under the spell of Wagner, its essential spirit was quite different from that of German music. Debussy summarized the basic traits as follows: "French music is clear-

ness, elegance, simple and natural declamation; French music wishes first
of all to give pleasure. Couperin, Rameau, these are true Frenchmen."
Furthermore, dance rhythms played an important part in French music
as they always had (cf. Plate 26). French composers in this period showed
a strong predilection for Spanish subjects and dances. In still other respects, French music presented a contrast to German music. Even when
chromaticism was used extensively, its application was quite different
(Franck and especially Debussy). In orchestration, far greater clarity and
color distinguish the French scores. Finally, there was a close relation
between the French poets, painters, and certain of the musicians, notably
Debussy.

CÉSAR FRANCK (1822–90)

César Franck was one of the most important composers of this period.
It was characteristic of the times that his instrumental work became
known only when Franck was well along in life. It is true that Franck
developed slowly, and his best works were composed in his later years. A
quiet and retiring man, he spent his days either in the organ loft or teaching at the Paris Conservatory. His qualities as a teacher can be measured
best by the devotion of his eminent pupils, among them D'Indy, Chausson,
and Duparc.

His style is a blend of Bach-inspired polyphony and chromaticism derived from Wagner and Liszt. In his music may be seen, too, the improviser at the church organ and a composer filled with devout spirit. His
chromaticism is individual and cannot be mistaken, but it is difficult to
describe its exact essence. The technique is one of chromatic alterations
and appoggiaturas imposed on chords of all types, and chromatic chords
are used in very free fashion. A kind of slippery and sliding chromaticism
results from these methods. Modulations are very free and fluctuating, a
typical modulation being to keys a descending third apart.

While his melodic material is sometimes lyrical, motives and rhythmic
patterns are more prominent. The structures are generally based on the
traditional instrumental forms, which are subject to considerable use of the
cyclic principle. Sometimes Franck changes the number and order of the
movements, and he sometimes telescopes two movements into one (cf.
Beethoven). His skill as a contrapuntist is evident in the canon in the last
movement of the Sonata for Violin and Piano (one of his best works) and
in the fugue in the String Quartet. Occasionally, the organist in Franck
shows in his orchestral music. The development sections, for example, are
sometimes reminiscent of the organist repeating a phrase while he changes
the manual. The same principle may also be seen occasionally in his orchestration. The best known works of Franck (in addition to those already
mentioned are his *Variations Symphoniques* (piano and orchestra), 1885;
Les Béatitudes (oratorio for soli, chorus, and orchestra), 1879; the Prelude,

Chorale, and Fugue for piano, 1884; and the Symphony in D minor, 1886.

The last mentioned is undoubtedly his most famous work, and it illustrates a number of the points mentioned above. The slow introduction contains two principal themes: the first one (Ex. 141a) is motivic, and the second (Ex. 141b), of contrasted, lyric character. The latter is also typical

Ex. 141

of Franck's chromatic harmonization. The opening theme of the introduction is used again for the beginning of the movement proper, but it is transformed in spirit by being played *allegro* (cf. Tchaikovsky's *Pathétique*). The first movement itself is in conventional sonata form, but the development section is notable for rather remote modulations. The coda uses a modulating ground bass (derived from a theme in the exposition); and it closes with a canonic statement of a theme heard late in the exposition proper.

Franck's symphony has only three movements because the "normal" second and third movements (i.e., the slow movement and the scherzo) are combined into one. The opening slow section, beginning with a lovely solo for English horn, is cast in the key of B-flat minor, a key a third below the main key of D minor. The two parts of the second movement are unified musically by combining the theme of the slow section with that of the scherzo at the end.

The last movement begins in D major, and for the contrasting key Franck does not use the dominant key typical of the Classic Symphony, but F major, again a key a third above the tonic note, D.[2] The rest of the last movement is a monument to the cyclic principle. After the statement of his two principal themes, Franck restates the English horn melody of the second movement. Following a development of the main themes of the third movement proper, two themes from the first movement are recalled, and, like the first movement, the third terminates in a coda using

---

[2] Neither the B-flat minor of the second movement nor the B major of the third are simple *diatonic* relations to the tonic D. Both are *chromatically* related.

a ground bass that modulates. A canon involving the first theme of the
last movement brings the symphony to its triumphant conclusion.

Suggested Listening

Franck, Sonata for Violin and Piano in A major (especially the last movement in canon).

Franck, Symphony in D minor.

Suggested Reading

Edward B. Hill, *Modern French Music*. Boston and New York: Houghton Mifflin Co., 1924.

GABRIEL-URBAIN FAURÉ (1845–1924)

In recent years the stature of Fauré has been increasingly appreciated
outside France. As a student, he came under the influence of Niedermeyer
and Saint-Saëns. He lived most of his life in Paris as an organist and a
professor of composition at the Conservatory (later, as Director, 1905–20).
As a teacher he exercised an important influence on Dukas, Enesco, Ravel,
Schmitt, Koechlin, and Nadia Boulanger.

The subtlety of Fauré's melodies and harmonies is remarkable. Their
suppleness owes something to his training in Gregorian chant and older
music at the Niedermeyer School. The use of modes mixed with major
and minor is typical. Thus the sharped fourth degree of the major scale
(i.e., the "Lydian" fourth or tritone) is common in his music. The leading
tone is often discarded in favor of the flat seventh degree to avoid the leading tone (sharped seventh) that contributes so strongly to the definition of
the major and minor and that also inhibits the possibilities of flexible
tonality. At the same time, Fauré uses the chromatic vocabulary of his
time. The exceptional character of his harmony depends less on the invention of a new vocabulary than on using the traditional resources in fresh
ways. Chords are combined with less attention to the usual voice leading
of counterpoint or harmony than to the sonorities of the vertical combinations. His tonalities are clear enough, but the flexibility of the lines and
harmonies gives the most subtle allusions through altered (chromatic)
chords to distant keys from which his special talents permit him to return
with the greatest ease (e.g., the song *"Le parfum impérissable"* in his
Third Collection of *Mélodies*). Like Wagner, although in a different way,
he regarded tonality as a very flexible affair. In the novel manner in
which he passes from one chord to another he is somewhat reminiscent
of Berlioz, but in his inexhaustible invention in fleeting modulation, he
is in a class by himself.

As a song composer, Fauré, together with Duparc and Debussy, made
an important contribution to the repertory. Duparc and Fauré transformed the French song (and also the lyrical piano piece). The song now

came to be called *Mélodie* as opposed to earlier types known as *Romance*. It ceased to be sentimental salon music, and was cast in a mold in which the piano and voice form a continuous and interlocked texture. These are also traits of the German Lieder (cf. Wolf), but the French songs, in their objective emotional tone, differ quite markedly from the German Lieder. The emotional restraint of a Fauré song is much closer to the Classic than to the Romantic spirit. In his beautiful chamber music, Fauré's concise, concentrated forms and vigorous rhythms are also reminiscent of the eighteenth century.

Fauré's music shows typical French qualities of refinement, simplicity, elegance, and emotional restraint. In these respects and in his freedom of harmony, Fauré exerted an important influence on Debussy and modern French composers.

Suggested Listening

Fauré, Songs: *"Lydia"; "Le parfum impérissable."* (For his Requiem, see p. 331.)

Suggested Reading

Norman Suckling, *Fauré.* New York: E. P. Dutton & Co., 1946.

Martin Cooper, *French Music from the Death of Berlioz to the Death of Fauré.* New York: Oxford University Press, 1951.

25. Impressionism: Debussy. Ravel.
Reactions: Satie.

IMPRESSIONISM: DEBUSSY

THE MOST DISTINCTIVE NEW MUSIC in France at the end of the nineteenth and the beginning of the twentieth century was related to *Impressionism,* an artistic movement that took various forms in painting, literature, and music. The term *Impressionism,* applied semi-derisively to Monet and his followers, was suggested by the title of Monet's painting "Impression: Sunrise" (1874). *See Plate* 26B. The first and greatest figure of musical Impressionism was Claude Debussy (1862–1918), whose work may be considered the musical counterpart of certain contemporary French painters and poets with whom he was in constant association. *See Plate* 29A.

The Impressionist painters Manet and especially Monet (the most influential), Pissarro, Sisley, and Renoir were first of all experimenters with light. They broke down the light spectrum into its primary colors, and the *impression* of objects and mixed colors was created by combining primary colors in juxtaposition. When these colors were put on canvas as small dots or points of pure color, the technique was known as *pointillism.* It was used especially by Seurat. *See Plate* 29B. The method of using blobs, patches, or points of color naturally tended to obscure sharp outlines, and the result was not only an impression of colors, but also an impression of the outlines and subjects portrayed—a somewhat blurred or out-of-focus effect. In Impressionist painting, the subjects were characteristically landscapes (sometimes flowers, persons, or even buildings), and various painters worked out of doors to capture the exact quality of light and to conform to their doctrine of "return to nature." Typical paintings showed the shimmer of light on the water or on the same subjects (such as haystacks) painted at different times of day to exhibit the effect of changing light. *See Plate* 26B.

At the same time, poets worked along lines related to the artistic ideas of the Impressionist painters. A group known as the *Symbolists,* which included such figures as Verlaine, Mallarmé, and the Belgian Maeterlinck, wished to substitute general truths and mystery for actuality. Mallarmé, inspired by Poe and Baudelaire, strove to enter the undefinable world of the dream, not through specific description, but through symbols that became an important means of conveying the truth. Mallarmé's poem *L'Après-midi d'un Faune* (*The Afternoon of a Faun,* 1876; Debussy's "Prelude" to the poem, 1894) is suggestive of the amorous play of two nymphs and a faun (a rural deity of human shape, but with ears, horns, tail, and the hind legs of a goat); but the symbolic and dreamlike quality of the language hints and implies rather than conveys a single, concrete interpretation. The poem begins:

> I would perpetuate those nymphs.
>
>   Their rosy
> Bloom's so light, it floats upon air drowsy
> With heavy sleep.
>   Was it a dream? [1]

The Symbolists favored lyric poetry, they placed special emphasis on the joint role of music and poetry in conveying emotions incapable of concrete representation, and they tried to create the *impression* of an emotion directly through sonority and rhythms of words rather than through the use of strict forms and phrases of definite meaning. Mallarmé experimented with deliberate dislocation of traditional grammatical construction—a process that tended to obscure the meaning of a passage or even make it incomprehensible. But obscurity was not a matter of concern to the Symbolists; on the contrary, it was proclaimed as a virtue in Mallarmé's famous words: "To name an object is to destroy three-quarters of the pleasure in it." Such ideas are peculiarly suited to the nature of music, the most indefinite of all the arts; and, for these reasons, the Impressionist musicians were closer to the poets than to the painters.

In the painting and literature of Impressionism, the suggestion and impression of an object are more important than the thing itself. Similarly, numerous pieces of music have titles that evoke the evanescent and intangible, such as Debussy's *The Sea, Clouds, What the West Wind Saw, Footsteps in the Snow, Fog, Sails, Moonlight, Gardens in the Rain,* and so on. Instrumental colors and sonority become increasingly prominent. Atmosphere, a mood, or reverie pervades the music. Emotionally, it is typically cool and detached when dealing with evanescent glimpses of the world of nature, which Debussy observed with so much admiration. ("There is more to be gained from seeing the sunrise than by hearing the 'Pastoral' Symphony," said Debussy.) However, in works with texts, as in

---

[1] Translation by Alexander Cohen. Reproduced from *Musical Opinion,* September, 1935. This issue is now out of print and unobtainable. For complete poem in translation, see Oscar Thompson, *Debussy* (Dover, 1967), pp. 313–16.

the beautiful songs and in the opera *Pelleas and Melisande,* the emotional tone is often more personal and intense because the composer has become involved with character and situation.

Debussy was trained at the Paris Conservatory, which in 1884 awarded him its coveted prize for study in Rome (*Grand Prix de Rome*). Earlier Debussy spent three summers (1880, 1881, and 1882) as tutor to the children of Madam Von Meck (Tchaikovsky's Russian patroness), and he became acquainted with Russian music, notably that of Borodin and Mussorgsky. (He never demonstrated any particular interest in Tchaikovsky.) In the summers of 1888 and 1889, Debussy made the fashionable pilgrimage to Bayreuth and heard Wagner's *Parsifal, Meistersinger,* and *Tristan.* About this time, he came into closer and closer contact with the Impressionists and the Symbolists, being especially fascinated by Mallarmé; and these relationships influenced and formed his mature style, which became evident about 1890.

In the next twenty years—a time of troubled personal life—Debussy produced his best-known works: his orchestral *Prelude à L'Après-midi d'un Faune* (1894, inspired by Mallarmé's poem); his only string quartet (1893); the best of the Verlaine songs (1891, 1892, 1904); the Baudelaire songs (1890); the *Chansons de Bilitis,* on poems by his close friend Pierre Louÿs (1898); the three Nocturnes for orchestra (*Clouds, Festivals, Sirens,* 1900–1901), his only completed opera, *Pelleas and Melisande,* on a play by Maeterlinck (1902); *The Sea* (three symphonic sketches, 1905); *Ibéria* (1908), from the orchestral suite *Images* (1906–11), *Children's Corner,* for piano (1908); and the first book of twelve *Preludes* for piano (1910).

Among his later works were: *Jeux* (1912, a ballet for Diaghilev's Ballet Russe with choreography by Nijinsky); the second book of twelve *Preludes* for piano (1913); and three sonatas as his "last will and testament"—one for cello and piano, another for flute, viola, and harp (both 1915)—and his final work, a sonata for violin and piano (1917).

Debussy's style was formed by intellectual and aesthetic notions similar to those of the Symbolist poets and the Impressionist painters. At the same time, his musical roots were deep in the past and in the scene about him. Among nineteenth-century musicians, Chopin, Fauré, and Mussorgsky were of special interest to him. Of earlier music, Debussy admired the works of Rameau, Palestrina, and Lassus, and the modal melodies of Gregorian chant. He was greatly attracted by the exotic scales, instruments, and dances of Java and French Indo-China, whose music he had heard at the 1889 International Exposition in Paris. Debussy was also fascinated by the dances, folk songs, and atmosphere of Spain (as were Georges Bizet and Maurice Ravel). The modern Spanish composer Manuel de Falla claimed that Debussy, without knowing Spain except through reading and listening, had succeeded marvelously in evoking its spirit by "his visionary genius" (cf. *Ibéria*). Moreover, the chromatic idiom of Wagner, especially in the operas *Tristan* and *Parsifal,* cast its spell over Debussy, although after 1889 Debussy reacted more and more against the powerful attractions he had felt previously in Wagner's music. Clearly realizing the magnitude of Wagner's genius and the dangers of imitating "the old poisoner," Debussy struggled to combat the prevalent Wagner cult in France and to resist the suffocating embrace of Wagner's chromatic style.

Debussy's style was new and distinctive, and in certain respects his harmony contained important implications for the future. Chords of all types (including seventh and ninth chords, and even elevenths and thirteenths) were used more as sonorities than as "functional" chords in the old sense of defining tonality (cf. Ex. 144b). Often Debussy manages to achieve a kind of coherence to progressions of such sonorities (or of more conventional harmonies) by constructing successive chords in parallel motion like the old organum (Ex. 142), parallel dissonant chords of

Ex. 142 * Debussy, *Preludes,* "The Sunken Cathedral," m. 1

Profondément calme

pp

* Permission for reprint granted by Durand & Cie, Paris, France, copyright owners; Elkan-Vogel Co., Inc., Philadelphia, Pa., sole agents.

various types, and even the old *faux bourdon* (parallel chords of the sixths; see p. 148 and Ex. 86). A bewildering variety of scales was basic to this music: the major and minor, the old modes, the whole-tone scale (Ex. 143), the pentatonic scale, and sometimes artificial scales. In essence, Debussy used a composite scale that included all the chromatic and enharmonic possibilities of the twelve half steps of the octave.

These developments were the manifestations of a revolution Debussy was creating in harmony and tonality, a revolution of such significance that it exerted a pivotal influence in leading the musician of the nineteenth century along new paths to the twentieth. In effect, Debussy rejected the old *dominance* of the major and minor scales, and he succeeded in blurring or "drowning" the tonality (*"noyer le ton"* in Debussy's words) by avoiding the type of scale, chord, or cadence that established the "tendency" or "leading" tone so essential in conventional tonality. Hence Debussy commonly resorted to the old modes (cf. Ex.

144a) or to the whole-tone scale (Ex. 143) which, having six equal tones, has no tendency to a tonality. Even when the common major and minor triads remained, their old function of establishing a key or tonality generally ceased to exist. In short, while Debussy did not *abolish* tonality by any means (a number of pieces begin and end on the same tone), he blurred and submerged tonality in the interest of a new freedom and variety of sonority.

Ex. 143 *   Debussy, *Preludes*, "Voiles," m. 1, 2

* Permission for reprint granted by Durand & Cie, Paris, France, copyright owners; Elkan-Vogel Co., Inc., Philadelphia, Pa., sole agents.

Debussy also "emancipated" the dissonance by not resolving dissonant chords or intervals to consonant chords or intervals, in this way destroying the old functional relationship of chords to tonality and essentially abolishing the voice-leading of counterpoint (cf. Ex. 144b). In effect, functional harmony was displaced in Debussy's music by progressions of *sonorities* and juxtaposition of chords often tonally unrelated or unresolved. Mallarmé's treatment of language, with its deliberately disordered structure and tenses, is analogous.

In Debussy's music, many elements combine to create the "impression." The melody itself tends not to sculptural lines but to vague contours. The intervals in the melodies are, so to speak, extracted from the harmony, and vocal lines with words often resemble a kind of recitative. Sometimes voices are used without words to sing neutral syllables, as in *Sirens,* where the female chorus is directed to sing "with closed mouth," thus making muted instruments of the voices.

The dynamics and nuance are as changeable as nature itself. The dabs of loud, soft, and the intermediary shades resemble the shooting fingers of the aurora borealis; or, in terms of painting, they are like blobs, patches, or points of color. Such fleeting dynamic impressions are characteristic not only of the orchestra, but also of the piano. Debussy was himself a pianist, and he (and Ravel, who anticipated him; see p. 388) demanded a new kind of playing which made extensive use of all three pedals in a manner more advanced than that of Chopin and Liszt. (Debussy wrote two books of études, each containing twelve studies, 1915.) The shimmering of the figuration against the notes held in the various pedals produced new effects of sonority and nuance, rivaling the resources of the orchestra.

In the orchestra, muted sounds are common. The harp suggests cool water and fountains, and a kind of haze or atmosphere is created as the background for the clear colors of the solo instruments. The use of a large number of instruments of low register permits many half shades and contrasts, particularly in the darker colors of the orchestra, which mutters in these deep and mysterious registers. Debussy was also master of the percussion instruments (including castanets and tambourine) and special effects in strings (cf. the guitar-like strumming by the violins playing *pizzicato* in *Ibéria*).

In a few works Debussy used traditional forms, such as sonata form and cyclic devices in the String Quartet. But as he gradually blurred the tonality, juxtaposed sonorities more freely, and devoted himself to the creation of mood and atmosphere suggested by texts or titles, Debussy turned to freer, individual types of formal organization better suited to the nature of his music. Never drawn to thematic development, Debussy gravitated naturally to the transformation of motive and theme (see the subtle transformations of the two motives in the piano prelude "The Sunken Cathedral"). On a somewhat larger scale, he was not averse to simple repetition and contrast of materials being used to delineate the mood or moods suggested by the title of the piece. The first of the "symphonic sketches" in *The Sea,* entitled "From Dawn till Noon on the Ocean," has a perfectly coherent form which embodies repetition and contrast of thematic material (though not beginning and ending in the same tonality), but the form is dictated more by the fluidity of the sea "from dawn till noon" than by the symmetrical repetition of material and unity of tonality, as in sonata form. *Festivals,* the second orchestral nocturne, incorporates a march whose coherence depends on the dynamic impression of the march getting closer and then fading away. Similar observations apply to the numerous piano pieces with titles, as in the two books of *Preludes,* where the particular form often results from the character, mood, or event implicit in the title. The form of "The Sunken Cathedral" differs from that of "Interrupted Serenade" if only because the form of the latter incorporates the "Interruption." In his remarkable songs and in his opera *Pelleas and Melisande,* the texts already provide a basis for coherence.

In discussions of Impressionism there is some confusion about "form" in general and about the role of form and color in art and music. Generally speaking, form is the element of order or coherence—the basic structure or framework—while color is a decorative element applied within the framework. In the traditional musical forms—ternary, rondo, sonata form, and the like—the most conspicuous formal principles are statement of material, contrast of material, and restatement after contrast; and the materials used to form the framework according to these principles are thematic materials which embody melody, rhythm, and harmony. In such forms the color of voice or instrument has traditionally been regarded as a secondary element of coherence. By analogy, a picture has the same form or framework, whether it is shown in color or in black and white; so in music, the *form* of a piece is the same whether played on the piano or by an orchestra. In our specific context, one can perceive that by blurring tonality and substituting sonorities for functional harmonies, Debussy uses fewer resources of coherence than those employed, for instance, by Beethoven. But this does not mean that Debussy's "fewer resources" are necessarily less effective than Beethoven's.

It is a debatable point whether Debussy achieves formal coherence by other means—tone color, for instance. To the Impressionist painters, color was inseparable from form, and through the substitution of color for line they were able to create the impression of a formal outline or framework because color itself defines space. But in music, the color of voice or instrument does not define or shape the musical space in the formal sense, the determining factors being rhythm, melody, and harmony. Consequently, it is only in connection with these elements that color or timbre takes on *formal* significance in music. The real point of Debussy's use of color is not its formal significance. Rather, it is that his use of voices or instruments for their color or timbre is a significant, even primary, factor in the musical *effect* of many pieces—doubtless much more so than in music before the advent of Impressionism.

PELLEAS AND MELISANDE

Debussy's opera is a masterpiece of Impressionist art based on an equally masterful play by Maeterlinck. These are the basic circumstances from which the plot of the five-act opera evolves: Prince Golaud, the grandson of the old and nearly blind King Arkel of Allemonde, first meets and then marries the beautiful, young, and mysterious Melisande of the innocent eyes and the long, golden hair. She is mutually attracted to Pelleas, the half-brother of Golaud, the latter being considerably older than either Pelleas or Melisande. In the life of King Arkel's old and gloomy castle, Pelleas and Melisande are drawn closer and closer together in episode after episode infused with erotic symbolism. The predictable happens—or seems to. Golaud's jealousy and suspicions increase until, finally, he surprises Pelleas and Melisande in a love scene (Act IV). Whereupon, he kills Pelleas and wounds Melisande slightly. In the end (Act V) she dies, not of her wounds, but of a broken heart. Golaud lives on, a broken man.

The love triangle of this story is a theme as old as man, and it has a certain resemblance to the ancient legend of Tristan and Isolde. The novelty of the libretto emanates from its impressionistic and symbolic character, which the music of Debussy accentuates. In Debussy's version, the work is characterized by an elusive twilight, half tones, mystery, and understatement. The shadowy and almost dreamlike character of the opera and of Melisande are reflected in her words in the last act: "Neither do I understand each thing that I say, do you see. . . . I do not know what I have said. . . . I do not know what I know. . . . I say no longer what I would."

Mystery and irrationality are everywhere evident. Allemonde itself is a mysterious country, and Melisande's origins, among other things, remain a mystery. Darkness and blindness are used as elements of mystery or fate. The king is almost blind, and there is a "Blindmen's Well." Water and the sea are elements of the vast and unfathomable.

The dramatic intensity of the opera is maintained, even progressively increased, from beginning to end largely by hints and symbolic actions. Melisande carelessly tosses her wedding ring over "Blindmen's Well" and loses it—a symbol of her casual attitude toward fidelity, which explains Golaud's extreme agitation at the ring's loss. Through numerous other symbols of like nature, used carefully and systematically, Maeterlinck suggests and hints at the truth to convey a continuing intensity to the drama.

In his musical setting, Debussy makes the voice sing the text in continuous declamation (at certain points of great intensity, he assigns the voice a lyric rather than a declamatory role, as in the love scene of Act IV). The orchestra underlines and supports lightly throughout, and the purely orchestral interludes further the musical continuity. The whole is tenuously held together by recurrent motives in the orchestra, and three of the most important of these are shown in Ex. 144: (a) *Fate,* harmonized in a modal progression; (b) *Golaud,* a motive of distinctive rhythm expressed in relatively complex chords of chromatic nature (note that the first chord does not "resolve" its dissonance and that it and the following chord may be heard in the whole-tone scale); and (c) *Melisande,* represented by a lyric, though static and somewhat ambiguous phrase, accompanied by animated whole-tone chords. The orchestra demonstrates its powerful ability to express feeling or situation directly, depicting Melisande so accurately in the first act that one perceives she is like a fluttering and frightened bird. The orchestration is marvelously suggestive. Darkness and the sound of fountains (Act II) are conjured up by Debussy's magic. Maeterlinck's play itself is full of imagery and personification. Pelleas says, "One can hear the water sleep"; and in the final love scene, so wonderfully set by Debussy, Pelleas says to Melisande: "One would think that your voice had come over the sea in the spring . . . it is as though it had rained on my heart."

Debussy's music is full of charm, poetry, and subtlety; and he exerted a great influence on his contemporaries, who recognized the freshness of his

Ex. 144 *   Debussy, *Pelleas and Melisande,* Act I, Scene 1

* Permission for reprint granted by Durand & Cie, Paris, France, copyright owners; Elkan-Vogel Co., Inc., Philadelphia, Pa., sole agents.

work. Moreover, it contained a number of new elements that were implicitly revolutionary. Debussy abandoned traditional tonality and functional chord progressions, dethroning the major and minor from their central position; and he blurred the conventional distinction between consonance and dissonance. All these changes undermined the traditional ways, suggesting new ideas and procedures to composers of the twentieth century. In these respects Debussy is often hailed as a revolutionary.

At the same time, he is also a transitional figure whose highly refined and vaporous Impressionism prompted a reaction in the direction of simplicity and clarity. The music of Erik Satie, for instance, stands as a parody of Impressionism, leading to Neoclassicism (see the last section of this chapter). Furthermore, Debussy's style was so personal and his technique so intuitive and empirical that few could follow him without sounding very much like Debussy. Although Debussy was a more progressive composer in 1900 than Schoenberg, the full realization of things to come had to await other developments, in particular Schoenberg's twelve-tone method, which allowed personalities of the most disparate idiom and feeling to compose with complete individuality.

Suggested Listening

Pelleas and Melisande (selections: opening scene; Act IV).

Preludes, Book I (piano): "The Sunken Cathedral," "Interrupted Serenade."

Suite Bergamesque (piano): "Clair de Lune."

Children's Corner (piano): "Golliwogg's Cake Walk."

The Sea (orchestra).

Nocturnes (orchestra): *Clouds* and *Festivals.*

Suggested Reading

Claude Debussy, *Monsieur Croche the Dilettante Hater.* New York: The Viking Press, 1928 (original French, 1921).

Maurice Emmanuel, *Pélleas et Mélisande.* Paris: Mellottée, n.d. (1929?).

Edward Lockspeiser, *Debussy: His Life and Mind* (2 vols.). London: Cassell, 1962–65 (paperback: Vol. I, New York: Crowell-Collier, 1962; Vol. II, New York: Macmillan, 1966).

Oscar Thompson, *Debussy Man and Artist.* New York: Dodd, Mead, & Co., 1937 (paperback: New York: Dover, 1967).

Leon Vallas, *Claude Debussy: His Life, His Works.* London: Oxford University Press, 1933.

RAVEL

Maurice Ravel (1875–1937) is often associated with Debussy, and they have certain features in common, such as Impressionist harmony and French refinement. Being part of the same Parisian environment, they were molded by similar influences, and Ravel himself speaks of his indebtedness to Fauré, Chabrier, Satie, Poe (who enormously influenced French literary figures), and Mallarmé. Both Debussy and Ravel were also interested in Borodin and Mussorgsky, in modal melodies and harmonies, and in the Oriental and the exotic.

However, Ravel's music is significantly different from Debussy's in a number of ways. As Ravel points out, his direction is "opposite to that of Debussy"; and he is distinguished from Debussy by other characteristics close to the spirit of the eighteenth century, notably by more clearly defined melodies and forms and by a somewhat more traditional usage with respect to tonality and dissonance. Ravel is, in fact, as much a Classicist as an Impressionist, especially in his later works. His melodies are much clearer *as melodies* than are Debussy's; they are typically as chaste and clear in form as any of the classics, and are lyrical and often diatonic or modal in character, although sometimes subtly tinged with chromatic harmony. The melody heard alone toward the end of "Ondine" is a case in point (Ex. 145). It begins in the pure Dorian mode, which is then subtly altered by the chromatic notes C sharp and G sharp.

Ex. 145 *

Ravel, "Ondine," from *Gaspard de la nuit*

* Permission for reprint granted by Durand & Cie, Paris, France, copyright owners; Elkan-Vogel Co., Inc., Philadelphia, Pa., sole agents.

There are still other distinctions. Ravel seldom resorts to melodies or harmonies based on the whole-tone scale beloved by Debussy; and when Ravel uses Debussy's repertory of chords (sevenths, ninths, elevenths, and even thirteenths), these elaborate harmonies can often be heard as quite simple combinations, even as triads, in which dissonances are imposed and then *resolved* by means of the moving voices of counterpoint. In this sense Ravel is closer to tradition than Debussy, who seldom resolves the dissonances in the more complex chords, simply juxtaposing them as sonorities. This is not to say that Ravel shrinks from using sharp dissonances, or at times unresolved dissonances, for the sake of sonorities (cf. the "cluster" chords in Ex. 146 from *Jeux d'eau*). Generally, Ravel's harmonic progressions establish a key or tonality, however much he may use modality, dissonance, or novel sonorities. There is relatively little of Debussy's ambiguity with respect to dissonance and tonality. Ravel's clarity of form is related to the type of melody and harmony just described not only in the traditional forms of instrumental music (as in his two piano concertos and String Quartet), but also in his music as a whole.

The broad range of Ravel's interests is reflected in the kinds and subjects of his musical compositions—characteristically dances, ballets, and subjects that are Spanish, exotic, or related to the past. Someone has said that Ravel's music springs from the dance, and the truth of this is

Ex. 146 *

* By permission of Associated Music Publishers, Inc., New York.

suggested by the numerous instances of specific dances and formal ballets: *Daphnis and Chloe* (1912), a ballet for Diaghilev's Ballet Russe (later as two suites for orchestra); *Boléro* (1928), originally a ballet and later one of his most famous pieces in an orchestral arrangement; *La Valse* (1920) for orchestra and also as a ballet. Specific dances are "Malagueña" and "Habanera" from *Rapsodie espagnole* (*Spanish Rhapsody*) for orchestra (1908); and the "Pavane pour une Infante défunte" ("Pavane for a Dead Princess," 1899). That some of these dances are Spanish in character is hardly accidental. Ravel's mother was Basque, and Ravel himself was born near the seacoast town of Saint-Jean-de-Luz, not far from the Spanish border (the family moved to Paris when Ravel was three months old). Indeed, his Spanish background is suggested in various other works, such as *L'Heure espagnole* (*The Spanish Hour*, 1911), his amusing one-act opera. Ravel's fascination with the world of the exotic and the fanciful emerges in works like "The Empress of the Pagodas" from the *Mother Goose* Suite (1908). This particular piece incorporates the exoticism of the pentatonic scale and especially the sounds of the Javanese *gamelan* (orchestra), showing that the Paris Exhibition of 1889 made as deep an impression on Ravel as on Debussy. Ravel evokes the spirit of the past in works like *Le Tombeau de Couperin* and *Daphnis and Chloe;* and he breathes the spirit of the future in the three Mallarmé songs (1913). Finally, Ravel's capacity for wit should not be overlooked, an excellent example being his one-act fantasy *L'Enfant et les sortilèges* (*The Child and the Sorcerers*, 1925, sometimes translated as *The Dream of a Naughty Child*).

In all his music Ravel exhibits a meticulous craftsmanship and, in his piano or orchestral works, a very special talent for idiomatic and virtuoso scoring. In *Jeux d'eau* (1902), the first of the virtuoso piano pieces, he anticipates the later piano style of Debussy. In "Ondine" (from *Gaspard de la nuit*, 1908), Ravel calls for the use of all three pedals of the piano (including the "middle" pedal) to produce sonorities that are truly orchestral in effect. Significantly, three staves of piano score are required to carry the notes and to indicate the desired effects. Ravel understood the orchestra as well as Richard Strauss and Mahler, and he achieves an extraordinary range of brilliant and telling effects in his own works (for example, *Daphnis and Chloe* and the *Mother Goose* Suite) and in arrangements of other composers' music, especially Mussorgsky's *Pictures at an Exhibition,* which was orchestrated by Ravel on a commission from Koussevitsky (1922). Ravel's special knowledge of the orchestra and the piano doubtless prompted him to orchestrate many of his own piano works and also to arrange orchestral works of his own or others for piano.

To many of his contemporaries, Ravel stood in the shadow of Debussy as an Impressionist. This judgment, which persists today, is unfair to Ravel's work as a whole; and it was a factor that clouded the personal relationship of the two composers. Ravel never was, and never pretended to be, an Impressionist or Symbolist like the Debussy of *Pelleas and Melisande.* Yet he could and did write masterly Impressionist pieces, especially in his early years. At the same time, Ravel's music, though not copious, shows a variety of styles of which Impressionism is only one. There is also the Classicism of his chamber music, the "blues" of jazz in his Sonata for Violin and Piano (1927), and the throbbing rhythms of *Boléro.* Doubtless, Debussy's influence on twentieth-century composers was greater with respect to freedom of tonality, dissonance, and sonorities. Ravel nevertheless remains today one of the best loved and most played of "modern" composers. His music embraces a wide variety of moods and formal settings, invariably composed with meticulous craftsmanship and scored with the touch and virtuosity of a master.

Suggested Listening
Mother Goose Suite (orchestra).
Rapsodie espagnole (orchestra).
Jeux d'eau (piano).
Gaspard de la nuit (piano): "Ondine."

Suggested Reading
Roland Manuel, *Maurice Ravel,* trans. by Cynthia Jolly. London: Dennis Dobson, 1947.
Vladimir Jankélévitch, *Ravel,* trans. by M. Crosland. Many illustrations. New York: Grove Press, 1959 (paperback: Evergreen).

REACTIONS: SATIE

The music of Erik Satie (1866–1925), as curious and fascinating a figure as the history of music affords, may be regarded as a reaction to Impressionism in certain particulars. Yet—in a typical Satie contradiction—he supported Debussy and in some instances employed similar harmonic devices. Satie practiced a studied simplicity in rhythm (including barless notation), melody, and harmony. This simplicity may be deceptive. Simple chords, for instance, are not related to each other in simple or conventional ways: a melody of nonchalant simplicity may be accompanied by unexpected, even polytonal, harmonies. Nevertheless, Satie represents a clarity and precision of sorts that in itself is a negation of Debussy's Impressionism. On the other hand, Satie claimed that he persuaded Debussy to give up his early interest in Wagner and to turn to a "music of our own—without sauerkraut if possible," and to a musical Impressionism inspired by such models as Monet. At times, Satie does what Debussy does, employing parallel ninth chords, unresolved chords, and a loosened tonality.

Satie's brand of humor was original, to say the least: "My humor resembles that of Cromwell. I also owe much to Christopher Columbus, because the American spirit has occasionally tapped me on the shoulder and I have been delighted to feel its ironically glacial bite." There was also something satirical or disconcerting about his humor. When Debussy complained of a lack of form in Satie's music, Satie brought him *"3 Morceaux en forme de poire (à 4 mains)"* (1903), meaning literally: *"3 Pieces in the Form of a Pear (for 4 Hands)."* But *poire* is also a slang word for "hoax," which casts another light on the meaning. A prickly fellow, Satie had more than a trace of the prankster in his makeup; and it says something for Debussy and Ravel that they helped to make his works known. Debussy, for instance, orchestrated two of Satie's *Gymnopédies* (originally for piano).

Satie was linked to the anti-Impressionists by Jean Cocteau (1891–1963), a poet, playwright, and artist. In his book *Coq et Arlequin* (1918), Cocteau repudiates Wagnerism and also Debussy's Impressionism, which he regarded as a French counterpart of Wagnerism. At the same time, Cocteau singles out Satie as an apostle of his creed: clarity, order, and precision; or, put another way: "After the music with the silk brush, the music with the axe" (Cocteau). Two of Satie's works of that time were good ammunition for Cocteau: the ballet *Parade* (1917) and the "symphonic drama" *Socrate* (1918). *Parade,* written for Diaghilev's Ballet Russe, brought together Satie, Cocteau (whose idea it was), Massine as choreographer, and Picasso, who used Cubism on the stage for the first time in this work. *See Plates 31B and 31A.* Whatever its artistic intent or merit, *Parade* shocked the public by its mocking tone at a time when World War I was in one of its most critical phases.

Satie has never appealed to the public at large, but there is no doubt that he exerted considerable influence on the younger French composers —"The Six" (see Chapter 31) and others in the 1920's. With Cocteau, Satie was the spiritual father of Neoclassicism.

Suggested Listening
Gymnopédies

Suggested Reading
Rollo H. Myers, *Erik Satie*. New York: Dover, corrected edition of 1948, paperback.

Impressionism may be viewed partly as a continuation of certain features of nineteenth-century Romanticism (such as subjectivity and dependence on effect) and partly as a reaction to it, leading to something quite new in the twentieth century. In this sense, musical Impressionism played a pivotal and transitional role, and Debussy's position was somewhat similar to that of Monteverdi and Beethoven in earlier times, both of whom bridged two centuries and two different cultural eras.

In any case, Romanticism had come to an end. The old system of tonality had been thoroughly explored and the seemingly infinite horizon pointed out by Beethoven had been reached. After Brahms, Wagner, and Verdi, any music conceived in their terms seemed an anticlimax compared with their achievements. By the opening years of the twentieth century a change was due, and during its first decade the old lights were going out one by one, just as they were on the political scene. For better or worse, something new had to come. It was already in the air, and the Romantic era, having run its splendid course, yielded to music of totally different character, reflecting a new time and feeling.

Suggested Reading
For further reading on the nineteenth and early twentieth century as a whole, see:

Gerald Abraham, *A Hundred Years of Music* (Third edition). Chicago: Aldine Publishing Company, 1966.

Alfred Einstein, *Music in the Romantic Era*. New York: W. W. Norton & Company, 1947.

Donald J. Grout, *A Short History of Opera*. New York: Columbia University Press, 1947.

Ernest Newman, *Stories of the Great Operas*. New York: Garden City Publishing Co., 1943. Available in paperback under the title *Great Operas*, Vol. I, New York: Vintage.

Ernest Newman, *More Stories of Famous Operas*. New York: Alfred A. Knopf, 1943. Available in paperback under the title *Great Operas*, Vol. II, New York: Vintage.

26. The Music of the Twentieth Century: An Introduction.

> There is no music worth hearing save only in the last forty years.
>
> TINCTORIS [1477]
>
> Succeeding generations are generally unjust to each other.
>
> ERNEST RENAN [1823–1892]
>
> If this is the music of the future, I pray that my maker will not let me live to hear it again.
>
> CRITICISM OF SCHOENBERG'S *Pierrot Lunaire,* 1912

THE COMPOSER AND THE PUBLIC

BY THE ADVENT of World War I, it was clear that music and art were undergoing a revolution. Matisse and his "Wild Beasts" were upsetting the world of painting; and the public felt so strongly about the music of Schoenberg and Stravinsky that the police sometimes had to restore order at performances. The *avant-garde* was changing traditional concepts so fast that laymen could not understand the "art of the future." Every "new" art is ahead of the public; it has to be, by definition. But in the early twentieth century the gulf was so wide that many musicians were apprehensive lest composers lose touch completely with their audience.

The quotations cited above represent general attitudes that can be found again and again in the course of the development of music. Tinctoris's view, expressed at the end of the fifteenth century, is that of the impatient *avant-garde.* The second quotation is a general commentary on the first, and as Renan rightly says, "succeeding generations are generally unjust to each other." The third quotation summarizes in extravagant form the outlook of the conservative critic and a considerable part of the public. The first and last of these views represent the extremes, the *alpha* and *omega* of the situation.

The present gap between the composer and the public began in the early nineteenth century and has been widening imperceptibly ever since. This all came about largely as a result of a series of social changes that created a situation in which the musical public had its feet firmly planted in the twentieth century but its ears tuned to the nineteenth. In the first place, the Romanticism of the nineteenth century was a two-edged sword. Romanticism reacted against the immediate past, and it revived a substantial amount of old music which it sometimes distorted to mirror its own image. This backward glance of Romanticism succeeded in enriching the repertory of music, but it also encouraged a kind of ancestor worship that made the public increasingly less sympathetic to the music of its own day.

At the same time, far-reaching transformations in society aggravated the situation just described. When the old patronage system came to an end at the beginning of the nineteenth century, the commercial concert took its place, and the audience that now paid the bills (and therefore largely determined what was played) was entirely different. Under the patronage system, music served a relatively small audience that was fashionable, somtimes frivolous, but often highly educated, highly intelligent, and interested in the latest thing. The new audience of the nineteenth century was drawn mainly from the middle class, much more conservative, less well educated, and less adventurous. It is human nature to like the "tried-and-true," and under the new conditions, a repertory of tried-and-true pieces developed—the "classics," which were played over and over again. Romanticism's backward glance and the natural tendencies of human nature, expressed in the commercial concert, gradually produced a time lag between the "standard" repertory and the work of composers who were trying to express the feelings of their own time. The situation was, and is today, further complicated by the growth of the star system, under which the most spectacular performers are paid huge sums to astound audiences—while the composer, thrown on the free market, survives by teaching, by what fees his compositions bring, and sometimes by private or state subsidies.[1]

By the early twentieth century, "modern" music was so far ahead of the average audience that Stravinsky's *The Rite of Spring* created a riot at its first performance in Paris (1913), and a year earlier the performance of Schoenberg's *Pierrot Lunaire* produced the remark quoted at the beginning of this chapter. And the situation got worse, not better, because the composer often mirrored in his music something of the uncertainty, the terror, and despair of the ensuing world catastrophes, depressions, and social upheavals, while the audience was seeking relief from these same forces through entertainment and escape.

At the same time, the musical system of tonality that had been developing for three hundred years had reached a point of exhaustion, and composers at the beginning of the twentieth century, reacting against a

[1] The economics of music is a fascinating, depressing, and eye-opening subject. See, among others, Paul S. Carpenter, *Music, an Art and a Business* (Norman: University of Oklahoma Press, 1950).

worn-out system, were obliged to create new methods of expression. Consequently, a bewildering array of new systems confronted the audience and, by the same token, a bewildering array of reactions confronted the composer: sometimes an enthusiastic and perceptive response on the part of the audience to a fresh and invigorated idiom of musical language, sometimes—doubtless more often—hostility to extreme dissonance and intricate rhythm. By any rational standard, the composer was simply reflecting either the crisis in music or the world-wide upheaval that was taking place in every walk of life. But the audience was not especially aware of the musical crisis and did not want to recognize the uncomfortable fact of the social crisis.

The composer was faced with a difficult situation. An old idiom was exhausted; it could not express his feelings, and something had to take its place. The search for new means of expression produced music whose novelty, variety, and difficulty confused many audiences. The composer was quite aware of this, and there were several alternatives open to him. The most congenial was to act according to his creative impulse, to seek a natural means of expression, come what might. For some composers, no hardship was involved in such a course because they naturally inclined toward the past or toward a style of expression pleasing to the audience. For other composers (Schoenberg, for instance) it would have been an impossibility to turn to the past. Still other composers tried to bridge the gap between themselves and the audience by writing in a deliberately simplified style, as Aaron Copland did at one period of his life (see Chapter 32). Similarly, Paul Hindemith inaugurated *Gebrauchsmusik* (meaning "music for use"), which served to introduce modern music to amateurs and schools through pieces whose forms, style, and technical demands were greatly simplified (see Chapter 29). But the simpler style in which Copland and Hindemith wrote for special occasions was something of a side issue in their work as a whole; and no composer who took his profession seriously could be expected to change his basic nature any more than the audience could reverse history or evade the social and spiritual facts of the twentieth century.

As a corollary, the majority of composers (and especially those of the *avant-garde*) had to deal with two durable and exasperating problems: getting a hearing and overcoming public incomprehension of a new idiom. These problems are closely related since one cannot comprehend what he does not hear; and repeated hearings of a piece are often essential to perceive in what particulars Weber and Webern differ other than in spelling. Getting a hearing in the regular concert hall and opera house was almost impossible for someone like the young Schoenberg in the early days in Vienna, and it is difficult for the young Schoenbergs of today. The large concert organizations still devote relatively little money and attention to new music because the directors and management think they cannot afford the necessary rehearsal time for new and difficult music, because the public does not like "this modern stuff" and it is not "good box office," or sometimes because managements themselves or even conductors do not really like music in new and experimental styles and support it only from a sense of duty. There are, of course, heartening exceptions to these generalities, but for the most part, the picture just painted is a valid one, and it implies stagnation of the new and frustration of its creators. This situation will improve when the public shows greater interest in the music of its own time and insists on large-scale financing from existing organizations or on a public subsidy.

Composers themselves are painfully aware of the need to be heard. A few, as explained above, have met the public more than half way by writing in a simplified style. Others, like Schoenberg, Webern, and Berg, in despair at the difficulty of securing public performances (and at the ensuing hostility of the public and the critics when they did), withdrew into themselves and formed a "Society for Private Musical Performances" in Vienna (1918). At these performances no applause was permitted, no critics were admitted, and the instrumentation was of the simplest, often being limited to the piano. Under such circumstances, the composer got a hearing of sorts that was undoubtedly of great value to him. Nevertheless, this solution created a species of cultural vacuum, and the music involved in such private performances had no meaning or relation to the public at large. A rather healthier development, aimed at bringing new music to a large public, was the formation of the International Society for Contemporary Music (ISCM) in 1922. Subsequently, a number of "Composers' Forums" were instituted in various localities, and they were often allied loosely to the ISCM. Festivals served similar purposes. In Germany, to mention one country, the summer festivals at Donaueschingen (1921–1926) were closely associated with the progressive young German composers and Hindemith in particular; today the festivals at Darmstadt (and Donaueschingen) serve a similar function. In the United States, Tanglewood (Lenox, Massachusetts) is a similar instance of a regular summer festival where, over the years, a number of young composers have been taught by European and American composers, among them Messiaen, Dallapiccola, Hindemith, Copland, and Sessions.

A number of these efforts to get a hearing were composer-generated, but composers were not without substantial help from a few publishers and performers. Universal Edition in Vienna was an early ally, especially after 1919, of the young "radicals" in Austria and elsewhere, Béla Bartók being an example of the latter. In San Francisco, Henry Cowell founded the *New Music Quarterly* in 1927 for the purpose of publishing ultramodern music (for example, the second movement of Charles Ives's Fourth Symphony). Among performers, the concert violinist Joseph Szigeti commissioned or regularly included works of contemporaries in his programs

—Bartók, Prokofiev, Cowell, Ives, Milhaud, and others—at a time when these composers were not the names they are today. A number of conductors also championed new works, sometimes under trying conditions, such as Pierre Monteux's historic performance of Stravinsky's *The Rite of Spring* (1913) or Dimitri Mitropoulos's performance of Schoenberg's Piano Concerto. Other conductors who have done much for new music are Stokowski, Koussevitzsky, Ansermet, Scherchen; and, more recently, Bernstein, Foss, Schuller, Samuel, Boulez, and Craft. In all this, it is important to stress that a new music often requires new breeds of performer and conductor who are technically and spiritually in tune with the music.

On the whole, the efforts of the large concert hall and opera house in the cause of new music have not been spectacular. Rather more support has come from the radio, television, long-playing records and concerts and opera workshops in colleges and universities. In Europe, the German Radio and the British Broadcasting Corporation (which claims to be the largest patron and performer of music in the world) have been great forces in performing and commissioning new works. In the United States, the situation has, in general, been a less happy one for composers. It is characteristic of the commercial *malaise* that the televised first performance of Stravinsky's *The Flood* (1962) was made possible through the sponsorship of a shampoo manufacturer, a fact not without its irony. However, television in this country has been responsible for at least one new medium, the television opera (for example, Gian-Carlo Menotti's *Amahl and the Night Visitors,* 1951); and the enormous educational potential of television is obvious, especially in programs prepared by a composer-conductor as gifted as Leonard Bernstein. It is probable that the most important single factor in the dissemination of new music was the advent of the long-playing record. Somehow, within the baffling mysteries of the recording industry, the long-playing record made such revolutionary economic changes that it was possible to record a large body of contemporary music with a reasonable expectation of profit—even the complete works of Webern!

The fact that there was a substantial market for contemporary music on recordings was due to public interest, and this interest in turn was aroused in part by instruction in educational institutions and the writing of composers themselves (cf. p. 130). Křenek and Schoenberg have written extensively about the problems of twelve-tone music; and, among others, Stravinsky, Hindemith, Sessions, Copland, and Honegger have discussed various aspects of contemporary music and the relation of composer to listener in their writings. All these efforts are interrelated. The efforts of schools, colleges, and universities to explain the composer to the public have been aided immensely by the long-playing record (and, more recently, tape) and by the fact that many composers have become teachers in colleges and universities. The latter have assumed a role in support of composers formerly played by the medieval Church and court.[2]

Some progress has undoubtedly been made in getting a hearing for new music and in closing the gap between composer and public. A new generation is growing up that listens to Schoenberg, Webern, Stravinsky, Bartók, Ives (and perhaps Boulez and Stockhausen) as naturally as an earlier "new generation" listened to Wagner, Strauss, Debussy, and Mahler. Still, we are not yet living in the best of all possible worlds. Although a great deal of music gets to the public, a great deal of *new* music does not. And one sad fact remains all too clear: for every composer (like Stravinsky) who can make his living *as a composer,* there are thousands who cannot and for whom the profession of composer has to remain secondary to some form of employment that returns a living wage.

THE REVOLT AGAINST ROMANTICISM. NEW DIRECTIONS: ATONALITY. PRIMITIVISM. FOLK-MUSIC IDIOMS.

In the first years of the twentieth century, the last masterworks of an aging Romanticism were produced at a time when the revolt against Romanticism was itself generating works of new and exciting character whose future potential was not clear and whose value was sometimes unappreciated. The operas of Richard Strauss were out-Wagnering Wagner in the psychological shock value of the violent themes treated in *Salome* (1905) and *Elektra* (1909), in the brilliance and size of his orchestra, and in the use of chromatic harmony and melody. Mahler's symphonies, although different in idiom, were drawn on the grandest scale, structurally and orchestrally; they were gigantic program symphonies combined with song elements; and they were romantic in their philosophical probings and their expansive emotional expressiveness. During the same period, Schoenberg and his colleagues wrote a series of "Expressionist" masterpieces in Vienna and Berlin (see Chapter 27), culminating in *Pierrot Lunaire* (1912); Stravinsky passed through an anti-Romantic stage to the primitivism of *The Rite of Spring* (1913); and Bartók produced a masterpiece of national folk style in *Allegro Barbaro* for piano (1911). French Impressionism had already attained full stature in a work like Debussy's *Pelleas and Melisande* in 1902 (see the preceding chapter).

The phenomenon of the old and the new existing side by side is by no

[2] The grants from private foundations to individual composers, orchestras, and institutions are often generous, but this support is necessarily sporadic and limited to relatively few persons and institutions.

means unprecedented.[3] Every movement eventually ages and decays, and its place is taken by something new, which may continue from the old or may emerge by a process of reaction against it. The story of twentieth-century music could be written in terms of continuations and reactions to the late stages of Romanticism, especially German Romanticism. The old lingers on as the new begins, both existing side by side for some time. This was the situation in the twentieth century, especially before 1914.

By the end of the nineteenth century, the more ambitious and, as it were, *avant-garde* outpourings of Romanticism proved too much of a good thing for a new generation seeking a change and a fresh outlook. Large-scale works became still grander in scale and more intense emotionally. The hero in Beethoven's Third (*Eroica*) Symphony grew to the super-hero in Strauss's tone poem, "A Hero's Life." In Tchaikovsky's Sixth (*Pathétique*) Symphony, the composer's feelings are made obvious enough to wring the last emotional drop from the audience. Strauss and Mahler called for enormous orchestras for new and still more overpowering effects, and the length of the works generally increased. The result was often loose and episodic structures.

To the younger generation of composers, much of this seemed overblown in sentiment and bombastic and pretentious in manner. Moreover, after the chromatic harmony of Wagner, Strauss, and Reger, there seemed little more that one could do following the same direction. Finally, Romanticism was basically German in origin, and the reaction to Romanticism was colored by anti-German feeling and by new nationalistic sentiments, both of which intensified after 1914, when World War I began.

Not surprisingly, the first reaction came in France, where in the 1890's Debussy had inaugurated a musical Impressionism comparable to like developments in literature and the fine arts (see the preceding chapter). For the overblown emotionalism of Romanticism, Debussy substituted reticence and understatement (compare the love scenes of *Pelleas* and *Tristan*) or, equally characteristic, the vagueness and mystery of Symbolism.

Debussy's new and distinctive musical style made a lasting contribution to the vocabulary of music. Nevertheless, its emotional range was not great, and other composers found it difficult to adopt Debussy's vocabulary without seeming to ape him. For these reasons, musical Impression-

---

[3] But this phenomenon is often inconvenient and troublesome for those who write about such matters and try to relate this composer or that to any particular movement, time, or "ism." The imprecision of labels or categories is only too well known to those who attempt to assign them; and every reader should be warned that any label, no matter how conscientiously defined, may contain some degree of error in its application. However, labels do suggest certain distinctions, aims, and even ways of composing; and they can be useful up to a point if not taken too seriously or applied too rigidly.

ism remained something of a one-man affair, and its duration was fairly short. It ceased to exert much influence on the generation of composers immediately following Debussy's death (1918), a number of whom, inspired by Satie (see the preceding chapter) reacted directly against Impressionism.

This is not to overlook Debussy's impact, direct or indirect, on certain composers. The early works of Ravel, for example, were indebted to Debussy, and others adopted Debussy's idiom in one degree or another. The American composer Charles T. Griffes (1884–1920) shows the influence of Impressionism in a work like the piano piece "The White Peacock" (1917). The Spanish composer Manuel de Falla (1876–1946), who lived in Paris from 1907 to 1914 and knew Debussy and Ravel, adopted the principles of Impressionism without giving up his folk-song heritage (see Chapter 31). Occasionally the works of the English composer Frederick Delius (1862–1934) are touched with an atmosphere characteristic of Impressionism (e.g., the opening of *Brigg Fair,* an English rhapsody for orchestra, 1907); or they may use such Impressionist devices as the whole-tone scale. Delius, however, was basically a Romantic composer (see Chapter 31). Doubtless more important in the long groundswell of musical development was the general influence Debussy exerted with respect to freedom of dissonance and the loosening of tonality. In this sense, composers like Bartók, Stravinsky, and Schoenberg were indebted to Debussy, though their mature styles were all quite different from his.

In terms of the truly new and durable, the twentieth century showed a certain reluctance to begin; and, for all practical purposes, three works already mentioned typify the strongest new currents of the opening years of the century: Schoenberg's *Pierrot Lunaire* (1912), Stravinsky's *The Rite of Spring* (1913), and Bartók's *Allegro Barbaro* (1911).

The Schoenberg work represents a landmark in the early use of so-called *atonality.* Starting with the chromatic scale and harmony in the tradition of Wagner, Schoenberg and his pupils Webern and Berg sought to use the twelve tones of this scale so that no tone should be more important than any other tone: in short, a music without tonality, or *atonal* music. Because of its free and empirical character, early atonal music is generally called *free* atonality. Characteristic of this music are unlimited dissonance ("emancipation of the dissonance"), jagged melodic lines, unpredictable rhythms, and a penchant for Expressionist texts—*Expressionism* being a movement in art and literature in which the internal world, the subconscious, and even the psychoanalytical are central. All these points are illustrated by *Pierrot Lunaire* (see Chapter 27).

A year later, Stravinsky's *The Rite of Spring* introduced a new freedom of dissonance, orchestration, and especially rhythm—all in the interests of a savage, primitive effect, corresponding to the theme of "The Rite of

Spring in Pagan Russia." This musical *primitivism* has its counterpart in Picasso's interest in African art. Stravinsky's music at this time is quite different in conception and idiom from Schoenberg's: It is basically diatonic, not chromatic; tonal, not atonal; and sometimes it is *polytonal* in that it uses two or more tonalities at the same time (see p. 432).

In Bartók's *Allegro Barbaro,* the twelve tones of the chromatic scale are used, but tonality is retained (sometimes polytonality is employed). The new elements are a "barbaric" insistence on rhythm, the percussive use of the piano, and the absorption of melodic and especially rhythmic elements from folk music into Bartók's idiom (for further discussion, see Chapter 29).

These three works have at least one negative attribute in common: they each break with the style of Romanticism and Impressionism. Of the three styles involved, the atonal idiom and especially its later manifestation (see pp. 511 ff) proved to be the most influential. Bartók continued to expand and mature the style predicted by the *Allegro Barbaro,* but his notion of absorbing certain traits of folk music into individual compositions had a limited application. Though the impact of *The Rite of Spring,* especially with respect to rhythm and orchestration, was great, Stravinsky's "primitive" phase was comparatively short. In the early 1920's he turned to Neoclassicism, and in the 1950's he confounded his followers and musicians generally by composing increasingly in an atonal idiom.

AFTER 1918: TWELVE-TONE MUSIC. NEOCLASSICISM. POST-WEBERN COMPOSERS. ELECTRONIC AND CHANCE MUSIC.

After World War I ended (1918), new political and social alignments influenced the development of the arts. The Russian Revolution (1917) established the new Soviet order, which believed in music for the masses and the artist as the servant of the state. While Russian composers enjoyed great freedom in the 1920's, hearing much "new" music from the West, the advent of Socialist Realism (see p. 461) early in the 1930's greatly inhibited the free development of Russian composers, eventually cutting them off from the mainstream of Western music. Only recently has this state of affairs begun to improve. Paris, as the most brilliant city of the victorious allies, became the center of the arts immediately after the war. But a surprising degree of activity also sprang up around new music in the defeated German countries, especially in Berlin and Vienna, even during the disastrous inflations and the great depression of the 1920's. The advent of the Nazis (1933) put a stop to any freedom of artistic activity, and it meant the persecution of the Jews and nonconformists. Many musicians left Germany, and a number of them (including Schoenberg and Hindemith) eventually came to the United States. These and other European musicians who came to this country in the 1930's and later helped it to continue to emerge from its cultural isolation in the arts. Directly after World War I, a number of young American composers went to Paris (rather than Germany as formerly) for their training, among them Copland, Piston, and Virgil Thomson. In Paris, Ravel, Satie, Stravinsky, and the celebrated teacher Nadia Boulanger influenced a whole generation of American musicians (the numerous pupils of Boulanger were called the "Boulangerie"). In the meantime, music that was native to America began to make its voice felt in the United States and abroad: the works of Charles Ives, for instance, and jazz, which greatly impressed European composers such as Stravinsky, Milhaud, and Hindemith.

World War I had disrupted the entire fabric of life, yet a number of musical trends that developed before the war continued to be strong after it. Simultaneously, certain quite peripheral movements had their brief day on the world stage. For example, products of the industrial and machine age, objective and unemotional things in themselves, became the subject of musical composition as in Honegger's *Pacific 231* (1923), a description of a locomotive, or Converse's *Flivver Ten Million* ("A Joyous Epic," ca. 1927), or Mossolov's *Steel Foundry* (1930). Noisy music of the same kind had a short-lived career under the name of *Futurismo* in Italy and *Bruitisme* in France.

Basically, the years between the two world wars were a time of consolidation of the developments and experiments that had taken place before 1914. From the many musical trends there emerged two main figures and two main styles with which the others could be related and contrasted: the twelve-tone music of Schoenberg in Vienna and the Neoclassic development, especially in Paris, centering about Stravinsky. Broadly speaking, Schoenberg was the key figure in the German chromatic, Expressionist trend toward a workable method of atonality. In close collaboration with Webern and Berg, Schoenberg succeeded (1923) in introducing system and order in the prewar "free" atonality by means of his "twelve-tone technique"—or more exactly, his "Method of Composing with Twelve Tones Which Are Related Only with One Another" (see Chapter 27). Stravinsky continued a French development begun by Satie and Cocteau: music essentially diatonic, tonal (or polytonal), relating subject and form to Classical ideals—a Neoclassicism, in short, with a reverence for order, clarity of form (especially the traditional forms of the eighteenth century), and a certain emotional detachment. There were many crosscurrents. Hindemith used the chromatic scale, as did Schoenberg, but he was not an atonalist; in fact, he had a strong bent toward Neoclassicism of a

German sort. Similarly, Bartók continued to write music that was often extremely chromatic, yet invariably tonal; above all, it was based on scales, rhythms, and motives derived from folk music.

After World War II little was to be the same, although this fact became apparent only gradually. A new *avant-garde* was displacing the old *avant-garde* of Schoenberg, Webern, Stravinsky, and Bartók. (Bartók and Webern died in 1945; Schoenberg, in 1951.) Pierre Boulez and others proclaimed the 1950's as "the age of Webern"; and as "post-Webern" composers, they extended Webern's principles of strict organization of tone (see Chapter 27) to other aspects of music (such as rhythm) or even to music in all its aspects ("totally organized music"). Neoclassicism was becoming a thing of the past, and in the 1950's Stravinsky gradually adopted the post-Webern style of atonality.

With the advent of electronic music in the 1950's, any conceivable sound could be produced by electronic generators and amplified by loudspeakers in any degree of pitch, color, loudness, or rhythm, giving composers a complete mastery of the sound spectrum. One of the chief exponents of electronic music is Karlheinz Stockhausen, who is also deeply interested in musical experiments involving space or time (see Chapter 33). Electronic production of sound is, of course, only a means to an end; and electronic sounds can be, and often are, mixed with sounds of voices and conventional instruments or with sounds derived from voices and instruments which have been manipulated by electronic means.

Electronic music, although so far rather limited in use, implies certain far-reaching changes: the abolition of the conventional performer, the need for a new and appropriate kind of concert hall for its performance, and the necessity of large and expensive laboratories for its composition. Electronic music also cannot be "read" from a score, which is essentially a set of directions to the electronic engineer(s); and often there is no score, the performance being "stored" on tape (for *musique concrète,* a kind of "tape" music, see Chapter 33). The unlimited potential of electronic music with respect to pitch, volume, and color has been used on occasion to make music of such unusual sonorities and overpowering loudness that certain questions have been raised about the distinction between music and noise. These distinctions are difficult to make, and they are not admitted at all by composers like Edgard Varèse, who "fathered forth noise," according to John Cage. Cage went in the opposite direction in some of his works, among them a piece entitled *4′33″,* consisting solely of four minutes and thirty-three seconds of silence ("played" by a pianist sitting in front of his instrument).

The use of silence and "noise" under the rubric of music raises the blood pressure of conventional musicians and members of the audience because it challenges the traditional notions of the nature of music itself. And there are other challenges: the introduction of the element of chance

33A   "Parade," designed by Picasso, music by Satie (1917).

B Kandinsky, "Improvisation 30"
   (expressionist painting; 1913

34A Anton Webern.

Stravinsky. *Orpheus*, autograph.
(1947).

35A Béla Bartók playing a folk instrument.

B Paul Hindemith with his viola.

36A Serge Prokofiev.

B Benjamin Britten.

37A Charles Ives and his wife.

B Roger Sessions.

Ex. 13. *Three chords from one fingering*

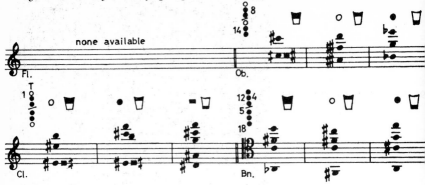

38A Bartolozzi. New sounds and chords on woodwinds (1967).

Foto Maria Austria, Amsterdam

B Pierre Boulez.

Réalités.

9A Karlheinz Stockhausen at work.

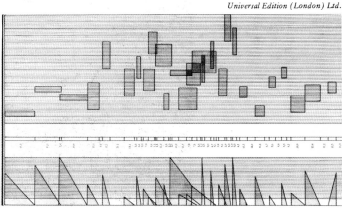

Universal Edition (London) Ltd.

B A score of electronic music: Stockhausen's *Electronic Study II.*

40A Jackson Pollock: "Number 1" (1948).

B John Cage.

and the idea of noncausality. In music involving "chance operations" (also known as "aleatoric" music), one or more elements of the piece is left to chance, as in Cage's *Imaginary Landscape No. 4* for twelve radios (see Chapter 33), where obviously what is on the radio determines the musical outcome. In noncausal music (also called "nonteleological," meaning "no end or purpose"), a sound is not considered part of the context of other sounds; each sound is an end in itself, and each sound is listened to for what pleasure it brings, unrelated to any other sound. Compositions of this kind are a series of individual "moments" that need have no relation to what precedes or follows (cf. Stockhausen's *Mixtur;* see Chapter 33).

All the ways of thinking and composing mentioned above are international in scope and adoption, and have reached countries that are relatively new participants in *avant-garde* music—Poland and Japan, for instance. The United States, which has participated in all these "new" tendencies in varying degrees, has made an additional and unique contribution through the various idioms of jazz from "rag" to "rock." Some composers like Gunther Schuller have sought to blend jazz and the modern idiom into a "third-stream" music.

These are some of the *avant-garde* directions of today. Needless to say, not all composers are *avant-garde;* and the chapters to follow are devoted to exploring the spectrum from left to right.

Suggested Reading
See the end of Chapter 33 (p. 527).

27. The New Vienna School of Schoenberg, Webern, and Berg. Expressionism and Free Atonality. The Twelve-Tone and Serial Techniques.

THE GRADUAL EMERGENCE of the new from the old is apparent in the continuation and transformation of German Romanticism by the New (or "Second") Vienna School of Arnold Schoenberg and his pupils Anton Webern and Alban Berg. Their early works contain reminiscences of Brahms and Wagner (among others), a good example being Schoenberg's String Sextet *Verklärte Nacht* (*Transfigured Night*, 1899).

About 1908 Schoenberg and his pupils pointed in a new direction. They sought to abandon tonality for *atonality* to achieve a type of music that had no tonal center. For this purpose, Schoenberg and his followers used the twelve tones of the chromatic octave freely in melodies and harmonies, trying to shun the old chords and cadencing devices used in traditional music to establish a tonal center or key. Because of its free and empirical nature, this type of atonality is called *free* atonality, as opposed to *twelve-tone music,* a later and highly disciplined variety of atonality (see p. 409).

At first music in free atonality was typically cast in the smaller forms of songs and piano pieces, such as Op. 19 of Schoenberg. Some "miniatures" of Webern lasted as little as fifteen seconds. The "orchestra" was often reduced to chamber-music combinations, as in Schoenberg's *Pierrot Lunaire.* Typical of this music were dissonant harmony and broken melodic lines (cf. Ex. 151), often with large leaps (Ex. 147). Sometimes chords

Ex. 147 * Schoenberg, Second Quartet, third movement

Nimm _____ mir die _ Lie - be

were built up by superimposed fourths, not by superimposed thirds as in conventional harmony. Dissonance—that is, dissonance by former, conventional standards—was "emancipated" since no dissonance of melody or harmony was ruled out provided the result was judged good by the composer's ear; and dissonances were not required, as formerly, to "resolve" to consonances. This was truly a period of fascinating experiments in harmony, in melody (such as *Sprechstimme;* see Ex. 151), and in various vocal and instrumental sonorities.

At this time Schoenberg and his circle were emotionally and aesthetically associated with the aims of *Expressionism.* The latter can be regarded as a continuation of certain trends of Romanticism and, at the same time, as a reaction to Impressionism. It was in the latter sense that the term "expressionism" was first used to describe a group of paintings in the Paris Salon of 1901. If Impressionism is basically French in spirit and origin, Expressionism is essentially German. Impressionism has to do with the artist's portrayal—his impression—of the *external* world. Expressionism has to do with the artist's portrayal of the *internal* world, not the ordinary emotional world of the nineteenth century, but an emotional world vastly intensified by the new discoveries of Freud in the realm of the subconscious—an undefined and even terrifying world like that of Kafka, where reality can hardly be distinguished from terrible dreams. Larger-than-life "expression" of an artist's feelings are characteristic of Expressionism. In painting, Expressionism is represented by Kandinsky (who founded "the Blue Rider" School, 1911-1914; *see Plate 33B*) and Kokoschka; in literature by Stefan George and Strindberg; and in music by Schoenberg, Webern, and Berg. Significantly, Schoenberg began to paint Expressionist pictures in 1907, about the time he turned to free atonality.

As Schoenberg increased the intensity of dissonance and chromaticism in free atonality, he raised the emotional temperature of the texts he used, and intensified the dreamlike fears of his characters on the stage. In his one-act opera *Erwartung* (*Expectation,* 1909), the subject is less like a dream than a nightmare, and the general effect is more morbid and shocking than Strauss's *Salome* and *Elektra,* written about the same time. A monodrama (that is, for a single character), *Erwartung* concerns the inner world of "a woman" (abstract and unidentified) who searches for her lover in a forest at night. In anguish and terror she sinks exhausted on a bench. She feels something with her foot. It is the dead body of the lover whom she seeks. She kisses the body. Then, in revulsion, she kicks it, thinking her lover has been untrue to her with another woman (that is, with Death). Again she kisses the body, and finally sings her farewells. "It is essential," writes Schoenberg, "that one sees the woman always in the forest to grasp that she fears it! *for the entire work can be conceived as a nightmare* (Angsttraum)." [Italics added.]

The poets had anticipated the musicians in voicing the hidden ferment of Expressionism. Consequently, it is not surprising that Schoenberg, Webern, and Berg turned to the "Expressionist" poets (such as Stefan George) for their early settings in songs and stage works in free atonality (for *Pierrot Lunaire,* see p. 414).

Later, Schoenberg, working closely with Webern and Berg, succeeded in introducing system and order in the prewar free atonality through his "Method of Composing with Twelve Tones Which Are Related Only with One Another." Characteristically, the first music embodying this "Method" was written for piano—the Five Piano Pieces of 1923 (although not all these pieces are in the new technique). The details of the twelve-tone method are described in the section on Schoenberg in this chapter.

The twelve-tone technique was essentially a systematic way of organizing what the atonalists had been doing in free atonality. In general, the style of atonal music—whether of the free or the twelve-tone variety—is characterized by dissonant harmony, strong interest in the most varied sonorities of instruments and voices, unpredictable rhythms, and jagged melodic lines. The last were often complex manipulations of basically simple motives by means of octave transposition. Webern used this technique to make a complex line (Ex. 148a) from the basically simple pattern shown in Ex. 148b.

Ex. 148 *

Webern, Op. 28, No. 3, m. 18–19

* By permission of Universal Edition, London, Vienna, Zurich, copyright owner; Theodore Presser Company, Bryn Mawr, Pa., agent.

The formal organization of atonal music is an especially interesting point, and it raises the question of how extensively the forms of tradi-

tional music can be continued or adapted in atonal music. Of the traditional forms, the variation is one of the most suitable and adaptable to the
new music. Because the twelve-tone technique repeats a basic tone series
as a pitch pattern over and over again, there is a basic affinity between this
technique and the procedure of variation; and significantly, one of
Schoenberg's best pieces from this period is the Orchestral Variations of
1928 (Op. 31).

Unlike the variation, however, many traditional forms rely heavily on
tonality for formal organization. Are such forms (for example, sonata
form), which are closely associated with tonality, adaptable to atonal
music, which *avoids* tonality? In point of fact, both Schoenberg and Berg
succeeded in adapting a number of the classic forms to atonal music (see
p. 417 for the discussion of sonata form in Schoenberg's Fourth String
Quartet). In Berg's Expressionist and freely atonal opera *Wozzeck,* the
traditional forms of instrumental music furnish the basic organization. By
way of contrast, Webern tended to less traditional forms; he broke his
basic tone series into short motives perpetually varied in a kind of
kaleidoscopic style—especially in his miniature forms. In his late style,
Webern preferred to write music reduced to the barest essence of tones,
and motives are heard alone or in the thinnest texture—a kind of pointillistic style in which the series is highly ordered and employed in a
complex web of counterpoint (see p. 424 for Webern's Symphony, Op.
21).

Schoenberg's innovations extended to many aspects of music, including
notation. After 1908 he abolished the key signature, marking instead all
accidentals. In later works, he distinguished in the score between the
principal voice   (H = *Hauptstimme*)   and   the   secondary   voice
(N = *Nebenstimme*). He also wrote all the transposing instruments at
pitch in his scores, a great boon to students and often to the conductor.
These reforms were adopted by a number of his followers.

While the twelve-tone technique would seem to be a highly disciplined,
even rigid, "method" of composing, in practice it proved extraordinarily
flexible and adaptable to the individual needs of composers of the most
diverse styles; and this freedom of individual usage was one of its greatest
attractions. Berg and Webern, the two most famous pupils of Schoenberg,
both used the technique while managing to sound quite different from
their teacher and from each other. Berg incorporated certain tonal elements into his music (as in the Violin Concerto); and Luigi Dallapiccola
(see Chapter 31), an important Italian follower of Schoenberg's method,
also used the series in tonal ways. Webern's use of the series suggested
new rhythmic and especially color possibilities, so that later composers of
electronic music trace some of their inspiration to Webern's ear for
instrumental and vocal sonority. Similarly, Webern's music suggested the
idea of serializing other aspects of music such as rhythm and tone color.

In certain works of Ernst Křenek and Pierre Boulez, among others, this "serial technique" is applied to *all* aspects of the music, which is then said to be "totally organized" (see Chapter 33).

SCHOENBERG

Arnold Schoenberg (1874–1951) is "the great troubling presence of modern music," to quote Paul Rosenfeld. Although the profound impact of the past is apparent in the influence of Brahms and Wagner on his earliest works, he and his pupils in Vienna gradually created a musical revolution of such world-wide significance that every composer today must come to grips with its implications in one way or another. Specifically, Schoenberg was among the leaders in showing the way to the "emancipation" of dissonance and to the freeing of music from its seemingly unshakable allegiance to tonality. These changes amounted to challenging three centuries of an established order in which consonance was clearly distinguished from dissonance and in which each piece of music generally focused around one tone—that is, music which was "tonal" or predominantly in one "key," as Beethoven's *Eroica* was in E-flat major.

Actually, there is no scientific basis for establishing an absolute division between consonance and dissonance. These distinctions were previously made on aesthetic grounds by any particular age or composer, a "dominant seventh" being dissonant to Palestrina in the sixteenth century but consonant to Monteverdi in the early seventeenth. By pointing out that "dissonant" notes can properly be called "less consonant," Schoenberg "emancipated" the dissonance theoretically by destroying the distinction between consonance and dissonance; and in practice, he used any combination of notes he considered appropriate, no matter how "dissonant" by previous standards (cf. Ex. 149a); and dissonance no longer had to resolve to consonance. In short, consonance and dissonance as such had ceased to exist for Schoenberg and his followers.

At the same time, proceeding from the chromatic scale and harmony established through usage by Wagner and others, Schoenberg gradually evolved a method of composing with the twelve chromatic steps of the octave in such a manner that *each tone remained as important as every other tone.* This method, finally clarified in 1923, was directly opposed to traditional tonality in which *one* tone was the center of musical gravity.

This "revolution" was regarded in quite different ways by various segments of the musical community. To most of the audience, music of unlimited "dissonance" and lacking a tonality was often an incomprehensible and ear-shattering experience; and significantly, Schoenberg and his circle had to found a "Society for Private Musical Performances" in

Vienna (1918) to secure a hearing for their new music. To professional musicians and especially to composers, the new possibilities created by the music of Schoenberg and his colleagues meant a revolution of almost infinite horizons. Schoenberg himself, however, denied that he was a revolutionist, claiming rather to be an "evolutionist." He had not invented the twelve-tone method, he said; it was simply there waiting to be discovered. His view was undoubtedly correct in the sense that he was extending the chromatic usage of Wagner and his successors. Nevertheless, from early in his career, Schoenberg's music *seemed* revolutionary to the audience in its extremes of melody, dissonance, and subject matter. And Schoenberg, no matter how clearly and correctly he saw his evolution from the past, was in fact an experimenter and innovator of such dimensions that the "Method of Composing with Twelve Tones" had to be viewed as new and path-breaking, even though it evolved as a later manifestation of his natural tendencies. In any case, whether engaged in evolution or revolution, Schoenberg clearly understood the importance of what he had done and intended to do; and in 1912 he predicted: "The second half of this century will spoil by overestimation what the first half has left of me through underestimation."

THE TWELVE-TONE METHOD

Although the developed "Method of Composing with Twelve Tones" required some years for its working out, it seems best to describe the essentials here for purposes of comparison. First a word of warning: these essentials simply afford a glimpse into the composer's workshop; they are not a blueprint for listening. From a composer's point of view, Schoenberg's technique is merely a way of organizing the texture or material to ensure an equal importance to each of the twelve tones. It is not an open sesame to composing by mere manipulation of tones; and Schoenberg, significantly, was thoroughly grounded in the classics and insisted on the same discipline from his students. From the listener's point of view, Schoenberg stressed time and again that his music was intended to be "expressive": "If a composer doesn't write from the heart, he simply cannot produce good music." The implication of this remark is that Schoenberg wanted his music to speak directly to the emotions of his listeners, not to their ability to follow the intricacies of counterpoint. In a letter to the violinist Rudolf Kolisch (1932), Schoenberg warns against technical analysis and says with some exasperation: "My works are twelve-tone *compositions,* not *twelve-tone* compositions." This is Schoenberg's way of saying: Listen to my compositions as music, not as constructional devices of twelve-tone music; listen to the sound of music as expressed by its melodies, rhythms, textures, dynamics, tone color of voice and instrument, harmony and counterpoint, and correspondence between music and text. If certain details of ordering or constructing a piece are not audible to the audience, one must assume that an "inaudible order" is the composer's intent, since it is his business to make clear to the audience whatever is essential in the communication of his thought and feeling.

In any case, the principal features of the twelve-tone method are the following: First, the composer formulates all twelve chromatic tones in a basic "series"—also called "set" or "row," [1] as in the opening of the Fourth String Quartet (Op. 37, 1936), shown in Ex. 149a. Once formulated, the order of any particular series is not changed in the piece, and individual notes of the series are not repeated in a given voice until the whole series has been stated. After its initial statement, the series is repeated over and over again continuously throughout the piece. *The basic series is not a theme* (although it may be used as such), because in later statements any rhythmic pattern may be applied, and any note may be sounded, at the octave(s) above or below its original pitch. Consequently, the same series may sound entirely different in later appearances. The inversion of the series (Ex. 149b) has a different *rhythm* from the opening statement (Ex. 149a), and it uses octave transpositions (Ex. 149b₁ also shows a simplified form *before* octave transposition). For these reasons, the inversion sounds entirely different from the initial statement.

The series is also used harmonically to furnish the "accompaniment." That is to say, the notes of the series may be used simultaneously. In the opening of the Fourth String Quartet (Ex. 149a), the first three notes of the series are accompanied by chords consisting of the following notes of the series: 4, 5, 6; 7, 8, 9; and 10, 11, 12.

An enormous variety is possible in successive statements of the series by using transposition and the devices of counterpoint. Any series may be transposed *as a whole* to any one of the twelve chromatic steps, and the "basic series" may occur in any one of four contrapuntal forms: (1) the original or basic form (Ex. 149a); (2) the inversion (Ex. 149b) of the original: that is, in a form in which an upward interval in the original becomes the same interval downward, and vice versa; (3) in retrograde form: that is, played backward from the end to the beginning (Ex. 149c); or (4) retrograde by inversion (not shown). By using the twelve possible transpositions in combination with these four contrapuntal forms, forty-eight statements of the basic series are possible. (For further details and implications of the twelve-tone system, see pp. 416–18.)

---

[1] The preferred terminology today is "series" or "set." "Series" will generally be used in this book.. "Tone row," a term formerly in great vogue, is used less nowadays because (among other reasons) "series" lends itself better to the prevailing and comprehensive term "serial music." The latter term refers collectively to music using "series" of tones and/or rhythms and/or timbres, and so on. For further reference, see the Index.

Ex. 149 *

Schoenberg, Fourth String Quartet, Op. 37, first movement

SCHOENBERG'S MUSICAL DEVELOPMENT

One can distinguish at least three periods in Schoenberg's musical development: (1) until about 1908, when his music is still tonal although often in a very dissonant idiom; (2) from about 1909 to 1922, a period of free atonality in which a tonality is no longer discernible in music of a free chromatic and dissonant idiom; (3) 1923 to his death in 1951, a period devoted mainly to twelve-tone composition. A "fourth" period is sometimes distinguished, beginning with his arrival in the United States (1933), in which some relaxation in the "method," or even a return to tonality, occurs (as in the Suite for Strings in G, 1934).

In his early life, Schoenberg lived mainly in Vienna and Berlin. He took composition lessons from Alexander Zemlinsky (whose sister he married), knew Richard Strauss and Mahler, and became acquainted with Debussy's music. Schoenberg experimented with different ways of writing, such as the use of unresolved dissonances and chords built on fourths (*Kammersymphonie,* 1906); and the types of music he wrote included songs with piano accompaniment, the symphonic poem *Pelleas and Melisande,* his well-known String Sextet *Transfigured Night,* and his Second String Quartet (1907), which uses the voice in the last two movements. *Gurre-Lieder,* based on a poem of J. P. Jacobsen and set for soloists, mixed chorus, and orchestra, surpassed in its orchestral demands those of the most extravagant works of Mahler and Strauss. (*Gurre-Lieder* was nearly finished in 1901, completed in 1911, and first performed in 1913.) In 1904 Webern and Berg became his pupils, a relationship that had a lifelong and mutual influence on all of them; and in 1907 Schoenberg began to paint "expressionist" pictures.

The second period of composition began about 1909 with the piano pieces of Op. 11. This is the period of free atonality, a term used to mean the absence of key and the free use of the chromatic scale. In essence, Schoenberg and a number of others had rejected tonality and were searching for a new order to replace the old system of tonality. Debussy and others like Scriabin and Roslavetz in Russia were seeking similar solutions. From 1908 until the advent of World War I must have been a time of intense work and excitement for Schoenberg and his pupils; and in the freshness and exhilaration of invention and discovery, this period is reminiscent of the spirit of the early seventeenth century compositions of Monteverdi and others.

The relationship of Schoenberg to his pupils was an unusually close one. A fascinating personality and an extraordinarily stimulating teacher, Schoenberg begins the preface to his *Harmonielehre* (1911) with these words: "I have learned this book from my pupils." The interplay of ideas and technique between master and pupils is suggested also by the similarity of types of works composed about this time: Schoenberg's songs of 1908 (Op. 14 and Op. 15—the latter on a text of Stefan George) were done about the same time as Webern's George songs (Op. 3 and Op. 4) and Berg's four songs of 1909. Again, Schoenberg's Five Pieces for Orchestra of 1909 (Op. 16) were followed by Webern's Six Pieces for Orchestra in 1910 (Op. 6); both were for very large orchestras. Berg finished his Three Pieces for Orchestra in 1914. Other significant works of this period were written by Schoenberg for the stage: *Erwartung* (Op. 17, 1909) and *Die Glückliche Hand* (*The Lucky Hand,* Op. 18, 1913), works that represent a parallel in music to the Expressionism in painting and literature.

Schoenberg's striking originality is demonstrated by two pieces from this second period. The first is entitled "Summer Morning by a Lake (colors)," the third piece from his Five Pieces for Orchestra (Op. 16). "Summer Morning" is especially interesting because it features Schoenberg's *Klangfarbenmelodie* ("tone-color melody"). Schoenberg has made the changes in tone color a central feature of the piece, the opening of which is shown in Ex. 150. Here a chord composed of one set of colors

Ex. 150 *

* With permission of the publishers, C. F. Peters Corporation, New York.

(two flutes, clarinet, and bassoon) is overlapped by the same chord but with another set of colors (English horn, muted trumpet, bassoon, and muted horn). This subtle procedure of tone-color melody gives variety, movement, and even a species of formal coherence. The movement begins very, very soft (*ppp*), and the dynamic register ranges from very soft (*pp*) to very, very, very soft (*pppp*)—a very low dynamic range. In this connection Schoenberg gives a most interesting direction in the score: "The change of chords in this piece has to be executed with the greatest subtlety, avoiding accentuation of entering instruments, so that only the difference in color becomes noticeable. The conductor need not try to polish sounds which seem unbalanced, but watch that every instrumentalist plays accurately the prescribed dynamics. There are no themes or phrases in this piece which have particularly to be brought out." When Schoenberg wrote this music, he was deeply engaged in painting, and "Summer Morning" is like a visual image transferred to sound. In addition to the changing chord, which is central to the tone-color melody, there are brief flurries of sound here and there, almost like the dots of pointillism in a Seurat painting.

Pierrot Lunaire (Op. 21, 1912), the second piece in question, is one of the landmarks of twentieth-century music and one of Schoenberg's best-known works. It is a setting in German translation of twenty-one Surrealist poems by Albert Giraud on the topic of "Pierrot touched by the moon." Pierrot is a jesting character, originally a stock figure in old French pantomime. The introspective, psychoanalytical, and even macabre aspects of Expressionism are demonstrated by these poems. In No. 13, for instance, Pierrot imagines that the moon is a glittering scimitar—the curved sword of Turkey—that is going to behead him.

The mood and variety of the poetry are matched by the variety of sounds and textures in Schoenberg's setting for female "reciter" and (in all) eight instruments played by five players. The individual settings are so varied that hardly two are the same. The extraordinary color of the music comes first of all from the "reciter," who half declaims and half sings in a way, especially invented by Schoenberg, called *Sprechstimme* ("speaking voice"; see Ex. 151, the beginning of No. 9, "Gebet an

Ex. 151 *

Schoenberg, *Pierrot Lunaire* (No. 9, *Gebet an Pierrot*)

Pierrot"). The *Sprechstimme* pitches (which are considered approximate) are given in the score by notes with crosses through their stems. The voice is accompanied essentially in chamber-music style, and each instrument is played by a soloist and treated soloistically. The instrumental parts are written in extraordinary ways from an instrumental point of view, and here again Schoenberg's acute ear for sonorities is apparent.

From the opening note of "Moondrunk," the first poem, our attention is immediately riveted on Schoenberg's setting, the voice of the "reciter" sounding disembodied or "out of this world." The music suggests no key, but rather a free atonality expressed in jagged chromatic lines. The voice parts are contrapuntal in effect, and each of the accompanying instru-ments in "Moondrunk"—flute, violin, cello, and piano—sounds in a differ-ent plane of sound color. The musical effect is in some mysterious way suggestive of the mood of the text, which begins:

> The wine that only eyes may drink
> pours from the moon in waves at nightfall.

For the listener, the strictness of some of the formal organization through-out *Pierrot* (such as the *passacaglia* in No. 8) is quite secondary to the effects of lines, colors, and harmonies in these amazing pieces.

During World War I, Schoenberg understandably wrote very little. Besides, it was then and for five years afterward that he was trying to formulate his new "method." After he succeeded (1923), Schoenberg composed mainly in the twelve-tone style described above. The Suite for Piano (Op. 25, 1924) is the first piece composed *completely* according to the twelve-tone method, although this technique is used partially in Op. 23 and Op. 24.[2]

Earlier composers had used "series" of one kind or another. Debussy, for instance, employed a whole-tone "series" in *Voiles* (cf. Ex. 143), one of the first set of his Preludes for piano (1910). But Schoenberg's usage dif-fered from previous methods in several respects: it involves *all* twelve tones of the chromatic octave, and *inclusiveness* and *equality* of all twelve tones are ensured by not repeating a note of the series until all twelve tones have been stated. An exception is made for the *immediate* repetition

---

[2] The problem of terminology for "atonal" music has not been completely re-solved. Schoenberg spoke of his "Method of Composing with Twelve Tones Which Are Related Only with One Another"—impossibly cumbersome as a descriptive phrase. "Twelve-tone music" (or "technique" or "method") is an acceptable abbreviation. "Atonality," a short and reasonably sensible word in common use, is a general term for any music that lacks a tonal center, twelve-tone music being a strict species of atonality. As a term, "atonality" has one important disadvantage: it is generally rejected by most composers and especially by Schoenberg, who sug-gested "pantonality." "Dodecaphony," favored in Europe, is simply Greek for "twelve-tone." "Serial music" is a general term that may imply more than "twelve-tone music," since, strictly speaking, the use of a series in twelve-tone music con-cerns only the pitch of the notes.

of a note, which is considered a rhythmic device (as in the third note of the series at the opening of the Fourth String Quartet; see Ex. 149a). Thus, the ordering of the tones of the series is a specific concept of Schoenberg to which (it should be added) his pupils and J. M. Hauer (1883–1959), a Viennese contemporary, contributed.

From a composer's point of view, the twelve-tone method was practical in that it was a basic way of organizing all the twelve tones while allowing complete freedom with respect to individual treatment of melody, rhythm, harmony, and so on. Unlike the style of Debussy, founded in the personal and empirical use of dissonance and harmony, the twelve-tone method permitted the most varied adaptations, as can be seen in Webern, Berg, and the later works of Stravinsky. In other developments, the twelve tones of the basic series were often broken into motives of smaller groupings. Even Schoenberg was fond of series that divided into two groupings of six notes (sometimes called "hexachords") with certain special properties.

The high degree of order imposed by the twelve-tone method is doubtless felt unconsciously by the audience, but the immediate aural impression of Schoenberg's twelve-tone music is, as before, one of novelty of tone color, disjunct melody, great variety of rhythm, a highly dissonant harmony, and density of texture. These characteristics and the various forms involved can be observed in a number of works from this last period of Schoenberg's composition, among them: Variations for Orchestra (Op. 31, 1928), the opera *Moses and Aaron* (1932, unfinished), the Violin Concerto (Op. 36, 1936), the Fourth String Quartet (Op. 37, 1936), the Piano Concerto (Op. 42, 1942), the String Trio (Op. 45, 1946), and *A Survivor from Warsaw* for speaker, male chorus, and orchestra (Op. 46, 1947).

This last period was punctuated by catastrophic events in Germany, and after Hitler became chancellor in 1933, Schoenberg settled in the United States (1933). He taught at the University of California in Los Angeles from 1936 to 1944, and in 1941 he became an American citizen.

TONE COLOR AND FORM. THE FOURTH STRING QUARTET.

Schoenberg had a most perceptive ear for tone color. In almost any of his scores, his interest in the timbre of voices and instruments is striking. The color of different registers of the voice and its particular properties can be examined in his songs and in *Pierrot;* and the particularly novel use of the *Sprechstimme* in the latter and the instrumental "tone-color melody" in Op. 16 have already been noted. Schoenberg exploited the particular properties of many of the instruments, the strings being a good example. (He played both the violin and the cello.) His astonishing cultivation of special string effects is particularly apparent in the String Trio (1946), where he calls for all sorts of *outré* effects by various combinations of artificial harmonics, mute, *sul ponticello, col legno, glissando, pizzicato,* and so on (for the technical terms, see the Glossary). Special effects are also used in piano music. In Op. 11, No. 1, Schoenberg writes chords for the left hand that look like held-out harmonies, labeled "pressed down almost tonelessly."

In his experiments leading from one period to another, Schoenberg often wrote songs or piano solos in the smaller forms, even in miniature forms (Op. 19, six short piano pieces), to clarify a new type of expression with the simplest means. In connection with such works, Schoenberg writes about "their extreme expressiveness and their extraordinary brevity. . . . Later I discovered that our sense of form was right when it forced us to counterbalance extreme emotionality with extraordinary shortness."

For larger structures, Schoenberg often relies on traditional forms, since the use of the series does not dictate a structure, but merely enforces the equality of the twelve tones within textures and themes. Perhaps significantly, the variation is typical of Schoenberg's larger forms, and in one sense the series itself and its possible transformations are one "perpetual variation." Still, there are a number of formal variations (such as the Variations for Orchestra). In certain of the traditional forms (as in the sonata form in the first movement of the Fourth String Quartet discussed briefly below), various means have to be employed, such as changes of tempo, dynamics, texture, or theme, to effect the sectional divisions formerly achieved by tonality. Schoenberg also experimented with "athematic" construction (that is, where no theme or motive is repeated, developed, or transformed) in *Erwartung,* but in this work the formal problem is already partially solved by the text itself.

The first movement of the Fourth String Quartet is composed entirely in twelve-tone technique; and, as a glimpse of the composer's working methods, we give details of the opening measures: the basic series and its harmonization (Ex. 149a), the inversion of the series (Ex. 149b), and the retrograde form (Ex. 149c). Paradoxically, it is best to forget these matters and listen to the development of the material as music, keeping in mind that listening to Schoenberg is difficult not because it is twelve-tone music, but because his music is generally concentrated in texture, jagged in chromatic lines, and dissonant in harmonies. In this movement, Schoenberg has helped the listener in several ways to hear the main outlines of the music. He does so by using the basic series as a theme at various points and by casting his material in a form resembling sonata form, whose main outlines he carefully distinguishes.

The treatment of the basic series as a theme here and there in this movement has the old-fashioned virtue that its recurrence *as a theme* is quite easily recognized by its rhythm, even in retrograde form. The repeated note in the "theme" is especially helpful as a device of recognition. Schoenberg also uses the basic series as a theme to help define the beginning of the main sections of the sonata form in this movement, especially at the beginning of the development (m. 95–96: Ex. 149d), where the inversion of the basic series in the cello is clearly recognized by the same distinctive rhythmic pattern heard in the opening statement (cf. Ex. 149a). Similarly, the opening of the recapitulation (m. 165) is clearly heard in Violin I as the return of the opening theme (although transposed to another pitch; see Ex. 149e). The beginning of the coda (or terminal development) is also recognizable rhythmically as a theme. The first half of the basic series returns in the cello (m. 239–40), and its inversion in the violin follows directly.

Schoenberg also takes pains to define the sections of his large structure in this movement. Lacking the tonality that had formerly been an important means of marking off large sections, he uses such resources as changes of dynamics, tone color, or tempo. The "second subject" (m. 62), for instance, is preceded by a section marked *"molto rit."* with a very pronounced change of sound: the first violin plays a cadenzalike figure (*ppp*), accompanied by the three lower instruments playing rapid string tremolos *sul ponticello* very softly. All parts terminate in a "hold" (⌒) just before the entrance of the "second theme" that is played alone and loudly in the cello with normal sound and bowing. The marked contrast of the section preceding the "second subject" has the effect of setting off and making a grand entrance for the latter.

Schoenberg is clearly one of the great ones of twentieth-century music, and through his own music and that of his pupils (especially Webern), his impact on other composers has been enormous. On the other hand, Schoenberg's effect on the public has been less, his music having proved relatively inaccessible to the mass audience. As far as the public is concerned, there is little evidence of that "overestimation" Schoenberg predicted for his music in the second part of the century. But no matter. Schoenberg's formulation of "The Method of Composing with Twelve Tones" was a discovery as important in its own way and context as Einstein's Theory of Relativity, and it opened comparable horizons to a new world and beyond.

Suggested Listening
Pierrot Lunaire: No. 1, 8, 9 (cf. Ex. 151), 15.
Five Orchestral Pieces (Op. 16), No. 3, "Summer Morning by a Lake."
Fourth String Quartet, first movement.
Six Little Piano Pieces (Op. 19).

Suggested Reading
Dika Newlin, *Bruckner, Mahler, Schönberg.* New York: King's Crown Press, 1947.

George Perle, *Serial Composition and Atonality* (Second edition, revised and enlarged). Berkeley: University of California Press, 1968.

Josef Rufer, *Composition with Twelve Notes,* trans. by Humphrey Searle. London: Barrie and Rockliff, 1954 (Third impression revised, 1965).

Arnold Schoenberg, *Style and Idea.* New York: Philosophical Library, 1950. Fifteen fascinating essays by Schoenberg, including the very important lecture (1941) concerning the gradual evolution of "Composition with Twelve Tones."

Arnold Schoenberg Letters, selected and edited by Erwin Stein, trans. by Wilkins and Kaiser. London: Faber and Faber, 1964.

WEBERN

Whatever may be said of Anton Webern's (1883–1945) reception by the public, he clearly exerted a great influence on later composers. Not for nothing were the 1950's labeled "The Age of Webern," and when Stravinsky was converted to serialism, his model was Webern. Webern opened many new vistas of method and sound and, unlike Schoenberg and Berg, he was an atonal composer "without tonal nostalgia" throughout his life. At the same time, it would doubtless have surprised him to be called the patron saint of electronic and "totally organized" music. So much has been attributed to Webern that Stravinsky once said with typical irony: "I would very much like to know if Webern himself knew who Webern was."

Whoever Webern was, there is very little in his lifetime to forecast so huge an influence after his death. His music was received with agonized cries from most of the critics and with complete bewilderment and other reactions by the majority of the public; and he played no major part in the musical life of Vienna. Indeed, Webern could scarcely support himself and his family, and the accounts of his financial plight are reminiscent of Mozart's in his last agonizing years. Webern's intimate relationship with Berg and Schoenberg was cut off prematurely by the latter's emigration to the United States in 1933 and by Berg's early death in 1935. Political events also cast a tragic shadow over the rest of his years. A lifelong conductor, especially of choral music, he gave up conducting and confined himself to teaching after the events of 1933–1934, when Hitler's assumption of power cast its baneful influence over Austria. His music was banned as "cultural Bolshevism" (bitterly ironic since Webern's music was not permitted in Russia until long after his death); and when the Nazis annexed Austria in 1938, all his income was cut off except that from teaching a few pupils. Shy by nature, he lived a life of introspection, revealing himself only to persons like Schoenberg, Berg, a few of his

musical and artistic friends and pupils, and his own family. *See Plate 34A.*
As the final tragedy, he was shot and killed in 1945, because of an
unintentional violation of military curfew, by an American soldier in
Mittersill, Austria.

If Webern's works have had a weighty influence, it is not because of
their extent, which is small indeed. The recording of the entire works (in
itself a tribute) can be played in well under four hours. Since the total
works comprise thirty-one opus numbers (mostly being subdivided into
separate pieces), each work is typically a miniature or a collection of
miniatures with respect to time. About half of his works are composed to
texts (songs, chorus), and most of his music is chamber music or in
chamber-music style.

As might be expected, Webern's music follows the same kind of
development as Schoenberg's: a first period of tonality, then one of free
atonality, then a final twelve-tone period. This was all preceded by his
studies as a musicologist in Vienna (Ph.D., 1906); and his investigation
of Heinrich Isaak (c. 1450–1517) gave him a profound insight into the
contrapuntal methods of the "Netherlanders" that greatly influenced his
own music and probably Schoenberg's too. In any case, his first work was
a *Passacaglia* (1908), apparently modeled on the last movement of
Brahms' Fourth Symphony. His period of free atonality extended from
about 1908 to 1924 (from Op. 3 to Op. 16). The early works of this period
are evidence of an intense, exciting time of experimentation with songs,
chamber music, and the orchestra; and Webern produced some extraordinary sounds, as in the String Quartet pieces of Op. 5 or the orchestral
pieces of Op. 6 and Op. 10. The lines are typically jagged, and the texture
often thick and dissonant (see the "Trakl" songs of Op. 14). Webern also
outdid himself in concentration and abbreviation. If his works as a whole
are miniatures, the instrumental works of Op. 9, 10, and 11 are "mini-miniatures." The individual movements in these works average about forty
seconds each, while one movement lasts only thirteen seconds (Op. 11,
No. 2). Since the logical continuation of such abbreviations would have
been total silence, Webern reversed his direction and returned to longer
settings involving texts (Op. 12–16).

In 1924 (Op. 17) he followed Schoenberg in adopting the twelve-tone
method of composition. Gradually Webern's style became calmer, simpler
in vocal and instrumental sound. The vertical combinations were much
thinned out, almost emaciated, in a kind of pointillistic style in which
Webern even composed the silences (cf. Op. 21, the symphony; see Ex.
155b). The material is presented in a terse, concentrated way, apparently
simplified in sound, but actually complex in conception (see below). His
last work, the Second Cantata (1943), is characteristic. It uses a vocal
polyphony of great complexity, but the vocal parts themselves are relatively easy and singable, and the orchestra simply doubles them.

Within the confines of his total work, Webern managed to deal with a remarkable variety and range of melodic types, dynamics, rhythms, harmonies, tone colors, and forms. It seems almost a paradox that a man who composed miniatures should have expanded the range of so much. Consider the "melodic" aspect of his work. Sometimes Webern's melodies have a real arch of line (Op. 12, No. 1), but more typically in his middle works the lines are jagged and "instrumental," whether for voice or instrument, often based on semitones in octave transposition. Ex. 152

Ex. 152 *

(from Op. 18, No. 2; 1925) shows a line for voice requiring immense agility and containing such intervals as minor ninths and major sevenths (through octave transposition of semitones). The vocal line of this example also has a compass in one direction of two octaves and a fourth (without octave transpositions this passage can be reduced to the compass of a sixth, and the difficult leaps reduced to simple semitones). In his last works, Webern's "melody" of short motives is fragmented and atomized so that it resembles discontinuous points of light or color (for example, the Symphony of Op. 21; the Concerto of Op. 24). Corresponding to the semitone melodic style just mentioned, Webern frequently used a harmony based on semitones. Ex. 153 shows this semitone harmony resulting, through octave transposition, in intervals of a major seventh and augmented octaves.

Ex. 153 *

Webern, Op. 8, No. 2, "Song"

Consider, too, other aspects of his style. Webern occasionally requires *fff,* but he has more generally considered a *pianissimo* composer; and his friends joked that he had invented a new term for the softest possible sound: *pensato,* meaning "thought of." Several rhythmic aspects are worth mentioning: his extensive use of triplets, his exactly notated *rubato* (Op. 7, No. 2), and his syncopations (cf. Ex. 148a).

In his treatment of voice and instrument, Webern seems to use all existing resources, including the extreme registers and virtuoso effects. The strings play *pizzicato* in dozens of ways and combinations (cf. the pieces for String Quartet, Op. 9); they are muted, play *col legno,* or make glassy *ponticello* tremolos or eerie harmonics. The brasses are typically muted. Flutter tonguing (see the Glossary) is a characteristic flute effect. Besides the usual percussion instruments, we hear in Webern's scores the cool sounds of celesta and glockenspiel; and bell-like sounds, even cowbells (Op. 10), remind us of the mountains that Webern loved. Doubtless some of these unusual sonorities resemble the effects of electronic music and inspired its composers.

In his orchestration Webern produces at times a kind of tone-color melody (chords at the opening of Op. 6, No. 4) on the model of Schoenberg's Op. 16. Also characteristic is a pointillistic orchestration in which melody is parceled out among several consecutive instruments. For example, in his arrangement of the "Ricercar" of Bach's *Musical Offering,* Webern breaks the fugue subject (which Bach gives as two phrases divided by a rest) into seven motives played by trombone, horn, trumpet, and harp. (Incidentally, Webern scores the second part of the subject in a *rubato* manner, speeding it up and slowing it down.) It is in his middle period that Webern used the coloristic effects of the instruments most intensely. In his later, pointillistic manner, he took to a cooler color palette, closer to the draftsman's black and white.

Webern's twelve-tone technique departs somewhat from Schoenberg's, the series often being broken into motives of six, four, three, or even two notes. The Concerto for Nine Instruments (Op. 24), for example, uses four "micro-series" of three notes each. Consequently, the textures are often woven out of smaller melodic particles, a method which lends itself to the bare-bones texture and transparent sound of his later pointillism (see the opening of Op. 21 in Ex. 155b).

Moreover, Webern's manner of using the twelve-tone series determines the formal construction to a greater extent than in Schoenberg's music. The constant manipulation of the motives is a perpetual variation, in itself a special formal construction. When segments of the series are used in these various and changing combinations, especially when garbed in the colors of instruments, the effect is kaleidoscopic. In any case, this use of segmented motives was not only a species of perpetual variation, but also a kind of repetition, which in Webern's view was one of the basic formal

principles. Webern's material, it must be admitted, is sometimes wonderfully concealed on repetition. The first movement of the String Trio (Op.
20, 1927) is said to be a rondo, but Stravinsky notes: "The music is
marvelously interesting, but no one could recognize it as a rondo." In his
shortest pieces, the single statement of the material may constitute the
form; and Webern once confessed he had the feeling that when the
twelve notes had all been played, the piece was over. Concerning his
Variations for Orchestra (Op. 30, 1940) Webern wrote Willi Reich
(1941): "Everything in this piece is derived from the two ideas stated in
the first two measures by the double bass and oboe." In themselves, of
course, texts lend an element of formal organization, but even in these
vocal pieces Webern frequently relies additionally on counterpoint. A
relatively simple example is Op. 16, Five Canons on Latin Texts (1924),
not in the twelve-tone technique. The first of these begins as shown in Ex.
154. The clarinet starts, the bass clarinet then imitates strictly by inversion

Ex. 154 *

* By permission of Universal Edition, London, Vienna, Zurich, copyright owner; Theodore
Presser Company, Bryn Mawr, Pa., agent.

(at the third below), and on the next beat, the voice comes in a second
above the original clarinet.

It is instructive to look at two orchestral works of Webern some twenty
years apart, one (Op. 6, 1909) in the early years of free atonality and the
other (Op. 21, 1929) in the pointillistic style of his twelve-tone maturity.
The Six Pieces for Orchestra of Op. 6, dedicated to Schoenberg, is a work
obviously inspired by Schoenberg's Five Pieces for Orchestra; and like
that work, it requires a very large orchestra (revised in 1928 for an
orchestra of regular size).

The fourth piece of Op. 6, set without strings, is especially interesting in
the character of sound of wind and percussion instruments, the clear
separation of melody and harmony, and the intensity of the final measures. Originally labeled "Funeral March," this movement evokes a corre-

sponding mood. It starts with a mysterious and barely audible roll of the bass drum. On this drum roll are superimposed the points of sound from the gong (*tamtam*) and then the deep chime (*tiefes Glockengeläute*). To this *continuum* of sound is added the kettledrums (m. 8). A measure later, chords are played in a declamatory rhythm successively by the flutes, then the muted horns, then the muted trumpets in tone-color melody fashion. Whereupon the E-flat clarinet plays a short melody accompanied by a static but rhythmically declaimed harmony in the muted trombones. The section is tapered off with four measures of percussion heard alone.

Next, a melody of three phrases begins, accompanied by punctuated chords of muted trombones and bass tuba. The opening phrase is stated very, very soft (*ppp*) in the lower register of the alto flute. A second phrase follows in the horn, articulating its first note *sforzando-piano*. The final phrase of the melody (*ppp*) is given to the muted trumpet again in a low register but in longer note values.

Meanwhile the chime and gong have resumed their patterned points of sound, joined by the roll of the small (snare) drum. A measure of rhythmic declamation in the woodwinds and muted horns is followed by the muted trombones and the tuba; and finally, the drum resumes its roll, the crescendo mounts in gong and chime, and the whole orchestra, in declamatory rhythms and intensified dissonant harmony, ends on an overpowering *fff*. The "March" concludes with two measures of the percussion mounting its own crescendo: *f–ff–fff*.

In this movement of Op. 6 there is a clear separation between melodic lines and accompaniment; and the accompaniment has massive chords which, in the final climax, attain full intensity through dissonant harmony and a very large orchestra. In the Symphony of 1928 (Op. 21), Webern has transported us to an entirely different world, fashioned in his pointillistic style and for relatively few instruments: clarinet, bass clarinet, two horns, harp, two violins, viola, cello (but no double bass). The "melody" as such has disappeared; it has been atomized into cells of sound which consist of segments of the basic series (Ex. 155a). These segments are emphasized by expressing them successively in the different tone colors of horn, clarinet, cello, and so on. Ex. 155a shows the series, the instrumentation, and the simplified form of the series. A full harmony is avoided—rather, a single note alone or two notes together are heard in fragmented points of sound, often in different instruments, giving the effect of tone-color melody in isolated tones (but not in chords as in Op. 6 or in Schoenberg's Op. 16). This apparently tenuous framework is held together by what is, in fact, a rigorously controlled manipulation of the series through the strictest contrapuntal means. To be exact: The first movement begins with a complex double canon by inversion. In Ex. 155b, the second line is in canon by inversion with the first line; lines three and

Ex. 155 *

Webern, Op. 21

* By permission of Universal Edition, London, Vienna, Zurich, copyright owner; Theodore Presser Company, Bryn Mawr, Pa., agent.

four form a second canon: line three is the retrograde inversion of the basic series and line four is the retrograde form. *These complex relationships, however, are essentially the composer's business.* What strikes the ear of the audience are successions of fragmented sounds in all their varieties, somehow with their own logic and unity—a perpetual kaleidoscope or variation of small motives ever changing in pitch, rhythm, and tone color.

Suggested Listening

Six Pieces for Orchestra (Op. 6), No. 4, "Funeral March."
Five Canons (Op. 16), No. 1, *"Christus factus est pro nobis."*
Symphony (Op. 21), first movement.

Suggested Reading

Walter Kolneder, *Anton Webern,* trans. by Humphrey Searle. Berkeley: University of California Press, 1968.

Willi Reich (ed.), *The Path to New Music* (Webern's lectures). Bryn Mawr, Penna.: Theodore Presser Company, 1963.

BERG

Anton Webern and Alban Berg (1885–1935) were Schoenberg's most distinguished pupils, yet they differed from each other in their pursuit of atonality and in their success with the public. Webern was completely uncompromising in his devotion to the twelve-tone technique, but Berg permitted himself backward and nostalgic glances to Wagner and Mahler, and even infiltrated the twelve-tone method with certain tonal devices in the interest of expression. Thus Berg quotes the opening of Wagner's *Tristan* in the last pages of his Lyric Suite (1926), the first movement of which has tonal aspects; and in the Violin Concerto (1935) he introduces Austrian dances and folk music and a Bach chorale, and uses the twelve-tone technique itself in ways suggestive of tonality. Consequently, in its organic blend of the old and the new, Berg's music is rather more accessible to audiences than that of either Schoenberg or Webern, and at least two of his major works, the opera *Wozzeck* and the Violin Concerto, have succeeded in entering the international repertory. In admiration of Berg's achievements, Sibelius once remarked that Berg was Schoenberg's best work.

Berg became a pupil of Schoenberg in the same year as Webern (1904), and from this time all three were close personal friends as well as professional colleagues. Berg maintained a voluminous and revealing correspondence with them. He also lectured and wrote in defense of the new ideas and theories. His relatively uneventful life was cut off prematurely at the age of fifty by blood poisoning (1935).

Berg was a far from prolific composer, but, unlike Webern's "miniatures," his works were on a traditional scale of size. Among them were *Wozzeck* (finished 1921), the Chamber Concerto (1925), the Lyric Suite for string quartet (1926), the Violin Concerto (1935, his last finished work), and the opera *Lulu.* The latter, not quite finished at the time of his death, is generally performed today in two acts and a final scene from the third act.

Berg possessed a lyric and dramatic gift of the first order. This gift was obvious enough in his stage work, but it was also a factor in some of his instrumental works. The Violin Concerto, for instance, is a kind of drama without words; and its form and certain of its details are determined by the fact that it was intended as a portrait of the life and death of a young girl (as explained below). The close relation between technique and the dramatic delineation of character and situation is explained by Berg himself in a lecture on *Wozzeck* (1929) in which he speaks of portraying folklike elements "with an easily recognizable primitive quality that is adaptable even within atonal harmony." Berg then goes on to cite, as particulars, harmonies in thirds and fourths, referring specifically to Marie's lullaby (with its chords constructed by intervals of fourths), melodies using the whole-tone scale and the perfect fourth, and also polytonality. Similarly, the voice and instruments are used with dramatic effect, and the orchestration at the end of the murder scene in *Wozzeck* (Act III, Scene 2) is a prime example (see below). Berg, like Webern and Schoenberg, had a highly developed ear for purely instrumental sonorities. The third movement of the Lyric Suite (entitled *allegro mysterioso*) is a drama of the wispy rushing of notes played *ponticello, pizzicato,* and *col legno,* among other devices; and if Bartók did not know the Lyric Suite when he wrote his Fourth String Quartet (see Chapter 29) two years later, Berg surely anticipated him.

Berg's *Wozzeck* (finished 1921, first performed 1924) is one of the most important operas of recent times. Based on a play by Georg Buchner (d. 1837), it is in three acts, each with five scenes connected by orchestral interludes (an idea derived from Debussy's *Pelleas and Melisande*). It concerns the tragedy of a poor soldier, Franz Wozzeck. His life is made miserable by his superior officer, by a sadistic doctor for whom he works, and by his mistress, Marie, by whom he has a child and who is faithless to him. In brooding despair, Wozzeck kills her and is himself drowned while searching for the knife with which he committed the crime.

An extremely effective score, it combines, in a highly dissonant idiom, elements of free atonality and other tonal means essential to the realization of the dramatic moment. Similarly, for dramatic ends Berg occasionally employs the *Sprechstimme* (modeled on Schoenberg's *Pierrot Lunaire*). The orchestra is a most powerful tool, following the lead of Wagner and Schoenberg. Throughout the murder scene (Act III, Scene 2), Berg uses a pedal tone, and as Marie dies, this tone is hushed to a single sound, very softly, then brought gradually to a frightening *fff* through the whole orchestra in unisons and octaves.

In its organization, *Wozzeck* is tightly constructed around the forms of instrumental music, significantly derived from the past. The five scenes of Act II, for example, comprise a sonata movement, a fantasy and fugue, largo, scherzo, and rondo. Each of the scenes in the other acts has its own distinctive form. Berg, however, regarded this unusual operatic construction as his private business as a composer. He maintained that others should not be aware of it, but only of "the idea of his opera, which transcends the individual fate of Wozzeck. And in this I believe I have been successful."

The Violin Concerto is an exceptionally good example of a novel construction in a concerto, its unusual form being explained by the circumstances of its origin. It was conceived as a Requiem to Berg's young friend Manon Gropius (Frau Mahler's daughter by a second marriage), whose tragic death at eighteen had greatly shocked Berg. The concerto is inscribed "To the memory of an angel," and the angel is symbolized by the solo violin part.

There are two main parts to the concerto, and each of these is divided into two sections: Part I is concerned with the character of Manon Gropius; it opens with an *andante,* which portrays the youthful charm of the young girl, and continues with a scherzolike *allegretto,* presumably reflecting her exuberance and joy of life. Part II begins with an *allegro,* which enunciates the catastrophe of her death, and consists of an elaborate and free cadenza accompanied by the orchestra. Then there follows a concluding *adagio,* which reconciles her death through religious faith, centering musically on a Bach chorale tune, the unspoken message of whose text begins: "It is enough! Lord, when it pleases you, free me from this earthly frame."

This is not a conventional concerto in form or idiom, although virtuoso demands are made on the soloist and on the orchestra. Its high degree of expressive individuality embraces both tonal and twelve-tone elements. The latter are formulated in the basic series (Ex. 156a), heard first on the entrance of the solo violin (m. 15); the tonal elements depend on waltz-like rhythms, on a Carinthian folk song, and on the Bach chorale in Bach's harmonization. Even the basic series is set out in the form of superimposed thirds which suggest broken major and minor triads (Ex. 156a). Moreover, the last four notes of the series are related by whole tones, which—by accident or design—are in the same relationship as the opening of the Bach chorale (cf. Ex. 156a and b). Perhaps the most eloquent moment of the concerto occurs at the opening of the final

Ex. 156 *

adagio, where the solo violin, in its lowest and richest register, in effect intones a prayer—the chorale and its implied message of sorrowful resignation: "It is enough! Lord. . . ."

This masterpiece, a memorial to Manon Gropius, was to be Berg's own Requiem. He died a few months after its completion.

Suggested Listening
Wozzeck (in whole or part).
Violin Concerto.

Suggested Reading
Willi Reich, *The Life and Works of Alban Berg,* trans. by C. Cardew. London: Thames and Hudson, 1965.

28. *Stravinsky. His Russian Background and Early Works. Neoclassicism in France. Neoclassic and Serial Works.*

IGOR STRAVINSKY (b. 1882), one of the greatest masters of the twentieth century, burst upon the international scene with his ballets on subjects and folk tunes drawn from his native Russia. An exile after the Soviet Revolution and a resident of France from 1920 to 1939, Stravinsky gravitated after 1920 toward a more "classic" style, becoming the most celebrated of the Neoclassicists through a large number of works of great variety and individuality. In 1940 Stravinsky settled in the United States, and for a dozen years thereafter the majority of his compositions continued to be basically Neoclassic in conception. After 1952 Stravinsky showed an increasing interest in the serial technique developed by Schoenberg and especially Webern. Thus, in the course of his long life, Stravinsky has embraced at least three main styles, confounding those who had previously considered two of them—Neoclassicism and atonality —to be mutually exclusive and contradictory.

Although clearly a phenomenon from his earliest years, Stravinsky was not a phenomenon isolated from tradition or events. Unlike Schoenberg, however, Stravinsky was not related at all to the tradition or musical lineage of Wagner, whose music he disliked; rather he was linked to the Russian nationalists—Borodin, Mussorgsky, and Rimsky-Korsakov. It was with the last that Stravinsky studied briefly (1907–1908) just before Rimsky's death; and from him the young Stravinsky received the legacy of the operatic tradition of Glinka, Russian folk music and legend, Russian Orientalism, and brilliant orchestration in the tradition of Berlioz. In later life, Stravinsky tended to react against the tradition of the nationalists, aligning himself with the tradition of Tchaikovsky.

Rimsky-Korsakov had a strong influence on a number of pupils, some of whom were prominent on the Russian musical scene in Stravinsky's youth. One was the symphonist Alexander Glazounov (1865–1936). Other figures were Ipolitov-Ivanov (1859–1935) and Reinhold Glière (1875–1956), both of whom wrote symphonies and operas in a style stemming from Rimsky-Korsakov. Another tradition, that of Tchaikovsky, continued in the able works of the celebrated pianist and composer Sergei Rachmaninov (1873–1943), whose symphonies and particularly piano concertos became world famous.

Alexander Scriabin (1872–1915) was another imposing figure of the Russia of the young Stravinsky. A curious and isolated figure, Scriabin stands somewhat apart from those just mentioned. His early work exhibits the influence of Chopin, but Wagner is clearly the central factor in his mature music, which explains why Stravinsky detested it. If anything, Scriabin goes beyond Wagner in his chromatic usage, sometimes carrying his music to the threshold of atonality and polytonality. Like Schoenberg, Scriabin experiments with chords of superimposed fourths; and one special chord of this kind, the so-called "mystic chord" (Ex. 157), fur-

Ex. 157

nished the harmonic foundation of his *Prometheus: The Poem of Fire,* a symphonic work (Op. 60, 1910). In this composition, Scriabin, inspired by Wagner and Mahler, strives for a kind of "union of the arts." Here, too, Scriabin exhibits a pronounced interest in mystical philosophy and religion, and he requires a "union" of diverse performing forces. Besides the orchestra, the piano has a prominent part, there is a chorus of mixed voices at the end, and—a true innovation—there is a special color keyboard to project changing colors of the spectrum, the precise colors and intensities being geared to the emotional situation. (It is a moot point whether the color keyboard ever took part in an actual performance.) Among Scriabin's other works are *The Poem of Ecstasy* (an earlier symphonic piece, 1908) and a large number of piano pieces, including ten sonatas. Scriabin was an innovator without real followers. If anything, he repelled composers, being a figure against whom the anti-Wagnerians (like Stravinsky) reacted. However, it is true that experiments in chord construction and free atonality, similar to those of Scriabin, were carried to a systematic conclusion by Schoenberg.

The true innovator who emerged from Russia in the early twentieth century was, of course, Igor Stravinsky himself. Stravinsky's early work is connected mainly with the Ballet Russe in Paris under the remarkable impresario Serge Diaghilev (1872–1929). The first of these ballets was *The Firebird* (1910), a fairy tale from Russian folklore which juxtaposes two types of magic beings: the Firebird, who embodies good; and the demon Kastchei, who embodies evil. Through the Firebird, the young prince of the fairy tale destroys Kastchei and wins a beautiful princess. *The Firebird* ballet was conceived under the influence of Rimsky-Korsakov and is strikingly original in its orchestration. It made Stravinsky an immediate reputation.

In the following year, the ballet *Petrushka* appeared, and it too created a sensation. *Petrushka* was full of tunes and dances, new and exciting in its explosive and irregular rhythms and sonorities; and its dissonant style derived partly from the use of polytonality (in Ex. 158 two keys, C and F

Ex. 158 *

sharp, are used simultaneously). Another feature is the considerable role Stravinsky conceived for the piano in the orchestration. Like *The Firebird*, *Petrushka* draws on Russian folk material. The central theme of the ballet concerns an old magician and his puppet show, which takes place in the midst of the lively events of the Shrovetide Fair in St. Petersburg during the 1830's. The three puppet characters—Petrushka (i.e., Pierrot), the Ballerina, and the Moor—act out a love triangle; and Stravinsky, besides vividly portraying the gay confusion and happenings of the fair, manages to endow the puppets with a true-to-life humanity. Consequently the audience is moved by the pathos of the ugly Petrushka, his hopeless love for the Ballerina, and his death by the sword of the Moor.

In 1913 the first performance of *The Rite of Spring* (subtitled *Scenes of Pagan Russia*) made Stravinsky famous. Perhaps more than any other, this work became the symbol of "modern" music. This ballet was shocking not so much in its subject as in the manner of staging and especially in its musical setting. The jarring dissonance, savage rhythms, changing meters and accents, and astounding orchestral effects set the members of the audience literally at each other's throats, and resulted in a riot. Musicians, especially of the older generation, found it hard going. Even Debussy had some doubts and allowed himself this slightly malicious comment: *"The Rite of Spring* is an extraordinarily savage affair. . . . it's primitive music with every modern convenience."

The subject itself was a species of musical primitivism, a counterpart of Picasso's cubism and the then-current interest in African art. *The Rite* is in two parts—"The Adoration of the Earth" and "The Sacrifice"—based on a theme which Stravinsky described as follows: "I saw in imagination a solemn pagan rite: wise elders, seated in a circle, watching a young girl dance herself to death. They were sacrificing her to propitiate the god of spring."

From the opening high note in the bassoon to the final chord at the end, *The Rite* is one masterly and innovative use of rhythm and of the orchestra (the largest for which he ever wrote), with special attention to the percussions. After the Introduction, the first real dance—"Auguries of Spring" (Dance of the Young Girls)—exhibits at once characteristic Stravinsky traits: an irregular accent of the rhythm and a polytonality of the harmony, in this case, two chords on roots a semitone apart (E flat

Ex. 159 *

and F flat). Ex. 159a shows the rhythmic pattern; Ex. 159b shows the polytonal chord of the harmony.

In 1914 Stravinsky finished his short three-act opera *The Nightingale.* Begun in 1908, when Stravinsky was still under the influence of Rimsky-Korsakov, it is a musical fairy tale based on a story by Hans Christian Andersen. *The Nightingale* was completed in Switzerland, where Stravinsky and his family made their headquarters during World War I. Under the changed economic conditions imposed by the war and its aftermath, Stravinsky composed several works on a much smaller scale: *The Soldier's Tale* of 1918, for narrator and seven players (one of the players, the percussionist, manages six percussion instruments); and later in the same year, *Ragtime* for eleven instruments, a piece which continued to explore the new jazz idiom first attempted by Stravinsky in the piece "Ragtime" in *The Soldier's Tale.* During his stay in Switzerland (1914–1920) and for a short time afterward, Stravinsky continued to compose on Russian subjects, examples being *The Wedding,* a cantata in four choreographic scenes (finished in short score, 1917; orchestration, 1923); and *Mavra,* his comic opera of 1922. However, Stravinsky's style was changing, and these were the last works on Russian subjects and the end of his "Russian" period.

STRAVINSKY AND NEOCLASSICISM

In 1920 Stravinsky and his family moved to France, although he did not settle in Paris until 1934 (the year he became a French citizen). Stravinsky's new style had marked affinities to classic ideals, and by the time of the Wind Octet (1923) he had clearly embarked on a *Neoclassic* style, a style that enjoyed a pronounced vogue in France during the 1920's and 1930's and even longer. Neoclassicism was, in fact, one of the two principal styles of European composition that were crystallizing in the early 1920's. These styles were quite different: In Vienna, Schoenberg was codifying the complexities of the twelve chromatic tones into a general twelve-tone "method" of composition (see Chapter 27); in France, Stravinsky and others gravitated toward a Neoclassicism that stressed simplicity and clarity of line and structure, favoring Classical subjects and forms reminiscent of the eighteenth century (for another important style, embodying folk-song elements, see Bartók, Chapter 29). Emotionally matter-of-fact and anti-Romantic, Neoclassicism was opposed to the programatic tone poems of Strauss and the vague atmosphere of Debussy's Impressionism. The lines and harmonies were generally diatonic and tonal, not chromatic and atonal as in Schoenberg. This modern diatonic style, sometimes called *pandiatonic* (i.e., all diatonic), is basically tonal without necessarily using the functional harmony of traditional tonal music. Sometimes not one, but two or even more keys were used—that is, bitonality or polytonality, respectively (see Ex. 158). The followers of Neoclassicism also favored economy of means in instrumentation, and the gigantic orchestra characteristic of Strauss or Mahler was replaced typically by a chamber music group or by a small orchestra, sometimes for reasons of economic necessity (as was the case with Stravinsky's *The Soldier's Tale*). Neoclassic forms were generally those of the "absolute" music favored in the Classic period. However, Neoclassicism was not merely a slavish imitation of the Classics. It was rather a matter of generalized notions of Classic ideals being translated by an artist into an organic, personal style of his own. One would never mistake Stravinsky's Neoclassic pieces for Bach or Mozart any more than one would confuse Picasso's work with the African art that inspired him at one time.

The simplified style of Neoclassicism had already begun in France with Satie, and under the guidance of Cocteau, it took the form of a reaction to Impressionism. It turned away from descriptive music and from Romanticism in general in favor of Classical simplicity and formal clarity (for Satie and Cocteau, see Chapter 25). The Neoclassicists also turned to the past for inspiration, taking as their models Mozart and J. S. Bach (hence another term: *Neobaroque*). A good example of "back-to-Bach" is Arthur Honegger, one of the group called "The Six" (see Chapter 31). In 1920 he wrote: "I attach great importance to the architecture of music and would not like to see it sacrificed to considerations of a literary or pictorial order. . . . My great model is J. S. Bach." A more general statement, clearly summarizing the aims of numerous contemporaries, was made in the same year by Albert Roussel (1869–1937): "The tendencies of contemporary music indicate a return to clearer, sharper lines, more precise rhythms, a style more horizontal than vertical; to a certain brutality at times in the means of expression—in contrast with the subtle elegance and vaporous atmosphere of the preceding period; to a more attentive and sympathetic attitude toward the robust frankness of a Bach or Handel; in short, a return, in spite of appearance and with a freer though still somewhat hesitating language, to the traditions of the Classics."[1] Roussel's statement is that of a Classicist, although he began as an imitator of Impressionism.

STRAVINSKY'S NEOCLASSIC WORKS

Stravinsky's inclination toward Neoclassicism became apparent in the *subject* of his ballet *Pulcinella* (1920), inspired by the music of Pergolesi,

[1] The Honegger quotation is taken from a letter to the music critic of *La Victoire* (September 1920). The Roussel statement is quoted in a lecture by Nadia Boulanger printed in the *Rice Institute Pamphlet* (April 1926), pp. 151–52.

literally thrust on Stravinsky by Diaghilev. But it was really with the Wind Octet (1923) that Stravinsky's Neoclassic *style* was inaugurated, showing a marked break with *The Rite of Spring* ten years earlier. Compared to the large orchestra of the latter and its varied tone colors, the Octet is reduced to the chamber-music proportions of eight solo instruments, and the tone color is limited to the dry and brilliant sonorities of the winds. In *The Rite of Spring,* the music is by turns rhythmically explosive, uninhibited in dissonance, savage in impact, and unfamiliar and even disturbing in its pagan theme. In the Octet all this is replaced by reverence for order, objective calm, and forms inspired by eighteenth-century models—forms notable for clarity and conciseness. In essence, Stravinsky returned to the eighteenth-century sonata and its various tonal and formal manifestations. The first movement opens with an introductory "Sinfonia" followed by a sonata form, the end of which is cast as a brilliant canon (see Ex. 160; for the meter changes and polyrhythm of this example, see p. 442). Stravinsky himself wrote of the Octet: "Composition, structure and form here are all in the line of the eighteenth-century

Ex. 160 *

* Copyright 1942 by Edition Russe de Musique. Revised version copyright 1952 by Boosey & Hawkes, Inc. Used by permission.

masters. . . . The allegro is a typical two-theme sonata allegro in the key of E-flat." The second movement of the Octet is a theme and variations—Stravinsky's first use of the variation form—on a singularly static subject. The final part of the variations calls on another formal device typical of the eighteenth century: the fugato. The third and last movement opens with an inventionlike section. However, these calculated structures and the seemingly abstract counterpoint do not prevent Stravinsky from establishing a mood—the first movement, for example, is one of nonchalant cheerfulness.

From the time of the Octet (1923) through *The Rake's Progress* (1951), a Neoclassic strain is central to a substantial number of Stravinsky's compositions. During these years, a new restraint, simplicity, and clarity are apparent in style and form. The Octet was followed by other "abstract" forms of traditional instrumental music—among them, the Piano Concerto (1924), the Piano Sonata (1924), the Violin Concerto (1931), the "Dumbarton Oaks" Concerto for sixteen stringed instruments (1938; clearly modeled on Bach's "Brandenburg" Concertos), the Symphony in C major (1940), and the Symphony in Three Movements (1945). A number of the ballets and works with texts are inspired by subjects from antiquity: *Oedipus Rex* (*King Oedipus*), an opera-oratorio derived from the play by Sophocles; the ballets *Apollon Musagète* (1928) and *Orpheus* (1947; *see Plate 34B*); and *Persephone* (1934), a stage melodrama with French text by André Gide. On the other hand, the plot of the opera *The Rake's Progress* is based on eighteenth-century scenes from Hogarth (libretto by W. H. Auden and Chester Kallman), and is realized musically in arias and recitatives, choruses, and ensembles "in the line of the classical tradition," as Stravinsky tells us. Then there are other works that do not fall into any of these categories: *The Circus Polka* (for young elephants of the Barnum and Bailey Circus, 1942), *The Ebony Concerto* (for Woody Herman's jazz band, 1946), and *The Card Party* (1936), a ballet "in three deals." Sacred texts are central to the *Symphony of Psalms* (1930; revised 1948) and the Mass (1948).

The *Symphony of Psalms* is one of Stravinsky's most impressive pieces. Commissioned by Sergei Koussevitzsky to celebrate the fiftieth anniversary of the founding of the Boston Symphony Orchestra, this remarkable work consists of three movements, each being a setting of a psalm for chorus and orchestra. Stravinsky uses the Latin version of the Vulgate for his texts:

I., from Psalm 38, begins *"Exaudi orationem meam"* ("Hear my prayer") and functions something like a prelude to the second movement.

II. is set as a double fugue on texts from Psalm 39, beginning *"Expectans, expectavi Dominum"* ("I wait patiently for the Lord").

III. uses all of Psalm 150, which begins *"Laudate Dominum"* ("Praise the Lord").

These settings are distinguished by a number of notable features. One is the remarkable sonority of the orchestra and chorus—consider the sound of the opening chord or the closing coda (see pp. 442–3 for comments on Stravinsky's orchestration). For another thing, Stravinsky evidently wished to achieve a high degree of counterpoint in the "symphony," and he placed the chorus and orchestra on an equal contrapuntal footing: in the double fugue of the second movement the first fugue subject is developed by the orchestra; then the second fugue subject is worked out by the chorus while the first subject continues in the orchestra. The third movement is distinguished by its sonorities, syncopations, wonderfully compulsive rhythm, and by an exceptionally impressive coda, $\frac{3}{2}$, *"Laudate Eum in cymbalis bene sonantibus"* ("Praise Him upon the high sounding cymbals"). This coda (see Ex. 161), one of the most remarkable

Ex. 161 *

passages in all Stravinsky's works, sounds its hypnotic and compelling theme again and again, with varied effect, over the bell-tolling *ostinato* figure in the bass. The ending adds the final touch to the aura of austere grandeur characteristic of this whole extraordinary work.

The *Symphony of Psalms* is a work of great impact, but it is detached emotionally in a way characteristic of Stravinsky, who does not believe that music is "expressive." It is the listener's business to respond in his own way; Stravinsky will not point out or dictate an emotional experience to him. In the *Symphony of Psalms,* Latin, the most universal of languages, is used to carry the sentiment of the words impersonally, not to impress the listener with Stravinsky's "expression" of the text through music. This is a detail typical of his attitude. According to Ansermet, "As Stravinsky . . . does not make of his music an act of self-expression . . . the *Symphony of Psalms* expresses the religiosity of others . . . but it must be agreed that the expression of this religiosity is itself absolutely authentic." [2] This detached emotional calm and the general qualities of proportion, clarity, and order anchor Stravinsky securely to Neoclassicism.

STRAVINSKY—PERFORMER, AUTHOR, COMPOSER

Stravinsky is a man of many parts and several countries. *See Plate 31A.* Born in Russia, he moved to France and became a French citizen. Later still, he settled in Hollywood (1940) and became an American citizen (1945). Hailed as a composer of genius before he was thirty, Stravinsky also exhibited other talents as a pianist, conductor, and author after he was forty. In the 1920's he began to play and conduct his works in public; and there has been hardly any composer since Wagner as expansive in print. His autobiography, *Chroniques de ma vie,* was published in two volumes in Paris (1935–1936), and it was translated as *An Autobiography* (1936; reprinted 1958; paperback, 1962). His Charles Eliot Norton lectures at Harvard (1939–1940) were given and published first in French (1942), and then published in English as *Poetics of Music* (1947). Later, after Stravinsky met Robert Craft (1948), who became his alter ego and assistant conductor, the two of them authored five volumes (to date) of "conversations" based on a question-and-answer format suggested by Craft: *Conversations with Igor Stravinsky* (1959); *Memories and Commentaries* (1960); *Expositions and Developments* (1962); *Dialogues and a Diary* (1963); *Themes and Episodes* (1966). The *Autobiography* and the *Poetics,* says Stravinsky, "are much less *like* me, in all my faults, than my conversations." In any case, Stravinsky's writings (or, more properly, those of "Craft-Igor"—to use Virgil Thomson's phrase) contain many rewarding insights presented with characteristic precision and wit, and sometimes with dogma or even a trace of malice.

Until the death of Schoenberg in 1951, he and Stravinsky were regarded by their followers, if not by themselves, as the irresistible twelve-tone force and the immovable Neoclassic object. And it is both strange and sad that these two great composers lived in Los Angeles within a few miles of each other for more than ten years (1940–1951) without meeting. Thus it was generally assumed that never the twain would meet, spiritually or otherwise, in this world or any other. However, this assumption reckoned without Stravinsky's curiosity, demonstrated capacity for change, or possibly his need of new resources. Then, too, there was Robert Craft, who after 1948 was a member of Stravinsky's household and a devoted admirer of the music of Schoenberg and especially Webern. However the change came about—and it was surely no greater than others that had taken place earlier between *The Rite of Spring* and the Octet—one can observe a new interest in counterpoint and especially in the use of serial processes, at least by the time of the Septet (1954).

[2] Ernest Ansermet, quoted in E. W. White, *Stravinsky* (Berkeley: University of California Press, 1966), p. 327.

At first the tone series is employed tentatively: in the Septet the serial technique is used only in the third movement (*Gigue*), and the tone series itself uses only eight of the twelve tones. The same tentative use of serial technique marks *Canticum sacrum* (*Sacred Song,* for Venice in honor of its patron Saint Mark, 1956) and the plotless ballet *Agon* for twelve dancers, consisting of twelve "abstract" dances (four groups of three dances each, punctuated by a prelude and two interludes, 1957). In the last two works, the music has a diatonic, tonal basis at the beginning and at the end, using chromaticism and serialism in the middle.

Threni (*Lamentations of the Prophet Jeremiah,* 1958) is the first work based entirely on the twelve-tone serial technique. In Stravinsky's serial music, the model is primarily Webern, canon is a typical contrapuntal device, and the music becomes characteristically more terse and concentrated. In 1957 Stravinsky said: "Nowadays my music is more compact. Certain parts of *Agon,* for instance, contain three times as much music, by the clock, as many of my earlier works." [3] More recent serial works include *The Flood* (a dance-drama first performed on television, 1962), *Abraham and Isaac* (a sacred ballad on a Hebrew text, 1963), *Variations* (in memory of Aldous Huxley, 1964), and *Requiem Canticles* (1966). With the possible exception of *Agon,* Stravinsky's serial works have been received by the general public with a degree of bewilderment similar to that accorded the early Neoclassic works.

STRAVINSKY'S STYLE

While it is impossible to discuss the style of Stravinsky's works as a whole within a manageable space, it may be useful to note certain general characteristics.

A typical Stravinsky melody is diatonic, limited in range, and often

Ex. 162 *

* Copyright 1921 by Edition Russe de Musique (Russischer Musikverlag). Copyright assigned 1947 to Boosey & Hawkes, Inc., for all countries. Reprinted by permission of Boosey & Hawkes, Inc.

[3] Quoted by Virgil Thomson in *The New York Review of Books* (Dec. 15, 1966), p. 3.

employs the interval of a third, in numerous cases alternating minor third and major third. Frequently repetitive in melodic pattern, a typical melody will as often seek a flexible rhythm to prevent a repetitive pattern from becoming static or monotonous. The opening of *The Rite of Spring* is a case in point (Ex. 162). Here the intervals of major and minor thirds predominate in the melody, the range is small, and the melodic pattern repeats with different rhythmic inflection emphasized by the *fermatas,* the meter change, and the phrasing. In Stravinsky, the literal repetition at the same pitch of a melodic fragment or figuration is more characteristic than the sequential repetition (that is, at different pitch) of motives or figurations, as is so common in earlier music. To cite the kinds of melodies just mentioned is not to suggest that Stravinsky did not use others—among them, catchy folk tunes (as in *Petrushka*), melodies of broken chords, those using larger intervals (such as sevenths or ninths), melodies which are more rhythmic than melodic, and figurations of rapid runs and arpeggios.

Like many composers in the twentieth century, Stravinsky has sought a flexible rhythmic style to avoid the so-called "tyranny of the bar line"—a tyranny that consists of a strong pulse at regular intervals of time (for example, every second, third, or fourth beat). An outward sign of Stravinsky's quest for flexibility is the frequent change of time signature. This may take the form of different time signatures used in succession (including such unconventional meters as $\frac{5}{4}$, $\frac{7}{16}$, and so on) to interrupt the regular recurrence of the strong pulse. Sometimes the same time unit of beat is retained, sometimes not. For instance, in successive measures marked $\frac{3}{4}$, $\frac{4}{4}$, and $\frac{7}{4}$, the strong pulse comes after the third, fourth, and seventh quarter note; there is no regular recurrence of strong pulse, but the quarter-note beat is common to all measures. However, the length of the beat itself may change. In successive measures marked $\frac{3}{16}$, $\frac{2}{8}$, and $\frac{5}{4}$, (as in a passage in the last movement of *The Rite of Spring*), not only is there no regular recurrence of strong pulse, but the time unit of beat changes successively from the sixteenth note to the eighth to the quarter. Changing the meter is one way to effect a flexible and irregular strong pulse. Another method is not to change the meter but to achieve irregularity of strong pulse by means of accent marks (Ex. 159).

Not being committed to regularity of strong pulse, Stravinsky is free to use an unexpected pulse or even a rest for explosive force or dramatic effect. In the instrumental opening of the *Symphony of Psalms,* for example, the distinctive and explosive initial chord is isolated by rests and, after interludes of sixteenth-note figuration, is repeated several times at irregular intervals, with marked effect.

In contrapuntal music Stravinsky may combine two or more lines, each of which is in a different meter or rhythmic pattern—in short, a *polyrhythm*. Such combinations take a number of forms—among them, two lines, each irregular in meter, may be combined; or, as in Ex. 160 (the end of the first movement of the Octet), one part of a regularly recurring pulse (the harmony of the lower parts in this case) may be combined with others of irregular pulse (here, the upper parts). In Ex. 160 the eight parts of the score are reduced to three for purposes of simplicity. The lowest part, of which only the rhythmic pattern is shown, represents the basic four-part harmony (two bassoons and two trombones). The melodic interest is contained in the brilliant canon between the trumpet and the flute. The barring and changing meters are fundamentally determined by the strong pulse required by the trumpet part which begins the canon; the flute part, which imitates the trumpet, simply accommodates itself to the trumpet part to simplify problems of ensemble. Against this canon, the players of the four-part harmony, indicated simply as a rhythm, play every other eighth note, and these parts are heard and could be written in $\frac{2}{4}$. (Like the flute part, they accommodate themselves to the barring of the trumpet part for purposes of ensemble.) The steady uniform rhythm of the harmony is a contrast to the flexible and deviating rhythm of the parts in canon. It is a remarkable study in polyrhythm, and the shifting of the rhythms, marching inevitably to the close, is ingenious and fascinating.

The explosive vitality and unpredictability of rhythm is one of the most exciting aspects of Stravinsky's music. Its complexity created some confusion at first—and not only for the audience. A number of musicians and ballet dancers had some difficulty mastering the intricacies of Stravinsky's rhythms on their first encounters with this novel music.

Until the advent of his serial music, written after 1952, Stravinsky's harmony was essentially tonal and diatonic. It was also relatively dissonant. Dissonance was sometimes achieved by polytonality, which generates considerable tension, typically involving chords or lines based on keys a semitone or tritone apart (see Ex. 159b and Ex. 158, respectively). Sometimes melodic lines are duplicated at a dissonant interval such as the seventh or second. Sometimes a clear chord is deliberately obscured by a dissonant note or notes.

The sound of Stravinsky's chords, however, often depends as much on the spacing or instrumentation of the component tones as on the actual harmonies themselves. Consider the E minor chord with which the *Symphony of Psalms* begins. Concerning another chord, Stravinsky once remarked: "How happy I was when I discovered that chord." In this case, Stravinsky was talking about a D major chord, and of course he was not saying that he had discovered the D major chord, but that he had found a spacing and sonority that gave the chord a unique sound. Similarly, the opening chord of the *Symphony of Psalms* has a unique sound because of spacing and instrumentation.

Two special devices of counterpoint are favorites of Stravinsky: the canon (especially in serial music) and the *ostinato* (see Ex. 161, at end of the *Symphony of Psalms*). The 'latter is in accord with Stravinsky's fondness for repeated melodic patterns, as explained above.

Stravinsky has always been a virtuoso orchestrator, and he has contributed much to the use of instruments both in orchestral combination and in the use of individual instruments. His early ballets demonstrated a virtuoso command of the large orchestra (over one hundred players in *The Rite of Spring*), and many of the instruments were used in novel ways (cf. the use of the high register of the bassoon in the opening of *The Rite,* shown in Ex. 162). Later works rarely used the full symphony orchestra, but the combinations of instruments and the use of particular instruments were almost always novel in effect. *The Soldier's Tale* makes a marked contrast to *The Rite*. The former has seven soloists: violin, double bass, clarinet, bassoon, cornet, trombone, and a percussionist who manages six percussion instruments. The "scratchy" way the violin is used is typical of Stravinsky's unconventional use of an instrument (though completely justified by the context). The use of percussion in this piece is also typical of his interest in percussion instruments and in a percussive style in general. Almost from the beginning, Stravinsky's orchestration has tended toward a dry, percussive, brilliant style rather than the lush orchestration typical of Romantic music. As part of this tendency, Stravinsky frequently introduces the piano into the orchestra, where it functions as a kind of percussion instrument; he does this, for instance, in *Petrushka,* the *Symphony of Psalms* (two pianos), and *The Wedding,* the latter being scored entirely for percussion instruments, including four pianos.

Another feature of Stravinsky's scores is a tendency to minimize the conventional dominance and expressive role of the strings, or to use them dryly or percussively. By the same token, the winds are emphasized more to achieve a dry and brilliant sonority. Sometimes no strings are used at all; sometimes the string parts are restricted: no violins or violas are used in the *Symphony of Psalms,* presumably to achieve a certain austerity or aloofness of tone.

A hallmark of Stravinsky's scoring is a clear texture and a bright sonority—"one could see through it with one's ears," said Diaghilev. In line with this clarity, Stravinsky may use instruments of different timbre to individualize the voice parts of chords.

Stravinsky, the most celebrated composer of modern times, is an old master who is always young at heart. His work, extending over more than sixty years of public performance, embraces an immense variety of musical forms and styles that reflect not merely changes of environment, but also his sympathy with the new and with the ideas of the young, his awareness of change, and his sensitivity to basic values. The "primitive" style of *The Rite of Spring* (1913) was succeeded quite naturally by the Neoclassicism emanating from Paris in the 1920's. In the 1950's Stravinsky's interest in the serial music *à la* Anton Webern represents less a faddish "Anton-olatry" than a desire to explore every basic resource. It is significant that Stravinsky, long vilified in the Soviet Union, finally accepted an invitation to visit Russia in 1962 on the occasion of his eightieth birthday, not because of "nostalgia" but because of "evidence I have received of a genuine desire or need for me by the younger generation of Soviet musicians."

For considerably more than half a century Stravinsky has been a recognized master who has turned out work after work, in each of which he achieves a uniqueness of style and solves a problem to which he seldom returns. This variety and change are very confusing to those devoted to tradition; and consequently each of Stravinsky's new works is viewed with alarm by those who have just accustomed themselves to his earlier style. As Stravinsky says: "On the next occasion, I do something different, and that bewilders them." The truth is, of course, that Stravinsky is simply being himself, and like every great artist, his style changes, as he does, from work to work. In any case, no matter how bewildering Stravinsky's changes may have been, no one has ever denied his consummate craftsmanship, his deep respect for the culture of the past and present, or his extraordinary impact on the music of the present day.

Suggested Listening

The Rite of Spring, especially "Introduction," "Dance of the Young Girls" and "Sacrificial Dance (The Chosen Victim)."

Octet for Wind Instruments.

Symphony of Psalms.

Agon.

Suggested Reading

Robert Siohan, *Stravinsky,* trans. by E. W. White. London: John Calder and Boyar, Ltd., 1965.

Roman Vlad, *Stravinsky,* trans. by F. and A. Fuller (Second edition). London and New York: Oxford University Press, 1967.

Eric Walter White, *Stravinsky.* Berkeley and Los Angeles: University of California Press, 1966.

For Stravinsky's own writings, including his *Autobiography, Poetics,* and various "Conversations," see above, p. 439.

29. Bartók and the Folk-Music Idiom.
Hindemith and Neoclassicism.

BARTÓK

UNLIKE STRAVINSKY, Béla Bartók (1881–1945) was brought up in the German tradition of Brahms, Wagner, Liszt, and Strauss. Early in the twentieth century, a new Hungarian nationalism in politics and art turned many young artists away from the dominant German influence; and Bartók, with his co-worker Zoltán Kodály (1882–1967), sought out the peasant music of Hungary for musical and nationalistic inspiration. Gradually the melodic traits, rhythms, dynamics, and inflections of Hungarian (and other) folk music became an organic part of Bartók's own style. At the same time, he was well acquainted with contemporary musical currents. By 1907 he knew some of Debussy's works (later he played Debussy's piano preludes constantly) and something of the music of Schoenberg and Stravinsky.

Unlike Schoenberg, Bartók composed music that remained basically tonal, although it is often extremely dissonant and chromatic. These traits are seen in his early style, which crystallized into an organic whole by the time of *Allegro Barbaro* (1911) and the Second String Quartet (1917)—music of strong, sometimes savage, rhythms and music whose melodic motives and intervals are typical of folk song (see below).

Bartók is the best example of the thorough absorption of folk-song elements into an organic style of composing "art" music. Kodály composed along similar lines. In other countries, folk songs, folk dances, and folk themes were sometimes used in this organic way or, perhaps more typically, quoted or used in some thematic fashion in the context of a composer's "regular" style.

In the first two decades of the twentieth century, Bartók's organic folk-music style is a third musical force, comparable in importance and distinction to the efforts of his contemporaries Schoenberg and Stravinsky

(Bartók was a year older than Stravinsky and seven years younger than Schoenberg). After World War I, Bartók and Hindemith (who belonged to a "younger" generation of "new" composers) represent important crosscurrents to the streams of "atonal" (twelve-tone) music and to a newly evolving Neoclassicism.

At the same time, the styles of both Bartók and Hindemith have certain elements in common with atonal and Neoclassic music. Schoenberg, Hindemith, and Bartók all used the chromatic scale as a basic resource. However, the results were quite different: Schoenberg evolved an atonal twelve-tone style, but both Hindemith and Bartók preserved tonality, sometimes expanding its horizon to polytonality. And Bartók often used modality as an additional resource. Stravinsky and Hindemith both wrote Neoclassic music inspired by love of order and clarity and by the styles and forms of earlier "classic" models, especially Bach and Mozart. Bartók was looking to a quite different and more primal source of inspiration— folk song in general and the peasant music of Hungary in particular—in order to infuse a twentieth-century style with the melodic and rhythmic traits long indigenous to a national culture. Bartók, however, thought that he and the Neoclassicists had one goal in common: In an interview published in 1928, he claimed that the Neoclassic trend and his alliance with folk music were both a rejection of Romantic music.

Bartók was a giant among composers of the twentieth century, and one of its most versatile musicians. *See Plate* 35A. A professional pianist of rare gifts and perception in playing music ranging from Bach to Bartók, he concertized widely in Europe and the United States; and though he steadfastly refused to accept students in composition, he taught the piano throughout his lifetime—his appointment to the Budapest Academy of Music as Professor of Piano lasted for nearly thirty years. From his piano teaching and playing came editions of music and teaching pieces, such as the six volumes of the *Mikrokosmos* (1926–1939), pieces graded from easy to difficult to introduce young pianists to the "world in miniature" of contemporary music. And naturally enough, he wrote extensively for the piano—more so than other important twentieth-century composers.

His lifelong passion for collecting the folk songs of Hungary and other nations was based on more than an ethnologist's interest; and as a composer he absorbed folk rhythms and melodies into an indigenous style of his own, a music of Hungarian nationalism. As Bartók said, "folk music will have significance for art only when it can permeate and in- fluence art music through a shaping genius." This genius was Bartók. In addition, he and Kodály recorded and transcribed the incredible number of some eight thousand peasant tunes; for good measure, they set a number of them for modern singers and players. Kodály was also a composer of distinction, although he never wrote music as powerful rhythmically or as uncompromising harmonically as did Bartók (but listen to Kodály's *Psalmus Hungaricus* of 1923, one of his best works).

Bartók was born in Hungary in the Torontál district, now part of Rumania. His early musical background, like that of Dohnányi and Kodály, his fellow students in Budapest, was the German music of Brahms, Wagner, Liszt, and Richard Strauss (whose music inspired him greatly at first). Moved by the newly awakened nationalism in Hungary shortly after 1900, Bartók and Kodály consciously rejected the German influences all around them. (As a political gesture, Bartók wrote a symphonic poem on the patriotic theme "Kossuth" [1903] in which the Austrian national anthem is caricatured.) Instead, they turned (1904) to the Magyar folk music of the Hungarian peasants, as opposed to the "Hungarian" music of Liszt (and Brahms), which was not real folk music but that of the city café. On the other hand, Liszt's virtuoso style made its impact on Bartók. Gradually, Bartók began to investigate other folk music: Rumanian, Slovakian, Wallachian, Turkish, and the Arabian folk music of North Africa.

This intense and quickening interest in folk music began a whole new period in Bartók's life as a composer, and it marked a new and pioneering milestone in folk-song investigation, especially because Bartók recorded the tunes on the wax cylinders of the Edison phonograph. In 1906 Bartók and Kodály published *Twenty Hungarian Folk Songs* (each composer arranged ten tunes), the first of a number of publications which had the twofold aim of being ethnologically accurate and of making musical settings for practical use. At the same time, folk rhythms, melodies, and scales were seeping into Bartók's blood. The result was the savage, throbbing rhythms of *Allegro Barbaro* for piano solo (1911) and the semitone usage of the melody and harmony in the Second String Quartet (1917).

Not all of Bartók's music, however, can be ascribed to folk influences. He knew some of Schoenberg's and Stravinsky's early works, and he was much impressed by Debussy. In 1939 Bartók stated that after Bach and Beethoven, Debussy had influenced him the most. His one-act opera *Duke Bluebeard's Castle* (1911) is colored by French Impressionism.

After the difficult times of World War I, Bartók traveled more and more as a concert pianist (including a tour of the United States, 1927), but his compositions were slow to be recognized. For one thing, he was at his most uncompromising in his music of the early 1920's. Indeed, the two sonatas for violin and piano (1921, 1922) come closest to departing from tonality in the use of dissonance and the different planes of sound. The Fourth String Quartet (1928) is more ingratiating, while displaying a high degree of formal order and tight construction. This and the Third Quartet also inaugurate a new species of sonority (see below).

In the 1930's there were more signs of recognition, Bartók's music being somewhat easier for the public. This was the period of *Music for String Instruments Percussion and Celesta* (1936), the Fifth Quartet (1934), Sonata for Two Pianos and Percussion (1937, which he and his second wife played), the Violin Concerto (1938), and the Sixth (and last) Quartet (1939). By this time, however, it was clear that Bartók's strong anti-Fascist stand and the approaching war would mean his leaving Hungary; [1] and in 1940 he and his wife left for New York. In the last five difficult years, ill (as he had been recurrently throughout his life), homesick, and in financial difficulty, he worked at transcribing Yugoslavian folk songs (on a grant from Columbia University) and completing commissions. The music of these sad years shows that the mastery of Bartók continued, especially in the Concerto for Orchestra (1944).

When Bartók speaks of folk music "permeating" art music, he does not mean the direct quotation of a folk song used in its entirety in a piece of art music. A number of composers quote folk songs directly in this way, often to make some patriotic reference, Brahms and Tchaikovsky being two of many examples. To Bartók, however, the "significant" use of folk music in art music meant the extraction of characteristic rhythms, melodic traits, and scales from folk music and their organic fusion in a composer's own style. He was uniquely equipped by temperament, gifts, and sympathy with the national aspirations of the time to be the "shaping genius" of an organic style of this nature; and he is one of the few examples of a composer of the first rank who has done so.

Rhythm is obviously central and greatly varied in its application. Following folk songs and dances, Bartók distinguishes two rhythmic styles: the relatively strict tempo of *tempo giusto;* and the free, varied tempo of *parlando rubato,* as in the third movement of the Fourth String

Ex. 163 *

Bartók, *Allegro Barbaro,* m. 76–84

* Copyright 1918 by Universal Edition; renewed 1945. Copyright and Renewal assigned to Boosey & Hawkes, Inc., for the U.S.A. Reprinted by permission.

[1] Because of Bartók's anti-Fascism and his strong folk-song interest, he was one of the few "advanced" Western composers whose music was allowed to be played in the Soviet Union after 1932.

Quartet (see below). Many pieces give the effect of pounding, repetitive rhythms (see Ex. 163 from the *Allegro Barbaro*); others are barred irregularly or accented irregularly to achieve rhythmic divisions of unequal length (cf. the opening of the fourth movement of the Fourth String Quartet). Then there are many syncopations and polyrhythms. Rhythmic motives are often as important as the melodic shapes with which they are entwined. Moreover, in Bartók's music, rhythm may take over a traditional function of harmony, which is to create tension through greater dissonance. Specifically, rhythm may be used to create points of tension and climax even though the harmony remains at the *same* level of dissonance. Similarly, the dissonance of the harmony may remain high while relaxation is produced by rhythmic means.

The Lydian mode, commonly used in Rumanian and Slovakian folk music, illustrates the point of extracting characteristic intervals from folk music and then applying them to art music. In this mode, embracing F–F on the white keys of the piano, the tritone interval (F–B), formed between the first and the fourth degrees, is characteristic of Bartók's melodic use. This melodic feature and another typical of Bartók are illustrated in Ex. 164, two excerpts from the second movement (*allegro*

Ex. 164 *

Bartók, Second String Quartet, second movement

molto cappriccioso) of his Second String Quartet (1917). In the first two measures the tritone is played in vigorous unison by the two violins (Ex. 164a). The theme proper commences a few measures later (Ex. 164b), beginning with a static insistence on the notes D and F. Then with a *sforzando* the F is changed to F sharp (effecting a change from a minor to a major interval), then back to F, followed by an augmented interval (D to G sharp). Throughout this passage, the accompaniment is a reiterated octave "D" in the second violin. This type of melody is motivic and plastic in effect. By way of contrast, a type of long "melodic" melody occurs in the Concerto for Orchestra, second movement ("Game of Pairs"). In *Music for String Instruments Percussion and Celesta,* the theme of the last movement begins with a Bulgarian rhythmic pattern, again using the Lydian mode. In another modal effect, the typical flat seventh degree is heard in the first melodic phrase of *Allegro Barbaro* (Ex. 163).

From the resources of new scales and modes, Bartók generated not only fresh-sounding melody, but also a new type of harmony. On the relationship of melody to harmony, he had some revolutionary ideas: "The simpler the melody, the more unusual may be its accompanying harmony," he said. This statement helps explain his freedom of harmonic treatment, including chord "clusters" composed of adjacent scale steps, diatonic or chromatic (Ex. 167, m. 4). With the resources of the chromatic scale, the whole tone, the pentatonic scale, and the "old" modes, almost any combination is possible.

The point must be emphasized, however, that no matter how dissonant or varied Bartók's music may be, there is invariably some sort of tonal center—a "free tonality" as opposed to the "free atonality" of the early Schoenberg works. Indeed, there are sometimes two clear tonal centers (bitonality or, more generally, polytonality). In the *Allegro Barbaro,* the melody is centered around "A," but the accompaniment is based on F sharp. Two chords may be in a similar bitonal relationship. Bartók also experimented with building chords by fourths; and he expanded melodic lines by the doubling of fourths, fifths, and octaves, as in the old organum. Bitonality (or polytonality) is also carried out in the contrapuntal sense of lines in two or more parts, a simple instance being the "Game of Pairs" in the Concerto for Orchestra. Here the "Game" is bitonal—the pairs proceeding to play a melody in parallel lines at the sixth, third, seventh, fifth, and second, which, carried out interval for interval, gives bitonality. In all this, counterpoint plays an important role.

Like other important composers of the twentieth century—for example, Schoenberg, Stravinsky, and Webern—Bartók exploited the capacities and sonorities of instruments (and voices) to the full. He was especially interested in percussion or percussive effects—a fact reflected in such works as the Sonata for Two Pianos and Percussion, in the percussive use of the piano, and in his "rebounding" *pizzicato* for stringed instruments. In the last mentioned effect, the string is plucked so hard that it rebounds from the fingerboard, a rather savage and startling sound. Apparently, this special type of *pizzicato* was invented by Bartók. In any case, he indicated its use by a special symbol (○).

From the time of the Third String Quartet (1927), Bartók was especially fertile in the use of color and special effects in strings. He contrasted passages in vibrato and nonvibrato (Ex. 167); he used the rebounding *pizzicato* and *pizzicato glissando* (for these and other technical terms, see the Glossary). Bartók even made the effect of upward *glissando* function as a structural device of imitation between the four parts of the string

Ex. 165 *   Bartók, Fourth String Quartet, second movement

quartet, as shown in Ex. 165, where the slanted lines indicate the pitch distance the finger of the player must glide (*glissando*) on the string. Among other devices are a number of natural and artificial harmonics, the *sul ponticello,* and the *col legno* (last movement of the Fourth String Quartet), and numerous combinations of all these effects. Bartók revels in great bursts of sonority by means of multiple stops. For example, the last movement of the Fourth String Quartet opens with three stringed instruments producing, among them, some eleven different pitches in a tremendous flood of sound. In the orchestra, Bartók shows the same attitude toward color, sonority, and experimentation. One typical example is his use of quarter tones in the solo violin part of the Violin Concerto.

Bartók also had a passion for exact information and notation. He supplies metronome markings and indicates how much time the whole piece ought to take. At the end of the piece he gives the place and date of completion. And so on. Nevertheless, one wonders why his notation is sometimes so complex. The opening melody of *Allegro Barbaro,* for example, can be written quite simply without flats or sharps, but Bartók notates it with all sorts of sharps, flats, even double sharps to make us see (if not hear) various augmented seconds and other chromatic intervals (see Ex. 163).

THE FOURTH STRING QUARTET (1928)

Until now, nothing has been said about structure in Bartók's music. The Fourth String Quartet, one of Bartók's best works, is an excellent example of his capabilities in this respect. Here one finds a fantastic degree of organization from the smallest motive to the largest aspects of structure. All five movements themselves are in an arrangement which involves a certain degree of symmetry, resemblance, and variety. The first and last movements are both in a species of sonata form, and they are directly related by the fact that the two main subjects of the first movement (Ex. 166a) are used in the last movement, but in reverse order (Ex.

Ex. 166 *

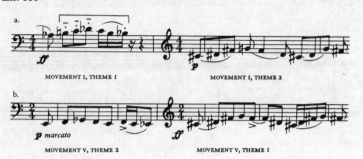

MOVEMENT I, THEME I   MOVEMENT I, THEME 2

MOVEMENT V, THEME 2   MOVEMENT V, THEME I

166b). The centerpiece is the remarkable third movement (see below); the second and fourth movements (*scherzi*) that enclose it have their own tenuous connections. Thus the five movements constitute a kind of "arch-form," A B C B′ A′, provided that movements two and four are regarded as related.

The third movement, the centerpiece, is music of quite special character and needs to be singled out for more detailed comment. The "cluster" chord with which it opens is produced by the successive addition of the upper three instruments, playing *nonvibrato* (Ex. 167). The whole cluster is then repeated, but with vibrato, the chord in consequence suddenly beginning to shimmer. In the middle of this dense cluster, Bartók craftily leaves a small vacuum of sound, a vacuum destined to be occupied by the first notes of the cello solo, which enters playing a magnificent long line of declaimed rhapsodic song in *parlando rubato* style. The accompaniment to the cello solo is the chord cluster, which continues to sound its static harmony. In the cello solo, the rather mournful, yet highly embellished, melody was probably inspired by music characteristic of the *tárogató,* a Hungarian instrument resembling a straight wooden saxophone. The opening of the melody centers on the tone D, typically alternating with semitones (and tones) above and below, as shown in Ex. 167. After the full sweep of its first long phrase, the cello stops for breath. The chord cluster ascends a semitone in pitch, and the cello begins another related phrase. Once more the cluster is raised a semitone, and a third time the cello voices its eloquent song.

The middle section of the movement begins with another static cluster, played by the three lower instruments. The first violin, now the soloist, devotes itself to birdlike chirpings in repeated notes, broken rhythms, accents, and broken octaves in a kind of *night music.* This term refers to a species of music of "nocturnal" sound that Bartók had begun to write two years earlier in *Out of Doors* (five pieces for piano, of which No. 4 is entitled "The Night's Music"). After a few measures, the lower voices

Ex. 167 *

stop holding the chord passively and instead make rapid *tremolos* and *pizzicatos*. The second violin breaks in with a rhapsodic reminiscence of the cello's song, the ensemble dissolving finally to the sound of a major third in the first violin. Thereupon there ensues a remarkable duet between cello and violin (the latter playing the inversion of the cello melody), and finally, the chirping of the night music returns in the first violin, which concludes the movement on a single high note (d³), "d" being the note about which the movement as a whole is centered.

This extraordinary quartet does not reveal itself at first hearing. Careful study and a process of horizontal listening by layers gradually disclose the full beauties of the work and reveal it as the masterpiece that it is.

Another masterpiece of the following decade is *Music for String Instruments Percussion and Celesta* (1936). Here is the same attention to the overall form that characterizes the Fourth String Quartet: some variant of the subject of the opening fugue (or allusion to it) plays an important role in each of the following movements. A striking feature of the work is the various sonorous combinations that Bartók extracts from the unusual instrumentation: a double string orchestra, a number of assorted percussion instruments under one player, and also timpani, xylophone, celesta, harp, and piano. In addition, Bartók induces a species of stereophonic effect by placing the strings in two different groups on the stage.

Each of the movements has a very special character. The masterly fugue of the opening movement is followed by a second movement in a species of sonata form. This movement is strongly rhythmic and percussive, including prominent use of the timpani, the piano, and *pizzicato* in the strings. The third movement is another species of "night music," strongly reminiscent of the third movement of the Fourth String Quartet. The extraordinary attention to color and sonority of the instruments begins with the opening bars of xylophone and timpani; and the "night sounds" in the middle of the movement are of an eerie kind that anticipates similar effects in electronic music (see Chapter 33). The last movement, rondolike in structure, is dominated by its opening theme cast in the Lydian mode and in a Bulgarian rhythm of great fascination.

Shy, sensitive, proud, and unswerving in principle, Bartók grew in stature with the years. At his death, he was deeply mourned by musicians throughout the world; but by one of those recurrent ironies of history, Bartók became famous only after his death to the public that had found him largely inaccessible in life.

Suggested Listening
Allegro Barbaro (for piano).
Out of Doors (five pieces for piano).
Twenty Hungarian Folk Songs (the first ten are set by Bartók).
Fourth String Quartet (movement three).
Music for String Instruments Percussion and Celesta (last movement).
Concerto for Orchestra ("Game of Pairs" movement).

Suggested Reading
Halsey Stevens, *The Life and Music of Béla Bartók* (Revised edition). New York: Oxford University Press, 1964.

HINDEMITH

Paul Hindemith (1895–1963) was the most distinguished composer of his generation to emerge in Germany. He was an immensely prolific composer in practically all styles and forms, and his early "radical" works show a preoccupation with chromatic lines and harmonies, *ostinato* figures, polytonality, and dissonant ("linear") counterpoint ("linear" counterpoint stresses the horizontal aspect of "line" at the expense of the vertical aspect of harmony). His later works are calmer and sometimes simpler, relatively consonant, and sometimes more diatonic; and he turns increasingly to the "absolute" species of music: the symphony, chamber music, and the sonata. Even in his first works Hindemith attracted attention by the vigor and persistence of his rhythmic patterns, his contrapuntal ingenuity, and the strength of his harmonies and melodies, in which the interval of the fourth is especially prominent.

The clarity of Hindemith's forms and his affinity for forms typical of the Classic and Baroque periods led inevitably to labeling his work as "Neoclassic," "Neobaroque," and "back to Bach." Hindemith himself was like the ideal of the composer-performer of earlier times, being a viola virtuoso, a player of numerous other instruments (including "old" instruments), and a conductor. *See Plate 35*B.

He also devoted some effort to writing music in a contemporary but simpler idiom for amateur players and beginners. This music, intended mainly for use at home or at school, is sometimes called *Gebrauchsmusik* ("music for use"), a term that came to annoy Hindemith. By writing sonatas for a number of instruments for which there was a very scanty repertory, Hindemith is owed a debt of gratitude by players of such instruments as the viola d'amore and the trombone. In a general sense, this filling of a vacuum in the repertory may be considered a "music for use."[2]

From Brahms, Strauss, and Reger, Hindemith inherited collectively a "romantic" tradition of strongly chromatic counterpoint and harmony, a love of things German (such as chorales and the works of Bach), and a preoccupation with the symphony, chamber music, and opera. As a reaction to his earliest "romantic" works in the style of Reger, Hindemith passed rapidly through various phases viewed as "anti-Romantic," "Expressionist," and even (mistakenly) "atonal." He also composed for the

[2] Carl Orff (b. 1895), a man of the same age as Hindemith, is another composer particularly interested in musical education in the sense of *Gebrauchsmusik;* and his *Schulwerk* (1930–1933), simply written and scored, contains music for beginners and amateurs. His calculated style of melodic and harmonic simplicity and a dominant rhythm established him as a popular composer, especially in one work, *Carmina Burana* (1936), a setting of twenty-four goliardic songs and poems from the thirteenth century.

cinema and experimented with jazz. Characteristic of these early works are the song cycle (with piano) *Das Marienleben* (*The Life of Mary,* on a text by Rilke, 1923; drastically revised, 1948), the opera *Cardillac* (1926), and the Third String Quartet (1922).

The last, typical of Hindemith at this time, employs a modern dissonant and chromatic style of considerable complexity and is cast in forms distinguished by variety and exceptional clarity. In particular, the first movement begins with a fugato on a chromatic subject and the harmony is dissonant in the manner of "linear" counterpoint. The second movement is typically energetic and insistent in rhythm, experimenting with polyrhythms to some extent (see Ex. 33, p. 45). The third movement employs polytonality as a basic resource; and the fourth movement is declamatory and rhapsodic, dissonant, and chromatic in texture. The final movement is a rondo whose opening subject illustrates Hindemith's use of the twelve tones as basic material for a "chromatic tonality" (Ex. 168).

Ex. 168 *

* Copyright 1923, B. Schott's Soehne, Mainz; by permission of Associated Music Publishers, Inc., New York.

This particular melody contains all twelve tones, some being used more than once; and it begins and ends on the same note, establishing a tone center of sorts. It is also neatly organized in two parts as antecedent and consequent, illustrating in miniature Hindemith's clear feeling for form.

But all this is a far cry from atonal or twelve-tone music in Schoenberg's sense; and no matter how chromatic or dissonant Hindemith's music may be, he continues to recognize the validity of tonality, the cadence, and the distinction between consonance and dissonance (for further detail, see his book mentioned on p. 457). The chromatic scale was basic to Hindemith's music; but contrary to Schoenberg's use of the twelve tones, not all the twelve tones are necessarily used by Hindemith in any given melody or series of harmonies, nor are the semitones in a melody arranged in an ordered series where no tone can be repeated before all the others have been used.

In 1927 Hindemith was appointed professor at the Hochschule für

Musik in Berlin (where Schoenberg was teaching at the time), and after this period his style became somewhat more diatonic and less dissonant—a fact the Nazi government (1933–1945) realized so little that they banned his music as "cultural Bolshevism" (cf. Schoenberg and Webern) and forced him from his position. Hindemith then went to Ankara (1935) to reorganize music education for the Turkish government. Later, he taught composition at Yale University (1940–1953) and, through his Collegium Musicum, gave valuable instruction to a large number of students in the music and instruments of past eras, including the Middle Ages and Renaissance, in which he had developed an intense interest. In his last years, Hindemith returned to Europe (1953), settling in Switzerland.

In pondering the long list of Hindemith's works, it is difficult to think of a species of composition for which he did not furnish at least one example. Of his stage works, the best known is the opera *Mathis der Maler (Matthias the Painter,* 1932–1934; generally performed in its symphonic extract of 1934); for the orchestra: Symphony in E flat major (1941) and *Symphonic Metamorphosis of Themes by Carl Maria von Weber* (1944); concertos for all sorts of instruments (for instance, the viola concerto *Der Schwanendreher,* 1935); ballets, for example, *Theme and Variations (The Four Temperaments),* 1944; a vast amount of chamber music of all sorts, including seven string quartets and a whole series of *Kammermusik* (chamber music) for varied combinations; solo works for piano and for organ; and a number of works for the voice (*Das Marienleben*) and chorus (e.g., his setting of Whitman's *When Lilacs Last in the Dooryard Bloom'd,* 1946). Hindemith's *Ludus Tonalis* (1943) is essentially a didactic work, modeled on Bach's *The Well-Tempered Clavier* and showing his constructive and contrapuntal ingenuity (the postlude is the upside-down version of the prelude). Hindemith's career as a teacher naturally suggested writing textbooks and especially a theoretical work, *The Craft of Musical Composition.*[3] His broader views are given in *A Composer's World* (1952).

The symphonic version of *Mathis der Maler* will serve as an example of Hindemith's mature style. Mathis, the hero of the opera, is in reality the famous artist Matthias Grünewald (ca. 1480–1528), who painted the Isenheim altarpiece (now in Colmar); and each of the three movements in the symphonic version is devoted to a theme of a panel of this work: (1) "Concert of the Angels," (2) "Entombment," and (3) "Temptation

---

[3] Translated from the original German edition of 1937 by Mendel and Ortmann (New York: Associated Music Publishers, 1941). In this book, Hindemith shows how any chord, no matter how complex, can be described by reference to its most important "fundamental" interval(s). The progression of chords is regulated by a system of tensions and relaxations worked out by Hindemith. Actually, Hindemith was seeking to evolve a method of analysis that could be applied to any music, present or past. In this he was not conspicuously successful.

of St. Anthony." The general theme concerns Matthias's part in the peasant revolt early in the sixteenth century and his reaction to authority —a theme much in Hindemith's mind at the time of Hitler's rise to power. Hindemith makes Matthias identify with St. Anthony, whose life and "temptations" he is to paint.

The opening movement reflects the radiant atmosphere of the "angel concert" by its "consonant" style (cf. the opening), the clarity of form, and the use of the old German tune "Three Angels Sang," first heard near the opening in the trombones. "Entombment," the second movement, is appropriately set in a very slow tempo. It begins with a passage (Ex. 169a) typical of Hindemith: note the "open"-fifth sound of the first and last chord quoted and the harmonies embracing the interval(s) of the fourth. Later, a melodic theme enters in the oboe (Ex. 169b), the two

Ex. 169 *

* By permission of Associated Music Publishers, Inc., New York.

consecutive melodic fourths with which it begins being a hallmark of Hindemith's melodic usage. The last movement portrays St. Anthony tempted and beset by an array of fantastic and monstrous creatures straight out of medieval demonology. The final part of this movement (which closes the symphony) begins with the busy counterpoint of a fugato. It continues with the introduction of a medieval Latin hymn, *Lauda Sion Salvatorem* ("Praise Zion the Savior"), and concludes with the choralelike "Alleluia." The latter suggests divine intervention and presumably a release of St. Anthony–Grünewald–Hindemith from the "temptation" of an active life among "the people," to devote himself instead to the life of an artist in the service of God.

As a musician there was almost nothing that Hindemith could not do or did not know. He was equally at home in the mysteries of counterpoint, the fingering of the viola (or, for that matter, ancient and obsolete instruments like the rebec and *Zink*), the theories of the Greek theoretician Aristoxenus, and conducting an orchestra. A man of broad outlook and sympathies, he was much concerned with closing the gap between composer, performer, and audience. Hailed as a "radical" in the 1920's, he later looked for inspiration, if not for idiom, more and more to the past of German and European tradition, composing in a simpler style of characteristic clarity and order, related to Neoclassic ideals. Hindemith's style was a distinctive one as befits a creative person of this magnitude, and he contributed important new works to the repertory of music. Yet he made relatively little impression on the composers of the following generations, especially after 1950. To young composers, Hindemith was an old "radical" of quite another time, and to them his music and theories had little to say or offer. Hindemith has retained a hold over a substantial public, however; and in works like *Mathis der Maler* he will doubtless continue to do so.

Suggested Listening
Third String Quartet.
Mathis der Maler (symphonic version).
Das Marienleben (version of 1948).

Suggested Reading
Heinrich Strobel, *Paul Hindemith* (Third edition). Mainz: B. Schott, 1948.
Paul Hindemith, *A Composer's World*. Cambridge: Harvard University Press, 1952.

30. *Music Under the Soviets:*
The Impact of the State on Music.
The Ballet. Prokofiev. Shostakovich.
Khachaturian.

IN THE HISTORY of music in twentieth-century Russia, two points deserve special emphasis: one is the pre-eminence of the ballet in Russia and as an international commodity; the other is the Soviet Revolution and the impact of the state on music. "Proletarian" music aimed to serve the needs of the masses, and a simplicity of idiom and emphasis on ideological themes were central considerations. The abstract, the experimental, and the individualistic were rejected. After the death of Lenin (1924) and the gradual concentration of power under Stalin, the artistic life of the country was correspondingly regimented. The Union of Soviet Composers, established in 1932, superseded all other professional organizations, and the doctrine of "Socialist Realism" was formulated.

All this took some time. Immediately after the Revolution and during the Civil War, mass songs or choral folk songs about the Red Army were prevalent. The Soviets took pains to see that musical education and culture were widespread: masses of people were brought to the opera house and concert hall, and music organizations were sent to outlying districts. An important organization at this time was the Proletkult (1918–1923), which was devoted to training workers and peasants in the writing and practice of the arts.

Lenin had said: "Art belongs to the people," but he neglected to say how to implement this ideal. Consequently, in music, as in art generally, a central question was: what music was to belong to the people? Or, restated, what music was to be understood and loved by the masses? Two organizations of quite different aims professed to have the answer. The first of these was the Russian Association of Proletarian Musicians or

RAPM, founded in 1923, partly as a successor to and partly as a negation of the Proletkult. The Proletkult believed in bringing workers and peasants to art, including contemporary art, but RAPM renounced contemporary music, considered the classics "bourgeois," and had little use even for national folk art. To RAPM, "Soviet music" was music immediately comprehensible to simple workmen or peasants.

The other organization was the Association for Contemporary Music (ACM), founded in 1924. ACM stood for "contemporary" in the international sense; it became closely associated with the International Society for Contemporary Music (ISCM); and it held that "music is not ideology." The presence of this group explains how so much "modern" music was heard in the Soviet Union in the 1920's and why music of such composers as Shostakovich had an *avant-garde* flavor until 1932 at least (see below). From 1925 to 1928, the period of greatest artistic freedom (especially in Leningrad), Russians heard, among other works, Prokofiev's *Love for Three Oranges* (at that time Prokofiev was living in Paris), Berg's *Wozzeck,* Honegger's *King David,* Stravinsky's *Mavra* and *Oedipus,* Křenek's *Jonny spielt auf,* and Weill's *Dreigroschenoper* (*Three Penny Opera*). The Persymphans (a conductorless orchestra based in Moscow, 1922–1925) played the classics and also the works of Bartók, Scriabin, Stravinsky, Honegger, Ravel, Falla, and Prokofiev.

For a variety of reasons ACM collapsed in 1931, but the triumph of RAPM was short-lived. The latter had become so intolerant and dictatorial that in 1932 the Communist Party stepped in and ended both "proletarian" art (RAPM) and "formalism" (ACM). The new party line was founded on Gorky's phrase "Socialist Realism," interpreted to mean generally that art must be understandable and loved by the masses, it must be worthy of its ancestry in classical Russian and world art, and it must help to build socialism by its strength and optimism.

RAPM was dissolved, and the Union of Soviet Composers was established in 1932 to implement Socialist Realism, which now became the one true musical Gospel of the Party. The musician's task—not an easy one as it turned out—was to interpret and implement this Gospel correctly.

In essence, Socialist Realism meant the use of a national or ideological subject related to the people and expressed in a melodious, easily comprehensible style of music. The "decadent" tendencies of the West (such as the Expressionism of Schoenberg or the Neoclassicism of Stravinsky) were labeled by such bugbear phrases as "formalistic antidemocratic music." The Soviet ideal, in short, was a kind of program music, music that tells a story (preferably an uplifting message with a moral), simple to comprehend, traditional in style and using traditional tunes such as folk songs, and typically Romantic in emotional character. Shostakovich's opera *Lady Macbeth of Mtzensk* was severely condemned (1936) and subsequently "withdrawn," not on grounds related to its musical qualities,

but because of its "decadent" subject matter and the "formalistic" discord-
ant style of the music. Immediately before this event, Stalin had formulated three necessary aims for the future of Soviet opera: (1) socialistic
subjects, (2) "realistic" musical language, and (3) the "positive" hero as
representative of the new socialist age. The "positive" hero implies a
mood in which optimism prevails over pessimism. These aims still guide
Soviet composers, although the range of subject matter has been expanded
to include a wider horizon of national history, as in Prokofiev's *War and
Peace* (1952).

The ideological gap between Russia and the West was strongly high-
lighted at the time of Shostakovich's Seventh ("Leningrad") Symphony
of 1941 (first performed in 1942). Ernest Newman, the celebrated English
critic, attacked this work on musical grounds, as a music critic in the
West normally would. To the Russians, this musical criticism was irrelevant, pointless, and almost criminally insensitive; and the Soviet press
attacked Newman not because of his musical criticism, but because he did
not appreciate the heroic defense of Leningrad and the immensity of
human suffering which the symphony commemorated. The real point in
Russian eyes was doubtless summarized in Shostakovich's own words
about this symphony: "No more noble mission can be conceived than that
which spurs us on to fight against the dark forces of Hitlerism. That is
why the roar of the cannon does not keep the muses of our people from
lifting their strong voices."

During World War II the old ideological struggles among Soviet
musicians were put aside. However, shortly afterward, in February 1948,
the most prominent Soviet composers were accused of "formalistic distor-
tions and antidemocratic tendencies" by Andrei Zhdanov, Stalin's com-
missar of culture. Among the offenders named were Shostakovich, Prokofiev, Khachaturian, Miaskovsky, and Shebalin (director of the Moscow
Conservatory). The decrees embodied in Zhdanov's criticisms reaffirmed
Socialist Realism and remained in effect until Stalin's death in 1953. Not
until 1958 were the personal criticisms of 1948 rescinded as "unfounded
and unjust." Although the composers who had been named as offenders
early in 1948 tried to conform immediately to meet the criticisms, not all
succeeded. In December of the same year the Union of Soviet Composers
engaged in nine days of discussion, after which they commended some
composers for mending their ways while condemning others, including
Prokofiev, for traces of "unregenerate formalism." After 1953 and especially after 1958, something of a thaw in the cold war of culture set in, and
the music of composers like Hindemith, Stravinsky, Bartók, Britten, and
Milhaud was studied and played. Nevertheless, those Western composers
connected with twelve-tone music or with the most *avant-garde* tendencies were still considered beyond the pale. However, a few of the young
and more adventurous Soviet composers, such as Valentin Silvestrov (b.

1937) and Alfred Schnitke (b. 1934), have begun to write in the more advanced Western idioms.

The Soviets had, of course, inherited a brilliant ballet tradition from the past. At first, it was an imported culture, relying on the great Italian and French dancers and their traditions. All this began about the middle of the eighteenth century. It was not, however, until late in the nineteenth century that native Russian dancers began to compete on equal terms with the Italians. But while the ballet in the Soviet Union was preoccupied with the beautiful production of the old-fashioned repertory (e.g., Tchaikovsky), the modern ballet was being born in Paris with new scores by Debussy and Stravinsky (among others) and being produced by Russian dancers who were members of Diaghilev's famous Ballet Russe (1909–1929). It is significant that the early Stravinsky ballets were all performed for the first time by Diaghilev's troupe in Paris, not in Moscow or in St. Petersburg (later renamed Leningrad).

Under the Soviets, the ballet continued to flourish, and the dancers received superb training at the various schools of ballet, especially in Moscow (Bolshoi) and Leningrad (Kirov). The repertory consisted of traditional ballets like *Giselle, Les Sylphides* (music by Chopin), and *Swan Lake* (Tchaikovsky); and a number of ballets by outstanding Soviet composers: Glière's *Red Poppy* (1927), Prokofiev's *Romeo and Juliet* (1940) and *The Stone Flower* (1950), but not his ballets composed for Diaghilev in Paris; Khachaturian's *Gayane* (1942) and *Spartacus* (1954); and Asafiev's *Flames of Paris* (1932), whose theme is the French Revolution.

The restraining precepts of Socialist Realism apply of course to the ballet, and the weight of old traditions is sometimes heavy. The incredibly beautiful and finished dancing is often wedded to the most traditional staging, costuming, and music. Possibly for this reason, very few ballets by Soviet composers have found a place in the international repertory. For example, Khachaturian's ballet *Spartacus* (set to rather romantic and sentimental music) was received badly in New York. On the other hand, Russian ballet troupes (especially the Bolshoi) have danced a classical repertory in this country to sold-out houses.

The careers and music of three celebrated Russian composers—Prokofiev, Shostakovich, and Khachaturian—make a fascinating counterpoint to the ebb and flow of the general developments described above.

PROKOFIEV

Sergei Prokofiev (1891–1953), the most gifted of Soviet composers and one of the most distinguished musicians of the twentieth century, was born in southern Russia (near Ekaterinoslav) and educated under the old regime. *See Plate 36A.* In 1918 he left Russia, and only later in life (1933) became a Soviet convert.

One of the few musicians of modern times to enjoy an equally high international reputation as a pianist *and* composer, Prokofiev demonstrated early in childhood his extraordinary capacity in both directions, guided at first by his mother, a good amateur pianist. In 1904 Prokofiev passed his entrance examinations for the St. Petersburg Conservatory, and the Examining Board was staggered by the amount of music submitted by this young prodigy, aged thirteen: four operas, a symphony, two sonatas, and a pile of piano pieces.

At the Conservatory Prokofiev came in contact with Glazounov and Liadow in composition, and with Rimsky-Korsakov in orchestration; and he studied the piano with Esipova. His fellow students included two lifelong friends and important figures in Russian music: Boris Asafiev, a composer and prominent Soviet theorist, and Nicolai Miaskovsky, one of the most prolific symphonists of modern times (twenty-seven symphonies).

At the end of his ten years at the Conservatory, Prokofiev had received a thorough exposure to the classics of Russia and the West and the new music of the future. To the latter, he was an intensely partisan contributor himself. Essentially antagonistic to Romantic and Impressionist music, Prokofiev was not drawn to Tchaikovsky, Rachmaninov, or Debussy, but rather to composers like Glinka, Borodin, Mussorgsky, and Rimsky-Korsakov; and, among "Western" composers, to Beethoven, Schumann, Brahms, and Ravel. Of the "futurists," Prokofiev knew the works of Scriabin, the young Stravinsky, and even Schoenberg—Prokofiev played Schoenberg's Op. 11 publicly at the St. Petersburg "Evenings of Modern Music" during the 1910–1911 season.

Prokofiev's strong personality, sometimes stormy temperament, and natural sympathies with "modern" music often brought him into conflict with the traditionalists at the Conservatory and elsewhere. Their values were not always his, and they were not endeared to Prokofiev's dissonant harmony, his distinctive but unconventional melodies, driving rhythms, percussive style of piano playing, and penchant for music of a witty, satirical, sarcastic, or even grotesque character. On the other hand, these same qualities and the originality of his style enchanted the *avant-garde;* and before he left the Conservatory (1914), Prokofiev was already regarded as a "futurist." All this time his piano virtuosity kept pace, and at graduation he received the first ("Rubenstein") prize.

Prokofiev's education was furthered by trips to the West. The first, on the eve of World War I, took him to London and Paris (1914), where he heard some of Stravinsky's early works and met Diaghilev, the ballet impresario. During the next years he gave concerts and composed energetically in spite of the war, finishing his first numbered symphony, the

"Classical" Symphony in 1917. This work, like Shostakovich's First Symphony later on, gave him a reputation abroad and doubtless suggested the possibility of further conquests in the West. In his early piano pieces and in works like the *Scythian Suite* (1915) and the "Classical" Symphony, Prokofiev already displays an original, personal style. The latter work, for instance, demonstrates the attractiveness of his gentle mockery and satire, being a model of "classic" form, melody, and harmony that is humorously "classical."

During the crucial time of the Russian Revolution in 1917, Prokofiev, unlike Shostakovich, showed no discernible political interest; and in 1918, evidently not encouraged by the prospects for music under the Soviets, applied for permission to travel abroad to pursue his career as a composer and pianist. The permission was granted, and Prokofiev went first to the United States (via Siberia and Japan) and afterward (1920) to Paris, the center of his life for the next dozen years.

During this second ("Western") period (1918–1933), Prokofiev lived in the midst of the Neoclassic development in Paris, whose tenets were fundamentally sympathetic to his own. There was no pronounced break with the first period in style of activity. He was earning his living as a pianist, and composing as much as he could. In Paris he was influenced, as well as overshadowed, by Stravinsky without losing his personal style or even without liking all of Stravinsky's works. Among Prokofiev's well-known works of this periods are the opera *Love for Three Oranges,* composed and performed in the United States (Chicago, 1921), the Third Piano Concerto (1921), and the ballet *Le Pas d'acier* (*The [Dance] Step of Steel,* 1925), written for Diaghilev in Paris (although on a Soviet theme).

In 1927 Prokofiev made the first of his return trips to the Soviet Union, where he was received with great enthusiasm. The warmth of this welcome, a natural longing for his native soil, and (one suspects) only moderate success in the West persuaded Prokofiev to return to his native land for good (1933). From then until his death twenty years later, he dominated the Soviet musical scene, his eminence being severely challenged only at the time of the official censures of leading Soviet composers by Zhdanov in 1948. In this last period, after his permanent return to the Soviet Union, Prokofiev's earlier satirical, dissonant, and percussive style was subordinated to one more lyrical in melody and more traditional in harmony, partly as a result of the natural attrition of age and maturity, partly through the sedate restraints of Socialist Realism. An impressive example of this lyrical style is the Second Violin Concerto (1935), the first important work after his return to the Soviet Union (cf. the earlier Third Piano Concerto of 1921). Prokofiev also turned to a greater use of folk material (e.g., the Second String Quartet) and themes of national history, as in the film *Alexander Nevsky* of 1938—the Teutonic Knights invade

Russia, seen as a prophecy of the Nazi invasion—and the gigantic panorama of his opera *War and Peace* (1941–1952) based on Tolstoy's novel.

During these last twenty years of his life, Prokofiev composed a number
of his best works. Besides those just mentioned, one might single out the
Fifth Symphony, the ballets *Romeo and Juliet* and *The Stone Flower*
(1950), music for the film *Lieutenant Kije* (1933; suite, 1935), the comic
opera (a rare species in Russia) *The Duenna,* and the piece known all
over the world: *Peter and the Wolf,* a "symphonic fairy tale" to introduce
children to instruments of the orchestra (1936).

Throughout his life Prokofiev composed in a variety of mediums, a
central place being occupied by works for his own instrument: nine
completed piano sonatas and five piano concertos, among other works.
Then there were concertos for other instruments (two for violin, one for
cello), seven symphonies, chamber music, seven ballets, eight operas, film
music, and instrumental suites extracted from his ballets and films.

Prokofiev made every effort to come to terms with Socialist Realism—
the lyrical emphasis of the Second Violin Concerto is an example—but he
did not succeed completely in satisfying the demands of Socialist Realism
for the optimistic, the heroic, and the melodic. In 1948, fifteen years after
his permanent return to the Soviet Union, he was accused of obscure,
Expressionist tendencies; and Tikhon Khrennikov, the rising and powerful head of the Composers Union, wrote about Prokofiev's new opera *The
Story of a Real Man:* "In the modernistic, antimelodic music of his opera,
the composer remains in his old positions, condemned by the Party and by
Soviet Society"—this in spite of the fact that Prokofiev, in accepting
criticism earlier that year, had pointed to the Fifth Symphony as an
example of having freed himself from Western music.

Prokofiev's work is an unusual combination of the simple and the
complex in style and in theme, the latter ranging from those of childhood
(as in *Peter and the Wolf*) through those of the fantasy world, to the
ugly, harsh, and satirical. The composer himself has said a good deal
about his own ideals and aims, the general ones being clarity of presentation and economy of expression—basically classical ideals. To commemorate his fiftieth birthday (1941), he wrote an account of his "five lines of
development," which are:

1. Classical: that is, traditional.
2. Innovatory: new harmonic idioms and mediums.
3. Toccata: rapid, rhythmically precise motion.
4. Lyrical.
5. Scherzo-humorous.

In his comments on these five, Prokofiev says he is paying increasing
attention to the lyrical side. In discussing "scherzo-humorous," he objects
to being labeled "grotesque," and suggests as more appropriate "jesting,"

"laughing," or "mocking"—terms aptly descriptive of that side of the composer which appears so often (for instance, in the second movement of the Fifth Symphony).

Prokofiev's style is a distinctive one, a prominent feature being melodies that are sometimes angular and exaggerated (see Ex. 170, the second theme of the first movement of the "Classical" Symphony) and sometimes quite vocal in character. The Second Violin Concerto contains good

Ex. 170 *

examples of "vocal" themes: the first and second theme of the first movement (Ex. 171) and the opening of the second movement have this lyrical aspect. Another typical trait of his melodies is a kind of melodic shift through the introduction of notes that may or may not be transient ("transient modulation"), suggesting a key fairly remote from the main key (m. 3–7 of Ex. 171). Sometimes folk material is used, and sometimes the melodies are strongly rhythmic, typically in dance melodies, marches, or fast movements. His driving rhythms are often present not only in marchlike and dancelike themes, but also in figurations and runs in concertos and sonatas (i.e., the toccata style). The pagan rhythms of the early

Ex. 171 *

Scythian Suite recall Stravinsky, as do passages which alternate unusual meters: for instance, the $\frac{7}{4}$ and $\frac{5}{4}$ in the last movement of the Second Violin Concerto.

In spite of his long exposure to Western music, Prokofiev never flirted seriously with the atonal idiom, and the twelve-tone technique left him quite cold. Like the Neoclassicists, his harmony, though frequently noisy and dissonant, was basically tonal. Often constructed of simple triads, it generally sounded fresh and unexpected in its use of the transient modulations suggested by the melodies (cf. Ex. 171). His favorite key was C major adorned with these typical transient and decorative modulations. In essence, his harmonic style and texture are transparent and relatively simple, with sophisticated additions. However, for certain effects, especially those of satire or humor, Prokofiev was capable of using a harmony that was incongruous with the melody—in the sense of polytonality, for instance.

A transparency, similar to the harmony, distinguishes his scoring, which is brilliant in the tradition of Rimsky-Korsakov, whose pupil he was. Unlike the nebulous effects of Impressionism, Prokofiev's music is sharply etched with tones of clear, hard instrumental colors, including those of the piano, often used percussively. Prokofiev knew the orchestra and the piano thoroughly, and although he wrote to the normal limit of their capacities, he did not require performers to exceed these limitations, which partly explains the popularity of his concertos. *Peter and the Wolf* is an example of a simple yet brilliant use of the orchestra and its capacity for characterization. Early in his career (1913), Prokofiev also simplified his scores, writing all instruments at *sounding* pitch (as Schoenberg did).

In a composer like Prokofiev, whose aims are clarity of expression and economy of presentation, it is not surprising to find transparency of harmony and orchestration and a preponderance of the classic forms of instrumental music. The "Classical" Symphony was doubtless something of a satire on the classic symphony of Haydn's time, but the sonata form of the first movement seems a natural manner of expression for Prokofiev. The same might be said of a number of later pieces (cf. the opening movement of the Second Violin Concerto, nearly twenty years afterward). The variation technique is another traditional form used by Prokofiev. To be sure, there are unusual forms among Prokofiev's pieces, but he reverted again and again to the traditional ones.

By a curious stroke of fate Prokofiev died on the same day as Stalin (March 5, 1953), which momentarily obscured the impact of his death. But not for long. Arthur Honegger, his French contemporary, wrote: "He will remain for us the greatest figure of contemporary music." Never a theorist or teacher, Prokofiev left an important legacy of works and style as a composer and pianist. Exposed for his whole formative life and early maturity to Western influences, Prokofiev was accepted with some reserve in certain quarters in the Soviet Union during his life. Since his death, this reserve has largely vanished. Characteristic of this change was the posthumous award (1957) of the Lenin Prize for his Seventh Symphony (1952). In the Soviet Union today, Prokofiev is viewed retrospectively as a classic figure among great modern composers and as one of the greatest pianists of recent times, worthy of his illustrious tradition.

Suggested Listening
"March" from the *Love for Three Oranges* (suite).
"Classical" Symphony (1917).
Fifth Symphony (1944) (second movement).
Peter and the Wolf (1936).
Piano Concerto No. 3 (1921).
Violin Concerto No. 2 (1935).

Suggested Reading
Israel V. Nestyev, *Prokofiev,* trans. by Florence Jonas. Stanford, Calif.: Stanford University Press, 1960.

SHOSTAKOVICH

Dmitri Shostakovich (b. 1906) is one of the Soviet Union's most honored citizens and is generally regarded by his countrymen as the foremost living Soviet composer. He was born in 1906 in St. Petersburg; and in 1919, in the troubled times shortly after the Revolution, he entered the Leningrad (Petrograd) Conservatory at the age of thirteen. Glazounov, the director, recognized his great talent and encouraged him; and Maximilian Steinberg, the pupil and son-in-law of Rimsky-Korsakov, taught him composition. As a graduation piece (1925), Shostakovich wrote his First Symphony at the age of eighteen. First performed in 1926, this astonishingly fresh work proclaimed a composer of exceptional gifts, and made him an international reputation overnight.

Unlike Prokofiev, Shostakovich is entirely a product of Soviet culture. He came of a family devoted to revolutionary aims and ideals, and he became one of the chief artistic spokesmen of the new Soviet government. The Soviets were delighted at the advent of a composer of such great promise (he was also an excellent pianist) at a time when many prominent musicians had left the country—Stravinsky, Rachmaninov, Prokofiev, and (later, in 1928) Glazounov. But although Shostakovich is a product of a new era, he had many musical ties to Russian composers of an earlier time: in the Conservatory, to Glazounov, Steinberg, and the still-fresh aura of Rimsky (d. 1908); and, through his schooling, to many others like Tchaikovsky. In the 1920's, Shostakovich was able also to hear a substantial amount of new music from the West through the Association for Contemporary Music, which played works of Prokofiev, Berg, Honegger, Stravinsky, Mahler, and others. Not until 1932, when the Union of Soviet Composers was established to propagate Socialist Realism, were Russian composers cut off from the main streams of the new in Western culture.

Ironically, it was the performance of a work by Shostakovich that heralded a new intensification of conformity to Socialist Realism. His opera *Lady Macbeth of Mtzensk,* composed between 1930 and 1932, dealt with the theme of adultery, murder, and corruption in an earlier Russian bourgeois society; and it was composed in a style influenced by Western standards of dissonance. *Lady Macbeth* was produced successfully and without incident in Moscow in January 1934; and in the next two years, it was given with growing success within and without the Soviet Union (e.g., Metropolitan Opera House, New York, February 1935). Then, on January 28, 1936, *Pravda,* the journal of the Communist Party, in an article entitled "A Mess Instead of Music," severely censured the opera and its composer as antimelodic and as a tool of Western modernism. The arbiters of Socialist Realism, including Stalin himself, who had just seen the opera, had clamped down. Shostakovich accepted the criticism humbly and promised to do better. In effect he did so in his Fifth Symphony (1937), on the score of which he wrote: "A Soviet Artist's Practical and Creative Reply to Just Criticism." This work was hailed as "Shostakovich's first appearance as an avowed artist-realist" and his "first address to a broad audience in clear, simple, and expressive language, and not to a narrow circle." In a word, Shostakovich was restored to favor. The critic in *Izvestia,* the journal of the Supreme Soviet, commented: "The Soviet listener is incapable of absorbing decadent, somber, pessimistic art, but he responds enthusiastically to all that is joyful, optimistic, self-asserting." Shostakovich himself, however, speaks of both optimism and tragedy: "The finale of the Symphony resolves the tense tragedy of the early movements on an optimistic plane," and he goes on to affirm the right of Russian tragedy to exist. In effect, he is enunciating what came to be the doctrine of "optimistic tragedy," a phrase often used in Soviet criticism. In this doctrine, tragic elements are permissable provided that optimism prevails in the end. (For further comment on the Fifth Symphony, see below.)

For the next ten years, Shostakovich's star rose. He became Professor at the Leningrad Conservatory in 1937 and at Moscow in 1943. In 1940 he was awarded a Stalin Prize of 100,000 rubles for his Piano Quintet. During the fearful siege of Leningrad, he was a volunteer air-raid watcher but was evacuated to Kuibyshev to finish his Seventh ("Leningrad") Symphony, which he did at the end of 1941. This work became the symbol of the patriotic war in the Soviet Union and even in the United States, being performed in New York (summer 1942) by Arturo Toscanini and played throughout the United States.

However, not long after the war (1948), the leading Russian composers, including Shostakovich and Prokofiev, came under the severe criticism of Zhdanov, Stalin's commisar of culture, who sternly urged composers to write music the masses could understand. Thereupon much self-criticism and breast-beating took place. Most composers took to writing with the most studied simplicity, or they simply became cautious. Shostakovich did not release his new Violin Concerto (finished 1948) until 1955, and from 1947 to 1951 wrote mainly film music. The repressive atmosphere of 1948 was not eased until the death of Stalin in 1953, and a number of the composers censured were not rehabilitated until 1958.

Shostakovich's reaction to the criticisms of 1948 was characteristic, outwardly at least. He responded in his usual humble way; and almost as a patriotic duty and with renewed expression of faith in the regime, he resolved on "new compositions that will find their path to the heart of the Soviet people." However wounded Shostakovich himself may have been from the Zhdanov censures, his career seems to have suffered no noticeable setback; and he sounded more and more like an apologist for the official Soviet view. In 1949 he was sent as a World Peace delegate to New York, to which city he was restricted because of the political climate (his cross-country visit to the United States in 1959 was a much happier occasion for him). In 1956, on his fiftieth birthday, he was awarded the Order of Lenin; and he has won at least six Stalin Prizes.

The question of the good or bad effect of Socialist Realism on the quality of Shostakovich's music is meaningless to Russians, since value judgments of art on its own terms, considered basic to the Western mind, are irrelevant to the purposes of Soviet art (cf. Ernest Newman's criticism of Shostakovich's Seventh Symphony, mentioned earlier). However, it is almost certainly true that Socialist Realism was the controlling factor that caused Shostakovich to write different things and in a different style than he would have done otherwise. Under other circumstances, for instance, it seems most unlikely that Shostakovich would have resorted to such frequent use of "programs" of a patriotic or ideological nature in his symphonies, in some of which the program relegates the music to an incidental role more suited to a film than to a symphony (e.g., the Second, Third, Eleventh and Twelfth Symphonies). On the other hand, the Fifth Symphony, written to conform to the tenets of Socialist Realism, is surely one of Shostakovich's best works. If the last movement seems vulgar and overblown here and there, the same may be said for passages in Tchaikovsky, among others. The whole issue will always remain unanswered and unresolved.

The pity is that a social revolution should require so rigid an adherence to the concept and practice of art in the traditional image of the past. At the same time, it must be said that Soviet Russia has performed heroic tasks in educating her people in the "classics," and her system of musical education, especially in the performing arts, is without peer in the West.

The works of Shostakovich are extensive, embracing various mediums, but a central place is occupied by his thirteen symphonies (1925–1962), which run the gamut of his style and development, and demonstrate his successes and failures (see below). In addition, there are numerous works for piano solo and a substantial amount of chamber music, including twelve string quartets (1938–c.1968), two sonatas for violin and piano, and the Piano Quintet, mentioned earlier. Among his concertos are the Violin Concerto, two for piano and two for cello.

For the stage, Shostakovich has written three ballets, incidental music for plays, an early opera *The Nose* (1928–1929), and of course *Lady Macbeth of Mtzensk*. In 1962 the latter work was revived with some changes as *Katerina Izmaylova,* and in 1967 it was made into a film. Shostakovich has also composed songs, choruses, and music for a number of films.

Although Shostakovich admired the revolutionary spirit of Beethoven and thought of him as a general model, there is little resemblance between the symphonies of the two composers beyond the heroic tone of some of them and the program character of others. Beethoven described his only program symphony (the Sixth or "Pastoral") as "more the expression of feeling than painting," while Shostakovich's program symphonies are sometimes almost visually explicit. Patriotic and ideological programs attract Socialist Realists, but they often distract others. Ernest Newman spoke of locating a Shostakovich symphony on a musical map "between so many degrees longitude and so many degrees platitude."

The First Symphony (1925) was brilliant and successful, and it had no program. If it showed the influence of Prokofiev and older Russian composers, it succeeded in combining the traces of its origin into an organic and personal style that displayed a remarkable formal sense, brilliance and clarity of orchestration, and a kind of sardonic and parodistic cast of melodic phrase reminiscent of Prokofiev. The next two symphonies were both programmatic. The Second Symphony (1927) commemorated the October Revolution, and the Third Symphony (1929) was entitled "First of May." Neither was successful in grafting and reconciling "people's music" with his earlier style. Each had a single movement with a final chorus.

The Fourth Symphony (1936), a gloomy and introspective work, was withdrawn by Shostakovich and not performed until much later. By way of contrast, the Fifth Symphony (1937), discussed below, is among his best and best-known works. If Shostakovich ever approached Beethoven in epic and heroic tone, it is here. At the same time, this symphony satisfied the tenets of Socialist Realism, and the tragic overtones of the first three movements are resolved in the optimistic finale. The Sixth Symphony (1939), originally planned as a musical portrayal of Lenin "as a great son of the Russian people and a great leader and teacher of the masses," has in reality nothing to do with Lenin, nor has it a "program." It is, instead, a symphony of somewhat novel plan in three movements: a lengthy opening *largo* followed by a scherzolike *allegro* and a saucy *presto* that is probably satirical in intent—there are references to themes of Rossini and Mozart, among others. Little noticed when first performed, the Sixth Symphony has since achieved a certain popularity in spite of its lack of unified mood and its excessive spinning out of the melodic materials of the opening *largo*. The Seventh ("Leningrad") Symphony of 1941 and the Eighth Symphony of 1943 are heroic works on an immense scale, both programmatic expressions of the war and its agony. In the Seventh, according to Alexei Tolstoi, Shostakovich "rested his ear against the heart of his country and heard its mighty song"; and it is irrelevant to those under the impact of such emotions that this symphony is too long for its substance and uneven in quality.

The Ninth (1945) and Tenth (1953) Symphonies are the complete antithesis of the preceding two. The Ninth, a piece of Classical simplicity, could almost have been written by Haydn—or Prokofiev. Its reception, however, was cool; perhaps the audience was in no mood for so light-hearted a piece at the end of the war. The Tenth Symphony, begun shortly after Stalin's death in 1953, was completed and performed at the end of that year. In this work, the composer struggled to come to terms with the central problem of a work of art: the proper form for a given substance and manner of expression. One of his best works, this symphony won the New York Critics Award for that year. As might be expected, his foes accused him of "formalism."

Like the Second and Third Symphonies, the Eleventh (1957) and Twelfth (1961) are programmatic, both depicting revolutions: the Eleventh is entitled "The Year 1905," and the Twelfth, "The Year 1917." Both works were intended to appeal to the masses, and they did so, but not to the Western critics. The latter thought the "programs" loomed far too large for the music, which might better have been film music to a subject treated visually.

The Thirteenth Symphony was first performed in December 1962, and then withdrawn (it is recorded, however). It is essentially a symphonic cantata in five movements. Each movement is based on a poem by Yevtushenko, and is for baritone, male chorus, and orchestra. The sentiments expressed in these five poems doubtless led to the withdrawal of the work: the first is "Babi Yar," in which the poet protests against anti-Semitism; the last is "Career," a tribute to a "nonconformist."

THE FIFTH SYMPHONY (1937)

The Fifth Symphony is a large-scale work, popular in tone and easily grasped in style. It is also notable for the care with which the material is worked out, for a number of passages of special beauty, and for the sureness of the orchestration.

Indeed, taken as a whole, this symphony could serve as a compendium of Shostakovich's moods and traits of style. In mood it ranges from caricature to the heroic, from brassy and vulgar banality to deeply felt lyricism. Its themes and rhythms reflect a similar variety, as Ex. 172–176 demonstrate. Both melodies and harmonies are tonal (or modal), but they also use the "transient modulations" so characteristic of Prokofiev and so unsettling, momentarily at least, to key. Shostakovich is partial to contrapuntal textures, and the symphony begins with a passage in imitative counterpoint. In spite of such integrating devices, Shostakovich's larger forms are apt to be loosely sectional (many are three-part forms); and as a unifying device he sometimes uses the cyclic procedure of recalling earlier themes in later movements. Shostakovich was accustomed to a large orchestra, and he used the full ensemble with great effect, *à la* Rimsky-Korsakov. At the same time, he handles individual instruments with finesse. He is an orchestral colorist who can highlight a woodwind instrument against a neutral background (e.g., the oboe solo in the third movement). Like Mahler, Shostakovich also contrasts the full orchestra with soloist orchestration, where a chamber-music ensemble comprised of soloists is heard as a foil or substitute for the full orchestra with its customary thicker doublings of two or more instruments on each voice part. As in this symphony, Shostakovich often calls for a large number of percussion instruments, including the piano.

The first movement (*moderato*) opens and closes in D minor, and it is cast in sonata form. The two principal themes of the exposition are shown in Ex. 172 and Ex. 173. The first theme is treated in imitation (a frequent device in Shostakovich), and the theme itself has the type of melodic shift, characteristic of both Shostakovich and Prokofiev, that carries the melody momentarily out of the key (m. 2–3). Actually, Ex. 172 is the first of a series of melodic fragments that follow each other to make up the first "group" of themes. Ex. 173, the first of the second group of themes, is a type of subject of large range and large leaps, a slow subject in the context of a faster rhythmic accompaniment. Played softly, this theme is a striking contrast to the subjects of the first group. The development section is notable for its various restatements and contrapuntal combinations of the melodic fragments of the first group in varied and increasingly brilliant orchestration. The recapitulation is especially effective. Ex. 172 returns *fortissimo* in a higher register than at the opening and is now scored for woodwinds as well as strings. A few measures later the second subject (Ex. 173), conspicuously absent from the development, is introduced *fff* in

Ex. 172 *

the brass, against the continuing figures of Ex. 172. After an extended treatment of this kind, the second subject is heard in a manner analogous to the exposition, but now in D major, its effect being heightened by being restated as a canon between flute and horn (with string accompaniment). The movement ends quietly, a mood underlined by a muted solo violin in the high register, followed in the last measure by upward chromatic passages in the celesta.

Ex. 173 *

The second movement (*allegretto*) shows Shostakovich in a jocose mood—a scherzolike movement with a number of highly contrasted subjects and many amusing bits of whimsy. The movement starts in an unusual way with a bass line heard alone in the Phrygian (E) mode. Then the first of the whimsical themes is heard starting in unison, high in the woodwinds. The opening bass line is repeated in varied form and instrumentation and is followed by a boisterous theme in the minor mode, first heard high in the woodwinds. A real contrast is afforded by the following theme in the major mode for two horns, reminiscent of a jolly day in the country. The next theme (Ex. 174) is a complete contrast and

Ex. 174 *

one of the most amusing moments of this movement—Shostakovich's parody of a waltz or *Ländler à la* Mahler. Played by a solo violin, the melody is accompanied lightly by harp and cello *pizzicato,* a passage typical of a chamber-music style of scoring that Shostakovich may have learned from Mahler. A final master touch: the "schmaltzy" use of the *glissando* in the solo violin. This theme (C major) and its repetition act as a middle section to the piece. Then the opening bass theme returns, the movement ending in A minor.

The third movement (*largo*) in F sharp minor, is a moving piece, marvelously scored for divided string orchestra, woodwinds, timpani, two harps, celesta, and piano (the piano often appears in Shostakovich's orchestra). It is also a masterpiece of scoring for the solo woodwinds, including an important oboe theme (in the middle of the movement), accompanied only by the first violin playing tremolo. This movement is full of imaginative touches. Much of the material is derived from the opening theme, the beginning of which is shown in Ex. 175. In addition, there is a reference to a theme in the first movement, and there are chromatic passages in which echoes of Wagner's *Tristan* can be heard. The last page of the score recalls the oboe theme, now scored for celesta doubling harmonics in the harp—an extraordinary idea. The string choir

Ex. 175 *

is heard alone at the close in a hushed chord altered from the expected minor to major, the sound dying away to nothing.

The last movement (*allegro non troppo*) is music that pulls out all the stops in the orchestral sense of Tchaikovsky. The vigorous, bombastic, and marchlike theme which dominates the movement is shown in Ex. 176. It is announced in unison in the brass, *fortissimo,* against the pound-

Ex. 176 *

ing of the timpani. Beginning in D minor, a fragment of the theme is transformed in the last pages to an "optimistic and grandiose close in D major."

Many pages of this work show Shostakovich in his best light: on the one hand, the jesting theme of parody, the driving theme and savage rhythm, and the brilliant orchestration; on the other, the quiet and deeply felt, the delicately and lightly scored, and the carefully worked-out part writing.

Shostakovich, a composer now venerated in the Soviet Union, has never been greeted with unqualified enthusiasm by Western critics. His First Symphony was a brilliant beginning, but his later music has been curiously uneven in quality. It is easy to blame Socialist Realism as a scapegoat, yet the fact remains that Prokofiev, working under the same system and under much the same restraints, was able to produce compositions consistently higher in quality. Shostakovich, however, is undoubtedly a natural musician of great gifts. In his best works, his music has the flow and sound of a man working in his natural medium. Yet his musical ideas often lack depth and are sometimes commonplace; and the organization of his material is often loosely conceived.

It was in just these matters of depth and organization that Beethoven's music was so impressive in his own time, and so lasting. That Shostakovich should look to Beethoven as a model is both ironic and understandable: Beethoven, who embodied the revolutionary ideal to be emulated, although never achieved, by Shostakovich. Beethoven was a revolutionary who looked to the future, and the example of his music influenced the course of composers who followed him in the nineteenth century; it is unlikely that history will render such a verdict on Shostakovich, the composer of another revolution and one of its most ardent and persuasive apologists. As admirable as some of Shostakovich's works are in themselves, they can hardly be expected to exert an influence on the future development of music. With a few early exceptions, his music represents a backward glance, and those works of Shostakovich that remain in the world repertory will be regarded as an extension of the ideals of the past.

Suggested Listening
First Symphony.
Fifth Symphony.
String Quartet No. 1 (second movement).

Suggested Reading
D. Rabinovich, *Dmitry Shostakovich, Composer*. Moscow: 1959.

KHACHATURIAN

Aram Khachaturian (b. 1903) was born of Armenian parentage in Tiflis, Georgia, far south of Moscow and Leningrad. Khachaturian's natural style is much closer to the accepted notions of Socialist Realism than that of either Prokofiev or Shostakovich. His melodies are derived from the folk songs of the Armenians and related peoples, and his luxuriant harmony is in the brilliant, Romantic tradition of Russian Orientalism (cf. Rimsky-Korsakov). Lavish orchestral colors and powerful rhythms are his forte. Nevertheless, certain "modernistic" tendencies brought his music under the censure of Zhdanov in 1948. Like the other censured composers, Khachaturian admitted his deviation from the proper style and came to terms with the authorities, apparently without artistic damage. At least in 1954 he could write that Socialist Realism "presupposes the free expression of creative individuals." Among his best known works are the ballet *Gayane* (1942), which includes the popular "Saber Dance"; the Violin Concerto (1940), and the Cello Concerto (1946).

Suggested Listening
Cello Concerto.
Gayane [*Gayne*] (ballet suite).

Suggested Reading
Grigory Shneerson, *Aram Khachaturyan.* London: Central Books, 1959 (in English).

31. *Other Leading Composers and Other Countries*

T HE LAST FEW chapters have dealt with the leading composers and the principal developments of the twentieth century to approximately 1945: atonality, Neoclassicism, and folk-song nationalism. (In Soviet Russia, Socialist Realism is a species of nationalism whose musical idiom characteristically looks backward to the nineteenth century.) The following two chapters are devoted to a discussion of the relationship of other leading composers in Western Europe and in the "New World" to the developments just mentioned.

FRANCE: "THE SIX"—HONEGGER, MILHAUD, POULENC

In France, the composer who best represented Neoclassicism was Stravinsky, but there were others who, in one way or another, followed its general tenets. Among them was a group of young composers dubbed "The Six Frenchmen" (usually abbreviated to "The Six") by the French critic Henri Collet (1920). This label stuck, although it was of no real significance and even became a source of annoyance to the composers concerned, especially to Darius Milhaud (b. 1892). Arthur Honegger (1892–1955), Francis Poulenc (1899–1963), and Milhaud were the most important of "The Six" who (according to Collet) "have, by magnificent and voluntary return to simplicity, brought about a renaissance of French music, because they understood the lesson of Erik Satie and followed the very exact precepts of Jean Cocteau." At first "The Six" were against Debussy, and they delighted in jazz and in the music of the Parisian music hall. Actually the mature styles of these composers diverged sharply from one another.

Honegger should not have been included in this group at all. He was

Swiss, his background was essentially German, and he opposed the harmonic simplicity of Satie, claiming that previous harmonic idioms should be used where possible "as a basis for lines and rhythms." *See Plate 30A.* Honegger is the best example of the back-to-Bach spirit among them (as his statement on p. 435 suggests); and his oratorio *King David* (1921), a work that made him famous, has passages of Bach-like rhythm and counterpoint. Much later, Honegger turned toward the style of Prokofiev (as did Poulenc), whom he professed to admire above all other contemporaries; and certain passages of Honegger's late works (the scherzo of his Fifth Symphony, the "Symphony of the Three D's," 1951) remind one of Prokofiev. His book *I Am a Composer* is a bitter commentary on a composer's lot. Although his career was outwardly successful, Honegger was deeply pessimistic about the state of new music and its creators. He said, "The most important attribute of a composer is that he be dead."

Milhaud, prodigiously prolific and versatile, is far too strong a personality to be influenced more than temporarily by any doctrinaire attitude emanating from Satie, Cocteau, or anyone else. Like Stravinsky, whom he greatly admires, he experiments in many mediums, and his particular works show the same kind of marked individuality. Milhaud is particularly facile as a melodist—he himself speaks of his "Mediterranean lyricism"—and his early work shows a considerable interest in polytonality, which he used to distinguish the melodic lines from each other and the melodic lines from the harmony. His Fourteenth and Fifteenth String Quarters are examples of his virtuoso technique: they can be played either separately or together as an octet.

Milhaud's association with French literary figures, notably Cocteau (1889–1963) and Paul Claudel (1868–1955), produced fruitful results. When Claudel went to Brazil as French ambassador (1917), Milhaud accompanied him as his secretary, returning to Paris in 1918 by way of New York, where he was overwhelmed by the jazz he heard in Harlem. Milhaud soaked up the popular music of Brazil—its tangos, rhumbas, and sambas—and this popular music was put to good use in the ballet *Le Boeuf sur le toit* (*The Ox on the Roof,* given in London as *The Nothing-Doing Bar*), which he did with Cocteau (1920). Claudel furnished the libretto for Milhaud's opera *Christophe Columb* (1928), one of his most ambitious works. The ballet *The Creation of the World* (1923) shows Milhaud's fascination with the jazz idiom (Ex. 177). About this ballet Milhaud wrote: "I adopted the same orchestra as used in Harlem, seventeen solo instruments, and I made wholesale use of the jazz style to convey a purely classical feeling."

At the beginning of World War II, Milhaud came to the United States, and today he divides his time between France and the United States.

Ex. 177 *

DOUBLE BASS (SOUNDS AS WRITTEN)

* By permission of Associated Music Publishers, Inc., New York.

In certain respects Poulenc remains the most faithful to the supposed ideals of "The Six" and is closest in spirit to Satie and Ravel. Poulenc is the most determinedly anti-Romantic—note his interest in street songs and the circus, for instance—the most humorous, and the simplest in style. On closer examination, however, this simplicity reveals its deliberate and sophisticated character, a reaction against the complexities of Romanticism. Poulenc's music, which embraces a large variety of types, exhibits a spontaneity of melodic invention (notably in the large number of songs) that is especially attractive. An intense seriousness, however, pervades his full-length opera *Dialogues of the Carmelites* (1956), as befits the subject. The setting is the French Revolution; and the story concerns the aristocrat Blanche, who becomes a Carmelite nun and accepts death with her sister nuns rather than return to the world.

Suggested Listening
Honegger, *King David.*
Milhaud, *The Creation of the World.*
Poulenc, *Dialogues of the Carmelites.*

Suggested Reading
Arthur Honegger, *I Am a Composer,* trans. by W. O. Clough and A. A. Willman. London: Faber and Faber, 1966 (original French, 1951).
Darius Milhaud, *Notes without Music* (autobiography), trans. by D. Dobson. New York: Alfred A. Knopf, 1953.
Gertrude Stein, *The Autobiography of Alice B. Toklas.* New York: Vintage Books, 1955 (original edition, 1933).

ITALY: MALIPIERO. DALLAPICCOLA.

In Italy, traditionally the home of the opera, opera dominated the musical scene in the nineteenth century. It continued to do so in the early years of the twentieth century in the works of Giacomo Puccini, most of whose operas fall in this period, but whose style was not in the *avant-garde* of musical development (for details on Puccini, see p. 370). A composer who understood the theater completely and captivated the public with his melodies, Puccini became the acknowledged leader of the Italian musical stage, and his operas were played all over the world, rivaling the popularity of Verdi's. Other well-known opera composers of the time were Ermanno Wolf-Ferrari (*The Secret of Susannah,* 1911) and Italo Montemezzi (*The Love of Three Kings,* 1913).

However, there was a new force abroad in the land of opera. In the last years of the nineteenth century a school of instrumental composers emerged and continued into the twentieth, the most important of whose members were Ottorino Respighi, Ferruccio Busoni (one of the greatest pianists), Ildelbrando Pizzetti, Alfredo Casella, and Gian Francesco Malipiero.

Gian Francesco Malipiero (b. 1882) is probably the most important of these composers. The diatonic scale is basic to his "pandiatonic" style, which also employs the old modes and modern harmonic resources. He is fond of elaborate *ostinato* figures and a rather static harmony; virtuosity in orchestration is a marked characteristic. He returns to the past for stanza schemes of older forms, and, typically, tune after tune is joined together in a sectional form. In keeping with such forms, Malipiero gave certain of his works titles of old stanzaic poetry, such as *Rispetti e Strambotti* (String Quartet, 1920). Malipiero also made extensive opera reforms by trying to achieve a close alliance between mimic action, text, and music. He is celebrated, too, for his critical writings and editions of older Italian music (critical editions of the works of Monteverdi and Vivaldi).

Luigi Dallapiccola, born in the twentieth century (1904), is the most distinguished Italian twelve-tone composer. One of the first in Italy to be influenced by Schoenberg, he owes more to Berg and Webern. Dallapiccola describes his own rather clandestine visit to Webern in the midst of World War II (1943) as a turning point in his life. A melodist like Berg, he characteristically tempers the twelve-tone technique by using "singing" melodies and sometimes by applying tonal or modal devices within the framework of twelve-tone music. Like Malipiero, Dallapiccola uses forms of early Italian music, such as the old dance forms or the *passacaglia* in his Partita for Orchestra (1933). Among his best known works are the opera *The Prisoner* (*Il Prigioniero;* 1948) and Variations for Orchestra (1954), the latter commissioned by the Louisville Symphony Orchestra. Dallapiccola has summed up his outlook in these words: "I personally am *for* tradition . . . but I am *against* traditionalism."

Suggested Listening
Malipiero, *Rispetti e Strambotti*.
Dallapiccola, Variations for Orchestra.

Suggested Reading
Arthur V. Berger, "Gian Francesco Malipiero," in *The Book of Modern Composers* (Second edition), edited by David Ewen. New York: Alfred A. Knopf, 1950.
Luigi Dallapiccola, "The Genesis of the *Canti di Prigonia* and *Il Prigioniero:* An Autobiographical Fragment," in *The Musical Quarterly* (1953), p. 355.

SPAIN: FALLA

The modern Spanish school dates from Felipe Pedrell (1841–1922). Like that of Balakirev in Russia, Pedrell's influence on younger composers was of considerable importance in creating a new nationalism in Spanish music. Pedrell believed that the salvation of Spanish music lay in using the material of genuine folk songs. He also revived music of the past (complete edition of the sixteenth-century Spanish composer Victoria).

The best-known composers of modern Spain are Isaac Albéniz (1860–1909), Enrique Granados (1867–1916), and, the most important, Manuel de Falla (1876–1946). Falla came under the influence of French Impressionism (he lived in Paris from 1907 to 1914), but he did not give up his own style, which was solidly founded in Spanish folk music and the Spanish art music of the past. Like that of Albéniz, his instrumental style is based on the Spanish dance with its conflicting rhythms and characteristic syncopations, on effects derived from guitar style, and on the melodic phrases of folk music. His harmonic vocabulary is more modern. In later works, such as the Harpsichord Concerto, Falla turned more to the concise forms and idioms of the Neoclassic style.

Suggested Listening
Ballet *El Amor Brujo* (*Love, the Magician*); No. 7 is the popular "Ritual Fire Dance."

Suggested Reading

Gilbert Chase, *The Music of Spain.* New York: W. W. Norton & Company, 1941.

FINLAND: SIBELIUS

Jean Sibelius (1865–1957) is the only Finnish composer who has attained an international reputation. Although Sibelius did not use folk song as such, he may be called a nationalist composer because he stirred the Finnish people by suggesting the special character of their land, history, and legends. He drew on the Finnish epic *Kalevala* for a number of tone poems (e.g., *The Swan of Tuonela,* 1893), and some of his music has become part of the national consciousness (*Finlandia,* 1902). Outside Finland, however, Sibelius's reputation rests largely on his Violin Concerto and on his symphonies, whose musical interest transcends the specifically national.

His symphonies are highly individual creations which show immense variety and differences among themselves. This is true with respect to the emotional atmosphere as well as the forms. The Fourth Symphony, for instance, is terse and gloomy, almost a reflection of the Arctic night. The Fifth regains a cheerful mood. The form of the First Symphony, a conventional sonata, is in striking contrast to the experimental nature of the Seventh Symphony, where a single movement is used. A very spare, condensed form characterizes the Fourth Symphony (probably his best). Another method is employed in the Second Symphony, where fragments are gradually pieced together like a mosaic until a complete statement of the theme is achieved. This construction is novel, but it has the disadvantage of obscuring the direction of the piece and cutting it up into episodes.

Sibelius's style is marked by energetic and virile rhythms, often persistent and syncopated. The melodies in his early work often resemble folk songs and sometimes the melodies of Tchaikovsky; in other works (especially the later ones), short, concentrated motives, such as the melodic tritone that is central to the Fourth Symphony (Ex. 178), are more

Ex. 178 *

Tempo molto moderato, quasi adagio

(CELLOS, BASSES, BASSOONS)
con sordino

dim.

* With permission of Breitkopf & Härtel, Wiesbaden.

characteristic. The dynamic nuances are very changeable. A *crescendo* on a single chord may be followed dramatically by a sudden *piano* or a rest; sometimes he ends a piece softly (Fourth Symphony). The harmony is typically spare, hollow, almost bleak in sound. Conservative by modern standards, Sibelius's harmony specializes in modal effects and skillful progressions of common triads. He favors pedal points of different kinds and also sustained doublings of lines in thirds and sixths. The orchestration tends to emphasize the hollow effect of the harmony by doublings, sometimes several octaves apart. Sibelius was also fond of the *pizzicato* and the string tremolo (sometimes of whole chords), and he scored delicately for the soloists, particularly solo woodwind instruments over a neutral string accompaniment. Sibelius was not timid about the unconventional. The second movement of the Fourth Symphony ends with two timpani strokes heard alone.

Sibelius is something of a solitary figure, standing apart from the experiments, "isms," and mainstreams of the twentieth century as they are viewed today. But in the 1930's, before these "mainstreams" were at all clear, Sibelius had a devoted following, especially in England and America; and certain English critics, such as Constant Lambert (*Music Ho!: A Study of Music in Decline,* 1934), detected in Sibelius's music a "mainstream" of the future. In retrospect, this view cannot be maintained, since Sibelius's musical idiom is clearly related to that of the nineteenth century. Moreover, after 1929 he ceased to compose, and his last important composition—one of his best—was the tone poem *Tapiola* (1925). Yet one must give Sibelius his proper due: He absorbed the past in a unique personal idiom of his own, combining the emotional heritage of his native land and the deep brooding of his inner self.

In 1897, early in his career, the Finnish government showed its enlightened policy toward great talent by settling on Sibelius an annual stipend, freeing him to work solely on musical composition. For more than thirty years, Sibelius requited this trust, his work became part of the national heritage, and after a long life, he died a hero to his countrymen.

Suggested Listening
The Swan of Tuonela.
The Fourth Symphony.

Suggested Reading
Gerald Abraham (ed.), *The Music of Sibelius.* New York: W. W. Norton & Company, 1947.
Harold E. Johnson, *Jean Sibelius.* New York: Alfred A. Knopf, 1959.

ENGLAND: DELIUS. VAUGHAN WILLIAMS. BLISS. WALTON. BRITTEN.

In contrast with the very Englishness of Elgar, Frederick Delius (1862–1934) was a curious combination of English and "foreign" strains. Delius was born in England of German parentage, traveled to the United States and elsewhere, and lived most of his life in France (after 1889). Some of his works are touched with Impressionism, but basically he was a Romantic composer of somewhat venturesome chromatic and dissonant harmony who was inspired by folk song, poetic texts (*Sea Drift,* 1903, on a poem by Walt Whitman), and evocative titles (*On Hearing the First Cuckoo in Spring,* 1913). Delius's music is of a poetic kind, a music of "distance, of background rather than foreground."

After Elgar and Delius, a fresh era in English music of the twentieth century began with Gustav Holst (1874–1934) and particularly with Ralph Vaughan Williams (1872–1958), the foremost English composer of his time. Vaughan Williams was firmly convinced that music should be related to life and to the people, and he identified himself with English nationalism, joining the English Folk Song Society (1904) in which Cecil Sharp was a prime mover. Like Bartók, Vaughan Williams collected folk material, assimilating folk-song elements into his style. He made numerous settings of folk melodies, his melodic style in general was determined by the character of English folk song, and sometimes he set whole works in folk-song style (the opera *Hugh the Drover,* 1911–1914). Vaughan Williams also returned to the past and adopted modal procedures and rhythms of the sixteenth century and the parallel chords of the still older organum. His admiration for the great English composers of the sixteenth century like Thomas Tallis and William Byrd affected the character of his polyphony, as in his *Fantasia on a Theme of Thomas Tallis* (1910) for string quartet and double string orchestra. However, he is not limited to folk-song or modal style. Consider his nine symphonies. His Fourth Symphony (1935) is an amazing contrast to his earlier symphonies. To go from *A London Symphony* (1914) to the Fourth Symphony twenty years later is to enter another world: The latter is one of sharp dissonance, terse motives, concise expression, and dynamic power; the former is that of folk song and modal music, not unreminiscent of certain works of Sibelius, of whom Vaughan Williams was a great admirer.

Other noted English composers of the present include Bliss, Walton, and Britten. Arthur Bliss (b. 1891) writes in a dissonant, vigorous style.

Among his copious works are ballets (*Checkmate,* 1937), orchestral pieces, chamber music, concertos, and film music (*Things to Come,* 1935).

William Walton (b. 1902) is a facile melodist and brilliant orchestrator who made an early name with his Viola Concerto (1929). Of a long list of later works, three important examples are *Façade* ("entertainment" for speaking voice and instruments, set to poems by Edith Sitwell, 1923), *Belshazzar's Feast* (oratorio for baritone, chorus, and orchestra, 1931), and his opera *Troilus and Cressida* (1954).

Benjamin Britten (b. 1913) is the best known and most important of living English composers. *See Plate 36B.* A prodigy, he began composing at eight. Today, as composer, solo pianist, and conductor, Britten dominates the English musical scene; and Aldeburgh, where he lives, is the center of an important festival.

Britten's early work immediately attracted the public because it combined lyrical qualities, flexible rhythm, and a harmonic style that was modern enough to be interesting without being baffling. In addition, Britten handled the orchestra brilliantly—natural enough for a man of his great knowledge of the capabilities of instruments and his intuitive grasp of orchestration. These qualities are apparent in Variations on a Theme of Frank Bridge, an early work (1937) that was his first real success. Britten learned much about instruments, including how to make the maximum sound from few resources, in his work with documentary films after his graduation from the Royal College of Music. In instrumental music Britten is attracted more to sectional forms like the variation than to the sonata and the symphony. Besides the Bridge Variations just mentioned, Britten chose to set a theme of Purcell to variations (with concluding fugue) in his *The Young Person's Guide to the Orchestra,* a piece used to introduce the instruments of the orchestra (1945), probably Britten's most played work (originally the music was for a film, *The Instruments of the Orchestra*). The *passacaglia* is another form of variation favored by Britten and used in his opera *Peter Grimes.*

However skillful his use of instruments in orchestra or chamber music, Britten's interest in the voice is central to his music—in songs, song cycles, choruses, and especially operas. He chooses texts that range over the past three centuries—from Donne to his contemporaries Auden and Spender; and his strong interest in the English past, in Elizabethan music and Purcell particularly, is evident in the flexibility of declamation, pliable rhythm, and effective use of the chorus. For the latter Britten has written such works as *A Ceremony of Carols* for boys' chorus and harp (1942) and the *War Requiem,* composed for the dedication of the rebuilt Coventry Cathedral (1962). The *War Requiem* is an important work on a large scale, written for soloists, choruses, and orchestra. It combines the Requiem text (sung by a regular chorus, a boys' chorus, and a soprano solo) with war poems of the English poet Wilfred Owen (sung by tenor and baritone, representing two soldiers). Altogether an extraordinary conception and an extraordinary work.

One of the most prolific of opera composers in modern times, Britten is undoubtedly the most important composer of English opera since Purcell. Britten's success in the theater rests on a genuine dramatic and lyric gift, on the central and effective role of the voice (both as solo and in the chorus) in his works, and on the exceptional sonority that he creates from a small orchestra. This chamber orchestration explains the numerous performances of Britten's operas outside the large opera houses. His first operatic success was *Peter Grimes* (1946), a grim tale of a bitter, lonely, and unyielding fisherman pitted against the townspeople of the "Burough," to whom he is an outsider. Certain resemblances to the general subject and the lyrical aspects of Berg's *Wozzeck* have not escaped notice. Among Britten's later operas are: *The Rape of Lucretia* (1946); *The Little Sweep* (children's opera, 1949); *The Turn of the Screw* (1954), based on a Henry James story and one of his most interesting scores; and *A Midsummer Night's Dream* (1960).

Suggested Listening

Vaughan Williams, *Fantasia on a Theme of Thomas Tallis*.
  Fourth Symphony.
Walton, *Belshazzar's Feast*.
Britten, *Peter Grimes*.
  War Requiem.

Suggested Reading

Eric Fenby, *Delius as I Knew him*. London: G. Bell and Sons, Ltd., 1936 (Reprinted by Icon Ltd., London, 1966).

Alan Frank, *Modern British Composers*. London: Dobson, 1953.

Michael Kennedy, *The Works of Ralph Vaughan Williams*. London: Oxford University Press, 1964.

Donald Mitchell and Hans Keller (eds.), *Benjamin Britten: A Commentary on His Works, from a Group of Specialists*. London: Rockliff, 1952.

32. Music in the New World:
The United States. Latin America.

THE UNITED STATES

THROUGH THE EARLY YEARS of the twentieth century, the United States was essentially a cultural province of Europe. The large opera house was dominated by the international repertory of Wagner, Verdi, and Puccini (things have not changed much today). The concert hall emphasized the German classics until 1914, and later there was a vogue for the French Impressionists. A large majority of performers were European, and American composers went to Europe to study as a matter of course when they could. The strong German influence at the end of the nineteenth century left its imprint on a composer like Edward MacDowell (1861–1908), who studied in Germany, just as French Impressionism influenced Charles Griffes (1884–1920) a generation later.

Before World War I, new European music made some impression in this country. Stravinsky's ballet *Petrushka* (1911) received a generally warm welcome, although the new "atonal" music of Schoenberg found practically no audience here. At the same time, at least one native composer of distinction went unhonored at home. Charles Ives was already writing music of great inventiveness and complexity before 1914 (see below), celebrating the local scene, but he remained quite unknown and unplayed in the first quarter of the century.

After World War I, the French influence on music increased on the international scene. Many American composers went to Paris to study in the 1920's, where they came in contact with Stravinsky, "The Six," and the various types of Neoclassic and twelve-tone music, the latter gradually seeping out of Vienna and Berlin. The phases of new European music influenced American composers as much as they influenced the Europeans. Besides, certain eminent European composers taught in the United States, one of the first and most influential being Ernest Bloch. The year Hitler came to power (1933) marks the beginning of large-scale migration of European musicians to this country. Many of them became citizens (among them, Hindemith and Schoenberg), and in the capacity of teachers they influenced younger composers. At the same time, native American composers, most of whom had received at least part of their training abroad (for instance, Sessions and Piston), began to play an equally—or perhaps more—important part in training native talents, especially in the universities. The number of American composers rapidly increased, and, more important, among them were composers of marked musical individuality.

American music, in short, gradually ceased to be a mere appendage to the European scene. While well aware of the European tradition, the American composer awoke to his own capacity and to the vast latent resources of the country. Like Ives, some composers were attracted by the immense reservoir of folk song, dance, and legend;[1] others found their inspiration in the rhythm, color, and improvisations of jazz. But what most composers actually found was themselves—not only a new nationalism or the heritage of folk song or jazz—and they sought to discover the kinds and means of expression, whatever its source, best suited to their own temperaments.

To Europeans, jazz was the most original American contribution,[2] both as music and as an influence on composers. Jazz made a pronounced impact on Milhaud's early music (see Chapter 31). Similarly, Stravinsky wrote *Ragtime* (1918), and Ravel and Hindemith, not to mention American composers like Copland, enjoyed a brief flirtation with jazz.

The invention of the phonograph enabled people all over the world to listen to successive phases and styles of jazz: among them the old "blues" and the "ragtime" of the original Dixieland (New Orleans) style dating back to the first years of the twentieth century. The phonograph record also permitted the public to listen in on the "jam session," essentially small groups improvising for themselves after regular hours of work in dance bands. "Swing" became the thing in the 1930's with famous names like Duke Ellington, Benny Goodman, and Louis Armstrong. Ellington used material that was basically composed, but "Bebop" was generally improvised, the high priest of this style being a saxophonist, Charlie Parker (b. 1920), known as "Bird" and often considered the greatest genius of jazz. "Cool" jazz (Miles Davis) takes off from Parker, and "West Coast" or "Progressive" jazz followed in the rein of cool jazz. More recently there is the vogue of the "Beatles" (more "popular" music than jazz)—not to

---

[1] The large amount of regional, occupational, and racial folk material is, in the aggregate, the national folk music of the United States. See, for instance, the recordings of authentic folk music released by the Library of Congress in Washington. (Cf. also pp. 135-37 in this text.)

[2] See Leonard G. Feather, *The Encyclopedia of Jazz.* New York: Horizon Press, 1966; and Marshall W. Stearns, *The Story of Jazz.* New York: Oxford University Press, 1956; revised edition, 1958. See also Gunther Schuller, *Early Jazz.* New York: Oxford University Press, 1968.

mention other groups with picturesque names like "The Rolling Stones," "Jefferson Airplane," and "The Grateful Dead"—and the various shades of "rock" (rock 'n roll), "the sacred squeal of now," which in its "harder" forms leads to "total immersion"—sound amplified electronically to ear-splitting levels. "Rock" today comes not only from the jazz tradition but also combines blues, "big beat," and country and "Western" styles.

Jazz at its best has added something new and vital to music through its rhythms and syncopated beat, the variety and novelty of its instrumental and vocal sound, and the revival of improvisation as an art. These are musical values. Jazz is also the product of an environment: it is dance; it is sex; it is the symbol (as it was from the beginning of jazz) of the alienation and struggle of despairing minorities against social and economic injustice.

BLOCH AND IVES: A STUDY IN CONTRAST

Ernest Bloch (1880–1959), an important composer and teacher, first came to the United States in 1916. Born in Switzerland, he became an American citizen and was intimately associated with American musical life. In 1917 he settled in New York and taught at the Mannes School. Later, he was director of the Institute of Music in Cleveland (1920–1925), director of the San Francisco Conservatory (1925–1930), and then (in the 1940's) a teacher at the University of California at Berkeley. The number of American composers who studied with him is quite astonishing, including Roger Sessions, Douglas Moore, and Randall Thompson.

Bloch's music is rhapsodic and passionate, full of fluctuating meters and rhythmic life. His idiom is rather romantic and ornate in style, although somewhat dissonant. An innate preoccupation with Jewish subjects is shown by the titles of certain of his works: *Schelomo: A Hebrew Rhapsody for Violoncello Solo and Full Orchestra* (1916); *Sacred Service* (1930–1933); and *Israel* (symphony with voices, 1912–1916). Other notable works include the opera *Macbeth* (1909), the Violin Concerto (1938), and a variety of chamber music, including five string quartets (No. 5, 1956).

Bloch and Charles Ives (1874–1954) are poles apart as regards their backgrounds, their style of music, and their acceptance by the American public. Bloch, a Swiss by birth and a composer in the tradition of a modernized Romantic idiom, had no difficulty finding either an audience or pupils when he came to the United States. On the other hand, Ives, a native American who dealt with many traditional aspects of the American scene, used a musical language so daring and novel that he had practically no audience in his own country until he had ceased to compose. One of America's most inventive musicians and born in the same year as Arnold Schoenberg, Ives was composing polytonal and atonal music, writing complex rhythms and harmonies, and even using quarter tones by the first years of the twentieth century—music as advanced as any music anywhere. *See Plate* 37A.

All this is a tragic illustration of how an advanced language of expression may serve as a barrier, often alienating an audience from the substance of a composer's thought. Ives's *language* was far too complex for most Americans of the early years of the twentieth century to grasp, yet the *substance* of what he wanted to express was as American as Stephen Foster, the transcendentalism of Emerson, or popular tunes and hymns, all of which Ives utilized in his music. Ives has gradually come into his own, and his influence has been felt in various ways and degrees by Henry Cowell, Elliot Carter, John Cage, and Lou Harrison, among others.

Ives was born in Danbury, Connecticut, the son of a most unconventional bandmaster who encouraged his son to experiment with dissonance, polytonality, and quarter tones. Young Ives learned to play the drums, piano, cornet, and organ; and he listened to village concerts. All this provided him with a repertory of hymns, marches, and popular tunes— bits of Americana and the local scene that he used copiously in his works later on. By the time of his graduation from Yale College (1898), it was perfectly clear to Ives that he could not hope to earn a living as a composer. Consequently, he entered the insurance business, relegating his composing to evenings and weekends. In his business Ives became rich, but as a composer he could scarcely get a public hearing. By 1921, a few years after suffering a serious breakdown (1917) from the strain of pursuing two professions, he had virtually ceased to compose.

Ives was a "national" composer in the sense that virtually everything he wrote was stamped with a national or regional character either through titles, literary allusions, or through literal quotations of hymns, popular tunes, marches, or snatches of ragtime. Sometimes the character or intent of the piece is obvious in the title: for example, *Three Places in New England* (for orchestra, 1903–1914), *General William Booth Enters Heaven* (a song; also for chorus and brass band, 1914), the Piano Sonata No. 2, "Concord, Mass., 1840–60" (see below). Ives also used a number of borrowed tunes in his four symphonies (1896–1916). The Fourth Symphony has at least twenty-five popular melodies, including *Nearer, My God, to Thee* in the first and fourth movement, and *From Greenland's Icy Mountains* as a fugue subject in the third movement. However, in a work like this symphony (and especially in the last movement), the immediate association of the tunes is secondary to Ives's general expression and interest in the transcendental, an interest verging on the visionary or mystical.

If Ives's melodic material is derived largely from traditional tunes (and occasionally from the classics, such as Beethoven or Brahms), his harmonic, rhythmic, and orchestral treatment was so original in technique and method as to anticipate the new European developments. One of the features of Ives's music is the striking contrast between the simplicity of the borrowed material and the astounding complexity of the music which surrounds it. His harmonic constructions, for example, include tone clusters (see Ex. 179), chords constructed by fourths, parallel chords of dissonant character, and quarter tones. The improvisational character of his music is reflected in the irregular barring or even no barring at all (opening of the "Concord" Sonata). Sometimes no meter is indicated, or unconventional meters are used. He pioneered in polyrhythm or polymeter: in *March 1776,* two march rhythms are combined in the "velocity ratio" of 4 : 3.

Ives also rather liked the idea of flexibility in a work, often specifying interchangeable and optional instrumental parts. This fluid concept may also have suggested the "chance" event introduced into the second movement of the Fourth Symphony. In this work there is also a contrast of tone colors and spatial grouping of orchestra and chorus, including a "distant choir" of five violins, viola, harp, and optional flute. In these notions of "chance" and "space" Ives anticipates by half a century the *avant-garde* of today.

The "Concord" Sonata (1909–1915) must have been a favorite of Ives. It was privately published by him (1919) and carefully revised in 1947. He also wrote an elaborate commentary on it (*Essays Before a Sonata,* 1920), which explains many of his specific ideas about the work. "The whole," says Ives, "is an attempt to present (one person's) impression of the spirit of transcendentalism that is associated in the minds of many with Concord, Mass., of over a half century ago" (i.e., 1840–1860). In "Emerson," the first movement, Ives introduces, shortly after the opening, the opening motive of Beethoven's Fifth Symphony, which he uses again in the third and fourth movements. "Hawthorne," the second movement, is a work of great technical difficulty, relieved by the introduction of a simple hymn tune in the middle. Among the particularly interesting harmonic features are two types of tone clusters. One, shown in Ex. 179a, is to be played by pressing down all the successive black keys of this "group chord." To do this, the player is instructed to use "a strip of board 14¾ inches long and heavy enough to press the keys down without striking." These "group chords" embrace two octaves and a tone (or minor third), and some of them are on successive white keys. Another type of cluster is shown at Ex. 179b—five-note "group chords" which "may, if the player

Ex. 179 *

Ives, "Concord" Sonata, Hawthorne movement

* © 1947 by Associated Music Publishers, Inc., New York. Used by permission.

feels like it, be hit with the clenched fist." The "Alcotts," the third movement, is a picture of the domestic life of that celebrated Concord family, with allusions to various tunes and songs, including a version of the Beethoven theme at the beginning. The last movement, "Thoreau," is concerned with a day in the life of the philosopher of Walden Pond. The Beethoven motive is heard once again at the end.

It is not easy to make a balanced judgment of Ives. One of the most original musicians who ever lived, he could hardly be considered a composer of the first class. Possessing no special gifts of melodic invention, Ives leaned too heavily on borrowed tunes and, by association, on programmatic elements. Nevertheless, he possessed an inventiveness and imagination of the first order, and his technical advances in harmony, rhythm, and instrumentation are almost unprecedented. Finally, the character of a remarkable human being shines through his essays and the music which they illuminate.

Ives has been considered in some detail not merely because of the belated recognition now accorded his music, but because he represents three points of importance in the discussion of other composers in the section that follows: namely, an experimental *avant-garde* idiom, a nationalism which uses native tunes and subjects, and the intangible matter of individuality.

To take the last point. Ives was, first of all, a composer who was being himself, just as Stravinsky, in his various facets of change in style, was being himself. All exceptionally creative persons have to be themselves, more or less implicitly by definition. Whether a composer creates in a conservative, *avant-garde,* or other kind of style is a matter of temperament and conviction; and it is only to give a certain perspective and order in the large canvas of an era that we indulge in categories at all. As Schoenberg said, "I compose twelve-tone *compositions,* not *twelve-tone* compositions." It is the composition, not the category, one must keep in mind, no matter whether the idiom is Neoclassic, twelve-tone, electronic, or that of folk-song nationalism. The important thing is the validity of the individual art work in its own terms and in its context, not its fashionable (or, for that matter, unfashionable) adherence to a current fad or "ism."

Suggested Listening
Bloch, *Sacred Service.*
    Schelomo.
Ives, "Concord" Sonata.
    General William Booth Enters Heaven (song).
    Fourth Symphony (second movement).

Suggested Reading
"Ernest Bloch," article in Oscar Thompson, *International Cyclopedia of Music and Musicians.* Ninth edition, New York, 1964.
Henry and Sidney Cowell, *Charles Ives and His Music.* New York: Oxford University Press, 1955.
Charles Ives, *Essays Before a Sonata,* privately printed, 1920. Available in paperback, New York: W. W. Norton & Company, 1961.

THE AVANT-GARDE. COWELL.

The experimental and forward-looking in Ives had its counterpart in a few contemporaries whose music generally met the same fate of rejection. Carl Ruggles (b. 1876) is an instance of a man who was trained in this country, who uses an atonal idiom, and whose few works have been rarely performed. Wallingford Riegger (1885–1961) received considerable training in Europe and lived there for some time. An excellent craftsman who wrote in a number of advanced styles, including atonality, he also worked with electronic instruments. Like Ives he received recognition later in life: his Third Symphony received the New York Music Critics Circle award in 1948. (The advanced and original music of Edgard Varese, born in France, will be considered in the last chapter.)

The man in the generation following Ives and most inspired by his example and outlook was probably Henry Cowell (1897–1965), the first to publish Ives's music in a regular publication (1929) and the co-author (with his wife) of a study of Ives's life and music. Cowell was a most original composer of marked experimental tendencies, and he formed a direct link between Ives and the *avant-garde* of today—John Cage, for example (see Chapter 33). One of the most prolific innovators of the century, Cowell elaborated on the notion of clusters of tones begun by Ives (cf. Ex. 179). He used the fist and forearm to produce clusters chords and special sonorities and percussive effects on the piano. On one of his five European tours playing his own piano music (he made twelve American tours), he met Bartók (1926), who was fascinated by the cluster technique and borrowed certain aspects of it from Cowell after asking his permission. Cowell also "played" the piano in an entirely new manner, plucking and stroking the strings inside the piano, sometimes scratching, strumming or scraping them in a vast number of ways and utilizing all sorts of new sound possibilities in connection with the pedals. (All this, of course, required a new kind of notation.) Cowell also investigated new rhythmic relationships, and he collaborated with the Russian Leon Theremin in inventing the *Rhythmicon,* which reproduces accurately some sixteen different rhythms (1931). He also founded the *New Music Quarterly* (1927) to publish *avant-garde* music, editing it until 1936. Later Cowell became interested in folk music, non-Western sources (the music of Bali, for instance), and percussion instruments and ensembles from Mexico and Cuba. He considered all music throughout the world as material on which to build a *new* music of our own time.

Cowell composed an astounding number of works—perhaps a thousand in all—including at least fourteen symphonies, numerous piano pieces, choral works, songs, chamber music, and pieces for band. Ironically, his most successful works were based on traditional tunes: *Tales of the Countryside* (for piano and orchestra, 1941); *Hymn and Fuguing Tune,* No. 1–8, (1943–1947, based on fuguing tunes of Billings, an eighteenth-century composer of hymns and anthems of most original cast).

Suggested Listening
Carl Ruggles, Organum for Orchestra.
Wallingford Riegger, Fantasy and Fugue for Orchestra and Organ.
Henry Cowell, *Hymn and Fuguing Tune,* No. 1–8.
  Quartet No. 3 ("Mosaic").
  Piano music (twenty pieces played by the composer), Folkways Records, No. FG 3349.

Suggested Reading
Henry Cowell, *New Musical Resources.* New York: Alfred A. Knopf, 1930.

THE NATIONALISTS: HARRIS. HANSON. GERSHWIN. MOORE.

The whole vein of Americana exploited by Ives was followed in one way or another by a number of composers, most conspicuously by Roy Harris, Howard Hanson, George Gershwin, and Douglas Moore.

Roy Harris (b. 1898), a pupil of Nadia Boulanger in Paris for a short time, is often considered the composer most representative of American nationalism. His titles refer to aspects of Americana ("When Johnny Comes Marching Home," 1934), and his style is calculated to suggest the barren stretches of the Great Plains by an open-fifth and open-fourth harmony and by typical declamatory and unaccompanied melody. A kind of expanding tonality permits considerable variety in creating a long "arch of melody" (see the opening of the Fifth Symphony, 1942). His use of modes also adds to the variety, and furnishes him with the material for one of his theories: the modes are scaled in light values from the darkest, most subjective (Locrian) to the lightest, most objective (Lydian). Harris's work is curiously uneven in quality, but in his Third Symphony (1937), he wrote a piece of music of compelling freshness and vitality, a highly unified one-movement form within which both *ostinato* and *fugue* occur. It is by far his best-known work. There are ten symphonies altogether, the Tenth—the "Abraham Lincoln" Symphony—appearing in 1965. Harris has also composed a considerable amount of chamber music.

Howard Hanson (b. 1896) was long the director of the Eastman School of Music. As an educator and conductor, he has been tireless in the cause of American music. His own music is in a conservative, Romantic vein. His Second Symphony is characteristically subtitled "Romantic." His works include numerous songs and piano works, choral pieces (*Lament for Beowulf,* 1925), an opera (*Merry Mount,* 1932), symphonies, and symphonic poems. A recent work is *Song of Human Rights* (1963).

George Gershwin (1898–1937), whose home was Broadway, occupies a special place in American music midway between "light" and "serious" music. His great gift for melody established him immediately as a popular song writer. He turned to jazz, and in the *Rhapsody in Blue* (commissioned by Paul Whiteman, 1924) he created "symphonic jazz," a kind of new, polite jazz that combined jazz rhythms with more elaborate forms and orchestration. Gershwin's *Porgy and Bess* (1935) is a folk opera using jazz rhythms. In the span of his lamentably short life, he created a real genre of the lighter forms of jazz and musical comedy.

Douglas Moore (1893–1969), well known as composer, teacher, and author, came from a background quite different from the three composers just discussed. His training and background were more cosmopolitan and European, and he studied with Ernest Bloch and Nadia Boulanger. Nevertheless, he turned primarily to national subjects and legend, and his characteristic mode of expression was the musical theater. His operetta *The Headless Horseman* (1937, text by Stephen Vincent Benet after

Washington Irving) concerns an American subject. It was written expressly for high school performance, an example of "music for use" (*Gebrauchsmusik*). His folk opera *The Ballad of Baby Doe* (1956) scored something of a "hit." Unpretentious, lyrical, and conservative in musical idiom, the theme of the opera concerns a true legend: how silver in the Rockies made and ruined Horace Tabor and his "Baby Doe."

Suggested Listening
Harris, Third Symphony.
Hanson, *Lament for Beowulf.*
Gershwin, *Porgy and Bess.*
Douglas Moore, *The Ballad of Baby Doe.*

Suggested Reading
David Ewen (ed.), *The Book of Modern Composers* (Second edition). New York: Alfred A. Knopf, 1950.

INDIVIDUALISM AND EUROPEAN CURRENTS: SESSIONS. THOMPSON. COPLAND. PISTON. THOMSON.

A number of the generation of composers born in the decade 1890–1900 studied with European teachers and participated in the general currents of European composition; yet they retained their own individuality in various idioms ranging from the twelve-tone technique to Neoclassicism to folk-song nationalism. Roger Sessions and Randall Thompson (as well as Douglas Moore), for instance, studied with Bloch in this country, and both lived and worked abroad for considerable periods of time; yet their own styles of expression were quite different—Sessions using a chromatic and eventually twelve-tone style as compared to the relatively conservative diatonicism of Thompson. A number of other composers were French-oriented, at least at first, studying in the 1920's in Paris with Nadia Boulanger: Copland, Piston, and Virgil Thomson are instances. Again, each wrote music of quite individual cast with crosscurrents of different idioms (sometimes in the same composer), as will be apparent below.

Roger Sessions (b. 1896), a major figure among composers and a powerful voice in American musical life, studied with Horatio Parker and Ernest Bloch. *See Plate 37B.* Then with the aid of two Guggenheim Fellowships (and other grants) he studied and composed in Europe for eight years (1925–1933), living not in Paris, as many American composers did at the time, but mainly in Florence, Rome, and Berlin. On his return to this country he taught at Princeton, Berkeley, and the Julliard School. He has a strong personal following of pupils; and his linear chromaticism has influenced the music of a number of younger American composers, some of whom have studied with him—notable examples are Andrew Imbrie (b. 1921), Leon Kirchner (b. 1919), and Seymour Shifrin (b. 1926). Sessions also exercises a wide influence by his writing and lectures; and, like Copland, he has been active in musical organizations of many sorts. Early in life he and Copland organized the "Copland-Sessions Concerts" of modern music (1928–1931), which attracted considerable attention.

Sessions is a man of marked originality and uncompromising musical ideals whose music must be accepted on purely musical grounds. The complex texture of his music results from intense contrapuntal activity— "total melody," someone has called it, which must be heard horizontally —highly dissonant harmony, and combinations of different rhythms. A long lyric melody is characteristic of slow sections. Some forms resemble those of the sonata, while others are like Bach arias that evolve from germinal motives contained in a condensed initial statement (Second Symphony, first movement). Sessions' own remarks on "form" are illuminating. About his Second Symphony, Sessions says in part: "The music took the shape which it had to take—I strove, as I always do, to be simply the obedient and willing servant of my musical ideas." About the first movement of the Second String Quartet (1951): "I did not set out to write a double fugue. I do not mean I was unaware that I was using fugal processes, but rather that these were in no sense *a priori;* the combinations . . . were not determined in advance but introduced in response to the demands of particular moments in the music. . . ."

Sessions' early work is reminiscent of Stravinsky (for example, *The Black Maskers,* incidental music to Andreyev's play, 1923; orchestral suite, 1928). Later he favored, successively, a free chromaticism and finally the twelve-tone technique of Schoenberg. This has all been a perfectly natural development. As Sessions himself stated it (1933): "I am not trying to write 'modern,' 'American,' or 'neoclassic' music. I am seeking always and only the coherent and living expression of my musical ideas. . . . I accept my musical ideas without theorizing."

The number of Sessions' works is not great, but it is not small either, and there are no "little" works among them. To mention a selected list: eight symphonies (Eighth Symphony, 1968), two string quartets (and other chamber works), the Violin Concerto (1935; one of the most difficult in the repertory), the Piano Concerto (1956), two piano sonatas, the *Idyll of Theocritus* for Soprano and Orchestra (1954), the one-act opera *The Trial of Lucullus* (1947), and the full-length opera *Montezuma* (1964), which Sessions considers his most important work.

Randall Thompson (b. 1899) is particularly distinguished as a choral composer (*The Peaceable Kingdom,* 1936; *Requiem for Double Chorus,* 1958; *The Passion According to St. Luke,* 1965). His innate sensitivity to words and poetry is apparent in the care he devotes to English declamation; and his vocal music is remarkable for its sonority and the combination of modal and modern harmony in which it is cast. He has written, besides, an opera (*Solomon and Balkis,* 1942), symphonies, chamber music, and songs.

Aaron Copland (b. 1900), one of the best known and most admired of American composers, studied with Nadia Boulanger in Paris (1921–1924). His early works reflect the variety of idioms to which he was exposed: jazz rhythms in the Piano Concerto (1927) and a rather austere emphasis on construction in the Piano Variations (1930). About 1934 he became increasingly concerned with narrowing the gap between the composer and the audience,[3] and in certain works he used a somewhat simpler style in melody and harmony. He wrote music for schools (*Second Hurricane,* 1937), and he has often chosen subjects related to the national scene here or elsewhere: the American theme in his ballets *Billy the Kid* (1938), *Rodeo* (1942), and *Appalachian Spring* (1944); Latin American material in *El Salón México* (for orchestra), one of his most popular and appealing works. In addition, he had composed much for the radio and especially for films (*Our Town,* 1940). At the same time, Copland is equally at home in advanced and sophisticated styles. His Piano Quartet (1950) uses a modified twelve-tone series as the basis of the piece.

The ballet *Appalachian Spring* (*see Plate* 30B), on a regional subject, is probably Copland's best known and generally admired work. It was composed for the dancer Martha Graham and first performed by her and her company in Washington, D.C. (1944). The original instrumentation called for a chamber ensemble of thirteen instruments; it was enlarged for a regular orchestra by the composer in a symphonic arrangement in 1945, which represents a slight condensation of the music of the regular ballet. The ballet has to do with "a pioneer celebration in spring around a newly-built farmhouse in the Pennsylvania hills in the early part of the last century. The bride-to-be and the young farmer-husband enact the emotions, joyful and apprehensive, their new domestic partnership invites. An older neighbor suggests now and then the rocky confidence of experience. A revivalist and his followers remind the new householders of the strange and terrible aspects of human fate. At the end the couple are left quiet and strong in their new house."[4] An especially attractive part of the ballet music is the last part (scene 7) where "the couple are left quiet and strong in their new house," and Copland creates this mood by means of a

---

[3] See his book *Our New Music.* New York: McGraw-Hill Book Co., 1941.
[4] From the Preface to the score, published by Boosey and Hawkes, 1945.

theme and five variations on a Shaker melody "The Gift to Be Simple" (Ex. 180). The music ends with a coda (scene 8).

Ex. 180 *

An economy of means and transparency of texture distinguish Copland's scores; and large melodic leaps, jazz rhythms, and irregular meters are typical. His music is basically tonal and diatonic although, as mentioned, he sometimes uses a modified twelve-tone style. In addition to the works already noted, Copland has composed symphonies, concertos, piano music, choruses, and chamber music.

Copland has been a mainspring of the American musical scene for some years not only as a composer but also as a pianist, conductor, lecturer, author, and board member of many organizations. His honors have also been many. He was the first composer to receive a Guggenheim award (1925–1927), and he received the Pulitzer Prize in 1945 for *Appalachian Spring.*

Walter Piston (b. 1894) is highly respected as a composer, teacher, and theorist. A composer of Neoclassic bent, Piston writes music that exhibits a notable degree of economy and concentration, liking for polyphonic forms, and vigorous syncopated rhythms. He is also partial to the forms of "absolute" music (symphonies, sonatas, concertos). His music is dissonant but tonal. An expressive style is sometimes apparent in his slow movements and in his later works. A pupil of Nadia Boulanger in Paris in the early 1920's, Piston returned to teach at Harvard until his retirement (1960). His books on harmony, counterpoint, and orchestration have carried his influence as a teacher far beyond the classroom. His works include a ballet (*The Incredible Flutist,* 1938), the impressive number of eight symphonies (1937–1965), a substantial amount of chamber music (Sonata for Violin and Piano, 1939; five string quartets, among others), and several concertos, including the Viola Concerto (1958), the Second Violin Concerto (1960), and the Cello Concerto (1967).

Virgil Thomson (b. 1896), also a pupil of Nadia Boulanger in Paris (where he lived for ten years) is equally noted as composer and critic. Formerly chief critic of the *New York Herald Tribune* (1940–1954), he is widely admired for the brilliance and penetration of his articles. The spiritual influence of France is strong in his works, and like Poulenc, he combines simplicity and sophistication. His early training as an organist and choirmaster has left certain imprints on his style: a hymnlike character of melody and diatonic harmony (some chromatic elements in later works). Among the most attractive of his numerous works are two operas and music for films. *Four Saints in Three Acts* (1934), an opera originally performed by an all-Negro cast, is a unique example of sophisticated simplicity and unworldliness well suited to the extraordinary libretto of Gertrude Stein. The music he wrote for government documentary films is exceptionally apt and interesting (*The Plough That Broke the Plains,* 1936; and *The River,* 1937). Some recent works are *Missa pro Defunctis* (1960), and *The Feast of Love* (1964).

Suggested Listening
Sessions, *The Black Maskers.*
  The Second Symphony.
Thompson, *The Peaceable Kingdom.*
Copland, *El Salón México.*
  Appalachian Spring.
Piston, Fourth Symphony (1951).
Thomson, *The Plough That Broke the Plains* (suite for orchestra).

Suggested Reading
Arthur V. Berger, *Aaron Copland.* New York: Oxford University Press, 1953.
Aaron Copland, *Copland on Music.* Garden City, N.Y.: Doubleday, 1960.
Aaron Copland, *Music and Imagination.* Cambridge. Mass.: Harvard University Press, 1952.
David Ewen (ed.), *The Book of Modern Composers* (Second edition). New York: Alfred A. Knopf, 1950.
Roger Sessions, *The Musical Experience of Composer, Performer, Listener.* Princeton, N.J.: Princeton University Press, 1950.

THE "YOUNGER" GENERATION: SCHUMAN. BARBER. MENOTTI.

The generation of composers born a decade after Aaron Copland no longer felt, or could follow so easily, the same urge to go abroad to study.

Times had changed. For one thing, the Great Depression occurred at the time of their formative years of instruction; for another, European teachers came to this country, and native composers began to teach more widely among the younger generation. Examples of the "younger" generation that illustrate these points are William Schuman and Samuel Barber. Gian Carlo Menotti is an especially interesting case, having come from Italy to study here. (For Carter, Kirchner, and others, see Chapter 33.)

William Schuman (b. 1910), a pupil of Roy Harris, is a composer whose work has attracted attention by its freshness and vitality of rhythm, long melodic lines, and dramatic intensity. For some years President of the Juilliard School of Music, Schuman has exercised an important influence on American musical education. Among his best-known works are: *American Festival Overture* (1939), Symphony No. 3 (1941), and the ballet *Undertow* (1945). Some recent works are: Eighth Symphony (1962), *Sons of Orpheus* (Fantasy for Cello and Orchestra, 1963), and Ninth Symphony (1968).

Samuel Barber (b. 1910) was educated at the Curtis Institute of Music in Philadelphia, studied with Scalero, and later taught there (1939–1942). His early style shows a marked lyricism in *Dover Beach* (for voice and string quartet, 1931) and especially in *Adagio for Strings* (1938, arranged from his String Quartet of 1936). The latter work, written in a cantabile and sonorous style, enjoyed a considerable vogue after it was first played by Arturo Toscanini and the NBC Symphony (one of the few "modern" American works played by that classics-minded maestro). Barber's later works are in a more astringent style, sometimes verging on atonality. His textures are often polytonal, and he is fond of counterpoint that features canonic and fugal elements. Among his works are: *Medea* or *Cave of the Heart,* a ballet written for Martha Graham (1946); *Excursions* for piano (1945) and Piano Sonata (1949); the operas *Vanessa* (1958, libretto by Menotti) and *Antony and Cleopatra* (1966); concertos; and songs.

Gian Carlo Menotti (b. 1911), born in Italy, came to the United States in 1927 and (like Barber) studied at the Curtis Institute (1927–1933). Many Americans had gone to Europe to study music, but it was unusual for an Italian to reverse the process. Menotti spends most of his time in the United States, but he is still an Italian citizen. Menotti is practically unique among "American" composers in that he has created a body of operatic works in English appealing enough to the public to gain a place in the "permanent" repertory. He is his own librettist, and he thinks English is an ideal language for opera. In his serious operas he favors a strongly dramatic content related to the spirit of the Italian *verismo* (see

Chapter 24). His is the manner of Puccini; sometimes, however, when the occasion requires, he employs polytonal or atonal styles. Menotti's powerful sense of the possibilities of the theater is accompanied by a realization of practical limitations and considerations. By scoring all his operas for small orchestra in chamber-music style and by virtually eliminating the chorus, Menotti doubtless assured himself of many more performances than would have been the case with operas requiring expensive orchestral and vocal forces. His principal operas are: *Amelia Goes to the Ball* (one-act *opera buffa,* 1937); *The Old Maid and the Thief* (1939); *The Medium* and *The Telephone* (1947), generally performed as a double bill; *The Consul* (1950); *Amahl and the Night Visitors* (Christmas Eve performance, 1951; television opera for NBC); *The Saint of Bleecker Street* (1954); *Help, Help, the Globolinks* (1968), an opera "for children and those who love children."

Suggested Listening
William Schuman, Symphony No. 3.
Barber, *Adagio for Strings.*
Menotti, *Amahl and the Night Visitors.*

Suggested Reading
Gilbert Chase, *America's Music from the Pilgrims to the Present.* New York: McGraw-Hill Book Company, 1955.
John Tasker Howard, *Our American Music* (Third edition, revised). New York: Thomas Y. Crowell Company, 1954.
Wilfrid Mellers, *Music in a New Found Land.* New York: Alfred A. Knopf, 1964. Up-to-date and stimulating account of "themes and developments in the history of American music."
Claire Reis, *Composers in America* (Revised and enlarged edition). New York: The Macmillan Company, 1947.

COMPOSERS IN LATIN AMERICA: VILLA-LOBOS. CHÁVEZ.

Two outstanding figures in Latin American music are the Brazilian Heitor Villa-Lobos (1887–1959) and the Mexican Carlos Chávez (b. 1899).

Villa-Lobos, probably the best known of Latin American composers, was early influenced by Debussy and especially Ravel, but his mature music shows great originality and creative force, and an extraordinary imagination for instrumental and vocal combinations. Powerfully attracted to folk music, he identified himself so strongly with it that he claimed: "I am folklore; my melodies are just as authentic as those which emerge from the souls of my people." Among the immense number of his works (said to total two thousand) are twelve symphonies, other large pieces for orchestra (*Chôros* No. 8, 1925), nine *Bachianas Brasileiras* (1930–1945, combining Brazilian folk music with Bach-like polyphony), concertos, operas, ballets, choral works, chamber music, piano music, and songs. Villa-Lobos had many ideas about musical education for his country, and he had a great influence in Brazil. In 1932 he was appointed Superintendent of Musical Education in the federal district of Rio de Janeiro, and in 1942 he established his own *Conservatorio Nacional de Canto Orfeônico.*

Chávez is the leading conductor and composer of Mexico. He has at times been an exponent of musical nationalism and is an important educator (Director General of Fine Arts). He founded the Symphony Orchestra of Mexico. Initially Chávez wrote in a Romantic and Impressionist style; then he turned to the native music and national themes of Mexico. Without abandoning the latter, his later music sometimes showed Neoclassic tendencies. He has written four ballets, choral works, works for orchestra—for example, *Sinfonia de Antigona* (1932), Symphony No. 2 (1933), *Sinfonia India* (1935), Toccata for Percussion (1942), and Symphony for Strings (1953)—concertos, chamber music, piano music, and songs. Chávez considers himself an experimentalist, and his book *Toward a New Music* (New York, 1937) explains his theories.

Suggested Listening
Villa-Lobos, *Bachiana Brasileira,* No. 1 (for eight cellos).
Chávez, *Sinfonia de Antigona.*

Suggested Reading
David Ewen (ed.), *The Book of Modern Composers* (Second edition), New York: Alfred A. Knopf, 1950. Chapters on Villa-Lobos (Weinstock) and Chávez (Cowell).
Nicolas Slonimsky, *Music of Latin America.* New York: Thomas Y. Crowell Company, 1945.

33. *The Avant-garde*

> *History has a way of leaving behind those who cannot accommodate the new.*

THE HOLOCAUST OF World War II ended in 1945, but no such clear break marks the evolution of music and its changing condition. Nevertheless, 1945 is as acceptable a date as any to signify the beginning of an era in which continuity of tradition is paralleled more strongly than ever before by new directions and experiments. The coexistence of the new and old has been noted again and again in our account of the development of music, yet what has happened since 1945 is quite unprecedented taken as a whole: the development of new physical means of sound production so far-reaching that literally *any* sound can be produced in *any* degree of pitch, tone color, rhythm, or loudness; and the propagation of new attitudes on the part of certain composers that represent a break with centuries of Western tradition. The musical horizon, accordingly, is now bounded only by the physical capability of the human ear to receive significant "signals" from this new music and the flexibility of the mind to encompass or accept new concepts of the nature and limitations of music itself.

Immediately after World War II a casual observer would have scarcely noticed a change. The same "fifty pieces" of the classics were played everywhere; and, as far as "new" music was concerned, Stravinsky, Prokofiev, Bartók, and Berg were being played more, but others, like Sibelius and Hindemith, were being played rather less, especially after 1950. The favorites of the audience were not necessarily the same as those of the composers, especially the younger composers. The latter were particularly interested in the twelve-tone technique (or, more generally, serial technique) and in the whole new sound world of tape and electronic music. The ephemeral universe of "chance" ("aleatory") music (see p. 524), among other types, implied an entirely new philosophic concept of the art of music. To a new generation of composers, the great figure in serial music was not Schoenberg, the prime mover, but Webern his pupil, and the 1950's inaugurated the "Age of Webern." In order to achieve a "totally organized" music, the post-Webern composers proceeded to apply serial technique to other "parameters" (i.e., elements) of music, such as rhythm, tone color, and dynamics.

NEW SOUNDS, INSTRUMENTS, AND INSTRUMENTAL USAGE. NEW DIRECTIONS.

While most serial music was composed for existing instruments (or for voices), an entirely new area was opened up by *electronic music*. The latter is produced by an oscillator, amplified through loudspeakers, and often (although not always) recorded on magnetic tape. (For electronic *instruments,* such as the theremin or the Hammond organ, see below.) By electronic means a composer can now utilize any sound whatever within the audible range of pitch or loudness, including any microtone (that is, a fraction of a semitone, such as a quarter, a sixth, a hundredth or even an "irrational" part of a semitone) in any tone color or rhythm, no matter how complicated. For years past, a number of composers had experimented with microtones and new sonorities, but mostly within the boundaries of conventional instruments or voices. With the advent of electronic music, every sound in every gradation is theoretically available to every composer. In practice, only a few composers have access to the relatively few institutions or laboratories equipped with the expensive and elaborate electronic equipment necessary. Moreover, while electronic music does away with the performer (always a troublesome fellow for the composer), the composer is left at the mercy of the mathematician or the engineer unless he has an aptitude for mathematics himself.

If elecronic music abolishes the performer, so-called "chance" music sometimes puts him on a higher pedestal than ever before (the same could be said about jazz). In music involving "chance operations," composers like Cage and Stockhausen abdicate their role as composers in varying degrees, leaving more and more to the performer, who does as his artistry bids him within a certain framework established by the composer. Sometimes a piece is left entirely to "chance," as in Cage's piece *Imaginary Landscape No. 4* (1951) for twelve radios operated by twenty-four "players" who, under a conductor's direction, turn the radios on and off according to Cage's "score," the results being entirely dependent on the "chance" of what is being broadcast at the moment. The point is illustrated by the first performance (May 2, 1951), at which a lengthy delay occurred, and many radio stations had gone off the air before the piece was performed. Asked what would have been his reaction if *no* stations were on the air, Cage is said to have replied: "I love silence."

The numerous new sounds of electronic music have a counterpart in a number of developments in conventional instruments. Fascinating new ways of playing the piano and new types of piano sound were discovered by Henry Cowell. The jazz players have been extremely ingenious in inventing new effects on various instruments. Virtuoso players like Louis Armstrong, for instance, improvise cadenzas that use the high registers, the vibrato, and the slide (*portamento*) in a way that shows a whole new technical and expressive side of the trumpet. Similarly, the blues singer and the percussionist showed the way to new effects of color, pitch, and rhythm.

In addition, there are electronic instruments (not to be confused with electronic music) that apply electronic devices to conventional instruments: for instance, the electronic piano, organ, and steel guitar (important for jazz and popular music). Such instruments are used mostly within the chromatic scale common to Western music and within the limitations of a tone color associated with the particular instrument in question. The *theremin* is an instrument invented in 1928 by Leon Theremin; it consists of a rod whose electronic generation of sounds is controlled by the motion of the hands of the players in space, the sounds resembling those of a cello. Probably the most important of these electronic instruments are the electronic guitar and the electronic organ. The latter has the advantage of portability, relative cheapness of initial cost and upkeep, and constant accuracy of intonation. Certain disadvantages of tone and limited color have been partially overcome.

For some years, twentieth-century composers have treated the strings in a variety of new ways (cf. Schoenberg and Bartók). Nothing comparable happened to the woodwinds until 1967, when the Italian composer Bruno Bartolozzi suggested a new and revolutionary technique for them.[1] In his book, Bartolozzi proposes fingerings and embouchures that would permit: (1) the playing of *chords* by a single woodwind instrument (*see Plate 38A*); (2) the production of quarter tones; and (3) a new variety of tone colors and sounds (not all beautiful) on a *single* pitch (cf. Schoenberg's *Klangfarbenmelodie*). Previously (as Bartolozzi points out), fingerings were standardized to give a single tone of the purest sound and the securest pitch. By using a variety of fingerings, intermediate pitches and relatively ugly sounds are also possible. Just as Schoenberg emancipated dissonance by obliterating absolute distinctions between consonance and dissonance, similarly Bartolozzi seeks to emancipate tone by using these new ways of playing woodwind instruments to obliterate absolute distinctions between "beautiful" and "ugly" sounds. To Bartolozzi, in short, all sounds are "sound phenomena" to be used as needed. This novel technique naturally requires a new notation to indicate varieties of fingering, pitch, and tone color.

With practically infinite resources of sound and technical possibility at his disposal, the composer is beset by an embarrassment of riches. His problem has become one of selectivity and definition. Stravinsky commented on this difficulty some time ago in the *Poetics of Music* (1947), remarking that he was terrified before "the infinitude of possibilities"

---

[1] Bruno Bartolozzi, *New Sounds for Woodwind,* trans. by Reginald Smith Brindle. London: Oxford University Press, 1967.

until he had defined and limited the problem sufficiently to focus his efforts toward a solution. "My freedom," he says, "thus consists in my moving about within the narrow frame that I have assigned myself. . . ."

For the audience, the new music after 1945 posed at least two difficulties. One concerned the ear: the age-old difficulty of getting used to a new idiom from one generation to the next. There was also something new in the attitude of certain composers that the audience had rarely, if ever, encountered before, something that involved the basic nature of music and posed the fundamental question: To what limits, if any, can "music" be extended before it reaches "nonmusic"? More specifically, is there a valid artistic (or even scientific) distinction between music and noise? Or can a piece of "silence" be music? John Cage wrote a piece entitled *4'33"* (four minutes and thirty-three seconds), and described it as follows: "This is a piece in three movements during all three of which no sounds are intentionally produced."

And what of "non-teleological" music—that is, music which is not seeking "an end," but only sets forth successive moments of sound unrelated to each other, each sound-moment existing only for the "pleasurable" impression which it affords in itself, unrelated to what precedes or follows? Music of this sort is related much more closely to notions of Eastern philosophies than to that of the West, since the whole development of Western music has been "teleological" in the Aristotelian sense of the unities of time and the continuity of an art work in which some relation of the parts to the whole is assumed as essential. Today Eastern philosophy (such as Zen) and the use of Oriental sounds and instruments (the sitar, for instance) are factors to deal with in the music of the West.

After World War II, Neoclassicism declined in favor, and the chromatic scale, especially the serial technique as practiced by Webern, was adopted by more and more composers, even by Stravinsky after 1952. A number of composers were also attracted by the resources of tape or electronic music, or those of "chance operations." Moreover, the geographical distribution had widened and changed. In certain Iron Curtain countries, notably Poland, an *avant-garde* group flourished: for instance, Witold Lutoslawski (b. 1913), Tadeusz Baird (b. 1928), and Krzysztof Penderecki (b. 1933). Even in the Soviet Union, a handful of composers has experimented with Western *avant-garde* idioms in the last few years. In Greece there is a school of modern composition which dates back to Nicos Skalkottas (1904–1949), a pupil of Schoenberg. The best-known contemporary Greek composer, however, is Yannis Xenakis (b. 1922), who lives in Paris and who is an experimenter in "chance" music.

Musical activities have also greatly increased in the United States. Besides the postwar compositions of established figures like Copland and Sessions, other pieces of composers like Carter, Kirchner, Babbitt, and Cage (see later sections of this chapter) have attracted a great deal of attention.[2] Jazz and "rock" have gone electronic ("total immersion" means electronic amplification to ear-splitting levels), and sometimes incorporate elements of Oriental music and sometimes the "far-out" sounds of serious music like Webern's. On the other hand, some composers sought to amalgamate jazz and the music of the concert hall or opera house. Gunther Schuller (b. 1925), for instance, speaks of an accommodation of jazz and art music as the "third stream"; and his successful opera *The Visitation* (1967) combines jazz and twelve-tone technique. Lucas Foss (b. 1922) stresses the element of improvisation, so central to jazz, in his Concerto for Improvising Solo Instruments and Orchestra (1960).[3]

THE SPREAD OF SERIAL MUSIC. THE POST-WEBERN COMPOSERS. TOTAL ORGANIZATION. LEIBOWITZ. BOULEZ. MESSIAEN. BABBITT.

In another geographical change, the twelve-tone technique widened its area of influence, securing a strong hold over young composers in Italy and France. Before 1945, Italian composers (with the exception of Dallapiccola) had shown little interest in the twelve-tone method of Schoenberg, and France was the center of Neoclassicism. A key figure in the change was the Frenchman René Leibowitz (b. 1913). He studied with Schoenberg and Webern before the war, and as a composer, conductor, and author[4] exercised a considerable influence on Boulez and the young Italians and Germans.

Pierre Boulez (b. 1925), the best known of the new generation of French composers, entered the class of Olivier Messiaen in 1942. *See Plate 38b.* He reacted strongly against the Neoclassicism of Stravinsky, and after the war he studied Schoenberg's music with Leibowitz in Paris. A factor of great importance in the spread of the influence of Schoenberg and especially Webern was the international summer courses in contemporary music given at the Kranichstein Institute in Darmstadt (Germany), beginning in 1946, the first director being Hindemith. From about 1949 on, the influence of the Schoenberg school became dominant through Leibowitz, who taught and lectured there. The students who gathered in Darmstadt constituted the young *avant-garde* of the future: among them, Pierre Boulez from Paris, Bruno Maderna (b. 1920) and Luigi Nono (b. 1924) from Italy; and Hans Werner Henze and Karlheinz Stockhausen from Germany.

[2] For European developments since 1945, see *Contemporary Music in Europe,* an entire issue of *The Musical Quarterly* (January 1965).

[3] For other developments in the United States since 1945, see Wilfrid Mellers, *Music in a New Found Land.* New York: Alfred A. Knopf, 1964.

[4] For example, *Schoenberg et son école,* Paris, 1947; English translation, New York: Philosophical Library, 1949.

The first piece by Webern was played for the first time in Darmstadt in 1948, and by 1951 his influence there was clearly greater than that of Schoenberg, who died in that year. In 1952, Boulez published an article entitled "Schoenberg Is Dead" (intended no doubt in the French sense of "The King is dead, long live the King"), rejecting Schoenberg as an old-fashioned composer who had not created a really new music but had confined the twelve-tone technique, and impeded the formation of a music that was genuinely new, by retaining the old baggage of tonal music: namely, repetition and development of themes and motives, traditional forms and rhythms, and a clear separation of melody and accompaniment. Boulez proceeded to "correct" these failings, taking as his point of departure the late (pointillistic) style of Webern (e.g., the Concerto for Nine Instruments). Boulez went beyond Webern by applying the serial technique to *all* the elements of music, making a "totally organized" piece. The same serial organization that had formerly been applied only to pitch was now extended by "post-Webern" composers like Boulez to include duration, loudness (dynamics), tone color (timbre), and even method of attack and density of texture. This extension of a serial organization to the various "parameters" of music was adopted in one degree or another by a number of composers such as Ernst Křenek, Karlheinz Stockhausen (*Zeitmasse,* 1956, for woodwinds), and Luigi Nono.

Boulez had already been anticipated by his teacher Messiaen and by Milton Babbitt. Olivier Messiaen (b. 1908), the celebrated organist in the Church of the Trinity in Paris, used Gregorian modes and "modes" of the Orient; and he was fascinated by the rhythms of India and (for their new sonorities) by exotic percussion instruments and electronic wave-generators (*ondes Martenot*). In 1949 Messiaen published *Four Studies of Rhythms,* of which the second is entitled *"Mode de valeurs et d'intensités"* (for piano), a work that applies serial organization to *duration* and *loudness* as well as to *pitch.* A year earlier (1948) in the United States, Milton Babbitt (b. 1916) had already gone further toward "total organization" in his Composition for Four Instruments, which applies the serial technique not only to pitch but also to "durational rhythm, dynamics, phrase rhythm, timbre, and register."

In any piece of music, no matter how fascinating the complications or "total organization," we must (as Boulez says) "very much distrust confusing composition with organization" (cf. Schoenberg's similar remarks, p. 409). In other words, the serial technique is a method of organization, not a style, and will solve no problems of expression. The "total serial organization" may quite likely be a "totally inaudible organization" to many listeners. Schoenberg made the general point more vividly when he remarked: "A Chinese philosopher speaks, of course, Chinese; the question is, what does he say?"

So the question is: What does Boulez say? What does he say in his most celebrated piece, *Le Marteau sans Maître* (*The Hammer Without a Master,* 1954)? This is an elaborate piece of nine movements based on three short Surrealistic poems by René Char, set by Boulez for alto voice and a group of six instruments. These six instruments are flute in G, viola, guitar, xylorimba (combination of xylophone and marimba), vibraphone, and percussion group played by the sixth player: drum, bongos, maracas, claves, bell, triangle, suspended cymbal, two small cymbals, gong, high and low tam-tam.

Of course Boulez is not saying anything in particular in *Le Marteau* (what is Beethoven "saying" in the Fifth Symphony?), but in general he might be saying something to the listener by way of directions: Listen to the extraordinary sound of this moment and that moment, to the ever-changing kaleidoscope of sound of voice and instrument; consider the virtue of unpredictability, the immediacy of direct expression, and the novelty of tone, timbre, and rhythm unrelated to the expected and to tradition. Listen to each *moment* for what it is, not for what precedes or follows it.

The kind of sound in Boulez' setting is related to the poem in the same manner of hallucinatory mood as the music of Schoenberg's *Pierrot Lunaire* is related to its poems. But Boulez' musical realization is rather that of the pointillist Webern after a longish period of residence in Bali! To show the character of the poetry, the first poem is quoted in translation:

> *The Furious Artisans*
> The red van by the prison's edge
> And a corpse in the hamper
> And draft horses in the horseshoe
> I dream, my head on the point of my Peruvian knife.[5]

These violent and discontinuous images are set to jagged lines of voice and instruments, accompanied by bell-like sounds reminiscent of the Orient, by points and splashes of sound, and by the numerous and varied resonances of percussion instruments against the shimmer of the vibraphone. The twang of the guitar, the low register and flutter-tongue of the flute, and the timbre of the viola are other features. Here there are no themes in the conventional sense, only sound-cells set to the most astonishing sonorities, colors, and diverse moments of sound. New types of rhythms are introduced in No. 4, a continual *accelerando* and *ritardando;* and in No. 5, an unstable tempo is used with a tempo change in nearly every measure.

Although many of these sounds seem to be discontinuous, the internal structure is actually highly organized by serial means; externally there are

[5] Author's translation.

nine interlocked and related movements, of which four use the voice and five are for instruments alone. Each of the movements has a completely different instrumentation. Indeed, *Le Marteau,* in its parts and as a whole, has a special sound and a special character, just as *Pierrot Lunaire* has, and it is a model of its genre.

Boulez also composed with electronic and tape resources (*Poésie pour pouvoir,* 1958), and he used chance operations in certain works (Piano Sonata No. 3, 1957). Since 1961 he has composed less and conducted more (recently he was appointed conductor of the New York Philharmonic Orchestra), often playing works of those composers whose influence he has acknowledged as decisive in his own music: Debussy, Stravinsky, and Webern. Boulez has also explained his own music and ideas in a book, *Penser la musique aujourd'hui.*

Suggested Listening
Babbitt, *Composition for Four Instruments* (1948).
Boulez, *Le Marteau sans Maître.*

Suggested Reading
Pierre Boulez, *Penser la musique aujourd'hui.* Mainz: Editions Gonthier, Schott, 1963.
See also the list at the end of this chapter.

NON-SERIAL CHROMATICISTS: CARTER. KIRCHNER.

In 1952 Boulez wrote: "Since the discoveries made by the Viennese, all composition other than twelve-tone is useless." This doctrinaire *pronunciamento* cannot be taken seriously: There is more than one road to Rome, and there are plenty of composers capable of musical eloquence and coherence without speaking twelve-tone Viennese. Two such composers are Elliott Carter (b. 1908) and Leon Kirchner (b. 1919), both Americans.

Carter studied with Piston and Boulanger; and he knew and admired Ives as a man and as the embodiment of idealism and experiment. Beginning to compose in a diatonic and modal vein, Carter wrote for a time in a Neoclassic style and then in various styles of free chromaticism. But he is hardly a twelve-tone composer, and his "other than twelve-tone composition" is far from "useless"! On the question of twelve-tone technique, Carter says: "I have studied the important works of the type and admire many of them a great deal. I have found that it is apparently inapplicable to what I am trying to do, and is more of a hindrance than a help. Its nature is often misunderstood, it is a building material and not the building. . . ." Carter also speaks of the dangers of fashion: "Each of the trends of our recent past—primitivism, machinism, neo-Classicism, *Gebrauchsmusik,* the styles of Bartók and Berg and now those of Schoenberg and Webern—has left and will leave in its trail numbers of really gifted composers whose music, skillful and effective as it is, is suffocated, at least for a time, by its similarity to other music of the same type. Of course, ultimately this faddishness is trivial, but its mercurial changes today have made the life of many a composer a great trial. . . ." [6]

Since his first String Quartet (1951), Carter's music has been increasingly admired by musicians and the public. While not prolific as a composer, Carter has produced one score after the other of great individuality, distinguished by virtuosity of instrumental treatment, intricate rhythm, and variety of the individual solutions.

The Variations for Orchestra (1955) is a case in point. An elaborate piece for full orchestra, it consists of an introduction, theme, nine variations, and finale, which is similar in external plan to Schoenberg's Variations for Orchestra (Op. 31, 1928). But, though highly chromatic and contrapuntally elaborate, it is not a twelve-tone work, and it has two points of special interest (among others) that give it a particular individuality: the first is Carter's notion of what constitutes a "variation" in this work. In the conventional scheme of theme and variations, each successive variation generally uses the same number of measures as the theme, and each variation has its own particular figuration or character maintained through the entire variation. Carter, however, uses a "dynamic" approach: the individual variation itself is subject to variation and to contrasted mood *within the limits of the single variation*—in short, dynamic variation(s) within each "variation." In this particular work, the technique of "dynamic" variation accounts also for the varying number of measures in individual variations: for instance, the theme has 46 measures, but there are 39 measures in Variation 1 and 71 measures in Variation 6.

A special rhythmic device which Carter calls *metrical modulation* is used in Variations 4 and 6. Metrical modulation is essentially a continually changing pulse or tempo achieved in the score through "metrical" notation (that is, through the length of the notes and their subdivisions) or through metronomic indications. Variation 4 uses the latter type. Here there are a number of sections, each being four measures long and each consisting of a gradual slowing down, in such a manner that the end of the passage is played at half the speed of its beginning. Carter's language in the score is more explicit: "The *ritardando* extending over each group of four measures should be a very regular one, each time starting at quarter-note = 200 and slowing down to half that speed" (in the score Carter gives an exact metronome marking for the beginning of each measure, thus: 200, 168, 141, 119; and at the end of the last measure the speed is 100; then, of course, it returns to the 200 rate). The reverse occurs in Variation 6, where a speeding up in the proportion of 1 : 3 (80 : 240) takes place. Again, Carter gives directions: "The *accelerando* extending over each group of six measures should be a very regular speeding up from quarter note = 80 to three times that speed each time" (and the metronome marks at the beginning of each measure are: 80, 96, 115, 139, 166, 201). There are besides all sorts of proportional relationships of tempi among the individual variations, which (as a result) tend to fall into three groups of three each. An impressive and lengthy finale concludes this remarkable work.

In his Second String Quartet (1960), Carter has differentiated the character of each part within a very intricate structure. He describes the first violin part as "fantastic, ornate, and mercurial"; the second violin "has a laconic, orderly character which is sometimes humorous." The various parts are also differentiated by the character of the intervalic and rhythmic structures employed. To emphasize the individuality of each part, Carter suggests that the players sit farther apart on the stage.

This extraordinary work won Carter the Pulitzer Prize. Two years later he received an accolade from Stravinsky in connection with the Double Concerto for Piano, Harpsichord, and Small Orchestra (1961). Stravinsky wrote that it was a masterpiece and the most interesting piece of American music he had heard.

Leon Kirchner (b. 1919) is another composer who gives the lie to Boulez' dictum that "all composition other than twelve-tone is useless." Kirchner drank at the sacred spring—he studied with Schoenberg and Sessions as well as Bloch—but the musical visions that came to him as a result were by no means projected exclusively in the twelve tones. At base, he is not a twelve-tone composer. Nevertheless, his music embodies the utterances of a strong personality that are artistically convincing.

Some fifteen years ago (1954) Kirchner wrote: "Many of us, dominated by the fear of self-expression, seek the superficial security of current style and fad-worship and make a fetish of complexity. . . . Idea, the precious ore of art, is lost in the jungle of graphs, prepared tapes, feedbacks and cold stylistic minutiae. An artist must create a personal cosmos. . . ." [7] The key words in this credo are "expression," "idea," and "personal cosmos"—all applicable to his Piano Concerto (1953), which brought Kirchner his first great success on the occasion of its first performance by the New York Philharmonic (1956), with Kirchner as soloist.

On hearing this and later works, the listener is aware of a composer seeking a vehicle of intense and individual expression: no cool detachment here, rather a great conviction that reflects a deep emotional involve-

[7] From the record jacket notes to his Trio for Violin, Cello, and Piano (1954), written especially for the issuance of this recording.

ment. Expression in Kirchner may find its outlet in a quiet lyricism in the slow sections of his music; or, more characteristically, in fast movements in pounding rhythmic figures, driving and savage rhythms (*à la* Bartók) —all this volcanic in energy (as in the last movement of the Piano Concerto). In the two-movement Trio for Violin, Cello, and Piano (1954), the expressive contrast from one part to the next is reflected in the composer's own marking: for instance, "wild," *"appassionato,"* "reflective," "lyrically-tenderly." In the service of so wide an emotional range, Kirchner calls on the full range of virtuosity from his players. The mode of all this "expression" is a free chromaticism, often highly dissonant in harmony yet tonal in end-effect, especially in final cadences, which generally focus on a tone center (as at the end of the Trio just mentioned, which focuses on "A").

The musical kernel which transmits the idea sometimes takes the form of free and improvisatory figuration, sometimes as interval encased in a rhythmic motive. The minor second and its transformations in the beginning of the Piano Concerto are examples. The idea, embodied in figurations, lines, motives, and harmonies, is amplified and extended to sections and movements, characteristically through a process of perpetual variation. Yet such sections of "perpetual variation" do not preclude juxtaposition of sections of quite different character. For instance, after the opening fast section of the first movement of the Piano Concerto a slow section is juxtaposed, all within the first (fast) movement.

Kirchner has created "a personal cosmos," highly individualistic and highly charged emotionally. Its ecstatic, rhapsodic qualities have often been noted—sometimes to the annoyance of the composer. In any case, the full intensity of these qualities is best realized in a personal way—in Kirchner's own performances as a virtuoso pianist, or under his direction. Kirchner could have written of his works, as Berlioz did a century ago, "To render them properly, the performer, and especially the conductor, ought to *feel* as I do." For his String Quartet No. 3 (1967), Kirchner won the Pulitzer Prize.

Suggested Listening
Carter, Variations for Orchestra.
Kirchner, Toccata for Strings, Winds and Percussion (1956).

MICROTONE MUSIC: BARTH. HÁBA. CARRILLO. PARTCH.

Electronic music is capable of producing *any* gradation of pitch and timbre. By way of comparison, the conventional semitone system and the tone colors available in existing instruments seem quite limited; and it is not surprising to find that attempts to overcome these limitations are not new. For more than a century, in fact, composers and others have sought to create a music based on microtones (intervals smaller than the semitone), and sometimes new tone colors have been generated in the process of producing new instruments to play microtone music.[8]

As a first step toward microtones, quarter tones were an obvious resource worth exploring, and a number of composers made limited use of them, especially where the complications were minimal, as in the stringed instruments. Ives was a pioneer in using quarter tones, and Bartók employed them in his Violin Concerto (1938), as did Ernest Bloch in his Quintet for Piano and Strings (1923). However, quarter tones present insurmountable difficulties for the full orchestra as it is presently and conventionally constituted. On the other hand, quarter-tone pianos have been specially constructed, among them a two-manual piano by A. Förster (Prague, 1923). Hans Barth (1897–1956) exhibited a quarter-tone piano in New York in 1925 and later wrote a Concerto for Quarter-tone Piano and Orchestra (1930). Alois Hába (b. 1893), a Czech composer, produced a Quartet in the quarter-tone system (1919), and established a class in the Prague Conservatory for quarter-tone techniques (1923). Later (1927) Hába expanded his notions to include sixth tones and twelfth tones, an example being his interesting *Duo in the Sixth-tone System,* significantly for two violins. In Mexico Julián Carrillo (b. 1875) claimed that since the 1890's he had composed with eighth tones and even sixteenth tones—that is, forty-eight and ninety-six to the octave, respectively.

The microtone systems mentioned above were all effected by simple arithmatic divisions of the existing semitone (twelve-tone) scale. Others were more radical in their approach to the octave and its subdivisions. The American composer Harry Partch (b. 1901), for example, worked out a system of forty-three microtones to the octave; and he built various instruments capable of playing in this system, including a reed organ called "Ptolemy" (1935) and others with exotic sounds and with exotic names like "cloud-chamber bowls" and "chromelodeon." Partch's most impressive work in this microtone system is *King Oedipus,* a setting of the Yeats version of the *Oedipus Rex* of Sophocles.

Today it is theoretically possible to achieve all conceivable microtones by electronic means, but it is not clear whether electronic music will entirely supplant those microtone pieces that are linked to the human performer for their realization.

Suggested Listening
Hába, *Fantasy for Violin Solo in Quarter-Tones* (Op. 9a).

[8] For a list illustrating events connected with more than a century of microtones, see William Austin, *Music in the Twentieth Century,* New York: W. W. Norton Company, 1966, pp. 381–83.

FORERUNNERS OF ELECTRONIC SOUND. VARÈSE. "NOISE" AS RAW MATERIAL.

Microtone music anticipates in a limited way the ability of electronic music to produce infinite gradations of pitch. Similarly, a few composers, using conventional instruments, have forecast some of the sounds that later came to be associated with electronic music. Webern is a case in point. Some of his scores (e.g., Op. 6, fourth movement) have moments of such unusual sound combinations that he is seen in retrospect as a spiritual ancestor of electronic music. Another instance is Edgard Varèse (1885–1965), a composer who produced all kinds of sounds so unconventional by ordinary standards that they can be viewed as a glimpse of the new horizon of electronic sounds. Varèse was born in France, and he was educated partly there and partly in Italy and Germany. In 1915 he came to the United States, where he remained for the rest of his life. One of the boldest innovators of twentieth-century music, Varèse was already writing music in the 1920's and 1930's that was prophetic of electronic music. John Cage claimed that Varèse "fathered forth noise," anticipating a potential of electronic music. By blurring the distinction between "music" and "noise," Varèse foresaw, in principle at least, all the possible raw material of sound later available through electronic means. Long before electronic music became a reality, Varèse's works display an intense preoccupation with sound in general—any sound, including what would conventionally be called "noise." In *Ionisation* (1931), written for percussion instruments and two sirens, Varèse produced a large variety of "sounds" which could as well be called "noises," including ear-splitting effects with sirens.

As early as 1915 Varèse abandoned such traditional concepts of composition as thematic development and the consonant harmony in which he had been trained. Rather, he thought of his music as "organized sounds" in terms of rhythms and sonorities, including the shrill sounds of unresolved dissonance; and he described himself as an "engineer of rhythms and timbres." After 1945, Varèse's music sometimes combined electronic means with conventional instruments, and it sometimes relied entirely on electronic means. An example of the former is *Déserts* (1954) for wind and percussion with interspersed recordings of industrial noises; an example of the latter is *Poème électronique,* a work created to be heard in the Phillips pavilion, designed by Le Corbusier, for the Brussels World Fair in 1958. Varèse's *Poème* was played by four hundred loudspeakers for those who walked through the pavilion, exciting, in one way or another, an "audience" that averaged some fifteen thousand persons daily for six months.

Varèse was a bold innovator in music. But innovation is not the same thing as experimentation, and Varèse had some well-chosen words to say to those who confused the two. "I do not write experimental music," said Varèse. "My experimenting is done before I make the music." Not a man to be taken in by prevailing platitudes, Varèse also observed: "Contrary to general belief, an artist is never ahead of his time, but most people are far behind theirs."

Suggested Listening
Varèse, *Déserts* (1954).

ELECTRONIC MUSIC. TAPE-RECORDER MUSIC. MUSIQUE CONCRÈTE.

The term *electronic music* refers to music that is produced by electronic generators and amplified over loudspeakers. This process automatically eliminates the human performer. Electronic music may be, and generally is, recorded on magnetic tape—the best way to "store" the music. The tape may then be the only record of the piece, there being no "score" in the musical sense. A "score" of an electronic piece, if the composer retains it, is essentially a set of technical and electronic directions. (For a "score" of electronic music, *see Plate* 39B.)

Tape-recorder music is a term that includes taped electronic music (of the sort just described) and also *musique concrète*. The latter is tape-recorder–loudspeaker music, but it is not electronic music since the basic sound material is taken from nature, not generated electronically: for instance, a musical sound, a dog's bark, or the slamming of a door. These "natural" sounds are then recorded on tape and manipulated by such devices as dubbing, splicing, running the tape faster or slower (to raise or lower the pitch), filtering the sounds, and so on. The result is a kind of sound montage that is generally a far cry from the original sounds employed. Tape manipulation, often a "hand operation," can be greatly speeded up by means of a *synthesizer* or, to some extent, a *computer*. *Musique concrète* was first composed by Pierre Schaeffer (b. 1910) in 1948, using the facilities of the Paris Radio Studio (Radio–Diffusion Française; Messiaen and Boulez also worked there). In 1949, Schaeffer and Pierre Henry (b. 1927) composed *Symphony for One Man*, an important milestone in this type of music. *Musique concrète*, which predates pure electronic music by a few years, showed that every sound or noise was possible raw material, through manipulation, for the "art work of the future."

Electronic music proper began in the 1950's with the establishment of electronic studios. The first was founded in 1951 in Cologne by Herbert Eimert (b. 1897) and others as an electronic studio of the West German Radio. The most celebrated name connected with this studio was Karl-heinz Stockhausen (see the next section). In 1952 an electronic studio was set up at Columbia University by Otto Luening (b. 1900) and Vladimir Ussachevsky (b. 1911); and shortly afterward Luciano Berio (b. 1925) and Bruno Maderna (b. 1920) founded the electronic *Studio di Fonologia* in Milan. A sophisticated step forward occurred in 1959 when the RCA Electronic Sound Synthesizer was established at the Columbia-Princeton Music Center, whose central figure was Milton Babbitt (Composition for Synthesizer, c. 1961). This list is, of course, only partially complete for the 1950's and does not give any of the studios established in the 1960's.

Electronic music opened an immense new horizon which is still to be fully explored. By means of electric generators it is easy to produce any pitch within the limitations of human audibility—under optimum conditions, from about 20 to 20,000 frequencies. By way of contrast, the standard piano keyboard today has 88 semitones, ranging from about 27.5 to 4186 frequencies. Furthermore, any degree or effect of duration (rhythm), volume, or tone color can be produced. Tone, for instance, may be infinitely varied from "pure" tone (no overtones)—a so-called sine wave or *sinusoidal* tone—to the most complex mixtures of them all: "white" sound analogous in its complexities to "white" light, being made up of an infinite number of sounds over the entire spectrum.

Pure electronic sound does not need any musical performers for its generation, and therefore electronic composers can work directly with their medium just as a painter works directly with paint on canvas. Nevertheless, the electronic process in music is far from a simple one, and it has certain defects of its virtues. With all its potential, the electronic medium has an aspect and a sound, characteristic of the machine age, that is impersonal, mechanical, and (as it were) dehumanized. These characteristics are especially noticeable in concerts of electronic music given in the conventional concert hall where the audience faces a stage filled with loudspeakers, not with living musicians. Recognizing this situation, Stockhausen recommended special halls for electronic music in which the audience is seated on a platform in the middle of the hall and surrounded by loudspeakers mounted in the walls on all sides. (For a new type of concert-hall construction for the presentation of conventional concerts and orchestras, *see Plate* 32B.)

Whether it is the "dehumanized" aspect of electronic music or the complex and expensive equipment necessary for its production, the fact is that "pure" electronic music has made relatively little headway in the concert hall. It has proved more fruitful for use in films or radio studios;

and in its most natural form of preservation on tape or phonograph disc, it is readily accessible to home or classroom.

STOCKHAUSEN

Karlheinz Stockhausen (b. 1928) is closely identified with electronic music and the West German Radio Studio at Cologne. *See Plate 39A.* Actually, Stockhausen, like Boulez, is an international figure who works in various mediums, and (like Stravinsky) he seldom uses a musical solution a second time. His earliest works were influenced by Schoenberg, but after a summer at Darmstadt (1951), where he met Boulez and Messiaen, he turned to Webern, whose works he increasingly admired. During 1951–1953 he worked in Paris with Messiaen and Milhaud and in Schaeffer's *musique concrète* laboratory. He also studied acoustics and related disciplines at Bonn with Meyer-Eppler. Returning to Cologne in 1953, Stockhausen joined the newly founded electronic laboratory, producing two pieces of pure electronic music: *Electronic Study I* (1953), using sine waves (pure tones) exclusively; and *Electronic Study II* (1954), the first electronic work to be published in "score"—actually a diagram of directions for the electronic realization of the piece. *See Plate 39B.* In this score, the upper part, calibrated from 100 to 17,200, is concerned with pitch and tone color. There are eighty-one pitch steps related by the interval ratio $\sqrt[25]{5}$ (the ratio of semitones on the piano is $\sqrt[12]{2}$), the former ratio being slightly larger. One hundred and ninety-three mixtures are constructed from these eighty-one steps. The heavy horizontal lines show the high and low frequencies of the first sound mixtures. To this, another overlapping mixture is added. In the middle of the page are shown the duration of the sounds measured in centimeters of tape moving at the indicated speed of 76.2 centimeters per second. The shapes at the bottom show the volume in decibels.

At the same time (1953), Stockhausen wrote *Kontra-Punkte,* a one-movement piece for ten instruments. In this work, although abandoning electronic sound momentarily, Stockhausen had something new in mind: There is "no repetition," wrote Stockhausen, "no variation, no development, no contrast. . . . Not the same shapes in a changing light. Rather this: different shapes in the same light that penetrates everywhere." Again in 1956, Stockhausen produced three pieces of great interest, each entirely different. In *Gesang der Jünglinge (Song of the Youths)*, one of his best works, he incorporates distorted vocal sounds into a piece of electronic music. *Gesang* is performed with five different loudspeakers "spaced" throughout the room, and it is one of the first of his pieces to employ the so-called space concept. In *Zeitmasse (Tempos)*, the second piece in question, Stockhausen used five wind instruments (oboe, flute, English horn, clarinet, and bassoon) to explore different levels of time or rhythm of great complexity. The third piece, *Piano Piece No. XI,* is an aleatory ("chance") excursion: it consists of nineteen fragments irregularly placed on a single large sheet of paper (about 21 × 37 inches), which may be played in any order, using any of six given articulations, dynamic levels, and tempos. Hence there is no "closed" form, but an "open" form depending on the selected pieces, order, and other factors.

In the 1960's Stockhausen has shown a great interest in "space" compositions, among them *Carré (Square; 1960)* and *Mixtur* (1965). *Carré* is a piece requiring large forces in which "space" effects are derived from four orchestras and chorus. The four groups, each with its own chorus, are placed against the four walls of the square hall, the audience being in the middle. *Mixtur* is written for "Orchestra, Sine Wave Generators, and Ring Modulators." A sine wave generator is used to produce a pure tone. When two different sounds are fed into a ring modulator, the resulting sounds are formed from the sums and differences of the frequencies of the two original sounds.

The composer requires the orchestra for *Mixtur* to be divided into spatially separated groups: wind instruments on one side, brass on the opposite side, two divided strings groups (one playing *pizzicato*) in the middle, and three percussion setups in the back. (This for a conventional stage; where possible, the audience should be in the middle, the four groups of the orchestra seated around the audience.) All groups play into separate microphones—one microphone per stand of two musicians. The sound of the percussion instruments (cymbals and gongs) is transmitted into contact microphones. The sound emitted by the various groups is then electronically altered by means of the sine wave generators and ring modulators; and the audience hears, in effect, both the original sound and the altered sound simultaneously.

The composition is a series of "moments," each written on one or two huge music sheets. Each "moment" represents a totally different sound picture. Various arrangements are possible, giving the conductor considerable freedom of choice, and the unorthodox musical notations give the players a certain amount of leeway within a strict framework of pitch, range, and time. *Mixtur,* whatever its musical virtues may be, is a fascinating combination of "space," "chance," and "non-teleological" principles; and it focuses the performer and the orchestra as the central raw material for electronic manipulation, presumably reconciling man and machine.

Stockhausen's pieces vary immensely in their methods and resources from "total control" to "chance" pieces, from conventional instruments to pure electronic pieces, from "space" experiments to combinations of various of all these possibilities. Besides, Stockhausen has written extensively about contemporary music. Among other things, he was co-editor (with H. Eimert) of *Die Reihe,* a quarterly review devoted to contemporary music (since 1955). At a relatively early age, he has emerged as one of the most original and influential of composers, a prophet of the *avant-garde.*

Suggested Listening
Gesang der Jünglinge.
Carré.

ALEATORY ("CHANCE") MUSIC. JOHN CAGE AND OTHERS.

"Totally organized" (or controlled) music is the direct opposite of "aleatory" music (*alea* = dice). In the latter, some or all of the music is uncontrolled or left to "chance." Both types of music appeared about the same time, at the beginning of the 1950's. In aleatory music, the composer introduces "indeterminate" elements into music, the disposition of chance being made by the performer or by circumstances. In Cage's *Imaginary Landscape No. 4* (1951) for twelve radios (see p. 508), the circumstance of what is "on the radio" at the moment of performance determines the outcome; in Stockhausen's *Piano Piece No. XI* (see p. 523), the performer exercises certain options given him by the composer, and the performer's choice is decisive in the result, the music varying from one performance to another according to chance. By its very nature, music of this kind cannot be "fixed"; it must be indeterminate or open in character by its very nature. Someone has aptly noted that chance music is rather like the mobiles of Calder; and in its randomness, chance music has another visual parallel in certain works of Jackson Pollack. *See Plate* 40A.

Other composers have approached the problem of chance music in different ways. The Greek Yannis Xenakis composes stochastic music of true randomness by means of a computer. (*Stochastic* denotes a variable function determined by random phenomena in time.) In New York a group of composers—Morton Feldman (b. 1926), Earle Brown (b. 1926), and Christian Wolff (b. 1934)—are interested in enlarging the role of the performer in chance music by increasing the number of possible "chances" open to him during a performance.

John Cage, who invented music involving "chance operations," has also brought his original mind to bear on a number of other areas, including philosophy of a sort. The results often suggest possibilities more exciting than Cage's own music, his genius being to point out new paths without necessarily providing the brightest illumination for them. Some of these paths, one is bound to add, may lead to dead ends.

Cage, born in Los Angeles in 1912, studied the piano with Richard Buhlig and composition with Henry Cowell and Arnold Schoenberg. *See Plate 40B.* Schoenberg thought Cage more of an inventor than a composer; and Cage thought Schoenberg's insistence on a conventional grounding in harmony and counterpoint excessively old-fashioned, at least for him. Nevertheless, Cage's earliest works (1933–1938) were influenced by Schoenberg and make some use of the twelve-tone technique. On the other hand, Cowell's original methods of utilizing the piano impressed Cage and may well have suggested the idea of the "prepared" piano, an invention of Cage's early in his career (1938). *Amores* (1943) is an instance (it is recorded). It consists of two solos for prepared piano, the piano being "prepared" as follows (according to the *Catalogue of Cage's Works,* p. 15):

Nine screws, eight bolts, two nuts and three strips of rubber, acting as mutes, were placed between the strings pertaining to eighteen keys. Upon this instrument an attempt was made to express in combination the erotic and the tranquil, two of the permanent emotions of Indian tradition. The second solo is written in the rhythmic structure 3, 3, 2, 2.

The result of this preparation is less like a piano than a gamelan orchestra of Bali. It resembles a percussion band of varied sonority. Indeed, *Amores* has two additional "Trios" for percussion requiring tom-toms, pod rattle, and woodblocks. Percussion instruments, as a matter of fact, have been an abiding interest of Cage, his earliest composition being for percussion in connection with modern dance groups.

The dance and rhythm have been other central interests, and he has written a large amount of dance music, especially for the dancer Merce Cunningham. A case in point is the ballet *Seasons* (1947) for orchestra (written for Cunningham). As in *Amores,* Cage mentions the Indian background and rhythm: "The *Seasons* is an attempt to express the traditional Indian view of the seasons. . . . The rhythmic structure is 2, 2, 1, 3, 2, 4, 3, 1." This preoccupation with rhythm gradually developed "to a point of sophistication unmatched in the technique of any other living composer" (Virgil Thomson in the *New York Herald Tribune,* 1945).

Cage, again, was one of the first in the new field of tape music (since 1951), and he has often used chance operations in conjunction with tape. *Fontana Mix* (1958) for magnetic tape, for instance, is "a composition indeterminate of its performance," written for the *Studio di Fonologia* of the Milan Radio.

Cage is not satisfied with the simple notion of chance but divides his progress in aleatory music according to subcategories and dates: for example, "composition using chance operations (1951—); composition using observation of imperfections in the paper upon which it is written

(1952—); composition without a fixed relation of parts to score (1954—); composition indeterminate of its performance (1958—)." He was doubtless led to chance operations through his long fascination with Oriental music, literature, and philosophy. The part played by *I-Ching* (*The Book of Changes*) in the "unpredictability" aspect of *Imaginary Landscape No. 4* and of *Music of Changes for Piano* is described in *Silence,* a book of essays Cage published in 1961 (p. 57 ff). A devotee of Zen Buddhism, Cage makes numerous references to Oriental (and especially Indian) culture and ideas in his works (cf. the quotation from *Amores,* above). These interests and sympathies are in line with the "non-teleological" (no end or purpose) character of many of his works, which consist of a series of moments, each moment being unrelated to what precedes or follows. By *reductio ad absurdum,* the noncausal relationship—or rather, nonrelationship—of one sound to another (or one moment to another) is ultimately best expressed as silence, as in his piece (for any instrument or instruments) entitled *4′33″* (1952), consisting of that length of silence.

The non-teleological aspects of Cage's works have wide implications for other arts, especially literature and painting; and Cage has himself engaged in a "literary" venture along these lines in *Indeterminacy: New Aspects of Form in Instrumental and Electronic Music* (1959). In spite of the explicit title, this "work" is actually 90 [funny?] stories read by John Cage with occasional fragmentary bursts of electronic music furnished by his friend, the pianist David Tudor. Each story lasts one minute; and consequently, the long stories are read very fast, and the short stories very slowly. An example of the short "stories" follows:

> A beautiful   woman   [pause]
> who   gives   pleasure   [pause; electronic effects]
>   to men   [long   pause]
> serves only to frighten   [pause]
>   the   fish   [long pause]
> when she jumps   [pause]
>   in the water.

In his notes to the recording of *Indeterminacy,* Cage says: "My intention of putting ninety stories together in an unplanned way is to suggest that all things, sounds, stories (and by extension, beings) are related and that this complexity is more evident when it is not over-simplified by an idea of relationship in one person's mind."

Cage can be counted on as a reliably unorthodox "composer." He is as complete a paradox as the age which produced him; and it is hardly possible to understand him on purely rational, evolutionary, or even musical grounds. In effect, he has abandoned historicism and Western culture and is impatient with its traditions. This point is emphasized by an incident related in *Silence* (p. 73):

Once in Amsterdam, a Dutch musician said to me, "It must be very difficult for you in America to write music, for you are so far away from the centers of tradition." I had to say, "It must be very difficult for you in Europe to write music, for you are so close to the centers of tradition."

Cage exerts a great influence on the young and on a considerable sector of the *avant-garde* scene, especially in Europe, where he is one of the few American composers to whom any attention is paid. Paradoxically, Cage is now a composer who no longer composes, being preoccupied with silence, mushrooms, "waking up to the very life we're living," and other philosophic concepts. However, if Cage the composer is presently submerged in Cage the philosopher and mycologist, one must remember a citation, accompanying his award from the National Academy of Arts and Letters in 1949, which read: "for having thus extended the boundaries of musical art."

Suggested Listening
Cage, *Amores for Prepared Piano and Percussion* (1943).

Suggested Reading
A *Catalogue of the Works of John Cage* is published by Henmar Press, Inc., (New York, 1962), and distributed by C. F. Peters Corp.

John Cage, *Silence*. Middletown, Conn., 1961; paperback, Cambridge, Mass.: M.I.T. Press, 1966.

John Cage, *A Year From Monday*. Middletown, Conn., 1967. In connection with this book, it is interesting to note that the publishers set the price "semi-arbitrarily"—not a chance operation—at $7.92. (Review in *Perspectives,* Summer 1968, p. 183).

Suggested Reading—Twentieth-century Music
1. On twentieth-century music as a whole:

William Austin, *Music in the 20th Century*. New York: W. W. Norton & Company, 1966.

Arthur Bliss, *As I Remember*. London: Faber & Faber, 1970.

Pierre Boulez, *Boulez on Music Today*. London: Faber & Faber, 1971.

János Démeny (ed.), *Béla Bartók Letters*. London: Faber & Faber, 1971.

A. E. F. Dickinson, *Vaughan Williams*. London: Faber & Faber, 1963.

Bernard Grun (ed.), *Alban Berg: Letters to his Wife*. London: Faber & Faber, 1971.

Peter S. Hansen, *Twentieth-Century Music* (Second Edition). Boston: Alleyn & Bacon, Inc., 1967.

Everett Helm, *Bartók* (Great Composer series). London: Faber & Faber, 1970.

Imogen Holst, *Britten* (Great Composer series). London: Faber & Faber, 1970.

Michael Hurd, *Vaughan Williams* (Great Composer series). London:
    Faber & Faber, 1970.

Harold E. Johnson, *Sibelius*. London: Faber & Faber, 1960.

Joseph Machlis, *Introduction to Contemporary Music*. New York:
    W. W. Norton & Company, 1961.

Vincent Persichetti, *Twentieth-Century Harmony*. London: Faber &
    Faber, 1962.

Eric Salzman, *Twentieth-Century Music: An Introduction*. Englewood
    Cliffs, N.J.: Prentice-Hall, Inc., 1967.

Murray Schafer, *British Composers in Interview*. London: Faber &
    Faber, 1963.

Erwin Stein (ed.), *Arnold Schoenberg: Letters*. London: Faber & Faber,
    1964.

Igor Stravinsky and Robert Craft, *Dialogues and a Diary*. London:
    Faber & Faber, 1968; *Expositions and Developments*. London: Faber
    & Faber, 1962.

E. W. White, *Benjamin Britten: His Life and Operas*. London: Faber
    & Faber, 1970; *Stravinsky*. London: Faber & Faber, 1966.

2. On developments since 1945:

Contemporary Music in Europe. Various authors in an entire issue of
    The Musical Quarterly for January 1965. New York: G. Schirmer.

3. On developments in the United States:

Wilfred Mellers, *Music in a New Found Land*. New York: Alfred A.
    Knopf, 1964.

Appendixes and Index

I. *Notation: How Music Is Written Down*

1. *NOTATION OF PITCH*

THE NOTATION OF PITCH can best be explained by referring to the keyboard of the piano. Example 181a shows part of the piano keyboard, which is composed of white keys and black keys. The black keys are arranged in alternate groups of twos and threes. The white key immediately to the left of any group of two black keys is called "C"; and the white keys that follow, counting to the right, are D, E, F, G, A, B, and C. This pattern is then repeated, above and below, so that every white key, in whatever register of the keyboard, is called by one of the letter names just mentioned. The distance from a note to its repetition above or below is called an "octave" because of the eight white keys encompassed.

WHITE KEYS

When one plays successive white keys on the piano, the pitch of the note is higher if the white key to the right is played; and lower, if to the left. Successive white keys raise (or lower) the pitch by an interval called a "whole tone," except that playing the white keys E—F or B—C produces a half, not a whole, tone. Thus if the white-key octave C to C is played, using each key in order, the following successive rise in pitch occurs (1 indicates a whole tone; ½, a half tone):

$$C \quad D \quad E \quad F \quad G \quad A \quad B \quad C$$
$$1 \quad 1 \quad \tfrac{1}{2} \quad 1 \quad 1 \quad 1 \quad \tfrac{1}{2}$$

BLACK KEYS

These keys are used to play the half tones between the whole tones. For example, the note found a half tone above C is called C sharp (C♯). The note found a half tone below D is called D flat (D♭). On the keyboard of the piano, D flat and C sharp are represented by the same black key, and, in the same way, D sharp and E flat share the same black key, etc. When

Ex. 181

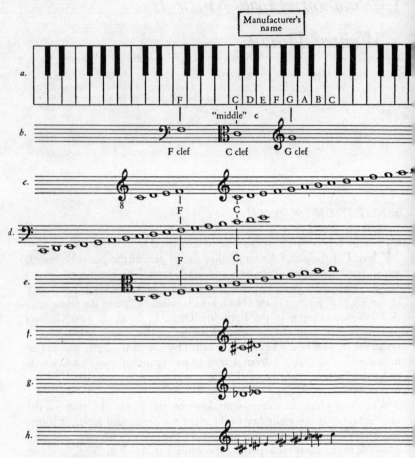

notes sound the same but are called by different names or are written differently, they are said to be "enharmonic" to each other (Ex. 181 f,g).

The half tone is the smallest pitch distance that can be played on the keyboard and the smallest that can be represented by our usual system of notation. To play a series of successive half tones in the same direction (that is, a "chromatic" scale), one plays successively the white and black keys in the order of occurrence. E—F, and B—C, already representing half tones, are played successively just as they appear on the keyboard (Ex. 181h). Hence, paradoxically, within the "octave" on the piano there are twelve half tones if all the black and white keys are used once in succession. The octave from C to C, using only the white keys, gives five whole tones and two half tones (Ex. 181a).

THE STAFF

In order to indicate the pitch of a note desired, a five-line staff is used (see Ex. 181b). The pitch of the notes placed on this staff is fixed by a "clef," which indicates the position of a particular note associated with the clef in question. The three most commonly used clefs are:

1. *The C clef* (𝄡). The line indicated by the middle of this clef is "middle" C. This particular note is the C of the central octave of the piano and is usually found just to the left of the manufacturer's name, as shown in Example 181a. In Example 181b the middle of the C clef comes on the third line of the staff. Hence middle C is found on the third line. If the middle of this clef came on the fourth line of the staff, then middle C would be found on the fourth line.

2. *The G clef* (or *treble clef*). This clef is the commonest of all clefs. It fixes the position of the G above middle C on the second line of the staff (Ex. 181b).

3. *The F clef* (or *bass clef*). This clef indicates that the F below middle C is fixed on the fourth line of the staff (Ex. 181b).

The most common clefs are the G clef and the F clef. The C clef on the third line is used today principally in writing for the viola (alto violin). The fourth-line C clef is used for the higher registers of certain instruments, for example, the cello and the bassoon. The G clef with the 8 below it (Ex. 181c) means that the note sounds an octave below the pitch indicated by the G clef. This clef is often used for the tenor part in the chorus.

Originally (probably in the eleventh or twelfth century), the F clef and C clef (and later the G clef) were affixed to the beginning of each line of the staff by the simple letters F, C, and G respectively. Gradually, idealized shapes evolved so that today the clefs shown in Example 181b are used. The pitch represented is indicated in relation to the piano keyboard.

Different clefs are necessary to avoid using more than a five-line staff and to avoid using ledger lines (lines added above or below the five-line staff; see Ex. 181d). The staff was limited to five lines because it was found difficult to read and distinguish notes at a glance on a staff with more lines. In addition, the use of more lines tended to waste paper—an important consideration in the days of very expensive parchment.

LINES AND SPACES

To indicate successive white keys on the piano, one writes notes on the staff from successive line to space, or from successive space to line. Example 181c shows this process using the G clef; Example 181d shows the use of the F clef; and Example 181e, the C clef. Examples 181c and

181d, taken together, show the notation of four octaves of white keys and their corresponding position with respect to the keyboard of the piano.

SHARPS, FLATS, ACCIDENTALS

A sharp (a half tone higher) or flat (a half tone lower) is indicated by placing a sharp (♯), or flat (♭), as the case may be, before the note affected. See Examples 181f and 181g. A natural sign (♮) indicates that the note is to be played in its "natural," that is, white-key, form. This sign is used most often to "cancel" a sharp or a flat. In Example 181h the natural before the next-to-last note indicates that the flat of the previous B is canceled, and that B natural (that is, the white note) is to be played.

The collective name for sharps, flats, and natural signs is "accidental(s)." An accidental retains its force throughout the rest of the measure in which it occurs.

KEY SIGNATURE

When certain notes are to be sharped or flatted regularly in a piece of music, the flats or sharps in question are indicated at the beginning of the piece (and on each successive line of music), and the note(s) concerned are thereafter sharped or flatted throughout *in whatever octave they occur,* unless contradicted by some accidental in the course of the piece. Such sharps or flats at the beginning of a piece, placed directly after the clef, are called the "key signature." In Example 182a the sharp placed on the F, immediately following the G clef, means that F, in whatever octave it occurs, must be played as F sharp. Hence the second note is played F sharp; but the fourth note is played as F natural, since the natural sign cancels the sharp in the key signature.

Ex. 182a

Suggestion for Study

Learn to recognize the notes on the G clef and F clef as shown in Examples 181c and 181d.

MATERIAL FOR FURTHER STUDY

Because E—F and B—C are already half tones, E sharp and B sharp are played as F and C respectively; and, in the same way, F flat and C flat are played as E and B respectively (Ex. 182b). Under certain conditions, a double-sharp (x) or a double-flat (♭♭) is used. The double-sharp means that the note is raised, not by one half tone, but by two half tones. C double-sharp, for instance, would be played as D; G double-flat would be played as F (Ex. 182b).

Ex. 182b

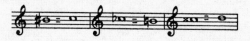

To distinguish the octave to which a note belongs, and to do so without the labor of writing out the staff and the clef, a letter notation is sometimes used. There are various such schemes. One of the most common and the one that will be used here, is as follows (Ex. 182c): the central octave

Ex. 182c

upward from middle C is distinguished by c^1, d^1, etc.; the next higher octave, by c^2, d^2; and so on, as shown. The octave below the central octave by c, d; the octave below that by C, D; below that, by CC, DD; and so on. The sign 8va--------- (or 8) means to play all notes under this indication an octave higher than written (Ex. 182c). The same sign below notes means to play them an octave lower.

2. *NOTATION OF TIME*

The pitch of a note is indicated by its position on the staff in relation to a clef. The duration of a note is shown by the particular symbol used. If nothing is to be played, the length of the silence is indicated by a "rest" of a particular shape. Example 183 shows the symbols used for the different kinds of note values and their corresponding rests.

Ex. 183

Note values:

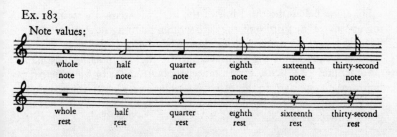

In this scheme the subdivisions are duple: two half notes equal a whole note, two quarter notes equal a half, four quarters equal a whole, in the manner of common fractions. The rests follow the same scheme. Example 184 shows the whole note and how smaller note values are

Ex. 184

The Rhythm Tree

related in the graphic form of a "rhythm tree." If one wishes to indicate a division that is not by two, a special device is used (Ex. 185). In this way

Ex. 185

three quarter notes are played in the time of a half note, three eighth notes are played in the time of a quarter note, and five sixteenth notes in the time of a quarter note, and so on.

Groups of individual eighth notes and notes of smaller values are often written, especially in instrumental music, by connecting the stems of the individual notes by a horizontal bar:

Ex. 186

For notes below the third line of the staff, the stems are written pointing up; above the third line, they are written pointing down; on the third line, they may be written up or down, whichever looks best. This convention simply keeps the stems within the staff as much as possible.

Sometimes two parts, for instance, soprano and alto voice parts, are indicated on one staff. In this case the soprano part *always* has stems going up, whether below the third line or not, and the alto part *always* has them going down.

DOTTING

Adding a dot after a note or rest increases by one half the original length of the note or rest concerned. For example, adding a dot to a whole note is equivalent to adding a half note to its time value. If a whole note indicates a duration of two seconds, a dotted whole note (○·) indicates a duration of three seconds. If the whole note represents four "beats" (see below), a dotted whole note represents six beats.

Sometimes a double dot (♩..) is used. The same rule applies: the second dot adds half the value of the first dot to the dotted half (♩.).

MEASURES, BAR LINES, AND TIME SIGNATURES

Notes are grouped into measures (sometimes called "bars"), indicated by vertical lines, called "bar lines," drawn through the five lines of the staff. Each measure contains a certain number of beats fixed by a "time signature." The latter is given at the beginning of a piece directly after the clef and after the key signature. The time signatures most commonly used are: $\frac{4}{4}$ (often written C), $\frac{3}{4}, \frac{2}{4}, \frac{6}{8}$.

In each case the lower number, the denominator, indicates the kind of note that receives one "beat"; the upper number, the numerator, indicates how many beats there are in a measure. Thus in $\frac{3}{4}$ time:

$$\frac{3 = \text{three beats in a measure}}{4 = \text{a quarter note receives one beat}}$$

In this kind of time there are three quarter-note beats, or their equivalent in duration. In the same way $\frac{6}{8}$ means that there are six eighth notes, or their durational equivalent, in a measure. Other time signatures are $\frac{3}{8}$, $\frac{9}{8}, \frac{12}{8}$. The sign ₵ is called *"alla breve"* (literally, counting "to the *breve*") and means $\frac{2}{2}$ (sometimes $\frac{4}{2}$). In this kind of time the beat is the half note, not the quarter note of the time signature C $\left(\frac{4}{4}\right)$. In music today, more complex signatures are often found, for instance $\frac{5}{8}, \frac{7}{4}$, and so on (cf. Stravinsky).

METER. THE SLUR

The time signature indicates the "meter," or measuring, of a piece. The ear distinguishes the meter by hearing a more or less regularly recurring accent, that falls, in theory at least, on the first beat ("downbeat") of the measure. In a measure of two beats the ear may distinguish an accent every second beat; in a measure of three beats, every third beat. In a four-beat measure the first beat is accented as usual, but there may also be a slighter, subordinate accent on beat three.

The first beat of the measure is the one normally accented. If another beat is to be accented, a special accent sign (>) is placed above or below the note concerned.

In Example 187 each measure receives the equivalent of three quarter notes, as required by the time signature. The number of beats proper to each note or rest is indicated immediately below the example, and, below that, the manner of counting. A special stress on beat three in measure three is indicated by the accent sign.

Ex. 187

Number of beats	2		1	3		1½	½	1 + 1	1	1	1	2		2 + ½
Count:	1	2	3	1	2	3	1	2 (+) 3	1	2	3	1	2	3	1	2	3
								"and"									

The new symbol in measures 3 to 6 of Example 161, the curved horizontal line, is called a "slur." If the slur connects two notes of the same pitch, as in the last measure of Example 161, it is called a "tie," and the notes are said to be "tied." The first note is held for the combined value of both without repeating the second. Several notes may be connected in this manner. When the slur connects two or more notes of different pitch, as in the next-to-last measure of Example 187, the notes involved are played "legato," that is, the notes are connected as smoothly as possible.

Suggestions for Study

1. Example 188 contains a tune in the G (treble) clef (for one in the F [bass] clef, see Ex. 22). Work out the pitch and the duration of the notes. If possible, play the notes on the piano, or, better, sing them. (For an explanation of the incomplete measures with which these pieces begin, see below.)

2. Try to write out the rhythm of a tune or tunes that you know, for example "America," and/or "The Star-Spangled Banner." In these two tunes, note that one begins on the first beat of the measure and the other on the "upbeat."

INCOMPLETE MEASURE. UPBEAT AND DOWNBEAT

A piece may begin, not with the first beat of a measure (and hence not with an accent), but with one or more unaccented notes. "America the Beautiful" (Ex. 188) begins on the fourth beat of the measure. The first accented note of this piece is the second note, the one that begins the first full measure. The last measure of this piece has only three beats. The fourth beat is supplied by the first note of the next stanza when the music is repeated. This is simply a convention. In this example the last

Ex. 188

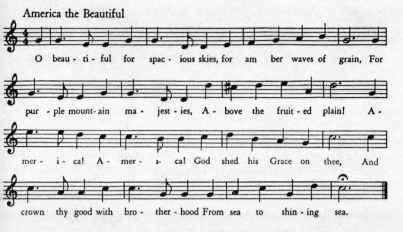

note is shown optionally extended by a "hold" or *"fermata"* (⌒), which means simply to hold out at will.

When a piece begins on the last beat of a measure, as in the case of Example 188, it is said to begin on the "upbeat," because the conductor's arm motion for this beat is invariably "up." Similarly, when the piece begins on beat one, one may say that it begins on the "downbeat" because the conductor's arm motion is "down."

The conventional gestures of conducting a piece in 2, 3, and 4 beats to the measure is shown in Example 189. These gestures also serve for rapid

Ex. 189

compound time: $\frac{6}{8}$ is conducted in two time; $\frac{9}{8}$ in three; and $\frac{12}{8}$ in four.

The conductor must give one "warning" beat to express to the players the exact speed of the unit of beat. Thus in Example 188 the conductor would beat "warning" beat three (of the four-beat gesture) to bring the singers or players in on beat four. In a piece starting on beat one, the conductor would give the upbeat as a warning beat to bring them in on beat one.

As explained above, the meter impresses itself on the ear by a regularly recurring pulse or accent that marks the beginning of each measure (sometimes there are subordinate accents within the measure as well). In Example 190 an impulse indicated by accent marks is transmitted to the ear at every fourth beat. Hence it is in "four time." One could not

Ex. 190

say that it was in $\frac{4}{4}$ time (as it is notated here) without seeing the score.
It might be $\frac{4}{8}$ or even $\frac{4}{2}$, but $\frac{4}{4}$ is the commonest time for moderate speed,
and that has been used here.

Suggestions for Study

1. In Example 191 insert the bar lines at the proper places, as suggested by the accent marks, and insert the proper time signature at the beginning. Clap the rhythm.

Ex. 191

2. Listen to various pieces. Try to determine the basic kind of time and also whether the pieces begin with the complete or the incomplete measure. If incomplete, does the piece begin on the upbeat?

3. Conduct simple tunes, for example, "America" and "The Star-Spangled Banner." Conduct accurately and rhythmically with clear and pronounced beat. One can also practice conducting gestures by following pieces on the phonograph. The Minuet from Haydn's "Drum Roll" Symphony is a good example for triple time.

4. Meter and accent become real in proportion as they are felt physically. Clapping to music, moving to music as in dancing, conducting, singing, and playing are all means to this end. The more this kind of exercise can be done, the more the rhythmic flow of music will become a part of an individual. Those who have never played instruments may wish to

experiment with relatively simple types of instruments such as the recorder (wooden flute), on which one can learn simple tunes in a few weeks. This instrument is quite inexpensive.

5. Watch the conductor at a symphony concert. His beat is often a highly individual form of the standard beat given above. Listen to the music first for the basic meter; then watch the conductor beat the downbeat, the upbeat, and the other beats. Compare different conductors.

2. *The Order of the Mass.*
The Complete Text of the Ordinary.

THE FOLLOWING shows the usual order of the Mass. When the Mass is sung (as it is in High Mass), the parts marked "Sung" are sung, usually in Gregorian Chant, by the choir (including soloists). The other parts are intoned or spoken by the priest. The Ordinary texts do not change. The Proper texts are appropriate to the time or season. In a polyphonic Mass, only the Ordinary is set.

	SUNG		*INTONED OR SPOKEN*
	ORDINARY	PROPER	PROPER
I.		*Introit*	
2.	*Kyrie*		
3.	*Gloria*		
4.			*Collect (prayers)*
5.			*Epistle*
6.		*Gradual*	
7.		*Alleluia or Tract*	
8.			*Gospel*
9.	*Credo*		
10.		*Offertory*	
11.			*Secreta*
12.			*Preface*
13.	*Sanctus*		
14.	*Agnus Dei*		
15.		*Communion*	
16.		*Post-Communion*	
17.	*Ite Missa Est*		
	(dismissal; from which the Mass or Missa *gets its name)*		

TEXT AND ENGLISH TRANSLATION OF THE ORDINARY OF THE MASS

1. KYRIE

Kyrie eleison.	*Lord, have mercy on us.*
Kyrie eleison.	*Lord, have mercy on us.*
Kyrie eleison.	*Lord, have mercy on us.*
Christe eleison.	*Christ, have mercy on us.*
Christe eleison.	*Christ, have mercy on us.*
Christe eleison.	*Christ, have mercy on us.*
Kyrie eleison.	*Lord, have mercy on us.*
Kyrie eleison.	*Lord, have mercy on us.*
Kyrie eleison.	*Lord, have mercy on us.*

2. GLORIA

Gloria in excelsis Deo, Et in terra pax hominibus bonae voluntatis.	*Glory to God in the Highest, And on earth peace to men of good will.*
Laudamus te.	*We praise thee.*
Benedicimus te.	*We bless thee.*
Adoramus te.	*We adore thee.*
Glorificamus te.	*We glorify thee.*
Gratias agimus tibi propter magnam gloriam tuam.	*We give thee thanks for thy great glory.*
Domine Deus, Rex coelestis Deus Pater omnipotens. Domine, Fili unigenite, Jesu Christe. Domine Deus, Agnus Dei, Filius Patris.	*O Lord God, heavenly King, God the Father almighty. O Lord, the only begotten Son, Jesus Christ. O Lord God, Lamb of God, Son of the Father.*
Qui tollis peccata mundi, miserere nobis. Qui tollis peccata mundi, suscipe deprecationem nostram. Qui sedes ad dexteram Patris, miserere nobis.	*Who takest away the sins of the world, have mercy upon us. Who takest away the sins of the world, receive our prayer. Who sittest at the right hand of the Father, have mercy upon us.*
Quoniam tu solus sanctus. Tu solus Dominus. Tu solus Altissimus, Jesu Christe.	*For thou only art holy, Thou only art the Lord. Thou only art most high, O Jesus Christ.*

Cum Sancto Spiritu, in gloria Dei Patris. Amen.

Together with the Holy Ghost, in the glory of the Father. Amen.

3. CREDO

Credo in unum Deum Patrem omnipotentem, factorem coeli et terrae, visibilium omnium, et invisibilium.

I believe in one God the Father almighty, maker of heaven and earth, and of all things visible and invisible.

Et in unum Dominum Jesum Christum, Filium Dei unigenitum. Et ex patre natum ante omnia saecula. Deum de Deo, lumen de lumine, Deum verum de Deo vero. Genitum non factum, consubstantialem Patri: per quem omnia facta sunt. Qui propter nos homines, et propter nostram salutem descendit de coelis.

And in one Lord Jesus Christ, the only-begotten Son of God, born of the Father before all ages; God of God, light of light, true God of true God; begotten, not made; consubstantial with the Father; by whom all things were made. Who for us men, and for our salvation, came down from heaven.

Et incarnatus est de Spiritu Sancto ex Maria Virgine; et homo factus est.

And was incarnate by the Holy Ghost of the Virgin Mary; and was made man.

Crucifixus etiam pro nobis: sub Pontio Pilato passus, et sepultus est.

He was crucified also for us, suffered under Pontius Pilate, and was buried.

Et resurrexit tertia die, secundum Scripturas. Et ascendit in coelum: sedet ad dexteram Patris. Et iterum venturus est cum gloria judicare vivos, et mortuos: cujus regni non erit finis.

And the third day He rose again according to the Scriptures; and ascended into heaven. He sitteth at the right hand of the Father; and He shall come again with glory to judge the living and the dead; and His kingdom shall have no end.

Et in Spiritum Sanctum, Dominum, et vivificantem: qui ex Patre, Filioque procedit. Qui cum Patre et Filio simul adoratur, et conglorificatur: qui locutus est per Prophetas.

And in the Holy Ghost, the Lord and giver of life, Who proceedeth from the Father and the Son, Who together with the Father and the Son is adored and glorified: Who spoke by the Prophets.

Et unam sanctam catholicam et apostolicam Ecclesiam.	*And one holy catholic and apostolic Church.*
Confiteor unum baptisma in remissionem peccatorum.	*I confess one baptism for the remission of sins.*
Et expecto resurrectionem mortuorum.	*And I await the resurrection of the dead.*
Et vitam venturi saeculi. Amen.	*And the life of the world to come. Amen.*

4. SANCTUS

Sanctus, Sanctus, Sanctus Dominus Deus Sabaoth. Pleni sunt coeli et terra gloria tua. Hosanna in excelsis.	*Holy, Holy, Holy, Lord God of Hosts. Heaven and earth are full of Thy glory. Hosanna in the highest.*
Benedictus qui venit in nomine Domini. Hosanna in excelsis.	*Blessed is He that cometh in the name of the Lord. Hosanna in the highest.*

5. AGNUS DEI

Agnus Dei, qui tollis peccata mundi, miserere nobis.	*Lamb of God, Who takest away the sins of the world, have mercy upon us.*
Agnus Dei, qui tollis peccata mundi, miserere nobis.	*Lamb of God, Who takest away the sins of the world, have mercy upon us.*
Agnus Dei, qui tollis peccata mundi, dona nobis pacem.	*Lamb of God, Who takest away the sins of the world, grant us peace.*

3. *Glossary*

THE GLOSSARY includes definitions of terms that, for one reason or an-other, have not been defined in the text; it is essentially an adjunct to the text proper. However, all terms, whether defined in the text or in the Glossary, will be found in the Index. In the following Glossary, terms of expression are generally followed by their abbreviations in parentheses. For other musical terms, consult a dictionary of music—for example, *Grove's Dictionary of Music and Musicians; Baker's Biographical Dictionary of Musicians; Apel's Harvard Dictionary of Music* (no biographies).

A cappella. Choral music without instrumental accompaniment.

Accelerando. Increase the speed gradually.

Acoustics. The science concerned with the property of sound, including (1) the nature of music (vibrations of tone-producing bodies, intensity, pitch, harmonics, and timbre); and (2) the application of this science to (a) music (intervals, concepts of consonance and dissonance), (b) construction of instruments, and (c) architectural problems.

Adagio. Very slow.

Ad libitum (ad. lib.). "At will"; usually, in free as opposed to strict time.

Air. Song or melody. *See also Aria.*

Allargando. Slowing down gradually.

Allegretto. Moderately fast.

Allegro. Fast. Literally, "cheerful."

Allegro ma non troppo. Fast, but not too fast.

Andante. At a moderate speed. Literally, "going." Slower than *allegretto*.

Animato. Animated.

Antiphonal. Two choruses singing "against" each other (i.e., alternating or together). By extension, two (or more) instrumental choirs opposed to each other.

Appoggiatura. An accented, dissonant note in a melody. See also the Index.

Arco. Literally, "bow." Used after the word *pizzicato* (plucked) to direct the string player to resume playing with the bow.

Aria. "Air." Song or melody, often elaborate (as in *da capo* aria). See also *Arioso* and *Recitative.*

Arioso. A recitative with some qualities of an aria: more melodious than a recitative and less melodious than an aria. Unlike the recitative, the *arioso* is often set to measured rhythms (especially in Bach).

Arpa. Harp.

Arpeggio. In harp or "broken" style: playing the notes that comprise chords, not as chords, but one after the other.

Assai. "Very." As in *allegro assai,* very fast.

A tempo. Return to the normal tempo after such deviations as slowing down or speeding up.

Bagatelle. A short piece, usually for the piano, especially characteristic of the nineteenth century. Literally, a "trifle."

Ballade. A form of trouvère poetry and music. In Machaut (fourteenth century), the ballade is set polyphonically, the form usually being A A B. In the nineteenth century, poetic ballades of the time were often set as songs by such composers as Schubert (e.g., his setting of Goethe's *Erlkönig*). Chopin and Brahms (among others) wrote ballades for piano in which, typically, dramatic and lyrical elements are contrasted as representations, respectively, of knightly heroics and love.

Ballet. Group dancing on the stage with costumes and music. Often connected with the opera.

Bar (form). See the Index.

Berceuse. Lullaby or cradle song, usually in $\frac{6}{8}$ time.

Brio. See *Con brio.*

Broken chord. The tones of a chord played in succession rather than simultaneously as a chord.

Cantabile. In singing style.

Cantata. Originally (seventeenth century), a vocal piece (*cantare,* to sing) as opposed to "sonata," an instrumental piece (*sonare,* to sound or play). In its developed form, the cantata was usually composed of several sections or movements consisting of recitatives, arias, choruses, and so on. An unstaged work for church or chamber. See the Index.

Cantus Firmus (*C. F.*). See the Index.

Cembalo. Harpsichord.

Chanson. Song. For French *chanson,* see the Index.

Chorale. The hymn tunes of the German Protestant Church, dating back to Martin Luther in the sixteenth century.

Chord progression. A succession of chords one after the other.

Chromatic. Melodies or harmonies based on the chromatic (semitone) scale.

Church year. Collectively, the times (and names) of the year according to the Church calendar: for example, Advent (the four Sundays before Christmas), Lent, Easter, Whitsuntide, and so on.

Clavecin. Harpsichord. See Index.

Col legno. "With the wood." An indication directing the string player to strike the string with the wood, not the hair, of the bow.

Coloratura. Brilliant runs, trills, and other devices used in virtuoso style. Thus: *coloratura soprano.*

Con brio. With fire.

Conductus. Latin song of the twelfth and thirteenth century. The polyphonic settings were generally characterized by note-against-note (chordal) style.

Conjunct. Proceeding by step, as in a conjunct melody.

Con sordino. With mute.

Cornett. Not to be confused with the modern cornet. The cornett (or *cornetto*) flourished in the Renaissance, and thereafter gradually became obsolete, although it was still used occasionally by J. S. Bach. The body of this instrument was made of wood (sometimes, ivory), straight or slightly curved with six finger holes cut in the sides. A special feature was the cup-shaped mouthpiece as in brass instruments. Made in various sizes.

Crescendo (cresc.). Make louder by degrees.

Decrescendo (decresc.). Make softer by degrees.

Détaché. A bowing direction to the string player. Literally, "detached," that is, played short. Also a single note played by a single bow stroke. In the eighteenth century, synonymous with *staccato* or *spiccato.*

Diatonic. A regular major or minor scale of seven tones as distinguished from the chromatic scale of twelve tones (cf. pp. 30–31).

Diminuendo (dim.). Make softer by degrees.

Discant (descant, discantus). A general term for thirteenth-century polyphonic music in which all the parts move together approximately in the same rhythm (as opposed, for instance, to one florid part being accompanied by a slow-moving part or parts). The term may also mean "treble" or "soprano" in part music, as in "descant viol."

Disjunct. Proceeding by leap or skip, as in a disjunct melody.

Divisi (div.). "Divided." A direction to a *section* of string players in an orchestra (e.g., violin I) to divide into two (sometimes more) bodies when playing passages that consist of two or more simultaneous-sounding notes (e.g., chords). Cf. Ex. 67. Otherwise, each player plays the passage in "double stops." (See below).

Dotted (-note) rhythm. A rhythmic pattern in which "dotted notes" (i.e., dotted quarters, dotted eighths, etc.) are prominent. For "dotting," see p. 537.

Double stops. In the strings, more than one note played at the same time. Literally, double stops mean "two notes"; but the term is sometimes used to mean two, three, or even four notes at the same time.

Enharmonic. A chord, note, or interval that sounds the same as another chord, note, or interval that is written differently (e.g., on the piano, C sharp and D flat are enharmonic to each other).

Ensemble. Literally, "the whole." The term refers either to (1) a group of players such as a quartet, quintet, or opera "ensemble" (q.v.); or (2) the performance, in the sense of the players being together in "good" or "bad" ensemble.

Entr'acte. A piece played "between the acts." Sometimes used as synonymous with intermezzo.

Estampie. Important instrumental (dance) music of the thirteenth and fourteenth centuries. It generally consists of four to seven sections, each being repeated: a a, b b, and so on. *Stantipes* is a similar form.

Etude. "Study." Usually devoted to some technical problem for the instrument concerned.

Figuration. Stereotyped figures such as arpeggios or running passages of notes. Cf. p. 79, Ex. 56, line 2.

Flutter tonguing. A special type of tonguing used by the flute, requiring a rolling movement of the tongue. This tonguing gives a curious "flutter" effect to the tone.

Forte (*f*). Loud.

Fortissimo (*ff*). Very loud. Still louder is indicated by *fff*, and so on.

Fuoco. Con fuoco. Fiery. With fire.

Glee. A type of unaccompanied choral music for men's voices, prevalent in the eighteenth century. Thus a "Glee" Club was originally intended to sing glees, not merely mirthful tunes.

Glissando. "Sliding." Rapid scales executed by a sliding movement of the finger or hand, especially on the piano or harp. Cf. *portamento*.

Glockenspiel. An instrument with horizontal rectangular steel plates of different lengths, arranged like a piano keyboard and struck with two wooden (or composition) hammers.

Grace note. An ornamental note printed in fine type, indicating that its duration is not reckoned as part of the measure but as part of the note which it (usually) precedes. So called because the term "grace" refers to an ornamental note in general.

Grave. Solemn. Slow.

Harmonics. Harmonic overtones. See the Index.

Harmonics (on stringed instruments). A note produced by touching the string lightly (not pressed down) at a particular ("nodal") point on the string, producing a light, "fluty," ethereal sound. Also called "flageolet" tones.

Intermezzo. Same as *Entr'acte.* Intermezzo also refers to a type of piano piece common in the nineteenth century (e.g., Brahms). See also the Index.

Intonation. Good or bad intonation refers to playing in or out of tune respectively.

Ländler. Austrian dance like a slow waltz, popular in the early nineteenth century.

Larghetto. Less slow than *largo.*

Largo. Very slow and broad.

Legato. Smooth and connected.

Lento. Slow.

Libretto. "Little book." The text of an opera; sometimes applied to the text of an oratorio or cantata.

Lied (plural, *Lieder*). Song(s). For German *Lied,* see the Index.

Madrigal (fourteenth century). A form of pastoral poetry, consisting of two or three strophes of three lines each plus a final two-line strophe called the *Ritornello.* In the musical form, the initial strophes were set to the same music but the *Ritornello* were set generally to contrasted music. Hence the musical form: A A (A) B. The madrigal of this time was set for two or three voice parts, the soprano often being of ornamental character. For the sixteenth-century madrigal, see p. 156.

Ma non troppo. "But not too much." See *Allegro ma non troppo.*

Marcato. Marked; with emphasis.

Marimba. A musical instrument resembling a xylophone, consisting of hard wooden bars, usua.'y with resonators beneath, played by being struck with small hammers.

Martelé. "Hammered." In stringed instruments, a special type of heavily accented bow stroke.

Mazurka (Mazur). A Polish dance in triple time, executed at moderate speed. An accent frequently occurs on the second or third beat (cf. Chopin).

Mezzo forte (mf). Mezzo piano (mp). Mezzo means "half" or "moderate." Hence *mezzo forte* means moderately loud; *mezzo piano,* moderately soft. The latter term, however, is ambiguous. It usually means a little louder than *piano* and a little softer than *mezzo forte.* But it sometimes means a little *softer* than *piano.*

Moderato. At a moderate tempo.

Monodrama. A term used by Schoenberg to describe his opera *Erwartung,* whose cast consists of a single character.

Mordent. A musical ornament. The *true* mordent is a rapid alternation of the written note with the note a tone or semitone below. Its typical sign is (⑃). Cf. Example 103.

Multiple stops. On the stringed instruments, a collective term for double, triple, and quadruple stops; that is, two, three, or four notes played simultaneously by a single player.

Mute. A device for muffling or dampening the sound of instruments. On the strings, the usual mute is a pronged clamp placed on the bridge. In the brass, a pear-shaped piece of wood or metal is inserted into the bell of the instrument.

Nocturne. "Night piece." A kind of piano piece popular in the nineteenth century. Typically melancholy with expressive melody (cf. Chopin).

Note and Tone. In strict usage, *note* refers to the written symbol of a sound on a page of music; *tone* refers to the sound itself. However, the two terms are often used interchangeably.

Nuance. Fine shades of expression in general. Used particularly in connection with subtle gradations of loud and soft, tempo, and phrasing.

Obbligato. An independent part, usually for instruments, as a *violin obbligato* is an independent, often florid, part for violin which accompanies the ensemble. Although *obbligato* means obligatory or indispensable, some modern usage has twisted this meaning to denote an accompanying part that may be omitted.

Opus (Op.). "Work" of a composer. The numbers used with Opus (e.g., Op. 4) indicate the chronological position of a composition, usually with respect to publication.

Oratorio. An extended setting of a text, generally religious in character, on a large scale for soloists, chorus, and orchestra. An oratorio may be dramatic in text or setting (including styles and forms typical of the opera, like the *da capo* aria), but the oratorio is not costumed or staged, being given in concert form in a concert hall or church. See also the Index.

Ornaments. Collective name for ornaments of expression. Usually indicated by specific signs in the score. See under *Trill, Mordent,* and *Turn.* For a list of some of these and their graphic signs, see Apel's *Harvard Dictionary of Music,* article "Ornamentation." For an exhaustive list of signs, see *Grove's Dictionary of Music,* Fifth Edition (1954), article "Ornaments"; the list of signs occurs on pp. 441–8. Cf. Ex. 103, p. 223, above.

Overture. A piece played before the opening (F. *ouvert* = open) of the curtain before an opera (or one of its acts). In short, the music played before the curtain goes up. By analogy, the piece which begins an oratorio (or parts of it). See the Index for *Overture* and *Concert Overture.*

Parlando. Literally, "speaking." The term refers to rapid speaking style in singing, as in Rossini. A derived type is the "patter" song in the operettas of Gilbert and Sullivan.

Partita. A term used in the seventeenth and eighteenth centuries to mean suite or variation.

Pianissimo (pp). Very soft. For still softer, the following are used: *ppp, pppp,* and (rarely) *ppppp* and *pppppp.*

Piano (p). Soft.

Pizzicato (pizz.). To pluck rather than bow the string of an instrument.

Plainsong. A name for Gregorian chant (see the Index). Derived from *cantus planus* ("plain song")—that is, free or unmeasured chant—as opposed to *cantus figuralis* ("figured song")—that is, polyphonic, exactly measured, music.

Polka. A nineteenth-century dance originating in Bohemia. Fast duple time. It became extremely popular in European society.

Polonaise. Polish dance of moderate triple time. It originated in court ceremonials, and dates back at least to the sixteenth century.

Ponticello. See *sul ponticello.*

Portamento. A sliding between two pitches without distinguishing the intermediate tones. Characteristic of the voice, strings (especially violin), and trombone. *Glissando* distinguishes all the intermediate half steps between two pitches. Thus the piano and harp can play *glissando* but not *portamento*. The voice, violin, and trombone can produce either, but the *glissando* is far more difficult for them. *Portamento* is a legitimate effect. Sometimes, however, it is the sign of faulty technique —when uncontrolled.

Presto (prestissimo). Very fast (very, very fast).

Rallentando (rall.). Gradually slower.

Range. The limits of a voice, instrument, or melody with respect to pitch.

Recitative. A reciting, declamatory style of vocal music in imitation of speech. It originated in the early seventeenth-century opera. For "measured" recitative, see p. 173, Ex. 91.

Register. A certain part of the range of a voice or instrument. Also, in the organ, a set of pipes controlled by one stop.

Resolution. The consonance that follows a dissonance is said to be its resolution.

Responsorial. A type of singing (especially in Gregorian chant) in which a soloist(s) is answered by the choir, or vice versa.

Ritardando (rit.). Gradually slower.

Ritenuto. Immediately slower. Sometimes the same as *ritardando.*

Rondeau. A form of medieval French poetry whose musical setting is based on a complicated repetition of two fairly short melodic segments (a, b). If A B stands for the same music as a b, but contains the refrain of the initial text, the form is: A B a A a b A B (the opening refrain being repeated at the end). Used in solo songs as well as in polyphonic settings.

Rubato (i.e., tempo rubato). "Stolen time." Slight deviations from strict time. *Rubato* may refer to tempo deviations of the melody alone (the other parts being in strict time) or to the stolen time of the whole. For Chopin's variety, see *Chopin* in the Index.

Sautillé. In the strings, a type of bow stroke in which the bow rebounds lightly "off" the string. See also *Spiccato.*

Sforzando (sf). A sudden forcing of tone giving the effect of a strong accent.

Siciliano. Originally a dance in $\frac{12}{8}$ or $\frac{6}{8}$ time, moderate tempo. Occurs in instrumental and vocal music of the seventeenth and eighteenth centuries (e.g., *Erbarme Dich* from Bach's *St. Matthew Passion*).

Sonatina. A "small sonata," typically having fewer or shorter movements, simpler style, or less demanding technical requirements than the sonata proper.

Sonority. Said of a sound in general. In modern music, "sonority" or "sonorities" may be used as a term to describe chords or any complex of simultaneous sounds that cannot otherwise be described with the terminology of conventional harmony.

Sordino(i). Mute(s).

Sostenuto. Sustained.

Spiccato. Same as *sautillé.* Earlier (eighteenth century), same as *détaché.*

Spinet. From *spina,* a thorn, the terms refer to thornlike points or quills or leathers used in the harpsichord. Strictly speaking, "spinet" refers to the harpsichord mechanism (*cf. Plate 14*B) enclosed in a box that is shaped roughly like a triangle. In modern usage, "spinet" is incorrectly used to mean a small upright piano.

Staccato. Disconnected. Usually indicated by a dot over (or under) a note. In the strings, it means a number of *martelé* strokes played rapidly with a single bow stroke. See also *Détaché.*

Stantipes. See *Estampie.*

Stretto. Stretta. See the Index.

Suite. An instrumental form consisting of a series of dances or dancelike movements generally in the same key (or parallel major or minor). See the Index.

Sul G. On the G string of the violin (*cf. Ex. 20*c).

Sul ponticello. "On the bridge." In the strings, a bowing done very close to the bridge, giving a thin, glassy sound.

Temperament. Any system of tuning whose intervals deviate from acoustically pure systems. In the latter, the size of the half and whole tones vary. In equal temperament (used on the piano), each half and whole tone is equal to every other half and whole tone.

Tone. See *Note and Tone.*

Transpose. Transposition. Putting a piece in another key (i.e., at another level of pitch).

Tremolo. See the Index.

Trill (*tr.*). A musical ornament, consisting of a rapid alternation of a (written) note with the note a tone or semitone above. Usually indicated by *tr* or by a graphic sign such as (∿) . Today the trill begins with the written note. In the eighteenth century, it typically began with the note above the written note. Cf. Ex. 103.

Troppo (*ma non troppo*). "Too much." See *Allegro ma non troppo*.

Turn. A musical ornament consisting of four or five notes "turning" around the main (written) note. Cf. Ex. 103.

Una corda. "One string." A direction meaning to depress the soft (left) pedal of the piano, thus shifting the striking mechanism so that the hammer hits one string (*una corda*) instead of two or three. In the modern piano, depressing the soft pedal results in striking two of the normal three strings (in the lower registers, one instead of the normal two).

Vibraphone. A musical instrument resembling the marimba but with electrically operated valves in the resonators, producing a gentle vibrato. In vogue in certain *avant-garde* scores for its special quality of sound.

Vibrato. See the Index.

Virginal. Sixteenth-century term for a type of harpsichord encased in an oblong box. The term is commonly used as "pair of virginals," the origin of which is uncertain. "Virginal" may be derived from *virga* (the "jack" of the harpsichord) *See Plate 14B*.

Virtuoso. A performer of great technical skill.

Vivace. Rapidly. Lively.

Word painting. A term used to mean the depiction of a text by some appropriate musical means to underline or emphasize the thing or sentiment in question. See the use of a dissonance to underscore the word "weeping" in Ex. 77, p. 116.

Xylophone. A musical percussion instrument consisting of a series of wooden bars graduated in length so as to sound the notes of the scale when struck with small wooden hammers.

Abgesang, 144

Absolute music: problems of, 56; defined, 115; titles given to, 124

A cappella, 159; defined, 546

A cappella Masses, 330

Accelerando, 546

Accent, 12; types of, 19–20; agogic, 16; sign for, 538

Accidental(s), 534

Acoustics, defined, 546

Adagio, 546

Adagio-composer (Bruckner), 311

Addison (and Steele), 196

Ad libitum (ad. lib.), 546

Aeolian (minor) mode, 35, 154

Aesthetics, *see* Beauty; Quality in art

"Affections," 164; Doctrine of, 190, 231

African tribal music, 136

Age of Reason (eighteenth century), 230

"Age of Webern," 402, 419, 507

Agnus Dei (Mass), 137; text of, 545

Agogic accent and agogics, 16

Air (aria): in comic opera, 270; defined, 546; *see also* Aria

Aix-la-Chapelle, Peace of, 201 n11

Albeniz, Isaac, 360 n1, 484

Alberti, Domenico, 235

Alberti bass, 235

Albinoni, Tomaso, 213, 215

Aleatoric (aleatory) music, 403; defined, 524

Alexander II (Tsar), 282, 359

Alfano, Franco, 370

Algarotti, Francesco (Count), 265

Alla breve, 537

Allargando, 546

Allegretto, 546

Allegro, 546

Allegro assai, 15

Allegro ma non troppo, 546

Alleluia (Mass), 137, 542

Allemande, 183

Alpine horn, 136

Altered chord, 53

Alto (voice), 85–6

Alto flute, 96

Alto oboe (English horn), 97–8

Ambros, A. W., 151 n12

Ambrose (Saint), 137

Ambrosian (Milanese) chant, 137

Amen (church) cadence, 50

"America," 18, 23; melodic contour of, 24

"America the Beautiful," 538

Andante, 546

Anderson, Emily, 277 n6

Anderson, Marian, 84

Anerio, Felice, 175

Animato, 546

Ansermet, Ernest, 396

Answer (of a fugue), 62; real and tonal, 65 n4

Antecedent, 28

Anthem, 154; verse anthem, 177

Antiphonal, 546

Apel, Willi, 187 n3

Appoggiatura, 52, 233; defined, 546

Appreciation (music), early history of, vii–ix

Aquinas, St. Thomas, 141

Arbeau, Thoinot, xxv, 158 n14

"Archform," 452

Architectural music (Berlioz), 323

Arco, 93, 547

Aria (air), 169; *lamento,* 171; *da capo,* 193–4; composite, 270; in rondo form, 270; "tinsel," 353; defined, 546; *see also* Da capo aria

Arietta, 270

Arioso: in Monteverdi, 169; in Schütz, 177; in J. S. Bach, 208 n14; in Verdi, 353; defined, 547

Aristoxenus, 459

Armstrong, Louis, 280 n8, 508

Arne, Thomas (autograph), Plate 20

Arpa, 547

Arpeggio, 547

Ars Antiqua, 156, 233

Ars Nova, 146–7, 233

Asafiev: *Flames of Paris,* 463; 464

Assai, 547

Association for Contemporary Music, 461

Arpeggio, 547

Athematic construction, 417

Atonality, 399, 401, 404; *see also* Twelve-tone technique

Atonal music: style of, 406; forms, 406–7; terminology, 411, 415

Atonement (J. S. Bach), 205

Auber, D. F. E., 334

Auden, W. H., 437

Aufklärung (Enlightenment), 230

Augmentation, 63

Augmented: interval, 40; chord, 53

Augustine (Saint), 126

Augustus III (King-Elector of Poland-Saxony), 209

Aulos, 134

Auric, Georges, 411 n3, Plate 30A

Austin, William, 518 n8

Authentic: cadence, 50; mode, 138

Auxiliary note, 51–2

Avant-garde, 402, 507ff

Avant-garde music, in Poland and Japan, 403

Babbitt, Milton: use of "total organization," 512; 521

Babble songs (children), 133

Bach, C. P. E., 245; sonatas, 231; *Versuch,* 245 n8; fantasias, 246 n9; mentioned, 233, 239, 240, 242

Bach, J. C., 260; mentioned, 239, 240

Bach, J. S.: as a church musician, 204; church cantatas, 204ff; evolution of cantata, 205; use of chorale, 204–5; theology, 205; organ, characteristics of, 222 n9; B-A-C-H as an autograph, 222 n10; compared with Handel, 225–8; orbit in church, chamber, and organ music, 226; harmony and polyphony in, 227; autograph, Plates 8A, 20; portrait, Plate 22D; mentioned, vii, 173, 209 n16, 225

    WORKS: *Chaconne,* 16, 113, 224, Plate 8; Orchestral Suite No. 1 in C, 17, 46; *The Well-Tempered Clavier,* 22, 46, 221–2; "Goldberg" Variations, 44, 60, 225, 291; *The Art of the Fugue,* 63, 64–7, 222; *St. John Passion,* 118; Toccata and Fugue in D minor, 182; organ chorale preludes, 207; *Durch Adams Fall* (chorale prelude), 191; *Christ Lag in Todesbanden* (cantata), 205–6; *Wachet Auf* (cantata), 206;

Bach (*continued*)

St. Matthew Passion, 207–8, 226; O Sacred Head now wounded (chorale), 208–9; Mass in B minor, 118, 191, 209–11, 275; "Brandenburg" concertos, 17, 214; Italian Concerto, 216; concertos (violin, harpsichord), 216; sonatas, 111, 218–19; suites, 219 n6; "English" and "French" suites, 224; organ fugues, 222; Passacaglia (organ), 224

Bach-Gesellschaft, 205 n13, 226

"Back to Bach," 455

Bagatelle, 284; defined, 547

Bagpipe, 136

"Bagpipe" scale, 37

Baïf, J.-A. de, 156

Baird, Tadeusz, 510

Balakirev, Mily, 360, 361, 362; "Group," 360; "Free School," 364

Balfe, William, 335

Ballade, 144, 146; Schubert, 294; defined, 547

Ballad opera, 200

Ballata, 146

Ballet, 172, 266, 333; Russian, 463; repertory in Soviet Union, 463; defined, 547; Plates 18A, 30B

Ballet Russe, 432, 463

Ballett (balletto: vocal form), 157

Bar (measure) and bar line, 12; defined, 537

Barber, Samuel: style and works, 504

Barcarolle, 296

Bardi, Giovanni (Count), 167

Bar form, 34, 144

Baritone (voice), 85–6

Baroque: characteristics of, 161ff; seventeenth-century background, 162ff; derivation of term, 162 n1; the art of, 163–4; musical characteristics, 164–7; function of music,

Baroque (*continued*)

165–6; orchestra in, 166–7; opera sets, Plate 17; architecture of, Plate 21A

Barth, Hans, 518

Bartók, Béla, 456ff; quarter tones, 37; music characterized, 402; folk-music style, 445; interest in folk music, 446; neoclassic elements, 446; quoted on folk music, 446; versatility, 446; life and works, 447–8; folk-music investigator, 447; influence of Debussy, 447; parlando rubato, 448, 452; last years, 448; organic folk-music style, 448; rhythm, 448; tempo giusto, 448; use of modes, 449; melody, 449–50; bitonality, 450; "free tonality," 450; glissando, 450; harmony, 450; instrumental sonorities, 450; pizzicato, 450; pizzicato glissando, 450; "rebounding" pizzicato, 450; notation, 451; structure, 451; "archform," 452; "night music," 452; non vibrato, 452; táragató melody, 452; "night sounds," 454; portrait, Plate 35A; mentioned, 135, 136, 395, 396, 399, 462, 518

WORKS: Allegro Barbaro, 397, 399, 400 (discussed), 445, 447, 449, 450, 451; Fourth String Quartet, 427, 447, 449, 451–3 (analyzed); Second String Quartet, 445, 449 (discussed); Mikrokosmos, 446; Kossuth, 447; Twenty Hungarian Folk Songs, 447; Duke Bluebeard's Castle, 447; Music for String Instruments Percussion and Celesta, 448, 449, 454 (discussed); Concerto for Orchestra, 449, 450; Sonata for Two Pianos and Percussion, 450; Third String Quartet, 450; Violin Concerto, 451; Out of Doors, 452

Bartolozzi, Bruno: woodwind technique, 509; new sounds and chords on woodwinds, Plate 38A

Bass (voice), 85–6

Bass clarinet, 99, Plate 4A

Bass clef, 533

Bass drum, 102

Bass flute, 96

Basso continuo, 165

Bassoon, 98, Plate 3B

Basso ostinato, see Ostinato

Bass viol, 159

Baton (conductor's), 109

Baudelaire, Charles, 378

Bayreuth: theater at (Wagner), 345, Plate 25B

BBC Symphony Orchestra, Plates 2B, 3A & B, 4A, 5B, 6A

Beat, conductor's, 537; "warning," 539

Beat: "strong," 12; "weak," 12

"Beatles, The," 491

Beaumarchais, P. A. (dramatist), 230, 271

Beauty: nature of, 126; criterion of, 126

"Bebop," 491

Beethoven, Ludwig van, 286ff; attitude toward program music, 124; knew C. P. E. Bach's *Versuch,* 245 n8; his importance, 286; new attitude toward society, 286; three styles, 287; the Romantic and Classic in, 287–8; influence of symphonies, 288; development of material, 288; use of *sforzando,* 288; emotional intensity, 288; *Heiligenstadt Testament* of 1802 and his deafness, 288 n4; modulations in, 289; dissonance in, 289; rhythm, 289; organic conception of music, 290; themes described by Ernest Newman, 290; notebooks, 290; method of composition, 290; forms,

Beethoven (*continued*)
290–1; scherzo, 290; use of orchestra, 290, 291; use of cadenza, 291; fugue, 291; variation, 291; mixture of forms, 291; increased size of orchestra, 291; powers of fantasy and improvisation, 291; attitude toward the text, 329–30; portrait, Plate 24B; mentioned, 239, 298, 299, 302, 303, 311, 312, 338, 352, 366

WORKS: Third Symphony (*Eroica*), 20, 32, 57, 59, 124, 243–5; Fifth Symphony, 29; Sixth ("Pastoral") Symphony, 124, 288, 291, 299; Ninth Symphony, 126, 288, 299, 320; "Diabelli" Variations, 60, 291; F major Variations, 291; piano sonatas, 124, 246; *Prometheus* (ballet), 244; chamber music, 250, 254–5; Quartet (Op. 59, No. 1), 17–18, 254–5; Quartet (Op. 59, No. 2), 22–3; *Great Fugue,* 249, 291; Quartet (Op. 132), 255; "last" quartets, 288; Quartet (C-sharp minor, Op. 131), 291, 299; Fourth and Fifth Piano Concertos, 290, 291; overtures and concert overtures, 316–17, 339 n3; *Fidelio,* 270, 339 (discussed); *Missa Solemnis,* 275, 330 (analyzed); Mass (C major), 330

Begas (lithographer), Plate 24C

Beggar's Opera, The, 200

Bel canto, 194, 335

"Believe me if all those endearing young charms" (Irish folk song), 26–8 (analyzed), 135

Bellini, Vincenzo, 336–7; influence on Chopin, 296 n9; influence on Tchaikovsky, 309; *Norma,* 336; mentioned, 352

Bells (orchestra), 102

Bembo, Pietro, 156

Benevoli, Orazio, 176

Benucci (singer), 273

Beowulf, 111

Berceuse: in Chopin, 296; defined, 547

Berg, Alban, 426ff; indebted to Wagner and Mahler, 426; compared to Webern and Schoenberg, 426; close relationship to Schoenberg and Webern, 426; early death, 427; lyric and dramatic gifts, 427; mentioned, 395, 416, 419, 470

   WORKS: *Wozzeck*, 407, 426, 427–8 (described), 428 (forms of instrumental music), 461, 489; Three Pieces for Orchestra, 413; Lyric Suite, 426, 427; Violin Concerto, 426, 427, 428 (analyzed); *Lulu*, 427

Berio, Luciano, 521

Berlin Philharmonic Hall (1963), Plate 33A

Berlioz, Hector: *Mémoires* (quoted), 110; influenced by Beethoven, 288; program symphony, 299, 318ff; importance of program, 319; *idée fixe*, 318, 319; his ideal orchestra, 321; abilities with the orchestra, 321; father of modern orchestration, 321; *Treatise of Modern Orchestration and Instrumentation*, 321; importance of the literary element in the works of, 321; a misunderstood composer, 322; estimate of, 321–2; literary sensibilities and talent, 322; Berlioz on his own music (*Mémoires*), 322–3; architectural music, 323; autograph, Plate 20; portrait, Plate 28c; mentioned, 124, 284, 320, 323, 344, 352, 361, 375

   WORKS: *Symphonie Fantastique*, 123, 318–20; *Harold en Italie*, 288, 320 (discussed); *Symphonie Funèbre et Triomphale*, 320, 323;

Berlioz (*continued*)
   Roméo et Juliette, 320–1, 323; *Les Troyens*, 321, 334; *Béatrice et Bénédict*, 321; *La Damnation de Faust*, 321, 323; *Le Spectre de la Rose*, 322; Requiem, 323, 331; *The Infancy of Christ*, 323

Bernard de Ventadour, 144

Bernini, G. L. (sculptor and architect), 164

Bernstein, Leonard, 396

Bertran de Born, 144

Béza, Theodore, 154

Bible, music in the, 133

Binary form, 34

Binchois, Gilles, 148

Bitonality, 450; *see also* Polytonality

Bizet, Georges: *Carmen*, 6, 283, 334 (discussed), 370; mentioned, 372, 379

Black keys, 531

Bliss, Arthur, 487

Bloch, Ernest: use of quarter tones, 37; career and influence as a teacher, 492; compared to Ives, 492; style and works, 492; mentioned, 490, 498, 518

Blow, John, 177

Blue Danube Waltz, 22

"Blues," 18, 136, 491

"Blues" singer, 509

Boccaccio, Giovanni, 145, 146

"Boehm" system (for woodwinds), 95, 98

Boieldieu, F.-A., 334

Boito, Arrigo, 353, 355

Borodin, Alexander, 360, 361, 362, 363, 379, 430

Bortniansky, Dmitri, 332

"Bouffon" war, 269

Boulanger, Nadia, 375, 401, 435 n1, 498, 501, 502, 503, 514

"Boulangerie," 401

Boulez, Pierre: proclaims "age of Webern," 402; article "Schoenberg is Dead," 512; as conductor, 514; quoted, 514; electronic and "chance" work, 514; portrait, Plate 38B; mentioned, 396, 397, 511, 520

    WORK: *Le Marteau sans Maître* (discussed), 513

Bourbons (French), 229

Bourrée, 183

Bow (violin), 91

Bow strokes (strings), 93

Boyce, William, 240

Brahms, Johannes, 304–8; influenced by Beethoven, 288; disciplined Romantic style, 304; rhythmic patterns, 304–5; syncopations, 305; polyrhythms, 305; scoring for piano and for orchestra, 305; harmonies, 305; cyclic devices, 305; use of motto, 305; use of Classic forms, 305; Romantic lyrical expression, 305; themes and rhythms, 306; use of Phrygian mode, 306–7; terminal development, 307; use of *chaconne (passacaglia),* 307–8; mentioned, 226 n12, 284, 313 n4, 315, 348, 365, 369, 408

    WORKS: songs, 294; First Symphony, 305; Third String Quartet, 305; Third Symphony, 305; Fourth Symphony, 306–8; Requiem, 331

Brass instruments: in general, 94–6, 99–102; limitations of, 99; harmonic series of, 99; crooks, 100; hand stopping, 100; valves, 100; *see also* Plate 6B

Brentano, Bettina, 286

Bridge (in sonata form), 69

Britten, Benjamin: discussed, 488; chamber orchestration, 489; liking for variation forms, 488; style and orchestration, 488; vocal music and

Britten (*continued*)

    operas, 488; portrait, Plate 36B; mentioned, 462, 488

    WORKS: *War Requiem,* 488; *Peter Grimes,* 489; *The Turn of the Screw,* 489

Broken chord, 547

Brown, Earle, 524

Bruch, Max, 315

Bruckner, Anton, 310–11; characteristics, 311; use of *adagio,* 311; cyclic finale, 311; mentioned, 299, 331, 369

Bruitisme, 401

Buchan, John, quoted, 21

Buchner, Georg, 427

Buhlig, Richard, 525

Bukofzer, Manfred F., 113, 187 n3

Bull, John, 124

Bull, Ole, 367

Bülow, Cosima von, 341

Bülow, Hans von, 365

Burney, Charles, vii, 197

Busenello (librettist), 168

Busnois, Antoine, 151

Busoni, Ferruccio, 483

Buxtehude, Dietrich, 177, 181, 220

Byrd, William: on singing, 85; *The Bells,* 124; *Ave Verum* (motet), 155; meter and rhythm in, 395, 487

Byron, George Gordon (Lord), 283, 335

Cabaletta, 353 n4

Caccia, 146

Caccini, Giulio: *Euridice,* 120; *Le Nuove Musiche,* 161, 164, 167 (quotation)

Cäcilienverein, 329

Cadence: melodic, final, intermediate, 30; harmonic, 49; types of, 50

Cadenza, 216; in Classic concerto, 256; written out in Beethoven, 291

Cadenza (*continued*)
in nineteenth century, 313; vocal, 336–7; accompanied (Berg), 428

Cage, John: earliest works, 525; "prepared" piano, 525; categories of "chance" music, 525; rhythm and dance music, 525; interest in Oriental culture, 525–6; *Silence* (book), 526; an estimate, 526; quoted on *Indeterminacy*, 526; quoted on tradition, 527; his influence, 527; portrait, Plate 40B; mentioned, 402, 508, 524

    WORKS: *4' 33"*, 402, 510; *Imaginary Landscape No. 4*, 403, 508, 524, 526; *Amores* (description), 525; *Indeterminacy* (a short story from), 526

Calder, Alexander, 524

Calzabigi, Ranieri di, 265

Canon: defined, 43; in fourteenth century, 146; in Franck, 373, 374; in Stravinsky, 442; *see also* "Sumer is icumen in"

Cantabile, defined, 547

Cantata: chamber, 198; of Alessandro Scarlatti, 198; of Rameau, 198; church (J. S. Bach), 204ff; defined, 547

Canterbury Tales, The (Chaucer), 111

Cantus firmus: defined, 140 n6; in fifteenth century, 151 n11; 154

Cantus-firmus Mass, 154

Canzona: instrumental, 158, 180, 181, 221; in comic opera, 270

Capriccio, 284

Carissimi, Giacomo, 176, 200

Carpenter, Paul S., 393 n1

Carrillo, Julián, 37, 518

Carter, Elliott: style, 514; quoted on twelve-tone technique, 514; metrical modulation, 515; Variations for

Carter (*continued*)
Orchestra (discussed), 515; Second String Quartet (discussed), 516

Casella, Alfredo, 483

Cassation, 248 n11

Castrato, 194, 196 (in Handel opera)

Catch (caccia), 146

Catherine the Great (of Russia), 360

Cavalieri, Emilio del, 176 n4

Cavalli, Pietro, 171, 172

Cavatina, 353 n4; defined, 270

Cavour, Camillo Benso di (Count), 351

C clef, 533

Cecilia (St.) Society, 329

Celesta, 103, 422

Cello, 92, Plate 2A

Cello concerto, 315

Cembalo, see Harpsichord

Cent (to measure intervals), 37

Cesti, Marc'Antonio, 171, Plates 17A & B, 19A

Chabrier, Alexis-Emmanuel, 334, 372

Chace, 146

Chaconne: defined, 60, 187; use in Brahms, 307

Chalumeau (clarinet register): 98, 248; use in Weber, 340

Chamber cantata, 198

Chamber concerto, 213

Chamber music, 180, 246ff; defined, 247; compared with orchestral music, 247; types of, 248ff; *see also* Duo; Trio; Quartet; etc.

Chamber-music orchestration (Mahler), 312

Chamber sonata, 185–6; *see also* Sonata da camera

Chambonnières, Jacques, 183

"Chance" ("aleatory") music, 507, 508; defined, 524

"Chance operations," 403, 508, 510

Chanson (= song), 120, 148, 151–
2, 155–6, 159; see also French
chanson; Mélodie

Chant: Gregorian, 137ff; Ambrosian,
137; for the Office, 137; for the
Mass, 137; see also Gregorian
chant

Chapel: Dijon, Papal (Rome), St.
Mark's (Venice), 153

Char, René, 513

"Character" piece (piano), 293

Character variation, defined, 60

Charles II (King of England), 162,
394

Charpentier, Gustave, 334

Charpentier, Marc-Antoine, 177, 190
n3

Chaucer, Geoffrey, 145, 146

Chausson, Ernest, 372, 373

Chávez, Carlos: style and works, 505;
conductor and educator, 506; Toward a New Music, 506; mentioned, 360 n1

Cherubini, Luigi, 231, 269, 333, 338

Chimes (in orchestra), 102

Choir: vocal, 85; orchestral, 90ff

Choir organ, 106

Chopin, Frédéric, 295–6; relation to
Romanticism, 295; his Polish nationalism, 295; Bellini's influence,
296 n9; piano music, 295–6; style of
piano playing, 296; his rubato, 296;
poetic imagination, 296; mentioned,
284, 295, 304, 315, 315 n5, 336, 376,
379, 381

"Chopsticks," 46

Choral color, 87

Chorale (German), 153 n13; use in
cantata, 204–5; use in Alban Berg,
428; defined, 547

Chorale cantata, 205

Chorale prelude, 177, 207

Chord: definition, characteristics,
types of, 48; degrees, 49; classified

Chord (continued)
as to major, minor, augmented, and
diminished, 52–3; diatonic, chromatic, altered, 53

Chord progression, 547

Chordal style, 151

Chori spezzati, 153

Choron, Alexandre, 329

Chorus, see Choir

Chotzinoff, Samuel, xxiii

Christiana Musical Society, 267

"Christ ist erstanden" (Christ is
arisen), 134

Chromatic, 547

Chromatic alteration, 40

"Chromatic" scale, 532; defined, 30–
31

Church, importance in medieval life,
143

Church cantatas (Bach), 204ff; see
also Bach, J. S.

Church concerto, 213

Church sonata, 184–6

Church year, 205; defined, 548

Cimarosa, Domenico, 268

"Circle of fifths," 38

Clarinet, 98–9, 237, Plate 4A

"Classic" (term), 233 n3

Classicism (eighteenth century), 232f

Classic period: background in politics,
229; reform ideals of the philosophers, influence on middle class,
229–30; Age of Reason, 230; art
and letters, 230; parallels in music,
231; relation of music to social
changes and French Revolution,
231

"Classics," the, 126, 393

Classic style: early, 231–2; of Haydn
and Mozart, 234ff; texture of, 236

Claude Le Jeune, 156

Claudel, Paul, 481

Clavecin, see Harpsichord

Clavichord: vibrato on, 104; description and mechanism, 158, Plates 13A and 14A; in rococo music, 237

Clavichord player, Plate 13A

Clef, kinds of, 533

Closing theme (sonata form), 69

"Coast of High Barbary" (folk song), 36, 135

Cobbett, Walter W., 248 n12, 250 n13

Cocteau, Jean: relation to Satie, 390; *Coq et Arlequin,* 390, Plate 30A; mentioned, 401, 435, 480, 481

Coda: of a fugue, 63; of sonata form, 68, 71

Codetta (sonata form), 71

Coleridge, Samuel Taylor, 283, 290 n5

Collect (Mass), 542

Col legno, 422; defined, 548

Collet, Henri, 480

Coloratura, defined, 548

"Colossal" style (in baroque music), 176

Comic opera, *see* Opera, comic

Commercial concert, 285, 393

Communion (Mass), 137, 275 (Requiem), 542

Compline, 137

Composer, relation to the public in twentieth century, 392ff

"Composing with the twelve tones," *see* Twelve-tone technique

"Composite" aria, defined, 270

Composite finale, 270

Composite forms: instrumental, 73–4; vocal, 121 n1

Computer (in tape music), 520

Con brio, defined, 548

Concert, commercial, 285, 393

Concert-halls, new types of, 521, Plate 32B

Concertato, sixteenth century, 159

Concertato style, seventeenth century, 168, 169, 175

Concertino, 212

Concert master, 89

Concerto: sixteenth century, 159; baroque *concerto grosso,* 212–14; baroque solo concerto, 215–17; Classic, 256ff; nineteenth century, 312–15

Concerto da camera, 213

Concerto da chiesa, 213

Concerto grosso, 180, 212ff

Concert overture: in Beethoven, 316–17; in Mendelssohn, 317

Conductor (orchestral): responsibilities and functions, 108; gestures of, 539

Conductus, 143; defined, 548

Con fuoco, see Fuoco

Congreve, William (dramatist), 201 n10

Conjunct, defined, 548

Conrad, Joseph, quoted, 3

Consequent, 28

Consonance, defined, 46–7

Con sordino, 93, 548

Continuo (basso), 165

Contrabassoon, *see* Double bassoon

Contralto (voice), 85–6

Contratenor, 149

Contredanse, Plate 26A

Converse, Frederick S., 401

Copland, Aaron: style, 394, 502; variety of idioms, 501; a mainspring of the American musical scene, 502; *Appalachian Spring,* 501 (discussed), Plate 30B; mentioned, 395, 396, 401, 501

"Copland-Sessions Concerts," 500

Cor anglais (English horn), 97–8

Cordier, Baude, manuscript of chanson, Plate 11B

Corelli, Arcangelo: sonatas, 183–4, 185, 186; *concerti grossi,* 213, 214

Cornet (valve), 101

Cornett, 177; defined, 548

Corno di Bassetto, *pseud.* for G. B. Shaw, 286 n3

Costeley, Guillaume, 156

Council of Trent, 121, 140, 154

Counterexposition (fugue), 62

Counterpoint (contrapuntal): defined, 42–3; devices of, 63; linear, *see* Linear counterpoint; *see also* Polyphony

Counter-Reformation, 152, 154

Countersubject (fugue), 62

Couperin, François: quoted, 182; suites, 223; mentioned, 231, 233, 373

Coupled (organ term), 106

Couplet (rondo), 58

Courante, 183

Cowell, Henry: *New Music Quarterly,* 395, 497; clusters, 496–7; relation to Ives and *avant-garde,* 496; interested in folk music, 497; piano playing, 497; a prolific composer, 497; mentioned, 396, 496, 508, 525

Craft, Robert, 396, 439

Credo (Mass), 137, 544 (text)

Crescendo: sign for, 25; continuous (in Mannheim orchestra), 237; in Rossini, 336; defined, 548

Crescendo pedal, 106

Critic, *see* Music critic

Crook (brass instruments), 100

"Cross" accent, 16–17, 20

"Cross relation," 155

Crusades, 143

Cubism, 390, Plates 31B and 33A

Cuckoo call (fugue subject), 124

"Cue" (signal), 108–9

Cui, César, 360

Cyclic: principle, 299; principle in César Franck, 373; forms in Bruckner, 311; relationships in Mahler, 312

Cymbal (percussion instrument), 102, Plates 5B, and 6B

Czerny, Carl, Plate 28c

Da capo (D.C.), defined and related to minuet, 58, 193

Da capo aria, 190, 193–4, 265

Daiches, David, xxii

Dallapiccola, Luigi: discussed, 483; influence of Webern, 483; twelve-tone composer, 483; forms, 483–4; quoted, 484; *The Prisoner,* 484; mentioned, 395

Damper pedal (piano), 105

Damrémont (General), 311 n2

Dance: Morris, Sword, 136; Ländler, 136; medieval, 143; sixteenth-century keyboard, 159; Plates 11A, 16A, 18A & B, 26A & B, 27A, 30B

Dance form, definition and diagram, 34

Dante Alighieri, 111, 145

Da Ponte, Lorenzo, *see* Ponte, Lorenzo da

Dargomijsky, Alexander, 360

Darmstadt (festival), 395, 511, 512

Darwin, Charles, 283

David, Ferdinand (violinist), 313 n4

David, J. L. (painter), 232

Davis, Miles, 491

D.C., *see* Da capo

Debussy, Claude, 377ff; on French music, 372–3; relation to poets and painters, 377; admiration of nature, 378; life and works, 379; works enumerated, 379; style, 379, 380; influence of Wagner on, 380; variety of scales, 380; revolution in harmony and tonality, 380–1; dynamics, 381; melody, 381; piano playing, 381; whole tone scale, 381; color as a function of form, 382; forms, 382; use of orchestra, 382; musical position summarized, 384,

Debussy (*continued*)
391; Monsieur Croche, 386; portrait, Plate 29A; mentioned, 372, 373, 375, 398, 412, 416, 445, 463, 480
   WORKS: *Pelleas and Melisande*, 49, 140, 379, 382, 383–4 (discussed), 397, 427; *The Sea (La Mer)*, 123, 382; *Prélude à L'Après-midi d'un Faune*, 327, 378; "The Sunken Cathedral," 364, 382; G minor Quartet, 367, 379, 382; *Sirens*, 381; *Festivals* (second orchestral nocturne), 382; *Iberia*, 382; "Interrupted Serenade," 382; *Preludes* (piano), 382; *Voiles*, 415

Deceptive cadence, defined, 50
Declamation, defined, 121–2
"Declamatory" song (Schubert), 294
Decrescendo, defined, 548
Delibes, Leo, 334
Delius, Frederick, 399, 487
Dent, E. J., 271 n2
De Quincey, Thomas, 319 n1
Descant, 140, 149
Descartes, René, 230
Descriptive music (eighteenth century), 129
Des Prez, Josquin, *see* Josquin des Prez
Détaché, 548
Deus ex machina, 266
Development: sonata form, 68, 70; terminal, 80
Devices of counterpoint, 63
Diaghilev, Sergei P. (choreographer), 432, 436, 463
Diapason (Organ), 106
Diatonic, defined, 548
Diatonic scale, defined, 30
Diderot, Denis, 230, 269
Die Reihe (periodical), 524
"Dies Irae" (Requiem Mass), 275, 319 (Berlioz), 331

Diminished: interval, 40; chord, 53; seventh, 53
Diminuendo: defined, 548; sign for, 25
Diminution, 63
D'Indy, Vincent, *see* Indy, Vincent D'
Discant, 548
Discantus, 143
Disjunct, 548
Dissonance: defined, 46–7; harmonic and melodic dissonances distinguished, 47; "emancipation" of, 381 (Debussy), 399, 405 (Schoenberg), 408
Divertimento, defined, 248 n11
Divisi, 93, 309; defined, 548
"Doctrine of the Affections," *see* "Affections," Doctrine of
Dohnányi, Ernst von, 447
Dominant (the), 38, 49; seventh (chord), 49, 53; chord, 52
Donaueschingen (festival), 395
Donizetti, Gaetano, 337–8, 352; operas, 337; "remembrance" tunes, 337; librettos, 337–8; use of chorus, ensembles, and orchestra, 338
Donne, John, 164
Dorian (mode), 35, 138
Dot: after a note, 537; double, 537; above a note, *see* Staccato
Dotted-note rhythm, defined, 548
Double (in Suite), 224
Double bass (stringed instrument), 92–3, Plate 2B
Double (contra) bassoon, 98, Plate 3B
Double-chorus style (*chori spezzati*), 153, 155
Doubled (doubling), 157; defined, 48
Double dot, 537
Double exposition: of Classic concerto, 257ff; diagram of, 257; relation to sonata form, 258; evolution

Double exposition (*continued*)
 of, 258; relation to baroque con-
 certo, 258–9; after Beethoven, 313
Double flat, 534
Double fugue, 221 n7
Double period, defined, 26
Double sharp, 534
Double stops (strings), 93–4; defined,
 549
"Double variation" (Haydn), 79, 242
Doublings (octave), in Berlioz, 321
Dowland, John, 157, Plate 12A
Downbeat, 537, 539
D'Oyly Carte Company, 335
Drama: liturgical, 140; French *bour-
 geois,* 230, 269
Dramma per musica, 167
Drum, Plate 5B
Drum sticks, 103
D.S. (*dal segno*), 193
Dufay, Guillaume, 120, 148, 149
Dukas, Paul, 327, 372, 375
Duke de Joyeuse, Plate 16A
Dumas, Alexandre, 335, 353
Dumka (*pl. Dumky*), 366
Dunstable, John, 148
Duo, 248
Duparc, Henri, 373, 375
Duple time, 12
Durante, Francesco, 192
Duration (of a note), 535
Durchkomponiert, see "Through-
 composed"
Durey, Louis, Plate 30A
Dvořák, Antonín, 315, 365–6; style,
 366; use of dances, 366; use of folk
 song, 366; music, 366; "New
 World" Symphony, 365, 366 (dis-
 cussed)
Dykema, Peter, ix
Dynamics: defined, 25; use in Classic
 period, 236–7

Earhart, Will, ix
Economics of music, 393 n1
Editor, relation of, to performance,
 112
Egypt, music in, 133
Eichendorff, Joseph, 369
Eighth note, 536
Eimert, Herbert, 521, 524
"Ein' feste Burg," 153
Einstein, Alfred, 251
Eisler, Hanns, 402
Eleanor of Aquitaine, 144 n7
Electronic guitar, 509
Electronic instruments, 509
Electronic music: implications, 402;
 its potential, 402; defined, 508; a
 new horizon, 521; mentioned, 520,
 521
Electronic organ, 509
Electronic piece, score, 520, Plate 29B
Electronic sound synthesizer, 521
Electronic studios, 521
Electronic Study II, score described,
 522, Plate 39B
Elements of music, defined, 10–12
Eleventh chord, 48
Elgar, Edward, 371–2, 487; influenced
 by Wagner and Richard Strauss,
 370; style, 371–2; works, 371–2
Elizabeth I (Queen of England), 157,
 162
Ellington, Duke, 491
"Emancipation" of the dissonance,
 381, 399, 405 (explained), 408
Embouchure, defined, 96 n4
Emerson, Ralph Waldo, 57
Encyclopedia, French, 230
Encyclopaedia Britannica, 230 n1
Encyclopedists, 266, 269
Enesco, Georges, 375
English Folk Song Society, 393
English horn: discussed, 97–8; used
 by César Franck, 374; Plate 3A
Enharmonic, 39, 430; defined, 549

"Enlightenment" (*Aufklärung*), 230

Ensemble: in opera, 270; defined, 549

Ensemble accent, 12

Ensemble finale, 199, 270, 335

Entr'acte, 549

Episode: in rondo, 58; in fugue, 63, 66, 221

Epistle (Mass), 542

Ernst, Wilhelm (violinist), Plate 28c

Esipova, Annette, 464

Estampie, defined, 549

Esterhazy family, 277

Étude: in Chopin, 296; defined, 549

Exposition: of a fugue, 62; sonata form, 68, 69; double, *see* Double exposition

Expression, defined, 25

Expressionism: defined, 399, 401; mentioned, 414, 461

"Fa-la" refrain, 157

Falla, Manuel de, 360 n1, 379, 398, 484 (discussed)

Fancy (instrumental form), 180

Fantasia, 180, 181, 246 n9

Fauré, Gabriel-Urbain, 375–6; Requiem, 331–2; as a song composer, 375–6; style of harmony and modulation, 375; chamber music, 376; mentioned, 329, 371, 372, 379

Fauves, Les ("Wild Beasts"), 392

Faux bourdon: explained, 148–9; in Russian music, 364; in Puccini, 370; in Debussy, 380

Favart, Charles Simon, 269

F clef, 533

Feather, Leonard G., 491 n2

Feldman, Morton, 524

Fermata, 16; to indicate cadenza, 257; defined, 539

Fétis, François-Joseph, viii n1

Fiddle and "Fiddling," 136

Field, John, 296

Fielding, Henry (novelist), 269

Fifteenth chord, 49

Figuration, defined, 549

Figured bass: defined, 165; obsolete, 235; texture, 236

Final (of a mode), 138

Finale: ensemble, 199, 270, 335; composite, 270

Fine, 193

First desk (stand) in orchestra, 89

First-movement form, 68

First theme (sonata form), 69

Fitzwilliam Virginal Book, 135, 159

"Five, The," 360–1; their careers, 361; style of music, 363

Flat: meaning, 531; indicated, 534; double, 534

Flaubert, Gustave (novelist), 283, 370

Flower, Newman, 196 n7

Flute, 96, 134, 136, Plates 5A, 9B; *see also* Recorder

Flutter tonguing, 549

Flying buttress (picture), Plate 10A

Folia (follia), defined, 187

Folk dance, 136

Folk instruments, 136

Folk music, 134ff; in Norway, 367; in Brazil, 505–6; in Spain, 484; in the United States, 491 n1

Folk opera (Gershwin), 498

Folk song: definition and origin, 134; character of different nations, 135; used by composers, 135–6; "seepage" theory, 136; Russian, 362; editing of in England, 371

Fontenelle, Bernard le Bovier de, 192

Form: defined, 55; in dance music, 56; determined by text, 56; and content, 189 n1; *see also* Forms; Sonata form; Rondo; Motet; etc.

Formalism: in the Baroque, 189–90; in Russia, 462

Formal principles, 33

Forms: smaller, 33–4; larger, 57ff; composite instrumental, 73–4; vo-

Forms (*continued*)
  cal, 118ff; composite vocal, 121 n1;
  changed by Beethoven, 290–1
Forsyth, Cecil, 81
Forte and *Fortissimo,* 549
Foss, Lucas, 396, 511
Franck, César, 372, 373–5; style, 373;
  use of cyclic principle, 373, 374;
  works, 373–5; Symphony in D
  minor, 299, 374–5 (analyzed)
Frederick the Great, 232
"Free" atonality: characterized, 404;
  defined, 412; mentioned, 399, 401,
  404
"Free" cadenza (Bartók), 428
"Free" forms (seventeenth century),
  180; *see also* Prelude; Toccata
French chanson, 151–2, 155–6; *see
  also* Chanson
French comic opera, 269, 334
French horn, 95, 101, Plate 6A; *see
  also* Horn
French music, basic traits summa-
  rized by Debussy, 372–3
"French-Netherland" style, 151, 153
French overture, *see* Overture, French
French Revolution, 229, 231, 281
French vs. Italian music, 192
Frescobaldi, Girolamo, 181, 182
Frets (on stringed instruments), 158
Freud, Sigmund, 283, 405
Froberger, J. J., 181, 183
Fugato, 62
Fugue, 57, 61–4, 67, 222–3, 291, 358,
  373, 400; one-subject, 221; double,
  221 n7, 222, 276; triple, quadruple,
  221 n7, 222; *see also* Bach, J. S.
Function of music (seventeenth cen-
  tury), 165
Fundamental, 37
Fundamentals of music, defined, 9
Fuoco (con fuoco), 549
Furiant (dance), 366
Futurismo, 401

Gabrieli, Andrea, 154, 155
Gabrieli, Giovanni, 154, 155, 159, 176
Gade, Niels, 366
Galliard, xx, 158, 159, 183
Galuppi, Baldassare, 268, 360
Gaultier, Denis, 183
Gavotte, 183
Gavotte en Rondeau, 261 n14
Gay, John, 200
G clef, 533
Gebrauchsmusik, defined, 394
Geminiani, Francesco, 219; quoted,
  110
George, Stefan, 405, 406
George I (King of England), 195
George II (King of England), 203
Gershwin, George: "symphonic jazz,"
  498
    WORKS: *Porgy and Bess,* 498;
    Rhapsody in Blue, 498
Gibbons, Orlando, 156
Gigue (jig), 14, 183, 184
Gilbert, W. S., 335; and Sullivan, *see*
  Sullivan, Arthur
Giotto (painter), 111, 149
Giraud, Albert, 414
Glazounov, Alexander, 431, 464, 469
Glee, defined, 549
Glière, Reinhold, 431; *Red Poppy,* 463
Glinka, Michail, 360, 430
Glissando, defined, 549
Glockenspiel, 422
Gloria (Mass), 137, 543 (text)
Gluck, Christoph Willibald (Ritter
  von): reform of *opera seria,* 265;
  Preface to *Alceste,* 265–6; role in
  French opera, 266; characterization
  in opera, 266; operas, 265–6;
  Orpheus and Eurydice, 116, 265,
  266, 267–8 (plot and analysis);
  mentioned, 56, 232, 269, 333
Goethe, Johann Wolfgang von, 232,
  284, 286, 287, 293, 369
Gong (orchestra), 102

Good taste, 126–7

Gorky, Maxim, 461

Gospel (Mass), 542

Gossec, François-Joseph, 240

Goudimel, Claude, 154

Gounod, Charles-François, 22, 334, 330

Grace note, defined, 549

Gradual (Mass), 137, 542

Graham, Martha (dancer), 501, Plate 30B

Granados, Enrique, 360 n1, 484

"Grand Concertos," *see* Concerto grosso

Grand opera, 333

Graun, Karl Heinrich, 276

Graupner, Christoph, 226

Grave, 549

"Great Eighteen" (chorale preludes, J. S. Bach), 207

Great organ, 106

Greece (ancient), music in, 133–4

Gregorian chant, 137ff, 542; liturgical aspect of, 137; musical aspect of, 138; forms of, 138; development in Middle Ages, 140; nineteenth-century interest in, 329; in Liszt, 331; *see also* Chant

Gregory "The Great" (Pope), 137

Gretchaninov, Alexander, 332

Grétry, André-Ernest-Modeste, 269

Griller Quartet, Plate 2A

Grieg, Edvard, 315, 366–7

Griffes, Charles, 399, 490

Gropius, Manon, 428

Ground, defined, 60

Guilmant, Alexandre, 329

Guitar: electronic, 509; seventeenth-century, Plate 16B

Hába, Alois, 37, 518

Half cadence, defined, 50

Half note, 536

Half tone, 531

"Hallelujah" Chorus: in Purcell, 178; in Handel, 203

Handel, George Frideric: progressive tendencies in orchestra, 166; use of French overture, 173; opera in England, 174; "borrowings," 209 n16; career and music compared with J. S. Bach, 225–8; an international figure, 226; harmony and polyphony in, 227; two portraits, Plate 23; autograph, Plate 20; mentioned, 219, 245, 435

  WORKS: Italian operas, 195–7; *Rinaldo,* 195–6, 200; *Giulio Cesare,* 119, 196–7; oratorios, 200–3; *Messiah,* 118, 201–3; *Music for the Royal Fireworks,* 201 n11; Grand Concertos, 214; organ concertos, 216; suites (lessons), 224; *Passacaglia* in G minor, 224; "Harmonious Blacksmith" Variations, 124, 225

Hand stopping (French horn), 100, 238

Hanslick, Eduard (critic), 129, 304, 365

Hanson, Howard, 498

Harmonic overtones, 37

Harmonic rhythm, defined, 53–4

Harmonics (strings): in Bartók, 397; defined, 549; *see also* Harmonic overtones

Harmonic series, 38

Harmony: defined, 42; "upbeat," 45–6; in different periods of music, 145, 147, 148, 155, 165, 190, 233, 235–6, 285, 388–92

Harp, 103–4, Plate 4B

Harpsichord, 158, 160, 237, Plate 13B; mechanism, Plate 14B

Harris, Roy: style, theories, and works, 498; mentioned, 360 n1, 504

Hasse, J. A., 265

Hauer, J. M., 416

Hauptstimme, 407

Haydn, Franz Joseph: thematic motives, 235, 236; development of the symphony, 240; article on, 248 n12; compared with Mozart, 276ff; their mutual influence, 277; stature and musical contributions, 277–8; style, 278; orchestration, 278; originality, 278; character, 278; humor, 278; edition of works, 278; mentioned, 124, 245, 249

    WORKS: "Drum Roll" Symphony, 13, 44, 74–82, 240ff; String Quartets Op. 33, 235–6; sonatas, 239ff; chamber music, 250; sacred music, 274–6; oratorios, 276

Heifetz, Jascha, 84

Heine, Heinrich, 283, 293

Henry II (King of England), 144 n7

Henry IV (King of France), 167

Henry VIII (King of England), 162

Henze, Hans Werner, 511

"Hexachords," 416

Hiller, J. A., 269, 129 n2

Hindemith, Paul, 455ff; fascinated by fourteenth-century music, 147 n10; *Gebrauchsmusik*, 394, 455; associated with Donaueschingen, 395; neoclassic elements, 446; background, 455; neoclassic forms, 455; "chromatic tonality," 456; compared to Schoenberg, 456; life, 456; "linear" counterpoint, 456; polyrhythms, 456; polytonality, 456; *A Composer's World*, 457; *The Craft of Musical Composition*, 457; "cultural Bolshevism," 457; works, 457; position summarized, 458–9; portrait, Plate 35B; mentioned, 128, 395, 396, 401, 446, 462, 491, 511

    WORKS: *Cardillac*, 456; *Das Marienleben*, 456; Third String Quartet, 45, 46, 456 (discussed);

Hindemith (*continued*)
    Ludus Tonalis, 457; *Mathis der Maler*, 457 (discussed)

Historicus, 176

Hitchcock, H. Wiley, 191 n3

Hitler, Adolf, 416, 419, 458, 462, 490

Hofmannsthal, Hugo von, 349

Hogarth, William, 437

Hold, *see Fermata*

Holst, Gustav, 487

Holy Alliance, 282

Homophonic, defined, 43

Honegger, Arthur, 480–81; quoted, 435 (on Bach), 468 (on Prokofiev); *I am a Composer* (autobiography), 481; portrait, Plate 30A; mentioned, 396, 470, 480

    WORKS: *Pacific 231*, 401; *King David*, 461, 481; Fifth Symphony, 481

Horn: Alpine, 136; "natural," 238; *see also* English horn; French horn

Horn, "hand stopping," *see* Hand stopping

Hotteterre, *"Principes"* (1708), Plate 15B

Hugo, Victor, 319 n1, 324, 335, 353, 353 n3

Hüller, J. A., *see* Hiller, J. A.

"Humanistic" music, 331

Human voice, 85–7

"Humoresque," 43

Hundred Years' War, 148

"Hungarian" scale, 37

Hypodorian, 138

Hypolydian, 138

Hypomixolydian, 138

Hypophrygian, 138

Ibsen, Henrik, 370

I-Ching, 526

Idée fixe, defined, 318

Imbrie, Andrew, 500

Imitation: strict and free, 43; in fifteenth century, 150; in sixteenth century, 152

Imitative counterpoint, *see* Imitation

Imperial Conservatory, St. Petersburg, 364

Impressionism, 377ff; forecast by Grieg, 367; in music, 377, 378–9; in painting, 377, Plate 26B; in poetry, 377–8; transitional role, 391; in Falla, 484; in American music, 490; mentioned, 377, 405

Impromptu, 284, 296

Indo-China, music of, 376

Industrial Revolution, 282

Indy, Vincent D', 329, 372, 373

Inquisition, the, 154

Instrumental effects in jazz, 398

Instrumentation, defined, 106–7

Instruments: in general, 87; tone color of, 87; folk, 136; illustrations of, Plates 1–6, 9A & B, 12B, 13A & B, 14A & B, 15, 16B

Instruments of the Orchestra (a film), 88

"Integrated" ballet, 266

"Integrated" introduction, *see* Introduction

Intermezzo: comic opera, 199; defined, 550

International Society for Contemporary Music, 395, 461

Interpretation: importance of, 110ff; criticizing, 128; *see also* Performance

Interval: melodic, 23–4; simple and compound, 23 n2; harmonic, 24; irrational, 37; general and specific names for, 40; *see also* Cent

Intonation, defined, 550

Introduction (sonata form), 68; "integrated" (Haydn), 74, 241

Introit (Mass), 137, 542

Inversion: explained, 63; in twelve-tone music, 411, 417

Inverted (chord), 48

Ionian (major) mode, 35, 154

Ipolitov-Ivanov, Mikhail M., 431

Irish Washerwoman, The (jig), 14

Isaak, Heinrich, 152, 420

Italian overture, *see* Overture, Italian

Italian vs. French music (eighteenth century), 192

Ives, Burl, 135 n2

Ives, Charles: advanced idiom, 493; early education, 493; influence, 493; lack of recognition, 493; a "national" composer, 493; use of popular and hymn tunes, 493; "chance" elements, 494; melodic material, 494; harmonic constructions, 494; rhythmic originality, 494; a judgment, 495; portrait, Plate 37A; mentioned, 396, 401, 490, 491, 492, 514, 518

  WORKS: Fourth Symphony, 395; "Concord" Sonata, 494–5 (discussed)

Izvestia (newspaper), quoted, 470

Jack (of harpsichord), Plate 14B (caption)

Jacobsen, J. P., 412

"Jam" session, 491

Janáček, Leoš, 399

Jannequin, Clément, 116, 151–2

Japan, avant-garde music in, 403

Java, music of, 376

Jazz: rhythm in Stravinsky, 434; rhythm in Milhaud, 480 (Ex. 177); "cool," 491; development and varieties of, 491; "progressive," 491; the product of an environment, 492; "symphonic" (Gershwin), 498; new effects in, 508–9; mentioned, 17, 401, 403, 480, 491, 511

Jesuits (order), 163

Jig, *see* Gigue

Joachim, Joseph (violinist), 257, 304, 313 n4, 315

John Lackland, *see* Lackland, John

Jommelli, Nicola, 192, 265

Jongleurs, 144

Josquin des Prez, 7, 116, 150, 151, 153

Judgment: defined, 127; standards of, *see* Quality in art

Kafka, Franz (novelist), 405

Kallman, Chester, 437

Kandinsky, Wassily, 405; "Improvisation 30," Plate 33B

Kant, Immanuel, 230

Kelly, Michael, 273

Kettledrums, *see* Percussion

Key, defined, 32

Keyboard (piano), 531, 532 (Ex. 181)

Key signature, 33, 534 (explained)

Khachaturian, Aram, 462, 479 (discussed); use of folk songs, 479; quoted on Socialist Realism, 479
    WORKS: *Spartacus* (ballet), 463; *Gayane,* 463, 479

Khrennikov, Tikhon, 466

Kirchner, Leon, 516–17; his credo quoted, 516; characteristics of music, 517; mentioned, 500, 514, 516
    WORKS: Piano Concerto (discussed), 516; Trio for Violin, Cello, and Piano (discussed), 517

Kirkpatrick, Ralph, quoted, 12

Klinger, Friedrich Maximilian von, 232 n2

Kodály, Zoltán, 360 n1, 445, 446
    WORKS: *Psalmus Hungaricus,* 447; *Twenty Hungarian Folk Songs,* 447

Koechlin, Charles, 375

Kokoschka, Oskar, 405

Kolisch, Rudolf, 409

Koussevitzky, Sergei, 396, 437

Kranichstein Institute (Darmstadt), 511

Krehbiel, H. E., ix

Kreisler, Fritz, 5, 257

Křenek, Ernst, 396, 512; *Jonny spielt auf,* 461

Kuhnau, Johann, 205

Kyrie (Mass), 137, 542, 543

Lackland, John, 144 n7

Lalo, Edouard, 315, 372

Lamartine, A. M. L. de, 324, 325

Lambert, Constant, 486

Lamento aria, 171; *see also* Aria

Landini, Francesco, 111, 146

Ländler (dance), 136, 293, 311; defined, 550

Lang, Paul Henry, 283 n1

Langer, Susanne K., 129 n2

Larghetto, 550

Largo, 550

Lasso, Orlando di (Orlandus Lassus), 154, 155, 156

Leading motive (*Leitmotiv*): in Wagner, 324, 347; defined, 343; in Richard Strauss, 349

Leading tone, defined, 30

Leading-tone chord, 52

"Learned" style, 233

Leclair, Jean-Marie, 191, 219

Le Corbusier, 519

Ledger lines, 533

Legato: indicated by slur, 25; defined, 550

Legno, see Col legno

Leibowitz, René, 511

Leitmotiv, see Leading motive

Le Jeune, Claude, 156

Lenin, Vladimir Ilyich, 460, 473

Lento, 550

Lenz, Wilhelm von, 287

Leo, Leonardo, 192

Leonardo da Vinci, 7, 111, 152

Leoncavallo, Ruggiero, 370

Leopold (Prince of Anhalt-Cöthen), 204

Leopold I (Emperor of Austria), Plate 17 (caption)

Lesson (in Handel), 224

Letter notation, 535

L'Homme armé, 134

Liadow, Anatol K., 464

Liber usualis, 138

Libretto, defined, 550

Lied (*pl.* Lieder): in the fifteenth century, 152; compared with French song in the nineteenth century, 376; *see also* Song; Schubert; Wolf; etc.

Lilienchron, Rochus von, 135

Line (staff), 533

Linear counterpoint, 456

Liszt, Franz: orchestral sonority on piano, 285; influenced by Beethoven, 288; on Schubert, 304; program music, 324-7; piano playing, 315, 381; symphonic poems as a model, 327; "humanistic" music, 331; mentioned, 124, 284, 285, 304, 312, 336, 341, 344, 361, 373, 447; autograph, Plate 20; portrait, Plate 28c

    works: Les Préludes, 123, 324-7; B minor Sonata, 299; *Transcendental Études,* 315 n5; piano concertos, 314-15; symphonies, 321; symphonic poems, 324-7; sacred music, 331

Liturgical music, Russian, 332

Lochheimer Liederbuch, 134

Locke, John (philosopher), 230

Locke, Matthew, 174

Locrian mode, in Roy Harris, 498

Logroscino, Nicola, 268

London Symphony Orchestra, Plates 1, 4B

"Lorelei, Die," 135

Loud (damper) pedal, on piano, 105

Louis VII, 144 n7

Louis XIV, 163, 166, 172, 229, Plate 18A; portrait, 19B

Louis XV, 232

Louis XVI, 229, 230

Louis Philippe, 282

Lowes, John Livingston, 290 n5

Luening, Otto, 521

Lully, Jean-Baptiste, 172-4, 200; ballet, 172; *tragédies lyriques,* 172; subjects treated in opera, 172; orchestra, 173; French overture, 173; Plate 18A (caption)

Lute: described, 158-9, 160; notation of, Plate 12A; illustrated, Plates 15C, 16B

Lute player, Plates 9B, 15C

Luther, Martin, 153

Lutoslawski, Witold, 510

Lydian mode, 35, 138; in Fauré, 375; in Harris, 498

Lyre, 134

MacDowell, Edward, 490

Machaut, Guillaume de, 146, Plate 11A

Macpherson, Stewart, ix

Maderna, Bruno, 511, 521

Madrigal: fourteenth century, 146; sixteenth century, 156 (Italian), 156-7 (English); mentioned, 120, 159; defined, 550

Madrigalism, 156

Maeterlinck, Maurice, 378, 383

Magna Carta, 144 n7

Magyar folk music, 447

Mahler, Gustav, 310-12; relation to Bruckner and Beethoven, 311; literary elements, 311; philosophical ideas, 311; orchestral and vocal forces, 311; use of orchestra, 312, 398; as song composer, 311; cham-

Mahler (*continued*)
ber-music orchestration, 312; character of his symphonies, 312; cyclic relationships, 312; "progressive" tonality, 312; mentioned, 124, 299, 312, 349, 371, 397, 398, 412, 431, 470

Major chord, 53

Major interval, 40

Major mode: defined, 31; represented by letters, 31; represented graphically, 31

Malipiero, G. Francesco: style and works, 483; writings and editions, 483; *Rispetti e Strambotti,* 483

Mallarmé, Stéphane (poet): obscurity of language, 378; treatment of language, 381; *L'Après-midi d'un Faune,* 378; mentioned, 378, 379

Mälzel, J. N. (metronome), 15

Mandyczewski, Eusebius, 241

Manet, Edouard, 377

Mannheim orchestra, 237

Ma non troppo, defined, 550

Manuals: on harpsichord, Plate 13B; on organ, 105

Manzoni, Alessandro (novelist and poet), 351

Marcato, 550

Marcello, Benedetto, 195, 265

Marcellus (Pope), 154

Marenzio, Luca, 156

Margarethe (Princess of Lorraine), wedding festivities of, Plate 16A

Margherita (Spanish Infanta), Plate 17 (caption)

Maria Barbara (Queen of Spain), 220

Maria de' Medici, 167

Marimba, defined, 550

Marmontel, J. F., 269

Marot, Clément, 154

"Marseillaise," the, 231

Martelé, 550

Marx, Karl, 282

Mary II (Queen of England), 178

Mascagni, Pietro, 334, 370

Masque (English), 174

Mass: chant for, 137; meaning of, 137; definition and scheme of, 137, 440; first complete polyphonic setting of, 146; style and texture of, 151; parody or transcription, 154; *cantus firmus,* 154; "instrumental," 275; settings of in eighteenth century, 274–6; *a cappella,* 330; text of, 542; mentioned, 120

Massenet, Jules, 334

Massine, Léonide, 390

Matins, 137

Matisse, Henri, 392

Mayrhofer, Johann, 293

Mazurka (*mazur*), 295; defined, 550

Mazzini, Guiseppe (Italian patriot), 351

Meaning of music, 128

Measure (bar), 537

Meck, Nadejda Filaretovna (Madame von), 379

Mediant (chord), 52

Meistersinger (song movement), 143

Melismatic (setting of text), 122, 138

Melismatic organum, 143

Mellers, Wilfrid, 511 n3

Melodic line, defined, 21

Mélodie, defined, 376

Melodrama: defined, 339 n4; in Weber, 340

Melody: defined, 21; rhythmic features of, 22; contour of, 24; range of, 23; "closed," 28; in fourteenth century, 147; "unending" (Wagner), 343

Mendelssohn, Felix: performance of Bach's *St. Matthew Passion,* 226; influenced by Beethoven, 288; program music, 317; mentioned, viii n1, 284, 299, 304, 348

Mendelssohn (*continued*)
  WORKS: Violin Concerto, 313–14 (analyzed); *Hebrides (Fingal's Cave)* Overture, 317; *Midsummer Night's Dream* (Overture), 317; *Elijah,* 331

Menotti, Gian-Carlo: *Amahl and the Night Visitors,* 396, 505; success in opera, 504; style and works, 505

Messiaen, Olivier: style and works, 512; mentioned, 395, 511, 520

Metastasio, Pietro, 192, 194

Meter: defined, 12; in twentieth century, 394–6; indicated by time signature, 537; *see also* rhythm

"Method of Composing with Twelve Tones Which are Related Only with One Another" (Schoenberg), 401, 406

Metronome and Metronome marking, 15

Metternich, Klemens (Prince von), 282

Meyerbeer, Giacomo, 333–4, 341, 352; *The Huguenots,* 333–4

Mezzo forte, 550

Mezzo piano, 550

Mezzo-soprano, 85, 86 (Ex. 60)

Miakovsky, Nicolai, 462, 464

"Micro-series," 422

Microtone and Microtone scale, 37; defined, 508

Microtone music, 517–18

Milhaud, Darius: discussed, 481; a melodist, 481; use of popular music and jazz, 481; portrait, Plate 30A; mentioned, 396, 401, 462, 480
  WORKS: *Le Boeuf sur le toit,* 481; *Christophe Columb,* 481; *The Creation of the World,* 481

Minnesinger, 143–44, Plate 9A

Minor chord, 53

Minor interval, 40

Minor mode: defined, 31; represented

Minor Mode (*continued*)
  by letters, 31; represented graphically, 31; derived from major, 31–32; parallel, 32 n4; relative, 32 n4; pure, 35; melodic, 35

Minuet, 57–58; in sonata form, 240; illustrated, Plate 18B; mentioned, 183

Missa, see Mass

"*Missa Brevis,*" defined, 330 n1

"*Missa Solemnis,*" defined, 330 n1; *see also* Beethoven

Mitchell, W. J., 245 n8

Mitropoulos, Dmitri, 396

Mixolydian (mode), 35, 138

Mobiles (Calder), 524

Modality, 36

Mode: defined, 31; church, 35; in sixteenth century, 154; use by Fauré, 375; use by Vaughan Williams, 487; *see also* entries on particular modes, as Dorian, etc.

Moderato, 550

"Modern" music and the audience, 393

Modified strophic form, 34, 294 (Schubert)

Modulation: defined, 33; melodic, 40; its importance, 50; explained by analogy, 51; in Beethoven, 289

Molière (dramatist), 163

Moment musical, 284

Mondonville, J.-J. C. de, 218 n4

Monet, Claude, 377; "Impression: Sunrise," Plate 26B

Monodrama (Schoenberg), 405, 550

Monody, 167

Monophonic, defined, 43

Monsigny, Pierre-Alexandre, 268, 269

Montemezzi, Italo, 483

Monteux, Pierre, 109 n1, 396

Monteverdi, Claudio, 168–71; madrigal of, 156; *concertato* style, 159; *stile concitato,* 169; edition of, by

Monteverdi (*continued*)

Malipiero, 413; portrait, Plate 22A; mentioned, 56, 353, 408

WORKS: *Orfeo,* 166, 168; *L'Incoronazione di Poppea,* 168; *"Lamento della Ninfa"* (from *"Non havea Febo ancora"* in the Eighth Book of Madrigals), 169–70; *Arianna,* 171; sacred music, including the "Vespers," 176

Moore, Douglas, 498; folk opera *The Ballad of Baby Doe,* 499

Morales, Cristóbal de, 154

Mordent, defined, 550

Mörike, Eduard, 369

Morley, Thomas, 157

Morris dance, 136

Moscheles, Ignaz, 296

Mossolov, Alexander, 401

Motet: thirteenth century ("Paris"), 140, 141, 149; sixteenth century, 151; mentioned, 120

Motetus, 141

Motive: defined, 26; *see also* Leading motive

Motto, in Brahms's Third Symphony, 305

Mouton, Charles (lute player), Plate 15C

Mozart, Leopold, 251

Mozart, Wolfgang Amadeus: sontata construction, 239–40; and the development of the symphony, 240; delineation of character by, 271; orchestral pun in, 274; compared with Haydn, 276; mutual influence with Haydn, 277; summary of career, 277; letters, 277 n6; style and forms, 279–80; way of composing, 280; appeal to primitive Indians, 280 n8; universality, 280; his character, 280; emotional range of music and life, 280; human understanding and insight, 280–1; as a

Mozart (*continued*)

child of his times, 281; as prophetic of Romantic period, 281; model for neoclassicism, 435; portrait, Plate 24A; mentioned, 194, 247, 249, 265, 270, 312, 352

WORKS: symphonies, 240, 242, 243; "Jupiter" Symphony, 242–3; sonatas for piano, 245–6; Piano Sonata in A major, 59, 239, 246; C minor Fantasia, 246; chamber music, 248, 250–4, 279; String Quintet in G minor, 240, 249, 252–4, 280; Quartet in G major, 251–2; Violin Concerto in A major, 260–1; Piano Concerto in D minor, 261–2, 313; concertos in summary, 262–3; *The Magic Flute,* 86, 270, 339; *The Marriage of Figaro,* 119, 265, 268, 270–4, 273 (Michael Kelly's account), 281, 336; *Don Giovanni,* 60, 268, 270, 280, 281; sacred music, 274–6; Requiem, 275–6

Multichorus style, 176

Multiple stops, 550

Murger, Henri (novelist), 370

Music: power of, 115; as language, 115, 128; "absolute," 115; illustrative, 115; with texts, 115; relation to text, 121; meaning of, 128; as a means of communication, 128; "power of uttering the unspeakable," 128; origin of, 133–4; in high civilization, 133–4; in the Orient, 134; life cycles of, 161

Music appreciation, early history of, vii–ix

Music critic, 285–6

Music education of public: in the nineteenth century, 286; through radio, phonograph, and television, 385; by schools and universities, 385

Music for use, *see Gebrauchsmusik*

Music printing, 153

Musique concrète, defined, 520

Mussorgsky, Modest: discussed, 360, 361–2; works corrected by Rimsky, 361, 361 n2; distinctive orchestration, 362; "crude" harmonies, 362; *Boris Godunov,* 359, 361–2, 363 (Ex. 139); songs, 362; relation to Debussy, 379; mentioned, 333, 379, 430

Mute: strings, 93; brass, 102; in Mozart, 253; defined, 551

"Mystic" chord (Scriabin), 431

Nägeli, H. G., viii

Napoleon (Bonaparte), 229, 282

Nardini, Pietro, 233

National Conservatory of Music, Paris, 231

Nationalism (musical), 359ff; meaning of, 359; influence of Romanticism and political events on, 359; self-conscious, 360; use of folk material, 360; in Russia, 360–4; and Russian opera, 361; in Bohemia, 365–6; in America, 366; in Scandinavia, 366–7; relation to German Romanticism, 367

"Natural" instrument (horn, trumpet), 95, 99

Natural sign (indication), 534

Nazis, and freedom of artistic activity, 400–1

Neapolitan opera (*opera seria*): recitative and aria scheme, 193–4; typical libretto of, 194; mechanics of, 194; abuses of, 195, 265; aesthetic scheme, 195; compared with comic opera, 199; reform by Gluck, 265; in nineteenth century, 355; *see also* Handel, Italian operas; Opera

Nebenstimme, 407

Neighboring note, 51–2

Neobaroque, 435, 455

Neoclassicism: described, 434; in Stravinsky, 434ff; in "The Six," 480; in Chávez, 506; mentioned, 400, 401, 461, 510

Neri, St. Philip, 176

Neumeister, Erdmann, 205

Neusiedler, Hans, 123

"New German School of the Future," 304, 330

Newman, Ernest: on "musical authorities," 127–8; on Beethoven, 290; on Shostakovich, 462, 472

"New" music (twentieth century), 392ff; *see also Ars Nova; Nuove Musiche, Le*

New Music Quarterly (Cowell), 395

New (or "Second") Vienna School, 404

Niedermeyer, Louis, and Niedermeyer School, 329, 332, 375

Nietzsche, Friedrich, 311, 341

Ninth Chord, 48

Nocturne, 293, 296; defined, 551

"Noise," 402, 519

Non-divisi (strings), 94

Nono, Luigi, 511, 512

"Non-teleological," 403, 526

Nordraak, Rikard, 367

Norwegian Academy of Music, 367

Notation: of pitch, 531ff; of time, 535ff; indicated by letters 535; to 1600 (manuscript), Plates 7A, 9B, 11A & B, 12A

Note and tone, distinguished, 551

Note values, 535

Notre Dame Cathedral (Paris), 141, 142, Plate 10A

"Notre Dame" motet, 141

Novalis, 283

Noverre, Jean-Georges (dancing master), 266

Nuance, 551

"Number" opera, 333, 335, 338, 342

Nuove Musiche, Le (Caccini), 161, 164, 167

Obbligato, 551

Oboe, 97, Plate 3A

Obrecht, Jacob, 151

Ockeghem, Johannes, 151

"Octave," defined, 531

Octave sign, 535

Octave transpositions, 411

Odhecaton (Petrucci), 153

Offenbach, Jacques, 334-5

Offertory (Mass), 137, 275 (in Requiem), 542

Office: chants for, 137; meaning of, 137

Ohl, John F., 64 n3

Opera: role of drama and music in, 56; baroque, 167ff; commercial, 169, 285; defined, 174; in England (seventeenth century), 174; comic, 199-200, 268-70, 334-5, *see also Ballad opera, Singspiel; opera buffa,* 199, 268, 335-6, 337; *opéra comique,* 269, 334, 338; *opera seria, see* Neapolitan opera; general traits, 264-5; in nineteenth century, 332ff; grand opera in France, 333; in Italy, 335-8; in Germany, 338-40; in Russia, 361; television, 396; folk, 498; Plates 17, 19A, 21B, 25A & B; *see also* "Number" opera; individual entries for Strauss, Verdi, Wagner, etc.

Opera house: first public in Venice, 169; in Vienna, Plate 16A

Opus (Op.), defined, 551

Oratorio, 176, 274, 276, 331; defined, 551; *see also* Carissimi; Handel

Orchésographie (Arbeau), xxv, 158 n14

Orchestra: choirs of, 88; size and

Orchestra (*continued*)

composition, 88; seating, 88-9; in ancient civilization, 133; baroque, 166; Mannheim, 237; Classic, 237-8; modern divisions, 237-8; Plate 1; *see also* Berlioz

Orchestration: defined, 106-7; style of, in Classic period, 235, 237-8; Russian, 364

Ordinary (Mass), 137, 542-45 (complete text)

Ordres (suites of Couperin), 223-4

Orff, Carl, 455 n2

Organ: construction of, 105-6; electronic, 508

Organ concertos (Handel), 216

Organ point (in a fugue), 63

Organum: strict, 140; free, 141; melismatic, 143; in Russian music, 364; in Puccini, 370; in Debussy, 380; in Vaughan Williams, 487

Oriental music, 11, 36, 42, 126, 134

Origins of music, 133-4

Orlando di Lasso, *see* Lasso, Orlando di

Ornament, defined, 551

Ossian, 293

Ostinato: defined, 60, 187; in Purcell, 117; in Monteverdi, 187; in Brahms, 308; in Roy Harris, 498

"Outside" chair (orchestra), 89

"Overblow" (woodwind instruments), 96

Overtones (harmonic), 37

Overture: French, 173 (Lully), 195, 225 (Bach); Italian, 194-5; function in Gluck, 265; in nineteenth-century opera, 333, 335; defined, 551; *see also* Concert overture

Owen, Robert, 282

Pachelbel, Johann, 177, 181

Paganini, Niccolò: concertos, 314-15; mentioned, 320; portrait, Plate 24c

Paisiello, Giovanni, 360

Palestrina, Giovanni Pierluigi da, 46, 329, 408; style of, 154

Pandiatonic, 434, 483

Parameters (of music), 507, 512

Paris, National Conservatory of Music, 231

"Paris" motet, see Motet, thirteenth century

Parker, Charlie, 491

Parlando style (Rossini), 336; defined, 551

Parody Mass, 154

Parrish, Carl, 64 n3

Parry, C. H. H., 371

Partch, Harry, 518

Partials (upper), 38

Partita, 183 n1; defined, 551

Pasdeloup, Jules, 372

Passacaglia: defined, 60, 187; in Bach, 224; in Brahms, 307

Passepied, 183

Passing Note, 51-2

Passion-Oratorio, 276

Passion story, evolution of musical setting, 208; see also Schütz; Bach, J. S.

Pater, Walter, 283

Patronage system, 393

Pavane, xxi, 158, 159, 183

Pedal: piano, 105; harpsichord, Plate 13B (caption); swell (organ), 106

Pedal organ, 106

Pedal point, of a fugue, 63

Pedrell, Felipe, 484

Penderecki, Krzysztof, 510

Pentatonic scale, 36-7, 391

Pepusch, J. C., 200

Percussion (instruments), 88, 102; kettledrums (timpani), 102-3; illustrated, Plate 5B

Perfect (interval), 40

Performance: importance of, 110ff; dependence on notation, 111; role

Performance (*continued*) of the editor in, 112; role of individual artist in, 112; quality of, 128; manner of, in primitive music, 133; illustrated, Plates 1-6, 9A & B, 12A, 13A, 15, 16B, 24D

Pergolesi, G. B., 192, 199, 231, 233, 268; *La Serva Padrona,* 199 (discussed)

Peri, Jacopo, 120, 167, 264

Period, defined, 26

Persymphans (orchestra), 108, 461

"Pes," 113, Plate 7

Petrarch, 156

Petrucci, Ottaviano dei (printer), 153

Philidor (Danican-), F. A., 269

Philips, Peter, Plate 12B (caption)

Phrase, defined, 26

Phrygian (mode), 35, 138; in Brahms, 306-7

Pianissimo, 552

Piano (pianoforte): description and types of, 104-5; pedals of, 105; in Mozart's time, 237; keyboard of, 531

Piano (term), 552

Piave, Francesco, 353

Picasso, Pablo, 400, 433, Plates 31B, 33A

Piccini, Nicola, 265, 266, 268

Piccolo, 96-7

Pincherle, Marc, 215 n2

Pissarro, Camille (painter), 377

Piston, Walter: works, 502; style and form, 502; books, 502; mentioned, 401, 514

Pizzetti, Ildebrando, 483

Pizzicato: defined, 93, 552; in Bartók, 450

Plagal cadence, 50

Plagal mode, 138

Plainsong, 137, 151 n11; defined, 552

Plato, 126, 169

Playford, John, 167 n3

Plectrum (harpsichord), Plate 14B (caption)

Pléiade, 156

Poe, Edgar Allan, 319 n1, 378

Pointillism, 377, 414, Plate 29B (caption)

Poland, avante-garde music in, 403

Polka, defined, 552

Pollack, Jackson, 524, Plate 40A

Polonaise: in Chopin, 295; defined, 552

Polymeters, 45

Polyphony (polyphonic): defined, 42–3; text obscured by, 121; in medieval music, 145; in *Ars Nova,* 147; *see also* Counterpoint

Polyrhythm: defined, 45; use in twentieth century, 436, 442, 456

Polytonality (polytonal): defined, 53, 400; in Hindemith, 456; in Stravinsky, 433, 442; *see also* bitonality

Ponte, Lorenzo da, 270, 349

Ponticello, see Sul ponticello

Portamento, defined, 552

Post-Communion (Mass), 542

Post-Webern composers, 402

Potpourri, 333, 335

Potter, Stephen, quoted, 5

Poulenc, Francis: style and works, 482; *Dialogues of the Carmelites,* 482; portrait, Plate 30A; mentioned, 480, 482

Pratt, Waldo, viii

Pravda (newspaper), 470

Preface (Mass), 542

Prelude: seventeenth century, 181–2; and fugue, 182; eighteenth century, 220; nineteenth century, 293, 296

Preparation (of a suspension), 52

Presto (prestissimo), 552

Prima donna, 164

Primitive music, 17, 19, 42, 133; characteristics and manner of performance, 133

Primitivism (musical), 400

Principal (in an orchestra), 89

"Program" chanson, 151

"Program" concerto (in Vivaldi), 124, 214

Program music, 122–5; importance and depiction of the program, 123; the program and the form, 124; titles given to "absolute" music, 124; nineteenth-century orchestral, 316ff

Program symphony, 124, 318–21

"Progressive" jazz, 491

Prokofiev, Sergei, 463ff; an anti-Romantic, 464; a "futurist," 464; music characterized, 464; training, 464; returns to Soviet Union, 465; "Western" period, 465; "five lines of development," 466; relation to Socialist Realism, 466; works for piano, 466; style, 467; forms, 468; harmony, 468; scoring, 468; position summarized, 468; portrait, Plate 36A; mentioned, 396, 462, 470, 478, 481

    WORKS: *Love for Three Oranges,* 461, 465; *War and Peace,* 462, 466; *Romeo and Juliet,* 463; *The Stone Flower,* 463, 466; Alexander Nevsky, 465; "Classical" Symphony, 465, 468; *Le Pas d'acier* (ballet), 465; *Scythian Suite,* 465, 468; Second Violin Concerto, 465, 467, 468; Third Piano Concerto, 465; Fifth Symphony, 466; *Peter and the Wolf,* 466, 468; *The Story of a Real Man,* 466

Proletkult, 461

Proper (Mass): meaning of, 137; polyphonic settings of, 146 n9; scheme of, 542

Protestantism, rise of, 152

Puccini, Giacomo: leader of *verismo*

Puccini (*continued*)
  school, 370; style and works, 370; mentioned, 283, 334, 483

Puchsberg, Michael, 277

Purcell, Henry: declamation in, 122; use of *ostinato*, 175, 187; *Dido and Aeneas,* 117, 174–5, 191; operas, 174–5; anthems, 177–8; *fantasias,* 181; sonatas, 186; autograph, Plate 20; portrait, Plate 22B; mentioned, 163, 292

Pushkin, Alexander, 360, 361, 364

Quadruple fugue, 221 n7

Quadruple stops (strings), 93

Quality in art, 126

Quarter note, 536

Quarter tones, 518

Quartet: string, 248–9, Plate 2A; piano, 249–50

Quinault, Philippe, 172

Quintet, 249

Quodlibet, defined, 43

Rachmaninov, Sergei, 332, 431, 464, 469

"Rag" ("Ragtime"), 403, 491

Rallentando, 552

Rameau, Jean-Philippe, 197–8, 373; orchestration, 166, 198; critics of, 197
  WORKS: *Le Rappel des Oiseaux,* 123, 224; operas, 197–8; secular cantatas, 198; *Pièces de Clavecin,* 224

Range, defined, 552

Rank (organ), 105

Rapée, Erno, 190

Raphael, 152

"Rasoumovsky" quartets (Beethoven), 255

Rationalism (eighteenth century), 189–90, 231

Ravel, Maurice, 386ff; his background, 386; compared with Debussy, 386–7; kinds and subjects of music, 387; capacity for wit, 388; pentatonic scale, 388; piano style, 388; Spanish background, 388; orchestration, 389; position summarized, 389; mentioned, 379, 401, 482
  WORKS: *Jeux d'eau,* 387; "Ondine," 387; *Daphnis and Chloe,* 388

Realism (musical), in vocal music, 115–16

Realizing (the figured bass), 165

Rebec, 459

Recapitulation (sonata form), 68, 70

Récitatif mesuré (measured recitative), in Lully, 172

Recitative (*recitativo*), 122, 169, 172; *recitativo secco* (dry recitative), 193; *recitativo accompagnato* (accompanied recitative), 193; defined, 552

"Reciting" style, 138

Recorder, 96, 158 (described), 160, 166, Plate 15B

Redemption (in J. S. Bach), 205

Reformation (Protestant), 153–4

Refrain (in rondo), 58

Reger, Max, 368–9; admiration for Bach, 368; chromaticism, 368; works, 368–9; mentioned, 398, 455

Register, defined, 552

Registration (organ), 106

Reihe, Die (periodical), 524

"Remembrance" motive, 337, 340, 342

Renaissance: musical traits, 148–9; general characteristics, 152ff; mentioned, 120

Renan, Ernest, quoted, 392

Renoir, Auguste (painter), 377

Reprise (sonata form), 68

Requiem (Mass), compared with usual Mass, 274, 275, 331; idea of, in Berg, 428–9; *see also* Berlioz; Brahms; Fauré; Mozart; Verdi

Resolution (of a suspension), 52, 552

Respighi, Ottorino, 483

Responsorial, defined, 552

Rest, 535

Restoration (English), 174

Retrograde (in tone row), 411, Ex. 149

Retrograde by inversion, 411

Return (fugue), 63

"Return to nature" (Rousseau), 229, 232

Revolution of 1848 (in Europe), 365; *see also* French Revolution

Rhythm: defined, 12; accents of, 13–14; in primitive music, 17; related to polyphony and harmony, 44ff; harmonic, 53–4; in medieval music, 145; complexities of, in fourteenth century, 146–7; in sixteenth century, 155; in Beethoven, 289; in twentieth century, 441–2; *see also* "Cross" accent; Meter; Polyrhythm; Syncopation

"Rhythm tree," 536

Ricercar(e), 158, 180, 181, 187, 221

Richardson, Samuel (novelist), 230

Richard "the Lion-Hearted," 144

Richter, Jean Paul, 284

Riegger, Wallingford, 496

Rigaudon, 224

Rimsky-Korsakov, Nikolai, 360ff; revision of Mussorgsky's works, 361; *Principles of Orchestration*, 364; mentioned, 332, 349, 430, 431, 464, 469

Ripieno, 212, 213 n1

Ritardando, 552

Ritenuto, 552

Ritornello form, 215–16; 258

"Rock" ("rock 'n roll"), 403, 492, 511

Rococo, 232; melodies, 233; origins of style, 233; texture, 236; theater, Plate 21B

Roman (medieval), 283

Romance (French song), 376

Romantic period and Romanticism: political, social, and artistic background, 283–4; defined, 283; style and forms of music, 284–5; music and social changes, 285–6, 393; influence on nationalism, 359; its backward glance, 393; reaction against, 397ff

Rondeau, 58, 144, 146, 223, 261 n14; defined, 552

Rondo: form, 34; scheme of, 58, 240

Ronsard, Pierre de (poet), 156

Root (chord): defined, 48; related to key, 49

Rosenfeld, Paul, quoted, 408

Roslavetz, Nicolai, 412

Rossini, Gioacchino, 334, 335–6; style, use of *crescendo* and orchestra, 336; *Il barbiere di Siviglia*, 336; mentioned, 337, 352

Round, defined, 43

Rousseau, J. J.: quoted, 192; influence of ideas, 229; on counterpoint, 233; *Le Devin du Village*, 269; *Letter on French Music*, 269, 360; mentioned, 266

Roussel, Albert, quoted, 435

"Row" (tone), 411

Royal Institute for Classic and Religious Music, 329

Rubato (tempo), 16, 296; defined, 552

Rubinstein, Anton, 364

Rudolph (Archduke of Vienna), 286, 330 n1

Ruggles, Carl, 496

Russian Association of Proletarian Musicians, 460

Russian liturgical music, 332

Russian Musical Society, 364

Sachs, Curt, 17 n3

St. Cecilia Society (Cäcilienverein),
329

St. Mark's (Venice), Plate 10B

St. Peter's (Rome), 163, 164

St. Petersburg, Imperial Conservatory at, 364

Saint-Saëns, Camille, 315, 327, 372,
375

Salzburg Cathedral, 176

Sammartini, G. B., 240

Samuel, Gerhard, 396

Sanctus (Mass), 137, 542, 545 (text)

Sand, George, 297

Sandburg, Carl, 135 n2

San Francisco Symphony, Plates 5A,
6B

Sarabande, 16, 183 (described), 184

Sargent, Malcolm, 88

Satie, Erik, 389ff; relation to Debussy
and Ravel, 390; humor, 390; linked
to anti-Impressionism by Cocteau,
390; style, 390; mentioned, 401,
435, 480, 481, 482

    WORKS: *Parade,* 390, Plate 33A;
"3 Pieces in the Form of a Pear,"
390; *Socrate,* 390

Sautillé, defined, 553

Scale: defined, 30; diatonic, 30; chromatic, 30–1; whole-tone, 36; pentatonic ("bagpipe"), 36–7; Hungarian, 37; microtone, 37; *see also*
Mode

Scalero, Rosario, 504

Scarlatti, Alessandro, 193, 198

Scarlatti, Domenico, 34, 231, 242; sonatas, 219–20

Schaeffer, Pierre, 520

Scheidt, Samuel, 177

Schein, Hermann, 177

Scherchen, Hermann, 396

Scherzo: form of, 58; in Beethoven,
244, 290

Schiller, J. C. F. (von), 284, 287, 293,
353; *Ode to Joy,* 283

Schlegel, A. W. (von), 293

Schmitt, Florent, 375

Schnitke, Alfred, 463

Schoenberg, Arnold, 408ff; as an Expressionist, 401; as a painter, 405;
notation, 407; Orchestral Variations, 407; quoted, 409, 413, 417,
512; as evolutionist not revolutionist, 409; musical development,
412ff; "expressionist" pictures, 412;
three periods, 412; second period of
composition, 412; relation to his
pupils, 412; Webern and Berg become his pupils, 412; *Harmonielehre,* 412; *Klangfarbenmelodie,*
412; usage of twelve tone, 415;
characterization of twelve-tone
music, 416; special effects, 416; tone
color, 416; forms, 417; summary
of his position, 418; portrait, Plate
32A; mentioned, 347 n1, 392, 395,
396, 399, 401, 419, 439, 445, 491,
511, 525

    WORKS: *Pierrot Lunaire,* 393, 397,
399, 404, 414 (analyzed), 415 (No.
1: "Moondrunk," described), 513;
Op. 19, 404; String Sextet *Verklärte Nacht,* 404, 412; *Erwartung
(Expectation),* 405–6 (described),
413, 417; Five Piano Pieces, 406;
Fourth String Quartet, 21–2, 407,
410, 416, 417–18 (analysis of first
movement); *Gurre-Lieder,* 412;
Kammersymphonie, 412; *Pelleas
and Melisande,* 412; Second String
Quartet, 412; *Die glükliche Hand,*
413; Five Pieces for Orchestra, 413;
The Suite for Piano, 415; *Moses
and Aaron,* 416; Piano Concerto,

Schoenberg (*continued*)
416; String Quartet, 416; *A Survivor from Warsaw,* 416; Variations for Orchestra, 416; Violin Concerto, 416; Op. 16, 422

Schola Cantorum (D'Indy), 329

Schopenhauer, Arthur, 283, 311, 341

Schubert, Franz, 293–4, 300–3; influenced by Beethoven, 288; song texts and their representation, 293; role of piano, 293; the song cycle, 294; formal types of songs, 294; critical estimate of, 303–4; number of works, 303; early death, 303; mentioned, 284, 298, 304, 311, 330, 366

    WORKS: "Unfinished" Symphony in B minor, 16, 40; "Great" C major Symphony, 90 (Ex. 65), 300–2; *Wanderer Fantasie,* 299 n1, 324; String Quintet in C major, 302–3; songs, 293–4; *"Gretchen am Spinnrade,"* 119, 293; *"Erlkönig,"* 119–20, 294; *"Die junge Nonne,"* 293; *"Der Doppelgänger,"* 293, 294; *Die Winterreise* (song cycle), 293–4; *"Der Wegweiser,"* 34, 294; *"Die Krähe,"* 116, 293; *"Auf dem Flusse,"* 293

Schuller, Gunther, 396, 403, 491, 511

Schuman, William, 6, 504

Schumann, Clara, 304

Schumann, Robert: as writer and critic, 284; *The New Magazine for Music,* 284; influenced by Beethoven, 288; descriptive titles, 295; use of piano, 295; typical harmony and rhythm, 295; "New Paths" (article), 304; mentioned, 284, 295, 299, 304, 315, 367

    WORKS: *Fantasy Pieces,* 123, 284, 295; songs, 294–5; *Frauenliebe und Leben* (song cycle), 295, 299; Quintet for Piano and Strings, 299

Schütz, Heinrich, 162, 176–7; use of *concertato,* 176; *Seven Last Words,* 177; Passions, 177

Score, 90, 110

Scott, Walter, 283, 335; quoted, 14

Schweitzer, Albert, 191 n4

Schwetzingen, Rococo theater in, Plate 21B

Scriabin, Alexander: color keyboard, 431; "mystic chord," 431; *The Poem of Ecstasy,* 431; *Prometheus: The Poem of Fire,* 431; mentioned, 412, 431, 464

Scribe, Eugène (librettist), 333

"Second" theme (sonata form), 69

Secreta (Mass), 542

Secular cantata, 198

Sedaine, Michel Jean, 269

"Seepage" theory (folk music), 136

Sensibilité, 232

Senza basso (sonata): defined, 185 n2; in Bach, 219

Sequence, defined, 29

Serenade, 248 n11

"Series" (atonal): transposed, 410; contrapuntal forms, 410; used harmonically, 410

Sermisy, Claude de, 156, Plate 9B

Service (English), 154

Sessions, Roger: quoted on his own music, 500; pupils, 500; style and form, 500; works, 500; writings, 500; mentioned, 345, 396, 499; portrait, Plate 37B

"Set" (atonal music), 411

Seurat, George (painter), 377, 414, Plate 29B

Seventh chord, 48

Sforzando (*sf*): in Haydn, 82; in Beethoven, 243, 288; in Mozart, 254; defined, 553

Shakespeare, William: quoted, 14; used by Verdi, 355; mentioned, 157, 284, 353, 362

Sharp: explained, 531; how indicated, 534; double, 534

Sharp, Cecil, 371

Shaw, George Bernard, 286 n3

Shebalin, Vissarion, 462

Shelley, Percy Bysshe, 283

Shifrin, Seymour, 500

Shostakovich, Dmitri, 469ff; quoted, 462, 470 (on his Fifth Symphony); a product of Soviet Culture, 469; effect of Socialist Realism on, 471; reaction to the criticism of 1948, 471; compared to Beethoven, 472, 478; style, 474; position summarized, 478

   WORKS: *Lady Macbeth of Mtzensk,* 461, 470, 472; *Katerina Ismaylova* (film of *Lady Macbeth*), 472; Seventh ("Leningrad") Symphony, 462, 470; First Symphony, 469; Fifth Symphony, 470, 471, 472, 474 (analyzed); Violin Concerto, 471; Thirteen symphonies, 472 (discussed)

Sibelius, Jean, 485–6; forms, 485; style, 485; symphonies, 485; tone poems, 485; dynamic nuances, 486; harmony, 486; orchestration, 486; position summarized, 486; supported by Finnish government, 486

Siciliano, 553

Side drum, 102

Signature: key, 534; time, 537

Silence (as music), 402

Silvestrov, Valentin, 462

Simpson, Christopher, Plate 15A

Sinding, Christian, 367

Sine wave tone, 521

Sinfonia: in Schütz, 177; Italian opera, 194–5, 240

Singing allegro, defined, 233–4

Singspiel (German comic opera), 269–70, 338, 339, 340

Sinusoidal tone, 521

Sisley, Alfred (painter), 377

Sistine Chapel (Rome), 159 n16

"Six, The," ("The Six Frenchmen"), 490, Plate 30A

Sixteenth note, 536

Skalkottas, Nicos, 510

Slavic Congress, 365

Slide (*portamento*) in jazz, 509

Slur, 25; defined, 538

Smetana, Bedřich: universal traits, 365; use of national dances, 365; mentioned, 327, 333

   WORKS: operas, 365; *The Bartered Bride,* 365; *The Moldau,* 365

Smith, Adam, 230

Smithson, Harriet, 318

Socialist Realism, 460, 462, 463, 465, 470, 478, 479; defined, 461

Société Nationale de Musique, 372

Society for Private Musical Performances (Vienna), 395, 408

Soft pedal (piano), 105

Solesmes (monastery), 329

Solo concerto, *see* Concerto, solo

Sonata: defined, 68; baroque "solo," 185, 217, 219–20 (Scarlatti); *senza basso,* 185 n2, 219 (Bach); trio, 185, 218, 219; Classic, 238ff, 245–6, 248 n10; Romantic, 298ff; *see also* Corelli; Purcell; String quartet; Symphony

Sonata-allegro form, 68; *see also* Sonata form

Sonata da camera (chamber sonata), 180, 185–6

Sonata da chiesa (church sonata), 184–6

Sonata form: defined and explained, 67–71; relation to texture, 61, 67–8; sections of, 68; how to "tell," 71; "verbal," 72; sonata-rondo, 73, 240, 242; without development (abridged), 72–3, 240, 252, 271;

Sonata form (*continued*)
"archaic" type, 242; with fugato, 73, 242, 252; mentioned, 239

Sonata-rondo, *see* Sonata form

Sonatina, 553

Song: in nineteenth century, 293–5; *see also* Chanson; Lied; individual entries of composers

Song cycle: origin in Schubert, 294; transferred to piano, 295

Song (ternary) form, 34, 294

Sonority, defined, 553

Soprano (voice), 85–6

Sordino, 553

Sostenuto, 553

Sostenuto pedal (piano), 105

Sousa, John Philip, 280 n8

Space (on staff), 533

Spencer, Herbert (scientist), 283

Spiccato, 553

Spinet, 104, 158; defined, 553

Spirituals, Negro, 136

Spohr, Louis, 315

Spontini, Gaspare, 333, 338

Sprechgesang, 343, 347, 349

Sprechstimme (speaking voice), 416, 427; defined, 414 (Ex. 151)

Stabreim, 342, 345

Staccato: how indicated, 25; defined, 553

Staff, 533

Stalin, Joseph: formulates aims of Soviet opera, 462; mentioned, 460, 468, 471

Stamitz, J. W. A., 237, 239

Stanford, Charles, 371

Stantipes, defined, 553

Stanza(ic) form, 33

"Star-Spangled Banner, The" (national anthem), 23, 399 n12

Stassov, Vladimir, 360

Stearns, Marshall W., 491 n2

Steinberg, Maximilian, 469

Stem (of notes), 536

Stendahl (novelist), 127

Stile concitato (Monteverdi), 169

Stile rappresentativo, 167

Stile recitativo, 167

Stochastic, defined, 524

Stockhausen, Karlheinz: quoted on *Kontra-Punkte,* 522; works in various mediums, 522; "space" composition, 523; as editor, 524; portrait, Plate 39A; mentioned, 397, 402, 508, 511, 512, 521

    WORKS: Electronic Studie II, 522 and Plate 38B; *Gesang der Jünglinge,* 522; *Zeitmasse,* 522; *Mixtur,* 523 (described); Piano Piece XI, 523

Stokowski, Leopold, 89, 396

Stollen, 144

Stop (organ), 105

Stradivarius, Antonius, 91

Strauss, Richard: tone poems, 327–8; transformation of themes, 327; orchestra and orchestration, 328, 349–50; librettos, 349; characterization in operas, 349; musical style, 349; relation to Wagner, 349, 350; operas, 349; mentioned, 123, 124, 397, 398, 405, 412

Stravinsky, Igor, 430ff; as a neoclassicist, 401; quoted, 423 (on Webern), 433 (on his *The Rite of Spring*), 440, 444, 509; Russian background, 430; early work, 432; neoclassic style, 434ff; neoclassic works, 437; attitude toward "expression," 438; use of *ostinato,* 438; as author, 439; *An Autobiography,* 439; as performer, 439; "serial" compositions, 439–40; style, 440; flexible rhythm, 441; orchestration, 443; use of canon, 443; use of *ostinato,* 443; use of piano, 443; position summarized, 443–4; portrait, Plate 31A; mentioned, 392,

Stravinsky (*continued*)
396, 399, 401, 416, 445, 462, 463, 470, 481, 490
   WORKS: *The Rite of Spring*, 393 (creates a riot), 397, 399 (discussed), 400, 433, 436, 441, 443; *The Flood*, 396; *The Firebird*, 432 (described); *Oedipus Rex*, 437, 461; *Petrushka*, 432 (described), 441, 490; *Mavra*, 434; *The Nightingale*, 434; *Ragtime*, 434; *The Soldier's Tale*, 434, 435, 443 (use of instruments); *The Wedding*, 434, 443; Wind Octet, 434, 436 (discussed), 442; *Pulcinella*, 435; *Persephone*, 437; *The Rake's Progress*, 437; *Symphony of Psalms*, 437 (discussed), 441, 442, 443; the Septet, 439; *Agon*, 440 (discussed); early ballets, 463; *Orpheus*, 437, Plate 34B (autograph)

Stretta, 270, 353 n4

Stretto, 243; fugue, 63

Strindberg, August, 405

String quartet, 248–9, Plate 2A

Strings, 90–94; range and tuning of, 90–91; special effects, 93; bow stroke, 93; *see also* entries for individual instruments

"Strong" beat, 12

Strophic form, 33; *see also* Modified strophic form

Strunk, Oliver, 167 n3

Studio di Fonologia (Milan), 521, 525

Sturm und Drang, 232, 233, 245

"Style galant et touchant," 232

Subdominant, 38, 49, 52–3 (chord)

Subject (of a fugue), 62

Subtonic (chord), 52

Suite (of dances): seventeenth century, 183–4; eighteenth century, 223; defined, 553

Sullivan, Arthur, 335, 371

Sullivan, Louis, 55

Sul G, defined, 553

Sul ponticello, 418, 553

Sumeria, music in, 133

"Sumer is icumen in," 113, 145, Plate 7

Supertonic (chord), 52

Surette, T. W., ix

Suspension, 52

Süssmayer, Franz Xaver, 275

"Swanee River," 43

Sweelinck, J. P., 181

Swell organ and *Swell* pedal, 106

Swell shutter (organ), 106, 237

Swing, 491

Sword dance, 136

Syllabic setting, 122, 138

Symbolists, 378

Symphonic poem, 124, 324–7; *see also* Liszt; Strauss, tone poem

Symphony: Classic, 240ff; Romantic, 298ff; *see also* entries for individual composers

Syncopation, 20, 305–6; defined, 16–17

Synthesizer (in tape music), 520

Szigeti, Joseph, 395

Tallis, Thomas, 487

Tambourine, 102

"Tangent" (clavichord), 158, Plate 14A (caption)

Tanglewood (summer school), 395

"*Tannenbaum*," 135

Tape-recorder music, 520

Tartini, Giuseppe, 219

Taste, 127

Tchaikovsky, Peter Ilyitch: relation to Balakirev, 364; use of folk song, 364; mentioned, 298, 315, 327, 332, 336, 364, 379, 430, 431, 485
   WORKS: Sixth (*Pathétique*) Symphony, 13, 25, 29, 308–10 (analyzed), 316, 394; *Swan Lake*, 463

Tchesnokov, P. G., 332

Telemann, G. P., 226

Temperament (tuning), 553

Tempo: defined, 14; terms indicating, 15; terms modifying, 16

Tempo rubato, see Rubato

Tenor (voice), 85, 86

Tenor, in polyphony, 140; fifteenth century, 149; sixteenth century, 154

Terminal development, 80, 244

Ternary form, 34, 294

Text: descriptive settings, 115ff; and vocal forms, 118ff; relation to music, 121; syllabic and melismatic setting, 122

Texture: defined, 42; Classic, 235–36; figured-bass, early Classic and Classic compared, 236

Théâtre de la foire, 200

Thematic motivation, 70, 252

Thematic transformation (symphonic poem), 125, 324

Thematic variants, 187

Theme and variations: defined, 59; procedures, 59–60; in Haydn, 79–80, 242; in sixteenth century, 159; in seventeenth century, 179–80, 186–7; in Bach and Handel, 224–5; in Beethoven, 244, 291; mentioned, 239; *see also* Chaconne; *Character* variation; *Folia; Ostinato; Passacaglia;* Variation(s)

Thème Russe (in Beethoven), 255

Theremin (instrument), 509

"The Six," *see* "Six, The"

"Third-stream" music, 403, 411

Thirteenth chord, 48

Thomas, Ambrose, 334

Thomas of Celano, 275

Thompson, Randall, 501

Thomson, Virgil: music for government documentary films, 503; style and works, 503; *Four Saints*

Thomson (*continued*)
in Three Acts, 503; mentioned, 401, 525

Thorough bass, 165

Thorough-bass period, *see* Baroque (period)

"Three Blind Mice" (round), 43, 61

Three-part form, defined, 34

"Through-composed," 151; defined, 121

"Tie," 538

Tieck, Ludwig, 283

Timbre (tone color), 84

Time signature: compound, 14–15; defined, 537

Timpani, 102–103, Plates 5B and 6B

Tinctoris, quoted, 392

Toccata: sixteenth century, 159, 159 n15; seventeenth century, 181–2; eighteenth century, 220

Tolstoi, Alexei, 473

Tolstoi, Leo (Count), 282, 359

Tonality: defined, 30, 33, 36; "progressive," 312; *see also* Atonality; Bitonality; Polytonality

Tone, *see* Note and tone

Tone color: defined, 84; voices, 86; instruments, 87

Tone-color melody, 416

Tone poem, *see* Strauss, Richard

Tone row: defined, 411, 411 n1; contrapuntal forms of, 411; *see also* Twelve-tone technique

Tonguing, flutter, 549

Tonic: defined, 30; chord, 52; of mode, 138

Torelli, Giuseppe, 213

Toscanini, Arturo, xxv, 172, 471

"Total immersion," 511

"Totally organized" music, 408, 507, 524; defined, 512

Tourte, François, 91

Tovey, Donald Francis, 55, 248 n12, 258, 308, 313

Tract (Mass), 542

Traëtta, Tommaso, 265, 360

Tragédie lyrique (Lully), 172

Transcription Mass, 154

Transformation of theme, 324, 327

Transpose and transposition, 553

Transposing instrument, 95–6

Treble clef, 533

Tremolo, defined, 94

Triad, defined, 48

Triangle (instrument), 102

Trill, defined, 554

Trio: part of minuet, 58; in chamber music, 248

Trio sonata, *see* Sonata

Triple fugue, 221 n7

Triple stop (strings), 93

Triple time, 12

Triplum, 141

Trombone, 101–2, Plate 6B, Plate 29B

Troping (trope), defined, 140

Troppo (ma non troppo), 554

Troubadours, 143–4

Trouvères, 143–4

Trumpet: "natural," 95, 238; valve, 100–1, Plate 6B; long (in Verdi), 354

Tuba, 102, Plate 6B

Tudor, David, 526

Tunder, Franz, 205

Turn (ornament), 554

Tutti (concerto), 215–16, 257

Twelve-tone method: described, 409–10; practical aspects, 416

Twelve-tone technique: in Schoenberg, 409ff; in Webern, 419ff; in Berg, 426ff; used by various composers, 407; mentioned, 401, 408

Two-part (binary) form, 34

Una corda, 105; defined, 554

Union of Soviet Composers, 460, 462, 470

United States, music in: 418ff; avante garde, 403; backgrounds, 490–1; folk music, 491 n1; jazz, 491–2; *see also* individual composers

Universities, role in music education, 396–7

Upbeat, 539

"Upbeat" harmony, 45–6

Upper partials, 38

Ussachevsky, Vladimir, 521

Valse, see Waltz

Valved instruments, 100

Varèse, Edgard: style and works, 519; a bold innovator, 519; "fathered forth noise," 519; quoted, 520; mentioned, 402, 519

    WORKS: *Déserts,* 519; *Ionisation,* 519; *Poème électronique,* 519

Variation(s): "double," 79, 242; principle of, 187; in atonal music, 407; *see also* Theme and variations

Vaudeville, 200

Vaughan Williams, Ralph: use of folk music, 487; style and works, 487; mentioned, 36, 222 n10, 360 n1

Veracini, Francesco, 219

"Verbal" sonata form, 72

Verdi, Giuseppe, 351–8; relation to politics, 351; operatic career summarized, 351–2; importance of the voice and libretto, 352; list of operas, 352; recurrent motives (*Aida*), 352; letters, 352; librettos, 352–3; mechanics of Verdi's opera, 353; virtuoso "tinsel" aria, 353; style of melody, 353; orchestration, 353–4; means of characterization, 354–5; "remembrance" motives, 355; portrait, Plate 28B; mentioned, 5, 333, 337, 346, 370

    WORKS: "Manzoni" Requiem, 331; operas, 351–8; *Falstaff,* 351, 352, 353, 354, 355–8 (analyzed)

Verismo (opera), 283, 334, 353, 370–1

Verlaine, Paul (poet), 378

Versailles (court at), 163, 164

Verse anthem, 154, 177

Vers mesuré, 156

Vespers, 137

Vibraphone, 554

Vibrato: defined, 94; in jazz players, 509; on clavichord, Plate 14A (caption)

Victoria, Tomás Luis de, 154, 484 (edition of)

Vielle, Plate 9A

Vienna opera house, Plate 19A

Vieuxtemps, Henri, 315

Villa-Lobos, Heitor: attracted to folk music, 505; quoted, 506; works and influence, 506; mentioned, 360 n1

Vinci, Leonardo da, *see* Leonardo da Vinci

Viol and viol family (*viola da gamba*), 158, 159 (bass), 160, 180, Plate 15A

Viola, 92, Plate 2A

Viola clef, 533

Viola da gamba, see Viol

Violin: described, 91–2; violin family compared with viols, 158; idiomatic styles, 179, 184; Plates 2A and 16B

"Violinning," 136

Violino piccolo, 206

Violoncello: described, 92; concertos for, 315

Viotti, G. B., 315

Virelai, 144, 146, cf. Plate 11A

Virginal, 158; defined, 554

Virtuoso: traveling, 285; defined, 554

Vitry, Philippe de, 146

Vivace, 554

Vivaldi, Antonio, 213–14; program concerto, 124, 214; *concerto grosso,* 213; solo concerto, 213, 258; mentioned, 219; portrait, Plate 22C

Vocal color, 87

Vogl, J. M., 293

Voice (human), 85–7

Voice part, defined, 21

"Volta, La" (dance), Plate 16A

Voltaire, 229, 230

Vorspiel, 343

Wagner, Cosima, Plate 28A

Wagner, Richard, 341–8; on meaning of music, 128; seeking an alliance of all arts, 285, 299; influence of Beethoven, 288, 343; *Leitmotiv* (leading motive) technique, 324, 343, 347; relation to Romantic movement, 341; influence of, 341, 368; political significance of opera subjects, 341; and theoretical writings, 341, 342; subject matter, 342; debt to Weber, 342; *Stabreim,* 342, 345; orchestra, 342, 343, 344–5; overture (*Vorspiel*), 343; his own poet, 343; "unending melody," 343; *Sprechgesang,* 343, 347; harmony and dynamics, 344, 347; rhythmic patterns, 344; powers as a dramatist, 345; loosening of tonality, 347 n1; plan for Festival Theater at Bayreuth, Plate 25B; portrait, Plate 28A; mentioned, 56, 284, 304, 311, 324, 327, 332, 333, 336, 337, 338, 341, 342, 351, 359, 373, 375, 379, 397, 398, 408, 430, 431

    WORKS: *Tristan and Isolde,* 29, 118, 341, 343, 344, 346–8 (analyzed); *Lohengrin,* 120, 342, 345; *The Ring,* 312, 343, 345; *Parsifal,* 341, 343; *Meistersinger,* 343, 345; Tannhaüser, stage set for, Plate 27B

Walton, William, 488

Waltz: *Blue Danube,* 22; in Richard Strauss; *Valse* in Chopin, 296; illustrated, Plate 27A; mentioned, 293

Watteau, Jean Antoine, 232

"Weak" beat, 12

Weber, Carl Maria von, 339–40; "remembrance" motives, 340; characterization in, 340; use of overture, 340; use of orchestra, 340; romantic elements, 339, 340; *Der Freischütz,* 270, 284 n2, 339–40 (analyzed), Plate 25A ("Wolf Glen" scene); mentioned, 284, 332, 337, 341, 359, 394

Weber, Constanze, 277

Webern, Anton, 419ff; forms, 407; pointillistic style, 407, 420, 422; sketch of life, 419; Stravinsky quoted on, 419; development in three periods, 420; miniatures, 420; "mini-miniatures," 420; traits of early music, 420; works recorded, 420; melodies, 421; dynamics, 422; formal construction, 422; motivic series (micro-series), 422; notated *rubato,* 422; "tone-color melody," 422; treatment of voice and instrument, 422; twelve-tone technique, 422; quoted, 423; as forerunner of electronic music, 519; portrait, Plate 34A; mentioned, 394, 395, 396, 416, 426, 439, 444, 511, 512

    WORKS: "George" songs, 413; Six Pieces for Orchestra, 413, 423–4 (No. 4 analyzed); *Passacaglia,* 420; Second Cantata, 420; "Trakl" songs, 420; Concerto (Op. 24), 421; Symphony (Op. 21) analyzed, 421, 424–5; "Ricercar" of Bach's *Musical Offering,* 422; String Quartet, Op. 9, 422; Five Canons on Latin Texts, 423; Variations for Orchestra, 423

Weelkes, Thomas, 115–16, 157

Weill Kurt, 461

Wells, H. G., ix

Wesley, Samuel, vii

White keys, 531

"White" sound, 521

Whole note, 536

Whole tone, 531

Whole-tone scale, 36

Whole-tone "series," 415

Wieniawski, Henri, 315

"Wies" church (Bavaria), Plate 21A

Wilbye, John, 157

"Wild Beasts" (painters), 392

Willaert, Adrian, 153

William II (Emperor), 341

William IX (Count of Poitiers), 144

Williams, Ralph Vaughan, *see* Vaughan Williams, Ralph

Winckelmann, Johann Joachim, 232

Wind instruments, 94ff; *see also* Brass instruments; Woodwind instruments

Wolf, Hugo, 294, 369 (discussed), 376

Wolff, Christian, 524

Wolf-Ferrari, Ermanno, 483

Woodwind instruments, 94, 95, 96–9, 509 (revolutionary technique)

Word painting, 117, 120; defined, 554

Wordsworth, William, 283

Xenakis, Yannis, 510, 524

Xylophone, 102, 554

Yevtushenko, Yevgeny, 473

Young Person's Guide to the Orchestra, 88

Ysaÿe, Eugène, 112

Zemlinsky, Alexander, 412

Zen Buddhism, 526

Zeno, Apostolo, 194

Zhdanov, Andrei, 462, 471, 479

Zink, 459

Zola, Émile (novelist), 283, 334, 379

Coláiste Muire gan Smál,
Luimneac.